THE INCEPTION *of* MODERN PROFESSIONAL EDUCATION

STUDIES IN LEGAL HISTORY

Published by the University of North Carolina Press
in association with the American Society for Legal History

Daniel Ernst and Thomas A. Green, editors

THE INCEPTION *of* MODERN

BRUCE A. KIMBALL

PROFESSIONAL EDUCATION

C. C. Langdell, 1826–1906

THE UNIVERSITY OF NORTH CAROLINA PRESS

Chapel Hill

© 2009 The University of North Carolina Press

All rights reserved

Designed and set by Rebecca Evans in Whitman

Manufactured in the United States of America

The paper in this book meets the guidelines for permanence
and durability of the Committee on Production Guidelines for
Book Longevity of the Council on Library Resources.

The University of North Carolina Press has been a member of the
Green Press Initiative since 2003.

Library of Congress Cataloging-in-Publication Data

Kimball, Bruce A., 1951–

The inception of modern professional education :

C.C. Langdell, 1826–1906 / Bruce A. Kimball.

    p. cm. — (Studies in legal history)

Includes bibliographical references and index.

ISBN 978-0-8078-3257-8 (cloth : alk. paper)

1. Langdell, C. C. (Christopher Columbus), 1826-1906.

2. Law teachers—United States—Biography.

3. Law—Study and teaching—United States—History—19th century.

4. Professional education—United States—History—19th century.

5. Harvard Law School—History—19th century. I. Title.

KF368.L36K56 2009

340.092—dc22

[B]

2008053306

13 12 11 10 09   5 4 3 2 1

May 22, 2009

To ZACHARY *and* REBECCA,

raised amid the "brooding omnipresence" of C.C.L.

CONTENTS

ILLUSTRATIONS, TABLES, AND FIGURE

Illustrations

Tables

ACKNOWLEDGMENTS

In the years since I began archival research on C. C. Langdell in 1995, a great many individuals and institutions have provided invaluable assistance. Above all, I am deeply grateful to Daniel Coquillette and to David Warrington and the staff of the Harvard Law School Library Special Collections, who have been wonderful colleagues and sources of expertise and support throughout the research. I am also especially grateful to Christopher Tomlins and Daniel Ernst who have provided encouragement and editorial guidance over several years. I owe a special debt to my research assistants who coauthored articles on Langdell: R. Blake Brown, Pedro Reyes, and Brian Shull. I am also indebted to Kathleen Mahoney and William LaPiana for generously sharing their work on Langdell and James Barr Ames.

John Schlegel has been enormously helpful in reading and criticizing drafts of articles and chapters, and many others have provided valuable feedback at various points: Daniel Hamilton, Jay Hook, Stephen Siegel, David Seipp, Neal Duxbury, Tyll Van Geel, Mary Beth Basile, Hugh Hawkins, Thomas Grey, and Gail Hupper. I am very grateful to my research assistants over the years: Jason Blokhuis, Celeste Daise Wheeler, Paul Collins, Jeffrey Ellsworth, Teresa Anderson, Cynthia Nicoletti, Kevin Carboni, Molly McGinn Shapiro, Kenneth Miller, Erin Carroll, and Ben Johnson. My colleagues at the University of Rochester provided support and encouragement at key points: Randy Curren, Harold Wechsler, and Lynn Gordon.

I owe a special debt to William D. Mohr, retired Reporter of Debate, U.S. Senate, who translated the shorthand letters of Charles W. Eliot in the Harvard University Archives (boxes 302–331).

I am also deeply grateful to individuals at many different libraries and archival collections: Douglas Lind of the Georgetown University Law Center Library; Whitney Bagnall at Columbia University Law School Special Collections; Nancy Lyon at the Yale University Archives; David Schoonover of the University of Iowa Archives; Sean Monahan of the Bowdoin College Library; William Copeley and David Smolen of the New Hampshire Historical Society; Aurore Eaton of the Cambridge, Massachusetts, Historical Society; Edouard Desrochers of the Phillips Exeter Academy Archives; Brian Sullivan of the Harvard University Archives; Carol Roberts of the Wilton, New Hampshire, Town Library; Phylis Talarico of the Wilton, New Hampshire, Historical Society; Mary Hawkins of the Spencer Research Library at the University of Kansas; William Grace of the Kansas State Historical Society; Susan Flacks of the Presbyterian Historical Society in Philadelphia; Douglas Denne of the Hanover College Library; Elizabeth Moore of the Hampton, New Hampshire, Historical Society; Barbara Rimkunas of the Exeter, New Hampshire, Historical Society; Sarah Hartwell of the Dartmouth College Library; Ralph Caiazzo and Nancy Joseph of the New York Law Institute Library; Mindy Spitzer Johnston and David Ferris of the Harvard Law School Library Special Collections; Jeffrey Dawson of the State Historical Society of Iowa; Ruth Siems of the Registry of Deeds, Gage County, Nebraska; Kathryn Jagger of St. Peter's Episcopal Church in Hillsdale, Michigan; Nola Baker and staff of the Coldwater, Michigan, Public Library; Terry Kubasiak of the County Clerk Office in Coldwater, Michigan; Theresa Regnier of the Weldon Library at the University of Western Ontario; Louise Ambler of Episcopal King's Church in Cambridge, Massachusetts; Wilma R. Slaight of the Wellesley College Archives; Katherine Kominis of the Boston University Library Archival Research Center; Margo Hagopian of Boston University law school; Joy Sudduth and John Pritchard of the Westwood, Massachusetts, Historical Society; Kelly Spring of the Johns Hopkins University Library Special Collections; and Helen Conger of the Case Western Reserve University Archives.

In addition, I am grateful to the staff members of the First Presbyterian Church, Fort Scott, Kansas; the Public Library of Fort Scott, Kansas; the Whipple Free Library of New Boston, New Hampshire; the New Hampshire State Archives in Concord; the Manuscript Department of the New York Historical Society; the Manuscript Division of the U.S. Library of Congress; the Bryn Mawr College Archives; and the Radcliffe College Archives at Schlesinger Library, Harvard University.

I gratefully acknowledge the financial support for my research that I received at different points from the Spencer Foundation, the American Council of Learned Societies, the Law School Admissions Council, the American Philosophical Society, and the James Barr Ames Foundation. I am particularly grateful to the officers of the James Barr Ames Foundation, and especially Charles Donahue, who generously facilitated the funding of this research. The opinions and conclusions of the research are my own and do not necessarily reflect the positions or policies of those institutions.

Finally, I gratefully acknowledge that the Association of American Law Schools has granted permission to draw upon sections of the following publications: Bruce A. Kimball, "Young Christopher Langdell: The Formation of an Educational Reformer 1826–1854," *Journal of Legal Education* 52 (June 2002): 189–239; Bruce A.

Kimball, "Law Students' Choices and Experience during the Transition to Competitive Academic Achievement, 1876–1882," *Journal of Legal Education* 55 ([2006]): 163–207; Bruce A. Kimball and Brian S. Shull, "The Ironical Exclusion of Women from Harvard Law School, 1870–1900," *Journal of Legal Education* 58 (2008): 3–31. In addition, the *American Journal of Legal History* has kindly granted permission to draw upon sections of these publications: R. Blake Brown and Bruce Kimball, "When Holmes Borrowed from Langdell: The 'Ultra Legal' Formalism and Public Policy of *Northern Securities* (1904)," *American Journal of Legal History* 45 ([2003]): 278–321; Bruce A. Kimball and Pedro Reyes, "The 'First Modern Civil Procedure Course,' As Taught by C. C. Langdell, 1870–78," *American Journal of Legal History* 47 (2005): 257–303. The University of Illinois Press has kindly granted permission to draw upon these articles: Bruce A. Kimball, "'*Warn Students That I Entertain Heretical Opinions, Which They Are Not to Take as Law*': The Inception of Case Method Teaching in the Classrooms of the Early C. C. Langdell, 1870–1883," *Law & History Review* 17 (1999): 57–140; Bruce A. Kimball, "The Langdell Problem: Historicizing the Century of Historiography, 1906–2000s," *Law & History Review* 22 (2004): 277–337; Bruce A. Kimball, "Langdell on Contracts and Legal Reasoning: Revising the Holmesian Caricature," *Law & History Review* 25 (Summer 2007): 345–99. Finally, Blackwell Publishing has kindly granted permission to draw upon these articles: Bruce A. Kimball, "The Principle, Politics, and Finances of Introducing Academic Merit as the Standard of Hiring for 'the teaching of law as a career,' 1870–1900," *Law & Social Inquiry* 31 (2006): 617–48; Bruce A. Kimball and R. Blake Brown, "'The Highest Legal Ability in the Nation': Langdell on Wall Street, 1855–1870," *Law & Social Inquiry* 29 (2004): 39–104.

In closing, I wish to thank my wife, Lynne Karlson; my son, Zachary; and my daughter, Rebecca, for their abiding love and support during the long pilgrimage of this work.

A NOTE ON STYLE AND MONETARY VALUES

In the quotations from original sources, ampersands, abbreviations, punctuation, and capitalization have generally been converted to standard modern English. Points of uncertainty in deciphering the annotations are indicated by dashes or bracketed question marks. Translations of monetary values from the past into the present are based on Scott Derks, ed., *The Value of a Dollar: Prices and Incomes in the United States, 1860–2004* (Millerton, N.Y.: Grey House, 2004).

THE INCEPTION *of* MODERN
PROFESSIONAL EDUCATION

About fifteen leagues up the coast from Boston, near the border between Massachusetts and New Hampshire, the Merrimac River empties into the Atlantic Ocean close to the town where John Langdell was born in 1790. Descended from the Langdale family of England, John's father died within two years, and John's mother, Margaret, took her only child and followed the Merrimac into the interior. Thirty miles inland from its broad mouth, the river turns abruptly north near the falls where the Lowells and the Lawrences subsequently built their textile mills and family dynasties. Continuing along the Merrimac toward its source in the White Mountains, Margaret traveled with John another thirty miles, reaching the rocks and gravel bars of Manchester, New Hampshire, where John's children would later work in the massive brick mills. Leaving the river, Margaret and John trekked west for ten miles to the small farming town of New Boston.

By the 1790s old Boston had grown wealthy and liberal, both politically and religiously, while retaining the self-righteous and superior attitude of its Puritan founders. But New Boston, with its steep hills, fierce winters, and granite ledges pushing through the thin soil, held to the severe tradition of its namesake. In that unforgiving land Margaret established their home and raised John, who eventually bought a farm and married. On 22 May 1826, Margaret's grandson and John's son was born and named Christopher Columbus Langdell. This child grew into the man who established the modern paradigm of professional education in the United States. This book is the story of his life.

The story is a tragedy both in form and content. The drama begins auspiciously with a promising early childhood. But by age ten the protagonist is virtually orphaned and mired in rural poverty. Through remarkable effort, discipline, and talent, he overcomes nearly insuperable barriers and triumphs professionally, first in law and then in academe. Just at that point, however, he is betrayed—actually betrays himself—and his life's work in professional education is undermined in a way that even his many critics over the past century never appreciated, for to have done so would have called into question their own merit.

During his tenure as dean of Harvard Law School (HLS) from 1870 to 1895, Langdell conceived, designed, and built the system of academic meritocracy that became the normative model of professional education in the United States. He did not originate the central idea of academic meritocracy: that scholastic achievement determines, or should determine, one's merit in professional life. While Americans in the early 1800s construed merit largely in religious or moral terms,[1] the British universities of Oxford and Cambridge introduced competitive examinations that were gradually employed to evaluate candidates for public service and the professions.[2] Having embraced the central idea during the middle of the nineteenth century, Langdell made the conceptual innovation of integrating his commitment to fostering academic merit with the formalism of his legal expertise. Based on this conceptual formulation, he then designed and built a *"new system"*[3] of professional education: a formal system of rational, impersonal policies and rules advancing and guiding academic progress that could be measured objectively.

Langdell also posited a new set of legitimating relationships among a profession, its domain within society, the expertise of the professionals, and their education. Specifically, Langdell maintained that the just working of the legal system relies on the effectiveness of the legal profession, which depends on lawyers' expertise derived from their academic achievement in law school. These relationships among professional education, expertise, practice, and virtue presented a new understanding of professional legitimacy that was highly contested. By the time of Langdell's death in 1906, however, "both instructors and students in the Law School . . . [we]re firmly convinced that rank in the School furnishes the strongest evidence of the coming professional career."[4]

While establishing much higher academic standards for admission and graduation than any other law school or medical school in the United States, HLS grew to six hundred full-time students by 1900, making it the largest and wealthiest professional school in the nation with the highest academic standards. Langdell's system of academic meritocracy was so successful and prosperous that other university law schools began to adopt it. In 1898 Oxford professor Albert Dicey recommended importing Langdell's system into England, observing that "Harvard is quite ahead

---

1. Thernstrom, *Poverty and Progress*, 65; R. Bruce, *1877*, 25–26; Wylie, *Self-Made Man in America*, 8–9; Morison, *Three Centuries of Harvard*, 260; Allmendinger, *Paupers and Scholars*, 122–24.

2. Young, *Rise of the Meritocracy*, 17; Rothblatt, "Student Sub-Culture and the Examinations System," 281–90; Deslandes, "Competitive Examinations," 550–54; Montgomery, *Examinations: An Account of Their Evolution*, 7–14; Roach, *Public Examinations in England*, 3–21.

3. Emphasis in original. "Harvard College Law School," 67.

4. Lowell, Annual Report 1908–9, 8.

of the Universities of the U.S. . . ., and the Law School is their greatest triumph."[5] By the 1910s 40 percent of American law schools had adopted Langdell's system, and another 24 percent had partially accommodated it with the clear prospect of complete adoption on the horizon. Of the 36 percent of law schools that still rejected it, the great majority were marginal or rapidly losing influence in American legal education, and most of these would convert during the next decade.[6] The university law schools thus endorsed the view of Harvard president Charles W. Eliot that HLS provided "a better organization of professional education in the United States."[7]

Meanwhile, Eliot prodded Harvard Medical School in the same direction, which the medical school at Johns Hopkins University had already begun to follow. Traditionally, scholars have taken the founding of the Johns Hopkins University School of Medicine, which opened in 1893 with four students, as the starting point of modern professional education in the United States, and maintained that law schools experienced "a lag of three decades" behind medical schools thereafter.[8] However, while Johns Hopkins University pioneered graduate study in the arts and sciences, its medical school developed a generation after HLS, and even then the school did not willingly adopt such academic meritocratic standards as requiring a college degree for admission.[9] The Johns Hopkins trustees had consulted Eliot about hiring Daniel C. Gilman as their founding president in 1876, and Eliot, an eager proselytizer, subsequently advised Gilman on presidential matters ranging from getting enough rest, to buying a summer home, to hiring faculty, to managing the finances of the university, to the problems and successes of Harvard's law and medical schools. After retiring, Gilman dedicated his memoir, *The Launching of a University*, to Eliot as "a very slight expression of the long continued gratitude that I have felt for you."[10]

In 1904 Eliot testified that "the Law School is the most successful of the Univer-

5. A. V. Dicey to Elinor M. Dicey (13–14 Nov. 1898), quoted in Rait, *Memorials of Albert Venn Dicey*, 164. See Cosgrove, *Our Lady the Common Law*, 42–44.

6. See Kimball, "Proliferation of Case Method," 240–47.

7. C. Eliot, Annual Report 1893–94, 23.

8. Oliphant, "Parallels in the Development of Legal and Medical Education," 156. See 156–64; Shryock, *Unique Influence of the Johns Hopkins University*, 27n31; Ta. Parsons, "Professions," 543; Wiebe, *Search for Order, 1877–1920*, 113–23; Starr, *Social Transformation of American Medicine*, 17–29.

9. See Flexner, *Daniel Coit Gilman*, 40, 108–12; Rudy, "Eliot and Gilman," 307–18; Cordasco, *Shaping of American Graduate Education*, 78; Hawkins, *Pioneer: A History of the Johns Hopkins University*, 77; Hawkins, *Between Harvard and America*, 56–57, 65, 129; Ludmerer, *Learning to Heal*, 60, 75; Fleming, *William H. Welch*, 98–99.

10. Gilman to Eliot (28 Feb. 1906). See letters between C. Eliot and Gilman, in C. Eliot, Papers, boxes 114, 214, and Gilman, Papers, box 1.13.

sity's professional Schools. And if there be a more successful school in our country or in the world for any profession, I can only say that I do not know where it is. The School seems to have reached the climax of success in professional education."[11] Looking back in 1915, Eliot maintained that selecting Langdell was one of the three best things he did in his forty-year tenure as president of Harvard.[12]

Eliot was succeeded in the presidency by one of Langdell's students, Abbott Lawrence Lowell, who in 1919 appointed another HLS graduate and student of Langdell, Wallace B. Donham, to be dean of the fledgling Harvard Business School and charged him to establish the HLS model there. Over the course of the next century, each of these three major professional domains—law, medicine, and business, as well as the myriad of "semi" or "minor" professional fields springing from them[13]—adopted, insofar as they could, the system of academic meritocracy that Langdell designed and built between 1870 and 1895.

—◦◦◦—

Raised on a hardscrabble farm in a small New Hampshire town, Langdell watched his family and its fortunes disintegrate, and by his tenth birthday he was living in a "shattered home" in "a low, one-storied house on a small farm on the poorest soil of New Boston."[14] Through the unfailing support of his older sister, Hannah, and his own tenacious effort, he worked and scrimped his way through Phillips Exeter Academy, where he experienced the "dawn of the intellectual life."[15] Upon matriculating at Harvard College, however, he found a strange mixture of educational tedium and social revelry, exhausted his savings and those of his sister, and dropped out in his third semester. After an office education with distinguished attorneys in New Hampshire, he entered Harvard Law School and studied there for the unusually long period of three and a half years, departing at the age of twenty-eight.

Surviving and succeeding during those early years as one of the generation of "pauper scholars" in New England planted in Langdell the seeds of his interest in education and of the specific reforms that he would promote as dean of HLS. Above all, his deep commitment to a formal system of academic merit stemmed from the personal experience of advancing himself through self-discipline, adherence to the established rules, and academic achievement. He therefore left Harvard in

---

11. Eliot, Address 1904, 68. See Williston, *Life and Law: An Autobiography*, 206.

12. C. Eliot to Pritchett (13 Apr. 1915).

13. See Etzioni, *Semi-Professions and Their Organization*; Glazer, "Schools of the Minor Professions," 346–64.

14. M. Langdell, *Journey through the Years*, 55.

15. Langdell, quoted in Ames, "Christopher Columbus Langdell, 1826–1906," 469.

1855 with a profound commitment to the idea of academic meritocracy: that one advances personally and professionally by excelling within the established rules of the formal system of academic merit. Langdell's conviction that academic achievement should determine one's professional fortunes also entailed a commitment to "democracy,"[16] in the sense that there should exist equal opportunity to succeed at the bar. Consequently, academic merit, professional success, and democracy coincided, in Langdell's view.

His first dozen years practicing law in New York City confirmed this formulation. Impressed by his legal knowledge and diligence, leading attorneys recruited him to work on prominent cases, and he gained a reputation as a shrewd and effective attorney. By 1860 he had built a flourishing practice and was nearly overwhelmed by the press of routine and complex cases coming into his Wall Street office. Meanwhile, Langdell helped to establish a new role in litigation: crafting the extensive written brief that was beginning to displace the weight of oral argument in complicated cases arising from large and intricate commercial transactions. Some attorneys attributed to him "the highest legal ability in the country."[17]

But during the height of Boss Tweed's corruption in the late 1860s, Langdell became disaffected from the New York City bench and bar, abhorring the complicity of the judiciary and the eminent lawyers in that corruption. By the time he accepted a professorship at HLS in 1870, his experience in legal practice had strengthened and extended his view that professional success demands strong legal science acquired through rigorous legal education. He concluded that the just working of the legal system relies on the effectiveness and legitimacy of the legal profession, which depend on lawyers' expertise derived from their academic achievement in law school. Hence, the newly appointed Professor Langdell viewed academic merit as the means not only to elevate the legal profession, but also to safeguard the integrity of the legal system.

During the 1870s Langdell personally fulfilled his commitment to that vision by producing a body of distinguished scholarship that established him as one of the leading theorists of contracts in Anglo-American law. Notwithstanding his significant contributions to jurisprudence—indeed, partly because of his introduction of parsimonious abstraction—Langdell's scholarship has been pilloried in the standard historical account of American legal theory. Guided by the Procrustean interpretation of Oliver Wendell Holmes Jr., scholars have long associated Langdell with a sterile approach to legal study known as "legal formalism" or "classical legal thought." But Langdell's characteristic mode of reasoning in the field of contracts

16. A. Russell to Machen (1 May 1868).
17. Whiton to Lord (circa 1871).

and, more broadly, in jurisprudence is actually three-dimensional, exhibiting a comprehensive yet contradictory integration of induction from authority, deduction from principle, and analysis of justice and policy. The contradiction lies in Langdell's combining all three while claiming to emphasize logical consistency and to disregard justice and policy. Langdell's mode of reasoning therefore fits not Holmes's critique, but the "paradox of form and substance" that has been considered one of Holmes's greatest insights about judicial reasoning.[18]

Apart from his exemplary pursuit of scholarship in the original sources, Langdell also provided the HLS faculty with new models of pedagogy. As at other law schools and at medical schools, the HLS curriculum in 1870 amounted to a cycle of elementary courses, and the classroom teaching consisted of transmitting content to receptive students. In response, Langdell made three fundamental innovations implied by his vision of the law professor who cultivates academic achievement in students. First, he began sequencing coursework by developing a required foundational course and advanced electives in his teaching of civil procedure and other subjects. Second, he invented case method teaching and the genre of the casebook. Finally, consistent with the purposes of that inductive method of teaching, Langdell invented the form of examination requiring students to respond in writing to complex hypothetical problems concerning specific situations.

In order to institute his academic vision for legal education, Langdell needed a faculty who demonstrated and sustained their commitment to the academic meritocratic system by actively pursuing scholarship. But his experience at the bar convinced him that legal practice taught lawyers the arts of chicanery and self-promotion and ruined leaders of the bench and bar as potential faculty for law schools. He therefore decided to mold his own law professors by introducing the revolutionary principle of hiring faculty from among recent graduates based on their performance in professional school. Langdell's plan encountered fierce opposition from those who held to the traditional standard of hiring faculty who possessed outstanding professional experience and reputations. In fact, many believed that Langdell meant to establish himself as the model for a law professor, an approach that seemed arrogant, narrow-minded, and impractical. Consequently, during the contentious decades between 1870 and 1900, hiring decisions tipped in favor of Langdell's new principle only when financial considerations counterbalanced the traditional standard.

Meanwhile, Langdell's commitment to legal formalism—though contradicted by his own jurisprudence—led him to introduce an analogous approach to education. This educational formalism treated professional education as a system of

18. O. Holmes, "Common Carriers," 630.

rational, impersonal policies and rules guiding incremental progress that could be measured objectively. Langdell then dedicated this educational formalism to the goal of fostering academic merit, and proceeded to design and build his system of academic meritocracy. Consequently, HLS first and most fully embraced academic meritocracy among professional schools in the United States partly because the legal expertise of Langdell and his colleagues made them receptive to educational formalism. After adopting academic merit as the fundamental standard of success, Langdell and his allies gradually established systematic provisions to effect that standard.

That initial step of enshrining academic merit was vigorously contested because it required a fundamental shift in professional and educational ideology away from gentility. Gentlemanly culture did not comport with the relentless pursuit of academic merit either in style or in substance, and Langdell's revolution succeeded precisely because he did not act like a gentleman. With the help of President Eliot, Langdell crusaded relentlessly, ignoring widespread appeals to accommodation and moderation, and the seeming arrogance of this tenacity incited vehement opposition from students, faculty, alumni, and members of the bench and bar.

Nevertheless, between 1870 and 1886, Langdell introduced and established these elements of his "new system" of academic meritocracy: the admissions requirement of a bachelor's degree or its equivalent, the sequenced curriculum and its extension to three years, the inductive pedagogy of teaching from cases, the hurdle of written examinations in order for a student to continue or graduate, the written examination posing hypothetical problems, the program of study leading to academic honor, the independent career track for faculty, the transformation of the library from a textbook dispensary to a scholarly resource, and the national alumni association actively supporting the school.

In support of these new policies, Langdell and Eliot also introduced a new economic logic for professional education. Traditionally, professional school faculty maintained low standards and low tuition in order to attract students and obtain sufficient revenue to operate and earn some profit. Langdell and Eliot argued that education for and admission to a "liberal profession" should transcend the commercial pressures of the marketplace, while they also maintained, paradoxically, that a professional school devoted to academic merit would prosper. Higher standards would produce better graduates who would be more marketable, making the school more attractive to prospective students and elevating the standards in the profession.

This institutional system of academic meritocracy in professional education was established during Langdell's deanship by 1886. Yet, he concurrently began to violate its basic premises by elevating his own academic specialty of equity jurisprudence to the highest rank of academic honor. His insistence that the best students take his courses was not without academic justification, for he was the most demanding professor. Nevertheless, identifying his own specialty with academic honor introduced an element of self-interest that belied the formalistic commitment to determine academic merit by applying objective standards through neutral, impersonal policies.

By 1890 Langdell's "new system" had triumphed. HLS was exceeding all expectations in raising academic standards, attracting growing numbers of well-qualified students, and producing well-trained graduates desired by leading firms. During the 1890s the system of academic meritocracy began to proliferate across the nation, and students crowded into HLS, prompting efforts by the dean and the faculty to reduce enrollment, restrict admissions, and distinguish among applicants' bachelor degrees. Though evidence of the success of Langdell's system, these efforts occasioned its betrayal, by incorporating invidious discrimination.

Despite its universalist principle, the practice of educational formalism was "gravely unjust,"[19] because the meritocrats explicitly categorized certain people—particularly women and graduates of Catholic colleges—apart from the rest of the applicants and then treated those categories invidiously as a matter of policy. The meritocrats believed that they had not violated formal standards of academic merit because, according to them, the separate categories deserved distinctive treatment. Nevertheless, in these two cases, all the leading meritocrats contributed to embedding categorical discrimination in the academic meritocracy from its inception. Ironically, the "just" system[20] of academic meritocracy discriminated against certain categories of people during the very decade when the triumph of the system should have, in principle, opened the door to admit them.

Langdell retired as dean in 1895 and as a professor in 1900. Although that "poor, old . . . white-whiskers" seemed pathetic or eccentric to many observers,[21] he continued studying and produced the most prominent and controversial writings of his career. In fact, he addressed two of the most significant, and abiding, constitutional questions of the following century: whether the U.S. Constitution follows the flag to all lands acquired by the United States, and whether corporate mergers that reduce competition violate the Sherman Anti-Trust Act (1890).

Though Langdell was influential in the public, political, and juridical debates over these significant questions of policy, his enduring legacy lies in his system of academic meritocracy that proliferated throughout American professional edu-

---

19. J. Havens Richards to Charles W. Eliot (3 Aug. 1893), in Mahoney, Complete Primary Source, 23.

20. Jagemann to Eliot (6 Nov. 1899).

21. Frankfurter to Frank (18 Dec. 1933).

cation over the course of the twentieth century. Indeed, it is no exaggeration to say that every professional school in the United States since the mid-twentieth century has felt the impress of the system that Langdell invented and instituted between 1870 and 1886.

In recounting his life, this biography attempts to analyze how Langdell's system commenced, triumphed, and was betrayed. Inasmuch as "Mr. Emerson says that history is biography,"[22] this book seeks to explain the inception of modern professional education in the United States.

22. C. Eliot, Inaugural Address 1869, 5.

CHAPTER ONE

Boyhood and Youth, 1826–1854

In Langdell's youth lie the origins of his interest in education and the specific reforms in professional education that he advanced as dean of HLS. His encounters with John Locke's *Education* at Phillips Exeter Academy, with taxonomy and specimens in the natural history classes of Asa Gray and Louis Agassiz, with "office" education in a law firm, with the degree requirements at Harvard Divinity School, with other law students in table talk, and with eleemosynary aid for needy students contributed to principles and policies that he later instituted in professional education. Above all, his firm commitment to a formal system of academic merit originated in the experience of practicing self-discipline, following the established rules, and achieving academically. By this route, he gradually elevated himself from an impoverished and traumatic childhood to the threshold of the elite in the legal profession.

Boyhood, 1826–45

In the two decades after arriving in New Boston in 1792, John Langdell grew into a thrifty, industrious young man, and by 1814 had built a farm comprising three acres in pasture and tillage, two oxen, and twenty acres of unimproved land. Valued at $140 amid estates ranging in value from $25 to $975, the farm was modest, but certainly respectable for a twenty-three-year-old man without a father or an inheritance.[1] Meanwhile, he met Lydia Beard, whose "Scots-Irish" forebears had emigrated from northern Ireland in the 1760s and found their way to New Boston, where she was born in 1793. In 1820 Lydia and John were married and had their first child, a son. The valuation of the farm had increased to $904, including three acres of tillage and pasture, six large livestock, and thirty-four acres of unimproved

1. Data above and below about Langdell's family finances are drawn from M. Langdell, *Journey through the Years*, 7–25, 55–60, 79; New Boston, "Family Records" (1791–1860), 2:1–50; Johnston and Savoy, *Statistical Records, Town of New Boston*, appendix A; New Boston, Tax Inventory, north side for 1814, 109; for 1819, 236; for 1824, 350; for 1826 and 1828, s.v. "Langdell, John."

land.[2] Over the next fifteen years, the family's labors steadily improved the farm. In 1824 a daughter, Hannah, was born, and the farm was taxed at a value of $1,088. In 1826 the oldest boy was doubtlessly helping with chores, while the farm had grown to $1,298 in valuation. On 22 May 1826, a second son was born and named Christopher Columbus Langdell.

Why Lydia and John selected this name is a mystery. It did not fit the four naming traditions of New England families up to 1850: the English tradition yielding such names as John, Robert, Richard, or Henry; the Puritan-biblical practice of drawing names from the Old Testament; the kinship pattern of naming after parents or grandparents; or the minor tradition of choosing classical names from antiquity. In fact, due to their "papist" associations, neither "Christopher" nor "Christopher Columbus" appear in any tabulations of New England naming patterns prior to 1850. Nor do the names appear elsewhere in the Langdell family tree. Given the strength of Yankee tradition in New Hampshire towns and the seriousness devoted to naming children, especially older boys, the name of "Christopher Columbus Langdell" was remarkably unorthodox.[3] His parents' nonconformity and the example of his namesake set Chris, as the boy was known to townspeople, on a course to challenge convention.

In breaking with tradition, John and Lydia were perhaps emboldened by the auspicious increase in their family, their estate, and their social status. In 1828 John assumed his first role in town government by serving on the committee that assigned families to school districts. His property value rose to $1,480, near the median valuation in the town. Also in that year Lydia gave birth to a third son. Then, in 1829 misfortune began to envelop the Langdells. The third son died due to "cancer of the eye," perhaps foreshadowing the severe problem that Chris would have with his own vision. The value of John's property plummeted to $440, one-quarter of its previous value, and included no land and only one horse and one cow. The precipitous decline cannot be explained by a personal tragedy or a natural disaster, because John did not petition the town meetings for an abatement from taxes or for compensation—as did other residents, who cited fire, sickness, or support of an indigent neighbor.[4] He may have defaulted on a debt or mortgage, since tax records show that he had no cash savings to cover a bad agricultural year.

2. *New Hampshire Gazette*, 20 Apr. 1820; S. Atwood to Batchelder (8 Aug. 1906); Allen to Town Clerk, New Boston (28 July 1924). The name of the oldest boy is not recorded.

3. D. Smith, "Child-Naming Practices," 543–44; D. Smith, "Continuity and Discontinuity in Puritan Naming," 67–91; Dumas, "Naming of Children in New England," 199, 202–3; Main, "Naming Children in Early New England," 1–27; M. Langdell, *Journey through the Years*, 74–80.

4. Quotation is from New Boston, Town Records, Third Book, 64. See New Boston, Tax Inventory, north side for 1829, s.v. "Langdell, John"; Minutes of Town meetings of 11 Mar. 1829 and 15 Mar. 1830 in New Boston, Town Records, Third Book.

In 1830 the last child—a daughter named Mary Ann—was born, and the financial situation on the farm did not improve. In the following year, likely with the help of the oldest son and seven-year-old Hannah, the family tilled half an acre and added a few sheep. In 1832 and 1833 their small estate continued to grow, and the valuation climbed to $980. But this financial recovery was no less precarious than the original prosperity had been, and the sudden death of Lydia in 1833 brought the recovery to a halt. John managed to work the farm for a few more years as the valuation declined to about $600.[5]

Then, the oldest son, who was perhaps thirteen years old and likely felt the brunt of his mother's absence as his father became embittered, fled from home and drowned soon after. Unable to cope with the farm and three young children, John broke up the home in 1836 and sent nine-year-old Hannah to live with relatives in Massachusetts, and seven-year-old Chris and three-year-old Mary Ann to different families in New Hampshire. By 1839 John had lost all his property, livestock, and taxable possessions and became "more and more a recluse."[6] No records remain for assessing the effect of these events on the two sisters, but there are indications of the harmful impact on the seven-year-old boy.

Throughout the remainder of his life, Chris avoided addressing the death of any longtime friend or colleague—even if the deceased had been one of his closest friends (William Gibbons in 1855 or Theodore Tebbets in 1863), or when he was invited to provide a memorial statement for his college roommate and a published excuse had to be conjured in order to explain his refusal (Chauncey Wright in 1875),[7] or when it seemed incumbent on his position as dean of HLS to eulogize a colleague (Charles F. Dunbar in 1900 or James B. Thayer in 1902). Langdell apparently wrote only one such eulogy,[8] and his reluctance to memorialize friends or colleagues whom he had known for years suggests that the deaths of his mother and brothers had severely wounded him.

In addition, several observers describe his mature relations with his wife and closest adult friends as of a "tender, almost feminine nature."[9] Such terms were highly unusual to apply publicly to a distinguished man in the Victorian era, particularly a law professor from Harvard University, which cultivated an ethic of

5. New Boston, "Register of Interment," 21; New Boston, Tax Inventory, north side for 1830–36, s.v. "Langdell, John"; New Boston, "Family Records" (1791–1860), 2:412.

6. S. Atwood to Batchelder (8 Aug. 1906). See Allen to Town Clerk, New Boston (28 July 1924); M. Langdell, *Journey through the Years*, 55. Cf. Ames, "Christopher Columbus Langdell, 1826–1906," 466.

7. J. Thayer, *Letters of Chauncey Wright*, 23.

8. Langdell, Memorial for George Arnold (circa Dec. 1893).

9. Quotation is from Batchelder, "Christopher C. Langdell," 442. See Ames, "Christopher Columbus Langdell, 1826–1906," 488; C. Eliot, "Langdell," 524.

manhood.[10] Hence, Langdell may still have been searching for the intimacy lost through the death of his mother and the disintegration of his family.

Finally, these losses may have contributed to his lifelong reclusiveness, for he rarely entertained guests or visited others. Friendships brought the prospect of separation and of reliving the searing 1830s. His relationship to his hometown demonstrates the tension between insularity and loneliness in his life. Beginning in 1895, the townspeople of New Boston published a pamphlet describing their annual reunion, an event when former residents returned each summer to renew acquaintances. Both his sister, Hannah, and his wife, Margaret, observed that, to the end of his life, Langdell eagerly requested that each pamphlet be read to him "from the first to the last page." But he never agreed to attend the reunion, sending his regrets each year, even when the townspeople asked him to come and address them.[11] He enjoyed the reunion vicariously in print, but would not witness the reuniting and the separating in the place where he had lost his family.

Though wounded by the loss of his mother and siblings, Chris received little comfort from his father, who "gave his boys nothing but took all he could from them." Chris nevertheless exhibited an extraordinary sense of filial obligation and personal generosity, supporting his father throughout his life and loaning and giving money to friends, relatives, and acquaintances in need.[12] In 1840 fourteen-year-old Chris returned home to help his father, and over the next four years the farm expanded to twenty acres plus livestock, while the valuation rose to $450.[13] Meanwhile, Chris nurtured the ambition to continue his education.

Both he and Hannah displayed the interest in education that characterized his mother's family. His uncle, Jesse Beard, was a prominent educator who had taught school and served on the school committee for over twenty years.[14] During the 1830s Chris and Hannah attended the district schools in New Boston and, perhaps, an academy in Hancock, New Hampshire. According to Hannah, her brother "was not precocious, but studious and ambitious"; and in about 1842 sixteen-year-old Chris "opened his heart to me for the first time, and it was also the first time he had made known his aspirations to any human being. He told me that he had a very strong desire for a college education, but he did not see how it could be

10. Townsend, *Manhood at Harvard*, 80–158.

11. Quotation is from M. E. Huson to F. A. Atwood (1908), quoted in F. Atwood, *Old Folks' Day*, 22. See also 11–12; S. Atwood to Batchelder (8 Aug. 1906).

12. Quotation is from S. Atwood to Batchelder (8 Aug. 1906). See Langdell, Check Ledger 1871–75; Webb to Langdell (20 Mar. 1881).

13. New Boston, Tax Inventory, north side for 1844, s.v. "Langdell, John."

14. Cogswell, *History of New Boston*, 381.

accomplished." Hannah resolved to help and left Massachusetts to join Chris in teaching school in New Boston and neighboring towns.[15]

As in most district schools, Chris and Hannah were plagued by uncooperative students and parents, unsuitable textbooks, and dilapidated facilities.[16] But an unexpected benefit came when the teachers in New Boston were joined by David Cross, who had graduated from Dartmouth College in 1841 and from HLS in 1843. To support himself while establishing his law practice, Cross began teaching school in New Boston in 1843 and imparted to Chris the ideas to enter law and to approach it as a "learned profession," that is, by earning a college degree and a law degree. The advice and example of Cross inspired Chris to save more money, so he and Hannah began working in the Manchester mills, and Chris applied to Phillips Exeter Academy in order to prepare himself for college.[17]

Beyond the personal influence of Cross, larger social and economic forces induced Chris to take these two steps on a path followed by many New England boys of his generation. In the second quarter of the nineteenth century, moving from farm to factory was a common step for Yankee youths seeking to advance their prospects.[18] A further step for the most ambitious was to join the "pauper scholars" who attended New England colleges. Because the supply of good land was becoming exhausted and because fathers preferred to keep the family estate entire by bequeathing it to one or two eldest sons, the younger boys in New England farming families expected no inheritance and began flocking to colleges in the 1820s and 1830s as a means to advance themselves. Meanwhile, the traditional sources of philanthropy could not support this influx of poor students, many of whom were over the age of twenty, so they had to scrimp, work, and borrow in order to sustain themselves. This demographic development radically changed the culture at smaller, provincial New England colleges.[19] All these social and economic forces influenced Chris Langdell, the exemplar of the pauper scholar, but deeply personal characteristics also played a role because he was aiming for Harvard, the college least accessible or congenial to pauper scholars.

15. Quotations are from Ames, "Christopher Columbus Langdell, 1826–1906," 466–67. See J. Smith, "Christopher Columbus Langdell," 27; Cogswell, *History of New Boston*, 170.

16. Weare, N.H., School Committee, *Report 1853–54*, 7. See New Boston School Committee, *Reports* (1850s).

17. F. Atwood, *Old Folks' Day*, 6; Taggart, "David Cross," 434–43; Ames, "Christopher Columbus Langdell, 1826–1906," 468; S. Atwood to Batchelder (8 Aug. 1906). On the concept of "learned profession," see Kimball, *True Professional Ideal*, 99–102.

18. Thernstrom, *Poverty and Progress*, 59. See Prude, "Social System of Early New England Textile Mills," 90–127.

19. Allmendinger, *Paupers and Scholars*, 3–4, 8–22, 28–29, 41, 45.

Phillips Exeter Academy, 1845–48

In April 1845 eighteen-year-old Christopher matriculated at Phillips Exeter Academy in Exeter, New Hampshire, one member of a class of twenty-five students who ranged in age from eleven to twenty-three. To remain enrolled, Christopher needed to win one of the scholarships awarded in July, since he had been sending money to his father and had not saved enough to pay his own way. During that spring he adapted well to Academy life, and in the beginning of July was nominated to enter the Golden Branch Literary Society, whose members all ranked academically in the top fifth of the student body.[20]

One week later, however, he learned that his scholarship application had been denied because he was deficient in preparation and "slow of speech and hesitant in manner."[21] Stemming from the limitations and troubles of his background, this failure "was probably the keenest disappointment of his life. Heartbroken, he sat down upon the steps of the Academy building and burst into tears."[22] He was losing not only the opportunity for an education but also the companionship of his first group of like-minded peers: the members of the Golden Branch Literary Society. However, both his sisters, Hannah and Mary Ann, provided reassurance and financial help that enabled Christopher to remain at the Academy while living frugally, working menial jobs, and staffing the library. Excelling academically throughout the year, he won a scholarship in the following July, and his continued enrollment was assured.

The three-year preparatory course at Exeter was thoroughly classical, required, and cumulative. The three terms of the first year consisted entirely of Latin grammar and literature; at the beginning of the second year, Greek was added to the Latin studies. In the last term of the second year, students took mathematics in addition to Greek and Latin. The final term of the third year was augmented by a brief course in geography.[23] Any exposure to additional subjects came from a student's own initiative, which the Golden Branch Society was dedicated to support. This student literary society maintained an extensive library for its members, who were expected to write essays on controversial and timely questions and debate their views at meetings.[24]

20. Phillips Exeter Academy Dean of Students, *Register 1830–54*. The following account draws on Golden Branch Society, Records 1841–50.

21. Quotation is from F. Atwood, *Old Folks' Day*, 18. Cf. Starks, "Christopher Columbus Langdell."

22. Ames, "Christopher Columbus Langdell, 1826–1906," 468.

23. Phillips Exeter Academy, *Catalog 1847–8*, 7–8.

24. Shapiro, "'Discovered Places': A History of the Academy Library," 3–4.

From the time of his election as a member in September 1845, the Golden Branch Society became the focus of Christopher's attention outside of the classroom. As a novitiate, he waited until February 1846 for the opportunity to present his first argument, in response to the question: "Is Oregon worth a war?" Throughout the spring, Christopher was active in making proposals and nominations, and the Society elected him vice president at the meeting in May 1846 when Charles Dunbar and Theodore Tebbets were elected members.

Dunbar and Langdell would interact with each other as students and colleagues at Harvard for the next half-century, but it was Tebbets who became Christopher's most consistent friend during the formative two decades when he made the transition from Manchester mill hand to Wall Street lawyer. Though Tebbets was five years younger, their lives had taken similar turns. Born in 1831 and raised in a small New Hampshire town, Tebbets was thirteen years old when his father died and the family went bankrupt. Intent on becoming a lawyer, he entered Exeter in September 1845 and supported himself by means of a scholarship, menial jobs, and scrupulous thrift.[25] Their circumstances and studious natures drew Christopher and Theodore together while participating in the Golden Branch Society.

In June 1846, chairing the meeting in the absence of the president, Christopher assigned himself to debate on the Rousseauean question: "Does man possess a greater capacity for happiness in a civilized, than in an uncivilized, state?" Over the summer he examined and certified the records of the Society's secretary and librarian. In January 1847 he debated the question: "Is a protective tariff beneficial?", and his criticism of another member's essay at a subsequent meeting stimulated "a long and very interesting discussion." In March 1847 Christopher arranged for the Society to suspend its normal format and hold a moot court on a case known as the "Manchester Murder." He served as attorney general, Tebbets as solicitor, and Dunbar as clerk.[26] The moot court must have succeeded because Christopher was elected president of the Society at the following meeting.

Assuming office in May 1847, President Langdell "delivered a very fine address to which the members listened with earnest and due attention." In September 1847, after the assigned members debated the question: "Is the institution of slavery a greater evil to the U.S. than the use of alcohol?" President Langdell added "some very interesting remarks" that were not recorded. In his final act as president in December 1847, Christopher sought to rectify abuse of the library by moving that

25. Towne, *Memorial of Rev. Theodore Tebbets*, 12, 9–10. See "Theodore Tebbets," Harvard College Class of 1851, Class Book, 168–69.

26. Minutes of 6 June 1846, 9 and 23 Jan. 1847, 6 and 20 Mar. 1847, Golden Branch Society, Records, 1841–50.

delinquent borrowers have their privileges suspended. The motion was approved, and a new president was then elected.[27]

Access to the library was one of the greatest benefits of membership in Golden Branch, and Christopher's voracious appetite for study was already prompting Lincolnesque anecdotes of him sawing wood and reading at the same time.[28] The Golden Branch records reveal that, among the 115 students who borrowed books during the two years of Langdell's membership, he borrowed more than all but four of those students, one of whom was his friend Tebbets. For outside reading, Langdell most often chose English, American, and French poetry, plays, and novels. His second preference was for modern history or biography, including John Campbell's *Lives of the Lord Chancellors and Chief Justices of England* and the *Life of William Wirt*. The latter typified the antebellum genre of biographies that described orphan boys who overcame hardship to achieve honor, fame, and wealth through a career in the law.[29] Apart from those two books, however, Langdell's reading was not oriented toward legal or political issues. His other selections were drawn from Greek or Latin history or grammar, natural history, theology, and philosophy, which consisted of repeated borrowings of Ralph Waldo Emerson's *Essays*, Isaac Watts's *Improvement of the Mind*, and Francis Bacon's *Essays*.[30]

Christopher's reading thus exhibited broad interests, with a preference for belles lettres. His modest foray into the well-known logical works of Watts was typical of the day. The selection of Bacon's *Essays* is intriguing in view of Langdell's innovation of inductive case method teaching, but the choice of Bacon was certainly conventional. The surprising selection was *Some Thoughts Concerning Education* by John Locke, which Langdell borrowed in the fall of 1847.[31]

Locke's *Education* is noteworthy for a number of reasons. Though famous for his political philosophy, Locke expressed those views in other writings that

27. Minutes of 3 Apr. and 8 May 1847, 25 Sept. and 4 Dec. 1847, Golden Branch Society, Records, 1841–50. The volume containing Langdell's address is missing from Golden Branch records in the Academy Archives.

28. Ames, "Christopher Columbus Langdell, 1826–1906," 470; *Centennial History of the Harvard Law School*, 225.

29. This life of William Wirt apparently refers to the appendix written by Peter H. Cruse for the tenth edition of Wirt's *Letters of the British Spy* (1832). On this genre, see Bloomfield, *American Lawyers*, 163–90.

30. Langdell borrowed 157 books in total: 68 volumes of poetry, plays, and novels, 47 of modern history or biography, 22 in Greek or Latin history or grammar, 9 in natural history, 7 in philosophy, and 3 in theology. Golden Branch Society, Librarian's Book [1846–49]. Multivolume sets were counted as one book, as was the same book being borrowed again at a different time. My thanks to Zachary K. Kimball for tabulating the Golden Branch records in the Phillips Exeter Academy Library.

31. Golden Branch Society, *Librarian's Book* [1846–49], s.v. "Langdell, C. C.," fourth term Book, #527. The title is listed as *Some Thoughts About Education*.

Christopher did not borrow. Instead, he selected a treatise obviously intended for someone with a special interest in education. Unlike Jean-Jacques Rousseau's *Émile* or Plato's *Republic*, Locke's *Education* has little appeal for someone without a particular, even professional, interest in education, and does not appear commonly in catalogs of antebellum academies or colleges, notwithstanding its prominence in the previous century.[32]

Christopher's unusual choice of reading, coupled with the activities of the Beard family and his own experience as a school teacher, suggests that by this point Christopher was already developing a special interest in education. That incipient interest was then informed by Locke's *Education*, which expressed the central tenets that Langdell later instantiated in his case method teaching:[33] encourage students' autonomy, challenge them with advanced texts, work from the particular to the general, aim at imparting not content but a method of learning. Above all, Langdell adopted from Locke the cardinal recommendation to present students with original sources rather than abstract rules: "'The study... of the original text can never be sufficiently recommended. It is the shortest, surest, and most agreeable way to all sorts of learning. Draw from the springhead, and take not things at secondhand. Let the writings of the great masters be never laid aside; ... make it your business to so thoroughly understand them in their full extent and all their circumstances; acquaint yourself fully with the principles of the original authors; bring them to consistency, and then do you yourself make your deductions.'"[34]

During the academic year 1847–48 Christopher finished the three-year course of study at Exeter. Near the beginning of that final year at the academy, his younger sister, Mary Ann, died at the age of seventeen,[35] and his family was effectively reduced to his older sister, Hannah. The support of the community at Exeter therefore played a significant role, providing a collegial and intellectual home such as he had never known and would never know again. "To the end of his life, he retained vivid recollections of his life at Exeter, and a strong interest in the place and the school. Asked later in life what it was that he felt he owed to Exeter, he

32. After its original publication in 1693, Locke produced four more editions of *Some Thoughts Concerning Education*, the last of which was published posthumously in 1705. Axtell, *Educational Writings of John Locke*, 3. I have found no reference to the work in catalogs of antebellum academies and colleges, nor is it cited as a textbook in G. Brown, *Consent of the Governed*, 36, 15–106.

33. At a loss for an explanation, Harvard president Eliot later attributed Langdell's innovative pedagogy to "the educational theories or practices of Froebel, Pestalozzi, Seguin, and Montessori," with whom, however, Langdell "had no acquaintance," Eliot admitted. C. Eliot, "Langdell," 523.

34. Locke, *Some Thoughts Concerning Education*, §195. See also 71–76, 148, 163–69, 187–89, 195–98. Locke was quoting and endorsing the view of Jean de la Bruyère (1645–96), in *Les caractères, ou les moeurs de ce siècle* (1688).

35. New Boston, "Register of Interment," 21.

said, 'I was a boy. I had lived on a farm and as a mill hand at Manchester. I went to Exeter'—and then, after a pause, added with much feeling—'Exeter was to me the dawn of the intellectual life.'"[36]

Completion of the course at Exeter virtually entailed admission to Harvard College, and that was Christopher's next destination. In the summer of 1848 he likely returned for a final time to New Boston and helped his father on the farm, which recovered in the late 1840s, then slumped during the 1850s to thirty-six acres and a horse, assessed at about $500. Christopher was still trying to save money for his education, but the farm was a constant drain, forcing him, even with a scholarship, to scrape his way through Exeter by working menial jobs, scrimping on food, and sharing a bare room.[37] He received nothing from his father, and the best that he could hope for was to be left alone.

Harvard College, 1848–49

In August 1848 Langdell matriculated into the class of 1851 at Harvard College as a twenty-two-year-old "fresh-sophomore," a first-year student with second-year standing. In view of his poverty, Langdell's decision to enter college is highly significant because he was more than qualified to go directly to law school. Only a fraction of law students in the second quarter of the nineteenth century had earned a college degree. Langdell's three years at Exeter had prepared him better than most students at even the best law schools, which generally comprised only one or two professors and a few dozen students.[38]

That Langdell, older and poorer than nearly all his Harvard classmates, was willing to postpone his vocational goal indicates the enormous value he placed on a college education and the ideal of "a learned and liberal profession of the highest grade."[39] In fact, the requirement of a college degree—particularly a liberal arts degree—for admission to law school was to become a hallmark of Langdell's later reforms in professional education. It was the reform that he most obstinately advocated, that was most deeply resisted, and that required more than twenty

36. Ames, "Christopher Columbus Langdell, 1826–1906," 469. Langdell later served on the Committee to raise money to build the Third Academy Building after the Second Academy Building burned. Starks, "Christopher Columbus Langdell." He and his wife made Exeter the major institutional beneficiary in their wills.

37. Batchelder, "Christopher C. Langdell," 438; New Boston, Tax Inventory, [circa 1846–63].

38. Stevens, *Law School: Legal Education in America*, 20–36. In 1898 it was estimated that less than 20 percent of students in law school had earned a bachelor's degree, and the estimate overlooked proprietary schools and law students reading in offices. The comprehensive figure probably did not exceed 5 percent. McIntyre, "Percentage of College-Bred Men in the Medical Profession," 682; Baldwin, "Readjustment of the Collegiate to the Professional Course," 1–23; Ames, Annual Report 1897–98, 160.

39. Langdell, Annual Report 1876–77, 89.

years to see instituted at HLS, the first law school in the country to do so. Given his commitment, as well as his sacrifices, Langdell's three semesters at Harvard College were bittersweet.

The beginning was auspicious. Accompanying him to Harvard as a fresh-sophomore was his friend, seventeen-year-old Theodore Tebbets, with whom he shared a room in Massachusetts Hall. Charles Dunbar, former comrade in the Golden Branch Society, was also a member of the class of 1851, having entered as a true freshman in the previous year. Other Harvard classmates whom Langdell later encountered in law school and in professional life included George Shattuck, James Carter, Nicholas St. John Green, James Thayer, and Joseph Choate, as well as those who were not lawyers, Chauncey Wright and Ephraim Gurney. Finally, there was Langdell's classmate at Harvard College and at HLS: Jason Gorham.

Gorham kept a detailed journal covering the fifteen months that Langdell attended college, and the differences between him and the pauper scholar are revealing. Entering Harvard in August 1847 as the sixteen-year-old son of a well-heeled lawyer from western Massachusetts, Gorham graduated from Harvard College in 1851 and matriculated at HLS in 1852. Viewing law as a livelihood rather than a field of study, Gorham attended HLS for only one year and completed his legal education by reading in a law office before entering his father's practice.[40]

The college that Gorham and Langdell attended in fall 1848 was one of the largest in the country, comprising 279 undergraduates, 19 theological students, 96 law students, 139 medical students, and 22 special students and resident graduates. A faculty of ten, not including President Edward Everett, oversaw the undergraduate curriculum, which, though among the most progressive in the country, still comprised mainly classical letters and restricted "elective studies" to juniors and seniors, allowing little choice in practice even there. The prescribed curriculum for Langdell's sophomore class consisted of Greek, Latin, Rhetoric, Mathematics, Modern Languages, Philosophy (of Mind), History (of England), and Natural History.[41]

As in other antebellum colleges, the standard teaching method at Harvard was not the lecture[42] but the recitation, later described by President Eliot in these words:

40. Gorham, Diary (31 Oct. 1848); Gorham Biographical File.

41. Harvard University, *Catalog 1848–49*. See Potts, "Curriculum and Enrollment," 41.

42. After the regular subjects were listed, the use of lecturing was specifically noted, by way of exception, in the form of a separate list of "courses of lectures." Harvard University, *Catalog 1848–49*, 43–44. This was the conventional format in nineteenth-century collegiate catalogs because the lecture was regarded as a pedagogy for more mature minds, requiring greater powers of concentration and analysis. See Kiddle and Schem, *Cyclopaedia of Education*, s.v. "lectures"; Seeley and Petticrew, *Seeley's Question Book*, 386–87; Suzzallo, "Lecture Method," 671.

The university teacher at the end of the hour gave out a lesson in a text-book—so many pages—and expected his class to recite that lesson to him at the next meeting. Fifteen or twenty students [each individually reciting a separate section] would take part in this recitation, which was in the main an exercise of the memory. The student recited a bit of the book; the teacher ordinarily made no comment whatever on a good recitation, confining himself to efforts to extract some fragments of the text from the incompetent or neglectful members of the class. The good students could, of course, derive no profit whatever from such an exercise, except practice in making a brief statement from memory before the class. The poor students made public exhibition of their insufficiency; but were seldom either mortified or stimulated thereby, for experience taught them that the consequences of habitual failure in recitations were not serious ... if they were regular in attendance on prescribed exercises, both secular and religious.[43]

The antebellum recitation therefore aimed to transmit to students the content determined by the professor, who was the expert and authority. In addition, students did not investigate the content because inquiry ran in one direction: the professor questioned and the student answered. Furthermore, the recitation was not a corporate event but a series of individual events. Students did not address each other or each other's responses.

Gorham conveyed the practical import of the recitation for the college education that Langdell experienced in 1848. Daily preparation of a small amount of material in each subject was necessary for success. Because the tedium of the routine often led students to neglect their lessons and because not every student could be quizzed in every class period, recitations became a cat-and-mouse game in which the professor tried to catch the unprepared. When a student escaped, he rejoiced: "I was not taken up today much to my satisfaction for I should have deaded if I had been." When obliged to say "unprepared," the student despaired, unless the professor "excused me afterward."[44] In either the case, the instructor's authority was reaffirmed.

To encourage students to prepare, some professors tried to keep students guessing when and what they would be asked: "I did not expect to be taken up in Latin today; or [if so] ..., I supposed of course that it would be on the review, as I was taken up on the advance last Friday; [but I was asked about new material] and therefore did not make a very good recitation." Such capriciousness naturally incited resentment, and students often became distrustful, antagonistic, and unruly,

---

43. C. Eliot, "Methods of Instruction," 174–75.
44. Gorham, Diary (2 Mar. and 11 May 1849).

as in Gorham's botany classes conducted by the distinguished botanist Asa Gray.[45] In classes where instructors maintained strict discipline and grading prevailed, students often resorted to cheating. "This afternoon I wrote my Greek exercise or, rather, I copied little Brown's who copied his from a copy of the original" found in the library, recorded Gorham. On another evening, "I went over to Goodwin's room and got him to permit me to copy his exercise. I found Mead there upon the same errand also. I got Brown's exercise also, and between the two I rather think I had a pretty good one."[46]

This out-of-class deceit inevitably appeared within the classroom: "Recited in history and mathematics. I did not know anything about the problem, but Towle did it upon a paper and then thr[ew] it to me, and I copied it from that... and... immediately departed, fearing lest [the professor] should... ask me some questions concerning the manner of obtaining the result, of which important fact I had not the slightest idea."[47] Such collaborative cheating became routine in some situations: "The way that I and, in fact, by far the greater part of the class [prepare for botany], is to read their lesson over once and get [the answer] in the recitation room. The seats are so formed as to render this operation perfectly safe; and as we can tell about on what part we shall be taken, we can get that part perfectly and thus make a [high mark]."[48]

It is striking that Gorham, who sought to earn good grades, presents this behavior as widespread and never expresses any reservations about it. Langdell had certainly encountered the recitation at Exeter, yet the comparative youth of the students and the fact that the subject matter—classical grammar—lent itself to routinization discouraged the kinds of behaviors that occurred in Cambridge. To the notoriously straitlaced Langdell, whose "mind recoiled from temporizing or avoiding the real issue,"[49] it must have seemed that the Harvard recitation violated every precept in Locke's *Education*. Indeed, American colleges in the 1840s were practicing what Locke called "the vulgar method of grammar schools," requiring students "to learn by heart great parcels of the authors which are taught them; wherein I can discover no advantage at all."[50]

The educational lesson that Langdell drew from the Harvard College classrooms in the 1840s was, therefore, what to avoid. The rack of recitation twisted the dialogue of professors and students away from genuine communication. The

45. Gorham, Diary (8, 16, 25, 30, 31 May, 28 Sept. 1848).
46. Gorham, Diary (27 Oct. and 24 Nov. 1848).
47. Gorham, Diary (20 Mar. 1849).
48. Gorham, Diary (23 May 1848).
49. Fessenden, "Rebirth of the Harvard Law School," 505. See Ames, "Christopher Columbus Langdell, 1826–1906," 472; C. Eliot, "Langdell," 524.
50. Locke, *Some Thoughts Concerning Education*, §175.

questions were not real questions because the professors knew the answers, and the answers were not real answers because the student was only transmitting the view from another source, sometimes his neighbor. Beyond that, the great irony of the recitation is revealed in Gorham's philosophy class: "Dr. Walker announced a theory which was new and startling today.... I should have liked to have asked how it could be proved, but there was not time."[51] The recitation provided no time for genuine questions, particularly from the student to the professor.

In spring semester 1849 the seventy sophomores in Langdell's class were enrolled in nine subjects. As suggested by the widespread cheating and subterfuge, many students worried about their grades, even though they had little bearing on students' professional prospects. Gorham certainly attended to his grades, noting whether a professor "marked me justly (which by the way I don't believe he did)." At the beginning of each month, Gorham went to the president's house to obtain his grades for the previous month, and appealed to the president (unsuccessfully) when he felt a professor had been unfair and (successfully) when a behavioral infraction had caused him to be graded down.[52]

Langdell excelled academically. His contemporaries report that "he ranked second in his class" and "was the best scholar in his class,"[53] a judgment confirmed by the "aggregate marks" for Langdell and selected classmates during spring semester 1849, presented in table 1. His performance for this semester distinctly outranked those of Nicholas Green, who taught at HLS in the early 1870s, and Dunbar, who later served as the first dean of the Faculty of Arts and Sciences at Harvard. Langdell ranked no lower than fifth overall, and, apart from rhetoric, his general rank was near the highest in the class. He thus distinguished himself by excelling within the formal system of academic evaluation across a broad range of subjects.

Langdell's college studies also provided the source of often quoted analogies that he later made between law and natural science.[54] In particular, his taxonomic analogies to natural history, botany, and zoology originated in his natural history course during the academic year 1848–49. The first half of this course was conducted by the botanist Gray, who employed *The Botanical Textbook for Colleges, Schools, and Private Students* (1842), which he had written specifically for his teaching at Harvard. Although he taught primarily through lectures and recita-

---

51. Gorham, Diary (7 Mar. 1849).

52. Quotation is from: Gorham, Diary (31 May 1848). See Gorham, Diary (11 May, 5 Oct., 9 Nov., 12 Nov., 11 Dec. 1848).

53. Quotations are, respectively, from: Ames, "Christopher Columbus Langdell, 1826–1906," 469; J. Thayer, *Letters of Chauncey Wright*, 23.

54. See appendix 2.

TABLE 1   "Aggregate Marks" for Langdell and Selected Classmates during
Spring Semester 1849

Subject		Highest Mark	Langdell	Tebbets	Shattuck	Dunbar	N. Green
Mathematics	Score	761	728	486	457	367	336
	Rank		3rd				
Greek	Score	807	549	570	479	530	509
	Rank		20th				
Rhetoric	Score	656	181	245	262	252	221
	Rank		42nd				
Elocution	Score	140	88	65	128	70	26
	Rank		9th				
Philosophy	Score	539	539	458	531	401	362
	Rank		1st				
Latin	Score	520	483	494	477	368	420
	Rank		10th				
History	Score	390	390	382	385	323	268
	Rank		1st				
French	Score	815	809	686	647	756	430
	Rank		3rd				

Source: Harvard College, *Monthly Returns 1848–49.* Langdell also took Natural History, but no grade sheets survive.

tions, Gray also brought natural phenomena into the classroom for students to observe. In May 1848, for example, the students assembled "to hear the lecture on the proper method of preserving botanical specimens," which Gray "brought with him for examples."[55] This demonstration of specimens followed from Gray's responsibilities to oversee the Botanic Garden and pursue his research in botany, duties that were extremely unusual in American colleges at the time.

The other half of Natural History was devoted to zoology and taught by the dominating figure in the field: Louis Agassiz, a Swiss scientist who had assumed a Harvard professorship in spring 1848. In zoology the students usually recited from Agassiz's new textbook *Principles of Zoology* (1848),[56] but he likely presented specimens in class as well, because Harvard had recruited him, like Gray, by offering

55. Gorham, Diary (16 May 1848). See, too, Gorham, Diary (25 May 1848). Cf. Dupree, *Asa Gray*, 123.
56. Gorham, Diary (19 Oct. and 14 Dec. 1848).

the rare combination of a secure professorship and the opportunity to pursue his investigations in the newly established Lawrence Scientific School. Moreover, Agassiz rapidly established a museum of natural history at Harvard, followed in 1858 by the Museum of Comparative Zoology.[57]

This natural history course constituted Langdell's entire scientific education, and therefore determined his view of natural science, scientific research, and scientific teaching.[58] Consequently, Gray's botany and Agassiz's zoology provided the conceptual frame for Langdell's taxonomic analogies between law and natural science.

Botanical taxonomy, the paradigmatic antebellum science,[59] has sometimes been dismissed as a simple enterprise of categorizing phenomena, which Charles Darwin's theory of evolution outmoded by making all categories inconstant and indeterminate.[60] However, as known and practiced by such sophisticated scientists as Gray, taxonomy was more subtle and complicated, as was its relationship to evolutionary theory. In fact, "far from discrediting the old taxonomy, Darwin consummated it and vindicated its essential validity." Gray, in particular, recognized that *The Origin of Species* depended on "the quest for a natural system of classification," without which "the *Origin* would have lacked that connection with empirical evidence which gave it most strength." Consequently, "the goal of a phylogenetic arrangement Darwin firmly set, but the ability to realize it was so far away that the botanist with a respect for the data had no choice but to continue his craft unchanged. . . . The 1870s and 1880s were an Augustan age for taxonomic botany."[61]

Gray thus understood that one needed taxonomy in order to recognize evolutionary change. Without taxonomy, evolutionary theory merely proposed an undifferentiated Heraclitean flux in the face of the seeming constancy of species. Conversely, Agassiz, who was not distinguished in taxonomy, rejected Darwinism, believing that classification implied constancy.[62] Following Gray's understanding, Langdell linked his claim that "law, considered as a science, . . . has arrived at its present state by slow degrees; in other words, it is a growth, extending in many cases through centuries," to the taxonomic assignment "to select, classify, and arrange all the cases which had contributed in any important degree to the growth, development, or establishment of any of its essential doctrines."[63] Hence, Langdell's

57. Lurie, *Louis Agassiz*, 138–39, 145, 226–27, 267.

58. Cf. Schweber, "Before Langdell: The Roots of American Legal Science," 629–31.

59. Daniels, *American Science in the Age of Jackson*, 72.

60. Bozeman, *Protestants in an Age of Science*, 62. See Schweber, "'Science' of Legal Science," 426, 449, 456–59; Kalman, *Legal Realism at Yale*, 11.

61. Quotations are from Dupree, *Asa Gray*, 262, 386.

62. Lurie, *Louis Agassiz*, 205–7.

63. Langdell, *Cases on Contracts* (1871), preface.

taxonomic analogies between law and natural science reflected a sophisticated conception rooted in his natural history class during academic year 1848–49.

—⁓—

In September 1849 Langdell returned to Massachusetts Hall for his junior year and roomed not with his close friend Tebbets, but with Chauncey Wright, an underclassman previously unknown to Langdell. Coming from a background nearly as humble as Langdell's, Wright was known even then as a mathematical and philosophical genius, and later he became the intellectual mentor of Charles S. Peirce, William James, and Oliver Wendell Holmes Jr. in the circle in which Pragmatism arose in the early 1870s.[64] Langdell and Wright may have been attracted to each other by their mutual affinity for intellectual engagement, as well as their shared standards of domestic upkeep. An avid boxer, Wright kept his pugilistic gear hung about his room, while Langdell was well known for his "rustic manners."[65]

Another new figure in Langdell's life was Addison Brown, who, after spending a year at Amherst College, arrived at Harvard in August 1849 as a fresh-sophomore in the class of 1852. Brown's financial resources were nearly as modest as Langdell's, and by practicing careful economy, he made it through college, graduating second in his class. Brown later joined Langdell at HLS and attended for three semesters, from September 1853 through December 1854. After moving to New York City and entering the bar, he became Langdell's law partner in 1864.[66]

Beginning his second year in September 1849 with junior status, Langdell was entitled to exercise some choice apart from the required subjects of rhetoric, astronomy, history, and philosophy, and he elected more Greek and Latin instead of German, Spanish, or mathematics. But the grade reports for the semester reveal that Langdell participated in classes only through about mid-November.[67] His departure from college soon afterward is surprising in light of his excellent record.

As at Exeter, Langdell's academic achievement earned recognition from the faculty. At the end of his first academic year, he was awarded a book prize "for remarkable diligence in studies," inscribed by the newly arrived President Jared Sparks.[68] In September the faculty selected him to make an academic presentation before the entire college in mid-October along with eleven other "fortunate individuals," including several of Langdell's acquaintances: Dunbar, who prepared

64. A. Brown, *Autobiographical Notes*, 64; Wiener, *Evolution and the Founders of Pragmatism*, 31–69.

65. Quotations are, respectively, from A. Brown, *Autobiographical Notes*, 64; S. Eliot, "Some Cambridge Pundits," 29. See J. Thayer, *Letters of Chauncey Wright*, 23; Batchelder, "C. C. Langdell," 312n; Maury, *Collections*, 5.

66. A. Brown, *Autobiographical Notes*, 58, 98, 98n.

67. Harvard College, *Monthly Returns* (1849–50).

68. *Pró insigni in studiis diligentia*. Milton, *Poetical Works* (1848).

a Latin dialogue; Carter, an English oration; and Tebbets, a translation from Greek into Latin. Langdell was assigned to translate an essay by Edmund Burke into Greek, but unfortunately he became ill and could not present.[69]

The students also esteemed Langdell. He was elected to Alpha Delta Phi, a small, prestigious literary society that attracted influential students: Dunbar was president, Shattuck vice president, Thayer a member, and Eliot joined the following year and was elected president in 1853, as was James Barr Ames in 1867.[70] Nevertheless, in Alpha Delta Phi, Langdell seems to have run afoul of the social exclusivity that, a quarter century later, strengthened resistance to his academic reforms, and this encounter likely contributed to his decision to leave college.

The problem arose with William and Joseph Choate, two brothers from a prominent Salem family who were elected to the Society. After graduating first and second in the class of 1852, they both attended HLS with Langdell and became successful attorneys.[71] Langdell had little contact subsequently with William, but Joseph, whose distinguished career culminated in his serving as U.S. ambassador to Great Britain, persistently deprecated Langdell.[72] Joseph Choate's begrudging attitude toward the former mill hand apparently originated in fall 1849 when Addison Brown was proposed for membership in Alpha Delta Phi. Brown appeared to be an excellent candidate since he was bound for the law, would graduate second in the class of 1852 (tied with Joseph Choate), and would eventually become a federal judge. But, after Brown unknowingly gave offense to William, the Choates blackballed him from both Alpha Delta Phi and the Hasty Pudding dramatic club.[73] Langdell, whose background resembled Brown's, likely objected to this exclusion on social grounds and ignited Joseph Choate's persistent dislike.

By the same token, Langdell took no interest in the social diversions that attracted younger, well-to-do students like Gorham. The College holiday that the administration declared to allow students to join the festive celebration inaugurating a new water supply for Boston did not bring out Langdell, who afterward explained his absence: "I preferred to study."[74] This event, occurring early in Langdell's first

69. Gorham, Diary (8 Sept. 1849); Harvard College, "Performance for Exhibition" (16 Oct. 1849); Ames, "Christopher Columbus Langdell, 1826–1906," 469.

70. [Alpha Delta Phi], *A. D. Club*, 5, 9; Alpha Delta Phi, *Catalog* (1851), 8–9; James, *Charles W. Eliot*, 1:48.

71. [Alpha Delta Phi], *A. D. Club*, 5, 9; C. Warren, *History of the Harvard Law School*, 3:63–64.

72. Shattuck to Eliot (17 Dec. 1869); Morawetz to Thayer (15 Apr. 1882); Choate, Address 1895, 63; Fessenden, "Rebirth of the Harvard Law School," 513; Choate to Batchelder (18 July 1906); Choate to Warren (18 Oct. 1907).

73. *New York Times*, 10 Apr. 1913; A. Brown, *Autobiographical Notes*, 66.

74. Batchelder, "Christopher C. Langdell," 438. See Gorham, Diary (25 Oct. 1848, 4 Apr., 2, 15 May, 2 Sept., 11 Nov. 1849).

semester, struck some as peculiar, but a greater source of Langdell's alienation was unruly student behavior.

Hazing of freshmen, for example, was an endemic problem that the faculty tried to address. But they had little success, perhaps due to their tacit acceptance of the practice, as shown by President Everett's proclamation that students should cease hazing unless they could not refrain, in which case hazing should be aimed only at "the largest fellows in the class." The generational transmission of hazing is revealed by Gorham's report that his two freshmen neighbors were repeatedly hazed. Upon becoming sophomores, those two "hazees" then became leading hazers of the entering freshmen, until they were caught by the Junior Proctors, who had been leading sophomore hazers the year before.[75] Langdell evidently had no tolerance for the practice. After he became dean of HLS in April 1870, the mild hazing still occurring there was rapidly extinguished.[76]

Whatever alienation Langdell felt about the social exclusivity and unruly behavior, financial difficulties also forced him to leave college. He could not afford the $100 for annual tuition, $3 weekly for meals in a boarding house, and $80 average in dormitory rent, at a time when an unskilled laborer earned about $300 per year and an artisan or craftsman about $600 per year.[77] Consequently, Langdell left Harvard because the academic experience did not justify the expense.[78]

His departure began as a leave of absence granted to him and twenty-five classmates in late November 1849 to teach school. Many college students who needed additional money taught school during the winter, when children were free of most obligations, and Harvard had a policy condoning the practice. However, school teaching for many became an "unenjoyable experiment," in the words of Brown, who observed that "I had not the requisite patience to deal satisfactorily with the dull, lagging, and humdrum mental work, or no work, of [teaching] a promiscuous mass of children."[79]

Langdell's teaching in a district schoolhouse in Dedham, Massachusetts, during the winter of 1849–50 also turned out badly. Apparently referring to Langdell, the *Report of the School Committee* states, "A portion of the winter term, however, has been lost by an unhappy difference or misunderstanding between the teacher and district, or a portion of it, which resulted in the withdrawal of one Instructor

75. Quotations are from Gorham, Diary (13 Oct. 1848). See 3, 21 Oct. 1849.

76. Fessenden, "Rebirth of the Harvard Law School," 494, 496–98.

77. Harvard University, *Catalog 1848–49*, 38–39; Faler, *Mechanics and Manufacturers in the Early Industrial Revolution*, 77–99; Soltow, *Men and Wealth in the United States, 1850–1870*, 121–22, 159; Laurie, *Artisans into Workers: Labor in Nineteenth-Century America*, 56–61.

78. J. Smith, "Christopher Columbus Langdell," 28; Ames, "Christopher Columbus Langdell, 1826–1906," 469.

79. A. Brown, *Autobiographical Notes*, 62. Harvard University, *Catalog 1853–54*, 37.

Schoolhouse where Langdell taught in Dedham, Massachusetts, 1849–50.
Courtesy of Westwood Historical Society, Westwood, Massachusetts.

and the engagement of another."[80] The reasons are not given. Perhaps Langdell was inflexibly committed to unreasonable academic standards; maybe his legal training became a distraction; there might have been a salary dispute. In any case, this second brief stint of teaching school, in combination with his experience at Harvard College, likely later contributed to Langdell's dissatisfaction with pedagogy that treated law students as if they were schoolchildren.

The beginning of 1850 was therefore another low point for Langdell. He was doubtlessly broke and had spent his savings and those of his sister in climbing the mountain to reach Harvard College, where he had found a strange mixture of

80. Dedham, Mass., School Committee, *Report 1849–50*, 5. See Slafter, *Schools and Teachers of Dedham, Massachusetts*, 178. Langdell taught in the Clapboardtrees district of the West Parish of Dedham, which is now Westwood, Massachusetts.

academic tedium and social revelry rather than Olympian challenge. The attempt to find suitable employment near Harvard Law School had failed. His father provided no support. His mother and all but one of his siblings were dead. His sister and closest confidant, Hannah, left New England at about this time and joined the migration of pious, young female schoolteachers heading to the Midwest in hope of improving their prospects by escaping the common-law doctrine of "coverture" that prevailed in New England states. In the mid-1850s Hannah married a Presbyterian minister, and settled in "bleeding Kansas" amid the conflict between Free-Soilers and proslavers.[81]

One option for Langdell was to head back north to the mills of Manchester; another was to continue on to the hills of New Boston, where his father still tended the farm. All this was familiar but held little promise, and there is no evidence that he ever went to New Boston again. Instead, Langdell trekked northeast to the area near Exeter, where he had been happiest and most successful, though he was now returning downcast. Having dropped out of college and failed at teaching school, he was arriving almost penniless, nearly twenty-four years old, and past the point when young men with prospects would have begun their careers. It would be astonishing if Langdell, though tenacious as he was, did not doubt himself and suspect that Exeter had been the high point after all, that the dream of a college degree had been hopeless from the start, and that the prospect of law school was ebbing away.

Legal Education in Office and School, 1850–54

Arriving in the Exeter area early in 1850, Langdell served as a private tutor for a few months in Dover, and then clerked for eighteen months in the Exeter office of William Stickney and Amos Tuck, while supporting himself through manual labor and tutoring.[82] During 1850 and 1851 Langdell thus completed an "office education" that exceeded the educational attainments of most new attorneys and the educational requirements for legal practice in most jurisdictions in the country.[83]

81. Kaufman, *Women Teachers on the Frontier*, xxi–xxii, 13–19; Porter, "Biographical Sketch of the Pastors," 14–16; E. Robinson, *Ministerial Directory*, 1:527; [McCormick] Presbyterian Seminary, *General Catalog*, 73. The doctrine of coverture held that a husband had legal control of his wife's property.

82. Ames, "Christopher Columbus Langdell, 1826–1906," 469–70. See J. Smith, "Christopher Columbus Langdell," 28. The 1850 U.S. Census lists Langdell as a "student" living in Exeter. U.S. Census of 1850, New Hampshire, Rockingham County, Exeter, leaf 205r.

83. In 1860 merely one-quarter of the states and territories required any level of professional training in order to practice law. Kimball, *True Professional Ideal*, 186. The debate as to whether "the office" or "the school" provided a better legal education was intense at this time. Stevens, *Law School: Legal Education in America*, 20–28.

This apprenticeship helps to explain both his subsequent interest in addressing questions arising from specific cases faced by practicing lawyers and his effectiveness in representing clients upon leaving law school. Furthermore, the apprenticeship reveals that his deep commitment to law school education did not derive from lack of experience with office education.

Stickney and Tuck were personally and professionally prominent. As a member of the state legislature, Tuck had gained renown for his opposition to slavery and to the annexation of Texas, and was elected to the U.S. Congress in 1847, while Langdell was attending Exeter. During March 1851, while Langdell clerked in the office, Tuck ran his third, bitterly contested campaign for Congress, which was widely viewed as a referendum on his opposition to any national policy compromising with slavery. The leading political figures in New England—Franklin Pierce and Daniel Webster—marshaled their forces on opposing sides of the campaign. Tuck won a third term and helped to found the Republican Party, serving as a delegate to the Republican National Conventions in 1856 and 1860. Meanwhile, President Zachary Taylor appointed Stickney the U.S. district attorney for New Hampshire in 1849, and Stickney served throughout Langdell's clerkship.[84] Langdell could not have apprenticed himself to more prominent attorneys in New Hampshire.

After eighteen months, Langdell left the office in Exeter and headed south in fall 1851 to enroll in the law school of Harvard College, housed in Dane Hall. He did so, in part, because Stickney handled most of the cases in the office and was known for his diligence, but not his brilliance.[85] Langdell therefore may have yearned for more advanced instruction. In addition, Stickney and Tuck were college graduates, so the ideal of a learned profession was always before Langdell's eyes. Perhaps, too, the knowledge that his former college classmates were entering HLS that fall ignited his hopes, or his desperation, and stimulated him to return to Cambridge, thinking that he might never do so if he did not leap then.

It was, indeed, a leap of faith, for he arrived "unkempt and . . . pinched by want," with no place to stay. Shattuck "gave him a couch to sleep on," and he spent $2 per week for food.[86] Moreover, Langdell enrolled precisely on 6 November 1851, the midway point of the first semester. Because the anarchic enrollment policy allowed HLS students to begin the curriculum at any point in any term, and because students paid half-tuition of $25 for entering halfway through a semester

84. Corning, *Amos Tuck*, 57–58; Sterns, *Genealogical and Family History*, 12; Gregg and Hippauf, *Birth of the Republican Party*; *DAB*, s.v. "Tuck, Amos"; *Exeter News-Letter*, 23 Mar. 1888, 3.

85. *Exeter News-Letter*, 23 Mar. 1888, 3.

86. Quotations are from Maury, *Collections*, 5; Grafton to Warren (28 Oct. 1907).

or less, enrollment precisely on November 6 allowed the ever pinched Langdell to attend as early as possible for as little cost as possible and still gain credit for a semester's residency.[87]

Langdell was down to his last penny when his faith was rewarded in late December 1851. Based on his academic achievement, the faculty awarded him the very first tuition remission granted to a student at HLS, thereby eliminating his major expense. Here again, distinguishing himself through the formal system of academic merit provided the means to overcome the obstacles in his path. The award required Langdell to provide assistance to the faculty, and early in 1852 he was assigned to help Professor Theophilus Parsons with the research for his *Law of Contracts*, the first volume of which was published in 1853, followed by the second volume in 1855.[88]

To review six thousand cases for the treatise, Parsons hired a number of students and placed Langdell in charge of assigning the cases, evaluating the briefs submitted, and writing the notes that provided the documentation and elaboration for Parsons's doctrinal exposition. The other assistants concluded that the treatise "appeared to be mainly the work of Langdell," because the draft pages consisted of "a brief margin of text by Parsons, clearly and neatly written out at the head. Then three or four times the space in text and citations in the inky, strong hand of C. C. Langdell." Furthermore, many readers considered the notes more valuable than the doctrinal exposition.[89] This complementary arrangement of satisfying his financial needs and his appetite for legal research was replicated in Langdell's appointment as HLS librarian in the summer of 1852. He flourished in this office as well; the Harvard Overseers Visiting Committee gave the library glowing assessments during his tenure.[90]

By the end of his first academic year, 1851–52, Langdell had righted himself financially and completed the second year of the curriculum, since the program was organized as a two-year sequence that recommenced every other year and Langdell had happened to enter during the second year of the cycle. He could do this because the minimal admission requirements and the policy allowing students to enter at any point in any term resulted in maintaining all courses at an

87. Harvard University, *Catalog 1851–52*, 58–60. See C. Warren, *History of the Harvard Law School*, 2:176; Ames, "Christopher Columbus Langdell, 1826–1906," 470.

88. Th. Parsons, *Law of Contracts* (1853, 1855); C. Warren, *History of the Harvard Law School*, 2:176–77. See J. Smith, "Christopher Columbus Langdell," 28; Langdell, Annual Report 1880–81, 78–86; Harvard Law School, Faculty Minutes (12 Oct., 10 Nov. 1891).

89. Quotation is from Grafton to Warren (28 Oct. 1907). See Choate to Warren (18 Oct. 1907); Wilder to Warren (11 Oct. 1907); J. Smith, "Christopher Columbus Langdell," 28.

90. Harvard University, *Catalog 1852–53*, 12; C. Warren, *History of the Harvard Law School*, 2:335–36.

introductory level, even though the catalog announced a sequenced curriculum.[91] The catalog also disguised the fact that the courses were defined less by subject matter than by the prescribed textbook, inasmuch as the curriculum covered a set of standard treatises rather than conceptual fields of law.

In the classroom, Professors Parsons and Joel Parker and Lecturer Edward G. Loring—the three instructors during Langdell's attendance from November 1851 through December 1854[92]—spent most of the time lecturing, supplemented by some verbal quizzing that emulated the recitation.[93] Students therefore maintained that teaching in the law school "was dull and inert" and even "crude."[94] Thayer, who later joined Langdell on the HLS faculty, wrote in fall 1854: "Professor Parker [is] the very dullest lecturer I have ever heard. It is his aim to give you the law, and he does it, but in such an inanimate, monotonous, ill-digested, indifferent manner that one is lucky if he can fasten his attention."[95] In 1855 Emory Washburn was appointed a full professor, replacing Loring, and the triumvirate of Parsons, Parker, and Washburn reigned as the HLS faculty through the late 1860s. During this period, students found the teaching at HLS "perfunctory," because Parker, Parsons, and Washburn employed "the old methods" of the lecture and recitation.[96]

The HLS classrooms therefore provided little pedagogical inspiration for Langdell, and his fellow students later maintained that extracurricular activities stimulated his subsequent innovation of case method teaching. Charles Codman, who attended during Langdell's first year, wrote that Langdell "lived in the library, and there perhaps first got his idea of teaching law by cases, rather than by textbooks."[97] Others attributed the origins of this new approach to Langdell's incessant discussions with fellow students about the law: "There were about a dozen of us who took our hash together at a boarding house on Brighton Street, and of these Langdell was the presiding genius. At table, nothing was talked but shop. Cases were put and discussed, and I have sometimes thought that from these table discus-

91. Quotation is from James, *Charles W. Eliot*, 1:268.

92. Harvard University, *Catalog 1851–52*, 11–15, 59, 62–65. In 1851–52 Loring lectured on real property, Roman civil law, and arbitration; Parker lectured on bailments, domestic relations, wills and administration, equity jurisprudence, evidence, and practice, constitutional law, and jurisprudence of the United States; Parsons lectured on evidence, bills and notes, shipping and admiralty, Sales, partnership, Kent's *Commentaries on American Law*, and Blackstone's *Commentaries on the Law of England*.

93. A. Brown, *Autobiographical Notes*, 91; Choate to Warren (18 Oct. 1907); Granger to Warren (Oct. 1907); Wilson to Warren (3 Oct. 1907).

94. Quotations are from, respectively, Lothrop to Warren (1 Oct. 1907); Phelps to Warren (29 Sept. 1907).

95. J. Thayer to Forbes (15 Sept. 1854).

96. Quotations are, respectively, from: Long to Warren (7 Oct. 1907); Blake to Warren (9 July 1907).

97. Codman to Warren (24 Oct. 1907).

sions Langdell got the germ of the idea that he later developed into the case system of instruction which has made his name famous both here and abroad."[98]

Another student assisting with the research on Parsons's treatise recalled that Langdell "used to get me to read aloud with him evenings, along with Shattuck, for I had the small accomplishment of reading well. He taught us how, from his point of view, to study law. He began with the cases of leading import. We had to read them, and then state the points to him. Then [Langdell] made us read all the leading authorities on such cases, and so pounded certain principles of law into us. It was from this that he developed subsequently his book on 'Cases.'"[99]

By the beginning of his second year, 1852–53, Langdell had therefore established himself as "the presiding genius" among the students. His intellectual leadership had been prepared by his participation in the Golden Branch Society at Exeter and Alpha Delta Phi at Harvard College. In those literary societies, Langdell's intellectual energy and acumen elevated him among his peers, despite his reserved demeanor and lack of polish. At HLS, those qualities were strengthened by his practical knowledge from eighteen months of study in a law office. Langdell therefore assumed a didactic role among the law students, who included three future congressmen, two governors, two ambassadors, an Anglican bishop, several state supreme court justices, and leaders of the bar and business corporations.[100]

This influence was rooted in Langdell's chief characteristic: his "almost fanatical and somewhat contagious enthusiasm" for studying the law. This enthusiasm led to some unorthodox behavior, for "he used to shut himself in the library on Sundays, and read all day," and "he always wore over his eyes a dark shade with green lining. I don't remember ever seeing him without it."[101] Those who regarded this behavior as outlandish, particularly within the relaxed atmosphere of the antebellum law school, considered him "a 'dig' of the first rate" or "a book worm, if there ever was one," and joked that he slept in the library.[102] Nevertheless, "students had great admiration for his marvelous diligence and legal acumen," and he "was looked upon in the law school as a prodigy of learning and master of research."[103]

Despite his studious reserve and lack of interest in social affairs, Langdell was

98. Phelps to Warren (29 Sept. 1907).

99. Grafton to Warren (28 Oct. 1907).

100. Reid, "Life at the Law School," 9; Richardson, *William E. Chandler*, 21–22.

101. Quotations are, respectively, from Ames, "Christopher Columbus Langdell, 1826–1906," 471; Grafton to Warren (28 Oct. 1907); Phelps to Warren (29 Sept. 1907). The need for the shade may be due to Langdell's eyesight, which was already poor and deteriorated over time. Maury, *Collections*, 5.

102. Quotations are, respectively, from: Codman to Warren (24 Oct. 1907); Phelps to Warren (29 Sept. 1907). See Ames, "Christopher Columbus Langdell, 1826–1906," 471.

103. Quotations are, respectively, from: Grafton to Warren (28 Oct. 1907); Choate to Warren (18 Oct. 1907).

not unfriendly but rather "very pleasant" and "held in high esteem by all the students."[104] Even those who judged him "somewhat inclined to pedantry and not very broad-minded" considered him "gentle, modest, and obliging.... Everybody was fond of Langdell."[105] But he became close friends with only a few, particularly younger, serious students, such as William Gibbons and Charles Grafton.[106] This pattern fit his earlier experience at Exeter with Tebbets.

Langdell's devotion to legal scholarship enhanced his sociability in the law clubs, which constituted one leg of the educational tripod at HLS.[107] In these student-run clubs, "cases are argued before a judge, appointed by the club, and by the members in turn, two at a time. Each [club] has a meeting once a week in the evening. One student is liable... to a club case once in five or six weeks." From this experience of preparing and arguing cases, club members later said that they "derived equal benefit and even more enjoyment" than from professors' lectures.[108] Langdell was invited to join the Coke Club, one of the two most competitive and prestigious, whose membership included Carter, Arthur Machen, Joseph Choate, Shattuck, and William Chandler.[109] Hence, as at Exeter and Harvard College, Langdell was drawn into influential social circles despite his reticence and rustic manners.

The second leg of the HLS tripod was the moot courts, held twice weekly and argued before the professors by four seniors, who had been appointed and given the case a month in advance. After they argued the case, "the presiding professor delivered the opinion, which I fear he had drawn up before hearing the arguments." Nevertheless, compared to the lectures, "it was the moot cases which... were most alluring and instructive, and it was by them [students] made the greatest progress."[110] The third leg was, of course, the formal curriculum. Langdell completed the "first year" curriculum during his second year, 1852–53, when Parsons lectured on William Blackstone's *Commentaries*, evidence, insurance, James Kent's *Commentaries*, and contracts; Parker expounded on agency, corporations, common-law pleading, practice, and equity; and Loring lectured on real property, Roman civil law, and arbitration.[111]

104. Wilson to Warren (3 Oct. 1907).

105. Phelps to Warren (29 Sept. 1907).

106. Ames, "Christopher Columbus Langdell, 1826–1906," 472; Grafton to Warren (28 Oct. 1907).

107. In the 1850s the HLS education had three components: classroom lectures, moot courts, and student clubs, with the latter two being most valuable. Long to Warren (7 Oct. 1907); J. Thayer to Forbes (15 Sept. 1854); A. Brown, *Autobiographical Notes*, 91.

108. Quotations are, respectively, from: J. Thayer to Forbes (15 Sept. 1854); A. Brown, *Autobiographical Notes*, 91. See C. Warren, *History of the Harvard Law School*, 2:319–31.

109. Douglas to Warren (1908); Grafton to Warren (28 Oct. 1907); Codman to Warren (24 Oct. 1907).

110. Quotations are, respectively, from: Codman to Warren (24 Oct. 1907); A. Brown, *Autobiographical Notes*, 91. See Blake to Warren (9 July 1907).

111. Harvard University, *Catalog 1852–53*, 61.

In June 1853 Langdell therefore finished the two-year program, received the LL.B. degree, and was elected to Phi Beta Kappa.[112] This would normally have ended his enrollment at HLS, but students could remain beyond the required four semesters to pursue deeper study in the list of books that the catalog recommended for postgraduates. In September 1853 Langdell returned as a "resident graduate" for a third year while continuing as librarian and chief research assistant for Parsons.

By this time, Langdell had already conceived and practiced at least the rudiments of what later became his case method teaching. During this postgraduate year, the most significant events contributing to his development as an educational reformer were his encounters with Eliot, the future president of Harvard. In 1870 Eliot brought Langdell back to HLS and later attributed the original idea for choosing Langdell to these encounters in the early 1850s. Eliot famously announced all this in a speech in 1886:

> When I was a junior in college in the year 1851–52 and used to go often in
> the early evening to the room of a friend who was in Divinity School, I there
> heard a young man who was making notes to *Parsons on Contracts* talk about
> law. He was generally eating his supper at the time, standing up in front
> of the fire and eating with good appetite a bowl of brown bread and milk.
> I was a mere boy, only eighteen years old; but it was given to me to under-
> stand that I was listening to a man of genius. In the year 1870, I recalled the
> remarkable character of that young man's expositions, sought him in New
> York, and induced him to become Dane Professor. So he became Professor
> Langdell.[113]

An interpretation of Eliot's story must begin with Langdell's friend Tebbets, who, after Langdell left Harvard College in November 1849, was able to continue his education with the support of scholarships, loans, and odd jobs. One of his tasks was to read aloud to a freshman named Charles Eliot who had enrolled at the college in fall 1849 and was extremely nearsighted. By the time Tebbets graduated with his class in June 1851, he had become one of Eliot's best friends.[114] Meanwhile, Tebbets had shifted his vocational interest from the law, his deceased father's field, to the ministry. Upon graduating, he went to Harvard Divinity School for five months—from July to December 1851—and lived in Divinity Hall, where Eliot visited him both for friendship and for continued reading. In November 1851

112. *Boston Daily Atlas*, 22 July 1853; *New York Times*, 23 July 1853.

113. C. Eliot, Oration 1886, 61.

114. James, *Charles W. Eliot*, 1:42. See Harvard College Class of 1851, Class Book, 489; S. Eliot, "Some Cambridge Pundits," 22.

Langdell returned to Harvard to begin at the law school, so Langdell and Eliot must have met in Tebbets's room in Divinity Hall in late autumn 1851, before Tebbets left Harvard in December to teach for a year and a half.[115]

Nevertheless, Eliot conflated several meetings at different times into his famous 1886 anecdote,[116] drawing parts of his story from the academic year 1853–54 when Tebbets reenrolled in Harvard Divinity School and resided in Divinity Hall. Eliot had then finished college and was living in his father's house in Boston, while Langdell was enrolled as a resident graduate at HLS.[117] In the fall of 1853 Langdell's jobs as research assistant and librarian allowed him to relinquish first Shattuck's couch and then the garret over the library in Dane Hall and to rent a room in Divinity Hall.[118] One reason for his move was to live near Tebbets; another was that Divinity Hall attracted bookworms. Above all, the dormitory was affordable for frugal students. Among them was Brown, who economized by eating breakfast and lunch in his Divinity Hall room, while Langdell ate all three meals there, including his pauper's supper of bread and milk.[119]

Eliot's detail of Langdell standing by the fire can be similarly explained. Throughout Harvard, as fall and winter wore on and poorer students ran out of money to buy wood or coal, their rooms went cold, and they clustered in the rooms of the wealthier students. Well-heeled Gorham had fuel left even for an unseasonably cool day at the end of May, and Dunbar and others without fuel came by to warm themselves. For Langdell, it was not a matter of running out, because his room was doubtlessly unheated all year.[120] Langdell's eating his pauper's supper in front of his friend's fire in Divinity Hall epitomizes his continuing privations even as a resident graduate.

In the academic year 1853–54 Eliot and Langdell met again in Tebbets's room.[121] During that time Langdell worked as the chief research assistant on Parsons's *Law of Contracts* and developed the method of Socratic inquiry into original case reports in extracurricular discussion groups with fellow students. Hence, in 1853–54 he likely held forth to Eliot and Tebbets about the nature of law and "the ways in

115. Towne, *Memorial of Rev. Theodore Tebbets*, 9–10; James, *Charles W. Eliot*, 1:42; Harvard College Class of 1851, Class Book, 486–87.

116. S. Eliot, "Some Cambridge Pundits," 29.

117. Harvard University, *Catalog 1853–54*, 46; Hawkins, *Between Harvard and America*, 12–13.

118. Harvard University, *Catalog 1853–54*, 50; S. Eliot, "Some Cambridge Pundits," 29; Ames, "Christopher Columbus Langdell, 1826–1906," 471.

119. A. Brown, *Autobiographical Notes*, 58–59.

120. Quotations are, respectively, from: Gorham, Diary (24 May 1848); S. Eliot, "Some Cambridge Pundits," 29.

121. Ames, "Christopher Columbus Langdell, 1826–1906," 472; S. Eliot, "Some Cambridge Pundits," 29; James, *Charles W. Eliot*, 2:43–49, 56–59, 71–73.

which lawyers ought to be trained."[122] Here again, Langdell's attention to education was apparent and must have resonated with Eliot's interest in the subject. It is intriguing to consider what Langdell might have proposed about legal training beyond case method teaching. Some of his proposals are suggested by the resemblance between three cardinal policies that Langdell observed in the Divinity School and later instituted in legal education.

In 1853–54 Harvard Divinity School required that its applicants who did not hold the bachelor of arts degree pass entrance examinations in a set of texts and subjects equivalent to a demanding college curriculum of the day, including not only advanced Latin and Greek, but also algebra, geometry, logic, English rhetoric, Locke's *Essay on Human Understanding*, Dugald Stewart's *Elements of the Philosophy of the Mind*, and William Paley's *Moral Philosophy*. These admission requirements made the divinity program tantamount to a postgraduate curriculum at the same time that HLS had no academic criteria for admission beyond English literacy. Second, the divinity students were required to attend three years, whereas HLS students completed their program in two years, at most, and one year routinely. Finally, the divinity curriculum was sequenced, requiring students to enter at the beginning of the first term and proceed upward through the "*system* of theological education," whereas law students were allowed to enter any course at any point in any term, effectively reducing all courses to the introductory level.[123] Given that these three policies were core reforms advanced by Langdell soon after his arrival at HLS, it may be that, while expounding to Eliot and Tebbets his ideas about teaching inductively from cases, Langdell learned from divinity students the conception of a three-year, sequential, postgraduate, professional school curriculum.[124] It existed and worked in the Divinity School, which students such as his accomplished friend Tebbets attended.

That Langdell was prepared to embrace these three reforms by this point is suggested not only by his enrolling in Harvard College after Exeter, but also by the influence he exercised on others, such as his young friend Gibbons, whom he convinced to withdraw from HLS in order to earn a B.A. degree before reenrolling.[125] In demanding a bachelor's degree for admission, Langdell would later require what he had himself had not formally attained, although his voracious reading

122. S. Eliot, "Some Cambridge Pundits," 29.

123. Harvard University, *Catalog 1853–54*, 47–48. Emphasis added.

124. This comparison demonstrates that, on average, divinity schools were far wealthier and more rigorous than law schools or medical schools until the end of the nineteenth century. See Kimball, *True Professional Ideal*, 249–50, 280–88, 323.

125. See Ames, "Christopher Columbus Langdell, 1826–1906," 472; Tebbets, *Memoir of William Gibbons*, 5–8, 12–13, 23, 26–27; *New England Historical and Genealogical Register* (1863).

and diligent study had likely reached the same academic level. In recognition of this attainment and of his contribution to legal research, Parsons wrote to the president of Harvard in June 1854:

> Allow me to present the name of Mr. Christopher Columbus Langdell as a candidate for the degree of Master of Arts at the approaching Commencement. Of this gentleman's life and character before he came to the Law School you know as much as I do. He has been in the School between two and three years; most of the time he has held and now holds the office of Librarian. I believe all who are connected with the School will agree with me, that no one of our graduates, for some years certainly, surpasses him and few equal him. I have no hesitation in saying that for capacity, industry, acquisition, perfectly good conduct, and all the elements of merit which a candidate for this honor should present, I should consider him certainly the equal of any young man whom I know. It may be remembered also, that he would now have had this honor in due course, and with a high rank of scholarship, if he had not been compelled to leave his class by extreme poverty; from which he has now rescued himself by his own exertions.[126]

In view of Langdell demonstrating "all the elements of merit which a candidate for this honor should present," the degree was voted, and Langdell received the A.M. honoris causa at commencement in 1854, along with the members of the class of 1851, who, according to the practice of the day, received their A.M.'s "in course."[127]

In August 1854, after three years of study at the law school, Langdell returned again as a resident graduate and Librarian, even though he had "received propositions to go to New York and enter at once upon extensive business."[128] He was probably persuaded to stay by Parsons, who persistently cajoled his former students to continue as research assistants as long as possible, even in their early years of practice after leaving HLS. The young graduates found it difficult to refuse, particularly since Parsons was writing recommendations for them, and they all spent many months weaning Parsons away from their help.[129] Langdell thus remained at HLS during fall 1854 in order to help Parsons bring the second volume of *Law of Contracts* near to completion.

126. Theophilus Parsons to James Walker (3 June 1854), quoted in C. Warren, *History of the Harvard Law School*, 2:180.

127. C. Warren, *History of the Harvard Law School*, 2:180.

128. Theophilus Parsons to James Walker (3 June 1854), quoted in C. Warren, *History of the Harvard Law School*, 2:180; Harvard University, *Catalog 1854–5*, 50.

129. See Th. Parsons to Machen (13 Mar. 1855); Langdell to Machen (19 Mar. 1856).

DANE LAW-SCHOOL, CAMBRIDGE, MASS.

Dane Hall, Law School, Harvard College, 1850s. Courtesy of
Special Collections Department, Harvard Law School Library.

In December 1854 the twenty-eight-year-old law graduate finally left Dane Hall
to join the bar in New York City. He departed Harvard with a profound commitment to the idea that personal and professional advancement is achieved through
excelling within the established rules of the formal system of academic merit. By
demonstrating "all the elements of merit" within educational institutions over the
course of these formative years, Langdell blazed a new path to fulfill the traditional
American image of "the self-made man" who rises out of poverty and a rural childhood.[130] With the help of his sisters and eleemosynary aid at opportune moments,
Langdell's tireless academic efforts lifted him from an impoverished and traumatic
childhood on a hardscrabble farm in the north woods to the gateway of the legal
profession on Wall Street.

130. Wylie, *Self-Made Man in America*, 24. See Thernstrom, *Poverty and Progress*, 2, 57–58.

CHAPTER 2

Lawyer on Wall Street, 1855–1870

Entering the practice of law in New York City in January 1855, Langdell believed that a lawyer's "abilities, learning, or experience" would determine his professional success or failure, because law was not a matter of whim, caprice, or "private and other '*influences*' with the judges," but an apolitical science requiring devoted study. Langdell's conviction that academic merit determined one's professional fortunes also entailed a commitment to "democracy," as one friend remarked, in the sense that there existed equal opportunity to succeed at the bar.[1] Consequently, scientific expertise, academic merit, professional success, and equal opportunity coincided, in Langdell's view.

His first dozen years in New York City confirmed this formulation. Impressed by his legal knowledge and diligence, leading attorneys recruited him to work on prominent cases in the higher courts of New York State, and he gained a reputation as a shrewd and effective attorney. By 1860 he had already built a flourishing practice and was nearly "driven to death" by the press of routine and complex litigation flowing into his office at 16 Wall Street.[2] In 1869, when the founding president of the Erie Railroad and his family sought out "the highest legal ability in the country" to contest a will, they were referred by other attorneys to Langdell.[3] Beyond serving as a prominent, effective, and busy lawyer, Langdell helped to establish a new role in litigation: crafting the extensive written brief that was beginning to displace the weight of oral argument in complicated cases arising from large and intricate commercial transactions.

During the "Erie Wars" scandals of 1868 and 1869, however, Langdell became disaffected from the New York City bench and bar. In a city run by Boss Tweed of Tammany Hall, Langdell, like some of his associates, abhorred the corruption of the judiciary and the complicity of eminent lawyers in that corruption. By the time

1. Quotations are from A. Russell to Machen (1 May 1868).
2. Langdell to Webster (12 June 1858).
3. Whiton to Lord (circa 1871).

Langdell accepted a professorship at HLS and left Wall Street in 1870, his experience in New York had strengthened and extended his view that professional success requires strong legal science acquired through a demanding legal education. After practicing in the *cloaca maxima* of the legal world that was New York City, he concluded that the just working of the legal system relies on the effectiveness and authority of the legal profession, which depend on lawyers' merit that is derived from their academic achievement in law school. The newly appointed Professor Langdell viewed lawyers' acquisition of strong legal science through demanding academic study as the means not only to elevate the legal profession, but also to safeguard the integrity of the legal system.

Entering the Bar

Legal practice in New York City during the 1850s and 1860s was shaped by several contextual factors, above all the machinations and corruption of Tammany Hall, the political organization that met in the hall of the Tammany Society during the second quarter of the nineteenth century and that, by the 1850s, had become coextensive with the leadership of the emerging Democratic Party in New York County. By 1900 Tammany Hall was known as "the most powerful, efficient, corrupt political machine in the history of urban America."[4] Lawyers routinely encountered Tammany's degradation of law and politics, as did Langdell in representing a group of citizens who were challenging the price-gouging that had resulted from an apparently corrupt municipal contract.[5] During Langdell's residence in the city, public offices, franchises, and contracts were sold to the highest bidder by political bosses, such as Mayor Fernando Wood, and by the "forty thieves" of the bicameral city legislature, which comprised twenty-four councilmen and seventeen aldermen.[6] One alderman was William M. Tweed, who rose to become Boss Tweed of the Democratic Party during the late 1860s.

Another contextual factor was the transformation of the court system, which the new state constitution of 1846 had drastically reorganized above the level of original jurisdiction for small civil and criminal complaints. One major change was to establish the Court of Appeals as the state's highest court. Another was to eliminate separate courts of equity and vest their jurisdiction in a misleadingly

---

4. Alexander B. Callow Jr., introduction to *History of Tammany Hall*, by G. Myers, v. See Mushkat, *Tammany: The Evolution of a Political Machine*, 1–2, 7. See Callow, *Tweed Ring*, 4ff.; Mandelbaum, *Boss Tweed's New York*, 7–26.

5. *In the matter of Turfler* (1865).

6. Callow, *Tweed Ring*, 18; Bergan, *History of the New York Court of Appeals*, 30.

named New York Supreme Court,[7] which had appellate jurisdiction, as well as original jurisdiction in civil and criminal cases that fell outside the lower courts. Still another change was that all judicial offices were made elective. Finally, the standards of expertise for entering the New York bar became minimal, as the hierarchical ranks of attorney, solicitor, and counselor and the correlated series of demanding examinations were eliminated.[8]

The minimal standards for entering the bar and the popular election of judges contributed to the corruption of the lower courts. Observers criticized "the ignorance, incompetence, and pretension" of the judges and "their evasions of duty" in order to ensure their reelection. By 1867 the upper levels of the judiciary were plagued by "the utter incompetency of some of the judges...and the mediocre character, to say the least, of the majority of them." Even here, "in order to secure success before certain judges, it was necessary to employ certain lawyers having influence with them."[9]

In addition, the bar became increasingly stratified. The bottom tier consisted of a growing number of lawyers with little legal expertise, such as Edwin Bogardus, who served for seven years as the senior partner of Langdell's former classmate Addison Brown. "Lacking systematic training, either in college or law school," Bogardus "had a good high school education and much business tact; he was naturally shrewd and of quick intelligence.... His business was very varied, being in all the state and city courts. Much of it was simple collection business, on claims large and small." But when the collection suits became complicated by "debtors' conveyances in fraud of creditors," Brown's "superior training in equity pleading and practice enabled [him] to be of much service" to Bogardus.[10]

---

7. Apart from criminal law, the adjudication of disputes between two parties in Anglo-American law was traditionally divided into two broad domains with separate court systems—"common law" and "equity." These two domains were distinguished primarily by their historical origins, their remedies available to plaintiffs, and their separate procedural systems: civil procedure in the common law and equity procedure in equity. During the second half of the nineteenth century in most jurisdictions in the United States, the domain of common law gradually subsumed equity doctrine, and the field of equity therefore shrank and virtually disappeared. Meanwhile, the more flexible procedure of equity was incorporated into the codes governing common law that were adopted by many states over the same period. In addition, the flexible procedure of equity was adopted by the U.S. federal courts. Consequently, equity continued to exercise considerable influence even though it withered as a separate, formal domain. Subrin, "How Equity Conquered Common Law," 909–1002.

8. G. Martin, *Causes and Conflicts*, 32; Bergan, *History of the New York Court of Appeals*, 18–48; LaPiana, *Logic and Experience*, 71–73.

9. Quotations are from [Shearman], "New York City Judiciary" (1867), 164, 154, 159. See Strong, *Diary*, 3:28; Callow, *Tweed Ring*, 133, 149.

10. A. Brown, *Autobiographical Notes*, 105. Equity was often regarded as the more esoteric legal domain, whose procedure required formal study. The complication arose when a debtor conveyed his property to someone else in order to prevent his creditor from obtaining the property by suing to satisfy a debt.

If Bogardus stood in the bottom tier, then Brown belonged to the middle level, whose members "emphasized technical competence and a workmanlike approach to the business of lawyering." Working on cases that generally spanned less than a week, these lawyers provided the routine technical expertise that was lacking in the bottom tier, with whom they often partnered.[11] Finally, the upper tier comprised those who worked on complicated, lengthy, and prominent cases that often reached the upper courts and were included in court reports. It was here that Langdell made his reputation and contributed to pioneering a new role in litigation.

The increasing complexity of economic and social affairs in growing commercial centers, such as New York, complicated legal practice in which cases began to involve thousands of pages of documents. This legal complexity elevated the importance of preparing intricate written briefs, which began to supplant the influence of oral argument in deciding cases. While much of his practice involved middle-tier work like that of Brown, Langdell not only established a reputation in the upper tier as well but pioneered the new role of master craftsman of the written brief that began to be required in highly technical and weighty cases arising in major commercial centers. In this way, Langdell contributed to advancing a more sophisticated and technical conception of legal expertise and anticipated the shifting locus of elite legal practice from the courtroom to the law office during the mid-1880s.[12]

At the same time, however, the enactment in 1848 of a new code of civil procedure in New York appeared to detract from the value of technical expertise and to empower untrained judges and lawyers.[13] This "Field Code," named after its principal advocate and author, David D. Field, was intended to simplify the highly technical system of pleading in common-law courts that New York and other states had inherited from England. In order to "plead," or present, one's complaint in the proper legal form and thereby gain access to a court of common law, one had to select the correct written form, usually called a "writ" or "form of action," that suited the nature of one's complaint. Courts would not admit a

11. Quotation is from LaPiana, *Logic and Experience*, 38. See Bloomfield, *American Lawyers*, 151; Bryce, *American Commonwealth*, 2:666.

12. R. Gordon, "Ideal and the Actual in the Law," 59; Hobson, "Symbol of the New Profession," 3. I am grateful to John H. Schlegel for suggesting this insight about written briefs.

13. "An Act to Simplify and Abridge the Practice, Pleadings and Proceedings of the Courts of this State," chapter 379, §391, 1848 New York Laws 497. This 1848 act was a partial code that was amended in 1849. The completed procedural code, submitted to the New York legislature in 1850 was never enacted. Subrin, "David Dudley Field and the Field Code," 317. A parallel effort was made to simplify criminal procedure for the adjudication of criminal law.

complaint presented incorrectly, and selecting the correct form required detailed technical expertise. The Field Code therefore attempted to consolidate the various types of written forms into one uncomplicated "cause of action" through which all complaints could be presented.[14]

By thus displacing the writ system of common-law pleading—"this most recondite, most precious, most lawyerly area of law"[15]—the Field Code prompted opposition and resentment from highly skilled lawyers who took pride in this esoteric technical expertise.[16] Furthermore, these expert jurists continued to employ the logic of the writs while pleading through the single cause of action. Langdell was one of these, as he complained to a friend: "The legislation here in New York [enacting and amending the Field Code], which has followed the adoption of the new constitution in [18]46, is the most frightful mass of stuff . . . ever beheld. I have groaned under it every hour since I came here. Whether I shall ever get to feel at home in it, I don't know. If it were a necessary evil I could endure it; but where it [was] brought about [by] a miserable set of intermeddling outsiders, it is too much for human patience. But I will not enlarge upon so disagreeable a topic."[17] Nevertheless, Langdell became skilled at Code pleading and, in a twofold irony, later presented a technical argument to the New York Supreme Court in 1869 on behalf of the simplicity of Code pleading whose simplification he here lamented.

Legal practice in New York City during Langdell's time from 1855 to 1869 was thus influenced by the predominance of Tammany Hall whose corruption widely infected the judiciary; by the reorganization of the courts; by the new form of civil procedure instituted through the Field Code; and by the stratification of the bar into a tier of unlearned businessmen, a tier of technicians, who often partnered with the businessmen, and a tier of legal scientists, who worked on long, complicated cases in which the highly technical, written brief was coming to supplant the importance of oral argument. All these factors played a role in Langdell's experience at the bar.

—◦◦◦—

In December 1854 Langdell and his classmate and future colleague, Brown, departed HLS and embarked independently on their legal careers. Neither had much

---

14. Coquillette, *Anglo-American Legal Heritage*, 147–62; Subrin, "David Dudley Field and the Field Code," 315–27.

15. Friedman, *History of American Law*, 392.

16. LaPiana, "Just the Facts: The Field Code and the Case Method," 309. Cf. Subrin, "David Dudley Field and the Field Code," 312.

17. Langdell to Machen (19 Mar. 1856). See LaPiana, *Logic and Experience*, 74.

money or an established lawyer to sponsor him, as did their classmate Joseph Choate, whose famous cousin, Rufus Choate, wrote a letter of introduction to William M. Evarts, a New York lawyer and future U.S. attorney general and U.S. secretary of state.[18] In contrast, Langdell's strategy likely resembled Brown's:

> I knew of no person from whom I could expect law business to be entrusted to me except in and about Haverhill [Massachusetts]; and ... there was not much law business there, while much of what there was, was of petty criminal character and undesirable, with a number of lawyers to divide it already. In going away from home and among strangers, the alternative[s] seemed to be either to go far west and grow up with some new and rapidly rising community, or to remain east and settle in the midst of the largest and most varied business interests and take my chances with the rest. This pointed plainly to New York. ... New York also seemed to offer readier means for a frugal support. For it was understood that a law school graduate of good standing could there easily find a situation in an established law firm, where, as salaried clerk, he could earn his living expenses and at the same time learn the local law practice and also pick up some business acquaintances; and that this might be continued until he was prepared to launch out alone, or join, as often happened, some older practitioner who needed a partner. With these anticipations I chose New York City, and went there about December 1854.[19]

Brown quickly found a clerkship in a firm, where he was paid a salary of six dollars weekly, soon raised to ten dollars.

Langdell established himself rapidly as well. He was not without contacts, having received letters of introduction from his mentor, Theophilus Parsons, and invitations to join recent HLS graduates in practice.[20] By April 1855 Dorman Eaton, an 1850 graduate of HLS, had arranged a position for Langdell at the firm of Kent, Eaton, and Davis at 110 Broadway Avenue, where Langdell worked for three years. This firm was distinguished by its senior partner, William Kent, who had edited an edition of *Commentaries on American Law*, written by his famous father, James Kent. Kent, Eaton, and Davis developed a successful commercial practice in the

18. E. Martin, *Life of Joseph Hodges Choate*, 1:84–85, 93–94; G. Martin, *Causes and Conflicts*, 24–26; Bergan, *History of the New York Court of Appeals*, 99.

19. A. Brown, *Autobiographical Notes*, 93.

20. Theophilus Parsons to James Walker (3 June 1854), quoted in C. Warren, *History of the Harvard Law School*, 2:180; Wilder to Warren (11 Oct. 1907); Langdell to Machen (19 Mar. 1856).

1860s, and became widely known in New York for representing large companies, including the Erie Railroad. As an attorney at this firm, Langdell was admitted to practice before the New York Supreme Court in May 1855.[21]

Meanwhile, Brown and Langdell entered the frugal rooming house life common to young, unmarried lawyers who were trying to establish themselves. Though still on a tight budget, Langdell enjoyed socializing with the New York family of William Gibbons, his young protégé from Harvard.[22] He also began to develop the rooming house contacts that aided young lawyers in building their practice. Brown, for example, became good friends with William Stanley, his future partner.[23] Referrals from other cities were infrequent, unless the young lawyer, like Langdell, had a network of accomplished law school classmates. Arthur Machen in Baltimore and Langdell in New York represented each other's clients in middle-tier litigation, while Alfred Russell and Langdell did the same between New York and Detroit.[24] On behalf of attorney George Shattuck in Boston, Langdell "ascertained where the Illinois Central keep their funds, so that there will be no difficulty in attaching," and Shattuck reciprocated by arranging for Langdell the arrest of a negligent debtor in Boston who was staying "at one of the best Hotels, and has plenty of money."[25] It was by such informal contact with an Exeter and Harvard alumnus that Langdell landed his first major case.

Legal Advocate and Counsel

The complicated equity case concerned the virtually identical wills of an unmarried and childless brother and sister, Joseph and Mary Rowe, who lived together. Mary's will granted Joseph a life estate in all her real and personal property. Upon Joseph's death, all of Mary's and Joseph's property was to be distributed among their three nieces and the nieces' children. In addition, the will stated that if a niece died "childless," the portion of the estate given to that niece would be distributed among the remaining nieces and their children.[26] Dated the same day as Mary's,

21. *New York Times*, 29 May 1855; Th. Parsons to Machen (13 Mar. 1855); Langdell to Webster (4 Apr. 1856); *Dorman B. Eaton, 1823–1899*, 3; McFarland, "Partisan of Nonpartisanship: Dorman B. Eaton," 807; Kent, *Commentaries on American Law.*

22. A. Brown, *Autobiographical Notes*, 95, 98, 111; Ames, "Christopher Columbus Langdell, 1826–1906," 474; Langdell to Webster (23 May, 17 Aug. 1857); *Boston Post*, 20 Dec. 1855.

23. A. Brown, *Autobiographical Notes*, 98.

24. Langdell to Machen (19 Mar. 1856); A. Russell to Machen (1 May 1868).

25. Langdell to Shattuck (28 Apr. 1860).

26. A niece was considered "childless" until one of her children reached the age of 21 or married, at which point her share became vested, that is, owned unconditionally. Similarly, a share received by a child was contingent until that child turned 21 or married. *Kuhn v. Webster* (1858), 5, 16–17.

Joseph's will was practically identical, except that it gave a life estate to his sister. The amount at stake was considerable. Mary's estate at her death was appraised at about $64,000 and Joseph's at nearly $108,000. In total, the amount at issue was well over $4 million today.[27]

Mary died in 1852, bequeathing the life estate to Joseph, who died in March 1856. The trustee of Joseph Rowe's estate was Joseph Webster, Langdell's friend who had attended Exeter and studied at Harvard College while Langdell was at HLS.[28] Webster immediately wrote to Langdell, who agreed to take the case in April 1856. At that point, three nieces survived, and two had children:

1. Hannah Webster, a sixty-one-year-old widow, had one son, Langdell's client Joseph Webster (of age and married), and one daughter (unmarried and under age twenty-one);
2. fifty-two-year-old Penelope White and her husband had no children;
3. forty-nine-year-old Anne Payson and her husband had one eight-year-old daughter.

Though pleased to have this significant case in equity law, Langdell did not belong to the Massachusetts bar and refused to sail to Boston to meet with one client, so he asked Webster to send both wills to him and arranged for Webster to retain a distinguished Boston attorney to file the necessary papers. In addition, Langdell's reluctance to travel to Boston reflected his prescient view that, in complex cases, a learned lawyer prefers to argue the technicalities in a written brief. When the case ultimately went to the Massachusetts Supreme Judicial Court, Langdell proposed "to have the case submitted on printed arguments," because, due to the complexity of the case, "I think I might derive some advantages from that mode of arguing the case."[29]

At the end of April 1856 Langdell wrote a twenty-page letter to Webster explaining each provision of the will and analyzing the legal issues, based on an extensive investigation of the relevant cases.[30] The practical question was whether, according to the distribution clauses in the wills, each of the three nieces was to receive one-third of the estates to share with her children or whether the three nieces and the three children were each to receive equal shares. By the former

27. *Kuhn v. Webster* (1858). The following discussion simplifies the facts of the case. I am grateful to Daniel Ernst and an anonymous reviewer for clarifying the issues in the case, though any misinterpretations remain my own responsibility.
28. Webster studied at Phillips Exeter Academy 1849–51, and received an M.D. from Harvard in 1859.
29. Langdell to Webster (16 Feb. 1857). See 11 Oct. 1857, 4 Apr., 8 July 1856.
30. Langdell to Webster (30 Apr. 1856), 10. See also 22 Nov., 9 Dec. 1856.

interpretation, Langdell's clients, Joseph Webster and his sister, would each receive one-ninth of the two estates; by the latter interpretation, one-sixth.[31] Those were the two primary possibilities, but other interpretations of the complicated issues yielded other distributions.

The other parties involved in the case were also quick to consult legal counsel. The Paysons retained Emory Washburn, a former governor of Massachusetts who had joined the faculty of HLS in the previous year and whom Langdell did not regard as a formidable adversary. But the Whites were represented by wily Samuel E. Sewall, one of the leading estate lawyers in Massachusetts who, after graduating from HLS in 1819, practiced for sixty-seven years until his death in 1888.[32]

In May 1856 Langdell wrote another twenty-page letter addressing technical aspects of one fundamental legal question: whether (or which parts of) Mary's property passed to Joseph as a life estate or in fee simple. In the former case, Langdell's clients would profit; in the latter, that property would become "residue" of Joseph's estate, circumventing Langdell's clients and passing permanently to the three nieces according to the law of intestate succession.[33]

Langdell's meticulous analyses, thorough review of the relevant cases, and patient explanations to his client demonstrate his effectiveness as legal counsel, particularly since Webster was proving to be a difficult client. He did not manage the affairs of the estate effectively, failing to insure the property properly or set aside the rents from the property for whoever would eventually take ownership. In addition, he pestered his attorney with arcane, trivial legal issues. In response, Langdell solicitously explained that Webster had to manage the estate not with regard to "convenience," but in view of his legal obligations, and then Langdell fully and patiently addressed the questions that Webster raised repeatedly.[34]

Furthermore, Langdell did not counsel the Websters based solely on doctrine and logic. Indicative of his approach to legal advocacy, he advised his clients to stay out of court and settle the matter fairly and rapidly by not pressing all their legal claims. In June 1856 he wrote, "I am very glad to hear if there is a prospect of your obtaining a settlement without litigation. So far as your individual interests are concerned, I should think it would be advisable for you to release all claims upon the nieces' shares, upon the condition that you shall receive a full sixth part."[35]

31. Langdell to Webster (30 Apr. 1856), 10.
32. Langdell to Webster (15 May, 9 Aug., 22 Nov. 1856). On Sewall, see C. Warren, *History of the Harvard Law School*, 3:1.
33. Langdell to Webster (15 May 1856). Intestate succession refers to the distribution of property of a person who dies without leaving a legal will.
34. Langdell to Webster (15 May 1856).
35. Langdell to Webster (16 June 1856).

Langdell's proposal was eminently fair. Under the most plausible interpretation of the will, the childless Whites were to get nothing unconditionally, while each of the three Websters and the two Paysons were to receive no less than one-ninth initially and one-fifth eventually, after Penelope White died. If the Payson daughter did not reach age twenty-one or marry, the Websters would receive the entire inheritance. Instead, Langdell proposed that everyone receive permanently one-sixth, avoid family squabbling, and stay out of court. But neither the Paysons nor, surprisingly, the Whites heeded Langdell's appeal to compromise and practicality. Given the disagreement, Langdell advised the Websters to avoid any legal process, such as going to probate court, that could not resolve the dispute, and to let the estate administrator, G. H. Kuhn, initiate a suit to the state supreme court, sitting in equity, so that all parties could be joined and the entire matter resolved.[36]

Here again, Langdell advised his clients by attending not only to substantive doctrine but also to effective procedure and to prudent strategy. As he wrote to Webster in August 1856: "I am entirely satisfied that your better c[ourse] is to remain entirely passive, at least for the present. Various reasons might be given, *some of a prudential and some of a legal nature,* but I presume it not worth while to attempt to enumerate them. . . . I trust, however, that no suit will be necessary. I think Mr. White and Mr. Payson will be very unwise if they do not accept your terms."[37] Thus, Langdell's advice reflected the sound strategy that the Websters' cooperation in a truncated legal process made their settlement offer less appealing, whereas passivity and the prospect of full due process made the offer more attractive.

Nevertheless, the Whites, encouraged by their lawyer Sewall, sought to obtain absolute ownership of one-third of the two estates. In order to increase the size of their share, Sewall argued that Mary and Joseph meant "to divide the real and personal property . . . into three shares, corresponding with the number of nieces. . . . This is the most natural division." Next, in order to defeat the "childless" provision that would bar the Whites from taking possession unconditionally, Sewall conjured an argument that "childless" means having lost a child: "Mrs. White is not a mother, and cannot die childless within the meaning of the will."[38] Finally, Sewall tried to circumvent the distribution clauses altogether by arguing

36. Langdell to Webster (8 July 1856).

37. Langdell to Webster (9 Aug. 1856). Emphasis added. According to Massachusetts law at the time, a husband had legal control of his wife's property; therefore, Langdell assumed that the husbands are dictating the strategy.

38. *Kuhn v. Webster* (1858), 9, 10. The will stated that the share of any "mother childless" was contingent (5), and this phrase, taken literally, gave support to Sewall's argument. But his interpretation rewarded nieces who had not had children and jeopardized the shares of those who had, whereas the intent of the will was clearly to direct the inheritance to future descendants.

that, when Mary Rowe died, her property passed to Joseph who took ownership absolutely, in fee simple. By Sewall's interpretation, Mary's property would pass to the heirs as Joseph's residue, and, according to the law of intestate succession, each niece would then take a third of Mary's legacy.[39]

In responding to Sewall, Langdell showed himself to be shrewd, adaptable, and strong-willed. Responding to Sewall's manipulation of the distribution clauses, Langdell argued that "the will of Mary Rowe gave Joseph an estate for life only."[40] As to the size of the shares, Langdell maintained, "The property specified is to be divided equally among the nieces and their children per capita, and not per stirpes [by family]. When property is to be divised [sic] to several persons, as joint tenants or tenants in common, they will be held to take equally, per capita, unless the will clearly manifests a contrary intention."[41]

Finally, Langdell turned Sewall's "childless" argument in favor of the Websters, arguing that one could die childless until one's child successfully became an adult. Hence, Langdell maintained that, among the nieces, only Mary Webster, who had an adult son, and Joseph Webster, who had turned twenty-one, should receive their shares absolutely, while the nieces Penelope White and Anne Payson (who did not yet have children who had turned twenty-one or married) and Hannah Webster's and Anne Payson's daughters (who had not yet turned twenty-one or married) should receive their shares contingently.[42] By this gambit, Langdell opened the possibility for his clients to gain possession of both estates in their entirety, in the event that either Anne Payson or her daughter died before the latter reached age twenty-one or married. If Sewall and the Whites spurned compromise and became aggressively ingenious, then so would Langdell and the Websters.

As the parties dug in their positions during the summer of 1856, the Whites proposed to submit the matter to a referee. Langdell strongly advised Webster against following this route, objecting repeatedly in this case and subsequent cases based on his experience of legal practice in New York City. First, Langdell argued that it would be inefficient and expensive to appeal to a referee, who would charge a large fee, conduct a full examination, and likely require lawyers to appear, at greater expense.[43] On this point, Langdell was showing the influence of eighteen months of practice in New York City, where refereeing was the main vehicle of judicial corruption. Although the 1846 New York Constitution removed opportuni-

---

39. *Kuhn v. Webster* (1858), 12–13.
40. *Kuhn v. Webster* (1858), 10, 11–12.
41. *Kuhn v. Webster* (1858), 14.
42. *Kuhn v. Webster* (1858), 14–15.
43. Langdell to Webster (19 Aug. 1856).

ties for judicial patronage in order to reduce corruption, one of the major avenues remaining for judges was "full power to appoint their friends to very lucrative positions" as a referee, who "charges for every day in which he does anything in a cause, even if he merely adjourns it to another day.... [A] steady flow of such business would not be unprofitable, even at the usual rates. But in cases of importance...he can make his own terms...say fifty to one hundred dollars a day."[44] This contemporary description comports with Langdell's comment to Webster that "it is the uniform judgment of lawyers of experience that a referee is the worst mode in the world of deciding a controversy; and that nothing but very special circumstances will render it advisable."[45]

Langdell objected, secondly, that this form of process was simply ineffective: "Now if the matter should be submitted to a referee, and he should decide these questions in your favor, what would his decision be good for?" If the other party disagreed, "there would be no means of enforcing the decision of the referee. An authoritative decree of a court of equity is the only thing upon which any reliance can be placed in such a matter of trust." As Langdell maintained about probate court, if the parties could not agree among themselves, then why would they concur with an unenforceable decision against them?

Finally, Langdell objected to the quality of a decision that would come from an official whose criteria and rules for making a decision were ambiguous and uncertain.

> Do they propose that [the referee] should decide the case according to what his own private judgment may dictate, regardless of the law, except so far as he may choose to take it into consideration, or do they propose that he should consider the questions presented as strict legal questions, and be found to examine and decide them according to law, as the court would do? If the former, I would not listen to it for a moment; for although I should not...doubt...the conclusions at which a man of good sense would arrive, I would not run the risk. Besides, I should not like the idea of surrendering up rights of such importance to myself to the private judgment or will or whim or caprice of any man. If, on the other hand, the latter mode is proposed, I do not see that anything is gained.... After all is done, you only have

---

44. [Shearman], "New York City Judiciary" (1867), 153. See Lerner, "From Popular Control to Independence: Reform of the Elected Judiciary."

45. Here and in the next six paragraphs, the text draws and quotes from Langdell to Webster (19 Aug., 22 Nov., 12 Dec. 1856, 16 Feb., 30 Aug., 8 Oct., 15 Oct. 1857).

the judgment of one man instead of a full bench, and that too without the
responsibility of official position....

Despite Langdell's objections, the Websters agreed to submit the case to a referee who was a justice of the Massachusetts Supreme Judicial Court. After meeting
with the Websters in Boston to prepare, Langdell waited in late November 1856
"with a good deal of interest and anxiety" for the referee's decision in his first
major case as lead counsel.

Early in December, the referee delivered a mixed decision that apparently concurred with Sewall's view that Mary Rowe's estate was residual and with Langdell's
view of the distribution clause. Langdell was prepared to assent to the disappointing
outcome, stating that a lawsuit could be avoided if the Whites agreed. But he also
told Webster, "you may depend upon it [the referee] is wrong. I have almost as little
doubt of that, as of my own existence. My con[vic]tions are very much stronger
than when I wrote before. And yet we can have no certain assurance that the court
will not agree with [the referee]. I can only say that if they do, they will commit
a great outrage." Despite Langdell's belief that the Whites got more than they deserved from the referee, the Whites would not abide by the decision, confirming
Langdell's warning against appealing to a referee. In mid-February 1857 Kuhn, the
administrator, decided to initiate a lawsuit in order to obtain directions to settle
the estate. Again, Langdell regretted that the parties could not compromise for
"that would have been the fair thing."

The planning for the suit before the Massachusetts Supreme Judicial Court
further reveals Langdell's balanced attention to strategy and to legal doctrine. Opposing Sewall's suggestion that the case be submitted without argument, Langdell
explained to his client not only that the doctrinal complexity required clear and
complete analysis, but also that Mrs. White enjoyed the tactical advantage "of
being heir at law, as well as legatee. So that, if the court should decide any point
incorrectly, there is a strong probability that it would result, one way or the other,
in [her] favor, and against you.... Consequently, I think it is for your interest to use
every means to enable the court to understand the case thoroughly." Furthermore,
while the Whites, as heirs at law, would stand to receive more if they could get the
will declared invalid, they "would much prefer that it should be done without any
active agency on [their] part. I would not be giving [them] that advantage.... Let
[them] take the responsibility of that position."

Both Webster's tactical disadvantage and the prospect of arguing his first major
case reinforced Langdell's inclination to analyze the legal issues thoroughly. In
August 1857 he was still researching case reports and wrote to Webster, "I very
much want more time to study the case. I have had it in my hands a good while, I

know, but it requires an infinite amount of study. There is scarcely a difficult doctrine in relation to wills, which it does not involve in some of its phases. I would like to employ all my spare time upon it for a year to come. The reason it requires so much time and study is that it is necessary to master subjects of great extent and excessive difficulty."

But Langdell had an additional motive for this jolting request for an extensive delay. He went on to say that "the immediate cause of my writing" is that Charles O'Conor "requested me to assist him in preparing for the summing up in the Parish will case, which I presume you have heard aplenty about. It is a contest as to the validity of a will disposing of more than a million of dollars. They have been a year and a half in taking the testimony, which fills *two thousand printed pages*. . . . It would have been a serious sacrifice to decline the Parish case, both because it would pay well, and because the proposition came from Mr. O'Conor, who is the great man of the New York bar."

Here Langdell spoke not as a legal scientist but as a careerist. Remarkably, he was telling his friend, Joseph Webster, who had given him his first major case and was preparing to go to court after waiting eighteen months, that he wanted to delay Webster's case for a year because a more lucrative and prestigious opportunity had appeared. The surprising point, within the legal culture of mid-nineteenth-century Wall Street, is not that Langdell chose the more lucrative and prestigious opportunity, but that he told his major client the reason for the delay. Webster apparently objected to Langdell's proposal because, one week later, Langdell agreed to move forward without delay. Nevertheless, Langdell accepted O'Conor's proposition and worked feverishly for the next two months.

The case of *Delafield v. Parish* was indeed a great opportunity for Langdell, and demonstrates his contribution to establishing the new role in litigation of crafting long, written briefs in complex cases with extensive documentation. Henry Parish, a wealthy New York merchant, had died in 1856, leaving an estate valued at about $35 million today.[46] In the years before his death, three amendments, benefiting his wife and widow above the other legatees, were added to his will, although Parish, who had suffered a stroke, could not read or write. The central issue of the case, therefore, was whether Parish was capable of altering his will after his stroke.[47] The case attracted a great deal of attention in the New York and Boston newspapers, and prominent attorneys worked on the case. Representing the widow were Francis Cutting and Evarts, mentor of Joseph Choate; the attorneys for Parish's

---

46. *Delafield v. Parish* (1857), 53.
47. *Delafield v. Parish* (1857), 16–17.

two brothers were James Brady, one of the leaders of the bar, and O'Conor, the foremost member of the New York City bar in the late 1850s, famous for his meticulous preparation and extraordinary record of winning cases.[48]

Langdell met O'Conor in the New York Law Institute, whose membership comprised the intellectual leaders of the New York City bar, including David Field, Samuel Tilden, and Oakey Hall, as well as Brady, Evarts, Cutting, and O'Conor. At the Institute in the summer of 1857, Langdell was researching Webster's case at the same time as O'Conor was starting to synthesize the two thousand pages of testimony and countless case reports into a final argument for *Delafield v. Parish*.[49] Impressed by Langdell's expertise, O'Conor invited him to help, and Langdell worked exhaustively on the Parish case until the summation was due in late October 1857. Two months later, the court decided that the stroke had partially impaired the testamentary capacity of Parish and that only the first of the three amendments should stand.[50] In response to the mixed decision, O'Conor launched an appeal, but Langdell, having impressed some of the leading attorneys in the city, had already turned back to Webster's case.

In the intervening months, Langdell had written at length to Webster about various Boston lawyers and their fees in order to help him select a member of the Boston bar to file the appropriate papers and represent him in the Massachusetts courts. Ultimately, Webster retained the distinguished Boston attorney Peleg Chandler, along with his partner Shattuck, Langdell's classmate from college and law school and his fellow research assistant of Theophilus Parsons.[51] Progress on the case was slowed, in part, because the Whites and attorney Sewall were reluctant to divulge their answer to the suit, though they were obligated to do so. For his part Langdell repeatedly blunted and parried Sewall's sharp practice, but did not engage in such tactics himself, maintaining that "we should not prejudice our just claims by putting forward those which are not well founded."[52] At the end of October 1857 Langdell tried to expedite the suit by sailing to Boston to meet his client and the opposing counsel.

Over the next six months while the parties waited for a court date, Langdell and

48. George A. Miller, "James Coolidge Carter," in Lewis, *Great American Lawyers*, 8:8. See G. Martin, *Causes and Conflicts*, 4, 22; *DAB*, s.v. "O'Conor, Charles"; Bergan, *History of the New York Court of Appeals*, 28–29; E. Martin, *Life of Joseph Hodges Choate*, 1:113; LaPiana, "Just the Facts: The Field Code and the Case Method," 314n168.

49. New York Law Institute, *Catalog*, 1–5; Ames, "Christopher Columbus Langdell, 1826–1906," 473. See Langdell to Webster (15 Oct. 1857).

50. Langdell to Webster (30 Aug., 8 Oct., 15 Oct. 1857); *Delafield v. Parish* (1857), 128–29.

51. Langdell to Webster (11 Oct. 1857); O. Holmes, *Memoir of George Otis Shattuck* (1900), 9. On Chandler, see Ware, "Remarks," 16; Hoar, "Remarks," 10.

52. Langdell to Webster (12 Oct. 1857).

Webster corresponded little. New York and the entire nation were deeply troubled politically, economically, and culturally. In the wake of the 1856 conflict between Free-Soilers and proslavery advocates in "bleeding Kansas," the threats of secession and armed response heightened tensions between the North and the South. On 13 October 1857, a financial panic commenced in New York City when all but one of the fifty-eight banks ceased payments in specie, sending crowds of people into Wall Street rushing between banks and brokerage houses. In the ensuing months, property values plummeted, unemployment rose sharply, and businesses, broker-ages, and banks failed, while the panic spread across the country.[53]

Despite these troubles, Langdell's career blossomed, engulfing him in work. "I have been driven to death for the last two or three months," he wrote to Web-ster. "I have had another heavy will case, which occupied me constantly for two months, and in which I prepared a long written argument," he continued, likely referring to the contemporaneous appeal in the Parish case.[54] Meanwhile, after meeting Langdell at the New York Law Institute, the successful lawyer Stanley invited Langdell to become his partner. In August 1858 Langdell enthusiastically announced the opening of the firm Stanley & Langdell, No. 16 Wall St.: "You will see by this [letterhead] the nature of my new business arrangements. I think they promise very finely in a pecuniary point of view. . . . I must begin to put some money in my purse, or old age would overtake me without a cent ahead. We have just as much business as we can do; though I suppose we should do more, if we had it."[55] Due to the press of work, Langdell wrote to Webster rarely and hurriedly in the subsequent months and finally extricated himself from composing and editing the notes to Parsons's treatises.[56]

In June 1858 Sewall attempted another maneuver on behalf of his client by amending his original answer and claiming that a large amount of commercial stock was residue of the estate. This designation would circumvent the distribu-tion provision of the wills, and the stock would pass directly and permanently to the three nieces as heirs at law. Having anticipated this maneuver, Langdell

---

53. Museum of the City of New York, description of *Wall Street, Half Past Two O'clock, Oct. 13, 1857,* <http://www.mcny.org/collections/painting> (19 December 2006).

54. The quotation is from Langdell to Webster (12 June 1858). *Parish v. Parish* (1858), 279–80.

55. Langdell to Webster (6 Aug. 1858). Ames, "Christopher Columbus Langdell, 1826–1906," 473.

56. Wilder to Warren (11 Oct. 1907); Langdell to Machen (19 Mar. 1856). Also at this time, Langdell likely gave up the project of preparing "A Treatise on the Law of Corporations, Civil and Eleemosynary, Municipal and Private," which was being advertised by Little Brown Publishing Company during the late 1850s. See "Catalog of Law Books, 1858," in Little, Brown, Papers, box 5. This project must have been arranged by Theophilus Parsons who had been repeatedly urging Langdell and Alfred Machen to sign contracts with Little, Brown to produce treatises on various topics. See Th. Parsons to Machen (13, 25 Mar. 1855).

Wall Street, Half Past Two O'clock, October 13, 1857 (1858), painted by James Cafferty and Charles G. Rosenberg. Courtesy of the Museum of the City of New York.

immediately wrote to Shattuck, conceding the claim, in part, but stating that "it would be unfair for us to admit that 'a large amount'" was residue since no one knew the exact amount. He thus proposed a compromise to split the stock. Once again, the Whites and Sewall did not agree, and Langdell finally decided to oppose Sewall's amendment.[57]

In late October 1858 Langdell made one more trip to Boston to confer with Webster, and then prepared the written brief that he and Chandler presented before the court in November 1858. After the arguments, there was nothing to do but wait, and in the ensuing months Langdell periodically wrote to Webster asking for news, anxious to know the outcome of his first major case in which he had opposed a formidable veteran attorney.[58] The decision came down in June 1859, and Langdell won on all counts.

The court held that, when Mary Rowe died, her property became a life estate of Joseph, held in trust to pay the legacies and annuities. Second, the estates had to be divided six ways among the nieces and their children. Finally, the court accepted Langdell's argument that the shares of all but Mary and Joseph Webster were contingent and defeasible.[59] It was the best possible result for the Websters and the worst for the Whites, who had lost everything through Sewall's attempt to defeat the wills. Naturally pleased, Langdell did not pause to relish the outcome but immediately turned to the endgame: "We must try to get a decree to suit us in regard to the state of the property, and then our triumph will be complete." He therefore advised Webster to let the other parties bear the burden of proving that any of the stock was "after-acquired" and, hence, residual and liable to pass to the heirs at law.[60]

Just as Langdell suspected, this final decree took some negotiation as Sewall and the original referee tried to eviscerate the decision, leading Langdell to protest, "it is rather disgusting to have them putting their heads together." Above all, he warned Webster against the trap of agreeing to any provision whereby disputes over the state of the property would be submitted to a master for mediation. In this regard, Langdell unfurled his full complaint about the semilegal process of employing referees:

57. Quotations are from Langdell to Webster (4 June 1858); Langdell to Shattuck (4 June 1858). See Langdell to Webster (12 June 1858).

58. Langdell to Webster (27 Oct. 1856; 30 Apr. 1856, leaf 20; 28 Jan. 1859); *Kuhn v. Webster* (1858), 10–15.

59. In particular, "Mrs. White's share is contingent, liable to be divested and go to her sisters in case she should die childless." *Kuhn v. Webster* (1858), 16–17.

60. Quotations in this paragraph and the following are from: Langdell to Webster (8, 19, 26 July 1859). Emphasis in original.

I say, don't consent to Sewall's amendment [to go to a master for mediation.] I will send you . . . the legal reasons, which show that there is no foundation for it. The reason which weighs with me most practically is that it will give [the referee] and Sewall a chance to annoy us, and have reference to a master, and delay the settlement of the estate, *and make a little more money*, without being of any service to anybody. . . . I have no idea that they expect to accomplish anything by the amendment, and for that reason I think it is mean and disgusting. [The referee] hasn't done anything from the beginning, but put some money in his pocket and make trouble. . . . Resist by all means any thing which will carry the case before a master. There would be no knowing when we should see the end of it. . . . Upon going before a master, the question would at once arise in regard to the burden of proof; the master would decide it, and then there would be an appeal to the court.

Thus, Langdell evaluated legal process in terms of its effectiveness and efficiency, and despised attorneys or judges who extended or manufactured legal process in order to pad their fees.

Instead, Langdell adopted a "high-minded" ethic[61] of "just price" in setting lawyers' fees,[62] as reflected in his approach to charging Webster for his services: "As to what my charge will be, I hardly know what to say. . . . I will say that my bill for everything that I can do for you, without leaving New York, until the whole matter is settled, shall not exceed two hundred dollars. And if the matter should turn out that you should regard that figure as too large a sum, I certainly shall not be unreasonable. If the matter should stop here, I suppose I should charge about one hundred dollars. But at any event don't let this matter have any influence upon your communicating with me."[63]

Commensurately, Langdell decried contingency fees and the associated market forces that undermined the traditional just-price ethic. "No high-minded man would be willing to agree to charge nothing unless you won the case. It would look too much like speculating," he wrote, "Lawyers who do business in that way charge enormous fees in case of success, to make up for the risk."[64] By the same token, it was "mean and disgusting" for lawyers or court officials to extend or

---

61. Langdell to Webster (16 Feb. 1857).

62. Inherited from the Middle Ages and long persistent in New England, the ethic of "just price" was the charge "willingly paid by a person experienced in such matters and in need of the article but under no undue compulsion to buy." Bailyn, *New England Merchants*, 20–21. The traditional just-price ethic was reflected in the statutory regulation of lawyers' fees that continued through the 1840s. Kimball, *True Professional Ideal*, 175–79.

63. Langdell to Webster (19 May 1856).

64. Langdell to Webster (16 Feb. 1857).

manufacture legal process for the sake of increasing their fees. Just as opportunities for higher education should be determined by merit that is demonstrated by academic achievement, so professional rewards and advancement should be determined by merit that is evaluated by expertise and effort, not by market forces, he maintained.

When finally determining his fee two-and-a-half years later, Langdell adhered to his notion of setting his price justly rather than in relation to the market, that is, the amount that the Websters received. He wrote: "You advanced me a little over a hundred dollars. I think you had better let that go against my expenses and disbursements, and the various little odds and ends that I have attended to. . . . I think it would be a fair thing for you to give me seven hundred ($700) more. I might give various reasons for thinking that a moderate charge, but I don't think it necessary. When you consider the whole course of the litigation from the time when you first wrote to me, and the results of it, I think you will be satisfied that the charge is at least reasonable."[65]

More than reasonable, Langdell's fee was one of the great bargains in Wall Street litigation during the 1850s. For three-and-a-half years of counsel that secured his two clients well over $1 million—and the nearly inevitable prospect of close to a million more when Mrs. White died—Langdell charged a fee that would be about $20,000 today, or about 1 percent of the award. Of course, this just-price standard was easier to adopt in his first major case, which provided other kinds of compensation. "I almost regret to see the matter coming to an end," he wrote to Webster. "It was the first case of importance that I ever had charge of, and I never expect to have one that will give me greater satisfaction. Indeed, there has been a clamor about it which I never expect another case to possess."[66]

—◊◊◊—

Contributing to Langdell's satisfaction in October 1859, the distinguished attorney Edwards Pierrepont decided to join Stanley and Langdell. Having practiced with Stanley until being elected to the Superior Court of New York in 1857, Judge Pierrepont now returned as the senior partner and provided new contacts for the firm at 16 Wall Street. Soon after joining the firm, for example, Pierrepont was invited by William B. Astor, the wealthiest man in the United States, to join Governor Hamilton Fish, Evarts, O'Conor, and other notables at a dinner for the justices of the New York Court of Appeals. Langdell therefore crowed about Pierrepont's arrival and the prospects of the firm: "You will see by this [letterhead] that we have had a

65. Langdell to Webster (5 Oct. 1859).
66. Langdell to Webster (5 Oct. 1859).

change in our office; we intend that the world shall know it."[67] Commensurately, Langdell felt relieved of worries about money for the first time in his life, and he continued supporting his father financially on the farm in New Boston.[68]

But the outlook was bleak for the most of the city and the nation. The Panic of 1857 culminated in a depression that hit New York City hard due to its dependence on trade with Southern states. John Brown's raid on Harper's Ferry in October 1858 put the entire country on edge, and Abraham Lincoln's election in November 1860 prompted South Carolina to secede. When Confederate forces fired on Fort Sumter in April 1861, the Civil War commenced, and the ensuing hostilities touched Langdell's family. In 1862 his older sister and closest confidant, Hannah, and her husband, Rev. Austin Warner, went to serve a Presbyterian church at Fort Lincoln, Kansas, one of a series of Union forts guarding against Confederate raiders. In 1864 Austin Warner reported a raid on his family: "the rebels ... robbed me of a fine horse and three hundred dollars worth of clothing. They took bedding, blankets, comforters, and sheets—my own clothing and Mrs. W's except for what we had upon our backs and the material for the children's winter clothing."[69] Ever generous to his family and friends in need, Langdell sent money to his sister and brother-in-law throughout at least the early 1870s.[70]

In April 1863 the New York Supreme Court heard the second reported case in which Langdell participated. Pertaining directly to his central interest and expertise, the case went to the Supreme Court sitting in equity and unsuccessfully challenged the court's appointment of a replacement trustee for a trust created by a will.[71] Another reported case initiated in 1863 expressly listed as co-counsel Langdell and Brady, whom Langdell had favorably impressed in the Parish will case. Involving two separate litigations with two trials and four appeals over the next eight years, the Madison Avenue Baptist Church case addressed a dispute between two factions of a church over the disposition of church property.[72]

By this point, lawyers in Langdell's hometown ranked him among the few from New Boston who "have already gained, or are rapidly gaining, eminence in the profession." The committee planning the town's centennial celebration urged him

---

67. Langdell to Webster (7 Dec. 1860). Strong, *Diary*, 2:ix, 3:117; *DAB*, s.v. "Pierrepont, Edwards."

68. S. Atwood to Batchelder (8 Aug. 1906); Langdell, Check Ledger 1871–75; New Boston, Tax Inventory, 1861, 1862, 1863; "1871 Tax Inventory, School District 16," in New Boston, *Annual Report for 1871*, xv.

69. Warner, Report of Superintendent of Public Instruction 1864. See Porter, "Biographical Sketch of the Pastors," 14–16; E. Robinson, *Ministerial Directory*, 527; Kansas State Historical Society, *Transactions 1905–1906*, 9:566.

70. See Hannah (Langdell) Warner to Mildred C. Warren (1907), in F. Atwood, *Old Folks' Day*, 11–12; Langdell, Check Ledger 1871–75, no. 115.

71. *Milbank v. Crane* (1863).

72. *Madison v. Madison* (1863), 73.

to return and be honored at the festivities on 4 July 1863. But he declined because "my engagements are likely to be of such a character as to make it inconvenient, if not impracticable, for me to leave town during the early part of July."[73] Langdell was certainly busy with his law practice, and, if he had agreed to go, his plans may have changed in late June when the battle of Gettysburg began and widespread riots against the draft broke out in New York City. Yet, he characteristically avoided commemorative social obligations. His longstanding friend, Theodore Tebbets, lived in New York City between 1860 and 1863, while trying to recover from a severe pulmonary disease. When Tebbets died in January 1863, Langdell apparently failed to write a commemoration of his friend, as was customary at the time.[74]

In 1864 Pierrepont left the firm and entered national politics, ultimately serving as U.S. attorney general and then ambassador to Great Britain under President Grant. Pierrepont was replaced by Brown, Stanley's friend and Langdell's Harvard classmate.[75] Assuming senior status in the firm, Langdell became sole counsel in an appeal to the highest court in New York State of a case that Stanley had lost in 1859. But Langdell did not persuade the New York Court of Appeals that his client debtor was not liable to a new creditor for promissory notes that had been fraudulently obtained from the original creditor.[76]

A few months later Langdell opposed his sometime critic and former Harvard classmate and member of Alpha Delta Phi, Joseph Choate. Argued before the New York Supreme Court, this case arose when a Massachusetts firm gave promissory notes to a New York creditor, then went bankrupt, and was granted insolvency protection by a Massachusetts court, which appointed an assignee. The New York creditor, Choate's client, obtained an order in New York for a sheriff to seize the firm's assets in New York. But the Massachusetts-appointed assignee went to New York, retained Langdell, and claimed that the assets should be released to him. Facing two parties with contradictory claims, the sheriff brought suit in New York to find out who should take possession of the assets. The court ruled in favor of Langdell.[77]

73. Quotations are, respectively, from Dodge, "Lawyers of New Boston" (1864); Langdell to Cogswell (22 June 1863).

74. Harvard College Class of 1851, Class Book, 533; *New England Historical and Genealogical Register* (1863); Langdell to Webster (16 June 1860). See Bernstein, *New York City Draft Riots*.

75. *New York Times*, 10 Apr. 1913; *DAB*, s.v. "Pierrepont, Edwards"; Kimball and Brown, "Highest Legal Ability," 79–80.

76. *City Bank v. Perkins* (1859); *City Bank v. Perkins* (1864), 562–63.

77. *Kelly v. Crapo* (1864). After Langdell left New York, the decision was reversed by the New York Court of Appeals, with Stanley representing the Massachusetts assignee and Choate the New York creditor. *Kelly v. Crapo* (1871). In the U.S. Supreme Court, however, Edwards Pierrepont and Stanley prevailed over William Evarts, and Langdell's argument was upheld. *Crapo v. Kelly* (1872).

During spring 1865, as the Civil War drew to a close and Langdell prepared to summer in England, he was engaged in three reported cases. In March he and Stanley served as co-counsel in an appeal to the New York Supreme Court over whether a court-appointed receiver dishonestly profited from managing the property of a man who had died without a will.[78] The circumstances of the case and the disappearance of his client, the receiver, indicate that Langdell witnessed here some of the chicanery commonly practiced by receivers and referees in the New York City courts.

In May 1865 Langdell represented a group of citizens who were challenging the city assessors for overcharging on a municipal contract, which fit perfectly the pattern of Tammany Hall corruption at this time.[79] On appeal, the New York Supreme Court, headed by Judge Daniel P. Ingraham, determined that "the assessment made in this case was illegal, and that the order vacating it was right and should be affirmed."[80] In 1866 and 1867 the appeals in the Madison Avenue Baptist Church case began to unfold. Having argued as junior counsel before New York Superior Court Judge John H. McCunn in the trial,[81] Langdell now became leading co-counsel and James Brady secondary co-counsel, a transposition that demonstrated Langdell's rising status in the legal world. These appeals were unsuccessful, and Langdell, acting as sole counsel, appealed and lost again in 1869, when the court observed that Langdell was perseverating in the erroneous reasoning that McCunn had rejected.[82] Finally, in 1871, the case was appealed for a fourth time and to the highest court in New York State, the Court of Appeals. The argument of Langdell, who by that point had joined the faculty at HLS, carried the day: a religious corporation could alienate its real property only by way of a legislative statute, not through a transaction governed by common law.[83]

The late 1860s saw Langdell involved in several different kinds of litigation. In 1866 he successfully defended British creditor assignees against a demurrer to their bill in equity demanding the return of diamonds that an insolvent London merchant had sent to a New York merchant to be sold for a commission.[84] In April 1867 Stanley, Langdell, and Brown won an appeal in the New York Supreme Court on behalf of gold brokers who had been sued for executing a sale that lost money for their customers who were speculating on the gold market.[85] Later in

---

78. *Demarest v. Daig* (1865).
79. Strong, *Diary*, 2:114; Callow, *Tweed Ring*, 18; Bergan, *History of the New York Court of Appeals*, 30.
80. *In the matter of Turfler* (1865), 53.
81. *Madison v. Madison* (1865); *Madison v. Baptist* (1866); *Madison v. Baptist* (1867).
82. *Madison v. Baptist* (1869), 122–24.
83. *Madison v. Baptist* (1871).
84. *Hunt v. Jackson* (1866).
85. *Sterling v. Jaudon* (1867).

1867 Langdell and another attorney lost an appeal in equity that sought to block an injunction requiring stockholders of a bankrupt company to return dividends paid by the company. The opposing attorney was David D. Field, the most prominent lawyer in the state, if not the country.[86]

Langdell's practical experience as a lawyer, acquired through such cases, subsequently informed his teaching.[87] For example, these last three cases touched on the law of partnership and of bailments, concerning the obligations owed by someone entrusted to keep valuables for another. In spring 1870 Langdell lectured on partnership in the first course that he taught at HLS, and in the mid-1870s Langdell offered an advanced course on bailments. Similarly, the primary domain of Langdell's reported cases—equity procedure and jurisdiction—became the predominant subject of his teaching and writing at HLS.

In addition, Langdell's practical experience in equity law, as well as under the Field Code, exercised significant pedagogical influence by contributing to his longstanding interest in scrutinizing cases and, therefore, to his development of case method teaching. By contrast, the antebellum common-law attorney conventionally argued in the "grand style."[88] In this mode, "the lawyer ... relied on principles of law which he applied to the facts at hand, without much regard for decided cases ... [James C.] Carter was a brilliant practitioner of this method of argument, and in his pleadings and oral arguments he seldom bothered with cases. If the other lawyer offered a series of decisions against him, Carter simply argued more clearly and forcefully that the principles, when applied correctly, must produce the answer he advocated. ... This style of argument had evolved in a period when few cases were reported, and fewer still in full."[89]

Langdell's approach, even as a law student, differed radically from the grand style, and the nature of his practice enhanced his focus on precedents rather than general principles. Of Langdell's thirteen reported cases, only one fell under the traditional domains of common law governed by the forms of action: *City Bank of New Haven* (1864), which concerned bankruptcy and debt. *Madison Avenue* (1866, 1869) was brought on an action of ejectment, but was argued by Langdell as a matter of "special statutory authority" trumping the common law.[90] *Turfler* (1865) concerned municipal law; *Kelly* (1864) was a case in the interstate conflict of laws; *Sterling* (1867) concerned partnership. Six cases belonged to equity: *Kuhn* (1858),

---

86. *Osgood v. Laytin* (1867).

87. See Langdell, Lectures on Partnership and Commercial Paper, including his lectures on "Putting in Bail."

88. Llewellyn, *Common Law Tradition*, 62–75.

89. G. Martin, *Causes and Conflicts*, 195–96. See Grossman, "James Coolidge Carter."

90. *Madison v. Baptist* (1869), 113.

Madison Avenue (1863), *Hunt* (1866), *Milbank* (1863), *Demarest* (1865), and *Osgood* (1867), as did *Delafield* (1857). *Northern Railroad* (1869) was also brought on an equitable motion for a stay of proceedings, but was argued by Langdell as an issue of procedure under the Field Code.[91]

Practice in equity and under the Field Code directed lawyers' attention to the facts and decisions in prior reported cases. The Field Code, which substituted one "civil action" for the old forms of action in pleading, required that lawyers plead by fitting their case not to the requirements of the abandoned forms, but to the facts and rules of prior cases. Consequently, practice under the Field Code and in equity reinforced Langdell's disposition to scrutinize closely the facts and decisions of cases.[92] Also contributing to the shift in legal argument from invoking principles to citing precedents was the expanding publication of court reporters.[93]

These factors—the shift to Code Pleading, the predominance of Langdell's practice outside of common law, and the rise of case reporting—strengthened his established custom of analyzing precedents and, thus, contributed to his development of case method teaching after joining the HLS faculty in 1870. In addition, earlier factors had encouraged this development, including his reading of John Locke's *Education* at Exeter, his zoology and botany classes at Harvard College, his discussing cases with other students at HLS, and his research for Parsons's treatises.

Turning Point in 1868

By 1868, at age forty-two, Langdell had distinguished himself professionally, litigating a number of prominent cases that were heard by high courts in New York State and noted in the *New York Times*.[94] Compared to Brown, his HLS classmate and law partner who later earned distinction as a federal district judge, Langdell

---

91. *New York v. Northern Railroad* (1869), 104–24. In a detailed analysis of the contested section of the Code of Civil Procedure, Langdell identifies where the Code is inconsistent, where the Code is insufficient and still supplemented by past practice in Chancery, and where the Code contradicts the New York Constitution (107–10). By 1869, Langdell was quite prepared to argue, as sole counsel before the New York Supreme Court, about the proper interpretation of the Field Code.

92. LaPiana, "Just the Facts: The Field Code and the Case Method," 335; LaPiana, *Logic and Experience*, 70–74.

93. G. Martin, *Causes and Conflicts*, 195–96. Cf. Lind, "Economic Analysis of Early Casebook Publishing," 100–102.

94. Notices in the *New York Times* appeared on the following dates regarding *Kelly v. Crapo* (13 July 1864), 3; *Sterling v. Jaudon* (19 May 1865), 2; *Madison v. Madison* (3 May 1865), 2 (25 Jan. 1869), 5; *Hunt v. Jackson* (13 Aug. 1866), 3; *Osgood v. Laytin* (25 Apr. 1867), 2 (29 Mar. 1867), 2 (7 Feb. 1867), 3 (9 Feb. 1867), 3 (1 June 1867), 2 (27 Oct. 1867), 5 (12 Oct. 1867), 2.

appeared far more often in reported cases.[95] In the course of this work, he had prepared and argued cases with and against leading members of the bar, while developing a reputation for his expertise in commercial law, equity, and, especially, wills and estates. Langdell acquired skills of oral advocacy, as Judge Monell of the New York Superior Court observed: "It was earnestly contended by [Langdell], that this court was in error.... The confidence with which that position was attacked has led me to a further examination of the question."[96] Flushed with this success, Langdell became "an enthusiast... in his profession."[97]

The year 1868 marked a turning point. For the first time in six years, he did not litigate a reported case, and his interest in practicing law began to shift dramatically. One factor was the attraction of literary and scholarly endeavors, such as writing for John Bouvier's *Law Dictionary*. This publication was among the best of its genre, drawing eminent contributors, including Chancellors or supreme court justices from seventeen states; current or former U.S. senators from three states; law professors from Harvard, Columbia, Yale, New York University, Albany, Virginia, Cincinnati, and Tennessee; three federal judges and a U.S. Supreme Court justice; and two directors of federal agencies in Washington. The rest were leading practitioners, and nearly all the authors had published treatises on their topics.[98] Langdell was probably the least experienced or published of the ninety-five authors, and his six entries—actually, short essays, each averaging a full page—enhanced his reputation.

All six essays addressed marriage (Alimony, Condonation, Divorce, Nullity of Marriage, Separation *a Mensa et Thoro*, and Promise of Marriage), a subject that none of his reported cases had addressed. But the first five topics, concerning the ending of a marriage, fell under equity, in which he was becoming an expert. "Promise of marriage" was a contract issue that Langdell had addressed years earlier in a long letter to Webster.[99] In structure, each essay begins with a brief definition, then summarizes the governing principles and rules drawn from the case law and treatises. In substance, the essays provide historical background on the topics and search for legal rules and principles to resolve practical questions. Regarding permanent alimony, Langdell outlines four necessary conditions; in

---

95. Kimball and Brown, "Highest Legal Ability," 79–80. Official stenographers were authorized for the upper courts in New York only in 1865, and even then decisions were selectively reported in the upper courts for long afterward. G. Martin, *Causes and Conflicts*, 195–96; Lind, "Economic Analysis of Early Casebook Publishing," 100–101.

96. J. Monell in *Madison v. Baptist* (1869), 122.

97. J. Carter to Eliot (20 Dec. 1869).

98. Bouvier, *Law Dictionary*, 1:5–13.

99. Bouvier, *Law Dictionary*, s.v. "divorce," "separation." See Langdell to Webster (8 Mar. 1857).

discussing the validity of a divorce granted in one state for a marriage formed in another state, he specifies five important considerations. At the same time, he recognizes that rules are sometimes hard to discern, and that legal outcomes depend on the context. For instance, regarding the granting of divorce, there exist "few positive rules upon the subject, the matter being left to the discretion of the court, to be exercised according to the circumstances of each case."[100]

Langdell's interest in scholarship also found an outlet in voluntary associations. Soon after arriving in New York, he joined the New-York Historical Society as well as the New York Law Institute, established in 1828 "for literary purposes, the cultivation of legal science, . . . and the formation of a law library." In 1858 the *New York Times* announced that he had been elected an officer in the Institute, a role that occupied his free time thereafter.[101] In particular, Langdell worked to expand the holdings of the Institute's library with the help of English law book publisher and bookseller Robert Haynes, whom he visited in London in the summer of 1865.[102]

On returning to New York, Langdell reciprocated by providing Haynes with continued orders for the Institute's library as well as a network of contacts. These included leaders of the New York Law Institute, such as Brady, president from 1861 to 1868, and treasurer O'Conor, who succeeded Brady,[103] as well as HLS alumni in other cities, to whom Langdell wrote letters of introduction, particularly when Haynes made a tour of the United States in 1868.[104] Back in London, Haynes gratefully acknowledged Langdell's role in building the Anglo-American bibliographical network: "I have (thanks to YOU my friend) obtained not only the patronage but the approbation of the Library Authorities at Boston, Philadelphia, Baltimore, and Chicago."[105]

While these literary and scholarly endeavors were drawing Langdell away from legal practice by 1868, another factor was pushing him away, as was observed by Carter, an HLS classmate of Langdell and a leader of the New York City bar.[106]

100. Bouvier, *Law Dictionary*, s.v. "divorce." See also s.v. "alimony," "nullity of marriage," "separation *a mensa et thoro.*"

101. Quotation is from *New York Law Institute Library*, 3. See New York Law Institute, *Catalog*, 1–5; *New York Times*, 3 May 1858; New-York Historical Society, *Charter and By-Laws 1858.*

102. Langdell to Machen (26 Mar. 1868). Langdell describes his early activity in Langdell to Machen (18 Feb. 1858).

103. *New York Law Institute Library*, 3; New York Law Institute, *Catalog*, 1–5; Haynes to Langdell (10 Feb. 1870).

104. Langdell to Machen (26 Mar. 1868). Machen referred Haynes to a mutual friend in Detroit. A. Russell to Machen (1 May 1868).

105. Haynes to Langdell (10 Feb. 1870).

106. G. Martin, *Causes and Conflicts*, 173–74.

Langdell entered upon the practice of the law in this city with the high purposes natural to such a man. He would scorn to win, or to struggle for, any success which was not the legitimate reward of merit. . . . I think he soon conceived a hearty disgust for the means and methods by which business, place, and reputation are here [in New York City] gained. He was not suf- ficiently content to take the world as he found it, and the result has been a failure on his part to reach that place in the profession to which he would otherwise have easily risen. I think he must have felt, and perhaps still feels, much disappointment, and the effect of it may have been in some degree to impair the freshness and elasticity of his character and encourage a sort of dissatisfaction with himself and the world.[107]

What Carter perceived as Langdell's "failure" stemmed partly from their dif- ferent conceptions of legal expertise. Skilled in the "grand style," Carter relied on eloquent and persistent restatement of his basic principles in arguing cases and, commensurately, mastered "the popular manners and personal attractions and the arts of rivalry."[108] Langdell belonged to a new breed, armed with the highly technical expertise necessary for composing a long, thorough brief that synthe- sized a complex web of precedents and commercial transactions. Langdell took pride in his expertise and derided old-school lawyers, such as Washburn. But this difference alone does not explain Langdell's "dissatisfaction with himself and the world," because he likely realized that the future of legal practice lay with his new expertise, which was gaining value.

In addition, as Shattuck observed from Boston, Langdell "is out of relations with the present state of things in New York. He is disgusted with their courts and general mode of doing business."[109] Indeed, Alfred Russell, the U.S. district attorney for Michigan and an HLS classmate of Langdell, wrote in May 1868, "I saw Langdell not very long ago and found him . . . breathing out slaughter [sic] against the New York judicial system and judiciary. He declares counsel are retained in consideration of private and other '*influences*' with the judges and not in view of their abilities, learning, or experience! Democracy can reach no lower deep."[110] Langdell was indeed disgusted, and the cause was the corrupt relations among lawyers and judges that provided the "means and methods by which business,

---

107. J. Carter to Eliot (20 Dec. 1869).
108. J. Carter to Eliot (20 Dec. 1869).
109. Shattuck to Eliot (17 Dec. 1869).
110. A. Russell to Machen (1 May 1868). On Russell, see G. Reed, *Bench and Bar of Michigan*, 408–11; A. Russell, *Avoidable Causes of Delay*, 35.

place, and reputation are...gained" in New York. Nor was Langdell alone, for Russell recoiled as well.

The late 1860s corruption of the New York City bench and bar was spawned by the growing power of the Tammany Hall political machine, headed by Tweed and his cronies Peter Sweeney, Oakey Hall, and Richard Connolly. In fact, "the year 1868 was a turning point in the history of the Tweed Ring," because it gained control over state legislative committees through bribery and patronage, and became the most potent political force in the state.[111] A key instrument in the hands of the Tweed Ring was the manipulation of the judicial system, facilitated by two structural anomalies introduced by the Field Code of Procedure.

On the one hand, although the thirty-one Supreme Court justices were elected by voters in eight separate districts, the jurisdiction of each justice's actions in equity, such as issuing injunctions, extended throughout the state. The overlap of jurisdictions allowed for and even promoted conflicting judicial orders. On the other hand, judges had almost unlimited power to issue injunctions and appoint receivers in ex parte proceedings, in which only one side of a dispute is heard and the judge then decides if there is enough evidence and legal standing to order a full hearing.[112] By controlling a number of well-positioned judges and manipulating these two structural provisions, the Tweed Ring was able to secure injunctions and delays to block opponents' legal moves whenever and wherever it wished, as well as to arrange for the appointment of receivers and referees who creamed off and kicked back enormous fees into Tweed coffers.[113] Among the notorious Tweed-controlled judicial officials were Supreme Court Justices George Barnard and Albert Cardozo, Superior Court Judge McCunn, Clerk of the Superior Court Sweeney, and district attorney Hall.[114]

During 1868 and 1869 the self-enrichment of the Tweed Ring, its manipulation of the judicial system, and the complicity of prominent lawyers came into public view in the Erie Wars, a series of legal battles over control of the stock of the Erie Railroad. The first Erie War pitted the industrialist Cornelius Vanderbilt against the railroad's corrupt directors, James Fisk, Jay Gould, and Daniel Drew. The counsel for each side were drawn from the most eminent lawyers in the city. Vanderbilt's lawyers were led by O'Conor, who, with the aid of Boss Tweed, obtained from the

---

111. Quotation is from Callow, *Tweed Ring*, 207. See also 69–79, 146–48, 211–15; Mandelbaum, *Boss Tweed's New York*, 50–51.

112. New York State, *Code of Civil Procedure*, §§40–42, 545–46, 715.

113. G. Martin, *Causes and Conflicts*, 5; J. Gordon, *Scarlet Woman of Wall Street*, 162; Strong, *Diary*, 4:264.

114. Callow, *Tweed Ring*, 134–43; Ackerman, *Gold Ring: Jim Fisk, Jay Gould, and Black Friday*, 28–29.

notorious Justice Barnard the injunctions needed to stymie Fisk, Gould, and Drew. Meanwhile, those three retained forty-one lawyers, led by Field and including Evarts, Tilden, and Pierrepont, who parried Vanderbilt by securing injunctions from justices favorable to them. At the same time, Supreme Court Justice Ingraham was issuing injunctions on behalf of the honest stockholders.

A compromise and truce were ultimately worked out, but in the course of one month, "five judges had issued seven injunctions, all enjoining or commanding things wholly inconsistent," and the incoherence and complicity of bench and bar in the shenanigans had been blatantly exposed in the public press.[115] The first, month-long Erie War ended in a draw, but Fisk and Gould realized the advantage of having the Tweed Ring and its judicial contacts on their side, so they replaced Drew with Boss Tweed on the board. When a second Erie War erupted late in 1868, Field and his legal stable were able to ward off challenges to the stock manipulations of their clients through savvy employment of injunctions and ex parte hearings. They employed similar tactics in yet a third Erie War in 1869 that concerned a related railroad.

Langdell was not alone in recoiling from the corruption epitomized by the Erie Wars, and manifested in innumerable lower-profile cases as well. Early in 1868 Langdell's colleague Brady, the president of the New York Law Institute, amazed his colleagues when he erupted one day in court and accused Supreme Court Justice Barnard of being in league with a corrupt court receiver whom Barnard had appointed.[116] In April 1868, shortly after the first Erie War, the prominent Wall Street lawyer George Strong wrote in his journal: "Bench and bar settle deeper in the mud every year and every month. They must be near the bottom now. Witness the indecencies done and suffered by [David] Field, Barnard, Brady, Haskin, etc. in general term of supreme court, as reported in the newspapers . . . [in which] many bits of specially pungent Billingsgate are suppressed as too filthy to print. . . . The Supreme Court is our *cloaca maxima*, with lawyers for its rats. But my simile does that rodent injustice, for the rat is a remarkably clean animal."[117] Only a few weeks later, Langdell was "breathing out slaughter" against the New York judiciary to the U.S. District Attorney for Michigan.[118]

---

115. Quotation is from G. Martin, *Causes and Conflicts*, 5. Material about the Erie Wars is drawn from G. Martin, *Causes and Conflicts*, 4–12; J. Gordon, *Scarlet Woman of Wall Street*, 168, 226–29; Callow, *Tweed Ring*, 219; Bergan, *History of the New York Court of Appeals*, 38–39; Ackerman, *Gold Ring: Jim Fisk, Jay Gould, and Black Friday.*

116. G. Martin, *Causes and Conflicts*, 9–10.

117. Strong, *Diary*, 4:202. *Cloaca maxima* means, in Latin, "greatest sewer."

118. A. Russell to Machen (1 May 1868).

In October 1868 Charles Francis Adams Jr. pilloried the complicity of the bench and bar during the first Erie War in the *American Law Review* and followed with another article in the *North American Review* after the second Erie War.[119] He later famously elaborated these assessments:

> The degradation of the bench had been rapidly followed by the degradation of the bar. Prominent and learned lawyers were already accustomed to avail themselves of social or business relations with judges to forward private purposes. One whose partner was elevated to the bench was certain to be generally retained in cases brought before this special judge; and litigants were taught by experience that a retainer in such cases was profitably bestowed.... The debasement of the tone was not confined to the lower ranks of advocates; and it was probably this steady demoralization of the bar which made it possible for the Erie ring to obtain the services of Mr. David Dudley Field as its legal advisor.[120]

Consequently, Langdell was not without sympathizers or justification in expressing "hearty disgust" about the New York bench and bar in 1868 and 1869. In fact, he was closer to the problems than many, because the very success of Langdell's first dozen years in practice on Wall Street had personally acquainted him with many of the central figures in the Erie Wars and the Tweed Ring—both the whistle-blowers and the culprits or collaborators. Among the latter group were O'Conor, Judge McCunn, Field, Pierrepont, Evarts, Hall, and Drew, who ousted the first president of the Erie Railroad, Eleazar Lord, who retained Langdell as counsel in June 1869, as described below.

Among the whistle-blowers were Brady, Judge Ingraham, and, above all, Eaton. Having brought Langdell into his law firm in 1855, Eaton began representing Fisk and Gould in the first Erie War until he realized that they were as pernicious as Vanderbilt, at which point Eaton began a personal campaign against the Tweed Ring corruption. His crusade ended in February 1870 when he was brutally beaten by a gang of Tweed thugs.[121] Eaton may, in fact, have been the most direct or fervent stimulus of Langdell's disaffection from the New York bench and bar.

Langdell was therefore acquainted with many figures involved in the Erie Wars and the Tweed Ring, while he experienced in his legal practice the coordinate influences of corruption and Code pleading, as seen in his final reported case before he left New York, *State of New York v. Northern Railroad* (1869).

---

119. See C. Adams, "Erie Railroad Row"; C. Adams "A Chapter of Erie."

120. C. Adams and H. Adams, *Chapters of Erie*, 110.

121. McFarland, "Partisan of Nonpartisanship: Dorman B. Eaton," 809–10; J. Gordon, *Scarlet Woman of Wall Street*, 216; G. Martin, *Causes and Conflicts*, 40.

In the mid-1850s the Northern Railroad, located in upstate New York, had its mortgages fraudulently foreclosed by the mortgage trustees, who took control of the railroad. Under private legislative acts of 1857 and 1864, the trustees then improperly dissolved the corporation, assumed its franchises, and incorporated themselves as the Ogdensburgh and Lake Champlain Railroad. Three original directors of Northern Railroad tried to continue operating and soliciting investors,[122] and the New York attorney general brought an action in 1867 to dissolve Northern Railroad and to enjoin the original directors from trying to operate it.[123] The case was heard before Justice James of the New York Supreme Court in May 1868.

Representing the original directors, Langdell requested an equitable stay of proceedings, pending the outcome of the suit they had commenced earlier, alleging fraud on the part of the Ogdensburg directors, who "are the real plaintiffs in this suit" on whose behalf the attorney general had brought the action in order to correct the improper dissolution of the original corporation.[124] The attorney general replied that Langdell had not denied the allegations, and asked for a summary judgment on the pleadings.[125] Justice James decided for the attorney general on every count, and caustically derided Langdell's long, complex answer as "sham and irrelevant," saying that it admitted everything that the attorney general alleged, while also contradicting itself by trying to deny those same points.[126] James's rebuke, issued just as Langdell was "breathing out slaughter against the judicial system and judiciary" in May 1868,[127] surely added to Langdell's outrage. Moreover, James's refusal to consider his "equitable jurisdiction" and look behind the formal and fraudulent facade of events is consistent with what Langdell denounced: that influence peddling was rampant among the judiciary.

Whatever the extralegal influence on James, the original directors immediately appealed, with Langdell as their sole counsel. The appeal turned on the issue that the Code of Procedure had intended to make moot: whether the form of the directors' pleading was technically correct. In a twofold irony, Langdell was required to make a technical argument on behalf of the simplicity of Code Pleading, whose simplification he had previously lamented. The specific questions were whether Langdell's answer had actually denied the attorney general's allegations and, if not, what the court should have done in response, particularly given that the defendants had requested an equitable stay of the proceeding.

---

122. *New York v. Northern Railroad* (1870), 221, 224.
123. *New York v. Northern Railroad* (1870), 218.
124. *New York v. Northern Railroad* (1869), 105.
125. *New York v. Northern Railroad* (1870), 224–25.
126. J. James unreported opinion of May 1868, quoted in *New York v. Northern Railroad* (1869), 100.
127. A. Russell to Machen (1 May 1868).

Langdell argued, first, that the court should look behind the attorney general in order to see the effective plaintiff: the mortgage trustees and Ogdensburgh directors. If the court exercised its equitable jurisdiction in this way, it would see not only that the real plaintiffs were the mortgage trustees and Ogdensburgh directors, who sought to dissolve the Northern Railroad, but also that "the very acts and omissions . . . relied upon as a ground for" dissolving the charter of Northern Railroad "were caused by the fraud of" the trustees and Ogdensburgh directors.[128] Second, Langdell argued that Justice James should not have considered, let alone granted, the plaintiff's motion for judgment. Citing "the former practice in chancery" and the U.S. Constitution, Langdell maintained that the defendants did not receive proper notice and were entitled to trial by jury, and that the motion for judgment could only be heard in equity.[129]

Third, Langdell asserted that, if his answer was somehow not in conformity with the Code of Procedure, then an opportunity to amend it should have been offered. To dismiss his answer due to a procedural defect "is as hostile to the spirit of our present system of practice [under the Field Code] as it is inconsistent with every idea of natural justice."[130] In these words, Langdell underscored the irony that the fundamental rationale of replacing the forms of action with the Code of Procedure was being undermined by the procedural stringency applied to his client. Furthermore, "any admissions contained in the answer" did not warrant judgment for the plaintiff, because those admissions (and the seeming contradictions in the answer) arose by way of asserting that fraud had been perpetrated on the defendant.[131]

Fourth, Langdell argued that the franchises of the Northern Railroad could not be transferred to the Ogdensburgh Railroad by the legislative acts of 1857 and 1864, because "the Northern Railroad was a total stranger" to those acts, which were private acts and therefore could not impair the contractual rights of Northern Railroad, according to the U.S. Constitution. Fifth and finally, "the lower court had no authority to enjoin the defendants and appoint a receiver," because these actions were not provided in the governing section of the Code of Procedure.[132]

This appeal was heard in January 1869 by the New York Supreme Court, comprised of Justice James and three other justices. All four affirmed the substance and the tone of James's earlier decision. Langdell's "answer is stuffed with irrelevant and redundant matter," the court held; "there is no attempt at a specific denial of

128. *New York v. Northern Railroad* (1869), 107.

129. *New York v. Northern Railroad* (1869), 107–8.

130. *New York v. Northern Railroad* (1869), 108.

131. *New York v. Northern Railroad* (1869), 109.

132. *New York v. Northern Railroad* (1869), 109, 110; U.S. Constitution, art. 1, §10, cl. 1.

any allegation of the complaint; and the denial which follows a prolix and confused narrative . . . raise[s] no issue of fact in the case. . . ."[133] The court skirted Langdell's fourth argument, but, apart from that, his points were denied and derided. He immediately appealed to New York's highest court.

The New York Court of Appeals implicitly credited Langdell's fourth argument that the private legislative acts of 1857 and 1864 unconstitutionally deprived the Northern Railroad of its property and rights by conveying its franchises to the Ogdensburgh railroad. Although James had endorsed and invoked those acts, the higher New York courts wisely did not. In addition, Langdell's first, second, third, and fifth arguments began to be heard and credited, as Northern Railroad lost again, but barely. A majority of five justices concurred with the lower courts, while three judges would have overturned their decision.

Writing for the dissenters, Justice Foster opined that James's decision on Langdell's first argument was not reviewable, but likely incorrect. He then specifically agreed with Langdell's second, third, and fifth arguments, commending his reading of two cases which are "true exponents of the meaning of the Code in reference to such denials" of a plaintiff's allegations.[134] Foster also noted that the form of denying the plaintiffs' allegations adopted by Langdell, "which was in this case held to be incompetent and not authorized by the Code, is quite as common as any other form" appearing in cases before the Court of Appeals. Finally, Foster attributed some partiality to Justice James.[135]

In December 1870 the case was appealed to the U.S. Supreme Court, which held that it had no jurisdiction to hear the case. But the Supreme Court observed that if the lower court, unlike James, had rested its decision on the private legislative acts of 1857 and 1864, whose constitutionality Langdell challenged, then it would have asserted jurisdiction to hear the appeal.[136] In the end, therefore, all of Langdell's arguments were persuasive to a significant number of justices of the New York Court of Appeals. Nevertheless, the experience of litigating *Northern Railroad* surely exacerbated Langdell's already expressed outrage and contributed both to his alienation from the New York bench and bar and to his decision in December 1869 to leave New York and join the law faculty at Harvard.

During that same month, other lawyers also decided that they had had enough. Prompted by calls from the *New York Times* to form themselves into an association in order to resist Tammany's control of the judiciary, Carter and a few other

133. *New York v. Northern Railroad* (1869), 122.
134. *New York v. Northern Railroad* (1870), 232–40. Quotation is on p. 240.
135. *New York v. Northern Railroad* (1870), 241, 239–40.
136. *Northern Railroad v. New York* (1870).

eminent attorneys in mid-December 1869 circulated a request to elite lawyers of New York City to form a bar association. By the time Langdell left New York early in February, more than two hundred lawyers had responded affirmatively, and the New York City Bar Association was formed shortly thereafter as the first modern bar association in the nation.[137] When the Tweed scandals fully came to light in July 1871, the leaders of the New York City Bar Association headed up the Committee of Seventy that was formed to expose, prosecute, and extirpate Tweed's corruption.[138]

Paradoxically, the leadership of the New York City Bar Association and the Committee of the Seventy incorporated many eminent lawyers who had staffed the legal teams during the Erie Wars of 1868 and 1869, including Evarts, Pierrepont, O'Conor, and Tilden.[139] Although these lawyers and acquaintances of Langdell did not apparently engage in judicial corruption, they each received fees in the neighborhood of $20,000 to $30,000 (more than a half-million dollars today) for a few weeks work in the Erie Wars.[140] Consequently, these eminent lawyers rapidly transformed themselves from profiteers into prosecutors of Tweed's malfeasance, and their metamorphosis implies an additional explanation for Langdell's "hearty disgust for the means and methods by which business, place, and reputation are here gained."

Langdell, therefore, "was not sufficiently content to take the world as he found it," but Carter did not appreciate the reasons.[141] As with his friend Eaton, influence-buying, judicial corruption, and the associated confounding of legal doctrine and procedure explain Langdell's alienation from the New York City bench and bar beginning in 1868. Aside from actual corruption, an additional reason was the improper conduct of the eminent lawyers who underwent the metamorphosis from profiteers to prosecutors. Langdell felt "hearty disgust" for those who, though formally and technically untainted, increased their "business, place, and reputation" through involvement with Tweed corruption. Finally, beyond the corruption and the complicity, the extravagance of the lawyers' fees violated Langdell's notion of just price and "reasonable" fees befitting a "high-minded man."[142]

137. Powell, *From Patrician to Professional Elite*, xiv; G. Martin, *Causes and Conflicts*, 12–15.

138. G. Martin, *Causes and Conflicts*, 63–67; Bergan, *History of the New York Court of Appeals*, 41–45; Mandelbaum, *Boss Tweed's New York*, 79–81.

139. G. Martin, *Causes and Conflicts*, 15–18, 23, 63–67; Bergan, *History of the New York Court of Appeals*, 41–45; Mandelbaum, *Boss Tweed's New York*, 79–81; R. Gordon, "Ideal and the Actual in the Law," 57.

140. G. Martin, *Causes and Conflicts*, 8–9.

141. J. Carter to Eliot (20 Dec. 1869). Carter's temporizing language and ambivalent role in responding to the Tweed Ring comport with his "legal Mugwumpery" (Grossman, "James Coolidge Carter," 580), with which Langdell had little patience.

142. Langdell to Webster (16 Feb. 1857).

Langdell's continuing commitment to an ethic of just price appears in one of the last major cases that he handled during his time on Wall Street, the Lord case. Arising when the former president of the Erie Railroad challenged a large will, this case became Langdell's personal Erie War and provides a telling comparison with the Webster will case from the late 1850s. The Lord case reveals both remarkable consistencies and significant changes in Langdell's views during the prior decade. In addition to his commitment to just price, the Lord case demonstrates, through 1869, the vitality of Langdell's legal practice, his willingness to engage in the "arts of rivalry," his tactical shrewdness, his high reputation among lawyers, and his condemnation of referees and receivers and the associated judicial patronage. The consistency of Langdell's personal and professional relations is also evident, for O'Conor and John K. Porter, with whom Langdell worked on the Parish will case in 1857, appeared in the Lord case in 1869. Nevertheless, this last documented case in New York also discloses that Langdell was not untainted by his fifteen years on Wall Street.

Langdell's Erie War

In 1845 the directors of the Erie Railroad ousted the founding president, Eleazar Lord, who fell into debt and became destitute. But he had a wealthy, unmarried, older brother named Rufus, and expected that, when Rufus died in May 1869, his bequest would be Eleazar's financial salvation. However, the will provided only a small annuity for Eleazar and his wife, while naming Eleazar's two younger brothers executors and residual beneficiaries, who stood to split three-quarters of a total estate valued at about $400,000, or $10 million today.[143] The provisions were patently inequitable, and made suspicious by the facts that the two younger brothers, Thomas and David Lord, took immediate control of Rufus's papers, would not show Eleazar the will or communicate its terms, and did not read or reply to Eleazar's letters. By the beginning of June 1869, the eighty-one-year-old Eleazar was gravely ill, and his son-in-law, William Whiton, who had been supporting him and his wife, took up the cause as Eleazar's representative.[144]

Whiton learned that a number of Rufus's disappointed relatives planned to retain a law firm that was proposing the standard tactics of litigating financial transactions in Boss Tweed's New York City: charging a contingency fee, securing the appointment of a referee or receiver, and exerting judicial influence. By 1869

---

143. The will is not preserved; these facts are gleaned from the twenty-four letters to and from Langdell in the folder pertaining to the final will of Rufus Lord in Lord Family Papers.

144. Lord to Lord (18, 20, 24 May 1869); Whiton to Lord (25 May, 4 June 1869).

even a layman such as Whiton recognized the unethical congeries, stating that he wished to avoid "placing the matter in the hands of the law firm to deal with it as a speculation" or "to see this large estate placed in the hands of a Receiver, the result of which could only be very [hurtful?] and disastrous, looking to the way these Receiverships [a]re manipulated by the corrupt practices of the 'Ring' in this city." Wishing to prevent the case from falling "into the hands of lawyers rapacious and unscrupulous," Whiton and Eleazar "demanded . . . that it should be examined by the highest legal ability in the country."[145]

After making inquiries, Whiton was referred to Langdell, who agreed to represent Eleazar and a few other relatives and suggested retaining as well Porter, Langdell's co-counsel in *Northern Railroad*.[146] Within a week, Langdell met with Porter, submitted a petition to Surrogate Court challenging the will of Rufus Lord, and wrote to Whiton that he and Porter would each expect a retainer of $500.[147] Langdell also encouraged Whiton to meet with Thomas and David Lord to try to resolve the dispute privately.[148]

To this point, Langdell's approach resembled that in the Webster will case a dozen years earlier. His reputation and knowledge had grown considerably, but his basic plan was still to resolve the matter out of court, while devising a shrewd strategy without adopting the notorious tactic of tying up the estate with a referee on whom undue influence could be exerted. Moreover, his fee was to be determined by the energy and time expended on the case, consistent with his notion of just price. In these fundamental respects, Langdell's approach to the Webster case matched that in the Lord case. Nevertheless, experience on Wall Street induced Langdell to dilute his early, pristine sense of honorable practice with a tincture of expediency, and his sharp practice in the Lord case led his legal opponents to call him a "robber" and "swindler."

Responding to Langdell's request for the retainers, Whiton replied that Eleazar feared that he could not afford to sustain a long suit and that, without wanting to insult Langdell or Porter by proposing a contingency fee, he wished them to understand that "while the favorable issue of such a legal undertaking would certainly entitle advisors . . . to an ample, indisputable recompense, failure, from whatever cause, to secure that issue, would leave [Eleazar] and other heirs as plaintiffs, in pe-

145. Quotations are from Whiton to Lord (circa 1871).

146. Holden to Whiton (17 June 1869); Langdell to Whiton (22 June 1869). Having served as co-counsel with Charles O'Conor in the re-argument of the Parish will case in 1862, Porter had known Langdell for nearly a decade. *Delafield v. Parish* (1862).

147. Langdell to Whiton (22 June 1869). Langdell and Porter, "Petition of Eleazar Lord" (28 June 1869).

148. Whiton to Lord (16 July 1869); [Whiton], "Substance of the communication" (30 June 1869).

cuniary circumstances, so different . . . , that the most moderate payments for legal services would be the best that they can promise or could afford."[149] No subsequent discussion of compensation is preserved, but it appears that this semicontingency arrangement was agreed to.

In a similarly ambiguous vein, Whiton added that he and Eleazar Lord wished to avoid "any method of procedure . . . as an expedient, which should be incompatible with that standard" of "truth, right, and equity."[150] The foremost of such expedients was the appointment of a receiver, which Whiton and Lord had specifically rejected and which Langdell and Porter did not suggest. But what Langdell did recommend, at his very first meeting with Whiton, was to notify the brothers that Eleazar intended to request the appointment of a "collector" for the estate, a tactic that Porter supported. The collector would essentially act as an administrator for the estate, and all the attorneys agreed that the court would grant such a request made by a named beneficiary and next of kin.[151]

Although Langdell and Porter did not envision "influencing" such a collector in the corrupt fashion common among the Tweed judiciary, they conceived this tactic as a means of bleeding the estate and thereby forcing a compromise with Thomas and David Lord. This expedient strategy was acknowledged by Langdell in recalling how he, poker-faced, met one of the Lords' attorneys, who

> called upon me to see if some arrangement could not be made as to the motion for a collector. He stated frankly that they had no hope of successfully resisting the motion if we pressed it, said it would be a very serious expense and injury to the estate, and that his clients would much rather pay to their brother what a collectorship would cost the estate directly and indirectly at a liberal estimate, than to have a collector appointed. . . . I did not give him any encouragement that any proposition to settle the collectorship merely could be entertained by us, but . . . I expressed a strong wish that the whole controversy might be settled on some reasonable basis . . . and he expressed the opinion that a settlement of the collectorship would prepare the way for the settlement of the entire controversy.[152]

Langdell's approach here seems at odds with his condemnation of Sewall in 1856 for seeking to bring the Webster will case to a referee. The young Langdell believed that expedient tactics that subverted effective and efficient procedure

---

149. Whiton to Porter and Langdell (25 June 1869).
150. Whiton to Porter and Langdell (25 June 1869).
151. Langdell to Whiton (22 June 1869).
152. Langdell to Whiton (9 Oct. 1871).

were "mean and disgusting" and virtually prostituted the legal process. It is not hard to imagine the young Langdell rebuking the veteran Langdell for what the latter called "undoubtedly a pretty sudden and vigorous measure" of giving notice of the intent to request a collector.[153]

Nevertheless, Langdell had some justification for this tactic.[154] The apportionment of the bequest seemed patently unfair; the two younger brothers had made no effort to conciliate Eleazar and had acted secretively in regard to the will, raising suspicions about them tampering with Rufus's estate. However, since "our adversaries, and they alone, were in possession of all the facts," Langdell saw little hope of contesting the will directly.[155] Hence, the request for the collector was probably the most effective legal means for achieving what Langdell felt was a fair settlement for his client. In addition, the key distinction between the request for a referee in the Webster case and the request for a collector in the Lord case was that Langdell was evidently not seeking to enrich himself, whereas he suspected Sewall was.

Going down this path, however, led Langdell to another level of expediency and brought him face-to-face with his early mentor O'Conor, who had been retained as the senior counsel to Thomas and David Lord. Here is striking evidence of Langdell's ascent in the Wall Street world; he had risen from an unnamed assistant to O'Conor in 1857, to facing him as opposing lead counsel in 1869. In a series of meetings during July, Langdell found that O'Conor and his co-counsel were willing to make a liberal settlement in order to avoid the appointment of a collector. However, Langdell could make no headway in settling the entire estate, because O'Conor feared that any such settlement with Eleazar would invite suits from other legatees. O'Conor would countenance only a settlement structured as compensation for the costs of the collector that would otherwise have been incurred.

At that point, Langdell, again poker-faced, asked for the amount that would have gone to Eleazar had he been named a residual legatee like his two younger brothers: "I immediately stated to them that I thought it necessary to figure the amount [for the collector's expenses] up to one hundred thousand dollars, as I could hold out no encouragement that my clients would accept any less sum. Mr. O'Conor seemed rather start[l]ed at that, and expressed a very decided opinion

---

153. Langdell to Whiton (9 Oct. 1871).

154. I am grateful to William LaPiana for his observation that, due to Eleazar's advanced age, Langdell may have felt pressured to get as much money for his client as quickly as possible, so that Eleazar could possibly preserve at least some of it from his creditors. If Eleazar had died before the matter was settled, any recovery would have been an asset of his estate and presumably available to his creditors.

155. Langdell to Whiton (9 Oct. 1871).

that it would be impossible to bring the figures up to that point. Finally, I said that seventy-five thousand dollars was the smallest sum to which I could even attempt to procure my clients' consent, and that I could make no promise that they would accept that. Upon that, we went to work, Mr. O'Conor taking the most active part."[156] The lawyers then fabricated a list of expenses that a collector would have charged to administer the estate for eighteen months, and came up with the astronomical figure of $76,050, or nearly one-fifth of the estate. In effect, this was a settlement for the estate, but it was submitted to and approved by the court as a payment to Eleazar in consideration of his not requesting a collector.[157]

By this arrangement, Langdell's expediency went a step further in executing a legal agreement that belied its true purpose. Of course, such an arrangement was commonplace, and O'Conor himself had done most of the work of inflating the figures. Nevertheless, while forcing a settlement by threatening to request a collector was an extralegal tactic, executing a surrogate agreement subverted the legal process, a step that Langdell had disdained in the late 1850s.

Langdell then took another expedient step to secure the $25,000 by which he felt the settlement for the collector fell short of the full $100,000 due, in all fairness, to Eleazar as one of the three surviving brothers. To obtain that shortfall, Langdell proposed to capitalize at a greatly inflated value the small annuity provided for Eleazar in the will. One of O'Conor's junior co-counsels, Henry Day, had originally suggested this as a means to settlement and was willing to accommodate Langdell in this arrangement. However, O'Conor again demurred, because capitalizing the annuity at an inflated value would appear to be a separate settlement of the estate with Eleazar that would open the executors to suits from other legatees. Nevertheless, O'Conor "expressed a strong belief" that the Lord brothers would voluntarily capitalize the annuity at an inflated value after the estate had been settled.[158] Day went further, however, and obtained the assent of Thomas and David and arranged a separate agreement with Langdell, without O'Conor's knowledge.[159] In this fashion, Langdell arranged a side agreement to capitalize the annuity that he kept hidden from O'Conor, his early mentor.

But O'Conor had the last laugh. Over the next two and a half years, William Whiton, Eleazar Lord, Day, and Langdell exchanged letters attempting to persuade Thomas and David to follow through on the nonbinding agreement to capitalize

---

156. Langdell to Whiton (9 Oct. 1871).

157. Langdell and Lord, "Surrogate Court" (24 July 1869). The agreement provided that Eleazar pay one-third of the amount to other relatives who were also involved in the litigation.

158. Langdell to Whiton (9 Oct. 1871).

159. Langdell to Whiton (9 Oct. 1871).

the annuity. The brothers refused, however, maintaining that "the seventy-five thousand dollars paid as a compromise . . . was extorted by high-handed measures stamped with falsehood and malice."[160] In September 1871 Whiton reported to Langdell, "the Lords, David and Thomas, repudiate the whole thing, and . . . David N. Lord and perhaps Thomas Lord speak of you and of me as 'Robbers,' 'Swindlers' etc."[161] For his part, Langdell replied to Whiton: "I am forced to conclude that during the negotiations they practiced a deliberate and systematic deception, not only upon us but upon their own counsel."[162]

If so, the Lords were not the only ones to engage in deceit, for Langdell and Day had not only kept their agreement from O'Conor, but also had formed it despite his express disagreement. This deception demonstrates how much Langdell's tactics had changed by 1869 from those of the young attorney who had castigated Sewall. The change is magnified in view of Langdell's longstanding personal and professional acquaintance with O'Conor and the fact that Langdell owed to O'Conor his first entrée into the Wall Street legal elite. Given that he and Day deceived O'Conor on this point, it appears that Langdell, by 1869, was willing to breach personal and professional trust in order to win his case.

Yet, if this deception presents Langdell in the worst light, it did not appear unseemly on Wall Street, and that may be Langdell's excuse. When O'Conor later learned about the capitalization agreement from his clients, he seems not to have begrudged the secrecy of Day and Langdell, but merely advised his clients to remain passive in the face of the unenforceable agreement. Langdell's deception was parried by the Lords' bad faith, and none of the lawyers took offense at this outcome.[163] After all, "the means and methods by which business, place, and reputation are here gained" involved so much worse in the *cloaca maxima* of legal practice.

—◦◦◦—

By the end of his fifteen years in New York City, Langdell's attitude toward legal practice had changed dramatically. He was no longer "an enthusiast . . . in his profession." Rather, "scorn[ing] to win, or to struggle for, any success which was not the legitimate reward of merit,"[164] he was "breathing out slaughter" against those

160. Langdell to Whiton (9 Oct. 1871).
161. Whiton to Langdell (14 Sept. 1871).
162. Langdell to Whiton (9 Oct. 1871).
163. H. Day to Langdell (31 Jan. 1870); Langdell to Day (26 Jan. 1871); Langdell to Whiton (21 May 1871).
164. J. Carter to Eliot (20 Dec. 1869).

C. C. Langdell, circa
1870. Courtesy of
Special Collections
Department, Harvard
Law School Library.

on the bench and bar who transgressed those meritocratic principles, which even he had compromised in the Eleazar Lord case.

At the same time, these transgressions led Langdell to look beyond the personal implications of those principles and to consider their relationship to professional and social affairs. While witnessing the widespread complicity of leading lawyers and judges in the corruption of New York City courts by Tammany Hall under Boss Tweed in the 1860s, Langdell concluded that the just working of the legal system depends on the effectiveness and authority of the legal profession, which rests on lawyers' merit derived from their academic achievement in law school. More generally, students' academic achievement in professional school determines, or should determine, their merit in professional life; and "a learned and liberal profession of the highest grade" in law "render[s] to the public the highest and best service in the administration of justice."[165] This conception of academic meritocracy was founded in a commitment to "democracy," as Russell remarked, in the sense that there existed equal opportunity to succeed in the profession. It was this notion of a "democracy of scholarship,"[166] or a "democratic meritocracy,"[167] that Langdell brought to Harvard upon leaving Wall Street in February 1870.

165. Langdell, Annual Report 1876–77, 89, 91.
166. Beale, "Langdell, Gray, Thayer, and Ames," 389.
167. Auerbach, *Unequal Justice: Lawyers and Social Change*, 28.

CHAPTER 3

Scholar, 1870–1881

In the three decades after leaving New York City and joining the HLS faculty, Langdell made reforms in five distinct but interrelated areas. Each constituted a radical change; together, they initiated a revolution in American professional education. In scholarship he set a higher standard for the faculty; in the classroom he made enduring innovations in pedagogy; in hiring professors he introduced an unprecedented strategy and criterion; in academic administration he overcame determined opposition to establish meritocratic structures and policies; in the entwined issues of institutional finance and student recruitment and culture he reversed the prevailing logic and norms. The following five chapters relate the complicated story in each of these areas successively, though the reader should bear in mind that Langdell worked simultaneously on all these endeavors.

This chapter explores Langdell's scholarship during the 1870s when he produced closely related works on contracts and sales that exercised seminal influence both pedagogically and jurisprudentially.[1] The novel genre of his casebooks on contracts and sales introduced case method teaching into American professional education, while these works, together with his doctrinal summaries, placed Langdell with Frederick Pollock, William R. Anson, and Oliver Wendell Holmes Jr. as the leading theorists of contracts during its "golden age" in Anglo-American law.[2]

Specifically, Langdell made five signal contributions to jurisprudence through his writings on contracts in the 1870s. First, he sought to identify abstract, parsimonious dimensions of contract; second, he identified offer, acceptance, and consideration as those dimensions; third, he advanced the distinction between sales and contract in the United States; fourth, he refuted the will theory and

1. Further discussion and documentation on various points can be found in Kimball, "Langdell on Contracts and Legal Reasoning."

2. Quotation is from Friedman, *History of American Law*, 275. See Hurst, *Law and the Conditions of Freedom*, 10.

introduced the bargain theory of contract; and, fifth, he promulgated the distinction between bilateral and unilateral contracts.[3]

Notwithstanding these contributions—indeed, partly because of Langdell's introduction of parsimonious abstraction—Holmes famously charged that Langdell considered formal, logical consistency to be the sole standard in making or evaluating legal decisions. But Langdell's characteristic mode of reasoning in the field of contracts and, more broadly, in jurisprudence is actually three-dimensional, exhibiting a comprehensive yet contradictory integration of induction from authority, deduction from principle, and analysis of justice and policy. The contradiction lies in Langdell's combining all three while claiming to emphasize logical consistency and to disregard justice and policy. Langdell's mode of reasoning therefore fits not Holmes's critique but rather the "paradox of form and substance" that has been considered one of Holmes's greatest insights about judicial reasoning.

Langdell fell into this paradox fundamentally due to his desire to elevate and legitimate legal practice and the legal profession through demanding legal education. Believing that lawyers must acquire a strong knowledge of legal science, which he associated with logical consistency, Langdell presented legal arguments in formal terms, while he also considered, though sublimated, justice and policy, and recognized the fact that legal decisions sometimes incorporate fictions.

Casebooks on Contracts and Sales (1870, 1871, 1872)

In the late 1860s the long-reigning gentlemanly professors at HLS—Joel Parker, Theophilus Parsons, and Emory Washburn—were nearing the end of their triumvirate. Parker, the first to go, resigned in 1868 after twenty years of service and was replaced by Nathaniel Holmes, a justice on the state supreme court of Missouri. Judge Holmes extended the line of distinguished but unscholarly lawyers on the HLS faculty and enjoyed "very congenial intimacy" with Parsons and Washburn and with notable lawyers on the Harvard governing boards, such as George Bigelow.[4] But Holmes's appointment worsened the discontent already

3. Two decades later, Langdell produced one more writing on contracts ["Mutual Promises as a Consideration for Each Other" (1901)], in which he hotly rebutted the charge made by Samuel Williston ["Successive Promises" (1894), 35], that Langdell had overlooked the logical fallacy of "mutual promises [serving] as a consideration for each other." Frederick Pollock called Langdell's rebuttal "a masterly reply" in "Afterthoughts on Consideration" (1901), 422. But compare Bronaugh, "Secret Paradox of the Common Law."

4. Quotation is from N. Holmes, *Journal*, 276. See 273. No relation to Oliver W. Holmes Jr., Nathaniel Holmes graduated from Harvard College in 1837 and HLS in 1839, and built a successful legal practice in Missouri before joining the court. His only scholarly endeavor was an investigation into whether Francis Bacon wrote the works attributed to William Shakespeare. N. Holmes, Papers, box 1, ff. 6, 10, 11; *Centennial History of the Harvard Law School*, 220.

brewing among certain alumni about the low academic standards at HLS, and in 1869 the Overseers Visiting Committee to the Law School called for a thorough investigation of the school.[5]

The call was timely because the university was seeking a new president in 1869. The search was conducted by Harvard's two governing boards: the Corporation, whose decisions were legally binding on most issues and which comprised five Fellows in addition to the president and the treasurer, and the board of thirty-two Overseers, who annually evaluated the separate departments of the university but whose judgments were mostly advisory to the Corporation. The Corporation and the Overseers selected thirty-five-year-old Charles W. Eliot, and installed him as president in mid-October 1869 with a mandate to reform the university. Eliot immediately commenced a detailed inspection of all its units, including the law school.[6]

This inspection was unprecedented because governance of the law school, like other units of the university outside of the undergraduate college, had previously been left to the faculty, with the senior professor serving as primus inter pares. Thus, Nathaniel Holmes regarded Parsons as the head of the school, and Washburn assumed that he would become head after Parsons departed. But Parsons soon found that Eliot did not heed his advice and "Knew not Joseph," and, in protest, offered his resignation in December 1869, "not expecting it to be accepted, but it was at once accepted, and he retired."[7]

Eliot immediately began soliciting opinions about a successor to Parsons and inquired especially about Langdell,[8] recalling the radical critique of legal education that Langdell had expounded two decades earlier in Theodore Tebbets's dormitory room. Undertaking to turn "the whole University over like a flapjack,"[9] Eliot needed like-minded allies to support that transformation in the face of strong opposition from many faculty and alumni. Langdell fit the need perfectly, and in November Eliot traveled to New York to propose that Langdell consider joining the HLS faculty. "The proposal attracted him strongly,"[10] for Langdell was thoroughly disenchanted with legal practice on Wall Street by that point.

In early December Langdell agreed to become Eliot's candidate for the Dane Professorship and prospective ally on the HLS faculty, although both realized

5. Harvard University, Report of the Overseers Visiting Committee 1868–69, repr., C. Warren, *History of the Harvard Law School*, 2:358–59.

6. Bolles, *Harvard University*, 3; C. Warren, *History of the Harvard Law School*, 2:363.

7. Quotations are from N. Holmes, *Journal*, 272, 311. See 275, 311; E. Washburn, "Harvard Law School," leaves 3v, 11v; J. Warren to C. Warren (2 June 1908).

8. J. Thayer to Eliot (13 Nov. 1869).

9. The phrase of Oliver Wendell Holmes Sr. is quoted in C. Warren, *History of the Harvard Law School*, 2:357.

10. C. Eliot, "Langdell," 518. See C. Eliot, Oration 1886, 61.

that his "unusual candidature" might not be acceptable to the Harvard governing boards.[11] Though a busy and respected lawyer, Langdell was not a leading or convivial member of the bench or bar, and Eliot therefore sought additional evaluations from George Shattuck, James Carter, and Washburn, all of whom gave mixed or tepid support.[12] Reflecting "his determination to win only by sheer force of merit" rather than personal influence, Langdell refused to comply with requests from the Overseers to provide further references or to have dinner with them.[13] His customary "scorn to win, or to struggle for, any success which was not the legitimate reward of merit" had been heightened by "the means and methods by which business, place, and reputation are . . . gained" in New York City, Carter observed.[14] Although his unyielding refusal detracted from his candidacy, the Corporation nevertheless appointed Langdell as Dane Professor on 6 January 1870.[15]

———∞∞∞———

Upon returning to the law school, Langdell plunged into his scholarship, which had long attracted his interest while working in a number of roles: HLS librarian, chief research assistant for Parsons, "presiding genius" at discussions with fellow law students, officer of the New York Law Institute, attorney who devoted "infinite . . . study" to cases, and author for Bouvier's *Law Dictionary*.[16] Joining the HLS faculty provided him the opportunity to pursue that interest, as well as the obligation to set a new standard for the faculty.

Langdell's massive project of preparing the first teaching casebook in law or any other field yielded fruit in October 1870 when Little, Brown, Co. published the first half of his *Cases on Contracts*.[17] His reasons for choosing to teach from cases were suggested above: the reading of Locke's *Education* at Exeter, the exposure to specimens in his natural history course, the intellectual influence of scientific taxonomy in the mid-nineteenth century, the intense discussions of cases with HLS students outside of class, the research for Parsons's treatises, the shift to Code Pleading in New York that entailed new emphasis on appeal to precedents, the predominance of Langdell's legal practice in equity, and the increased reporting of

11. C. Eliot, "Langdell," 518. See Th. Parsons to Eliot (1 Dec. 1869).

12. Shattuck to Eliot (17 Dec. 1869); J. Carter to Eliot (20 Dec. 1869); E. Washburn, "Harvard Law School," leaf 2r.

13. Ames, "Christopher Columbus Langdell, 1826–1906," 475.

14. J. Carter to Eliot (20 Dec. 1869).

15. Harvard University, Corporation Records, 11:174 (6 Jan. 1870).

16. Quotations are from, respectively, Phelps to Warren (29 Sept. 1907); Langdell to Webster (30 Aug. 1857).

17. Langdell, *Cases on Contracts* (1870). On the originality of Langdell's casebook, see Kimball, "Langdell Problem," 335–37.

cases throughout the United States. Of course, these factors applied to many other law teachers at the time and do not explain necessarily why Langdell so completely and firmly subscribed to the inductive Socratic method of teaching. At root, he was intuitively fascinated with studying the law through cases. His reasons for compiling and publishing the casebook were more mundane. Such a collection was far more efficient for the students, who would, otherwise, all "want the same books [of case reports] at the same time."[18] In addition, publishing the casebook saved the library's copies of case reports from being "destroyed in a few years by excessive use upon a [small] number of pages."[19]

The choice of subject for the first casebook stemmed from his service as the chief research assistant for Parsons's massive, two-volume treatise, *Law of Contracts*, during the early 1850s. The original reports of more than six thousand cases were examined for the treatise by HLS law students whom Parsons hired to brief the cases and submit their work to Langdell for evaluation and synthesis.[20] Consequently, Langdell already knew these pre-1852 cases when he began preparing the casebook in the spring of 1870, and this made it possible to complete the first half of *Cases on Contracts* by the start of classes in October 1870.[21]

Langdell's practice of case method teaching is analyzed in the next chapter, but it is relevant here to note a few novel features of the casebook. One of the most arresting at the time—but so conventional today that it is overlooked—was the "chronological arrangement" of cases, as Oliver Wendell Holmes Jr. observed.[22] This arrangement revealed "the growth, development, or establishment of...essential doctrines" in the law.[23] "Decisions are made; principles live and grow. This conviction is at the root of all Mr. Langdell's work," observed Pollock.[24] Law is not static, but evolving. Another feature was Langdell's attention to historical situation, shown by his adding to the title and citation of each case the normally omitted information about location, court, and precise date of the case.[25]

A third novel aspect was the absence of headnotes or commentary, testifying to the inductive character of his teaching. This inductive approach contrasted with

---

18. Langdell, *Cases on Contracts* (1871), preface.

19. C. Eliot, Annual Report 1879–80, 16.

20. Th. Parsons, *Law of Contracts*, 1:x; Grafton to Warren (28 Oct. 1907).

21. Even with this head start, Langdell ultimately drew from Parsons's treatise only 35 percent of the cases (117/336) in the completed 1871 edition of *Cases on Contracts*.

22. [O. Holmes], Review (1871), 540. See also *North American and United States Gazette* (16 Dec. 1871).

23. Langdell, *Cases on Contracts* (1871), preface.

24. Pollock, "Vocation of the Common Law," 17.

25. For example: "*Payne v. Cave*. In the King's Bench, May 2, 1789. (Reported in 3 *Term Reports*, 148)." Langdell, *Cases on Contracts* (1870), 1.

the antecedent treatise tradition that endeavored "to render cases subordinate to principles, . . . to throw the main body of [cases] into the notes, and to incorporate those only in the text, which seemed to afford the best *illustrations* of the doctrine under consideration."[26] Parsons carried this subordination to an extreme by adopting "the rigorous exclusion from the text, of all cases."[27] In contrast, Langdell, rather than presenting cases *illustratively* to demonstrate previously announced principles, as found in the treatise tradition, intended "to compel the mind to work out the principles from the cases."[28]

A final innovation was the casebook's inclusion of overruled and conflicting cases. Through this material, Langdell pointed students toward the reasoning behind the cases rather than the prevailing rules, as shown by his own analysis of the casebook's opening cases. Regarding the second case concerning the question of how long a contractual offer is legally operant, Langdell observed that the King's Bench in 1790 held that an offer is good only at the time when first made. In the third case, the same court, twenty years later, in order to accommodate transactions through the mail, announced the new doctrine that a contractual offer continues indefinitely. In the fourth case, ten years later, the same court reverted to the earlier doctrine in order to protect the offeror. Meanwhile, in the fifth case, "another court was at a loss how to apply the doctrine of [the third case] thinking that it might involve the consequence of making an offer irrevocable during the period of its continuance."[29] Hence, Langdell's series of cases required students to focus on the underlying reasons and belied the prevailing "English attitude . . . link[ing] authority with judicial status."[30]

The lone review of the 1870 edition of *Cases on Contracts* appeared early in 1871 in the *American Law Review* and was the *Review*'s second anonymous commentary that referred to Langdell. Both commentaries were written by Holmes, one of the

26. Emphasis added. W. Story, *Treatise on the Law of Contracts*, v; W. Story and Bigelow, *Treatise on the Law of Contracts*, 1:xiii.

27. Th. Parsons, *Law of Contracts*, 1:viii.

28. Langdell, quoted in Note, *Harvard Law Review* (1891–92), 89. As authorization for his inductive method, Langdell quoted on the title page of *Cases on Contracts* a Latin maxim from Sir Edward Coke: "many times *compendia sunt dispendia* [shortcuts are a waste of time] and *melius est petere fontes quam sectari rivulos* [it is better to seek the sources than to follow the tributaries]." A few years later, Louis D. Brandeis testified, "Some of our professors are trying to inculcate in us a great distrust of textbooks, to prove to us the truth of the maxim—'*Melius est petere fontes quam sectari rivulas* [sic].' When one sees how loosely most text-books are written and how many startling propositions are unsupported by the authorities cited to sustain them—the temptation to become a Convert of Coke's is very great." Brandeis to Wehle (12 Mar. 1876).

29. Langdell, *Summary of the Law of Contracts*, 12, 11–12.

30. Simpson, *Legal Theory and Legal History*, 315.

Review's two editors.[31] The first, published in October 1870, sharply criticized the condition of HLS under Langdell's predecessors and added that "the learning and ability of [Langdell's faculty] warrant us in predicting that their labors will make Harvard Law School what it ought to be."[32] Continuing the support and praise of the dean's work, Holmes, in the 1871 review, commended the casebook as "original and instructive." In particular, he approved the inductive method that was reflected in the "wisely omitted" headnotes, and adjudged the developmental ordering of cases "most instructive and interesting."[33] Apart from the praise, Holmes offered a few recommendations, which Langdell embraced.

Holmes said that, on the subject of forbearance, the cases had been collected with "an overscrupulous minuteness" and recommended reducing the number of "contradictory and unreasoned" decisions. In the second edition, Langdell responded by excising twenty-five cases from the Forbearance section and noting the change in his preface. Secondly, Holmes suggested adding "a full index,"[34] and Langdell responded in 1871 by providing a thirteen-page index whose discursive entries extended for several lines, imparting rules, holdings, and cross-references to relevant cases in the casebook.[35]

Finally, Holmes justified his praise for Langdell's developmental ordering of cases by observing, "Tracing the growth of a doctrine in this way not only fixes it in the mind, but shows its meaning, extent, and limits as nothing else can."[36] The import of these words, if not some actual terms, seems to be echoed in the preface that Langdell wrote a few months later for the complete, first edition: "Each of these doctrines...is a growth extending in many cases through centuries. This growth is to be traced in the main through a series of cases."[37] Hence, Holmes's review may have inspired the evolutionary language in Langdell's preface.[38] Whatever the extent of this inspiration, both men were closely attuned to the developmental

31. O. Holmes, *Collected Works*, 1:243.

32. [O. Holmes], "Harvard University Law School" (1870).

33. [O. Holmes], Review (1871), 539–40.

34. [O. Holmes], Review (1871), 539–40. Langdell, *Cases on Contracts* (1871), index; Langdell, *Cases on Contracts* (1879), v.

35. Commensurate with the inductive character of his teaching, Langdell apparently referred to the index rarely in his own teaching, inasmuch as his students James B. Ames and William A. Keener made copious annotations throughout their personal copies but scarcely touched the index. See *ACon71*; *KCon71*.

36. [O. Holmes], Review (1871), 540.

37. Langdell, *Cases on Contracts* (1871), preface.

38. This possibility is strengthened by the converse suggestion that Holmes later borrowed Langdell's language for his own famous 1895 essay "The Path of the Law." Alschuler, *Law without Values*, 89–90. Of course, the language also reflects the "immediate and cataclysmic change in outlook" arising from the publication of Darwin's *The Origin of Species* in 1859. Ghiselin, *Triumph of the Darwinian Method*, 1.

TABLE 2 Geographical and Chronological Distribution of Cases in
Cases on Contracts (1871)

Geographical Distribution		Chronological Distribution		
Country or State	Cases	Period	Cases	Percentage
England	310	Pre-1700	136	40
Ireland	1	1700–99	40	12
Scotland	2	1800–51	114	34
France	1	1853–70	46	14
U.S. Supreme Court	2			
Massachusetts	10			
New York	8			
Connecticut	1			
Pennsylvania	1			
Total	336	Total	336	100

ordering of cases that Holmes found "most instructive." This mutually affirming relationship between Langdell and Holmes continued throughout the 1870s.

In October 1871 Little, Brown, Co. published the completed first edition of *Cases on Contracts*, subsuming the 1870 edition and adding a large section on conditional contracts along with the index and the preface that explained and justified case method in evolutionary and taxonomic terms.[39] This 1871 casebook distributed 336 total cases into three divisions: "mutual consent," with twenty-five cases and no subdivisions; "consideration," with 139 cases spread across ten subdivisions; and "conditional contracts," with 172 cases distributed into nine subdivisions. Within the doctrinal subdivisions, the cases were arranged geographically and then chronologically under each geographical area, with a few exceptions. This arrangement further demonstrates Langdell's attention to the historical situation, reflected in his adding the location, court, and date to the title of each case.[40] The cumulative geographical and chronological totals are reported in table 2.

As indicated by table 2, the great majority of cases in Langdell's casebooks were English, and most exceptions came from jurisdictions heavily influenced by England: Massachusetts and New York. This selectivity was dictated partly by the practical limitations: few case reporters existed, and Langdell was working without help under the pressure of a tight deadline. Over time, his choice of cases became

39. Langdell, *Cases on Contracts* (1871), 1022 pp.; "Manuscript Cost book for Little Brown. 1865–," Little, Brown, Papers, box 1, §L, 65.

40. Langdell also sometimes adverted to the geographical and chronological situation in his later *Summary of the Law of Contracts*, as on p. 13.

more American and contemporary. Beyond those limitations, Langdell focused on English, Massachusetts, and New York cases because the most important developments in contract law "had occurred since 1750 in the increasingly commercialized and industrialized society of England. In the United States, New York and Massachusetts were the premier jurisdictions of commercial and industrial expansion . . . and their courts had first and most continuously wrestled with the contractual problems presented by megabusiness and macroindustrialization."[41]

Among the few reviews of the 1871 edition,[42] the *American Law Review* again published one written anonymously by Holmes, who repeated his "very high opinion" of *Cases on Contracts*. On pedagogical grounds, Holmes endorsed the omission of headnotes and praised the thirteen-page index, which exceeded his hopes. Holmes expressed one reservation, "We do not agree with . . . his seemingly exclusive belief in the study of cases. . . . We think [a beginning student] would find the present work a pretty tough pièce de résistance without a text-book or the assistance of an instructor." In jurisprudential terms, Holmes reaffirmed "Mr. Langdell's learning and remarkable powers"[43] and pointed to Langdell's first scholarly contribution to the field.

Holmes extolled Langdell's abstraction of general dimensions of contract, observing: "There is nothing of . . . the 'manual method.' A contract concerning coal is not indexed under the head Coal, nor even under the popular name of the contract, as Charter-party or Insurance. The cases are referred to under the general principle of the law of contracts."[44] The "manual method" was employed by prominent writers such as Kent (1827), Story (1844), Metcalf (1867), Leake (1867), Parsons (1853, 1855), Hilliard (1872), and Bishop (1878), who organized their discussion of contracts around particular operational topics. For example, the different kinds of parties who might enter into contracts usually constituted separate doctrinal categories: contracts of innkeepers, contracts of drunkards, contracts of spendthrifts, contracts of seamen, contracts of slaves, contracts of infants, contracts of married women, and so forth.[45] Yet, even while presenting

41. Barnes, introduction, 15. See 18–20.
42. See, for example, *North American and United States Gazette* (16 Dec. 1871).
43. [O. Holmes], Review (1872a), 353–54. See O. Holmes, *Collected Works*, 1:273.
44. [O. Holmes], Review (1872a), 353–54.
45. An excellent discussion and demonstration of this point is found in LaPiana, *Logic and Experience*, 58–67. See Kent, *Commentaries on American Law*, 2:363–436; W. Story, *Treatise on the Law of Contracts*, vii–x; Metcalf, *Principles of the Law of Contracts*, 349–57; Leake, *Elements of the Law of Contracts*, vii–xxii; Th. Parsons, *Law of Contracts*, 1:xiii–xxviii; 2:iii–x; Hilliard, *Law of Contracts*; Bishop, *Doctrines of the Law of Contracts*. In the late 1870s HLS professor John C. Gray, whose appointment Langdell had opposed, still categorized contracts according to their subject matter: services, money, or property. Wigglesworth, *Agency and Carriers* 1877–78, 1–2.

such particularistic accounts, these writers recognized the need "to elucidate and systematize, as far as practicable, the general law applicable to the subject."[46] This need arose from the growing range and complexity of commerce, which increased uncertainty and led merchants to seek contractual agreements that anticipated unforeseen and unusual circumstances through their conceptual power. In addition, abstract rules tended to normalize doctrine so that the same rules applied to all parties regardless of station.[47]

Progress toward "conceptualizing contract" is credited to the small group of leading nineteenth-century contract theorists: Pollock, Anson, Holmes, and Langdell.[48] Among this group, Langdell, who preceded the other three by a few years, may even be considered "the first theoretician of contract law in the United States."[49] At the least, his attempt to identify abstract dimensions of contract, which Holmes praised again in 1886,[50] is Langdell's first significant contribution to contracts jurisprudence.

Holmes's review also extolled Langdell's complementary contribution of introducing parsimony as a guiding principle for abstracting dimensions of contract. As Langdell wrote in his preface, "the number of fundamental legal doctrines is much less than is commonly supposed; the many different guises in which the same doctrine is constantly making its appearance, and the great extent to which legal treatises are a repetition of each other, being the cause of much misapprehension. If these doctrines could be so classified and arranged that each should be found in its proper place, and nowhere else, they would cease to be formidable from their number."[51]

Endorsed by Holmes in 1872 and again in 1886,[52] Langdell's invocation of parsimony served to correct the multifarious nature of contract doctrine at the time. For example, William Story's 1844 treatise presented seventy-seven divisions and subdivisions of doctrine, some abstract such as "mutual promises," some opera-

46. W. Story, *Treatise on the Law of Contracts*, v. See Th. Parsons, *Law of Contracts*, 1:vii, xi; Siegel, "Joel Bishop's Orthodoxy," 216–17.

47. Teeven, *History of the Anglo-American Common Law of Contract*, 186, 198, 236–39.

48. Quotation is from Duxbury, *Frederick Pollock*, 191. On the association of these four jurists with each other and with conceptualizing contract law, see Bronaugh, "Secret Paradox of the Common Law," 193, 195n8; Farnsworth, "Contracts Scholarship," 1414; Teeven, *History of the Anglo-American Common Law of Contract*, 239; Gordley, *Philosophical Origins of Modern Contract Doctrine*, 158; Gordley, "Natural Law Origins of the Common Law of Contract," 428, 446; P. Kelley, "Critical Analysis of Holmes," 1696–97; Duxbury, *Frederick Pollock*, 191–201. Cf. Alschuler, *Law without Values*, 122–23.

49. LaPiana, *Logic and Experience*, 188n19.

50. O. Holmes, Oration 1886, 38.

51. Langdell, *Cases on Contracts* (1871), preface.

52. [O. Holmes], Review (1872a), 353–54; O. Holmes, Oration 1886, 38. Pollock also subsequently endorsed the principle of parsimony that Langdell expressed. Duxbury, *Frederick Pollock*, 303.

tional and particular such as "innkeepers," and both kinds overlapping. Melville Bigelow preserved this multitude in revising the treatise for publication in 1874.[53] In 1853 Parsons devoted 342 pages to the classification of parties to a contract, distinguishing joint parties, agents, brokers, servants, attorneys, trustees, executors and administrators, guardians, corporations, and so forth.[54]

In contrast to these many particular categories, Langdell parsimoniously identified the most salient abstract dimensions. He drew the great majority of his cases from a small fraction of Parson's treatise; of the 117 cases that Langdell selected, three-quarters (88) come from about 5 percent of Parsons's 1,500 pages. Compared to Parsons's treatise, Langdell's casebook presented a highly focused selection of the most important doctrinal categories. For example, Langdell gave particular attention to the cases in a five-page section that Parsons entitled "Contracts on Time."[55] This opaque category was refined and elaborated in Langdell's 1870 casebook into the first 160-page section on "Mutual Consent," that is, offer and acceptance. The other major section of the 1870 casebook was 245 pages devoted to "Consideration," which Parsons covered in forty-five pages.[56] Langdell thus abstracted from Parsons's sprawling treatise the most salient doctrinal dimensions—offer, acceptance, and consideration—which he refined and elaborated.

Consequently, the 1870 edition of *Cases on Contracts* became the first text on contracts published in the United States or in Britain that was organized around "the basic requirements of offer, acceptance, and consideration" or, more parsimoniously, "the two most important common elements, consideration and assent."[57] This was Langdell's second scholarly contribution.[58]

53. W. Story, *Treatise on the Law of Contracts*, vii–x; W. Story and Bigelow, *Treatise on the Law of Contracts*, vol. 1.

54. Th. Parsons, *Law of Contracts*, 1:xiv–xxii.

55. Th. Parsons, *Law of Contracts*, 1:403–8.

56. Th. Parsons, *Law of Contracts*, 1:353–98.

57. Quotations are, respectively, from P. Kelley, "Critical Analysis of Holmes," 1706; LaPiana, *Logic and Experience*, 59. On these common elements, see Friedman and Macaulay, "Contract Law and Contract Teaching," 812; Gordley, *Philosophical Origins of Modern Contract Doctrine*, 161–213; Simpson, *Legal Theory and Legal History*, 181–83; Atiyah, *Introduction to the Law of Contract*, 45; P. Kelley, "Critical Analysis of Holmes," 1750; Duxbury, *Frederick Pollock*, 201–8.

58. In the 1871 edition, Langdell added a third section on "Conditional Contracts," and divided "Consideration" and "Conditional Contracts" into nine and ten subsections respectively, while he also promised future volumes of *Cases on Contracts* and later elaborated the subdivisions in his *Summary of the Law of Contracts*, demonstrating that the categories of offer, acceptance, and consideration required augmentation. Nevertheless, the centrality of offer, acceptance, and consideration is shown by the fact that when Contracts was divided into "prescribed" and "not prescribed" courses in 1872–73 and 1873–74 academic years, the "prescribed" course was devoted to the first half of the casebook that addressed offer, acceptance, and consideration, while the second half of the casebook that addressed "conditional contracts" was relegated to the elective course.

—◦◦◦—

Even as Holmes praised Langdell's "most valuable" *Cases on Contracts* for a third time when reviewing a different work,[59] Langdell was completing *Cases on Sales*, published by Little, Brown, Co. in May 1872. Prepared for his course on sales during the 1872–73 academic year,[60] this was the first volume written in the United States on the distinct domain of sales, and its appearance, particularly in conjunction with a separate volume on contracts, was highly significant.[61] In England, the law of sales had originated in "law merchant"—the commercial law administered in medieval merchants' courts whose doctrines incorporated their customs and emphasized the concept of title to goods as well as a sense of fair play in an open market. In the seventeenth century, the common-law courts gradually usurped the authority of the merchants' courts and adjudicated disputes over sales through principles of contract, subtly emphasizing the intentions of the parties. Meanwhile, in 1677 Parliament enacted the Statute of Frauds, whose seventeenth section stipulated formal requirements for sales in order to remedy the increasing problem presented by fraudulent claims of sale. By the beginning of the nineteenth century, the confluence of merchant law, common-law doctrines derived mostly from contract, and case law decided under the Statute of Frauds had created a disparate jumble of doctrines that gradually coalesced through a series of cases during the 1800s.[62]

American treatise writers in the first half of the nineteenth century therefore made little distinction between contracts and sales. In 1827 Kent's entire discussion of contracts was conducted under the head "of the contract of sale." In 1844 Story incorporated "sale of personal property" into his treatise on contracts.[63] In the 1850s Parsons sprinkled discussion of sales throughout *The Law of Contracts* as "if that were the only or chief topic of the book."[64] In 1867 Theron Metcalf's

59. [O. Holmes], Review of *American Reports* (1871), 550. See O. Holmes, *Collected Works*, 1:249.

60. Langdell, *Cases on Sales* (1872), vol. 1, 1039 pp. Similar to the production of *Cases on Contracts*, a preprint of the first half of this volume was issued in February 1871 and may have been used in Langdell's 1871–72 course on Sales. "Manuscript Cost book for Little Brown. 1865–," Little, Brown, Papers, box 1, §L, 65. No copy of the preprint has been found.

61. By the twentieth century, the casebook was largely forgotten in prominent historical analyses of the subject and overlooked even when modern casebooks recount their antecedents. Llewellyn, "Across Sales on Horseback"; Llewellyn, "First Struggle to Unhorse Sales"; Friedman, "Formative Elements in the Law of Sales," 411n; Nelson and Howicz, *Williston on Sales*, 1–5; Honnold and Reitz, *Sales Transactions*, 1–7.

62. Statute of Frauds, 29 Car. II, ch. 3, §17 (1677). This account is drawn from Friedman, "Formative Elements in the Law of Sales," 458; Friedman, *History of American Law*, 262–63, 540; Nelson and Howicz, *Williston on Sales*, 2–5; Honnold and Reitz, *Sales Transactions*, 4–5.

63. Kent, *Commentaries on American Law*, 2:363; W. Story, *Treatise on the Law of Contracts*, 479–553.

64. Th. Parsons, *Law of Contracts*, 1:xi–xii.

Law of Contracts discussed sales under "acceptance of offer," "fraud," and "unlawful contracts."[65] Conversely, the two American treatises nominally devoted to the "law of sales" addressed the many operational categories and doctrinal rules found in contracts treatises.[66]

The first book devoted to distinctive legal issues pertaining to sales was published in 1845 by Colin Blackburn, a prominent English jurist. Blackburn confined his treatise to the effect of a sale on the property rights in the goods being sold. He chose this topic because, due to the increasing distance and complexity of commercial transactions, executory sales—in which the buyer receives title to, but not possession of the goods sold—were becoming common and creating uncertainty and disagreements about the property rights in goods sold. In 1868, building on Blackburn's work, the first comprehensive treatise on legal issues related to sales, as distinguished from contract, was published by Judah P. Benjamin, a former U.S. senator from Louisiana and prominent leader in the Confederacy who had emigrated to England.[67] *Benjamin on Sales* has therefore been called "the first treatise on the English law of sale."[68]

Two years later, in preparing the first volume published in the United States that was devoted solely to legal issues pertaining to sales, Langdell relied heavily on Blackburn and Benjamin. Printed notes in the text and handwritten annotations on students' copies of the casebook from Langdell's classes reveal that he frequently adverted to Blackburn or Benjamin for insights into doctrinal questions while also distinguishing his own views from theirs.[69] Nevertheless, Langdell still faced a significant challenge in distinguishing specific cases and issues in sales from those in contract. For example, the very first case in *Cases on Contracts*, *Payne v. Cave* (1789), appears to be a quintessential case of sale because it established the rule that, at an auction, the title to auctioned goods passes "when the goods are 'knocked down' to the buyer. But in *Payne v. Cave* the issue was not framed in terms of . . . title. The question was approached from the standpoint of mutuality of assent in contract. Such assent, said the court, was 'signified on the part of the

65. Metcalf, *Principles of the Law of Contracts*, 349–50, 355–57.

66. The only two American treatises appear to be: Hilliard, *Treatise on the Law of Sales* (1841); W. Story, *Treatise on the Law of Sales* (1847). See Marvin, *Legal Bibliography, or a Thesaurus of Law Books* (1847), 387.

67. Blackburn, *Treatise on the Effect of the Contract of Sale* (1845); Benjamin, *Treatise on the Law of Sale* (1868). See Meade, *Judah P. Benjamin*, 337; Holdsworth, *History of English Law*, 15:303–5.

68. Gruning, review (2001), 989.

69. See, for example, Langdell, *Cases on Sales* (1872), 95–96, 1026, 1033; ASal72, marginal notes on 404–5, and an additional copy annotated by an unidentified student (Special Collections, Harvard Law School Library), marginal notes on 153.

seller by knocking down the hammer. . . .'"[70] Hence, although the transaction looks clearly like a sale, Langdell's characteristic attention to underlying principles appropriately led him to categorize *Payne v. Cave* under contract.[71]

Langdell's effort to distinguish legal issues in sales complemented the project of abstracting fundamental categories of contract, and was subsequently embraced by Holmes, Anson, and Pollock.[72] Professor James Thayer recognized the novelty of Langdell's approach in 1876, upon assuming responsibility for teaching sales at HLS. He assigned Langdell's *Cases on Sales* and began the course by assuring the students (and, it seems, himself) that, although "the subject is [usually] treated as a branch of the law of contracts," it made sense to have a separate casebook and course devoted to sales, if the textbook "is one of a series" and if the course "is a part of *a series* or system of courses."[73] The publication chronology of Langdell's casebooks also demonstrates the originality of his complementary projects.

After publishing the first half of volume 1 of *Cases on Contracts* in October 1870, he completed the first half of volume 1 of *Cases on Sales* in February 1871. Turning back to the casebook on contracts, he produced the second half of the first volume in October 1871, and then issued the second half of volume one of *Cases on Sales* in May 1872. At that point he projected a second volume of *Cases on Contracts*, to be followed by a second volume of the casebook on sales.[74] In this way, Langdell alternately issued installments of casebooks in each domain as he parsed the cases into the two fields, thereby advancing the distinction between contracts and sales and making a third significant contribution to contracts scholarship in the United States.

Beyond that contribution, *Cases on Sales* demonstrates the development of Langdell's editorial principles in constructing casebooks. Though continuing to

70. Friedman, "Formative Elements in the Law of Sales," 455. See *Payne v. Cave* 3 *Term Reports* 148, in Langdell, *Cases on Contracts*, 1–3.

71. Attending Langdell's class in the mid-1870s, William A. Keener recorded about *Payne v. Cave*, "Prof. Langdell thinks that, on principle, the moment the bid was made and accepted . . . this was a contract, though not a sale. The fall of the hammer passing the property." KCon71, 2marg.

72. "Langdell and Holmes in the United States and Anson and Pollock in England . . . describe general contract law without trying to relate it to the law of sales, the law of leases, and so forth." Gordley, *Philosophical Origins of Modern Contract Doctrine*, 158; Gordley, "Natural Law Origins of the Common Law of Contract," 446.

73. Emphasis in original. J. Thayer, Sales Teaching Notebook number 1, leaf 1 (20 Sept. 1876). In contrast, Professor J. C. Gray, who did not embrace case method or the project of abstracting categories until the 1880s, told his students that sales belonged to the subfield of contracts concerning "property." Wigglesworth, Agency and Carriers 1877–78, 1–2.

74. See "Manuscript Cost book for Little Brown. 1865–," Little, Brown, Papers, box 1, §L, 65; Langdell, *Cases on Sales* (1872), preface. No copy of *Cases on Sales*, vol. 1, part 1, is extant; its existence is known only through the records of Little, Brown, Co.

omit headnotes, he responded to Holmes's call for editorial help for students by adding more and longer footnotes that explained editorial excisions and provided some commentary.[75] He continued to emphasize the historical situation of cases and the evolutionary growth of doctrine, first, by adding the date, court, and location of each case to its citation and, second, by adopting the geographical and chronological arrangement of the previous casebook. *Cases on Sales* divided each of its two chapters—"Statute of Frauds" and "Executory and Executed Sales"—into six subsections, which classified their cases geographically and then chronologically under each geographical area, with a few exceptions.

The selection of the cases also indicates the development of Langdell's editorial principles. *Cases on Contracts* had 336 cases; *Cases on Sales* had 252. In *Contracts* 92 percent of the cases were English; in *Sales* 78 percent. Pre-1800 cases constituted 52 percent in *Contracts*; 4 percent in *Sales*. Post-1851 cases amounted to 14 percent in *Contracts* and 28 percent in *Sales*. Thus, the collection in *Cases on Sales* was significantly more selective, American, and recent than in *Cases on Contracts*. All these points responded to Holmes's urging to reduce the "overscrupulous minuteness" of the selection in *Cases on Contracts*.

The topical index to the sales casebook also reveals the development of Langdell's editorial principles. More substantive than that in *Cases on Contracts*, the nineteen-page index in *Sales* was 50 percent longer for 25 percent fewer cases and contained longer entries, ranging up to thirty lines of text. Also more articulated, the index in *Sales* comprised eighteen alphabetical doctrinal headings and subheadings with 109 numbered paragraphs written in full sentences, with cross-references to case names and pages in the casebook.[76] Here, too, Langdell seemed to be responding to Holmes's call for more help for students.

Cases on Sales received another anonymous, complimentary review by Holmes, whose approval is not surprising, given that the inductive and evolutionary approach had impressed him from the outset and that Langdell had taken his earlier suggestions to heart. Holmes carefully counted and commended the number of cases on sales, reduced from the "overscrupulous" number in *Cases on Contracts*. Langdell not only provided an index, as Holmes had requested in the first review, but elaborated the prototype in *Cases on Contracts* (1871), and Holmes therefore extolled "the admirably constructed index" in *Cases on Sales*.[77] As of 1872 Holmes was enthusiastically encouraging Langdell in his novel genre.

75. Langdell, *Cases on Sales* (1872), 3n1, 92–93, 286n1.

76. Langdell, *Cases on Sales* (1872), 1021–39.

77. [O. Holmes], Review (1872b), 145–46. On Holmes's authorship, see Kimball, "Langdell on Contracts and Legal Reasoning," appendix 1.

Langdell and Holmes on Contracts, 1879–81

Langdell never completed the second volume of either casebook, after his work on contracts and sales was "interrupted and delayed"[78] in the mid-1870s by administrative burdens and by a shift in his scholarly focus to equity pleading. This shift stemmed from his personal interest and from new curricular requirements in equity at HLS, though his approach to the new topic did not vary from the pattern in contracts and sales. First, he issued a casebook in two successive parts in 1875 and 1876, then a 130-page "summary" of doctrine in 1877, and finally the entire casebook in one volume in 1878.[79]

Langdell's *Summary of Equity Pleading* prompted another highly favorable, anonymous review from Holmes, who wrote: "If we were to select any part [of the *Summary*] as of preeminent excellence, we should mention the [historical] introduction. The development of the ecclesiastical procedure as there unfolded, and the suggestion that [the procedure] of the common law is founded upon the assumption that the parties to an action owe no obedience to the court, with the subsequent explanation of equitable doctrines as the result of a procedure in which litigants are compelled to obey, will take the student farther into the heart of the subject than many a weary hour of reading elsewhere; and, under the author's hand, even the function of parchment in the time of Lord Eldon becomes instructive."[80]

Here Holmes applauded Langdell's historical and functional explanations for the nature of legal doctrine, which Holmes himself was working out in the middle and late 1870s.[81] In fact, Holmes's enthusiastic praise for Langdell's originality in the *Summary of Equity Pleading*—"there is not an argument or conclusion in the book, even upon familiar law, which does not throw a new and often brilliant light upon what it touches"[82]— suggests that in 1877 Holmes felt that his conclusions were finding confirmation in the inferences that Langdell was drawing from the inductive historicism of his casebooks.

This glowing review for the *Summary of Equity Pleading* extended the trajectory of Holmes's increasing praise for the supplementary material appended to Langdell's casebooks. From 1870 to 1871 to 1872 to 1877, each time Langdell had

78. J. Thayer, Sales Teaching Notebook no. 1, fly leaf (30 Oct. 1876).
79. Langdell, *Cases in Equity Pleading* (1875); Langdell, *Cases in Equity Pleading* (1876); Langdell, *Summary of Equity Pleading* (1877); Langdell, *Cases in Equity Pleading* (1878).
80. [O. Holmes], Review (1877), 763. On Holmes's authorship, see Kimball, "Langdell on Contracts and Legal Reasoning," appendix 1.
81. G. White, *Justice Oliver Wendell Holmes*, 132–38.
82. [O. Holmes], Review (1877), 763–64.

developed the supplementary material, Holmes had encouraged him more. Appreciating this, Langdell had sent Holmes page proofs of the *Summary of Equity Pleading* and a final copy when it appeared.[83] In addition to this positive response to his longest writing thus far, Langdell also received news at this point that *Cases on Contracts* was selling out and that the publisher desired a new edition.[84]

In 1878, soon after sending the full casebook on equity pleading off to the printer, Langdell therefore began to prepare a second edition of *Cases on Contracts*. He changed the organization and selection of cases very little. The basic divisions remained Mutual Consent, Consideration, and Conditional Contracts, while he added an eleventh subdivision to the "Consideration" section. He also eliminated twenty-eight cases, including twenty-five older ones from forbearance, and added eighteen new ones, none before 1700 and thirteen after 1869. These changes, along with the expansion of the topical index to nineteen pages, comport with feedback from Holmes's reviews of the 1870, 1871, and 1872 casebooks. But Langdell devoted most of his effort to writing a 131-page "summary of topics covered by the casebook," responding to Holmes's reservation that students would find *Cases on Contracts* "a pretty tough pièce de résistance without a text-book or the assistance of an instructor."[85]

In fall 1879 Little, Brown, Co. issued the second edition of *Cases on Contracts*, and in February 1880 a highly unfavorable, insulting review appeared in the *Southern Law Review*, located in St. Louis. The anonymous author deprecated case method teaching as Langdell's "hobby," ridiculed the omission of headnotes and inclusion of overruled cases, and concluded that legal treatises and digests "not volumes of cases without headnotes, are the law-books of the future."[86] In keeping with his custom, Langdell made no response,[87] but an extended rebuttal soon appeared in the *Southern Law Review*, maintaining correctly that the reviewer did not understand Langdell's inductive case method, whose purpose "is to teach the student the habit of legal analysis and synthesis, and not to make the student's

83. O. Holmes to Langdell (3 Mar. 1877).

84. Little, Brown, Co. had printed 1,500 copies of each of the first two casebooks. *Cases on Contracts* sold out in February 1878, while *Cases on Sales* sold more slowly, but steadily, until the supply was exhausted in 1892. "Copyright and Commission Accounts 1869," Little, Brown, Papers, box 11, leaf 12.

85. Quotations are, respectively, from Langdell, *Cases on Contracts* (1879), vi; [O. Holmes], Review (1872a), 354. Langdell's summary was appended to the casebook as pages 985–1116.

86. Review of Langdell's *Selected Cases on Contracts* (1880), 872–73. The author was likely the editor Seymour D. Thompson, "a self-taught man who worked at a dozen occupations" before being admitted to the bar in 1869 and elected judge of the St. Louis Court of Appeals in 1880. Paul, *Conservative Crisis and the Rule of Law*, 43n11. See Note, *Harvard Law Review* (1891–92), 89.

87. Schofield, "Christopher Columbus Langdell," 286; Ames, "Christopher Columbus Langdell," 213.

mind a mere dictionary of decisions."[88] Meanwhile, in March 1880 the distinguished English jurist Albert Dicey, with "the most unfeigned admiration," ranked Langdell's book among great American legal writings.[89]

The most noted review of the second edition of *Cases on Contracts* appeared anonymously in the *American Law Review*. Written by Holmes,[90] the review addressed *Cases on Contracts* (1879) together with *Principles of the English Law of Contract* by the distinguished English authority Anson. Holmes devoted but a paragraph to Anson's book, and suggested that "its more penetrating qualities" might be owed to reading Langdell's brief index to the first edition of *Cases on Contracts*.[91] Turning from this remarkable depreciation of Anson, Holmes then devoted two pages to Langdell's second edition, primarily the appended summary.

Calling the summary of "unequal value" in teaching students about the principles underpinning the law, Holmes wrote, "no man competent to judge can read a page of it without at once recognizing the hand of a great master. Every line is compact of ingenious and original thought." Indeed, "there cannot be found in the legal literature of this country, such a tour de force of patient and profound intellect working out original theory through a mass of detail and evolving consistency out of what seemed a chaos of conflicting atoms."[92]

Nevertheless, the appended summary was "equally extraordinary in its merits and its limitations," continued Holmes. He then let fly barbed criticism, which must have surprised Langdell, who likely conceived the summary as a natural extension of the topical indexes that Holmes had previously extolled. Holmes now construed the summary to reveal "the weak point in Mr. Langdell's habit of mind. Mr. Langdell's ideal in the law, the end of all his striving, is the *elegentia juris*, or *logical* integrity of the system as a system. He is, perhaps, the greatest living theologian. . . . If Mr. Langdell could be suspected of ever having troubled himself about Hegel, we might call him a Hegelian in disguise, so entirely is he interested in the formal connection of things."[93]

88. J. M[yers], "Langdell's 'Selected Cases on Contracts' [A reply]," 449. "M." is most likely James J. Myers, one of Langdell's students between 1871 and 1873, who also defended Langdell's educational reforms in the anonymous articles. [J. Myers], "'Law Schools vs. Lawyers' Offices'" (1, 11 Apr. 1873), and [J. Myers], "Harvard Law School" (5, 19 Feb. 1875).

89. Dicey, "English View of American Conservatism," 229.

90. [O. Holmes], Review (Mar. 1880), 233–35. See Touster, "Holmes a Hundred Years Ago: The Common Law," 695n91.

91. Anson, *Principles of the English Law of Contract* (1879); [O. Holmes], Review (Mar. 1880), 233.

92. [O. Holmes], Review (Mar. 1880), 233–34.

93. [O. Holmes], Review (Mar. 1880), 234.

This shift in Holmes's judgment and tone reflected two factors. First is that Langdell's appended summary of contracts did not adopt the historical and functional approach of the *Summary of Equity Pleading* (1877) that Holmes had so admired. Neither a historical introduction nor a functional organization of the content according to procedure appeared in the summary of contracts.[94] Instead, Langdell preserved the alphabetical organization of the topical indexes.

Secondly, Holmes's jurisprudential views had continued to develop significantly since 1877.[95] In the late 1860s and early 1870s, Holmes sought, like Langdell, to abstract principled order from the sets of inconsistent rules left from the demise of the writ system and forms of action in the common law. Beginning in about 1872, Holmes began to argue that particular historical circumstances had given rise to various rules, that many such rules had continued to function after their original generating circumstances no longer obtained, and that, as a result, legal fictions had been developed over the centuries to explain or justify these rules and doctrines. Hence, Holmes must have believed that Langdell's historical and functional approach in the *Summary of Equity Pleading* fit closely his views at that time. By the end of the 1870s, Holmes concluded that such rules and doctrines could not be made logically consistent and that jurists had to distinguish between parts of doctrine that could be logically systematized and parts that derived from historical circumstance or "policy." Consequently, Holmes likely concluded in 1880 that Langdell had retreated from the jurisprudential view that Holmes himself regarded as progressive in 1877. Whatever his reasons, Holmes's review gave rise to the later interpretation that, in the *Summary of Contracts*, Langdell formalistically attempted to build a deductive or geometrical pyramid of contract doctrine.

The separate publication of the summary in 1880 completed Langdell's decade of seminal publications on contracts and sales,[96] as well as equity pleading. The *Summary of Contracts* received a laudatory five-line notice by Holmes and some brief commending references.[97] Holmes saved a more extensive response for *The Common Law* (1881), whose evident borrowing from the *Summary of Contracts* reveals Langdell's additional scholarly contributions. His contributions are also shown by the fact that Langdell's writings were cited by counsel or justices in five

94. Compare Langdell, *Summary of Equity Pleading* (1877), 5n1.

95. The following interpretation relies on the magisterial interpretation of G. White, *Justice Oliver Wendell Holmes*, 116–38.

96. Only a few changes were made from the 1879 version. Langdell, *Summary of the Law of Contracts*, v.

97. [O. Holmes], Review (Sept. 1880). On Holmes's authorship, see Kimball, "Langdell on Contracts and Legal Reasoning," appendix 1. See Keasbey, "Origin and Nature of Consideration," 334.

different cases decided by the U.S. Supreme Court between 1879 and 1885, during an era when it was rare to cite authorities other than cases.[98]

—◊◊◊—

Comprising a series of lectures delivered at the Lowell Institute in Boston in November and December 1880 and published in March 1881, *The Common Law* includes three chapters on contract, and opens with a famous line drawn directly from Holmes's 1880 review of Langdell's *Cases on Contracts* (1879): "The life of the law has not been logic; it has been experience." From that starting point, the beginning pages of the first lecture set forth Holmes's thesis that legal rules emerge and develop in response to historical exigencies, and are later rationalized ex post facto to achieve a fictional logical consistency.[99]

Although this opening and thesis seem to target Langdell, *The Common Law* does not employ the barbs of the 1880 review. Of the nine explicit references to Langdell's writings on contracts, three are positive, and six respectfully object to Langdell's "ingenious" or "logical" analyses.[100] Apart from those explicit references, however, "Holmes borrowed, without attribution, Langdell's doctrinal insights" from the *Summary of Contracts*, notwithstanding Holmes's claims to originality, which have long been credited by historians.[101]

One reason for the borrowing is that Holmes needed the expertise, not having carefully studied the subject of contracts and being under a tight deadline to complete the lectures, scheduled for the fall of 1880.[102] In addition, Holmes greatly respected Langdell's knowledge of case law, as shown by his prior reviews. Finally, Holmes was virtually obliged to consult Langdell's *Summary of Contracts*, because it appeared at the end of June 1880 just as Holmes was beginning to write his three lectures on contract.[103] Holmes could scarcely ignore it, and upon completing his lectures in September, he published a brief, anonymous review of Langdell's *Summary*, closing with the freighted observation, "It may be desirable, at a proper time, to give some reasons for different conclusions on many essential points; but

98. Grafton v. Cummings (1879), 105; Davis v. Wells (1881), 166; Thompson v. Insurance Co. (1881), 256; Hart v. Sansom (1884), 155; Campbell v. Holt (1885), 625.

99. [O. Holmes], Review (Mar. 1880), 234; O. Holmes, *Common Law*, 1, 5.

100. The three: 297n2, 335n1, 337n1; the six: 286n3, 304n2–305nn1–2, 316n4, 317n1, 327n1, 329n2, 339n1, in O. Holmes, *Common Law*.

101. P. Kelley, "Critical Analysis of Holmes," 1756. Cf. Howe, *Justice Oliver Wendell Holmes*, 2:228–30, 241, 246; Horwitz, *Transformation of American Law, 1870–1960*, 37–38.

102. P. Kelley, "Critical Analysis of Holmes," 1746.

103. Langdell, *Summary of the Law of Contracts*, vi; G. White, *Justice Oliver Wendell Holmes*, 172.

that time is not the present."[104] Less than eight weeks away, the Lowell lectures provided the "proper time."

After delivering the lectures in November–December 1880 Holmes revised and published them in March 1881 as *The Common Law* (1881). In April Holmes wrote to Pollock urging that he read Langdell's *Summary of Contracts*, and equivocating between high praise and damning criticism, as in his published review. "A more misspent piece of marvelous ingenuity I never read, yet it is most suggestive and instructive," wrote Holmes. "I have referred to Langdell several times in dealing with contracts [in *The Common Law*] because to my mind he represents the powers of darkness. He is all for logic and hates any reference to anything outside of it. . . . But he is a noble old swell whose knowledge[,] ability and idealist devotion to his work I revere and love."[105] Among the "instructive" insights borrowed by Holmes was Langdell's fourth scholarly contribution: refuting the will theory and introducing the bargain theory of contract.

In the mid-nineteenth century, contract doctrine was still amorphous and marked by "a confused combination of subjective and objective thinking."[106] In particular, historians have debated the time and the process by which the "objective" view of contract superseded the "will theory." It is generally agreed that the "subjective" will theory—holding that contractual obligations derive from the subjective will or intentions of the parties—predominated early in the nineteenth century. By the end of the nineteenth century, the objective view—holding that the parties' word and behavior rather than their underlying intentions determine contractual obligations—prevailed. Beyond this general agreement, when and how the shift occurred are explained in different ways,[107] although Holmes has traditionally been credited with refuting the will theory.[108]

However, prior to Holmes's declaration, Langdell had expressly stated, "As to

---

104. [O. Holmes], Review (Sept. 1880), 666.

105. O. Holmes to Pollock (10 Apr. 1881).

106. J. Baker, Review, 469. See the different interpretations of intellectual influence in Gordley, *Philosophical Origins of Modern Contract Doctrine*, 161; LaPiana, *Logic and Experience*, 76–78; Sebok, "Misunderstanding Positivism," 2087; P. Kelley, "Critical Analysis of Holmes," 1687–89; Perillo, "Origins of the Objective Theory of Contract Formation," 429, 462.

107. See Perillo, "Origins of the Objective Theory of Contract Formation," 427–29, 463; Friedman, *Contract Law in America*, 87; Gordley, *Philosophical Origins of Modern Contract Doctrine*, 161–63; Horwitz, *Transformation of American Law, 1870–1960*, 36–39; P. Kelley, "Critical Analysis of Holmes," 1694–96, 1756–57; Duxbury, *Frederick Pollock*, 191–201.

108. See Howe, *Justice Oliver Wendell Holmes*, 2:232–33, 246; Gilmore, *Death of Contract*, 35; Farnsworth, "Contracts Scholarship," 1412; Horwitz, *Transformation of American Law, 1870–1960*, 37–38. As late as 1896, Holmes imputed the will theory to Langdell, thereby encouraging modern scholars to attribute to Langdell a "preoccupation with subjective consent." Seipp, "Holmes's Path," 526–27. For such an attribution, see Howe, *Justice Oliver Wendell Holmes*, 2:232–33.

the rule that the wills of the contracting parties must concur, it only means that they must concur in legal contemplation, and this they do whenever an existing offer is accepted.... In truth, *mental acts or acts of the will are not the materials out of which promises are made; a physical act on the part of the promisor is indispensable*."[109] Langdell thus refuted the will theory in his *Summary of Contracts* that Holmes had studied while preparing the contracts chapters for *The Common Law* in the summer of 1880. In fact, Langdell refuted the will theory in his classroom in the mid-1870s.

As a student at HLS from 1875 to 1878, William Keener recorded Langdell's words that directly anticipate the language of the *Summary of Contracts*: "The rule that the minds of the contracting parties must meet simply means that they must, in legal contemplation, concur; and this they do whenever an existing offer is accepted. Mental acts or acts of the will are not the essence of a promise. A physical act is indispensable, and when done, can only be undone by a physical act.... Upon mutual consent, law only regards consent manifested, not the abstract state of mind."[110] Consequently, already in the mid-1870s Langdell was announcing to his students that the will theory was a legal fiction.[111]

Commensurate with refuting the will theory of contract, Langdell introduced the bargain theory of contract. Scholars have conventionally credited this new conception to Holmes whose bargain theory rested on a putatively "new analysis of consideration," namely treating consideration as the sole inducement for each party.[112] In Holmes's often quoted words, "It is the essence of a consideration, that, by the terms of the agreement, it is given and accepted as the motive or inducement of the promise. The root of the whole matter is the relation of reciprocal conventional inducement, each for the other, between consideration and promise."[113] But, again, Holmes's view appeared first in Langdell's *Summary of Contracts*: "Every consideration is...the promisor's sole inducement to make the promise. As the law cannot see any inequality in value between the consideration and the promise, so it cannot see any motive for the promise except the consideration."[114] Holmes apparently borrowed his famous theory of consideration from Langdell.[115]

To be sure, imputing originality for the bargain theory is conjectural because

---

109. Langdell, *Summary of the Law of Contracts*, 244. Emphasis added.

110. *KCon71*, 3marg, 13marg.

111. Langdell's explicit refutation antedated Pollock as well. Duxbury, *Frederick Pollock*, 194–96.

112. Howe, *Justice Oliver Wendell Holmes*, 2:241. See also Gilmore, *Death of Contract*, 19–21; Farnsworth, "Contracts Scholarship," 1412; Atiyah, *Essays on Contract*, 60; Nyquist, "Contract Theory," 75–76.

113. O. Holmes, *Common Law*, 293–94.

114. Langdell, *Summary of the Law of Contracts*, 78–79.

115. See P. Kelley, "Critical Analysis of Holmes," 1722, 1757.

the nature of consideration was much debated during the nineteenth century.[116] But students' notes reveal that, already in the early 1870s, Langdell was teaching his classes that, in the sixteenth century "when [a] promise is first held to be a consideration," the cases make it appear that "the promise was of earnest to bind a bargain."[117] Moreover, Langdell's introduction of bargain theory is manifested in a more technical innovation.

"Consideration" was conventionally understood to comprise a "benefit" to the promisor and a "detriment" to the promisee.[118] This formulation required that the value of the benefit to each party be assessed in order to determine the equivalency of exchange. But this requirement posed a problem for the objective bargain theory because the determination of value of a benefit was inevitably subjective. "The value of most considerations...is a thing which the law cannot measure; it is not merely a matter of fact, but a matter of opinion," wrote Langdell. Consequently, in order to eliminate the parties' subjective motives, Langdell declared that "benefit to the promisor is irrelevant to the question of whether a given thing can be made the consideration," and that a "detriment to the promisee is a universal test of the sufficiency of consideration."[119]

This detriment-only formulation became normative with the rise of bargain theory,[120] and has been attributed to Pollock and to Holmes. But Langdell's priority appears in several ways. First, the textual evidence does not sustain the attribution to Pollock,[121] and Holmes's discussion begins with Langdell's detriment-only formulation, without attribution.[122] Second, HLS professor James Barr Ames explicitly identified the detriment-only formulation as original with Langdell.[123]

---

116. See Duxbury, *Frederick Pollock*, 163, 206–9; Friedman, *History of American Law*, 277; Atiyah, *Essays on Contract*, 68; Atiyah, *Introduction to the Law of Contract*, 124–60; Gordley, *Philosophical Origins of Modern Contract Doctrine*, 165–75.

117. *ACon71*, 411marg.

118. Metcalf, *Principles of the Law of Contracts*, 161–63; W. Story, *Treatise on the Law of Contracts*, 1:503; See Kent, *Commentaries on American Law*, 2:364–65; Pollock, *Principles of Contract*, 154–58; Anson, *Principles of the English Law of Contract* (1879), 61; Keasbey, "Origin and Nature of Consideration," 296.

119. Langdell, *Summary of the Law of Contracts*, 71, 82.

120. Gordley, *Philosophical Origins of Modern Contract Doctrine*, 173.

121. Gordley, *Philosophical Origins of Modern Contract Doctrine*, 173, cites the tenth edition (1936) of Frederick Pollock, *Principles of Contract*, while attributing "the core idea" to the first edition of 1876 (150–51), although Pollock does not there or elsewhere reduce consideration to detriment.

122. O. Holmes, *Common Law*, 290. Holmes proceeded to define consideration as whatever the parties declare to be the inducement for their promise (292). The fundamental point, which Langdell had introduced, was that the law would not try to determine the "actual" inducement apart from what the parties declare to be their inducements. P. Kelley, "Critical Analysis of Holmes," 1757. Cf. Gilmore, *Death of Contract*, 19–21.

123. Ames, "Christopher Columbus Langdell, 1826–1906," 479. See also Keasbey, "Origin and Nature of Consideration," 334.

Finally, an HLS student recorded in his class notes in October 1876 that, in the opening lecture to his contracts course, Ames told the class: "Consideration in law = detriment incurred by promisee at request of promisor."[124] This telling statement reveals that already by 1876 Ames was transmitting to students as established doctrine the detriment-only formula that he attributed to Langdell. Consequently, Langdell must have announced this formulation during the period 1870–73 when Ames attended Langdell's course on contracts, before Ames began teaching it in 1873–74. This chronology demonstrates that reducing consideration to "detriment to the promisee," identifying consideration as the sole inducement, and viewing contract as a bargain amount, collectively, to an original scholarly contribution that Langdell formulated in the early 1870s.

Langdell's fifth contribution was, in the words of Ames, his "emphasis upon and promulgation of the distinction between unilateral and bilateral contracts."[125] The centrality of this distinction for Langdell followed from his abstracting offer, acceptance, and consideration as primary, salient dimensions of contract. Langdell invoked the distinction throughout the *Summary of Contracts*, including the final sentence. Further, he emphasized the distinction in his teaching, as shown by the flyleaves from Ames's and Keener's copies of Langdell's *Cases on Contracts* (1871) used in Langdell's class during the early 1870s.[126]

The origins of unilateral obligations in nineteenth-century contract doctrine are obscure.[127] In 1862 the central problem in the kind of contract that Langdell subsequently defined as "unilateral" was addressed in the English case *Offord v. Davies*. But in 1867 Metcalf omitted the issue, and Leake in the same year discussed what Langdell called a "unilateral contract" under the heading "contracts arising upon executed consideration."[128] In 1874 Bigelow, in his revision of Story's prominent treatise, discussed "unilateral contracts," but his term was a misnomer, meaning simply an unaccepted offer, which, he admitted, "cannot properly be called a contract before acceptance."[129] As if recognizing Bigelow's misnomer,

124. Wigglesworth, Contracts 1876–77, leaves 1–2.
125. Ames, "Christopher Columbus Langdell, 1826–1906," 479. "The contract is unilateral, [if] consisting of a promise on one side, and something given or done (not promised to be given or done) on the other. If there is a promise on each side, and yet but one contract, the contract is bilateral; and if the making of a promise is the only thing given or done on either side, the contract is purely bilateral...." Langdell, *Summary of the Law of Contracts*, 102–3.
126. Langdell, *Summary of the Law of Contracts*, 253; ACon71; KCon71.
127. Perillo, "Origins of the Objective Theory of Contract Formation," 452.
128. *Offord v. Davies* (1862); Metcalf, *Principles of the Law of Contracts*, 191–220; Leake, *Elements of the Law of Contracts*, 26–38. Leake's term is operational, overbroad in some respects, and too narrow in others, whereas Langdell's unilateral/bilateral distinction is more precise and salient.
129. W. Story, *Treatise on the Law of Contracts*, 1:524.

Pollock in 1876 employed "unilateral promise" to mean what Bigelow called a "unilateral contract." Elsewhere Pollock briefly addressed, without naming, the situation in which "the proposal or acceptance of an agreement may be communicated by conduct as well as by words."[130] In 1879 Anson likewise noted that situation in passing, without naming or analyzing it.[131]

Consequently, Ames was correct in asserting that Langdell introduced and promulgated the distinction between bilateral and unilateral contracts in the early 1870s. While this distinction is overshadowed by his other four contributions,[132] it most clearly demonstrates Holmes's unacknowledged borrowing, because, in *The Common Law*, Holmes repeatedly adopted and elaborated the bilateral/unilateral distinction without crediting Langdell.[133] In this fashion, he borrowed from and built on Langdell's new distinction and terminology, while making Langdell's contribution appear deficient rather than original.

Langdell's Mode of Legal Reasoning

Notwithstanding the significant contribution made by Langdell's contracts scholarship during the 1870s, scholars through the beginning of the twenty-first century have considered him "one of the principal sources of the sterile formalism," or "classical legal thought," that predominated in American jurisprudence between 1870 and 1920. Legal formalism consisted in the view that deductive inference from objective, immutable legal principles determines correct decisions in legal disputes.[134] The locus classicus attributing this view to Langdell appeared in Holmes's 1880 review:

130. Pollock, *Principles of Contract*, 148, 27.

131. Anson, *Principles of the English Law of Contract* (1879), 23.

132. "The terms unilateral and bilateral are disappearing since the bifurcation does not encompass the formation of all contracts." Teeven, *History of the Anglo-American Common Law of Contract*, 179. Cf. Farnsworth, "Contracts Scholarship," 1410–11; Atiyah, *Introduction to the Law of Contract*, 46–48.

133. O. Holmes, *Common Law*, 335–39. See also, 287, 304–6, 319, 327; LaPiana, *Logic and Experience*, 120–21.

134. Quotations are, respectively, from: LaPiana, *Logic and Experience*, 3; Kennedy, "Toward an Historical Understanding of Legal Consciousness," 3. See Gilmore, *Ages of American Law*, 62; Wiecek, *Lost World of Classical Legal Thought*, 92–93; S. Smith, "Believing Like a Lawyer," 1077; Alschuler, *Law without Values*, 87; Horwitz, *Transformation of American Law, 1870–1960*, 9–31, 189; Simpson, *Legal Theory and Legal History*, 204; Grey, "Langdell's Orthodoxy," 36; Friedman, *Contract Law in America*, 212; Friedman and Macaulay, "Contract Law and Contract Teaching," 805–6; Teeven, *History of the Anglo-American Common Law of Contract*, 218; Patterson, "Langdell's Legacy," 198–201; P. Kelley, "Critical Analysis of Holmes," 1704–10, 1755–56; P. Kelley, "Holmes, Langdell, and Formalism," 35–40. On this terminology, see Siegel, "Joel Bishop's Orthodoxy," 216n6.

Mr. Langdell's ideal in the law, the end of all his striving, is the *elegentia juris*, or *logical* integrity of the system as a system. He is, perhaps, the greatest living theologian. . . . A single phrase [from Langdell's *Summary of Contracts*] will illustrate what is meant, "It has been claimed that the purposes of substantial justice and the interests of contracting parties as understood by themselves will be best served by holding etc. . . . and cases have been put to show that the contrary view would produce not only unjust but absurd results. *The true answer to this argument is that it is irrelevant*; but . . ."

Then Holmes continues:

The reader will perceive that the language is only incidental, but it reveals a mode of thought which becomes conspicuous to a careful student. . . . The life of the law has not been logic; it has been experience. The seed of every new growth within its sphere has been a felt necessity. The form of continuity has been kept up by reasonings purporting to reduce every thing to a logical sequence; but that form is nothing but the evening dress which the newcomer puts on to make itself presentable according to conventional requirements. The important phenomenon is the man underneath it, not the coat; the justice and reasonableness of a decision, not its consistency with previously held views. No one will ever have a truly philosophic mastery over the law who does not habitually consider the forces outside of it which have made it what it is.[135]

These words are always cited in support of the charge of formalism made against Langdell's mode of legal reasoning,[136] and it is important to clarify exactly the nature of the complaint.

Holmes's critique, when interpreted in light of Langdell's scholarly contribution of parsimonious abstraction, has often been understood to accuse the *Summary of Contracts* of building a systematic pyramid of contract doctrine from a few initial premises, as in Euclidean geometry. However, the book does not present an axiomatic, hierarchical framework, descending from basic definitions to principles to specific rules, as do the Roman law books that Langdell knew well.[137] In fact, the

---

135. Holmes inserted the emphasis in his quotation of Langdell. [O. Holmes], Review (Mar. 1880), 233, quoting Langdell, *Summary of the Law of Contracts*, 20–21.

136. The authority of Holmes's critique is traceable through the influential writing of Mark De Wolfe Howe, Grant Gilmore, and Thomas C. Grey. This lineage is discussed in Kimball, "Langdell Problem," 302–22.

137. I am grateful to Daniel R. Coquillette for this insightful comparison.

Summary of Contracts can scarcely be considered a "treatise," because Langdell arranged his subjects not hierarchically but alphabetically.[138] Thus, "the arrangement of subjects . . . indicates nothing as to the order in which they should be read, and every reader must exercise his own taste and judgment as to the order in which he will read them, or whether he will read them in any order," as Langdell wrote.[139] Furthermore, the *Summary of Contracts* "embraces only a part of the subject of Contracts" and does not cover "the subjects discussed."[140] It summarizes neither contract doctrine nor the topics addressed.

The *Summary of Contracts* consists of an alphabetized collection of "separable, brilliant doctrinal analyses"[141] arranged in 187 numbered paragraphs distributed under twenty-six headings: sixteen major headings and another ten subheadings under the general heading of "consideration."[142] All of these headings, with the exception of "debt," correspond to divisions or subdivisions of the casebook.[143] Consequently, a student or teacher could employ the alphabetical "summary" like an encyclopedia to find an interpretation of the cases related to a particular topic in the casebook. If, for example, a class were discussing cases in chapter 3, section 4, concerning "conditions subsequent" in the casebook, then the students or teacher could flip back to the appendix, find the alphabetized heading under that entry, and read the analysis of the cases.[144] Hence, the *Summary of Contracts* "was written for the sake of the Cases, and the two were designed to be companions. . . . The cases are constantly cited and discussed without any statement of them, it being always

---

138. See Langdell, *Summary of the Law of Contracts*, v; Schweber, "'Science' of Legal Science," 460; Siegel, "John Chipman Gray," 1516.

139. Langdell, *Summary of the Law of Contracts*, v.

140. Langdell, *Summary of the Law of Contracts*, iii, v.

141. P. Kelley, "Critical Analysis of Holmes," 1710.

142. Acceptance of Offer, Bidding at Auction, Concurrent Conditions, Conditions, Conditions Precedent, Conditions Subsequent, Consideration (Adequacy of consideration, Consideration and motive, From whom the consideration must move [in 1879 casebook], To whom the consideration must move, Mutual consent as an element of consideration, Relation in time of the consideration to the promise, Moral consideration, Consideration void in part, Mutual promises, Executed consideration) Debt, Demand, Dependent and independent covenants and promises, Mutual consent, Notice, Offer, Performance of conditions, Revocation of offer, Unilateral and bilateral contracts.

143. The correspondence holds if one subsumes under the casebook's undivided chapter on "mutual consent" the headings "acceptance," "bidding at auction," "offer," "revocation of offer," and "unilateral and bilateral contracts."

144. The availability of the summary had the potential of turning the case method from inductive into illustrative; and subsequent HLS professors felt that "too much help was thus given to the student by [Langdell's] summaries; and . . . the later Harvard case books contained no summary" with a few exceptions. *Centennial History of the Harvard Law School*, 81.

assumed that the reader has them before him."[145] The appended "summary" was clearly a pedagogical reference guide, as Holmes acknowledged.[146]

A narrower understanding of the formalism charge is that Langdell viewed law not as a geometrical pyramid, but as a purely deductive discipline, in which logical consistency is the sole criterion of validity. But Langdell was not exclusively deductive, for he induced the premises for his deductions from the cases, and always produced his summaries—on contracts, equity pleading, and equity juris-diction—a few years after his casebooks. He built the summaries on the casebooks, not vice versa, and his inductivism was praised by Holmes in statements from 1870 to 1886. Furthermore, because induction alone cannot lead to a comprehensive, coherent system, Langdell's writings on contracts and sales do not yield a deduc-tive system. Instead, these writings—including his *Summary of Contracts*—present abstract dimensions or categories (offer, acceptance, and consideration, above all) under which are collected separate analyses of technical questions,[147] reflecting the approach of a practicing lawyer who had handled technical questions in separate cases for fifteen years.

At its core, the Holmesian critique therefore asserts neither that Langdell was Euclidean nor that he was purely deductive, but that he neglected what Holmes called "the forces outside of" the law. Those forces have conventionally been con-sidered under the two categories of "justice" and "policy"—often called "fairness" and "convenience," respectively, in nineteenth-century writings. Taken together, justice and policy have been labeled concerns of "acceptability."[148] Holmes funda-mentally charged that Langdell dismissed acceptability in determining doctrine and analyzing decisions in cases. As his cardinal example, Holmes quoted Langdell's statement that "the purposes of substantial justice and the interests of the con-tracting parties ... [are] *irrelevant*" in legal analysis of the mailbox dilemma.

This dilemma posed the question of when a contract offer is legally accepted: upon the offeree's mailing the acceptance or upon the offeror's receipt of the mailed acceptance. The importance of this dilemma grew during the eighteenth and nineteenth centuries due to reliance on the mails amid the increasing dis-tance, complexity, and volume of commercial transactions. When and how could

145. Langdell, *Summary of the Law of Contracts*, v. The preface to the *Summary* implies that Langdell did not want to issue it separately and did so only at the urging of the publisher, which envisioned a separate market for it (iii–iv).

146. [O. Holmes], Review (Mar. 1880), 234.

147. See P. Kelley, "Critical Analysis of Holmes," 1710; LaPiana, *Logic and Experience*, 58, 65, 78.

148. "A legal system is *acceptable* to the extent that it fulfills the ideals and desires of those under its jurisdiction...." Grey, "Langdell's Orthodoxy," 10.

a manufacturer in England revoke offers to buy cotton from growers in Mississippi or Egypt? All these factors gave "rise to difficulties in practice" and to a vexing legal dilemma, according to Pollock in 1876.[149] Langdell's seven-page discussion of the dilemma consists of one page introducing the problem; three pages addressing authority, or case law; two pages addressing principle, or doctrinal logic; and one page addressing acceptability, or justice and policy.[150]

Authority presented two distinct resolutions of the mailbox dilemma for an American lawyer. In 1818 the King's Bench in England held in *Adams v. Lindsell* that a contract became effective when the offeree put the acceptance in the mail. Parsons and Anson invoked the authority of this case, and Pollock declared it to be "the first and perhaps still leading case on the matter."[151] Yet, the Supreme Judicial Court of Massachusetts in 1822 held oppositely in *McCulloch v. Eagle Insurance Company*: a contract was not formed until the offeror received the signed, accepted contract in the mail.[152] Hence, the rule of *Adams* did not prevail uniformly in leading jurisdictions in the United States, and even in England, Pollock stated in 1876 that "the actual state of the law cannot be laid down with much confidence" regarding the mailbox dilemma.[153] Given this indeterminacy, Langdell, in his three pages addressing authority, conducted a compact but thorough overview of fourteen leading cases and concluded that *McCulloch* was the only unconditional, unanimous decision directly on point.[154]

In the ensuing two-page analysis of principle, Langdell arranged the *Adams* argument "in the form of a syllogism" and concluded that "the fault of this syllogism is in the major premise, which is untrue."[155] Instead, Langdell argued, since "a letter of acceptance... contains by implication a counteroffer," and since "communication to the offeree is the essence of every offer" and since an unreceived offer is uncommunicated, then "a letter of acceptance... is accepted" when "the letter of acceptance reaches the original offeror."[156] While this conclusion supported the decision in *McCulloch*, Langdell's logical analysis of doctrine was no less susceptible to objection than his interpretation of cases. For example, he did

149. Pollock, *Principles of Contract*, 13.

150. Langdell, *Summary of the Law of Contracts*, 15–21.

151. *Adams v. Lindsell* (1818); Pollock, *Principles of Contract*, 13. See Anson, *Principles of the English Law of Contract* (1879), 20; Th. Parsons, *Law of Contracts*, 1:406–407nk.

152. *McCulloch v. Eagle* (1822).

153. Pollock, *Principles of Contract*, 13.

154. Langdell, *Summary of the Law of Contracts*, 16–18. All fourteen cases were included in *Cases on Contracts*.

155. Langdell, *Summary of the Law of Contracts*, 19.

156. Langdell, *Summary of the Law of Contracts*, 15, 21.

not indicate how an infinite loop of counteroffers and counteracceptances could be avoided. If Langdell actually drew his premises from a priori principle, uninformed by cases, then it seems surprising that he did not select the premises so as to avoid such circularity.

Hence, Langdell's preference for *McCulloch* could have arisen as easily through induction from cases as through deduction from a priori principle. But even if Langdell reasoned inductively in this fashion, he would still be examining only cases and treating acceptability—justice and policy—as "irrelevant," as Holmes contended[157] and later scholars agreed through the beginning of the twenty-first century.[158]

Nevertheless, if Langdell treated justice and policy as "irrelevant," this view was justified in at least three respects for a prudent lawyer and law professor in the 1870s. First, in commercial law businessmen valued uniform rules, believing that "no special, personal factors should influence the rational calculus" of the marketplace.[159] When forced into court, merchants and members of the growing commercial and industrial interests demanded that cases be conducted "by trained judges, under standardized procedures, and governed by known precedents," rather than by untrained justices seeking to do justice in individual cases.[160] Far from indicating "Platonic" affection for *elegentia juris*,[161] Langdell's "irrelevant" remark reflected both conventional wisdom of a powerful constituency and hardheaded advice derived from his fifteen years of practice on Wall Street.

More generally, Langdell's "irrelevant" remark reflected the fact that appeals to acceptability in court were ineffective, since contemporary judges firmly believed that "doing justice was not the job of the court if precedent demanded injustice." Early in the 1800s leading American jurisdictions endorsed this doctrine.[162] In the 1850s Theophilus Parsons observed that this remained "an old and deeprooted principle of the common law, and though it sometimes has the appearance

---

157. See S. Smith, "Believing Like a Lawyer," 1089; Grey, "Langdell's Orthodoxy," 16–24.

158. Howe, *Justice Oliver Wendell Holmes*, 2:243n50. See Touster, "Holmes a Hundred Years Ago: *The Common Law*," 695n91; Purcell, *Crisis of Democratic Theory*, 75; Grey, "Langdell's Orthodoxy," 13–15; Patterson, "Langdell's Legacy," 198; Siegel, "Joel Bishop's Orthodoxy," 221n23; Reimann, "Holmes's *Common Law*," 256n98, 261n148, 262n154; Siegel, "John Chipman Gray," 1524–26; P. Kelley, "Holmes, Langdell, and Formalism," 35–40. See Kimball, "Langdell Problem," 316–22.

159. Friedman, *History of American Law*, 539, 534–35.

160. Risjord, *Chesapeake Politics*, 182. See Roeber, *Faithful Magistrates and Republican Lawyers*, 112–202.

161. Gilmore, *Ages of American Law*, 62.

162. Quotation is from Perillo, "Origins of the Objective Theory of Contract Formation," 441. See 441–42, citing: *Beane v. Middleton* (1797), 78; *Wilkie v. Roosevelt* (1802); *Paul v. Frazier* (1807), 73; *Hallett v. Wylie* (1808), 46; *Banorgee v. Hovey* (1809), 23.

of harshness, it would be difficult to contend against it on principle."[163] In 1879 Anson did not consider acceptability while concluding that "neither principle nor authority" supported a view of revocations of offer that was closely related to the mailbox dilemma.[164] Thus, nineteenth-century legal scholars and jurists customarily distinguished between moral obligation and legal obligation in analyzing specific cases.[165]

Finally, Langdell's "irrelevant" remark may reflect the distinction between law and equity. Langdell devoted far more attention to equity than common law in his legal practice, teaching and scholarship, and a separate body of case law about contracts had arisen in equity,[166] where judges looked, in theory, to acceptability and were empowered with discretion to declare remedies. For example, addressing breaches of conditions in the *Summary on Contracts*, Langdell explained that "the rule in equity differs from the rule at law. . . . Equity can give relief on such conditions as it sees fit to impose."[167] Some remedies in common law were conventionally taught in a course by that name, while equitable remedies, such as specific performance, were usually taught in a course on equity.[168]

In sum, there are at least three respects in which Langdell's "irrelevant" remark expressed a well-established, prudent course for a lawyer in the 1870s. The distinction between law and acceptability was preferred by parties to commercial contracts, was commonly endorsed by courts in leading jurisdictions, and was consistent with the traditional distinction between law and equity. These three jurisprudential justifications are strengthened by the pedagogical nature of Langdell's remarks. In the 1870s Langdell's "irrelevant" remark expressed sound and practical doctrine for a law professor to convey to students.

By the same token, Holmes scarcely attended to acceptability in his analysis of the mailbox dilemma, confining himself to the single sentence: "if convenience preponderates in favor of either view, that is sufficient reason for its adoption." Nor did Holmes discuss case law. In fact, Holmes devoted the bulk of his discussion to "the merely logical grounds" of principle, rebutting Langdell's "most ingenious argument."[169] On this issue, as elsewhere in *The Common Law*, Holmes "may have

163. Th. Parsons, *Law of Contracts*, 2:33. See also 1:522–26.

164. Anson, *Principles of the English Law of Contract* (1879), 19.

165. Teeven, "Conventional Moral Obligation Principle," 715–16.

166. See, for example, Langdell, *Summary of Equity Pleading* (1883), §§109–11, 113, 119.

167. Langdell, *Summary of the Law of Contracts*, 208–9.

168. Farnsworth, "Contracts Scholarship," 1430–31. Ames, for example, credited Langdell with introducing and establishing the point that forcing "specific performance" on a contract in common law was a misnomer, drawn from equity, and actually referred to requiring "specific reparations" for breach of contract. Ames, "Christopher Columbus Langdell, 1826–1906," 479.

169. O. Holmes, *Common Law*, 305–7.

called for the replacement of 'logic' with evolutionary history, but he was not particularly inclined to practice evolutionary history as a methodology."[170]

Rather, it was Langdell who analyzed acceptability, beginning with the sentence quoted by Holmes: "It has been claimed that the purposes of substantial justice, and the interests of the contracting parties as understood by themselves, will be best served by holding that the contract is complete the moment the letter of acceptance is mailed; and cases have been put to show that the contrary view would produce not only *unjust* but *absurd* results. The true answer to this argument is, that it is irrelevant; but . . ."[171] In the italicized words, Langdell dismissed considerations of fairness and convenience, respectively.

Holmes stopped analyzing Langdell's text at the "but," while Langdell proceeded to consider hypothetically what he had just dismissed: "but, assuming it to be relevant, it may be turned against those who use it without losing any of its strength. The only cases of real hardship are where there is a miscarriage of the letter of acceptance, and in those cases a hardship to one of the parties is inevitable."[172] In other words, the appeal to acceptability is equivocal and indeterminate.

Among "those who use" the appeal, Anson likely stood foremost in Langdell's mind. Regarding the mailbox dilemma, Anson concurred with *Adams v. Lindsell* while also invoking both fairness and convenience. Anson held that offerees would unfairly "be exposed to serious loss" if they relied on a contract that they had accepted by letter but that was later determined not binding because the letter did not reach the offeror. In addition, if the offeree had to wait to act on the contract until confirming receipt of the mailed acceptance, that delay would not "conduce to the conduct of business."[173] Thus, Anson in 1879 addressed acceptability, but only from the offeree's perspective.

Langdell's appreciation of indeterminacy arose from considering the offeror's perspective, as well: "Adopting one view, the hardship consists in making one liable on a contract in which he is ignorant of having made; adopting the other view, it consists of depriving one of the benefits of a contract which he supposes he had made." Hence, for either resolution of the mailbox dilemma, "a hardship to one of the parties is inevitable."[174] Langdell's analysis was therefore more comprehensive

---

170. Quotation is from G. White, *Justice Oliver Wendell Holmes*, 152. See 171, 179–80; Gilmore, *Ages of American Law*, 52; Touster, "Holmes a Hundred Years Ago: The Common Law," 679–80; Alschuler, *Law without Values*, 86–107. In Robert Gordon's memorable phrase, "*The Common Law* . . . is a book at war with itself." R. Gordon, "Holmes's *Common Law*," 720–21.

171. Langdell, *Summary of the Law of Contracts*, 20–21. Emphasis added.

172. Langdell, *Summary of the Law of Contracts*, 21.

173. Anson, *Principles of the English Law of Contract* (1879), 20.

174. Langdell, *Summary of the Law of Contracts*, 21.

than that of Anson, who subsequently acknowledged the importance of treating the perspectives of both parties in the 1883 revision of his treatise.[175] Holmes in *The Common Law* also implicitly conceded Langdell's point by sidestepping acceptability in the single sentence: "if convenience preponderates in favor of either view, that is sufficient reason for its adoption."[176]

Then Langdell asserted that acceptability is, in fact, determinate and that fairness comports with the decision in *McCulloch*. Between "making one liable on a contract in which he is ignorant of having made" and "depriving one of the benefit of a contract which he supposes he had made, . . . the choice would seem to be clear: the former [*Adams* rule] is positive, the latter [*McCulloch* rule] merely negative; the former imposes a liability to which no limit can be placed, the latter leaves everything in statu quo."[177] Lastly, Langdell ended his analysis by considering convenience or efficacy, again from both perspectives. "As to making provision for the contingency of the miscarriage of a letter, this is easy for the person who sends it," that is, the offeree. But "it is practically impossible for the person to whom it is sent," the offeror.[178] Consequently, convenience also favors the rule of *McCulloch* that the contract is not binding until the offeror receives the acceptance.

Far from ignoring acceptability, Langdell therefore proposed several contradictory positions. He declared acceptability irrelevant, considered it anyway, showed it to be indeterminate, considered fairness with respect to both parties, examined convenience with respect to both parties, and concluded that justice and convenience favor the resolution that he had previously announced through an analysis of case law and then of principle. Compared to other leading contemporaries, Langdell's seven-page assessment of the mailbox dilemma was more comprehensive and thorough than either Anson's one-sided analysis or Holmes's narrow discussion of principle. Only Pollock's treatment approached Langdell's in compass and sophistication, and likewise fell into contradiction, favoring one view on the grounds of acceptability, which he declared to be relevant, and another based on authority, which he endorsed.[179] The mailbox dilemma seemed no more tractable for Pollock than for Langdell, who also had to contend with *McCulloch*.

Langdell's seven-page analysis was, in fact, the most comprehensive and thorough discussion of authority, principle, and acceptability related to the mailbox dilemma that appeared in the treatise literature to that point. Langdell's failing lay in expressing contradictory views or in not explaining his method of recon-

175. Anson, *Principles of the English Law of Contract* (1883), 30–31.
176. O. Holmes, *Common Law*, 305.
177. Langdell, *Summary of the Law of Contracts*, 21.
178. Langdell, *Summary of the Law of Contracts*, 21.
179. Pollock, *Principles of Contract*, 11–13. See p. 18.

ciling authority, principle, and acceptability. This contradiction and failure were apparent when Langdell addressed other topics, even as he repeatedly attended to acceptability.

———《》———

Apart from the discussion of the mailbox dilemma, Langdell's *Summary of Contracts* is studded with considerations of acceptability in regard to specific rules or individual decisions.[180] For example, Langdell stated that the law adopts fictions "to promote justice, i.e., in order to prevent some injustice or some inconvenience which would otherwise arise." Langdell here invoked acceptability specifically in regard to the "doctrine of relation," permitting the legal backdating of a transaction. Under this doctrine, Langdell specified bottom-level rules that are justified "to prevent some injustice or some inconvenience": "that every acceptance of an offer relates back to the time when the offer was first made," that "the ratification of a contract or conveyance made by an agent without sufficient authority" relates to the time of the making, that "the enrollment of a deed of bargain and sale" relates back to the time of the transaction, and that "a parol contract rendered invalid by the Statute of Frauds ... afterwards complied with by a memorandum in writing" relates back to the time of the original acceptance.[181] These are bottom-level rules, which Langdell justified by appeal to acceptability.

Another instance concerns the doctrine that "mental acts or acts of the will are not the materials out of which promises are made; a physical act on the part of the promisor is indispensable; and when the required physical act has been done, only a physical act can undo it." Exceptions are allowed, Langdell observed, "for purposes of justice and convenience," such as that promises signified by physical acts can be obviated when coerced, and that such promises can be terminated when actual consent would be impossible, as in the case of "the death or insanity of an offeror during the pendency of his offer." In addition to these bottom-level rules, Langdell cited examples from specific cases.[182]

Third, Langdell explained that where contractual covenants are to be performed on the same day, the law presumes that the promises "are to be performed at the same moment, and concurrently" as a way "of avoiding these opposing [practical] difficulties, of reconciling the just claims of both parties, and of doing

180. Quotation is from Grey, "Langdell's Orthodoxy," 15. Grey cites a number of the following instances of Langdell "appealing to considerations of justice or policy," but does not regard these as "justify[ing] a bottom-level rule or individual decision" (14, 13–14n50).

181. Quotations are from Langdell, *Summary of the Law of Contracts*, 8–9.

182. Quotations are from Langdell, *Summary of the Law of Contracts*, 244. Langdell references cases in *Cases on Contracts* (1879), 125, 129, 136, 156, 160–61.

perfect justice to each." This constructive dependency "is founded upon equality, which is justice" and so "is regarded by the law with favor." Here, again, Langdell proceeded in the next two pages to specify the application of this rule of constructive dependency by discussing five conditions and the related cases from his casebook.[183]

Fourth, regarding "mutual promises" serving as consideration for each other, Langdell held that an offer and acceptance will legally be considered simultaneous because this view is not only "rational" but "carries out the intentions of the parties." Langdell deemed such intentions irrelevant regarding the mailbox rule, but here he discussed how this rule of simultaneity applied to a series of cases.[184]

Another example is "whenever two mutual acts are incapable of being performed at the same moment, and yet no reason can be given for requiring one to be performed before the other." Langdell explained that the law treats the two acts as "mutually independent" and holds that "each must be performed at the proper time without regard to the performance of the other." Drawing on a specific decision in his casebook, Langdell justified this rule by invoking convenience. "It would be *absurd* to say that performance on either side was a condition precedent to performance on the other side," he wrote. "The performance of the plaintiff's covenant to raise the soldiers and bring them to the port, and of the defendant's covenant to find shipping and victuals for them, should be completed as nearly as possible at the same time. Each, therefore, was bound to proceed without waiting for the other."[185]

In another instance, Langdell noted practical constraints and set forth "one or two rules" appealing to fairness for both the offeree and the offeror in order to explain why the duration of an offer in a unilateral contract should be "less strictly limited by implication" than in a bilateral contract.[186] Appealing elsewhere to acceptability, Langdell observed that, if a conditional contract is made by a debtor to pay a debt, an action for debt will still lie "without regard to the condition."[187]

183. Quotations are from Langdell, *Summary of the Law of Contracts*, 169–70. Case references are made on 170–71.

184. Langdell, *Summary of the Law of Contracts*, 11.

185. Langdell, *Summary of the Law of Contracts*, 177. Emphasis added.

186. Langdell, *Summary of the Law of Contracts*, 201–2.

187. Otherwise, it would be "very harsh," or unfair, for the debtor to gain relief from the debt through an agreement intended to prevent payment of the debt. Applying the rule to a specific case "in building contracts," Langdell maintained that a condition, such as procuring "the architect's certificate," would be unfair if the architect is "employed...by the [owner] who makes the condition" and who seeks to avoid paying the builder by withholding the certificate. In this situation, "the court should not, therefore, give a condition such a construction, if it can fairly avoid doing so." Langdell, *Summary of the Law of Contracts*, 44–45.

Another instance is when courts read constructive conditions into a contract,[188] as well as when courts convert a condition precedent into a condition concurrent.[189] A further example is Langdell's treatment of privity and the rule that third-party beneficiaries could not maintain an action on a contract benefiting them.[190]

Not only did Langdell consider acceptability with respect to these bottom-level rules, but he also characteristically provided a more comprehensive analysis by examining the situation from the perspective of each party in the contract, as in the mailbox dilemma and in limiting the duration of offers in unilateral contracts. This attention to fairness from both parties' perspectives appears also in his discussion of when and why courts may impose implied conditions in a contract,[191] particularly in view of the prohibition that courts may not change express conditions.[192] Langdell similarly considered justice from both perspectives in explaining why an executor is liable "for a suit in equity to compel the application of the fund" to the legatee, but "there is no remedy at law to recover a fund, or any interest in it."[193]

In addition to such appeals to fairness, Langdell invoked other moral principles to justify bottom-level rules. "As the law will permit no man to take advantage of his own wrong . . ., it is always an excuse for not performing a condition of a covenant or promise that the covenantor or promisor prevented its performance."[194] Also, "the law . . . will compel no one to do vain and nugatory acts"; therefore, "if a covenantor or promisor, who is required to cooperate in the performance of a condition, has disabled himself from doing so, the covenantee or promisee need do nothing."[195] Furthermore, Langdell invoked "the maxim, 'an accuser ought not to be heard to the contrary,'" in order to explain why "a covenantor or promisor will

---

188. Langdell maintained that, in order to avoid "hardship," the court will read a condition subsequent into a contract when unforeseen dire events result in nonperformance. In circumstances such as the death of a covenanter or the destruction of the property to be conveyed, Langdell states, "the hardship of requiring a party to pay damages for nonperformance is so great as to raise a presumption that the event would have been made a condition subsequent if it had been foreseen." Langdell, *Summary of the Law of Contracts*, 54.

189. "The only security that one ever has, when he performs a condition precedent, that the covenant or promise will be performed, is an action for damages. . . . The only way in which the law can relieve a plaintiff [covenantor] from this hardship is by making the condition concurrent, and that the law does whenever it can." Langdell, *Summary of the Law of Contracts*, 228–29.

190. A sterile formalist would justify the rule by appeal to the logical principle that the third-party beneficiary was not a party to the mutual assent between offeror and offeree. But Langdell invoked fairness: a rule allowing third-party beneficiaries to sue exposes the promisor to extended liability, because "the promisor would be liable to two actions." Langdell, *Summary of the Law of Contracts*, 79.

191. Langdell, *Summary of the Law of Contracts*, 5–6, 135.

192. Langdell, *Summary of the Law of Contracts*, 209–10.

193. Langdell, *Summary of the Law of Contracts*, 95.

194. Langdell, *Summary of the Law of Contracts*, 225.

195. Langdell, *Summary of the Law of Contracts*, 226.

not be permitted to take two inconsistent positions in regard to the performance of a condition. If, therefore having a right to throw up the contract for a breach of condition, he elects to go on with it, he cannot afterwards set up the same breach in defense of an action on the contract."[196]

Throughout the *Summary of Contracts*, Langdell did, therefore, justify bottom-level rules and specific cases by appeal to acceptability, including justice and policy. This should not be surprising because Langdell devoted far less of his lawyering, teaching, and writing to contracts than to the fields of equity, procedure, and commercial law, which were suffused with appeals to fairness, convenience, and judicial discretion.[197] When teaching those fields, Langdell made such appeals even more emphatic.

For example, in Partnership and Negotiable Paper, the two courses that Langdell taught during spring 1870, he maintained that the legal doctrine of partnership, lying outside of common law, must be inferred from "careful observation" of extra-legal factors, including the practice of merchants. "Partnership is a thing created by the parties, and in that respect it differs from a corporation, which is created by the state.... Therefore, no court can take upon itself authoritatively to define a partnership, and then say that everything which comes within that definition is a partnership and nothing else is. The definition may either be erroneous or incomplete," Langdell continues, because "the mercantile community, their ideas and their practice, constitute the ultimate source of information on the subject. How could it be otherwise? Partnerships are created by them alone...and exist primarily for them alone; and the...object of the law is to deal with them as it finds them for the purpose of administering justice when called upon to do so."[198] Regarding negotiable paper, Langdell likewise observed that one must proceed both "theoretically and practically," inasmuch as "if you choose, in your declaration, to adopt the theory...perhaps you may do it...but this has never been the practice; nor would it generally be either convenient or advantageous."[199] This invocation of acceptability is unmistakable.

—◦◦◦—

196. Langdell, *Summary of the Law of Contracts*, 237. Langdell had invoked this principle in 1871–72 when he delivered a lecture at Columbia University law school. George A. Miller, "Summary by Professor C. C. Langdell, of Harvard Law School, of the law of dependent and independent covenants and promises," leaf 7, in Dwight, "Law Lectures 1871–2."

197. Grey, "Langdell's Orthodoxy," 13–14; Subrin, "David Dudley Field and the Field Code," 336–37. See Kimball, "Langdell Problem," table 1.

198. Langdell, Lectures on Partnership and Commercial Paper, vol. 1, leaves 9–11, 48–49.

199. Langdell, Lectures on Partnership and Commercial Paper, vol. 1, leaves 52v, 54v.

Given that the bulk of Langdell's lawyering, teaching, and writing was devoted to fields suffused with appeals to fairness and convenience, which he incorporated; given that Langdell's *Summary of Contracts*—conventionally considered his exemplary formalist work—is studded with appeals to acceptability; and given the absence of a Euclidean structure to his writings on contracts and sales, it is clear that Holmes's famous Procrustean interpretation in the 1880 review does not fit Langdell's mode of legal reasoning. Instead, a sound analysis must incorporate his inductive analysis of cases, his thorough discussion of principle, and his seeming contradictions about invoking acceptability. Indeed, these three elements constitute a telling pattern in Langdell's thinking. This is seen in his analysis of another contract problem that is often said to exemplify Langdell's lamentable formalism and neglect of acceptability.

The problem at issue is the revocation of unilateral contracts, which is significant not only because of the clarity of Langdell's supposed neglect of acceptability[200] but also because of the centrality of this issue in his doctrine. Just as Langdell's prominent and extensive attention to the mailbox dilemma stemmed from his emphasis on offer and acceptance as fundamental dimensions of contract law, so the revocation dilemma is magnified by Langdell's novel and sustained emphasis on the "many and important...consequences of a contract being unilateral or bilateral."[201]

A unilateral contract poses the problem of whether and when the offeror may revoke an offer if the offeree has begun to perform the act that, when completed, will constitute the consideration for the offer. In the early nineteenth century, this revocation dilemma most commonly arose over standing orders for goods, guarantees for products sold, or the hiring of a worker for a stipulated task.[202] By the middle of the nineteenth century, prevailing authority held that the offeror could legally revoke the offer before completion of the task, depriving the poor worker of any compensation for partially completed work. This rule prevailed in many cases in England and the United States even though "some of these cases are of great severity," wrote Parsons in 1853.[203]

200. Grey, "Langdell's Orthodoxy," 15.

201. Langdell, *Summary of the Law of Contracts*, 253. See Ames, "Christopher Columbus Langdell, 1826–1906," 479.

202. Th. Parsons, *Law of Contracts*, 1:516–17, 520–23. "Contracts arising from mutual promises are Bilateral. Contracts arising from shipment of goods by order, allotment of shares, guaranties, etc. are unilateral, binding offeror. . . . [In] ordinary unilateral contracts, e.g. those arising from shipment of goods according to order, the offeree is not required to give notice of the performance of the act requested...." *ACon71*, flyleaves; *KCon71*, marginal notes at 1, 3–6, 37.

203. Th. Parsons, *Law of Contracts*, 1:522–23. Langdell began his long accompanying note: "If this question is to be governed solely by the number of authorities, it would seem to be at rest" (522n1).

Having discussed over forty cases in more than two hundred lines in his foot-notes to Parsons's view in 1853, Langdell began his one-and-a-half-page discussion of the revocation dilemma in the *Summary of Contracts* by endorsing revocation in a two-sentence statement and citing the leading English case of *Offord v. Davies* (1862), included in his casebook. "As the performance of the consideration is what converts an offer into a binding promise, it follows that the promise is made . . . at the moment when the performance of the consideration is completed. It also follows that up to that moment the offer may . . . be revoked . . . , and the offeree thus be deprived of any compensation for what he has done."[204] In the next five lines, Langdell dismissed countervailing appeals to acceptability, just as he did regarding the mailbox dilemma: "As this [rule] may cause great hardship and prac-tical injustice, ingenious attempts have been made to show that the offer becomes irrevocable as soon as performance of the consideration begins; but such a view seems to have no principle to rest upon."[205]

The number of "ingenious attempts . . . to show that the offer becomes irre-vocable" amounted to only one: the losing counsel in *Offord v. Davies*. Even these lawyers invoked "hardship" only once in the course of quoting another case, and ar-gued against revocation fundamentally on the doctrinal grounds that the guarantee in question was actually a contract of suretyship. That Langdell could cite only one "ingenious attempt" is not surprising because other leading commentators gave no more attention, if any, to acceptability in examining the revocation dilemma. Parsons's *Law of Contracts* (1853) dismissed acceptability in a single phrase.[206] In 1867 Metcalf did not consider the problem of partial performance, and Leake did not address acceptability when invoking *Offord v. Davies* and the established rule. Nor did Bigelow deal with this issue in the 1874 edition of Story's *Treatise*. In 1876 Pollock invoked only authority when stating the rule that "conduct which is relied on as constituting the acceptance of an actual contract, must . . . be unambiguous and unconditional." In 1879 Anson did not consider the problem of partial perfor-mance or *Offord v. Davies*.[207]

Notwithstanding the neglect of acceptability by contemporary treatise writers, Langdell proceeded to consider acceptability even though he had dismissed it—just as he had regarding the mailbox dilemma. He began by declaring that appeals to

204. Langdell, *Summary of the Law of Contracts*, 3. See Langdell, *Cases on Contracts* (1879), 33–38; Th. Parsons, *Law of Contracts*, 1:517n, 522n–523n; *Offord v. Davies* (1862).

205. Langdell, *Summary of the Law of Contracts*, 4. As did Holmes, Grey treats Langdell's analysis as complete at this point. "Langdell's Orthodoxy," 15.

206. Th. Parsons, *Law of Contracts*, 2:33; 1:516–17.

207. Pollock, *Principles of Contract*, 29. Pollock did not cite *Offord v. Davies* (1862). See Metcalf, *Principles of the Law of Contracts*, 191–220; Leake, *Elements of the Law of Contracts*, 25; W. Story, *Treatise on the Law of Contracts*, 1:375; Anson, *Principles of the English Law of Contract* (1879), 23.

fairness were indeterminate, because "there may be hardship on the other side as well; for the offeree may at any stage refuse to proceed further in performing the consideration." Indeed, there are many circumstances in which the offeror would be worse off due to the partial performance of the offeree, such as when a construction crew leaves a job half finished. If the offeror could not revoke the offer after partial performance, then this irrevocability "would not...serve the purposes of substantial justice, as it would protect the offeree, while leaving the offeror wholly unprotected."[208]

Meanwhile, convenience should be considered, argued Langdell. The offeree "may die; and then the offeror will confessedly be without remedy." In addition, the parties have a practical option through which to avoid the revocation dilemma: "The true protection for both parties is to have a binding contract made before performance begins, by means of mutual promises; and if they neglect this precaution, any hardship that they may suffer should be laid at their own doors."[209] Langdell thus seems to conclude that the law must presume a certain amount of prudence on the part of every person; hence, fairness and convenience ultimately comport with authority and principle in supporting the view that performance constitutes the consideration, which converts the offer into a promise and seals the contract.

Notwithstanding this resolution, Langdell seems to reverse himself one more time and implicitly concede that the offeror more often receives a favorable outcome and, consequently, that the offeree deserves some protection. Thus, he argued subsequently that the continuance of an offer in a unilateral contract should be "less strictly limited by implication" than in a bilateral contract. In this regard, he set forth "one or two rules" appealing to fairness, as mentioned above.[210]

Overall, Langdell made the same contradictory moves on the revocation dilemma that he did on the mailbox dilemma. Beginning with his long footnotes in Parsons's treatise, he gave extensive attention to authority and to principle without indicating clearly which prevails. After denying the relevance of acceptability, he considered it anyway, and declared it indeterminate while also examining the perspectives of both parties. He then gave some attention to convenience, construing it to comport with his views on authority and principle. Finally, on balance, he eventually seemed to say that justice favors a particular side, and he interpreted doctrine to comport with that judgment.

A complete reading of Langdell's analyses of these key dilemmas not only be-

208. Quotations are from Langdell, *Summary of the Law of Contracts*, 4–5.
209. Langdell, *Summary of the Law of Contracts*, 4.
210. Langdell, *Summary of the Law of Contracts*, 202.

lies the caricature of him as a sterile legal formalist concerned with geometrical symmetry or logical consistency to the exclusion of acceptability, but reveals that Langdell gave *more* consideration to acceptability than did other leading commentators, such as Holmes, Anson, and Pollock. Contrary to the longstanding interpretation, Langdell exhibited a more comprehensive and thorough (and therefore inconsistent) discussion of authority, principle, and fairness and convenience.

Langdell's Paradox of Form and Substance

Far from conforming to a closed, formal system modeled on deductive logic or geometry, Langdell's mode of reasoning—even on the issues conventionally invoked to demonstrate his formalism—is three-dimensional, exhibiting a comprehensive yet contradictory integration of induction from authority, deduction from principle, and analysis of acceptability, which includes justice and policy. The contradiction lies in Langdell's combining all three while claiming to emphasize logical consistency and disregard justice and policy.

In one dimension, he extensively examined authority on the problem. This movement is shown by the fact that he always produced casebooks on a topic before writing his summary or survey, as seen in his work on contracts, equity pleading, and equity jurisdiction. In a second dimension, his inductions from authority led to reasoning about principle. This movement was certainly guided by deductive rigor, as shown by Langdell's arranging an argument "in the form of a syllogism" in order to demonstrate that "the fault of this syllogism is in the major premise, which is untrue."[211] The third dimension in Langdell's characteristic mode of reasoning was to consider justice and policy through a contradictory sequence of steps: denying the relevance of acceptability, considering fairness and convenience anyway, examining the interests of both parties, declaring acceptability indeterminate because those interests balance each other out, and finally indicating that acceptability preponderates in favor of one party. This third movement is usually "a model of brevity," reflecting his "pithy," "compact," "concise" style.[212]

Although the third movement is listed here last and is usually presented in the closing part of Langdell's discussion, its place in the temporal order of the three movements is not evident. The analysis of authority always seems to precede principle, following Langdell's inductive approach. Apart from that, it is not

---

211. Langdell, *Summary of the Law of Contracts*, 19.

212. The terms appear in [O. Holmes], Review (1877), 764; [O. Holmes], Review (Mar. 1880), 233; Ames, "Christopher Columbus Langdell, 1826–1906," 486; Kelley, "Critical Analysis of Holmes," 1708n106, 1710.

clear whether—as the textual order suggests—Langdell turned to acceptability at the end for confirmation or whether he moved back and forth among authority, principle, and acceptability in order to reach his conclusions.

This uncertainty about the order of Langdell's analysis indicates the ambivalence in his mind. Langdell evidently wanted to be, or felt he should be, a purely logical formalist. His "official" view was that acceptability did not matter. He not only disclaimed acceptability, but repeatedly tried to show that it was indeterminate and not worth considering, even if one wanted to. And his succeeding analyses of acceptability are highly compact and minimized, as though he were trying to hide or sublimate the discussion.

Nevertheless, Langdell attended to acceptability, and, ironically, his analyses were more comprehensive and thorough than those of contemporaries, such as Anson, who consulted fairness and convenience without reservation. When considering acceptability despite his unwillingness to do so, Langdell was more prepared to start afresh and consider all parties' interests and convenience, whereas other treatise writers tended to invoke the conventional acceptability concern that had predominated in prior discussion, such as the interest of the offeree in the mailbox dilemma or revocation dilemma. The irony is that Langdell generally presented a more comprehensive and thorough assessment of acceptability than other legal commentators on the same issue, who explicitly embraced acceptability concerns.

Furthermore, Langdell tried to harmonize authority, principle, and acceptability. He much preferred to say that all three domains concurred, rather than that one trumped the other, and this preference points to his desire for formal consistency. But the relative weight and order of consideration among the three domains appears indeterminate.

—◦◦◦—

In trying to understand Langdell's three-dimensional mode of reasoning within the context of the time, it is best to set aside Holmes's critique in his 1880 review of Langdell's *Summary of Contracts*, which has served as the premise for subsequent interpretations. Nevertheless, Holmes sheds light on Langdell in a more profound respect. Langdell's inconsistent three-dimensional mode of reasoning conforms to the "paradox of form and substance" that has been considered one of Holmes's greatest insights about judicial reasoning.[213]

Holmes proposed that, "while the logical symmetry of [legal] doctrines . . . was

213. O. Holmes, "Common Carriers," 630. See G. White, *Justice Oliver Wendell Holmes*, 139; S. Smith, "Believing Like a Lawyer," 1069–86.

retained on the surface over time to foster the impression of consistency and continuity, doctrines were under constant pressure to change...from contemporary notions of policy." The consistency in the logical "form" concealed the inevitable changes in the "substance" of law driven by emerging exigencies. In fact, "the form in which legal rules were articulated was designed to minimize or to conceal change, since the legal system had an investment in stability and continuity over time."[214] This "paradox of form and substance" was expressed in Holmes's 1880 review: "The form of continuity [in legal doctrine] has been kept up by reasonings purporting to reduce everything to a logical sequence; but that form is nothing but the evening dress which the newcomer puts on to make itself presentable according to conventional requirements. The important phenomenon is the man underneath it, not the coat; the justice and reasonableness of a decision, not its consistency with previously held views. No one will ever have a truly philosophic mastery over the law who does not habitually consider the forces outside it which have made it what it is."[215]

In fact, Langdell considered "forces outside" of logical consistency, as we have seen. Not only did he attend to fairness and convenience in specific cases, but he explicitly acknowledged this concern, as when he stated in regard to the doctrine of relation: "It is not, however, a conclusive objection to a relation that it is fictitious, for the law does sometimes create such relations; but it only does so in order to promote justice, i.e. in order to prevent some injustice or some inconvenience which would arise."[216] Langdell's inconsistent three-dimensional mode of reasoning thus exemplifies Holmes's paradox.

Indeed, Langdell virtually stated the "paradox of form and substance" in his lectures on Partnership and Negotiable Paper in spring 1870, when he made the most personal and explicit statement on jurisprudence in his extant writings.

> When one is considering what the law ought to be in respect to any feature of negotiable paper, the first thing to inquire into is the nature of the subject to which the law is to be applied; and until we understand that, rules of law will do us no good; for it has always been admitted that, upon the principles of the common law applicable to contracts and choses in action, bills of exchange could not exist at all;[217] and hence we have been obliged to import

214. Quotations are from G. White, *Justice Oliver Wendell Holmes*, 145, 150.

215. [O. Holmes], Review (Mar. 1880), 234.

216. Langdell, *Summary of the Law of Contracts*, 8.

217. A "chose in action" was a person's proprietary right to something not in the person's possession, "such as a debt owed by another person, a share in a joint-stock company, or a claim for damages in tort." Black, *Dictionary of Law* (7th ed., 1999). Langdell's point is that a bill of exchange, such as a personal check, would not have satisfied the prevailing common-law rules governing contract or choses in action.

the customs and usage of merchants in respect to [bills] and make that in fact the law, which merely means that we have studied the nature and functions of the instrument and the various uses to which it is put.

I have built up a system of [commercial] law upon that foundation, *using the well known principles of the common law when they served the purpose and establishing exceptions when they did not. This is what the courts have always professed to do and what they ought always to have done; but, for obvious reasons, they have often failed to do it, and have gone on applying the legal rules with which they were familiar without perceiving that they had no proper application to negotiable paper;* and I think the subject of consideration affords a striking instance of this.[218]

This pronouncement of Langdell in 1870 regarding commercial paper, virtually expresses the "paradox of form and substance" that Holmes stated several years later in regard to the common law.

Consequently, the difference between Langdell and Holmes lies in their normative conception of common-law jurisprudence. Langdell remained committed to the inductive and parsimonious abstraction that had been one of his scholarly contributions in the early 1870s. But he was too practical and prudent a person, a lawyer, and an administrator to neglect acceptability. Driven to attend to acceptability but unwilling to acknowledge it in common-law jurisprudence, Langdell adopted various contradictions, or legal fictions, in the third movement of his mode of reasoning. Meanwhile, "the Holmesian Revolution" was to identify the "fallacy and illusion" of reasoning from authority and principle and to declare that acceptability actually shaped legal doctrine.[219] Langdell had stated as much regarding commercial paper in 1870. Holmes's insight was to normalize this methodological fiction by declaring it integral and customary in the history of common law and, thereby, to legitimate the consideration of acceptability in common law.

Langdell exemplified the fiction that Holmes identified. But, mistaking form for substance, Holmes became the legal formalist in analyzing Langdell. Looking not to what Langdell was actually doing, but to the form of what Langdell said he was doing, Holmes focused on "the evening dress which [Langdell] put[] on to make [him]self presentable according to conventional requirements." Holmes thus violated his own admonition to Langdell: "the important phenomenon is the man underneath it, not the coat." Holmes's caricature of Langdell as the consum-

218. Langdell, Lectures on Partnership and Commercial Paper, vol. 1, leaves 56–60. Emphasis added.

219. S. Smith, "Believing Like a Lawyer," 1069n102.

mate legal formalist, ironically, reveals the formalism of Holmes, not of Langdell. Langdell wanted to become a formalist but could not. Holmes in trying to use Langdell to condemn formalism became one.

—⟶⟵—

Why did Langdell explicitly endorse formal consistency but paradoxically consider fairness and convenience as well? One reason is that this approach was "consistent with the way common-law judges, then and now, decide cases,"[220] inasmuch as fictions were notoriously employed throughout the law.[221] A second explanation may lie in Langdell's interest in highly technical legal questions, leading him to be "mainly a doctrinal writer rather than a philosopher."[222] This technical focus, combined with his frantic pace of work and heavy administrative responsibilities, may have prevented Langdell from addressing the latent paradox in his mode of reasoning.

Another explanation appears in his overall conception of dispute resolution. As a practicing lawyer, Langdell consistently maintained that parties to a dispute should employ common sense and resolve their disagreement outside of court. This informal process might require a lawyer's expertise in order to inform the parties about the risks and problems in submitting their dispute to law, but the process remains extralegal and aims to achieve substantive justice in the particular dispute. The alternative, in Langdell's view, was resort to the formal legal system which provides procedural consistency and evenhandedness, but does not aim at substantive justice in the particular dispute.[223]

Between the two alternatives stood semilegal process, such as appeal to referees, which Langdell and other lawyers abhorred. He maintained that, since referees are not bound by legal rules, the parties are merely subjecting themselves to the personal discretion of a third party, whom they could have consulted anyway without the expense. And, if the semilegal process follows legal rules, the referee has neither the professional accountability to apply the rules correctly nor the authority to enforce the resolution. Hence, the disputants are back to where they began. Consequently, Langdell's jurisprudential "paradox of form and substance" may reflect his desire to maintain a clear distinction between extralegal and legal

220. P. Kelley, "Critical Analysis of Holmes," 1755.

221. S. Smith, "Believing Like a Lawyer," 1069n102.

222. Grey, "Langdell's Orthodoxy," 3. See Teeven, *History of the Anglo-American Common Law of Contract*, 218; P. Kelley, "Critical Analysis of Holmes," 1709–10.

223. Langdell's view of this alternative resembles the view presented in Fried, "Lawyer as Friend."

process, stemming from his dismaying experience with semilegal process as a practicing attorney in New York City.

Finally, the most compelling explanation may lie in his concern about elevating and legitimating legal practice and the legal profession through strong legal science and legal education. In 1855 when Langdell left Harvard Law School and went to New York City, he carried with him a deep commitment to two related principles that had been forged during the arduous path of his youth: democratic advancement by merit and the value of legal study. In 1870, upon leaving New York to return to HLS as a professor, Langdell understood that success in legal practice, even among elite lawyers, did not necessarily depend on legal expertise and that, absent such dependence, the legal system and the entire polity were at risk. He therefore adopted the view that the justice and legitimacy of the legal system depend on the quality and legitimacy of the legal profession, which require, in turn, that lawyers acquire strong legal knowledge through a demanding legal education. This novel view spurred Langdell's educational reforms and, likely, his commitment to legal science, which he associated with formal consistency, leading to his paradoxical mode of legal reasoning.

CHAPTER 4

Teacher, 1870–1881

In addition to pursuing scholarship in the original sources, Langdell provided the faculty with new models of pedagogy while responding to several problems at HLS during the 1870s. As at other law schools and at medical schools, the Harvard curriculum consisted of a cycle of elementary courses and "worked like a merry-go-round.... When a student enrolled he got aboard at whatever point was passing at the moment, and sat down between men who had perhaps been reading and attending lectures for a whole year."[1] With students stepping on and off the merry-go-round, no advanced instruction was possible.

Another problem was that classroom teaching remained stultifying, even though the mind-numbing recitation had virtually disappeared by 1868 when Nathaniel Holmes replaced Joel Parker on the faculty.[2] During the 1860s the lecture had become "the principal means of instruction as the recitation was abandoned; but it was the unaided lecture in the least commendable forms," observed President Eliot, "the professors gave series of lectures which constituted treatises on the several branches of the law, and gave the same lectures year after year. They referred students to cases, but the attitude of the student was purely receptive; the student took no part in the exercise, he was merely listening and taking notes; and no pains were taken to make sure that he mastered, or even looked at, the cases referred to. When the law professor had published a series of treatises, his lectures often degenerated into running commentary on his printed books."[3]

In teaching his own courses, Langdell responded to these problems by making three fundamental innovations implied by his vision of the law professor who cultivates academic achievement in students. First, he began sequencing course-

---

1. James, *Charles W. Eliot*, 1:268. Among medical schools, only Lind University in Chicago had sequenced its curriculum, comprising two five-month terms. Ludmerer, *Learning to Heal*, 20–21.

2. N. Holmes, *Journal*, 273. See C. Warren, *History of the Harvard Law School*, 2:317.

3. C. Eliot, "Methods of Instruction," 178–79. See the corroborating account by students: Fessenden, "Rebirth of the Harvard Law School," 500; Sprague to Warren (20 Feb. 1908). See Carmalt to Warren (10 Oct. 1907); Crocker to Warren (30 Jan. 1908).

work by developing a required foundational course and advanced electives in his teaching of civil procedure and other subjects. Second, he invented case method teaching and the genre of casebook. By this "inductive method,"[4] Langdell required students to read original sources rather than textbooks, to analyze particular controversies rather than general propositions, to formulate their own interpretations in response to questions, and to respond to hypotheticals and opposing views. He also exposed himself to questions and challenges from students, and revised and corrected his own judgments in class. In this unprecedented fashion, Langdell sought to develop in students the independent, critical intellect that he himself modeled. Finally, consistent with the purposes of that new method of teaching, Langdell invented the form of examination that required students to respond in writing to complex hypothetical problems concerning specific situations.

Sequencing Coursework on Civil Procedure

Between 1870 and 1876 Langdell introduced a foundational course and advanced electives in civil procedure, thereby sequencing the coursework. This innovation, reflecting his higher academic expectations for law students, constituted a major reform in professional curricula generally, as well as a central feature of "the modern course in civil procedure" in particular. In addition, Langdell's courses in civil procedure display other "modern" features, such as focusing on procedure rather than merits of cases, conceiving procedure broadly, presenting a unitary system of procedure rather than hybrid variations, and incorporating practical issues and empirical materials.[5] In his lectures on civil procedure, Langdell explicitly advised students on "the *mode* of doing it . . . in modern times."[6]

Prior to 1870 the teaching of civil procedure in American law schools was confined almost entirely to pleading, as outlined in Blackstone's *Commentaries* and elaborated in Chitty's *Pleading* and Stephen's *Pleading*. Pleading was the process of presenting a client's complaint in the proper legal form in order to gain access to the common-law courts, which adjudicated civil cases. Pleading required the highly technical expertise of choosing the correct "writ" or "form of action" that fit the facts of the complaint. As the most arcane and marketable expertise of lawyers in the mid-nineteenth century, pleading demanded its own course and directed

---

4. [J. Myers], "Harvard Law School" (5, 19 Feb. 1875), 146–47; Ames, "Vocation of the Law Professor," 362.

5. Quotations are from McManamon, "History of the Civil Procedure Course," 27–29, which identifies these features but contrasts Langdell's teaching with "the modern civil procedure course." See also Carrington, "Teaching Civil Procedure." Further discussion and documentation on various points is presented in Kimball and Reyes, "First Modern Civil Procedure Course."

6. Langdell, "Civil Procedure," notebook 2, leaf 4r.

attention to the facts and merits of the dispute rather than other significant steps of procedure in a litigation—jurisdiction, trial, judgment, and execution of the decision—which were routinely neglected in law school.[7] In identical language throughout the 1850s and 1860s, HLS catalogs therefore prescribed "pleading" in their list of courses and the standard treatises of Joseph Chitty and Henry Stephen as textbooks.[8]

Though still conventional, this pleading course was becoming outdated by February 1870 when Langdell joined the HLS faculty, because the rules of pleading in civil cases were changing. Long attacked as artificial, inflexible, and arcane, common-law pleading in the United States began to be displaced in 1848 when New York State adopted the simplified "Field Code" of procedure, which consolidated the myriad common-law "forms of action" into one "cause of action." No longer was it necessary for a lawyer to choose the proper form that matched the facts of the complaint in order to gain access to the courts. Between 1848 and 1870 twenty-four other states and territories followed suit, often emulating the New York Code.[9] Nevertheless, code procedure was not taught at HLS or any other degree-granting law school in the United States in 1870.[10]

Langdell began to reform the teaching of civil procedure partly because his experience under the New York Code for the previous fifteen years contributed to his understanding of these new developments. In addition, he maintained a special interest in procedure, for he taught and wrote extensively about equity procedure and, more generally, his "explanations of the workings of the law are intimately tied to the peculiarities and technicalities of procedure."[11] Moreover, his introduction of case method when teaching Contracts and Sales in the early 1870s reinforced the need to teach procedure, he said, apparently because analyzing and discussing cases in class with students raised procedural questions.[12]

In 1870–71 Langdell began sequencing his courses by substituting an expanded foundational course—Civil Procedure at Common Law—for the traditional, narrow course on pleading.[13] In 1873–74 he cotaught Civil Procedure at Common

7. McManamon, "History of the Civil Procedure Course," 407, 407n35; Carrington, "Teaching Civil Procedure," 317. See Blackstone, *Commentaries on the Laws of England*, vol. 3 (1868); Chitty, *Treatise on Pleading* (1847); H. Stephen, *Treatise on the Principles of Pleading* (1859).

8. See Harvard University, *Catalog 1852–53*, 58, 60; Harvard University, *Catalog 1866–67*, 17–18, 22.

9. Clark, *Handbook of the Law of Code Pleading*, 24; T. White, Review (1901), 324; Subrin, "David Dudley Field and the Field Code," 312–22, 336–37. See C. M. Cook, *American Codification Movement*.

10. McManamon, "History of the Civil Procedure Course," 407, 413. During the 1860s New York Code procedure was apparently not taught even at Columbia University Law School. For reviewing its catalogs, I am grateful to Whitney Bagnall, Special Collections Librarian of Columbia University Law School.

11. LaPiana, *Logic and Experience*, 69. In 1873–74 Langdell began teaching procedure in equity, the legal domain complementary to common law.

12. Langdell, Annual Report 1870–71, 60.

13. Langdell, Annual Report 1870–71, 60.

Law with newly appointed Assistant Professor Ames. In 1874–75 Langdell introduced the first advanced elective—Process, Arrest, and Bail—in which he assigned cases and "no textbook." Ames alone taught the required first-year course, but reverted to the pre-1870 practice of assigning Stephen's *Pleading* while preparing his own first casebook, *Cases on Pleading*.

In the watershed year of 1875–76 Langdell resumed teaching Civil Procedure at Common Law, employing Ames's new casebook. He also taught the advanced elective, Process, Arrest, and Bail, while assigning *Forms of Procedure in the Court of King's Bench*, a collection of legal forms that he had compiled and published. Finally, he introduced a second, advanced elective: Procedure under the New York Code, assigning the Code of Procedure as textbook. This is one of the first instances of teaching code procedure at a degree-granting law school in the United States.[14] In 1876–77 Langdell again taught the entire sequence of the foundational course and two electives and assigned the same materials.[15] In 1877–78 Ames resumed teaching the first-year course, and Langdell taught the two advanced electives.

Beyond sequencing coursework in civil procedure, as well as other subjects mentioned below, Langdell introduced additional features that would come to characterize "the modern course" in civil procedure over the next century. In the opening lecture of Civil Procedure at Common Law, he broadened the subject matter by describing five stages of procedure: getting the defendant into court, pleading, trial, judgment, and execution of the court's decision.[16] Both the expanded scope and expansive title of this foundational course had no precedent in American legal education.[17] Conceiving civil procedure broadly entailed a second "modern" feature: emphasizing the purely procedural aspects of cases, rather than

14. In 1871–72 Theodore W. Dwight delivered "Lectures on the Code of New York." See Dwight, "Law Lectures 1871–72."

15. Langdell's teaching of the first course was recorded in Wigglesworth, Civil Procedure 1876–77. Langdell's own class notes from the elective on Process, Arrest, and Bail are recorded in Langdell, "Civil Procedure," notebooks 1, 2, 3. Handwritten and printed syllabi of the cases assigned in that course and in the second elective, Procedure under the New York Code, remain in Langdell, Papers. Only a few copies of *Forms of Procedure* are extant.

16. Wigglesworth, Civil Procedure 1876–77, leaves 1r–1v. Of these five stages, H. Stephen, *A Treatise on the Principles of Pleading* (1859) addressed only pleading in detail and gave cursory treatment to the remaining stages in one chapter. He ignored, for example, necessary procedural steps such as arrest and bail (5–26). Similarly neglecting the other stages, Chitty's *A Treatise on Pleading* (1847) focuses on the forms of action (94–212) after expounding the potential liability of various defendants—infants, lunatics, animal owners, married women, corporations, public officers, and others—in tort actions (76–85).

17. See McManamon, "History of the Civil Procedure Course," 407. Bibliographical searches have identified only a few treatises—apart from the codes themselves—that employed the term "civil procedure" in their title before or contemporaneous with Langdell's course. The only treatise that appears to be a possible textbook or a manual was published after the English Judicature Acts of 1873 and 1875: Roscoe, *Outlines of Civil Procedure* (1876). The first treatise with the term "civil procedure at common law" in the title appears to be A. Martin, *Civil Procedure at Common Law* (1899).

their merits, as did the traditional pleading course.[18] In this fashion, Langdell anticipated the "modern . . . vision of procedure as instrumental to a distinct body of substantive law," which gradually emerged over the next half-century.[19]

Langdell's more comprehensive conception of civil procedure—as well as another "modern" feature of incorporating practical issues and empirical materials—also informs his textbook *Forms of Procedure in the Court of King's Bench*. This work comprises 128 forms and their variants, covering the entire procedure of a hypothetical civil suit from the plaintiff's initiation through the execution of the court's judgment. In a chronological and systematic fashion, the enumerated forms mark the permutations of procedure that might occur depending on the circumstances and the strategies of the attorneys involved. Overall, the 128 forms and variant wordings mirror the broad conception of civil procedure that Langdell laid out in five stages in his opening lecture of "Civil Procedure at Common Law": getting the defendant into court (arrest and bail) is addressed in items numbered 1–43, which culminate in "putting in bail"; pleading in items 44–68, leading to the "issue joined"; trial in items 69–109, addressing juries, costs, evidence, and requests for judgment; judgment in items 110–15; execution of the court's decision in items 116–28, largely concerning the sheriff.

Langdell's practical and inductive approach is also shown by his turn to discussing cases after a few opening lectures. Most of these cases appear not in the assigned casebook, Ames's *Cases on Pleading*, but on a syllabus of supplementary cases that Langdell expected students to find themselves.[20] This supplementary syllabus further demonstrates Langdell's intent to broaden the foundational course beyond pleading, to which Ames confined his casebook. The attention to practical issues and inductive materials also appears in the advanced elective, Procedure under the New York Code. For a text, Langdell assigned the Code itself and sixty-two cases, whose distribution demonstrates the timeliness and relevance of his instruction: sixty were from New York, forty-two from the period 1848–60, and fifteen from 1860–75.[21]

18. McManamon, "History of the Civil Procedure Course," 427–29. Thus, a modern casebook focuses on procedure while treating civil procedure broadly, dividing it into at least three general sections: 1) jurisdictional issues (including personal jurisdiction); 2) the litigation process (including pleading, discovery, trial, appeal, and respect for judgments); and 3) joinder. See Yeazell, *Civil Procedure*.

19. Bone, "Mapping the Boundaries of a Dispute: Conceptions of Ideal Lawsuit Structure," 17.

20. At points, Wigglesworth noted "Can't find anything" or "No good" after a given case citation. Wigglesworth, Civil Procedure 1876–77. Moreover, one such handwritten syllabus, entitled "Class in Equity," announces, "The cases will be taken up in the following order," and lists forty-nine cases with page numbers in *Cases in Equity Pleading* (1878), indicating that Langdell jumped around Ames's casebook in a much different order than the published text.

21. A table of citations to the cases appears in Kimball and Reyes, "First Modern Civil Procedure Course."

The other advanced elective—Process, Arrest and Bail—also demonstrates the timeliness and practicality of Langdell's instruction, as well as the "modern" feature of presenting a single unitary system, rather than hybrid variations, of civil procedure. These points require some explanation because Langdell presented the steps and permutations of process in arrest and bail from the period between 1726 and 1832 in the court of the King's Bench in England.[22] At first glance, his course thus seems outdated and irrelevant to American students in the 1870s.

Arrest and bail had two cardinal purposes that Langdell identified: first, "to get the defendant into court so that the plaintiff could declare against him," thereby initiating the suit; second, "to get the security of the defendant's body for the satisfaction of the judgment which he expected to recover."[23] In the common-law system, arrest and bail thus constituted both the first stage in civil procedure[24] and the security for judgment.

That first stage began with the plaintiff filing an affidavit with the court, asserting facts as the basis of the arrest. The court officer then issued a written order authorizing arrest, which the plaintiff presented to the sheriff who issued a warrant to the bailiff who then arrested the defendant. The defendant either went to jail or filed bail bond to remain out of jail until the day when the sheriff officially returned the writ to the court and reported the defendant's status. The defendant then satisfied the bail-bond and, in order to remain out of jail until the judgment, put in bail by providing sureties who would satisfy any judgments that went against the defendant. At the same time, the plaintiff presented the complaint, and pleading began, which Langdell addressed in the foundational first-year course. This generic process of arrest and bail was subject to special conditions and arrangements in the King's Bench, to which Langdell gave detailed attention because plaintiffs generally preferred to bring defendants there.[25]

But why was Langdell teaching pre-1832 procedure in the King's Bench to students in the United States in the 1870s? This approach seems wholly impractical at a time when, for example, the University of Virginia law school was teaching "Virginia Pleading and Practice," and Columbia University law school

---

22. Langdell, "Civil Procedure," notebook 1, leaf 3r. A significant reform in English common-law process occurred in 1726 and obtained until the English Uniformity of Process Act in 1832. See 12 George 1, ch. 29 (1726); J. Baker, *Introduction to English Legal History* (1990), 80–81.

23. Langdell, "Civil Procedure," notebook 3, leaf 5v. See also notebook 1, leaf 29r; notebook 2, leaf 2r.

24. Gould, *Treatise on the Principles of Pleading*, 14.

25. Langdell, "Civil Procedure," notebook 1, leaves 3r–19r. The King's Bench offered trial by jury and had record-keeping provisions, and was therefore more popular than the other two superior English courts, the Court of Common Pleas and the Exchequer. See J. Baker, *Introduction to English Legal History* (1990), 44–62.

was teaching Pleading and Practice" in New York.[26] In his opening lecture in Civil Procedure at Common Law, Langdell stated "reasons why I should select some one system and adhere to it rigidly; reasons why I should resort to England for that system; why, in point of time, I should fix upon 1830 as the standard."[27]

The central problem faced by Langdell in planning his new approach to teaching civil procedure was the great variety in procedural systems in the United States. American jurisdictions had adopted English common-law procedure to different degrees and in different ways; consequently, common-law procedure in the United States had many variants.[28] The introduction of code procedure exacerbated the variety. Between 1848 and 1870 twenty-five states and territories enacted codes of procedure, which were nevertheless under incessant attack. A half-century later, the procedural systems among the states remained variegated and divided among code states, common-law states (numbering at least eleven), and quasi-code or quasi-common-law states (including at least eight). Even these categories were not discrete because, for example, some states that still distinguished between law and equity nevertheless allowed "equitable defenses" in actions at common law.[29]

Not only did the rate and extent of adopting codes vary, but, when adopted, their implementation was inconsistent, as in regard to the treatment of "special pleading."[30] Even within a single jurisdiction where uniformity might be expected, such as New York, the lack of experience with and resistance to the Code led nineteenth-century lawyers and judges to rely on the logic of the abolished forms of common-law procedure in order to achieve understanding and agreement about process. Therefore, the common-law forms of action, though officially abolished, continued to thrive inconsistently as legal concepts in the courts of New York and elsewhere.[31] As a result, the codes were blamed for increasing the variety and confusion in civil procedure that they had been intended to alleviate.[32]

Faced with this variation, Langdell said that he decided to "select some one system and adhere to it rigidly," rather than surveying systems in different juris-

---

26. Ritchie, First Hundred Years, 79–80. I am grateful to Whitney Bagnall, Special Collections Librarian of Columbia University Law School, for reviewing its catalogs.

27. Langdell, "Civil Procedure," notebook 1, leaf 3r.

28. Millar, Civil Procedure of the Trial Court, 79.

29. Clark, Handbook of the Law of Code Pleading, 24, 28–29. See Oakley and Coon, "Federal Rules in State Courts."

30. McManamon, "History of the Civil Procedure Course," 413n71. "Special pleading" refers here to a response to an allegation that does more than merely deny the allegation, "as by introducing new matter to justify an otherwise blameworthy act." Black, Dictionary of Law (7th ed., 1999).

31. LaPiana, "Just the Facts: The Field Code and the Case Method," 309. Cf. Subrin, "David Dudley Field and the Field Code," 312.

32. Thurston, Review (1901), 554; McManamon, "History of the Civil Procedure Course," 413n71.

dictions. In addition to this singular focus, he looked for a unitary system rather than a hybrid that had been melded from competing systems. "In order to teach or study practice to any purpose, it is necessary to have a fixed and definite system. In studying for practice, one's great object should be to acquire a knowledge of a system as such; every separate question should be considered with reference [to that]."[33] These two criteria would have been satisfied by teaching the procedural system of ancient Rome or Napoleonic France. But Langdell had a third factor in mind: he looked for a system that had influenced all the different hybrid systems in the United States. His choice was as obvious as it was sensible: the pre-1832 English procedure in common law, with its apex in the King's Bench. In fact, that system still provided the foundation for civil procedure in most jurisdictions of the United States in the 1870s. To see this point, it is necessary to understand the delays involved in effecting the reforms in civil procedure.[34]

First was the delay of formal adoption. The traditional legal forms officially persisted in the American colonies and the United States long after they had been formally superseded in the mother country. Langdell himself noted this lag in observing that, although the English process of arrest and bail had been changed in 1726, New York long resisted the innovation and persisted in the pre-1726 process.[35] By the same token, New York, the most progressive of the states in adopting a Code of Civil Procedure in 1848, had waited to do so until sixteen years after the 1832 enactment of the Uniformity of Procedure Act in England. Another telling example of the delay in formal adoption of changes in civil procedure is shown by pleading in the alternative, which was adopted in England in 1873, Rhode Island in 1876, Connecticut in 1879, New Jersey in 1912, New York in 1920, and most American jurisdictions thereafter.[36]

A second delay occurred between the formal adoption of a procedural reform and its effect in practice, two steps that must be carefully distinguished.[37] In the

33. Langdell, "Civil Procedure," notebook 1, leaf 2r. These sentences were subsequently overwritten.

34. Historical interpretations of procedure have often focused on reformers' theories or the officially adopted reforms without considering the delays or gaps in local practice. Cf. Subrin, "How Equity Conquered Common Law," 909–1002; Subrin, "David Dudley Field and the Field Code," 311–27; Bone, "Mapping the Boundaries of a Dispute: Conceptions of Ideal Lawsuit Structure," 1–118.

35. Langdell, "Civil Procedure," notebook 3, leaves 11v, 5v.

36. McManamon, "History of the Civil Procedure Course," 426. "Alternative pleading" means that "the pleader alleges two or more independent claims or defenses that are not necessarily consistent with each other, such as alleging both intentional infliction of emotional distress and negligent infliction of emotional distress based on the same conduct." Black, *Dictionary of Law* (7th ed., 1999). The term does not appear in the first edition, published in 1891.

37. On this general point, see J. Baker, *Law's Two Bodies*. Scholars have sometimes presumed that a state's adoption of a code of procedure immediately outmoded common-law procedure and that continuing to teach the latter implies that a law faculty was ignorant or neglectful. See McManamon, "History of the Civil Procedure Course," 421, 429; Yeazell, "Teaching Supplemental Jurisdiction," 242n4.

1870s New York lawyers still employed the logic of the common-law forms of procedure that had been superseded by the New York Code. In addition, certain common-law processes, such as commencing a civil action by arrest pursuant to a warrant, were still practiced in New York during the 1870s.[38] Virginia and Massachusetts also long preserved English procedural forms.[39] Through the 1920s, most Southern states—including Alabama, Georgia, Mississippi, Tennessee, Texas, Florida, Virginia, West Virginia, and Maryland—were regarded as quasi-code or common-law states. Law schools in such jurisdictions thus tended to require the study of both common-law and code procedure. Midwestern states often employed a revised and simplified procedure—such as substituting a writ of summons for a writ of arrest as the first step in a suit—but common-law procedure still endured in some jurisdictions.[40]

The practice of civil procedure thus lagged well behind procedural reform even after 1900, when but half of the states had adopted some form of code pleading.[41] In the 1870s English common-law procedure, as it stood prior to 1832, operated subliminally in the United States, particularly in leading legal jurisdictions, such as Massachusetts, New York, and Virginia. Langdell's experience at the bar in New York City prompted him to look beneath the formal changes and teach the single unitary system underlying operant procedure.

A third delay in the effect of changes made to civil procedure doctrine relates particularly to arrest and bail, the subject of Langdell's advanced elective. Given that the common-law forms guided procedure for lawyers and judges long after the enactment of the New York Code in 1848, arrest and bail persisted even longer in the traditional mode, because these two steps lay in the province of sheriffs and bailiffs, who tended to adhere to habit in conducting their business. Langdell knew well the customs of sheriffs and bailiffs from his experience in debt collection, the staple of legal practice for young lawyers in New York. For example, when he asked a Boston lawyer for help in arresting a delinquent New York debtor who was traveling through Massachusetts, Langdell followed the requirements later set forth in his lectures at HLS: supplying evidence that supported the plaintiff's

---

38. Wait, *Law and Practice in Courts of New York* (1874), 2:111. See also Gould, *Treatise on the Principles of Pleading*, 14–15, which describes the original writ as commencing all civil suits and as being directed to the sheriff of the county.

39. Millar, *Civil Procedure of the Trial Court*, 79.

40. Millar, *Civil Procedure of the Trial Court*, 79–82; Buswell and Walcott, *Practice and Pleading in Personal Actions*, 20; Clark, *Handbook of the Law of Code Pleading*, 28. See Ritchie, *First Hundred Years*, 79–80; Vanderbilt University Law Department, *Register 1904–1905*, 17–18; Lafferty, "Founding of the College of Law of the University of Kentucky," 58.

41. McManamon, "History of the Civil Procedure Course," 423.

claim for damages; satisfying the criteria that warranted arrest on the claim, such as the amount of damages; and establishing the legal standing of the plaintiff in the jurisdiction that provided the writ of arrest. These English principles regarding arrest and bail still obtained in Massachusetts in the 1870s.[42]

Consequently, Langdell taught pre-1832, English common-law process to students at HLS in the 1870s for a number of compelling reasons. Faced with a variety of hybrid systems of procedure, he decided to teach a single unitary system that influenced all the others. Despite the procedural variety resulting from delays of formal adoption, delays between formal adoption and practical effect, and delays of practical effect on the habits of sheriffs and bailiffs, Langdell identified a system that underlay most of the others. This system was the procedure of the English common law in the King's Bench prior to 1832. Furthermore, Langdell made this material relevant to American students in the 1870s by leading them through the numbered writs in his *Forms of Procedure* in highly specific and orderly steps in order to demonstrate exactly how the process worked.[43] He frequently indicated how English process deviates from process "here," and how pre-1832 practice departs from "the *mode* of doing it ... in modern times."[44] These clarifications explain why Langdell, though intending Process, Arrest and Bail to be relevant to practice, made the course elective. Arrest and bail were "less important now," he explained, because by the 1870s the writ of summons was beginning to replace the writ of arrest as the method of commencing a suit in the English and American legal systems.[45]

In this fashion, Langdell offered practical teaching informed by historical scholarship, believing that scholarly professors and courses could provide useful

42. Langdell to Shattuck (23 Apr. 1860); Buswell and Walcott, *Practice and Pleading in Personal Actions*, 20.

43. For example: "When you proceed by bill ... make out ... a bail price, No. 17, and take it with the intended bail to a judge's chambers, and deliver it to his clerk, who will administer to the bail the acknowledgment, No. 18, and procure the judge's signature to the caption of the bail price, No. 17, retaining it for that purpose. This constitutes putting in bail by bill. Having put in bail, you notify plaintiff's attorney in writing that you have done so. No. 23. If the latter is not satisfied with the bail, he may except to them any time within twenty days (No. 26), and give notice thereof to defendant's attorney. No. 27. If the bail are excepted to, but not otherwise, they must justify in open court within four days; and you must give plaintiff's attorney one day's notice of the time when they will justify. No. 28." Langdell, "Civil Procedure," notebook 1, leaves 9v, 32r; notebook 2, leaves 5r–6r. Langdell also stipulates the necessary form and location of certain phrases (notebook 1, leaves 15r–16r).

44. Langdell, "Civil Procedure," notebook 1, leaves 1v, 4r, 20r, 24r–25r, 28r–29r; notebook 2, leaves 4r, 15r; notebook 3, leaves 24r, 11v, 47r.

45. Quotation is from Wigglesworth, Civil Procedure 1876–77, leaf 2r. See Millar, *Civil Procedure of the Trial Court*, 78–80.

education for law students. Reflecting his higher academic expectations for legal education, he introduced the sequencing of coursework in civil procedure and in professional curricula generally between 1870 and 1876, by offering a foundational course and two advanced electives in civil procedure. In addition, Langdell's courses on civil procedure display other "modern" features, such as focusing on procedure rather than merits of cases, conceiving procedure broadly, presenting a unitary system of procedure rather than hybrid variations, and incorporating practical issues and empirical materials.

These innovations evidently discomfited many students because few enrolled in Langdell's upper-level courses,[46] which he ceased teaching after 1877–78.[47] One reason for these low enrollments was that case method rendered the courses notoriously difficult for the students, and Langdell was least compromising in the inductive approach. Another reason was that Langdell graded harder than the other professors.[48] In addition, given that Langdell's prescient distinction between procedure and substantive issues was only beginning to emerge, the underlying rationale for the sequence of courses may have seemed suspect to students who often heard criticism of Langdell for his unusual educational ideas. Finally, Langdell was engaged in heated disputes about faculty hiring and institutional reforms, so he may have decided to cut his losses here in order to develop and defend his other innovations. Nevertheless, he did not abandon the idea of sequencing coursework, for he introduced and maintained it in teaching contracts and equity.

The Langdellian Method of Teaching Law

Langdell's interest in inductive teaching reflected several factors in his educational and professional background, as discussed in previous chapters. At Exeter, he had read Locke's recommendations that teachers should present students with original sources rather than textbooks, work from the particular to the general, challenge students with the competence of those more advanced, encourage students' autonomy, and impart not content but a method of learning. Those points, obviating

46. In 1876–77, eighty-four students completed the required "Civil Procedure at Common Law"; four students, the advanced elective in "Civil Procedure at Common Law"; and six students, "Civil Procedure under the New York Code." Langdell, Annual Report 1876–77, 83.

47. Langdell, Annual Report 1877–78, 88. Beginning in 1878–79 Ames annually taught the first-year course. In 1892 Langdell arranged to hire a lecturer to resume teaching the New York Code at HLS, after students petitioned for the course and the faculty agreed to offer it. Langdell to Eliot (22 Aug. 1892); "Law School" (1892).

48. See Harvard Law School, Grade Records, vol. 0, 1869–76.

Classroom in Dane Hall, Harvard Law School, 1870s. This photograph
was taken later, after gas lighting was installed, but the furniture and
arrangement of the classrooms in Dane Hall changed little. Courtesy of
Special Collections Department, Harvard Law School Library.

the use of textbooks, were supported by Langdell's experience with demonstrations
in natural history class at Harvard College, his study and discussion of cases with
other students at HLS in the early 1850s, his research and writing of the notes for
Parsons's treatises, his practice under the Field Code, and his litigation in equity
and other extra common-law domains, which entailed the scrutiny of cases.

Upon joining the HLS faculty in February 1870, Langdell therefore intended
to teach inductively, and he proposed at a faculty meeting soon after his arrival
that all professors should assign cases, rather than textbooks, for students to study
and discuss in class. Although nearly everyone acquainted with Langdell admired
his energetic research and intimidating knowledge of cases, this proposal seemed
impractical and somewhat arrogant. Professors Washburn, Nathaniel Holmes, and
Parsons (who attended the meeting despite having retired) objected that teaching
entirely out of cases would be too slow to cover all the material. President Eliot,
also in attendance, endorsed Langdell's proposal, to which Parsons replied, "You
would not [agree]..., Mr. President, if you knew more of the subject." After some
discussion, "it was finally arranged that Prof. Langdell would pursue his own

method with his subjects, and that Prof. Washburn and [Holmes] should continue ... in the main as before."[49]

Langdell immediately began experimenting with inductive pedagogy in both courses that he taught during spring 1870. In Negotiable Paper, for example, he supplemented the lectures by posing hypothetical cases to the class:

> Put a case founded on *Munroe v. Bordies*, 1 Parsons 181, to wit: I am an importer of dry goods in New York, being indebted to Mr. John Bright, a manufacturer in Manchester, to the amount of ten thousand pounds. I purchase a bill for that amount of Brown Bros & Co., payable to the order of John Bright at 60 days sight, and immediately send it by mail to Mr. Bright in payment of my debt.... Being in good credit with Brown Bros. & Co., I pay them for the bills that I purchased of them on the next foreign postday after they are delivered. On the day after I purchase the bill in question, I suspend payment, not having paid for the bill; whereupon the drawers write to the drawees not to accept the bill or pay for it. In consequence of this advice, the drawees refuse acceptance, and Mr. Bright sues the drawer. Have they any defense? Refer to the opinion. Again, suppose Mr. Bright, being the holder of a large amount of 5/20 N.Y. bonds, sends me fifty thousand dollars with instructions to sell them and remit the proceeds to him in a bill on London. I execute the agency and purchase a bill, etc. Will the drawer [of the bill] be liable in that case?[50]

By posing such hypotheticals, Langdell required students to analyze legal disputes and evaluate decisions, rather than simply ingest legal rules related through lectures, as the veteran professors preferred.

Langdell's persistent, iconoclastic caseputting in spring 1870 stimulated great curiosity about his fall course on contracts, in which students expected "a new method. But no one had any conception what it would be until the students were given, in advance of the lecture, ... reprints of cases, the headnotes omitted, selected from various reports."[51] The case method revolution was underway.

---

49. N. Holmes, *Journal*, 275. This laissez-faire approach at HLS persisted throughout the long controversy over case method. See Harvard University, Report of the Overseers Visiting Committee 1873–74, 3–5; J. Thayer, Criminal Law Teaching Notebooks, 1:1–2 (2 Oct. 1876); J. Thayer, Correspondence and Memoranda, 1:9–10; Gray, "Cases and Treatises," 756–64. The criticism that case method prevented "coverage" of subject matter subsequently became one of the major objections to the new pedagogy. See Kimball, "Proliferation of Case Method," 226–27.

50. Langdell, Lectures on Partnership and Commercial Paper, vol. 2, leaves 76–78.

51. Fessenden, "Rebirth of the Harvard Law School," 498.

Langdell wrote little describing or explaining his method.[52] His most detailed description appears in a letter of 1878, possibly addressed to John B. Minor, distinguished professor of law at the University of Virginia, which the *Virginia Law Register* excerpted in 1895:

> The method of teaching by cases ... consists, first, in using a collection of cases on a given subject as a text-book, instead of using a treatise on the same subject. For each exercise the members of the class are expected to prepare themselves by studying thoroughly some ten or twelve pages of the cases. During the exercise each student has his volume of cases before him with facilities for taking notes. The instructor begins by calling upon some member of the class to state the first case in the lesson, i.e., to state the facts, the questions which arose upon them, how they were decided by the court, and the reasons for the decision. Then the instructor proceeds to question him upon the case. If his answer to a question is not satisfactory (and sometimes when it is), the question is put round the class; and if the question is important or doubtful, or if a difference of opinion is manifested, as many views as possible are elicited. The students also question the instructor and state their own views and opinions without being called upon. ... Before leaving a case, the instructor makes such comments and criticisms upon it as he thinks are called for. As the cases are always more or less conflicting (and frequently very much so), the instructor is compelled to deal with every question upon principle. If he says a decision is right, he has to support it against all attacks; if he says it is wrong, he has to meet all arguments adduced in support of it. In short, the instructor finds it necessary to have a sharply defined view of his own upon every question that arises, and to be prepared to maintain it against every variety of objection.[53]

Langdell's account is confirmed by the recollections of those who attended his classes, as well as by the types of marginalia that Langdell and his students wrote in their casebooks.

One type consists of declarative observations that explain, summarize, or elaborate points. For example, Langdell translates a Latin quotation, refers to another case, invokes an authority, or explains confusing circumstances about a case. In a second type, Langdell poses questions, some of which clearly have the didactic tone of an instructor testing students and expecting certain responses. Other questions

52. Ames, "Christopher Columbus Langdell, 1826–1906," 484; Schofield, "Christopher Columbus Langdell," 286; C. Warren, *History of the Harvard Law School*, 2:503.
53. Quoted in "Case System of Teaching Law" (1896), 299.

seek not to elicit a particular response, but to stimulate open inquiry: "When was the contract in this case completed, if at all, and why?" "How does this case differ from" other cases? In this vein, Langdell frequently notes in the margin: "*quaere de hoc.*"[54] Third, Langdell raises hypotheticals, some of which seem intended purely to test the students' knowledge. Other hypotheticals, however, posed problems for discussion: "If the son had been a minor and a member of his father's family, could Plaintiff have recovered [on the debt]; and if so, upon what theory?" "Would this case have been brought in England in a common law court or a court of equity and why? Could Plaintiff or not have had a specific performance and why?"

Fourth, Langdell expounds what he elsewhere called his "heretical opinions" about the cases.[55] These are sometimes laconic and unequivocal: "Correct," "not-law," "no," "Right," or "Wrong." Other times, they are nuanced and qualified: "That seems to be the wrong ground on which the decision can be supported, . . ." Or: "This case was decided correctly, but on erroneous grounds. . . ." Finally, Langdell frequently revises his opinion, crossing out and correcting his annotations,[56] and students sometimes explicitly note Langdell changing his mind, as seen below.

The fundamental goals of Langdell's method were, therefore, to develop in the student the expertise and self-confidence to infer, evaluate, and formulate legal doctrine and judgments autonomously, regardless of the weight of contrary authority. Given these aims, Langdell required students to read original sources rather than textbooks, to analyze particular controversies rather than general propositions, to formulate their own interpretations in response to questions, and to respond to hypotheticals and contrary judgments. He also exposed himself to questions and challenges from students, and revised and corrected his own views in class.

This approach discomfited most students in Langdell's early classes. Franklin Fessenden, who attended Langdell's very first class on contracts, observed that, initially, when "questions were put to draw out the views of the students as to the

54. "Ask about this." Quotations and examples in this paragraph are from *LCon70*, 5a, 12a, 20a, 24a–25a, 39a, 55a, 63a, 84a, 112a, 264a, 314a, 338a, 348a, 367a, 444a.

55. Langdell, Lectures on Partnership and Commercial Paper, vol. 2, leaves 55–56. In Partnership and Negotiable Paper, the two courses that Langdell taught during his first semester, spring 1870, his lecture notes explicitly recognize the contradictions and indeterminacy in legal opinions, including his own: "In offering such a test of . . . partnership as the foregoing, I admit that I have departed somewhat from the beaten track and that I cannot adduce a specific English or American authority in its support; also that there are numberless *dicta* and some decisions which cannot be reconciled with it. It is proper, therefore, that I should say something in justification of the view here advanced over and above a conviction of its correctness. . . . But all the authorities hold otherwise [from me]; and the best that I can say is that they proceeded originally upon an erroneous principle and must now be regarded as anomalous" (vol. 1, leaves 55–56, 68–70).

56. *LCon70*, 190a, 241a, 319a, 333a, 335a, 337a, 433a.

arguments and opinions . . ., it was almost impossible to get much expression, for it was evident that very few [students] had studied the case critically, and had had no thought of forming any judgment of their own. . . . It seemed to them the height of presumption to have, and much more to express, an opinion. It was to learn rules of law that they had come to the School. . . . They thought it absurd to undertake to give their thoughts about a subject of which they knew nothing. . . . [But] Langdell asked more and more questions. . . . The result of the method of Langdell was active search and inquiry; that of the other professors was passive absorption."[57]

James Myers, who also attended Langdell's first revolutionary classes, wrote, "the student is taken to the cases at the very beginning of his work, and is taught to analyze, criticize, and reason upon them for himself, while at the same time he is subjected to the criticism and suggestion of his instructor and fellow-students in doing so. His attention is constantly stimulated from the very first, and the consequence is that a quality of permanence is given to the knowledge acquired, which alone constitutes a strong argument in favor of the new system. In addition to this, he is made pains-taking, careful, and accurate, and above all thorough. He is taught how to work, and has aroused in him a genuine enthusiasm for the work."[58]

Along with directing new students immediately to the original sources, Langdell's most disturbing technique was to ask questions and demand to know the student's reasoning. In fact, "students soon learned that any position they might advance was pretty soon to be followed by the question 'Could you suggest a reason?'"[59] This "Socratic" emphasis on developing "an aptitude in original criticism" prompted divergent reactions.[60]

On the one hand, case method "was seldom mentioned except to be criticized" by faculty, alumni, and members of the bench and bar, and the number of students attending Langdell's courses dwindled to seven or eight.[61] On the other hand, this small group of devotees proudly assumed the eponym of "Langdell's freshmen" or

57. Fessenden, "Rebirth of the Harvard Law School," 499–500.

58. [J. Myers], "Harvard Law School" (5, 19 Feb. 1875), 146–47. See confirming judgments by other fellow students: "Harvard College Law School" (1874), 68; Ames, "Vocation of the Law Professor," 363.

59. Schofield, "Christopher Columbus Langdell," 275.

60. Quotations are, respectively, from "Harvard College Law School" (1874), 68; Harvard University, Report of the Overseers Visiting Committee 1873–74, 2. "Langdell was always worried about 'Why?' and 'How?' He didn't care particularly whether you knew a rule or could state the rule or not, but how did the court do this? And why did it do it? That was his approach all the time." Roscoe Pound, recalling his experience in Langdell's course in 1889–90, quoted in Sutherland, "One Man in His Time," 10.

61. Quotation is from Langdell, Address 1895, 46–47. See E. Washburn, "Harvard Law School," leaves 14r–16r; N. Holmes, *Journal*, 277–78; [J. Myers], "Harvard Law School" (5, 19 Feb. 1875), 8; C. Eliot, "Methods of Instruction," 202; J. Smith, "Christopher Columbus Langdell," 29; Schofield, "Christopher Columbus Langdell," 286; Everett to Warren (10 Feb. 1908); Fessenden, "Rebirth of the Harvard Law School," 503, 499.

"Kit's freshmen" and considered themselves the "best men" in the school, although they were sometimes ridiculed by others.[62] As a result, for several years the students "were divided into the Langdellians and the anti-Langdellians."[63]

Despite his support, Eliot grew concerned about the strong opposition to Langdell's teaching, and took the extraordinary step of calling some of Kit's freshmen individually into his office and soliciting their views. As one recalled: "President Eliot said, 'I want to know what you think of Prof. Langdell's lectures.' [Being] . . . a first-year student of about three months, [I] was flabbergasted, but . . . swallowed [my] astonishment and said, 'Well, Mr. President, I can go to Prof. Washburn's lectures and hear him read a chapter from his book on real property. I can go to Prof. Parson's lectures and hear him read a chapter from his book. But I learned to read before I came down here. When I go to Prof. Langdell's lectures I get something that I cannot find in any book.' 'Thank you,' said President Eliot."[64] Eliot regarded the students' "judgment as conclusive upon the matter" and never questioned Langdell's teaching again."[65]

Even when conceding that case method served these students, critics accused Langdell of fostering disrespect for courts, precedents, and judges. But this charge owed less to his Socratic technique than to the dismissive, even scornful, tone of Langdell's leading disciple, Ames. This tone appears persistently in Ames's marginal comments in the casebooks with which he taught,[66] and it initially surprised students, including Louis Brandeis who in 1876 wrote that "it seemed to be Ames's great aim and object to convince us that nine-tenths of the judges who have sat on the English bench and about ninety-nine-hundredths of the American Judges 'did not know what they were talking about.'"[67] But, after the initial shock, many students began to emulate Ames, offending members of the bench and bar, as well as Ames's colleagues at Harvard, who objected to his "intellectual arrogance and contempt" for the received opinions of judges.[68] The critics of this hypercritical hubris on the part of Ames and HLS students attributed it to Langdell, whose case method was said to make students "obstinate and unduly conceited."[69] But

62. C. Warren, *History of the Harvard Law School*, 2:373; Ames, "Professor Langdell," 13; Ames, "Christopher Columbus Langdell, 1826–1906," 484–85; Batchelder, "Christopher C. Langdell," 440–41; Fox, "Professor Langdell," 7.

63. Quotation is from Ames, "Professor Langdell," 13; Ames, "Christopher Columbus Langdell, 1826–1906," 484.

64. Grinnell, "Unpublished Conversation with President Eliot."

65. E. Washburn, "Harvard Law School," leaf 12r.

66. See *ACon71* or *ASal72*.

67. Brandeis to Wehle (12 Nov. 1876).

68. Gray to Eliot (3 Jan. 1883). See Fessenden, "Rebirth of the Harvard Law School," 503; Gurney to Eliot [3 Jan. 1883].

69. Fessenden, "Rebirth of the Harvard Law School," 513. See Choate, Address 1895, 63.

Langdell's comments were rarely scornful and typically of this tone: "Green v. Crosswell is wrong 'with all deference of course.'"[70]

The nature of Langdell's early case method appears in the following reconstructed class discussions from February 1872 and October–November 1875. These reconstructions weave together the annotations made by Langdell and his students in their surviving casebooks, incorporating the "dialectic between Text and Annotation" in annotated documents.[71] In the narratives, the quotations from contemporary sources are signified by italics and drawn from the handwritten glosses of the named participants, from words attributed to them by annotations in other casebooks, or from the printed case reports, which were quoted in class from time to time.[72] The quotations are supplemented by nonitalicized interpolations in order to complete the statements.

Inside Langdell's Classroom (February 1872)

Langdell began teaching from the complete first edition of *Cases on Contracts* immediately after its publication in October 1871, and the following dialogue reconstructs a class discussion that occurred in February 1872 concerning the question of whether and when the law may be considered doubtful.[73] The case at issue—*Longridge v. Dorville*, decided in England in 1821[74]—comes after 120 pages of cases that develop doctrine on the question of when forbearance from suing provides a sufficient consideration to support a promise and establish a bilateral contract. In other words, does your promise to pay me in return for my not suing you establish a legal contract between us? If my prospective suit has no foundation in fact or in law, then my not suing you is worthless, and I am giving no consideration sufficient to support the promise and establish a binding contract between us, according to the doctrine of the time. "Forbearance of an unfounded suit is no forbearance at all."[75] But the question in *Longridge* is more complicated, namely,

---

70. Langdell, "Lecture Notes in Suretyship Class, 1892–93," 62.

71. Quotation is from N. Davis, *Return of Martin Guerre*, 106. The methodological issues involved in this reconstruction are analyzed in Kimball, "'Warn Students That I Entertain Heretical Opinions,'" 77–94.

72. Citations to the annotations are indicated by the page number and the suffix "a," whereas quotations from case reports are cited by the page number alone. In addition to those annotations and case reports, the reconstructions draw on other primary sources such as letters from former students of Langdell and Ames and on accounts published by contemporaries. Since some of Ames's casebooks contain his annotations both as a student and as a professor, those annotations are found under either category.

73. The discussion can be dated in February 1872, between an early bound of "Jan '72" that Ames included in a gloss on a prior case and a later bound of "Mar. 4" that he noted subsequently (ACon71, 267a, 461a).

74. Langdell, *Cases on Contracts* (1871), 308–11.

75. Langdell, *Cases on Contracts* (1871), 291.

whether "the giving up of a suit, instituted to try a question respecting which the law is doubtful, is a good consideration to support a promise."[76] That is to say, if you promise to pay me for not suing you on grounds that are legally doubtful, is there still a contract established between us? This question raises the issue of whether and when the law may be doubtful.

One archival source for the dialogue is Langdell's annotated copy of the 1870 edition of *Cases on Contracts* (*LCon70*), which he continued to use in his teaching even after the complete 1871 edition appeared. Another source is the personal copy of the 1871 edition annotated by William Keener (*KCon71*), who attended Contracts during the mid-1870s.[77] The third is Ames's copy of the 1871 edition (*ACon71*), which he annotated at least seven times as a student or professor, reflecting his extensive collaboration in teaching with Langdell.[78] *ACon71* and *KCon71* are the sources for the student voices, which have been attributed to a number of anonymous students (Student1, etc.).

The narrative follows the annotated and printed cross-references in *LCon70*, *ACon71*, and *KCon71* indicating the path that Langdell and his students followed in the casebook. Thus, the reconstructed class discussion opens in the middle of the casebook at *Longridge*, jumps toward the front, and then moves back, following the annotated cross-references, the order of the casebook, and the doctrinal development. Finally, the discussion concludes where it began at *Longridge* with the provocative consideration of whether and when the law may be considered doubtful.

February 1872, Course on Contracts, Harvard Law School

LANGDELL: Gentlemen, before taking up the case of *Longridge v. Dorville* today, let us review the doctrine concerning "*consideration*," namely the *sole inducement to make the* contract.[79] What specifically may be regarded as a consideration, Mr. ———?

STUDENT1: *Justice Holroyd states in* Longridge *that Any act of the plaintiff... from which the defendant derives a benefit or advantage, or any labor,*

---

76. Langdell, *Cases on Contracts* (1871), 311.

77. I am grateful to David Warrington for alerting me to the existence of Keener's copy in the University of Virginia Law School Library Special Collections, and for arranging for me to examine it at Harvard Law School Library Special Collections, courtesy of the University of Virginia Law School Library.

78. The majority of glosses in the reconstruction come from the penciled annotations that are the earliest in the casebook, dating from the early 1870s when Ames was a second-year student and a Resident Bachelor of Laws. But some of Ames's comments in red pen, which belong to the mid-1870s when Ames taught Contracts, are also included. These comments are cited as "*ACon71*, red" below. On their collaborative teaching, see Kimball, "'Warn Students That I Entertain Heretical Opinions,'" 62–65.

79. Langdell, *Summary of the Law of Contracts*, 78–79.

detriment, or inconvenience sustained by the plaintiff, is a sufficient consideration to support a promise and thus establish a contract. (311)

LANGDELL: In what sense does forbearance from suing fit Justice Holroyd's conception?

[Student2 raises his hand.]

LANGDELL: Yes?

STUDENT2: *Justice Holroyd*, again, states, *the consideration of forbearance [from suing] is a benefit to the defendant.... The authorities cited proceed on that ground.* (311)

LANGDELL: Can you state the early authority of *Davis v. Reyner* (1671) in this regard?

STUDENT2: An individual *devised a legacy to [Davis], and made [Reyner] executor.* Later, upon Davis *intending to sue [Reyner] for the legacy, [Reyner] in consideration of forbearance promised to pay* Davis. But Reyner did not pay, so Davis then brought suit on the grounds that Reyner did not fulfill his promise to pay. (267)

LANGDELL: *Could you suggest a reason* for the ruling in favor of Davis? (Schofield, "Langdell," 275)

STUDENT2: Reyner had made *his own promise in consideration of forbearance, and a forbearance of suit for a legacy is a sufficient consideration* for a promise to pay. (267)

[Murmuring. Ames raises hand.]

LANGDELL: Mr. Ames?

AMES: But only last month, Professor *Langdell [you] thought this case could not be sustained.* (ACon71, 267a)

LANGDELL: Did I, Mr. Ames? *Could you suggest a reason* for that view?

AMES: You said that *there is no suit at Common Law for legacy,* but *there is in Spiritual court.*[80] (ACon71, 267a)

LANGDELL: I've *changed my opinion,* Mr. Ames. (ACon71, 267a)

[Some students smile, having seen this before. Ames notes in margin *Kit changes opinion.* (ACon71, 267a)]

---

80. Langdell occasionally employed the term "Spiritual court" interchangeably with "ecclesiastical court," which he considered to be the source of the procedure for courts of equity in England. Langdell, *Summary of Equity Pleading* (1877), xiii.

LANGDELL: But this is beside the central point that forbearance to sue is a good consideration for a promise, although matters are generally not this simple, as we see in *Longridge*. And where precisely?

STUDENT1: [Breaking in.] In Justice Bayley's opinion, where he states, *If it had appeared in this case that the [defendants] . . . could not have been liable at all, . . . the consideration [of forebearance] for the promise would have failed.* (311)

[Silence.]

LANGDELL: This is *not so*, Gentlemen. *There would be a good consideration even if it were admitted that there was no cause of action.* In this regard, *Longridge* is *not distinguishable from Smith v. Monteith [on] p. 220.* (ACon71, 311a) *Could you suggest a reason* why?

AMES: In *Smith v. Monteith [the] consideration was not forbearance at all, but discharge . . . from custody, which custody would have been illegal if [Smith] had known that he had no cause of action. Therefore, the discharge would have been no consideration.* (ACon71, 291a)

LANGDELL: Yes, the issue turns on the *knowledge of the Plaintiff*, although some courts have held that *Smith v. Monteith [is] distinguishable* and that in forbearance *knowledge of the Plaintiff [is] immaterial, for if [the suit is] not well founded, Plaintiff [has] no right to proceed.* (ACon71, 293a)

[Students write furiously. Ames notes, *Distinction important.* (ACon71, 291a)]

LANGDELL: Let us now consider when the grounds *may be doubted.* (213) This question brings us to *Smith and Smith's Case*, which is explicitly doubted in *Longridge*. You recall that *Smith and Smith's Case* was heard in 1583, and was the first in our discussion of *Sufficiency of Consideration in General.* (183) Please state the case, Mr.———?

STUDENT1: *Tho[mas] Smith . . . lying sick of a mortal sickness, [and] being careful to provide for his . . . children . . . constituted [John Smith] overseer of his will, and ordained and appointed by his will that his goods should be in the disposition of [John]. Furthermore, in consideration [that Thomas] . . . would commit . . . the disposition of his goods after his death . . . to him, [John] promised to [Thomas] to procure the assurance of certain customary lands to one of the children and to dispose of [Thomas'] goods after his death . . . for the education of the said children.* (183)

LANGDELL: And why would John Smith, the defendant here, agree to become the overseer and make the promise to dispose of the goods as stipulated?

STUDENT1: Because... as *Chief Justice Wray* says, such overseers [*of wills*] *commonly gain of such disposition.* (184)... And, in fact, *the goods [of Thomas]... came to [John's] hands to his great profit and advantage.* (183) But John Smith evidently did not dispose of the goods as he had promised, and the executor of the estate, Lambert Smith, filed suit. In the end, *Chief Justice Wray* and *Justice Ayliffe* held that John was not bound to dispose of Thomas's goods as he had promised because *there is not any benefit... that [is] a consideration in law to induce him to make this promise; for the consideration is no other but to have the disposition of the goods of [Thomas] pro educatione liberorum.* (183–84)

LANGDELL: Can you state this in your own words?

STUDENT1: [Triumphantly.] The *appointment of [John] to have control of [Thomas'] property* as overseer of his estate was *no good consideration* for John's promise to dispose of Thomas's goods in a certain way. (*ACon71*, red, 183a)

LANGDELL: Try again. *I should like a little more precision in the use of terms.* (Schofield, "Langdell," 275)

STUDENT1: The benefit of overseeing an estate is not a sufficient consideration to support a promise about disposing of the estate.

LANGDELL: *Could you suggest a reason* for the ruling, Mr. ——?

STUDENT2: As *Chief Justice Wray* says, the law *presumes every man to be true and faithful if the contrary be not shewed; and therefore the law shall intend that [John Smith] hath not made any private gain to himself, but that he hath disposed of the goods of [Thomas] to the use and benefit of [Thomas'] children according to the trust reposed in him.* (184)

STUDENT2: [Raising hand.] *Professor Langdell, [you] deemed this case bad law... on the ground that [John's] renunciation of a right [to appoint the overseer of his property] was a sufficient prejudice to him to make a good consideration. (ACon71, 183a)*

LANGDELL: So I did. Why is that, Mr. Keener?

KEENER: *At an early day in our law, the only consideration... was a consideration which would warrant a debt, and for which an action of debt would lie, a quid pro quo.... But today, when promisee owes anything at request of promisor, which he was not bound to do, he has, in legal contemplation, incurred a detriment, and it is a sufficient consideration.* (*KCon71*, 183a)

LANGDELL: Precisely. *Benefit to the promisor is irrelevant to the question of whether a given thing can be made the consideration,* because *detriment to the promisee is a universal test of the sufficiency of consideration.* (Langdell, *Summary of Contracts*, 82)

[Ames raises hand.]

LANGDELL: Yes, Mr. Ames?

AMES: *But if [John] might at any time have recalled the appointment, what right did he relinquish?* (ACon71, 183a)

LANGDELL: Can anyone answer Mr. Ames?

[Silence.]

LANGDELL: Granted, John may still *recall the appointment,* but to do so, he must undergo the labor and expense of renouncing the appointment that he has already made. Hence, *renunciation of a right* is still a *detriment.* (ACon71, 183–84a).

STUDENT1: So the *case [was] decided before [the] notion that detriment to Pl[aintiff] might be a good consideration* was understood? (ACon71, 184a)

LANGDELL: Yes. Remember that *each of these doctrines has arrived at its present state by slow degrees; in other words, it is a growth, extending in many cases through centuries.* (vi) And so we arrive at *Longridge v. Dorville* where *Smith and Smith's Case* is explicitly doubted. Mr. Keener, would you please state the issue, as *Justice Holroyd* defines it?

KEENER: Let's see. . . . *Now the consideration of forbearance [from suing] is a benefit to the defendant, if he be liable. . . . The authorities cited proceed on that ground. . . . This case differs materially from those; for here a suit . . . is given up . . . the final success of which was involved in some doubt.* (311)

LANGDELL: Why is the *final success . . . in doubt,* Mr. Keener? (311)

KEENER: I'm not sure.

LANGDELL: *See p. 290, note 8.* (LCon70, 308a)

KEENER: [Reading.] *In Longridge the matter in dispute was about to be decided in a tribunal governed by the civil law, with which the [common law] judges, [and, certainly] the lay parties to the [dispute], might be presumed to be unacquainted.* (290n8)

AMES: [breaking in]: *So doubtful means the judges are not presumed to know the civil law* pertaining to this case. (ACon71, red, 310a)

LANGDELL: Exactly.

AMES: But not knowing the law is different from doubting the law.

LANGDELL: True enough.

AMES: This note on 290 refers to not knowing the law. *But can the law ever be said to be doubtful?* (ACon71, 310a)

LANGDELL: Excellent question, Mr. Ames. Can the law ever be said to be doubtful? Let us *see p. 291* and the view of *Justice Maule.* (ACon71, 311a)

AMES: *Justice Maule says that Longridge is hardly consistent with some of the*

cases, wherein it has been laid down that no law is doubtful. Jones v. Randall
is the earliest case in which a question of law is admitted to be of doubtful
issue. (291)

LANGDELL: Very good Mr. Ames. Where did Justice Maule make this reference earlier?

[Uncomfortable silence.]

Turn to *Brooks* at p. 212. *[Justice] Alderson*, as well. (*ACon71*, 311a)
STUDENT2: *Justice Alderson* seems sympathetic to the reservations of Maule,
because he asks, *What is the ground on which giving up a doubtful point of*
law is a consideration? To whom must it be doubtful? (212)
STUDENT3: [Breaking in.] On the next page, *Justice Bosanquet* concurs, *A*
point may be considered [doubtful], on which learned men differ. (214)
STUDENT2: [Joining in.] *Lord Abinger*, too, because he says, *It is carrying fic-*
tion too far to say that the courts must always know how the law will be. (214)
AMES: Nevertheless, there are cases holding *that no law is doubtful*, as *Justice*
Maule says. (291)
LANGDELL: True, Mr. Ames, but *whether law is doubtful or not is a question of*
fact. (*ACon71*, red, 311a)
AMES: How does one know this fact? How does one *find out whether law is*
doubtful or not? (*ACon71*, 311a)

[Pause, as everyone looks to Langdell expectantly.]

LANGDELL: *To find out whether law is doubtful or not . . . [the] Judge*
looks into books to see what the opinions of learned men are. They may
differ . . . (*ACon71*, 311a)
AMES: But, Professor Langdell, what if *the opinions of learned men . . . differ*
while [the Judge] himself is perfectly clear? (*ACon71*, 311a)
LANGDELL: *While [the Judge] himself is perfectly clear, [s]till law may be*
doubtful. . . . Opinion . . . is simply evidence. . . . Whether law is doubtful or not is
a question of fact. (*ACon71*, 311a) As *Chief Justice Abbott* states in *Longridge*,
the law might fairly be considered as doubtful [when] there [are] contradic-
tory decisions on the subject. (310)

As for myself, Mr. Ames, I have tried to *warn students that I entertain*
heretical opinions, which they are not to take as law but as what I think the
law ought to be. Indeed, I specifically addressed *the subject of "Consider-*
ation" in this regard. (*LPar70*, vol. 2, leaves 55, 56) My judgment, like the
opinion of [the] parties . . . is simply evidence about *whether law is doubtful.*
(*ACon71*, 311a)

[Pause. Silence in class, while students take notes.]

LANGDELL: Gentlemen, the hour grows late. For our next class, we will consider the holding of *Justice Holroyd* that *the giving up of a suit instituted for
the purpose of trying a doubtful question . . . is a good consideration . . .* (311)

[Class adjourns, while students continue to write.]

Inside Langdell's Classroom (October–November 1875)

During the academic years 1874–75, 1875–76, and 1876–77, Langdell annually
taught the course Jurisdiction and Procedure in Equity, a subject in which he
became expert. In 1875 he published part 1 of *Cases in Equity Pleading*, followed in
1876 by part 2 with a 120-page appendix that was published separately in 1877 as
Summary of Equity Pleading. In 1878–79, though abandoning the advanced electives
in civil procedure, Langdell immediately began sequencing the coursework in
equity by dividing Jurisdiction and Procedure in Equity into two parts. In 1879–80
the first half, Jurisdiction and Procedure in Equity—Second Year, was taught by
Ames, employing Langdell's casebook, *Cases in Equity Pleading*. The second half,
Jurisdiction and Procedure in Equity—Third Year, was taught by Langdell, who
issued installments of his never completed *Cases on Equity Jurisdiction* between
1879 and 1883.

Drawing on five heavily annotated copies of *Cases in Equity Pleading*, the following dialogue reconstructs a memorable incident that occurred on 29 October
and 4 November 1875, in Langdell's original course, Jurisdiction and Procedure in
Equity. The procedural issue of equity pleading in the case of *Scott v. Broadwood*
(1846), which arose over a dispute about rightful ownership of real estate, was
whether a plea (defendant's response) to a bill (plaintiff's complaint or petition)
may be "double," that is, state more than one response. Longstanding doctrine
in equity jurisprudence permitted only one response to a bill and barred double
pleading.[81]

---

81. *LEq75* is Langdell's copy of Part I (1875); *AEq1* is Ames's copy of Part I (1875) and Part II (1876), bound
together. *VNEq75*, a third copy of Part I (1875), was annotated by student George W. Van Nest of New York
City, who attended HLS during the period 1874–76 and occasionally refers to his classmate, Charles Almy.
WEq75, a fourth copy of Part I (1875), was annotated by Charles L. B. Whitney, another classmate of Van
Nest and Almy. *AEq2*, a fifth copy of Part I (1875) bound together with Part II (1876) and the Summary
(1877), was also annotated by Ames in 1877 and 1878. In this reconstruction, *AEq2* is included as the voice
of Professor Ames, reflecting the arrangement of coteaching the course in 1877–78.

29 October 1875, Procedure and Jurisdiction in Equity, Harvard Law School

LANGDELL: Mr. *Almy,* please state the case of *Scott v. Broadwood* (1846). (*VNEq75,* 129a)

ALMY: In *Scott v. Broadwood the bill alleged that Sir Andrew Chadwick, being . . . in the actual possession and receipt of rents of a certain piece of ground . . . died on the 22nd March, 1768, intestate as to his real estate . . . and without issue.*[82]

LANGDELL: Note, gentlemen, that *from the time of Sir [Chadwick]'s death there were innumerable litigations up to this time as to who was his heir.* (*VNEq75,* 30a)

STUDENT1: *A long litigation,* indeed. (*AEq1,* 30a)

WHITNEY: [Whispering.] An *interminable litigation.* (*WEq75,* 30a)

ALMY: *after deducing the title . . . [to the land] from Thomas Chadwick, [the plaintiff] alleged that the premises . . . had come into the possession of the defendant Henry Broadwood . . . but the plaintiff had been unable to discover when the defendant obtained such possession, or from whom . . . he derived his title. . . . The plaintiff had commenced an action of ejectment against the defendants Broadwood and his partners, but . . . the plaintiff was unable to go to trial without a discovery of the contents of the leases.* (30)[83]

[Student raises hand.]

LANGDELL: Yes?

STUDENT1: *This is an insufficient allegation. [It] must show that contents [of the leases] will help [the] Plaintiff prove certain allegations.* (*AEq1,* 30a)

LANGDELL: True enough. Mr. Whitney, *could you suggest a reason?*

WHITNEY: It is *not enough to say that [the plaintiff was unable to go to trial without a discovery of the contents of the leases] merely. [The plaintiff] must allege that they are essential to proving some of his allegations; if he does that, then defendant must provide [discovery] unless defendant denies it in plea[ding].* (*CWEq75,* 30a)

LANGDELL: But how can the Plaintiff state what the leases will discover before seeing them, Mr. ———?

---

82. Chadwick died without leaving a will or having any children.

83. Thomas Chadwick claims to own the estate on which Broadwood resides. Before Chadwick can pursue an action (suit) of ejectment in a court of common law against Broadwood, Chadwick must go to a court of equity and win a bill for discovery to see whether Broadwood has a lease and what it says.

STUDENT1: At least, *the Bill [ought] to show the title [is vested] in the Plaintiff at the time the action was brought . . . that the Plaintiff maintains a sufficient title. (AEq1, 30a)*

LANGDELL: Well said. What exactly does the Bill allege, Mr. Almy?

ALMY: *the bill [in the court of equity] . . . prayed that the defendants might make a full and true discovery of [his lease] . . . in order that the plaintiff might give [it] in evidence at the trial* in common law. (30–31)

LANGDELL: What was the response to the bill, Mr. Almy?

ALMY: *The defendant, Broadwood, by an order of the court, had leave to plead two pleas in [response to] this bill and to support such pleas by such averments, by way of answer, as might be necessary.* (31)

LANGDELL: Gentlemen, what is the *confusion of ideas* here? *(LEq75, 31a)*

STUDENT2: *The double pleading here is multifarious . . . obviously. (AEq1, 31a,* pencil) Only one plea is allowed in equity.

LANGDELL: Mr. Van Nest?

VAN NEST: In fact, double pleading was *allowed rarely. [The] first order allowed was in 1820. (VNEq75, 31a)*

[Stamping of feet.]

LANGDELL: Well, Gentlemen, whose view is correct?

VAN NEST: [Continuing.] *Gibson v. Whitehead (4 Maddock 241) (1820) [was] the first case in which it was allowed to plead double. (VNEq75, 31a; AEq1, 31a) Later the Chancellor became more liberal. (VNEq75, 31a)*

LANGDELL: True enough. Double pleading was allowed in equity, though it was *not a matter of course as in Common Law. (VNEq75, 31a) Could you suggest a reason,* Mr. Van Nest? (Schofield, "Langdell," 275)

[Silence and shuffling.]

      Mr. ———?

STUDENT1: It was always considered *a privilege to plead at all at Equity. . . . [hence] Double pleading [was] allowed only by order and obtained with difficulty. (AEq1, 31a)*

LANGDELL: Very good.

[Class notes this in margin. *AEq1* overwrites his assertion that double pleading is *multifarious.* (31a)]

      Now, what does each of the two pleas address?

STUDENT2: *The first plea covers the whole bill. In the second plea, each part goes only to part of the bill. (AEq1, 30a)*

LANGDELL: Please tell us more about the nature of the first plea, Mr. Van Nest.

VAN NEST: The *first plea [is] affirmative* ... (*VNEq75*, 30a)

LANGDELL: Yes, *I think this [is] affirmative*. (*CWEq75*, 31a)

[Ames gestures.]

    Professor Ames?

PROF. AMES: I believe this is a *Negative Plea*. (*AEq2*, 31a)[84]

[Silence.]

LANGDELL: Well ... upon reflection, I think you may be right. Yes, *I think this [plea is] negative*. (*CWEq75*, 31a)

        Yes, in fact, this *negative plea affirms [a] negative —len!* (*LEq75*, 31a)

[Whispering:]

STUDENT1: What does he mean?

STUDENT2: The *Plea [is] negative*. (*AEq1*, 31a)

WHITNEY: *L[angdell] is changing his opinion*. (*CWEq75*, 31a)

[Van Nest crosses out *first plea affirmative* and glosses: *L[angdell]—neg.* on 30a, and *Negative plea* on 31a. Whitney does likewise. (31a)]

LANGDELL: *No, cross that out*. (Cross out on *LEq75*, 31a) Better to say: *the first plea is affirmative in form, being a plea of fine* ... *but it is negative in effect, being a denial of the plaintiff's title*.[85] (Part II, *Summary*, §109)

[Student raises hand.]

LANGDELL: Yes?

VAN NEST: So *the first plea [is] affirmative, being a plea of fine?* (*VNEq75*, 30a)

LANGDELL: *No, negative*. (*VNEq75*, 30a)

STUDENT2: But *a plea of fine is affirmative*. (*AEq1*, 31a)

---

84. A negative plea denies a "material allegation" in the plaintiff's bill. An affirmative plea does not deny an allegation, but avoids the bill (thereby implicitly conceding the truth of the bill) by asserting, for example, that the remedy is barred for some reason, such as because it would violate the Statute of Limitations. Langdell, *Summary of Equity Pleading* (1877), 61–65.

85. A "fine" in conveyancing was the "amicable" resolution of a suit "by which the lands in question become, or are acknowledged to be, the right of one of the parties." Black, *Dictionary of Law* (1891). Here the plea of fine seems to be the defendant's claim that he owns the land by virtue of such a fine in the past. Fines were abolished in England by the time of this suit.

LANGDELL: *affirmative in form…negative in effect.* (Part II, *Summary*, #109)
  Gentlemen, I should like a little more precision in the use of terms. (Scho-
  field, "Langdell," 275) Other points to note about the first plea?
VAN NEST: *This plea [is] a defense to the whole.* (VNEq75, 31a)
STUDENT1: [Breaking in.] That was already said.

[Clapping and stamping.]

LANGDELL: What is missing from the first plea, Mr. ——?
STUDENT2: *No answer [is made] in support of the first plea, as there should be.*
  (AEq1, 34a)
STUDENT1: [Breaking in.] Yes, *no answer in support* and *no order made [by the
  Vice-Chancellor] as to this Plea.* (AEq1, 30a)
LANGDELL: Very good, gentlemen. And *when we say [that a] negative plea
  needs [an] answer we mean* what? (CWEq75, interleaf 30–31)
WHITNEY: *We mean that the Bill is properly drawn and that [the] plea denies
  something actually in the Bill.* (CWEq75, interleaf 30–31)
LANGDELL: Well said. Let us conclude now, and begin with the second plea
  at our next class.

———

[Class Resumes. 4 November 1875 (VNEq75, 33a)]

LANGDELL: Mr. Van Nest, please explain *the substance of the [second] plea* in
  Scott v. Broadwood. (AEq2, 32a)
VAN NEST: *The second plea is a defense…being divided into two parts, the first
  paragraph being a plea to the first part [of the bill], and the second and third
  as to the rest.* (VNEq75, 33a)
PROF. AMES: [Breaking in.] But what is *the substance of the plea?* (AEq2, 32a)
STUDENT1: *The second Plea [is] in two parts. [The] first part [is] negative, [the]
  second affirmative.* [(AEq1, 30a)]
LANGDELL: Yes, *the first paragraph [of the second plea] is a negative plea to
  part of the bill.* (LEq75, 32a) Let us look more closely.

[Silence.]

PROF. AMES: *Much of this would not make a good plea.… The substance of the
  plea which negatives[?] to the Plaintiff is found only on page 32.* (AEq2, 32a)
LANGDELL: And why is that substance negative, gentlemen?
STUDENT1: *This is a negative plea, for [the] Statute of Limitations gives a title to
  defendant.* (AEq1, 31a)

STUDENT2: [Breaking in.] *But in choses in action [a] Plea of Statute of Limita-tions is affirmative as admitting a claim and avoiding it by [providing] a bar to remedy. (AEq1, 31a)*

VAN NEST: [Joining in.] *I agree. The Statute denies an allegation which [the] Plaintiff has to make, viz., possession within 20 years. (VNEq75, 33a)*

LANGDELL: Nevertheless, like the first plea, *the first paragraph of the second plea is also affirmative in form, being a plea of the Statute of Limitations or of adverse possession, but negative in legal effect, being a denial of the existence of the leases alleged in the bill. (Part II, Summary, #109)*[86]

[Pause, as students furiously take notes. AEq1 crosses out *this is a negative plea* and overwrites his annotations. (31a) Whitney notes: *Langdell now says affirmative.* (32a)]

LANGDELL: What of the second part of the second plea?

VAN NEST: *The second and third paragraphs are affirmative. (VNEq75, 32a)*

STUDENT2: [Joining in.] Yes, *the second part of the second plea is affirmative. This [is] clear from the effect of the . . . Statute [of Limitations] by which the Defendant must show affirmatively that he has been in actual receipt of rents for twenty years. (AEq1, 33a)*

LANGDELL: Well said, *the 2nd and 3rd paragraphs of the plea are an affirmative plea . . . affirmative in form and in legal effect. (LEq75, 32a; Part II, Summary, #109)*

[Pause.]

> Perhaps *the first paragraph [of the second plea] is a negative plea; but the two [paragraphs] . . . [go] to different parts of the bill, [so] there is no duplicity. The plea is properly one in form. (LEq75, 32a)*

[Pause. Ames gestures.]

> Professor Ames?

PROF. AMES: *This is erroneous. Both [pleas] are negative. (Part II, Summary, #109a]*

[Long pause. Students shrug.]

---

86. The effect of a plea either of the Statute of Limitations or of adverse possession is to say that the defendant, Broadwood, has resided on the estate so long that the plaintiff, Chadwick, has forfeited any claim he may have had to the real estate and that, therefore, Broadwood does not need to provide discovery of the leases in the court of equity, as Chadwick's bill requests.

LANGDELL: *Damn rot.* (VNEq75, 33a) Professor Ames is correct.

[Students exchange glances.]

VAN NEST: The *second and third paragraphs are negative?* (VNEq75, 32a)

LANGDELL: Yes. I now say *the plea was improperly one in form.* (LEq75, 32a)

STUDENT1: Professor *Langdell, [you seem to] change [your] ground and con-sider it improper to make two pleas.* (AEq1, 30a, 32a)

WHITNEY: Yes, Professor *Langdell, [are you] now saying the opposite?* (WEq75, 32a)

LANGDELL: I am saying that I *think it not proper to divide the second plea into two sep[arate] pleas.* (attributed to "Langdell" in WEq75, 32a)

PROF. AMES: So the *Summary #109 is wrong?* (AEq2, 30a)

LANGDELL: Precisely. We'll begin from here next class.

—⁓—

Class adjourns as everyone writes furiously. Langdell crosses out *but the two pleas… [go] to different parts of the bill, [so] there is no duplicity.* (LEq75, 32a) Van Nest crosses out *affirmative*, writes in *negative* (VNEq75, 31a), and Whitney inserts the word *Not* in the following statement: *Langdell thinks it Not proper to divide the 2nd plea into 2 sep[arate] pleas.* (32a)

The "Langdellian method of teaching law"[87] recreated in these dialogues was gradually adopted by Langdell in his other classes, as he had the time and oppor-tunity to develop appropriate material. In particular, his civil procedure courses illustrate the progressive steps from conventional lecturing to empirical dem-onstration drawing on specimen documents, to inductive teaching from cases assigned through a provisional list, and, finally, to the full and formal adoption of case method employing a published casebook.[88] Through these stages, his teaching on a particular subject evolved from exposition by lectures to case method.

Examinations Presenting Actual Problems for Solution

Thorough written examinations were a radical innovation in American profes-sional education in 1870. Previously, mere attendance, "without examination or inquiry of any sort," had served to qualify students for the LL.B. or the M.D. A few law schools and medical schools began to institute examinations as a degree

---

87. C. Eliot, Annual Report 1896–97, 25.
88. Kimball and Reyes, "First Modern Civil Procedure Course," 289–90.

requirement during the 1860s,[89] but these exams, patterned after the recitation, were "hasty, unequal, and unsubstantial as a guaranty" of educational attainment. President Eliot therefore convinced the Harvard Corporation in April 1870 to require a "thorough public examination" for every degree.[90]

The term "public examination" was drawn from the English precedent of requiring students to pass highly competitive examinations written in common, rather than in private, in order to earn honors at Oxford and Cambridge universities. Instituted at Oxbridge during the first half of the nineteenth century, these competitive examinations gained immense cultural authority and were extended to secondary education and to the civil service between 1850 and 1870. In subsequent decades, "public examination" became "the primary means through which academic success was measured and professional credentials were established ... among the Victorian and Edwardian elite in Great Britain."[91]

Notwithstanding this precedent, the institution of written examinations at HLS was novel in significant respects. Oxford and Cambridge regarded liberal education as the proper preparation for professions and therefore excluded or marginalized professional education, particularly the study of common law, through the end of the nineteenth century. Even in 1901 the English universities had no strong schools of common law, and many of the leading lawyers between 1850 and 1950 were not university graduates.[92] Hence, Harvard's requirement of 1870 introduced "public examination" into university-based professional education, and Langdell then embraced and transformed this innovation.

Upon becoming dean in September 1870, he announced that HLS examinations culminating the degree course "will be of a thorough and searching character."[93] In September 1872 the examination requirement was extended to each course, and Langdell informed entering students who sought to qualify for one year of

89. Quotation is from Langdell, Annual Report 1875–76, 72. See C. Eliot, Annual Report 1873–74, 30; E. Brown, *Legal Education at Michigan*, 182–83; C. Warren, *History of the Harvard Law School*, 2:364; Ludmerer, *Learning to Heal*, 63.

90. Quotations are, respectively, from C. Eliot, Annual Report 1873–74, 29; Harvard University, Corporation Records, 11:196 (8 Apr. 1870). See C. Eliot, Annual Report 1869–70, 17; Goebel, *History of the School of Law, Columbia University*, 50; Ritchie, *First Hundred Years*, 54–56.

91. Deslandes, "Competitive Examinations," 544, 550–51. See Roach, *Public Examinations in England*, 3–4; Soffer, *Discipline and Power, 1870–1930*, 136; Montgomery, *Examinations: An Account of Their Evolution*, xi, 14.

92. Ames, "Vocation of the Law Professor," 357; J. Thayer, "Teaching of English Law," 169–70; Hill, *Harvard College*, 253, 265; J. Baker, *Introduction to English Legal History* (1979), 149. See Roach, *Public Examinations in England*, 14; Cosgrove, *Our Lady the Common Law*, 42–44.

93. Harvard University, *Catalog 1870–71*, 72.

advanced standing that they would have to pass the first-year examinations.[94] The *American Law Review* and the Harvard Overseers' Visiting Committee applauded these moves, and some observers later considered "the series of severe annual examinations required for a degree" to be the most important reform at HLS during the 1870s.[95] In response, students became increasingly diligent, and by the early 1880s an ambitious student typically noted in his casebook: "Be P[retty] D[amn] careful that you know exactly what this case decides. You may be asked that question on Exam Paper."[96]

Meanwhile, Langdell transformed the nature of the examination questions, which at English universities had often been criticized for requiring rote memorization or formulaic learning and for promoting "cramming" rather than deep learning. This criticism applied even to the famous Mathematical Tripos at Cambridge that was justified as a "gymnastic" of the mind.[97] Also susceptible to this criticism, the older HLS faculty in the early 1870s prepared their examinations according to a fairly uniform format of posing about fifteen questions that asked for general definitions or specific rules. For example, in Evidence Charles Bradley asked, "Give the rule as to a modification of a written contract by oral evidence." In Criminal Law Edmund Bennett asked, "What is the criminal liability of infants?" In Real Property Washburn put a three-part question: "What is an estate in Fee Simple? What word is essential to create such an estate at common law? What are the incidents of such estate?"[98] These kinds of questions were characteristic of legal examinations generally, whether in works such as Baylies's *Questions and Answers for Law Students* (1873), intended for "the solitary student in the office of the practicing attorney," or in Dowley's *The Law in a Nut-Shell, comprising concise and lucid answers to five hundred leading legal questions* (1878), which provided "answers to all questions propounded to law students at the prize examinations of Columbia College."[99]

Some of Langdell's early exam questions follow this pattern, but he soon intro-

94. See Langdell, Annual Report 1872–73, 62; Langdell, "Memoranda Concerning Law School Students," 56, 60, 66.

95. Quotation is from Gray, "Cases and Treatises," 762. See [O. Holmes], "Harvard University Law School" (1870), 177; Harvard University, Report of the Overseers Visiting Committee 1873–74, 3; Batchelder, "1906—Notes for Langdell art[icle]"; C. Warren, *History of the Harvard Law School*, 2:390; Fessenden, "Rebirth of the Harvard Law School," 497–98.

96. PSal72, 195marg.

97. Soffer, *Discipline and Power*, 135–37, 159; Searby, *History of the University of Cambridge*, 181–86.

98. In Harvard Law School, Annual Examinations, see Charles S. Bradley, "Examination in Evidence," (June 1871) question 12; Edmund H. Bennett, Criminal Law (June 1871), question 6; Emory Washburn, Real Property, Elective (June 1871) question 3.

99. Baylies, *Questions and Answers for Law Students*, v; Dowley, *Law in a Nut-Shell*, iii.

duced a new form of question to assess whether students could infer, evaluate, and formulate legal doctrine and opinions. These were the capacities that he intended to develop in students through his new case method, so instead of asking for a general definition or legal rule, Langdell began posing particular hypothetical situations that required students to identify the legal question at issue, generate the legal principle, and apply it correctly to the situation. For example, his Contracts exam in 1871 asked, "An offer is sent from Boston to New York by mail on Monday, and an answer accepting it is received on Wednesday at 10 A.M., but in the meantime another letter withdrawing the offer has been sent on Tuesday, and received on Wednesday at 9 A.M. Is there or not a contract between the parties, and why? If there is, what was the *punctum temporis* at which it was completed?" In Negotiable Paper he asked, "If A gives a note to B and B at the same time gives a note to A, for the same amount, and payable at the same time, the transaction being for their mutual accommodation, can they or not sue each other on such notes, and why? Will it make any difference whether or not the plaintiff in such an action has paid the note given by him?"[100]

In 1873 Langdell began to pose more complex hypotheticals, and the average number of questions for each examination was reduced from fifteen to ten. In first-year Contracts he asked, "A, of Bordeaux, having a quantity of brandy in New York, wrote to B, in New York, to whom the brandy had been consigned, offering to sell it to him on specified terms. B accepted the offer by letter, and immediately resold the brandy on his own account at a considerable profit. After the sale of the brandy by B, and before his letter of acceptance reached A, the latter died. Was there, or not, a contract of sale between A and B, and why? If there was, was it unilateral or bilateral and why?" Another question asked, "A vessel was chartered to proceed in ballast from London to Jamaica, and there receive a return cargo of sugar, which the charterer agreed to furnish at a stipulated rate of freight, 'provided she arrives out and ready by the 25th of June.' Was the charterer, or not, bound to furnish cargo, and why? Would it, or not, have made any difference if, instead of the above proviso, the charter-party had contained a stipulation that the vessel should arrive out and be ready to load by the 25th of June? Why?"[101]

While harking back to caseputting at the inns of court in London, such questions posed by written examinations in university-based professional education presented a remarkable innovation consistent with the principles of Langdell's case

100. In Harvard Law School, Annual Examinations, see Langdell, Contracts Special Paper Exam (June 1871) question 10; Langdell, "Negotiable Paper" (June 1871) question 2.

101. In Harvard Law School, Annual Examinations, see Langdell, Contracts, First Year (June 1873), questions 4, 10.

method. He was testing students' capacity to analyze particular legal situations and problems, rather than their recollection of definitions and doctrinal rules. As with his case method, however, most students did not respond positively to this innovation during the early 1870s. One of Kit's freshmen reported:

> Langdell's [examination] papers did not call for statements of the rules of law, but were designed to ascertain whether the students understood the principles sufficiently to apply them to supposed cases. Although they contained only matters which had been considered in his courses, they were considered "stiff" and even unfair. Many of those who had not attended his lectures failed to pass and were deeply disappointed, some openly indignant. They had passed the other examinations. It was discovered that a few who had not attended some of the other courses but had read the textbooks used, passed the examinations in those courses, receiving excellent marks.... Predictions of future disaster for the School were renewed with an increasing force. The year ended with a general belief that the new way was impracticable and impossible.... There was much interest in what Langdell would do. Those who had thought he would modify his method were disappointed. He made no change. This was attributed pretty generally to obstinacy; for it was felt, notwithstanding the enthusiasm of his followers, that the past year had demonstrated the folly of his way. He persisted, and indeed at no time made any modification whatever of his method of teaching [or examination] until in later years.[102]

Langdell's obstinacy was beneficial. As Roscoe Pound later observed, "Langdell's conception of an examination in the form of hypothetical cases calling for reasoned solutions has proved one of the most fruitful features of his method of teaching,"[103] and that conception gradually became the norm at HLS and in legal education generally. In this fashion, Langdell introduced into law schools—and university professional schools generally—the form of examination which "presented actual problems for solution."[104]

———≈———

During the 1870s, while exemplifying the pursuit of scholarship as a professor, Langdell fostered academic achievement among students through three signifi-

102. Fessenden, "Rebirth of the Harvard Law School," 506–7.
103. Pound, "Law School, 1817–1929," 495.
104. Batchelder, "Christopher C. Langdell," 441.

cant reforms in teaching his own courses. First, he introduced the sequencing of coursework by developing a required foundational course and advanced electives in teaching civil procedure, as well as contracts and equity. In addition, Langdell invented the pedagogy of case method and the genre of casebook. Through this inductive method, Langdell required students to read original sources rather than textbooks, to analyze particular controversies rather than general propositions, to formulate their own interpretations in response to questions, and to respond to hypotheticals and contrary judgments. He also exposed himself to questions and challenges and revised and corrected his own views in class. In this unprecedented fashion, Langdell sought to develop in students the independent, critical judgment that he himself modeled. Finally, Langdell introduced examination questions that required students to respond in writing to complex hypothetical problems. In this way, he assessed students' capacity to analyze particular problems, rather than recall general rules.

Despite vociferous disapproval from most students, alumni, and colleagues, Langdell obstinately and rapidly instituted these changes within his own classroom and courses during the 1870s. Establishing a schoolwide "system" of academic merit would entail an even more contentious process.

CHAPTER 5

Faculty, 1870–1900

Though elected dean in September 1870 and empowered by President Eliot to institute his vision for legal education, Langdell still needed a faculty committed to the idea of academic meritocracy: that scholastic achievement determines, or should determine, one's merit in professional life. But his work on Wall Street had convinced Langdell that contemporary legal practice cultivated in even the best lawyers sharp and deceptive tactics that ruined leaders of the bench and bar as potential faculty for law schools. He therefore needed a new source of law professors and decided to grow his own by introducing the revolutionary principle of hiring faculty according to their academic merit, as determined by their performance in professional school. If leading judges and lawyers were unsuited to be professors, then HLS would have to intercept "the very first men in [their] class"[1] before the bench and bar corrupted them.

President Eliot initially embraced the traditional standard of hiring law professors according to their professional experience and reputation, but Langdell soon persuaded him to adopt the new principle. Most observers, however, continued to object strongly, although they admired Langdell's deep commitment to legal scholarship. But this admiration turned to indignation at points when he appeared to be establishing himself as the model for a law professor, an approach that seemed arrogant, narrow-minded, and impractical. The new principle was also opposed by those objecting to Langdell's other reforms or to Eliot's procedural missteps in selecting candidates. Consequently, it was only when financial considerations counterbalanced the traditional standard that hiring decisions tipped in favor of Langdell's new approach during the contentious decades between 1870 and 1900.

Meanwhile, Langdell refined his view after initially regarding the two hiring standards as incompatible. He remained wary of the corrupting influence of con-

1. Langdell to Eliot (22 Nov. 1897).

temporary professional practice, but he had always believed that, properly conducted, a learned profession was perfectly consistent with, indeed required, high academic standards. As a result, he eventually decided that faculty candidates with extensive experience were acceptable so long as their commitment to his academic norms could be trusted. It was only in the early 1900s, when Langdell's students assumed control of the HLS faculty, that his original principle was unequivocally established as policy in the school. In this way, the new generation of academic meritocrats sought to replicate and validate themselves.

The New Hiring Standard of Academic Merit

In April 1870 the Harvard Corporation established in each faculty of the university the new office of dean, "whose duty it is to keep the records of the faculty, to prepare its business, and to preside at its meetings in the absence of the president."[2] Previously, HLS "had been managed by the faculty by mutual consultation.... There was no dean and very rarely any formal meeting of the faculty." The most senior professor, Theophilus Parsons, had served as effective head of the school, and the faculty expected that the next in line, Emory Washburn, would succeed Parsons.[3] But they knew that changes were afoot when Eliot nominated Langdell to replace Parsons.

During spring and summer 1870, Washburn, who had expressed reservations about hiring Langdell, found himself increasingly isolated, so the faculty meeting scheduled for late September 1870 to elect the first dean of HLS therefore promised to be contentious. However, Washburn immediately nominated Langdell and, joined by Nathaniel Holmes, voted him in, while Langdell said nothing and abstained. This move by Washburn and Holmes seems puzzling, particularly given Washburn's later complaint that this election was the turning point after which Langdell usurped control of the school. But in 1870 no one knew exactly what a dean did, and Washburn and Holmes assumed that the office was essentially clerical and took no interest it, while Eliot intended to empower Dean Langdell to reform the school. As a result, Washburn later alleged that Langdell and Eliot used the new office illegitimately to "usurp" control of the school, as epitomized by the offensive act that the HLS catalog began listing Dean Langdell right after the president and before Washburn.[4]

2. Harvard University, Corporation Records, 11:196 (8 Apr. 1870).
3. Quotation is from E. Washburn, "Harvard Law School," leaf 11v. See 3v; N. Holmes, *Journal*, 311.
4. E. Washburn, "Harvard Law School," leaf 3v. See C. Eliot, "Langdell," 519; Harvard Law School, Faculty Minutes (27 Sept. 1870).

Emory Washburn,
circa 1870. Courtesy
of Special Collections
Department, Harvard
Law School Library.

In hiring faculty, Langdell's ultimate objective was to establish "the teaching of law *as a career*,"[5] that is, a full-time vocation distinct from the practice of law. To be sure, Parker, Parsons, and Washburn had served as full-time, salaried professors at HLS, but this arrangement resulted from circumstance rather than policy. Only a few other schools paid regular salaries to law faculty. Nearly all law professors in the United States maintained a legal practice and taught part-time, receiving compensation directly from students' tuition. Langdell thus stood at the forefront of the professionalization of university faculty that evolved in the United States between the Civil War and World War I. Within that broad movement, the professionalization of faculty at Harvard and, more generally, in the social sciences buttressed Langdell's effort at the law school.[6] But the professionalization of faculty in law, medicine, engineering, and other professional domains faced powerful opposition from practitioners in the field who had traditionally filled the faculty role and thereby gained additional status and compensation. Despite this opposition, Langdell established the profession of law teaching by the end of his twenty-five-year tenure as dean at HLS, and other institutions followed the School's lead.

5. Langdell, "Harvard Law School, 1869–1894," 497–98. Emphasis in original.
6. See Buck, *Social Sciences at Harvard 1860–1920*; Haskell, *Emergence of Professional Social Science*;

The most significant aspect of this innovation lay in Langdell's new principle that full-time, permanent faculty should be hired according to their academic merit as determined by achievement in professional school. If accomplishment at the bench or bar qualified one to profess the law, then the emergence of "the teaching of law *as a career*" meant merely a difference in role within the same profession. Instead, Langdell repeatedly insisted about candidates for positions on the HLS faculty "that we ought to employ a man who... has received our honor degree."[7] Indeed, "a candidate for a professorship in the Law School... is required as a sine qua non to distinguish himself in the Law School... [by] being one of the very first men in his class."[8]

Not only was experience on the bench or at the bar therefore *insufficient* to make a law professor, but Langdell went further to maintain that such experience was *not necessary* for a law professor: "What qualifies a person, therefore, to teach law is not experience in the work of a lawyer's office, not experience in dealing with men, not experience in the trial or argument of causes—not experience, in short, in using law, but experience in learning law."[9] In fact, Langdell proceeded to the extreme heresy that accomplishment in legal practice was *not beneficial* to the professor and may, in fact, be *detrimental*. He believed that purity of academic merit was required of those who profess the law.

Langdell's extant writings never explicitly deprecate practice, yet his closest allies and sharpest critics attributed to him the view "that success at the Bar or on the Bench was, in all probability, a disqualification for the functions of a professor of law."[10] His critics thus warned that Langdell would hire faculty guided by "the idols of the cave which a school-bred lawyer is sure to substitute for the fact."[11] This hearsay evidence is credible because, during his fifteen years practicing in New York City, Langdell had expressed disgust at various points that success at the bar could be achieved through corruption, through personal favoritism, through incompetence by opposing counsel or by judges, through "sharp" tactics or improper use of procedural maneuvers, or through arts of rhetoric. Even without stooping to these measures, the practicing lawyer was inevitably compromised

Ross, *Origins of American Social Science*; Johnson, *Schooled Lawyers*, 21; Kimball, *True Professional Ideal*, 198–300.

7. Langdell to Eliot (22 Aug. 1892). See Harvard University, Corporation Records, 13:428–29 (19 Apr. 1886), a vote of the HLS faculty applying this standard.

8. Langdell to Eliot (22 Nov. 1897).

9. Langdell, Address 1886, 50. See Langdell to Eliot (22 Aug. 1892); Langdell, "Harvard Law School, 1869–1894," 495.

10. C. Eliot, "Langdell," 520.

11. Gray to Eliot (3 Jan. 1883).

by them, believed Langdell, who was fiercely committed "to win only by sheer force of merit."[12]

During the first two years of his administration in 1869–71, President Eliot enthusiastically hired at HLS part-time "lecturers who are engaged in the active practice of the profession."[13] But Langdell soon convinced Eliot that "the teaching of law is a difficult and honorable profession in itself, and cannot often be combined with . . . the practice of law, another absorbing profession."[14] Consequently, in the second year of Langdell's deanship, Eliot began to call for hiring "young men fresh from their studies, possessed of the most recent methods of instruction."[15]

By December 1874, Eliot, who remained committed to clinical education in other professional domains, had fully embraced Langdell's position, asserting: "*Law is to be learned almost exclusively from the books* in which its principles and precedents are recorded, digested, and explained. . . . The successful practitioner may or may not have the knowledge, tastes, and mental powers which go to make a good teacher of law, and the chances are against his having them. A good teacher of law in any high sense must be a thorough student by nature and habit; but it is well understood that a practitioner engrossed in business can hardly study any large subject with thoroughness, so manifold are the questions in quick succession brought to his attention."[16] Eliot repeatedly named Langdell as the source of his new conviction that "the teaching of law . . . cannot often be combined with, or late in life taken up in exchange for, the practice of law, . . . which appeals to different motives, develops different qualities, and holds out different rewards."[17]

Eliot's endorsement was necessary because he exercised significant control over faculty hiring, which followed a customary process at HLS between 1870 and 1900.[18] First, a candidate for an opening was suggested to Eliot or came directly to his notice, as did Langdell. Next, Eliot began to consult the dean and other senior faculty, as well as key members of the Corporation and Board of Overseers. If the candidate seemed worthy of further consideration, Eliot or an HLS professor who knew the individual well ascertained his interest in a professorship. At some point, the candidate was discussed at a faculty meeting where, by the 1890s, a

---

12. Ames, "Christopher Columbus Langdell, 1826–1906," 475.

13. C. Eliot, Annual Report 1869–70, 17. See C. Eliot, Annual Report 1870–71, 15.

14. C. Eliot, Annual Report 1881–82, 31.

15. C. Eliot, Annual Report 1871–72, 23.

16. C. Eliot, Annual Report 1873–74, 26–27. See E. Washburn, "Harvard Law School," leaf 7r. Emphasis added.

17. C. Eliot, Annual Report 1881–82, 31. See C. Eliot, Address 1895, 70; C. Eliot to Langdell [1892?]; C. Eliot, "Langdell," 520.

18. This uncodified process is revealed in the correspondence concerning individual appointments.

vote was taken. If there was agreement on all sides, Eliot sent a written offer; and if the candidate accepted, then Eliot proposed the candidate to the members of the Corporation. If they approved, the candidate responded with a final written acceptance. Meanwhile, the Corporation communicated its decision "to the Board of Overseers that they may consent thereto if they see fit."[19]

—*∿∿*—

Langdell's principle of hiring faculty according to their academic merit, uncontaminated by experience, was soon given effect. In spring 1872, Nathaniel Holmes recalled, "President Eliot called on me at my home, and said . . . that it was 'his painful duty' to inform me that the Corporation had voted that they would accept my resignation" for "'the good of the school.'" However, "interrupting him there, I remarked that I had my own opinions about that, which were not likely to be changed, and it was enough for me to know that they were willing to accept my resignation, and I would at once make way for a better man."[20]

Meanwhile, an unorthodox candidate, wholly opposite to Holmes, was emerging. After graduating from Harvard College in 1868 and teaching school, Ames had spent a year traveling and studying in Europe. He then attended HLS during Langdell's first two full academic years on the faculty, 1870–72. Earning excellent grades, particularly in Langdell's courses, and receiving the LL.B., Ames stayed for a third, postgraduate year at HLS.[21] In June 1873 twenty-seven-year-old Ames—at the urging of Langdell, with the concurrence of Eliot, and with the reluctant approval of the Harvard Corporation and Overseers—was given a five-year appointment as assistant professor of law, the first law professor in the United States who had never joined the bar or practiced law.[22]

Washburn "did not think it advisable" to replace Holmes with Ames,[23] and other senior HLS professors subsequently objected to hiring recent law graduates with little or no experience, as did influential members of the Harvard College administration, the Corporation, and the Board of Overseers. After all, "if you

19. Harvard University, Corporation Records, 12:18 (8 Dec. 1873). Records of the Corporation meetings often relate little more than their final, formal actions. In particular, the Corporation records do not usually include debate about subjects, since, "by tradition," the Corporation always acted in unanimity. Finding Aid to Harvard University Corporation Records, Harvard University Archives.

20. N. Holmes, *Journal*, 278. See E. Washburn, "Harvard Law School," leaf 7v. See *Centennial History of the Harvard Law School*, 220.

21. *Centennial History of the Harvard Law School*, 175–76; Harvard Law School, Grade Records, vol. 0, 1870–71, 1871–72.

22. C. Eliot, Annual Report 1872–73, 16–17; C. Eliot, "Langdell," 520.

23. E. Washburn, "Harvard Law School," leaf 8v.

James Barr Ames, circa 1874. Courtesy of Special Collections Department, Harvard Law School Library.

would teach baseball you would select not merely a teacher who knew the laws of projectiles, but one who had played the game himself."[24] This principled objection to Ames's appointment was surely strengthened by the sentiment of Washburn, Parsons, Holmes, and others that the forced resignations of Parsons and Holmes had violated the genteel norms of academic culture.

The factor outweighing these objections for the Corporation, the Overseers, and the president was money. Subject to the review of the Corporation, the president decided all financial matters relating to faculty appointments. Dean Langdell sometimes discussed salaries with prospective faculty out of convenience,[25] but he always referred the candidates to Eliot or the Corporation for definitive information. Even compensation for part-time lecturers was determined by Eliot.[26] By 1890 Eliot had established an unofficial policy that guided salaries and professorial promotions:

> The tenure of assistant professors is for five years. At the end of that time he ceases to be a member of the University, unless reappointed or promoted. The salary is $2,000 in the College; but in the Law School it is $2,250 a

24. Harvard University, Report of the Overseers Visiting Committee 1882–83, 2. This comment was made in a later episode of the same controversy, but because Ames had been a prominent baseball player at Harvard, the metaphor seems to indicate lingering resentment at his appointment. I am grateful to an anonymous reviewer for suggesting this link to Ames.

25. See Keener to Eliot (28 Dec. 1882); Wambaugh to Eliot (30 May 1892).

26. See C. Eliot to Brandeis, [1893]; C. Eliot to Langdell [circa 1894a].

year.... If you succeed as assistant professor, you may reasonably expect at the end of five years to be made a full professor; but the Corporation do not propose hereafter to pay a young man just made professor at the same rate that they pay the older professors.

The Corporation have laid down no rules, however, with regard to rates of salary for professors in the Law School. Within the past twenty years they have had at different times three grades of salary, $4,000, $4,500, and $5,000, the $5,000 salary having been reached only [in 1890]. I believe that they would pay a former assistant professor, when first made professor, a salary of $4,000, and that this salary, after a moderate number of years, would be advanced to $4,500, and later to $5,000; but the Corporation have not laid down a rule in this respect.

The amount of [teaching] expected of an assistant professor or professor in the Law School is six hours a week, but this amount has not been fixed by any action of the Corporation, and is only determined by custom—a custom of the professors themselves. All the present professors in the School have from time to time done more than six hours' work a week.[27]

These salaries were substantial. In 1890 assistant professors earned about fifteen times the annual tuition at HLS, and eleven times the average annual earnings of public school teachers, five times that of all nonfarm employees, and two-and-a-half times that of highly skilled workers. Full professors earned commensurately more: at least thirty times the annual tuition at HLS, and twenty-two times the average annual earnings of public school teachers, ten times that of all nonfarm employees, and five times that of highly skilled workers.[28] In relative terms HLS professors were paid very well.

But they focused on the fact that they "would receive in [legal] practice a very much larger income than their present salaries."[29] During the 1870s a successful lawyer in Boston made two to three times the salary of HLS professors. In 1890, when the Corporation raised the salary of full professors with ten years of tenure to $5,000, a successful lawyer in Boston or New York made at least three or four times that amount.[30] Furthermore, the annual income necessary to maintain a genteel lifestyle surpassed the salaries of Harvard professors during this period.

27. C. Eliot to Williston (23 Apr. 1890).
28. Kimball, *True Professional Ideal*, 254–70.
29. Ames to Eliot (7 Aug. 1903).
30. Gawalt, "Impact of Industrialization on the Legal Profession," 99; F. Parker to Adams (18 Dec. 1882); Ames to Eliot (7 Aug. 1903); Kimball, *True Professional Ideal*, 256–57.

In 1895 a Boston probate judge wrote a series of articles in *Scribner's Magazine* about the difficulty of living like a gentleman on an annual income of $10,000. In the 1880s his family had maintained their household and employed four maids on an annual income of $6,500 to $7,500. But "within the space of a decade, three amenities the gentry had previously taken for granted—servants, spacious housing, and superior private schooling for their children—were jeopardized by the rising cost of living," and "the gentry were rapidly being squeezed out" of their privileged place in American society.[31] HLS professors were falling even further behind the expectations of a genteel life.

Every full-time HLS professor directly or indirectly expressed dissatisfaction about these shortfalls at some point during the final third of the nineteenth century, and that financial constraint influenced faculty hiring no less than did the principled debate over whether professional experience or academic merit should determine faculty appointments. Further complicating these circumstances was the fact that Eliot veiled the financial considerations and, if forced to hire an inexperienced professor at a lower salary, cited instead Langdell's principle of hiring according to academic merit.

Eliot encountered, but did not mention, the financial constraint when he hired Langdell at an initial salary of $4,000. In late 1869 Eliot was seeking to replace Parsons, and an HLS alumnus and leading member of the New York bar observed to the president that Harvard did not pay enough to attract a top lawyer from an elite practice: "If you had the whole world to choose from, you could find a better man than Langdell, but your list must be a limited one."[32] The point was not confined to major cities. Another HLS alumnus refused to leave his lucrative practice in Providence, Rhode Island, to replace either Parker in 1868 or Parsons in 1869.[33]

Similarly, when Eliot consented to Langdell's recommendation to hire Ames based on his academic merit, the president had scarcely any other choices. Not only did Eliot realize that few leading lawyers or judges would accept a professor's salary, but HLS did not even have sufficient revenue to offer a full professor's salary to those few, due to "the shrinkage in the number of law students which resulted from the adoption of the Langdell case system" of teaching.[34] Consequently, the appointment of Ames as assistant professor had three expedient advantages for President Eliot: supporting his new dean, making a provisional appointment of

31. Persons, *Decline of American Gentility*, 102–3. See Grant, "Art of Living" (1895), 3–15, 615–27, 760.

32. J. Carter to Eliot (20 Dec. 1869). See Langdell, Check Ledger 1871–75. At some point after he was elected dean in fall 1870, the university provided Langdell with a house in which to live on campus.

33. J. Thayer to Eliot (13 Nov. 1869).

34. C. Eliot to Lane (2 Oct. 1922).

five years, and doing so at $2,000, rather than $4,000 per year. Eliot of course recognized, but never explicitly acknowledged, the financial constraints in connection with Ames's appointment.

Disputing the New Standard

In the ten years after 1873 HLS had four opportunities to replicate Ames's appointment, and each time selected instead a professor "from the ranks of the active profession."[35] The first was James B. Thayer who in fall 1874 assumed duties as a full professor. After graduating from Harvard College in 1852 and HLS in 1856, Thayer had practiced law for eighteen years and in his spare time written for major literary magazines. In addition, he contributed to legal scholarship and in 1870 agreed to edit the twelfth edition of Kent's famous *Commentaries on American Law*.[36] This appointment of an established, albeit scholarly, practitioner violated Langdell's principle of hiring young faculty according to their academic merit achieved in professional school.

Thayer's appointment and tenure also reveal how financial considerations weighed against the hiring of distinguished practitioners. Having declined a professorship in rhetoric at Harvard College in 1872 due to the salary, he was likewise reluctant to accept the law professorship,[37] and over the next twenty-five years complained more about finances than any other professor. Coming from a modest background, Thayer continually found himself torn between scholarship and writing "that will bring in money. Probably I shall have to print some learned stuff first, then the money-making thing."[38] In 1884 he inquired of Eliot whether he could apply for a scholarship for his son, Ezra, to attend Harvard College, and in 1890 the raise in full professors' salary to $5,000 largely resulted from Thayer's insistent prodding of Eliot.[39]

In fall 1874 a fifth full-time professorship became available to supplement Langdell, Washburn, Ames, and the newly hired Thayer. Langdell and Eliot desired to replicate the appointment of Ames, who "sympathized with Langdell in everything" and "was the subject of constant and extravagant eulogy on the part of the president," grumbled seventy-five-year-old Washburn. The dean and the

---

35. C. Eliot, Annual Report 1881–82, 31.

36. Hook, "Brief Life of James Bradley Thayer," 1–8; James P. Hall, "James Bradley Thayer," in Lewis, *Great American Lawyers*, 8:345–84.

37. J. Washburn to Thayer (5 Dec. 1873); Bradley to Thayer (9 Dec. 1873).

38. James B. Thayer to Sophy Thayer (17 June 1883), in J. Thayer, Correspondence and Memoranda, vol. 6, leaves 4–5.

39. C. Eliot to Thayer (16 Oct. 1884); J. Thayer to Eliot (10, 16 Oct. 1889).

president therefore preferred young Joseph D. Brannan, who had graduated from Harvard College in 1869, attended HLS with Ames during 1871–73, and was an excellent student and "a full believer in Langdell's case method." Washburn, feeling increasingly marginalized, favored John C. Gray, who had been teaching as a part-time lecturer since Langdell's first semester, spring 1870.[40]

After graduating from Harvard with a B.A. in 1859 and an LL.B. in 1861, Gray formed a law firm and served in the Union Army during the Civil War. He then practiced law and pursued scholarship on the side, founding and editing the *American Law Review*. A member of a wealthy mercantile family in Boston, Gray was well connected with the legal and social elite. His half-brother, Horace Gray, was named chief justice of the Massachusetts Supreme Judicial Court in 1873 and later associate justice of the U.S. Supreme Court. Having attended HLS in the late 1840s, Horace was one of those who, in the early 1870s, "predicted that Langdell would ruin the School."[41] This background incited Langdell's opposition to John, but attracted the favor of the Harvard Corporation, which rejected Brannan and appointed Gray a full professor in March 1875.[42]

Gray's appointment demonstrates again that professional reputation out-weighed Langdell's principle in hiring if the dissatisfaction with faculty salaries could be addressed. Gray never complained about compensation, because he was the only full-time professor at HLS who continuously practiced law for the next three decades, thus demonstrating indirectly that a law professor's salary was unsatisfactory.[43]

These two appointments in the mid-1870s tipped the five-member HLS faculty against Langdell and Ames. To be sure, Gray and Thayer had higher scholarly standards and aspirations than Washburn, and spent "the first year or two" sizing up the situation at HLS. But Washburn concluded that "Gray's views coincided substantially with Mr. Thayer's and my own," and "I became satisfied that Thayer and Gray's views were conservative and would not be [changed?] by Langdell."[44]

In April 1876 Washburn resigned, presenting the opportunity to Langdell and Eliot to shift the balance on the five-member faculty by hiring another recent graduate purely on the basis of academic merit. Washburn reported that, "in choosing

40. Quotations are from E. Washburn, "Harvard Law School," leaf 15v. See leaves 10v, 12r–v.

41. Fessenden, "Rebirth of the Harvard Law School," 508. See *Centennial History of the Harvard Law School*, 205–14; Siegel, "John Chipman Gray," 1527–29.

42. E. Washburn, "Harvard Law School," leaf 15v; Harvard University, Corporation Records, 12:105 (18 Mar. 1875).

43. C. Eliot to Lee (13 Mar. 1897). Gray spent one highly remunerative day a week in his office, administering the estates of wealthy Bostonians whom he knew through his social connections. Beale, "Langdell, Gray, Thayer, and Ames," 388; Siegel, "John Chipman Gray," 1528.

44. E. Washburn, "Harvard Law School," leaves 16r, 15v, 16r.

[my] successor the president was still anxious to select one who . . . would not vote against Langdell."[45] But the dean's critics saw the situation no less clearly, and moved quickly to propose the candidacy of Charles S. Bradley, who had attended HLS in 1840–41, developed a successful practice in Providence, and served as chief justice of Rhode Island's supreme court. Like Gray, Bradley had been lecturing at HLS since Langdell's first semester, spring 1870. But unlike Gray, Bradley gave little attention to scholarship or his lectures.[46]

Eliot opposed Bradley's candidacy, as doubtlessly did Langdell. Gray's position is not reported, and he may have avoided the dispute, having recently joined the faculty. The genial Thayer was Bradley's "dear cousin," and likely did not provide any opposition.[47] The leading advocate for Bradley was George Bigelow, a business associate of Washburn and a Fellow of the Harvard Corporation whose career was the antithesis of Langdell's vision. After graduating from Harvard College in 1829, Bigelow read law in his father's office and rose through legal practice to become chief justice of the Massachusetts Supreme Judicial Court from 1860 to 1868. Led by Bigelow, a majority of the Corporation approved Bradley who accepted the position of full professor in June 1876.[48] Bradley's appointment, following Gray's, was a second, even more resounding defeat for Langdell, Eliot, and Ames, the three advocates of establishing academic merit as the standard for hiring faculty. Here again, professional reputation trumped Langdell's principle in hiring because the financial constraint was alleviated. Bradley had a lucrative practice that he intended to sustain, so he was willing to join the faculty despite the relatively low salary.

Disgusted by Bradley's appointment, Ames submitted his resignation in March 1877 to take effect in the following September, one year before his original five-year contract as assistant professor was to end. The Corporation responded by promoting Ames to full professor in June 1877, having no other choice without repudiating the reforms that Langdell and Eliot had instituted in the law school over the previous seven years.[49] Langdell conveyed his disapproval of the Bradley

45. E. Washburn, "Harvard Law School," leaf 16v. See E. Washburn to Eliot (1 Apr. 1876).

46. Bradley to Eliot (2 June, 12 July 1870); *Centennial History of the Harvard Law School*, 198.

47. Quotation is from Bradley to Thayer (9 Dec. 1873). See E. Washburn, "Harvard Law School," leaf 16v.

48. E. Washburn, "Harvard Law School," leaf 16v. See Bradley to Eliot (27 June 1876); W. Davis, *Bench and Bar of Massachusetts*, 1:172.

49. Harvard University, Corporation Records, 12:254 (26 Mar. 1877); 12:273 (25 June 1877). Ames may have also felt a particular distaste for Bradley's jurisprudence. Louis Brandeis believed that "Ames and Bradley" represented the two "extremes" of the HLS faculty, the former being "the inflexible professor of the deductive method" and the latter a pure moralist. "Between these extremes, Ames and Bradley, there are . . . the views of the three other Professors"—Langdell, Thayer, Gray. Brandeis to Wehle (12 Nov. 1876).

appointment by omitting it from his annual report for the academic year 1876–77 and, again, for the academic year 1878–79, when Bradley resigned to return to practice full-time. As far as Langdell was concerned, Bradley was never on the HLS faculty.

Bradley's departure stemmed directly from his dissatisfaction with the faculty compensation. After indicating repeatedly in the late 1860s his reluctance to surrender his lucrative practice for a professorship, Bradley expressed to Eliot in the early 1870s that teaching as a part-time lecturer "take[s] too much time away from [my] practice for too little money."[50] During his three-year tenure as a full-time professor, Bradley commuted to Rhode Island in order to maintain his law practice, and "his lectures were frequently jotted down on the backs of envelopes during his train journey from Providence the same morning."[51] Thus, Bradley, like his cousin Thayer and, implicitly, like Gray, was not satisfied with the HLS salary. But rather than complain about it like Thayer or keep his supplemental work at a reasonable level like Gray, Bradley shirked his duties and eventually stepped down.

Bradley's resignation turned his appointment in favor of Langdell's principle. Even the dean's strongest critics at Harvard had to concede that Bradley's interest in practice had detracted from his professorial duties and that the appointment had been a mistake, and Langdell was not about to let them forget it. With unusual, if not singular, sarcasm, he later wrote, "it might have been thought best to leave [Washburn's] professorship vacant for a time.... However, an opportunity offered to make a brilliant and attractive appointment—one also which was urged by a strong and unanimous public in the legal profession of Boston—and accordingly the vacancy was filled" by Bradley.[52] Consequently, those proposing to hire experienced practitioners thereafter had to rebut the counterexample of Bradley.[53]

Bradley's departure at the end of the 1878–79 academic year brought the number of full-time professors down to four, but the declining enrollments and precarious finances at HLS precluded filling the vacancy. In fall 1881 enrollments had still not improved, yet Eliot received "certain assurances, as he supposed, that the money for a new endowment for a [fifth] professorship would be forthcoming," and he approached Oliver Wendell Holmes Jr. about his interest in joining the faculty in September 1882.[54] Eliot's choice is somewhat perplexing, even though Holmes was the son of a famous author and influential Harvard professor, Oliver

50. Quotation is from Bradley to Eliot (19 July 1870). See Bradley to Eliot (28 Apr. 1871, 2 Oct. 1872); J. Thayer to Eliot (13 Nov. 1869).

51. *Centennial History of the Harvard Law School*, 98. See Gurney to Eliot [3 Jan. 1883].

52. Langdell, Annual Report 1880–81, 76.

53. See Gurney to Eliot [3 Jan. 1883].

54. J. Thayer, Correspondence and Memoranda, 3:103.

Wendell Holmes. Nevertheless, Eliot's selection of the son was inconsistent with the Ames model, with Eliot's statements in favor of hiring recent law graduates, and with his support for Langdell.

Holmes fit the profile of Thayer and Gray because he was forty years old, had practiced law for fifteen years, and had pursued complementary scholarship by editing the twelfth edition of Kent's *Commentaries* and serving as editor of the *American Law Review*. His recently published *The Common Law* (1881) had not yet attracted much attention.[55] In addition, Holmes was "intimate" with Gray and was a colleague of Thayer,[56] and only a year earlier had insulted Langdell in a book review and then, without acknowledgment, borrowed and published many of Langdell's doctrinal insights on contracts in *The Common Law*. Thus, Holmes, though endorsed by recent HLS alumni who supported Langdell's reforms,[57] was aligned with Gray and Thayer, who by 1881 were warring with Langdell and Ames over academic reforms at HLS. Any new HLS professor would be forced to choose between the two entrenched camps, and, knowing all this, Eliot selected an ally of Thayer and Gray.

Eliot's reversal in choosing Holmes likely stemmed, in part, from the financial pressure on the school, whose enrollment was sinking ever lower. Before approaching Holmes, Eliot had not actually secured the endowment for a new professorship. After Holmes accepted Eliot's offer of a position in early November 1881, the supposed endowment did not appear, and Eliot began to approach Holmes's friends and supporters to raise the money. Upon learning this, Holmes retracted his acceptance two weeks later, embarrassed that the professorship might appear to be the result of personal influence rather than merit.[58]

Eliot's plan from the start may thus have been exactly what embarrassed Holmes. Eliot could not afford to hire another professor for HLS because enrollment had continued to drop. Holmes had many supporters on the bench and bar, and was well connected among elite Bostonians. A professorial chair for him was eminently fundable—as it turned out to be—so, if he agreed to come, then raising the endowment would not be difficult. But Holmes would not want his friends and supporters to be solicited on his behalf, so Eliot had to tell Holmes initially that he had virtually raised the endowment, that is, he "had certain assurances, as he supposed, that the money...would be forthcoming."[59] Such a strategy of

---

55. G. White, *Justice Oliver Wendell Holmes*, 149.

56. Quotation is from J. Thayer, Correspondence and Memoranda, 3:140. G. White, *Justice Oliver Wendell Holmes*, 113, 125–26.

57. J. Thayer, Correspondence and Memoranda, 3:103–7.

58. O. Holmes to Eliot (1, 18 Nov. 1881).

59. J. Thayer, Correspondence and Memoranda, 3:103.

exploiting support for Holmes to secure a professorship for HLS helps to explain Eliot's selection of Holmes.

Whether or not the president was responding to the financial constraint on the school, Holmes himself brought up the issue of faculty salaries, prompted by conversations with Thayer. Holmes wrote to Eliot that the HLS professorship "will involve a pecuniary sacrifice which ... would probably be considerable," and he wanted to be assured "that as soon as any law professor's salary is raised mine should be."[60] In response, Eliot explained the policy on faculty raises and rebutted Thayer's claim, reported by Holmes, that a raise was forthcoming.[61] Holmes did not stay long enough for salary to become a point of contention, but clearly the seeds of a dispute were sown in these negotiations about his appointment.

Apart from the financial constraints, Eliot's selection of an ally of Gray and Thayer was complicated by the procedural misstep that he seems not to have consulted Langdell or Ames before choosing Holmes. As a result, when Eliot asked at an HLS faculty meeting in January 1882 after Holmes withdrew, whether anyone was willing to seek an endowment for a professorship for Holmes, he was met by silence. Then Langdell opined that raising such an amount would be impossible, and Ames concurred.[62] Thayer, however, said that he would try to solicit the funds, and did so within a few days. With the endowment in hand, Eliot again offered the professorship, to begin September 1882, and Holmes accepted a second time on very attractive terms. He was put on the payroll six months early and, while other full professors were assigned an overload of seven class hours weekly for the 1882–83 academic year, Holmes was given four-and-a-half weekly hours.[63] The entire arrangement was another major defeat for Langdell and Ames, who were marginalized throughout the process.

Then, early in December 1882, Holmes abruptly resigned after one semester to accept an appointment to the Massachusetts Supreme Judicial Court. Eliot, Thayer, and Gray were stunned and found the outcome "highly disagreeable."[64] Thayer observed, "my experience with [Holmes] ... which I had been willing to forget, comes all back again—that he is, with all his attractive qualities and his solid attainments, wanting sadly in the noblest region of human character—selfish, vain, thoughtless of others." Langdell, who on short notice had to teach Holmes's courses in the spring, conveyed his disgust by treating the appointment like that of Bradley and

60. O. Holmes to Eliot (1 Nov. 1881).

61. C. Eliot to Holmes (4 Nov. 1881); J. Thayer, Correspondence and Memoranda, 3:141–42.

62. J. Thayer, Correspondence and Memoranda, 3:103–4.

63. Harvard University, Corporation Records, 13:115 (23 Jan. 1882); J. Thayer, Correspondence and Memoranda, 3:104–8, 141–42; Harvard Law School, *Catalog 1882–83*.

64. J. Thayer, Correspondence and Memoranda, 3:140.

omitting it from his annual report for 1882–83.[65] To the end of his career, "Langdell was never reconciled" to Holmes's resignation, Eliot later recalled.[66] Holmes had deserted the School at its most vulnerable moment, with enrollment at its lowest point, after special accommodations had been made to hire him.

———∿∿∿———

The debacle of the Holmes appointment vastly worsened and complicated the disagreement over Langdell's new standard for hiring law faculty. More than ten years had passed since Eliot had commended hiring "young men fresh from their studies, possessed of the most recent methods of instruction."[67] Ames was no longer such a young man, and no similar appointment had been made. Meanwhile, since Washburn's retirement in 1876, the attempts to fill the vacant fifth professorship while placating those demanding experience in legal practice had resulted in two disasters. Given all this, Langdell surely felt that Eliot owed him a chance to hire according to the Ames model. Moreover, Langdell and Ames argued that the resignation of Bradley, and perhaps Holmes, confirmed the reasons for hiring recent, meritorious graduates.[68] Bradley and Holmes had vastly different interests. One had chosen the remuneration of the bar; the other the public stature of the bench. Yet, common to both was a lack of commitment to the School and to "the teaching of law *as a career*." HLS had been injured precisely because it had not hired recent law graduates qualified by and committed to academic merit demonstrated purely by achievement in the classroom.

Eliot was quickly persuaded to reverse course once again. Still feeling "very annoy[ed]" at Holmes a month later,[69] Eliot likely wanted to make amends with Langdell and signal his strong support for the dean he considered most successful. Perhaps, too, Eliot concluded that Langdell's principle had more to recommend it than he had realized. Hence, scarcely two weeks after Holmes's stunning resignation on December 9, Eliot tried to replicate the Ames appointment by offering a full-time assistant professorship to William A. Keener, who had graduated from Emory College in 1874, earned an LL.B. from HLS in 1877, studied for a third year as a resident bachelor of laws in 1877–78, and then practiced in New York City for four years. On 28 December 1882 Keener accepted the nomination in writing.[70]

65. J. Thayer, Correspondence and Memoranda, 3:143–44. See Langdell, Annual Report 1882–83, 90–95.

66. C. Eliot to Holmes (28 Mar. 1924).

67. C. Eliot, Annual Report 1871–72, 23.

68. Gurney to Eliot [3 Jan. 1883].

69. C. Eliot to Dunbar (11 Jan. 1883). See C. Eliot to Holmes (28 Mar. 1924).

70. Harvard Law School, Grade Records, vol. 0, 1874–75, 1875–76; Keener to Eliot (28 Dec. 1882); *Centennial History of the Harvard Law School*, 222–23.

While changing course again by making a selection "which was practically decided the other way in the nomination of Holmes,"[71] Eliot made a procedural error that indicated his eagerness to atone for the Holmes appointment. First, the normally patient and deliberate Eliot moved unnecessarily fast. Second, while directly involving Langdell,[72] Eliot did not consult Gray or Thayer. Thus, on the very same day that Keener wrote to Eliot accepting the nomination, Gray wrote to Eliot urging patience in naming a candidate to replace Holmes.[73]

As a result, Eliot's selection soon unraveled. On 2 January 1883, at an HLS faculty meeting attended by all four professors, Eliot announced that Keener had been offered and had accepted the nomination. On the same day, Eliot completed the draft of his annual report for the previous academic year, 1881–82, and forecast the appointment of Keener by announcing Holmes's resignation and arguing the merits of hiring assistant professors with academic merit and little experience.[74] Eliot read this section of the draft to Ephraim Gurney, his longtime friend and principal adviser, who had clashed with Langdell while serving as dean of Harvard College in the 1870s and would be named a Fellow of the Harvard Corporation in 1884.[75]

In the week after the January 2 faculty meeting, Gray, Gurney, and Thayer separately protested against the process and substance of Keener's appointment. Far from disillusioning them about hiring experienced practitioners, Holmes's appointment had seemed to inspire them with the prospect of outvoting Langdell. Liberation from Langdell's "ruinous follies" was within reach. On January 3 Gray wrote to Eliot "that students of law should be taught . . . by men who ha[ve] considerable practical experience" and "that to choose an inexperienced assistant professor would be . . . most injurious" because "a school where the majority of the professors shuns and despises contact with actual facts, has got the seeds of ruin in it and will go and ought to go to the devil."[76]

Gurney also preached doom: "Langdell, running the School at his pleasure, would wreck it. . . . His ideal is to breed professors of Law, not practitioners; erring as it seems to me, on the other side from the other schools, which would make only practitioners. . . . If the appointment of Keener—of whom I never heard till yesterday . . . —means that the School commits itself to . . . breeding within itself

71. Gurney to Eliot [3 Jan. 1883].
72. Keener to Eliot (28 Dec. 1882).
73. Gray to Eliot (28 Dec. 1882).
74. Harvard Law School, Faculty Minutes (2 Jan. 1883); C. Eliot, Annual Report 1881–82, 32.
75. *Boston Evening Transcript*, 13 Sept. 1886; Gurney to Eliot [3 Jan. 1883].
76. Quotations are from Gray to Eliot (3 Jan. 1883). This letter is undated, but Gray wrote "to say what I could not well say last night" at the faculty meeting, which occurred on January 2.

its course of instruction and thus severs itself from...the courts and the bar, it commits the gravest error of policy which it could adopt."[77]

On January 7 Thayer took the even more radical step of going over Eliot's head and complaining directly to John Quincy Adams Jr., one of the five Fellows of the Harvard Corporation. Adams replied sympathetically and evidently persuaded Eliot to allow Thayer, Gray, and others the opportunity to find a distinguished practicing lawyer to fill the vacancy left by Holmes. On January 9 Eliot withdrew the offer to Keener, who agreed to be held in reserve.[78] For the next five months various Overseers, Corporation Fellows, and HLS alumni tried "to secure as [Holmes'] successor someone of large experience in the practice of the law and, if possible, of wide reputation in the profession."[79] Joseph H. Choate of New York, Jeremiah Smith of New Hampshire, and Louis Brandeis of Boston were suggested, among others.[80] No suitable and willing candidate appeared, so on May 14 the Corporation appointed Keener an assistant professor for five years on a salary of $2,250.[81] Though concurring a month later, the Overseers regretted this outcome and encouraged "continued efforts...in filling the [full] professorship still vacant" with an experienced practitioner.[82]

In this confrontation between advocates of the two hiring standards—complicated by opposition arising from Langdell's curricular reforms and Eliot's lack of consultation—financial considerations ultimately tipped the balance in favor of Langdell's principle. As Corporation Fellow Adams wrote to Thayer, defending the choice of Keener: "There are two cogent arguments which are most difficult to answer so far as I am personally concerned. 1st, [HLS] funds are too low to pay the full professorial staff from lack of [students]. 2nd. I am at my wits end to find a man...willing to take the place who could do us any good."[83] Financial constraint thus trumped the principle of hiring a distinguished lawyer or judge. Even the academic star and recent graduate Brandeis could not be enticed from his lucrative law practice to join the faculty as an assistant professor at a salary of

77. Gurney to Eliot [3 Jan. 1883]. Gurney's undated letter was written after the announcement of Keener's appointment to the Harvard Law School faculty (Jan. 2) and before a month had passed after the resignation of Holmes (Dec. 9).

78. J. Adams to Thayer (9 Jan. 1883); Keener to Eliot (11 Jan. 1883).

79. Harvard University, Report of the Overseers Visiting Committee 1882–83, 2.

80. Gurney to Eliot [3 Jan. 1883], leaf 9; Noble to Eliot (20 Apr. 1883); Brandeis to Brandeis (30 May 1883).

81. Harvard University, Corporation Records, 13:214 (14 May 1883). See Scudder to Hoar (9 June 1883).

82. Harvard University, Report of the Overseers Visiting Committee 1882–83, 2. See Harvard University, Overseers Records, 3:244 (15 June 1883).

83. J. Adams to Thayer (9 Jan. 1883).

$2,250.[84] Advocates of practical experience or academic merit might argue passionately about the appropriate standard for hiring, but in the end the list of available candidates had to "be a limited one."[85] After only a few years in practice, even a recent graduate, such as Keener, hesitated to come to HLS due to "the sacrifice from a pecuniary standpoint," and requested that his starting salary be raised so that "I would be relieved from no little anxiety."[86]

Keener's concern about salary soon led to his resignation. In the mid-1880s enrollments rose dramatically, and in 1888–89 HLS enjoyed "a third year of decided prosperity" and accumulated a significant budget surplus. At that point, Eliot worsened the dissatisfaction over salaries by announcing in his annual report that "the time is approaching when the teaching staff can be again enlarged."[87] Thayer requested that, instead, "the salaries of the professors be now increased to 5,000 dollars."[88] A few months later, in 1890, the Corporation granted the increase for full professors, but did not include Keener because he had been promoted to full professor only two years earlier in 1888. Believing that a salary increase had been promised him upon his hiring, Keener angrily resigned in March 1890 and moved to Columbia University law school.[89]

Dissatisfaction with salary thus limited not only hiring but also retaining faculty, and the limitations were compounded by Eliot's desire to sublimate the financial issue. Without spending much more money, Eliot could have alleviated dissatisfaction by taking the initiative, moving sooner, and expressing concern rather than reticence about salaries. In any case, the pattern of hiring the seven full-time professors between 1870 and 1889—Langdell, Ames, Thayer, Gray, Bradley, Holmes, and Keener—indicates that Langdell's principle of hiring according to academic merit, though supported by Eliot, was outweighed by the hiring standard of professional experience and reputation, unless financial considerations counterbalanced that traditional standard and tipped hiring decisions in favor of academic merit.

84. F. Parker to Adams (18 Dec. 1882); Brandeis to Brandeis (30 May 1883); Auerbach, *Unequal Justice: Lawyers and Social Change*, 67–73.

85. J. Carter to Eliot (20 Dec. 1869).

86. Keener to Eliot (28 Dec. 1882).

87. Quotations are from C. Eliot, Annual Report 1888–89, 20. In private correspondence with President Daniel C. Gilman of Johns Hopkins University, Eliot had indicated earlier that Harvard would not pay the higher salaries being offered by Hopkins because that would entail "making a considerable reduction of force." C. Eliot to Gilman (23 Mar. 1876).

88. J. Thayer to Eliot (10 Oct. 1889), in C. Eliot, Papers, box 77.

89. J. Thayer to Eliot (16 Oct. 1889); C. Warren, *History of the Harvard Law School*, 2:444.

Langdell Refines His Standard

In response to Keener's resignation in March 1890, Eliot reversed himself yet again and stumbled in the procedure. He nominated a distinguished and gentlemanly practitioner, Jeremiah Smith, who had graduated from Phillips Exeter Academy, Harvard College, and then HLS in 1861 under the ancien régime. After serving as a justice of the New Hampshire Supreme Court, Smith practiced law for nearly twenty years. His background resembled most closely that of Nathaniel Holmes and Bradley, and his lack of scholarly background created difficulties for him in adjusting to his professorial role in the 1890s.[90]

In making this surprising nomination, Eliot again acted unnecessarily quickly, writing to Smith with the offer on the very same day that Keener submitted his resignation. In fact, Smith asked Eliot for "a little time for consideration" because "I . . . can hardly decide in a moment whether to make such a complete change."[91] In addition, Eliot did not consult Ames, an important colleague who was likely to object. Ames was therefore upset at both the process and selection, leading him to conclude "that [Eliot] and I take mostly different views as to the function of the Law Faculty."[92]

Eliot evidently had consulted Langdell, who approved Smith's appointment, indicating a change, or refinement, in the dean's view. It is difficult to fathom Langdell's assent unless it stemmed from a long, personal relationship with Smith, which is indicated by several facts. During the bleak year of 1850 Langdell apparently served as a private tutor for Smith, then a thirteen-year-old Exeter student whose father was a prominent jurist in New Hampshire. In the early 1870s Langdell collaborated with Smith in a financial campaign for Exeter, and eventually named Smith in his will to be one of the appraisers of his estate.[93] Hence, the appointment of Smith—and of other faculty subsequently— indicates that, with his academic system firmly instituted at HLS after 1890, Langdell was willing to appoint distinguished practitioners who supported the HLS system. This was the distinction between Smith and either Bradley or Nathaniel Holmes.

Consequently, Langdell's principle of hiring faculty according to their academic

90. "Obituaries [of Jeremiah Smith]," 18–19; Williston, "Jeremiah Smith," 157; Beale, "Jeremiah Smith," 1–8.

91. J. Smith to Eliot (12 Mar. 1890). It is reported that Eliot was so impressed with a talk that Smith gave to Harvard undergraduates that Eliot decided to offer Smith an appointment. See Williston, "Jeremiah Smith," 157.

92. Ames to Eliot (10 Mar. 1890).

93. Ames, "Christopher Columbus Langdell, 1826–1906," 469; Langdell, Will (1906); "Obituaries [of Jeremiah Smith]" ; Starks, "Christopher Columbus Langdell."

merit, though consistent with devaluing practice, did not necessarily entail that corollary. In the 1870s and early 1880s Langdell's curricular system of academic merit was gradually instituted, and he believed that only those who had succeeded in the system could appreciate and support it. Hence, only recent stellar graduates—such as Ames, Brannan, and Keener—were acceptable candidates for the faculty. In the 1870s and early 1880s, having extensive experience implied lack of appreciation for Langdell's system of academic merit. After 1890 Langdell began to support the hiring of experienced practitioners whose commitment to academic merit he felt he could trust on the basis of either a personal relationship or achievement within the new academic system.[94]

In April 1890 Smith accepted the fifth full-time professorship.[95] Having accumulated considerable property in the practice of law, the fifty-three-year-old Smith expressed no concern about salary, and had no disagreement with Eliot on this issue.[96] As with Gray, Smith's situation implicitly confirmed that HLS salaries were satisfactory only for those with significant outside resources.[97] Perhaps Smith's financial security even contributed to Eliot's surprising selection of him.

Concurrent with the appointment of Smith, a sixth professorship opened in spring 1890 due to burgeoning enrollments, and Eliot nominated the third assistant professor, after Ames and Keener, to fit closely the model of hiring "young men of mark, who have shown a genius for law and a desire for the life of a teacher and student...at an early age."[98] After graduating from Harvard College in 1882 and HLS in 1888 as an excellent student and one of the founders of the *Harvard Law Review*, Samuel Williston served as a clerk for U.S. Supreme Court Justice Horace Gray and then joined a law firm in Boston. Williston immediately accepted Eliot's offer, and the Corporation made the appointment at the end of April 1890.[99] In this fashion, Langdell apparently insisted on quid pro quo in faculty appointments during the 1890s notwithstanding the refinement in his position: distinguished practitioners were acceptable if they had demonstrated their allegiance to the HLS system. At the same time, these appointments had to be balanced by hiring recent graduates.

Meanwhile, Eliot tried to alleviate faculty dissatisfaction about salary. First, he

94. Ames, however, remained committed to appointing only those like himself. Langdell's deviation from the model, first instanced in the appointment of Smith, may have caused a temporary rift between Langdell and Ames, which Eliot observed but Ames denied. Ames to Eliot (10 Mar., 28 Sept. 1890).

95. J. Smith to Eliot (10 Apr. 1890).

96. Putnam to Eliot (25 Apr. 1891); J. Smith to Eliot (4 Jan. 1907); C. Eliot to Smith (5 Jan. 1907).

97. See Ames to Eliot (7 Aug. 1903).

98. C. Eliot, Annual Report 1881–82, 31–32.

99. Williston to Eliot (22 Apr. 1890); C. Eliot to Williston (23 Apr. 1890).

attempted to clarify the issue when appointing assistant professors. After twenty years of addressing misunderstandings and false expectations, it seemed to Eliot "desirable to state to [a new appointee] just what an assistant professor of law may look forward to as an academic career."[100] While this approach reduced complaints from assistant professors, Eliot placated the full professors for the next decade by raising salaries in 1890. This raise to $5,000 turned out to be well timed because the deflationary trend in consumer prices over the previous two decades culminated in the recession of 1893. By 1896 the 52 percent deflation since 1873 meant that the purchasing power of the HLS professor's salary in 1896 amounted to about $7,500 in 1870 as compared to the $4,000 that Langdell had been paid.[101]

Nevertheless, salary negotiations with experienced lawyers remained awkward, as when a scholarly practitioner, loyal to Langdell's system, was appointed full professor in 1892. After graduating from Harvard College in 1876 and excelling as a student at HLS from 1877 to 1880, Eugene Wambaugh returned to his home state of Ohio and worked as a lawyer in Cincinnati for ten years. He then accepted a professorship at the University of Iowa law school, and led the conversion to case method teaching. In February 1892 Wambaugh was chosen to be dean of the new law school at Western Reserve University in order to install "the Harvard system."[102] While Wambaugh was negotiating with Western Reserve, HLS decided, due to enrollment increases, to break its first-year class into two divisions, doubling the number of first-year courses and necessitating the hiring of additional faculty. Consequently, the practitioners and the academicians on the HLS faculty united in endorsing Wambaugh because he was an accomplished lawyer who had demonstrated his academic merit and wholehearted commitment to "the Harvard system."[103]

In offering the professorship to Wambaugh during Eliot's absence, Langdell tried to explain "the present practice of the Corporation" regarding salary, cautioning that "some one representing the Corporation can alone speak with authority on the subject." Wambaugh later wrote to Eliot requesting "definite information" on his salary from "some one representing the Corporation," and asking "Am I right in believing that you are the person to whom I should apply?" Eliot replied at length that the Corporation had set Wambaugh's salary according to the

100. C. Eliot to Williston (23 Apr. 1890).

101. Langdell, Check Ledger 1871–75; Kimball, *True Professional Ideal*, 260–62.

102. Quotation is from Wambaugh to Thayer (17 Feb. 1892). See Wambaugh to Thayer (30 Mar. 1889). Beginning in 1891, Wambaugh had published several relevant works: *Cases on Evidence* (1891); *The Best Education for a Lawyer* (1892); *The Study of Cases: A Course of Instruction in Reading and Stating reported Cases* (1892).

103. Wambaugh to Thayer (17 Feb. 1892); Langdell to Wambaugh (26 Mar. 1892).

provisions stated by Langdell, and that Wambaugh could have contacted the Corporation treasurer with questions, though this would have been unprecedented. Thus, the dean pointed to the Corporation, including the president, who pointed back to the dean. No one, it seemed, wanted to tell Wambaugh directly and finally that his salary would be $4,000. Wambaugh replied by thanking Eliot for the information and apologizing for "the awkwardness of a person necessarily ignorant of the proper way to approach the Corporation."[104]

Consistent with the quid pro quo policy, a recent graduate with a background similar to Ames's was appointed assistant professor, complementing Wambaugh's appointment. After graduating from Harvard College in 1882, Joseph Beale taught secondary school for a year, entered HLS in 1884, and graduated in 1887, having helped to found the *Harvard Law Review*. After spending a few years in private practice, he became a lecturer at HLS from 1890 until 1892, when he was named assistant professor.[105]

With these appointments in mind, Langdell announced in 1894 that the Ames model "of recruiting the teaching force, and of filling professors' chairs, has become the settled policy of the School."[106] But he certainly exaggerated. The promotions of Williston in 1895 and Beale in 1897 to full professor demonstrated only that, after twenty-five years, the Ames model was an acceptable alternative for recruitment. HLS still sought academic practitioners, although financial considerations weighed against their appointment.

In 1897 HLS offered a full professorship to Blewett Lee, who had been a stellar student at HLS and moved to Chicago where he practiced full-time and taught as a full professor at the law school of Northwestern University. Lee did not accept the HLS offer because "to do so would involve some pecuniary sacrifice and giving up the practice of my profession to which I am considerably attached."[107] Balancing the offer to Lee, HLS hired an assistant professor, Frank Williams, who had graduated from HLS in 1895 and then served as an instructor during 1896–97.[108]

In spring 1898 HLS turned back to the model of academic practitioners and selected Brannan with the approval of Langdell, which demonstrates the refinement in his view. Twenty-five years earlier, Langdell had unsuccessfully advocated the hiring of Brannan, a classmate of Ames, over Gray. Brannan then returned

---

104. Langdell to Wambaugh (26 Mar. 1892); Wambaugh to Eliot (30 May and circa 5 June 1892); C. Eliot to Wambaugh [circa May 1892].

105. Williston, "Joseph Henry Beale," 686–89; Pound, "Joseph Henry Beale," 695–98; Frankfurter, "Joseph Henry Beale," 701–3.

106. Langdell, "Harvard Law School, 1869–1894," 495.

107. C. Eliot to Lee (13 Mar. 1897); Lee to Eliot (15 Mar. 1897).

108. *Centennial History of the Harvard Law School*, 286–87. Williams served only one year as assistant professor.

home to Ohio and became a prominent practitioner in Cincinnati, and taught at the University of Cincinnati law school in the mid-1890s, while maintaining his allegiance to "undoubtedly the best system of teaching law" at HLS.[109] In 1898 Brannan was nominated solely with the support of Langdell, Ames, and Eliot, since the other HLS faculty "did not know him."[110] Successful practice no longer disqualified a candidate in Langdell's mind, if he knew that the candidate had demonstrated allegiance to the HLS system of academic merit.

Consistent with that standard, the HLS faculty concurrently opposed hiring another distinguished practitioner who had fallen far short of the "sine qua non ... of being one of the very first men in his class."[111] After searching unsuccessfully for several years to fill a professorship in international law, Eliot offered the position to Edward H. Strobel, who had performed poorly as a student at HLS in the early 1880s, then practiced law in New York City for three years, and worked in the diplomatic service of the United States for thirteen years.[112] Evidently anticipating opposition from the HLS faculty, Eliot—as with the Keener and Smith appointments—avoided consulting those who would protest and secured the Corporation's approval in May 1898. But the academic meritocrats and scholarly practitioners on the HLS faculty closed ranks and protested the appointment of Strobel both on procedural and on substantive grounds. In a formal letter to Eliot and the Corporation, the law professors stated "that the Faculty should be consulted before the appointment of professors and instructors of Law" and that Strobel "is not qualified either by his legal training in the Law School, or by his subsequent legal experience, to conduct any of the courses in private law." Then the faculty detailed Strobel's inferior performance as a student at HLS.[113]

To balance Strobel, the HLS faculty then appointed Jens I. Westengard an assistant professor in May 1899. Born in Chicago in 1871, Westengard had entered HLS in the fall of 1895 by passing the admissions examination, since he had not completed a college degree. Westengard not only passed the higher academic requirements set for those entering by examination, but graduated second in his class of 129 in 1898.[114]

---

109. Brannan to Thayer (3 June 1897). See Taft to Thayer (11 June 1898); Wilby to Eliot (11 June 1898).

110. C. Eliot to Ames [circa June 1898]; "Record of the [Harvard Law School] Faculty voting on the appointment of Mr. Brannan," C. Eliot, Papers, box 268–269, f. June 1898.

111. Langdell to Eliot (22 Nov. 1897).

112. C. Warren, *History of the Harvard Law School*, 2:464–65; C. Eliot to Strobel (19 May 1898).

113. Langdell and Gray, leaders of the two factions on the Harvard Law School faculty, were absent, but doubtlessly concurred with the protest. Ames to Eliot (6 June 1898). See also J. Thayer, Papers, box 20, f. 2.

114. Beale, "Jens Iverson Westengard."

Overall, the full-time professorial appointments at HLS, listed in table 3, reveal the stiff opposition encountered by Langdell in establishing academic merit as the standard for hiring faculty. Until 1890 Langdell's principle of hiring according to academic merit, though supported by Eliot, was outweighed by the hiring standard of professional experience and reputation, unless financial considerations counterbalanced that traditional standard and tipped hiring decisions in favor of academic merit. When assistant professors in the Ames mold began to be hired after 1890, they were outnumbered by new appointments of practicing lawyers. The conflict between the two hiring standards is evidenced by the bimodal distribution of the faculty, all of whom had either more than ten years of experience or less than five years. It was only after 1900 that recent graduates like Ames became the norm for new faculty appointees.

Complicating the debate between 1870 and 1900 was Eliot's desire to avoid addressing or admitting the financial constraint on hiring faculty at HLS. Certainly, he knew the dilemma, for, like presidents of other leading universities, he received inquiries or nominations for professorships from distinguished judges or lawyers who, upon finding that "the salary was ridiculously small,...withdrew."[115] Yet, apart from his first annual report, Eliot scarcely acknowledged the financial limitation in his public statements about hiring faculty. In private correspondence, he even told the president of Johns Hopkins University in 1876 that he preferred enlarging the faculty to increasing salaries.[116] Although the Ames model was employed only twice between 1870 and 1890 and both times was resorted to when HLS could not afford a senior, experienced lawyer, Eliot repeatedly extolled Langdell's principle of hiring "young men of mark, who have shown a genius for law and a desire for the life of a teacher and student...at an early age."[117] Only once in his public statements promoting the Ames model did Eliot acknowledge in passing "the increasing difficulty of obtaining and retaining suitable professors" from the bench and bar.[118] Also complicating the process was the refinement in Langdell's view. After initially regarding the two hiring standards as incompatible, he decided in about 1890 that faculty candidates with extensive experience were acceptable so long as their commitment to the HLS academic system could be trusted and their appointments were balanced by young academic meritocrats in the mold of Ames.

115. Putnam to Eliot (25 Apr. 1891).

116. C. Eliot to Gilman (23 Mar. 1876). See C. Eliot, Annual Report 1869–70, 16.

117. C. Eliot, Annual Report 1881–82, 31–32.

118. C. Eliot, Annual Report 1881–82, 31. Cf. C. Eliot, Annual Reports 1872–73, 16–17; 1873–74, 27; C. Eliot, Address 1895, 70; C. Eliot to Langdell [1892?]; C. Eliot, "Langdell," 520.

TABLE 3 Full-Time HLS Professors Classified by Years in Legal Practice, 1870–1900

Academic Years	Faculty with Ten or More Years in Legal Practice	Faculty with Less than Five Years in Legal Practice	
		Names	Percentage
1870–71	*Langdell*, Washburn, N. Holmes		0
1871–72	Langdell, Washburn, N. Holmes		0
1872–73	Langdell, Washburn		0
1873–74	Langdell, Washburn	*Ames*	33
1874–75	Langdell, Washburn, *Thayer*	Ames	25
1875–76	Langdell, Washburn, Thayer, *Gray*	Ames	20
1876–79	Langdell, Thayer, Gray, *Bradley*	Ames	20
1879–82	Langdell, Thayer, Gray	Ames	25
1882–83	Langdell, Thayer, Gray, *Holmes*	Ames	20
1883–90	Langdell, Thayer, Gray	Ames, *Keener*	40
1890–92	Langdell, Thayer, Gray, *Smith*	Ames, *Williston*	33
1892–97	Langdell, Thayer, Gray, *Smith, Wambaugh*	Ames, Williston, *Beale*	38
1897–98	Langdell, Thayer, Gray, Smith, Wambaugh	Ames, Williston, Beale, *Williams*	44
1898–99	Langdell, Thayer, Gray, Smith, Wambaugh, *Brannan, Strobel*	Ames, Williston, Beale	30
1899–1900	Langdell, Thayer, Gray, Smith, Wambaugh, Brannan, Strobel	Ames, Williston, Beale, *Westengard*	36

Note: Emphasis indicates faculty newly appointed at the beginning of the period of academic years.

Notwithstanding these complications, Langdell had established "the teaching of law *as a career*" by the time of his retirement as dean in 1895.[119] In that year, Thayer presented a noted "justification for the professional role of the American law teacher" to the Section on Legal Education of the American Bar Association.[120] In 1898 the eminent English law professor Albert Dicey visited the United States and observed the "final triumph of the Harvard professoriate" in establishing the

119. See Harvard University, Report of the Overseers Visiting Committee 1896–97, 530.
120. Konefsky and Schlegel, "Mirror, Mirror on the Wall," 848. See Schlegel, "Between the Harvard Founders and the American Legal Realists," 316. See J. Thayer, "Teaching of English Law," 169–84.

Harvard Law School faculty, circa 1900. Top row, left to right: John C. Gray, Joseph D. Brannan, Jeremiah Smith, Samuel Williston, Eugene Wambaugh, C. C. Langdell. Bottom row, left to right: Jens I. Westengard, Joseph H. Beale Jr., Edward H. Strobel, James B. Thayer, James B. Ames. Courtesy of Special Collections Department, Harvard Law School Library.

academic profession in legal education.[121] In 1901 Ames proclaimed the "sound general rule that a law professorship should be regarded as a vocation and not as an avocation," inasmuch as "about one fourth of the law professors of this country give themselves wholly to the duties of their professorships, while three fourths of them are active in practice or upon the Bench. These proportions . . . are likely to be reversed in the next generation."[122] Consequently, by the time of his retirement from the faculty in 1900, Langdell's vision of a faculty composed of full-time, salaried professors hired on the basis of academic merit had taken hold at HLS and was proliferating to other university law schools.[123] Some historians consider this alone "the most important development" in legal, if not professional, education during the late nineteenth century.[124]

121. Dicey, "Teaching of English Law," 423–24.

122. Ames, "Vocation of the Law Professor," 361–62.

123. Schofield, "Christopher Columbus Langdell," 291; *Centennial History of the Harvard Law School,* 70; Auerbach, *Unequal Justice: Lawyers and Social Change,* 75, 74–101; Stevens, *Law School: Legal Education in America,* 38–39.

124. Johnson, *Schooled Lawyers,* 105.

CHAPTER 6

The First Dean, 1870–1886

Assuming his new administrative role in September 1870, Dean Langdell immediately began to extend the formal system of academic merit beyond his own
classroom to the rest of the school. Though accused of arrogance and obstinacy,
Langdell did believe that academic merit determines the effectiveness and integrity of the members of "a learned and liberal profession of the highest grade."
These professionals will then "render to the public the highest and best service
in the administration of justice."[1] Langdell's justification for the academic meritocratic model of professional education was thus self-serving to some extent, but
also functionalist in principle. He viewed himself as the exemplary law student,
lawyer, and professor, while he also believed that his approach served individual
professionals, the profession, and the public.

The design for the academic meritocracy derived from the nature of Langdell's
professional expertise. His commitment to legal formalism, though contradicted
by his own jurisprudence, led him to introduce an analogous approach to education. This educational formalism treated professional education as a formal system
of rational, impersonal policies and rules guiding incremental progress that could
be measured objectively. Langdell knew the law too well to instantiate his formalist
ideal in jurisprudence, but he understood education too little to doubt that the
ideal could be realized in that domain. By combining this educational formalism
with the goal of fostering academic merit, Langdell designed and built the system
of academic meritocracy. Thus, the legal expertise of Langdell and his colleagues
made them receptive to educational formalism. After adopting academic merit as
the fundamental standard of success, Langdell and his allies gradually established
systematic policies and structures to support that standard. As a result, HLS first
and most fully embraced academic meritocracy among professional schools in
the United States.

1. Langdell, Annual Report 1876–77, 89, 91.

But the initial step of enshrining academic merit required a fundamental shift in professional and educational ideology and thus ignited opposition and conflict. His revolution would have gone smoothly, said his critics, "if Mr. Langdell had been a gentleman."[2] In that case, however, there would have been no revolution, because Langdell's transformation entailed "the uncomfortable transformation of gentlemen into professionals."[3] The relentless pursuit of academic merit contravened gentility both in manner and substance, and Langdell's revolution succeeded precisely because he did not act like a gentleman. The dean crusaded relentlessly, ignoring widespread appeals for accommodation and moderation, just as he had in teaching and examining students, and the seeming arrogance of this tenacity incited vehement opposition in students, faculty, alumni, and members of the bench and bar.

If Langdell Had Only Been a Gentleman

The gentry in early nineteenth-century America "were a self-constituted aristocracy of the best," monopolizing culture, virtue, and power in America. The gentry initially competed with the wealthy, until the two factions gradually formed an "overlapping group" that was coextensive in Boston and personified by Oliver Wendell Holmes Sr., the noted author and Harvard medical professor who coined the term "the Brahmin caste of New England." Over the final third of the nineteenth century the gentry slowly surrendered their influence to the wealthy in mass society,[4] but in old Boston this "Brahmin aristocracy" persevered far longer, sustained by the cultural validation of Harvard.[5] Meanwhile, within Harvard, a distinction between the "Brahmin caste" and the "scholars," who were devoted to academic achievement, arose in the early 1800s and persisted to the end of the century. In 1878 Teddy Roosevelt crowed to his family that he ranked nineteenth out of 230 in his Harvard class, and that "only one gentleman stands ahead of me." As Roosevelt indicated, most high-achieving "scholars" simply did not count in the view of the genteel student body that was stratified by social clubs.[6]

These "Brahmin" gentry embodied "a curious compound of opposites: gentleness and valor, honor and self-effacement, tact and allegiance to principle, agree-

---

2. E. Washburn, "Harvard Law School," leaf 12v. See, too, Batchelder, "C. C. Langdell," 312n.

3. Persons, *Decline of American Gentility*, 247.

4. Quotations are from Persons, *Decline of American Gentility*, 3, 11, 46. See 276–77.

5. R. Story, *Forging of an Aristocracy*, 160–81.

6. Quoted in Horowitz, *Campus Life*, 47. See Allmendinger, *Paupers and Scholars*; Townsend, *Manhood at Harvard*, 92–94, 141.

ableness and pride."[7] Thus, a "chivalrous gentlemen," such as Oliver Wendell Holmes Jr., combined "'high breeding' with manliness, courage, suppression of 'needless display,' courtesy, dignity of manner, and even chivalry."[8] Further complicating this "curious compound of opposites," Langdell presented a mixed case between the gentleman and the scholar, as shown by contemporaries' equivocal evaluations of the dean.

In common with the Brahmin gentry, Langdell would "scorn to win, or to struggle for, any success which was not the legitimate reward of merit."[9] In addition, he demonstrated commitment, individualism, and self-reliance; he was "a noble old swell . . . whose idealist devotion to his work I revere and love," as Holmes testified.[10] Like a gentleman, Langdell was also averse to "needless display" and self-promotion, being "incorrigibly modest" and unwilling to engage in public controversy.[11]

Nevertheless, Langdell lacked the "high breeding" of old Boston and violated important norms of those in "the Brahmin class of New England," to which Gray, Thayer, Ames, Holmes Jr., and Ames belonged.[12] In daily behavior, his shortcomings appeared in "his awkward, countrified manners," revealing the absence of "gentlemanly training."[13] In speaking, the gentleman was unfailingly courteous and temporized or avoided points of dispute, whereas Langdell was singularly direct and free of "cant," "temporizing," or "guile,"[14] becoming at times dismissive toward those unsympathetic with his views.[15] Compounding these deficiencies was Langdell's insularity and reluctance to socialize with his colleagues. The gentlemanly professors and their families "were intimate and friendly," but never developed "any very congenial intimacy" with Langdell, who "seemed to be another sort of man altogether."[16]

7. Quotations are, respectively, from G. White, "Revisiting James Bradley Thayer," 55–60; Persons, *Decline of American Gentility*, 29.

8. G. White, *Justice Oliver Wendell Holmes*, 29, 28.

9. J. Carter to Eliot (20 Dec. 1869). See Ames, "Christopher Columbus Langdell, 1826–1906," 475.

10. O. Holmes to Pollock (10 Apr. 1881). See Persons, *Decline of American Gentility*, 3.

11. Quotations are from Fox, "Professor Langdell," 7. See Langdell, Address 1895, 46–47; J. Carter, Address 1895, 38–41; Schofield, "Christopher Columbus Langdell," 286, 291; Wambaugh, "Professor Langdell," 1; Ames, "Christopher Columbus Langdell, 1826–1906," 484; C. Eliot, "Langdell," 523–24.

12. Beale, "Langdell, Gray, Thayer, and Ames," 390.

13. Quotations are from, respectively, Batchelder, "C. C. Langdell," 312n; Persons, *Decline of American Gentility*, 36. See E. Washburn, "Harvard Law School," leaves 19Ar–20.

14. Quotations are from F. Atwood, *Old Folks' Day*, 21; Fessenden, "Rebirth of the Harvard Law School," 505; Wambaugh, "Professor Langdell," 4. See Ames, "Christopher Columbus Langdell, 1826–1906," 472; C. Eliot, "Langdell," 524; Fessenden, "Rebirth of the Harvard Law School," 513; Schofield, "Christopher Columbus Langdell," 275; Persons, *Decline of American Gentility*, 106.

15. E. Washburn, "Harvard Law School," leaves 2v–3r, 12v–13r; C. Eliot, "Langdell," 524; Shattuck to Eliot (17 Dec. 1869).

16. N. Holmes, *Journal*, 274, 276.

Contemporaries attributed his ungentle conduct to "Langdell's intellectual arrogance and contempt."[17] Notwithstanding his shy, self-effacing manner, the dean sought to dominate and control others, Washburn lamented.[18] Above all, Langdell was considered unduly relentless and uncompromising. To his credit, he had advanced himself through "invincible perseverance" and "indomitable will" and defended his views with "tenacious firmness."[19] But his Harvard colleagues considered him "as *intransigeant* as a French Socialist,"[20] because he violated the genteel expectation "to use restraint and good taste."[21]

Though ungentle, these characteristics suited Langdell's scholarly commitment to pursuing knowledge. Driven by "his passion for truth.... he was extremely modest, but extremely tenacious of his convictions," observed Ames. "This not from any pride of opinion, but because any one who would change his convictions, formed after painstaking examination and much reflection, must plough deeper than he had gone, and, by a wider generalization, expose the error of these convictions. Once convinced of error, no one was readier to admit it."[22] In contrast, gentlemanly Washburn was "the epitome of the old Harvard." His jurisprudence "was not science; it was amateur moralizing."[23] Already in 1856 Langdell had dismissed Washburn's counsel in *Kuhn v. Webster* as "an utter absurdity."[24] The ideal of broad, general knowledge long associated with the gentlemanly tradition had no place in the academic meritocracy. As Langdell had read in Locke's *Education*, the studies for "gentlemen" do not suit "scholars" who "have a mind to go deeper than the surface and get themselves a solid satisfaction and masterly insight in any part of learning."[25]

The new dean's administration might therefore have gone smoothly "if Langdell had only been a gentleman," as "one of the clique of courtly old professors at the Law School observed privately."[26] And the truth of these words lies deeper than Langdell's "rustic manner." The conflicts arose from the fundamental ideological

---

17. Gray to Eliot (3 Jan. 1883). See E. Washburn, "Harvard Law School," leaves 19Ar–20; Gurney to Eliot [3 Jan. 1883].

18. E. Washburn, "Harvard Law School," leaf 15r.

19. Quotations are from, respectively, Batchelder, "Christopher C. Langdell," 441; Brandeis, "Harvard Law School," 18; *Boston Herald* (7 July 1906), 6. See Maury, *Collections*, 5.

20. Quotation is from Gurney to Eliot [3 Jan. 1883]. See Fessenden, "Rebirth of the Harvard Law School," 504, 507; Fox, "Professor Langdell," 7.

21. Persons, *Decline of American Gentility*, 49.

22. Ames, "Christopher Columbus Langdell, 1826–1906," 487–88.

23. LaPiana, *Logic and Experience*, 137.

24. Langdell to Webster (9 Aug. 1856).

25. Locke, *Some Thoughts Concerning Education*, §195. See Persons, *Decline of American Gentility*, 297; Brauer, *Education of a Gentleman*, 52.

26. Batchelder, "C. C. Langdell," 312n.

opposition between gentility and academic meritocracy, each with its own manner, values, and purposes. The conflict was so deep that the two factions on the small HLS faculty, occupying neighboring offices in the same building, scarcely communicated with each other about significant issues during the 1870s and 1880s. Sometimes they did not communicate at all, even on topics of mutual self-interest, such as salary. When addressing contentious issues outside of faculty meetings, they often exchanged notes rather than talking face to face; within faculty meetings they endured awkward silences. Even when all four or five professors met together, they sometimes voted to canvass the views of each other privately.[27] Dean Langdell's push to institute a formal system of academic merit required a radical shift in the manner, values, and purposes of professional education, and it succeeded because Langdell never became a gentleman of old Boston.

———*∿∿*———

Kit gave it a try. Stirred perhaps by the memory of his undergraduate days, Langdell attempted to enter Harvard's professional and social circles upon returning to his alma mater in February 1870, and the Brahmin tried to accept him. In the early 1870s he faithfully attended the reunion dinners of his college class, and joined an Exeter alumni committee to raise funds for the academy. In the subscription campaign held by Harvard after a fire in 1872, Langdell stood fourth on the list of University contributors.[28] In 1873 he joined a group of prominent Boston literary and legal figures in signing a petition protesting a legislative proposal to stigmatize former Confederate soldiers serving in the Federal army.[29] Meanwhile, the American Academy of Arts and Sciences elected him a Resident Fellow,[30] and he became a governing trustee of Boston's Social Law Library, operated by a group of studious lawyers that included John Gray, John Ropes, Nicholas St. John Green, Holmes, Melville Bigelow, and Brooks Adams.[31] In addition, he joined the American Social Science Association (ASSA), and was named to its Department of Jurisprudence, which largely comprised HLS alumni living in Boston or Cambridge.

27. See J. Thayer to Eliot (16 Oct. 1889); E. Washburn, "Harvard Law School," leaves 2v–3r; C. Eliot to Brandeis (27 Apr. 1893); Gray to Thayer (27 July 1878); J. Thayer, Correspondence and Memoranda, 3:103–4; Harvard Law School, Faculty Minutes (4 Jan. 1876, 14 May 1878).

28. Starks, "Christopher Columbus Langdell"; Harvard College Class of 1851, Class Book, 553, 558; Harvard College Class of 1851, Records, box 55; C. Eliot, Papers, box 67, f. "Harvard 1872"; "Scrapbook of Clippings," in J. Thayer, Papers, box 27, f. 5, p. 11.

29. *Lowell Daily Citizen and News* (3 Mar. 1873).

30. AAAS, Proceedings (1873), 8:302, 316; AAAS Archives, box 13, vol. 8; Langdell, Check Ledger 1871–75, number 251.

31. Langdell, Check Ledger 1871–75, numbers 110, 209; Social Law Library, *Act of Incorporation and By-Laws*, leaf 4; Bellefontaine, "Social Law Library."

In March 1870 this ASSA department appointed him to a special committee to examine "the science of jurisprudence in the United States"; and at a meeting held in Langdell's absence, the special committee elected him secretary and Yale president Theodore Woolsey chairman, and assigned the two to plan a meeting of the entire Association "devoted exclusively to...the subject of education in jurisprudence." The planning languished, and in February 1871, Langdell sought to extricate himself from the committee assignment, writing to Woolsey a long letter that followed his standard mode of reasoning.[32]

Invoking a positivist distinction between law and jurisprudence, Langdell first argued that, in principle, the assignment was inappropriate for him because he worked on education for "law," not "jurisprudence." He then added that, lacking prior notification, his election as secretary was virtually invalid, because it occurred "at a meeting at which I was not present and without the slightest notice that anything of the kind was contemplated." Finally, he observed "that my other engagements should not permit me to take so active a part in the work for which the committee was formed."[33] Hence, principle, doctrine, and convenience—all of which had to cohere in Langdell's mind—pointed to the same conclusion that he should be excused from the special committee.

Yet, in keeping with his standard mode of reasoning, Langdell's presentation emphasized principle and authority, while sublimating convenience. He first expatiated on the positivist distinction and then addressed the precedent of giving prior notification, but his final, passing appeal to convenience was apparently the real determining factor. By February 1871 the new dean was besieged with administering the school, teaching his first case method class, completing his first casebook, fighting with senior faculty over academic standards, and initiating new reforms. The day after writing to Woolsey, Langdell wrote a similar letter ending his involvement in the Eleazar Lord case, while observing that he had just withdrawn from another longstanding litigation because "my engagements here are so pressing."[34] In 1871 he was already terminating outside professional obligations in order to focus on the looming battle in Cambridge. But rather than forthrightly say that he was too busy for the ASSA special committee, Langdell characteristically felt he had to convince Woolsey, and himself, that principle and authority dictated his resignation.

32. Quotations are from ASSA, "General Intelligence" (1873), 199. See ASSA, "List of New Members" (1870); ASSA, "Department of Jurisprudence" (1871). On Langdell's mode of reasoning, see chapter 3 above.

33. Langdell to Woolsey (6 Feb. 1871). Compare the interpretation of LaPiana, who discovered Langdell's letter. *Logic and Experience*, 77.

34. Langdell to Whiton (7 Nov. 1871).

While his participation in high-profile, national organizations was therefore limited, Langdell continued to develop his social circle by following the conventional path of a Victorian gentleman and accepting an invitation to join a social club. His choice was the small, informal Septem Club, formed in the 1850s by Charles Dunbar, Ephraim Gurney, George Shattuck, Chauncey Wright, Eliot, and Thayer. These men all had important offices or connections at Harvard, and Langdell's joining in 1871 demonstrates the efforts that he and others made to involve him in the inner circle of the university. In the early 1870s members of the Septem Club helped Langdell make the transition to Cambridge by advising him on choosing accommodations, boarding his pony, investing his money, and other personal matters.[35] Langdell's closest relationship was with Wright, "the most acute philosopher of his generation" in the United States.[36]

In fall 1849 Wright and Langdell had chosen to room together at Harvard College due apparently to their "rustic" standards of domestic upkeep and their mutual affinity for intellectual discussion. In addition, the two young men were alike in personality, for Wright, like Langdell, was "a peculiar boy, somewhat reserved.... His most noticeable peculiarity was his abstractedness, amounting to absent-mindedness.... Some looked upon this as evidence of something wrong—a screw loose somewhere.... Out of doors, he was a quiet boy, seldom joining in the boisterous school-boy games, preferring to wander away by himself and within himself." Nevertheless, each was "always well liked."[37]

Certain factors drew Langdell and Wright back together in 1870. After several years away, both were returning to Harvard and beginning to teach for the first time. Both could be engaging, even dominating, participants in personal conversation or small groups, but each was strongly criticized by students for their initial efforts in the classroom.[38] Although Wright had a minor appointment and Langdell a central position at Harvard, they interacted regularly over the next four years, as Langdell periodically lent money to Wright, who frequently sought financial help from his friends. In July 1872 the two sailed together to Ireland, sharing a stateroom paid for by Langdell. Wright reported that they conversed intensely on

35. J. Thayer, Correspondence and Memoranda, 2:26–27 (24 June 1878); C. Eliot to Thayer (30 Jan. 1874). See Langdell's checks written to Eliot, Shattuck, and Thayer in Check Ledger, 1871–75. On the Septem Club and social clubs, see Madden, *Chauncey Wright*, 10–14; Persons, *Decline of American Gentility*, 104.

36. Quotation is from Turner, *Liberal Education of Charles Eliot Norton*, 189. On Wright's philosophical stature, see Norton, *Philosophical Discussions by Chauncey Wright*, vii; Madden, *Chauncey Wright*, 22; Wiener, *Evolution and the Founders of Pragmatism*, 31–69.

37. J. Thayer, *Letters of Chauncey Wright*, 14. See S. Eliot, "Some Cambridge Pundits," 29; A. Brown, *Autobiographical Notes*, 64; Maury, *Collections*, 5.

38. J. Thayer, *Letters of Chauncey Wright*, 157–58, 175, 201, 213; Madden, *Chauncey Wright*, 24–27.

the voyage, likely addressing inductive method in law and legal procedure because Wright subsequently began to refer to these topics in his writings on evolution and scientific method. Langdell stayed in Ireland, perhaps visiting his mother's relatives, while Wright went on to England to meet Charles Darwin, who regarded Wright as his most sophisticated interpreter in the United States.[39]

After returning to Harvard, Langdell and Wright boarded at the same table, maintained by Harriet Jacobs, the famous African American author of *Incidents in the Life of a Slave Girl* (1861).[40] Also around Jacobs's table—"chosen for its intellectual superiority"[41]—sat several of the future "best men" of the Gilded Age.[42] J. R. Dennett taught rhetoric at Harvard and became the first editor of the *Nation*, to which Langdell subscribed. John Fiske taught history in the College and advocated Darwinism and an educational philosophy said to resemble Langdell's. Another boarder was James Myers, friend of Wright and one of "Kit's freshmen" at HLS, who wrote a series of articles defending Langdell's "new system" at HLS and later became speaker of the Massachusetts House of Representatives.[43]

Also boarding at the table was Henry Adams, who began teaching at Harvard concurrently with Langdell and Wright and then studied in Europe during 1872–73 while HLS student Ames taught his courses. When later describing his inductive method of teaching history, Adams employed the same metaphor about the "tangled skein" of human events that appeared in Langdell's famous preface to *Cases on Contracts* (1871).[44] Another boarder was Brooks Adams, a protégé of Oliver Wendell Holmes Jr., who subsequently wrote influential works on political economy and became a close adviser to President Theodore Roosevelt. After he and Myers attended Langdell's first class taught by case method, Adams recommended the method "with the highest praise" to future HLS professor Thayer. Upon leaving

39. Langdell, Check Ledger 1871–75, numbers 142, 227, 245; Wright to Charles Darwin (3 Sept. 1874), in J. Thayer, *Letters of Chauncey Wright*, 307. See also 31, 192, 246; Norton, *Philosophical Discussions by Chauncey Wright*, xvii, 169–70, 256–59, 368.

40. Langdell, Check Ledger 1871–75, numbers 104, 163, 188, 238; J. Thayer, *Letters of Chauncey Wright*, 38n, 49n–50n, 372. Cf. Yellin, *Harriet Jacobs*, 222–23.

41. Beringause, *Brook Adams*, 48.

42. Sproat, *Best Men: Liberal Reformers in the Gilded Age*, 4–6. Boarding did not necessarily entail lodging there. At some point after becoming dean in fall 1870, Langdell was provided a house on campus by the university, and he may already have been residing there.

43. "New system" is quoted from [J. Myers], "'Law Schools vs. Lawyers' Offices'" (1, 11 Apr. 1873); [J. Myers], "Harvard Law School" (5, 19 Feb. 1875). See "Pow Wow Records of Supreme Court 1870–82," 27–28; Langdell, Check Ledger 1871–75, number 272; J. Thayer, *Letters of Chauncey Wright*, 199n, 225, 230; Beringause, *Brook Adams*, 48; Stevens, "Law Schools and Legal Education, 1879–1979," 211.

44. Quotation is from H. Adams, *Education*, 302. See Beringause, *Brook Adams*, 48; Samuels, *Young Henry Adams*, 208–98; Samuels, *Henry Adams*, 90–124; H. Adams, *Letters*, 2:156n3.

HLS, Adams said that he wished to be remembered at the law school as a founding member of the student club formed by "Kit's freshmen."[45]

Beyond engaging these young "best men," Langdell's participation at Jacobs's boarding table may have induced the second African American graduate of HLS to enroll. Langdell recorded his matriculation on 26 September 1872, in the dean's registration book: "No. 39. Archibald Henry Grimké. Charleston, So. Car. A.B. Lincoln University, Chester Co. Penn. 1870. Has read law a little, but begins the course. 38 Divinity Hall." Grimké was the brother-in-law of Harriet Jacobs's close friend, and her link to the dean may have contributed to his enrolling at HLS.[46]

Jacobs closed her boarding house in April 1875, the point at which the documentary record of Langdell's personal activities virtually ends. Nevertheless, Langdell's efforts to join the Brahmin gentry at Harvard had already begun to languish. The burdens of the deanship, the radical nature of the project, his lack of gentility, and the barbs of his critics drove him back into his characteristic insularity once again.

The First Dean and His System

The purview of the new office of dean gradually became evident after Langdell's election in September 1870. The president retained authority over hiring and remunerating faculty, while the dean assumed responsibility for admitting and registering students, determining their standing,[47] and supervising their conduct.[48] The contested domain was academic policy which the faculty customarily governed

45. J. Thayer, Correspondence and Memoranda, 1:53 (27 Oct. 1874). See Langdell, "Memoranda Concerning Law School Students," 38; Batchelder, "1906—Notes for Langdell art[icle]"; Batchelder, "Christopher C. Langdell," 440–41; "Pow Wow Records of Supreme Court 1870–1882," 5–11, 39–40; Beringause, *Brook Adams*, 48, 76–78, 239, 243–44, 296–97.

46. Quotation is from Langdell, "Memoranda Concerning Law School Students," 90. See Yellin, *Harriet Jacobs*, 234–36; Langdell, Check Ledger 1871–75, number 276; J. Thayer, *Letters of Chauncey Wright*, 340. In 1870 and 1871 Grimké's aunts were trying to find a place for him to study law in Boston. D. Bruce, *Archibald Grimké*, 27–28.

47. For example, Langdell recorded in his register: "18 Sept. 1871. Daniel Boone Holmes, A. B. Kentucky University, 1870, Lexington, Ky. Wishes to be admitted to advanced standing; brings a proper certificate [of employment and character] from Messrs. Breckenridge and Buckner with whom he has studied. Am to inform him that he will be examined in both years studies. Informed him to that effect 25 Sept. 1871." Langdell, "Memoranda Concerning Law School Students," 43–44.

48. During Langdell's first semester, the new librarian, William A. Everett, who lasted one year, was unable to enforce the rules on a defiant student, and Langdell told him to appeal to Eliot to enforce the rule. Everett to Warren (circa 1907). Thereafter, Langdell never again "procured the enforcement of his wishes by an exercise of the President's authority" over students. C. Eliot, "Langdell," 522. Cf. C. Warren, *History of the Harvard Law School*, 2:486; LaPiana, *Logic and Experience*, 14; Everett to Warren (10 Feb. 1908).

and the new dean intended to transform. But how could Langdell carry out his revolution based merely on the Corporation's authorization to "prepare the business of the Faculty"?[49] To be sure, he had the backing of Eliot, who commenced to attend all the meetings of every faculty in the university, and who spoke and voted in favor of Langdell's initiatives at HLS faculty meetings. But Eliot's authority was subject directly to the Corporation and indirectly to the Overseers, and his own position was not yet secure, so transforming the school into an academic meritocracy depended on whether and how Langdell and Eliot collaborated and mollified, or co-opted, the gentlemen.

The two had much in common, despite the gulf between Langdell's difficult youth in New Boston and Eliot's Brahmin background in old Boston. Both were handicapped by weak eyesight, and both had been wounded as boys, Langdell by rural poverty and the loss of his family, and Eliot by the bankruptcy of his family during the Panic of 1857 and by the stigma of "the great red birthmark on one side of his face."[50] As a result, each was well defended and not given to levity, exhibiting a "characteristic reserve" and often saying little, but speaking directly and tactlessly when he did. As administrators, both were highly expedient and prudent, yet willing to take calculated risks.[51] Langdell had greater acumen in financial matters,[52] but sometimes neglected administrative detail, so Eliot often interjected himself into minor HLS matters, for he relished detail and was prone to micromanage the university, as he himself acknowledged.[53] Saddled with an "addiction to work," both were extraordinarily industrious and famously tenacious in pursuing their goals.[54] Being so unyielding, each was often criticized as an "autocrat," and Eliot acknowledged that he needed to be "more patient, conciliatory, and conservative."[55] Here lies the distinction that made for their successful collaboration.

49. See C. Eliot, "Langdell," 519.

50. S. Eliot, "Some Cambridge Pundits," 22. See James, *Charles W. Eliot*, 1:13–15, 308–15.

51. Quotation is from Hawkins, *Between Harvard and America*, 78. See James, *Charles W. Eliot*, 2:75–78; Batchelder, "Christopher C. Langdell," 441; Beale, "Professor Langdell," 9–11; *Centennial History of the Harvard Law School*, 34.

52. C. Eliot, "Langdell," 524; C. Eliot to Holmes (18 Nov. 1916). Langdell invested in railroad bonds and mortgages for farmland in the Midwest. See Langdell, Check Ledger 1871–75, numbers 153, 155, 207, 260; Langdell, Will (1906); Warranty Deed from Austin and Hannah Warner to Christopher C. Langdell (10 Feb. 1877).

53. Hawkins, *Between Harvard and America*, 75–76; C. Eliot to Dunbar (11 Jan. 1883). See Langdell to Eliot (14 Nov. 1893, 27 Apr. 1894, 6 May 1895); C. Eliot to Langdell [circa 1894b, circa 1895]; Petition to the Dean and Faculty of the Law School ([1894]), in C. Eliot, Papers, box 124.

54. Hawkins, *Between Harvard and America*, 77.

55. Quotations are, respectively, from E. Washburn, "Harvard Law School," leaf 13r; S. Eliot, "Some Cambridge Pundits," 27.

Compared to Langdell, Eliot was still a Brahmin gentleman, and the president often played good cop to the dean's bad cop, as when Eliot conciliated HLS professors complaining about Langdell's rude intransigence, but encouraged Langdell on the side. Though not deliberately staged, this "partnership of Eliot and Langdell" functioned extremely well,[56] and this complementary arrangement explains their successful collaboration as well as why Eliot valued Langdell so highly. No one at Harvard except Langdell—"a downright radical"[57]—made Eliot seem "patient, conciliatory, and conservative."[58]

Beyond making Eliot appear moderate, Langdell contributed conceptually to their collaboration by synthesizing the two basic principles of the academic meritocracy. On the one hand, Langdell aimed to promote higher academic achievement by the students and faculty; on the other hand, he designed the policies to fit into a formal "system." Initially, some, such as Nathaniel Holmes, did not understand that the individual changes belonged to a *"new system"* for the law school.[59] But already in 1871 Langdell was clearly announcing his educational formalism: "In order to teach or study practice to any purpose, it is necessary to have a fixed and definite system.... Every separate question should be considered with reference" to that.[60] Langdell's synthesis of these two principles—promoting academic achievement and establishing a formal system—was gradually recognized by critics such as Ephraim Gurney: "The whole tendency of [Langdell's] System would be, to build up a great school of Law as an exact science, and divorce it more and more from actual administration" of the law.[61]

Reinforcing Langdell's commitment to educational formalism, nineteenth-century Victorian culture exuded "moral certainty and love of order," leading Americans to "attribute omnipotence to abstractions" and formalization.[62] Enshrining statistics and bureaucratic organization, the nation developed "a more centralized,

56. R. Perry to Chafee (28 Feb. 1929); Chafee to Perry (6 Mar. 1929). See C. Eliot to Dunbar (11 Jan. 1883); C. Eliot to Fessenden (3 Mar. 1919); James, *Charles W. Eliot*, 2:62.

57. C. Eliot to Holmes (18 Nov. 1916).

58. In contrast, another prominent, reforming university president in the same era, Andrew D. White of Cornell, had no one to play the role of Langdell and lacked Eliot's commitment, leading him to compromise his desired reforms to a far greater degree than Eliot. Altschuler, *Andrew D. White*, 67, 70.

59. Emphasis in original. "Harvard College Law School" (1874), 67. See N. Holmes, *Journal*, 311.

60. Langdell, "Civil Procedure," notebook 1, leaf 2r. These sentences from his introductory lecture were subsequently overwritten. On Langdell's "system," see [J. Myers], "Harvard Law School" (5, 19 Feb. 1875), 8–9; "Higher Legal Education" (1876): 540; E. Washburn, "Harvard Law School," leaf 11v; Wambaugh to Thayer (17 Feb. 1892); Brannan to Thayer (3 June 1897); Schofield, "Christopher Columbus Langdell," 286; C. Warren, *History of the Harvard Law School*, 2:390, 393; Wigglesworth, "Law as a Profession" (1909).

61. Gurney to Eliot [3 Jan. 1883].

62. Quotations are, respectively, from Wise, *Italian Boy: A Tale of Murder and Body Snatching*, xiv; Wiebe, *Search for Order, 1877–1920*, 164.

urban, industrial society," dominated by regulated, systematic, impersonal administration. Large cities eclipsed the small, cohesive, personal "island communities" of the antebellum era. Small-scale familial workshops of artisans gave way to large-scale industries governed through bureaucratic management.[63] Epitomizing the new industrial model, railroads became the nation's cultural icon in the last third of the nineteenth century, even establishing its time zones, informing its vocabulary, and reshaping legal practice.[64] It was no coincidence that some of Langdell's most significant litigation, his experience of corruption of the bench and bar, and his major successful investments all involved railroads.

Contributing to their iconic role, "the operational requirements of the railroad demanded the creation of the first administrative hierarchies in American business." Following this track, business enterprise adopted the organization of the industrial corporation, comprising many distinct operating units distinguished by their rational function and "managed by a hierarchy of salaried executives."[65] Large corporate law firms began to organize themselves according to this model as well. These firms rose to the apex of the legal profession in the closing decades of the nineteenth century, as their number, size, and influence grew faster than the rest of the bar. Paul Cravath in New York and Louis Brandeis in Boston first organized the firm along the lines of the industrial corporation, establishing functional specializations of lawyers, hierarchical organization in the name of efficiency, and recruitment of top law students with the promise of rising up through the ranks.[66]

Leading lawyers increasingly adopted the bureaucratic rationality of the age partly because that ideology suited their own expertise. Legal formalism—the view that deductive inference from apolitical, abstract legal principles, by itself, yields correct decisions in legal disputes—coincided with the Victorian bureaucratic ideology and "search for order." In American jurisprudence, legal formalism, or "classical legal thought," thus predominated in the late nineteenth century, amid

63. Quotations are, respectively, from Walker, *Everyday Life in Victorian America*, 14; Laurie, *Artisans into Workers: Labor in Nineteenth-Century America*, 113, 118–23. See Wiebe, *Search for Order, 1877–1920*, 133–63.

64. W. Thomas, *Lawyering for the Railroad*, 247. See Walker, *Everyday Life in Victorian America*, 63; Wiebe, *Search for Order, 1877–1920*, 7.

65. Quotations are from Chandler, *Visible Hand: The Managerial Revolution in American Business*, 87, 1. On the complex relationship between the "national habit" of creating "regulated, systematic, impersonal bureaucracies" at the end of the nineteenth century and the rise of corporate capitalism, see Wiebe, *Search for Order, 1877–1920*, 164, 133–63; Zunz, *Making America Corporate, 1870–1920*; Roy, *Socializing Capital: The Rise of the Large Industrial Corporation*.

66. Hobson, "Symbol of the New Profession," 3–18; Gawalt, "Impact of Industrialization on the Legal Profession," 97–123; R. Gordon, "Legal Thought and Legal Practice in the Age of American Enterprise," 82; R. Gordon, "Ideal and the Actual in the Law," 51–74; Galanter and Palay, *Tournament of Lawyers*, 4–19.

analogous formalism that arose and flourished in economics, philosophy, ethics, psychology, and other fields of social thought.[67]

Though believing at some level that legal formalism was the proper and necessary approach to jurisprudence, Langdell understood too well the technical complexities of legal practice to reduce his analysis to this kind of approach. Hence, his jurisprudence is, finally, contradictory and paradoxical. In education, however, Langdell, the failed schoolmaster, attempted to institute his formalistic commitment to the "*logical* integrity of the system as a system."[68] His experience at the bar taught him that legal formalism did not actually work in practice, but, in applying the ideal to education, he had no reservations and championed the ideal to the end of his career, even as the educational formalism proved no less problematic than the legal and his system ultimately belied its own premises.

Langdell was not alone in pioneering educational formalism, to be sure. Bureaucratic "university management" emerged contemporaneously with the new business model of the industrial corporation.[69] As President Eliot prophesied in his inaugural address, "The principle of divided and subordinate responsibilities, which rules in government bureaus, in manufactories, and all great companies, which makes a modern army a possibility, must be applied in the University."[70] Lamenting the radical shift expressed in that view, traditional presidents, usually clergymen, such as Martin B. Anderson of the University of Rochester, opined about Eliot, "He is not a broad scholar, ... never teaches the students and has not the least formative control over their minds or characters. He is really a sort of general manager with duties analogous to those of a superintendent or president of a railroad."[71] By the end of the century, however, even clergymen leading major universities, such as William R. Harper of the University of Chicago, called for "the development of a system in our higher educational work." Classifying and stratifying colleges and universities, Harper averred, "will contribute toward a system of higher education ..., the lack of which is sadly felt in every sphere of educational activity."[72] Indeed, in American higher education "the years 1895 to 1920 can aptly be designated 'The Age of Standards'" due to the rise of accred-

67. Wiebe, *Search for Order, 1877–1920*, 111–63; M. White, *Social Thought in America: The Revolt Against Formalism*, 3–10; Purcell, *Crisis of Democratic Theory*, 75; J. Foster, *Ideology of Apolitical Politics*, 4–9; Kennedy, "Toward an Historical Understanding of Legal Consciousness," 3–24; Horwitz, *Transformation of American Law, 1870–1960*, 9–31.

68. [O. Holmes], Review (Mar. 1880), 234.

69. See Newfield, *Ivy and Industry*, 67–90.

70. C. Eliot, Inaugural Address 1869, 26.

71. Quoted in May, *History of the University of Rochester*, 101.

72. Harper, "Situation of the Small College" (1900), 388–89.

iting and professional associations, whose "frequent use ... of the word *system*" expressed "something talismanic."[73]

Thus, Langdell's commitment to educational formalism had antecedents and was informed by the cultural and academic context. But his designing and building academic meritocracy by fusing educational formalism and academic achievement occurred at HLS a generation earlier than at any other professional school in the United States. This innovation in professional education secured the preeminence of HLS, making it the most academic, most elite, and most influential professional school in the country by 1890. Moreover, Langdell's philosophy of professional education was deeply related to his jurisprudence. He fused the formalism of his unrealized jurisprudential ideal to his singular devotion to academic merit and thereby introduced into professional education the paradigmatic system of academic meritocracy.

Initial Steps toward Academic Meritocracy

Identifying and advocating the specific policies that constituted the system of academic meritocracy was Langdell's other major contribution to the collaboration with Eliot. The president had the general "disposition to work a complete revolution in the University," but the particular reforms followed "the lines originally laid down by Professor Langdell."[74] These policies were often criticized as impractical or too theoretical, criticism that even Eliot expressed privately in the early 1880s when attacks on the dean reached a crescendo and HLS enrollment fell to its nadir.[75] At that crucial point, Langdell abandoned his customary reserve to comment tartly in his annual report: "This School ... has suffered seriously in its material interests from a charge of being too scientific in its aims, too theoretical, and too little practical."[76] Apart from that comment, Langdell appeared oblivious in public to attacks, and persisted in proposing and instituting specific reforms.

Some of Langdell's new policies were discussed in previous chapters: that faculty in a professional school should be hired on the basis of academic merit and view their professorship as their career, and that students should be taught inductively, examined rigorously about their *understanding* of subject matter, and

73. Hawkins, *Banding Together: The Rise of National Associations*, 77.

74. Quotations are, respectively, from E. Washburn, "Harvard Law School," leaf 13r; Dunbar, "President Eliot's Administration," 464. See C. Eliot, "Langdell," 521; James, *Charles W. Eliot*, 1:270.

75. C. Eliot to Dunbar (11 Jan. 1883). See Harvard Law School, Faculty Minutes (5 Apr. 1886); Brandeis, *Letters*, 1:84–88, 113–17; Letters in C. Eliot, Papers, box 137 B, f. 1237; *Boston Evening Transcript* (6 July 1906): 8; Fessenden, "Rebirth of the Harvard Law School," 512.

76. Langdell, Annual Report 1880–81, 84.

offered the opportunity to pursue advanced study through sequenced coursework. Langdell personally adopted these reforms in his own professorial work while other HLS faculty, save Ames, largely resisted.

In his role as dean, Langdell meanwhile made a number of rapid changes, elevating the academic tone of the school. When meeting and matriculating new students at the beginning of the academic year, he interrogated each about his academic background, warning that "a person who had not received a sound preparatory training might find the courses very difficult." Commensurately, the mild hazing still occurring among HLS students rapidly ceased, and the dean prohibited the HLS faculty from delivering extracurricular, amateur lectures on nonlegal topics, even if requested by students. He also halted the longstanding, gentlemanly custom of delivering a welcoming lecture of paternal and professional advice to the entering students, after he heard Washburn's version.[77]

In addition, Langdell convinced the HLS faculty to cease awarding monetary prizes for student essays, based on judgments "by gentlemen, invited from abroad." Instead, these funds went to scholarships determined by the faculty under Langdell's preponderant influence, and the number of scholarships increased to eight by 1875.[78] Meanwhile, in organizing the core subjects of study, HLS catalogs began to minimize practical topics conveyed in manuals (such as pleading, domestic relations, and wills) and to emphasize emerging conceptual fields (such as civil procedure and torts). These early changes indicate the shift from gentility to academic meritocracy occurring across the school.

Still another rapid change was to develop the library "on Langdell's principles."[79] Throughout his education and career, Langdell had helped to support libraries: at Exeter, at HLS, at the New York Law Institute, at other law schools in conjunction with Robert Haynes of London, and at the Social Law Library in Boston. Bringing this deep interest back to HLS, Langdell found the library "nearly a wreck," in his phrase. Its collection was underfunded, poorly maintained, little supervised, and depleted each year through the practice of dispensing free copies of prescribed textbooks to students.[80] This situation required immediate attention because, in Langdell's view, the library was the heart of the academic system: "The most essential feature of the School, that which distinguishes it most widely from

77. Quotation is from Fessenden, "Rebirth of the Harvard Law School," 496–97. See 494, 498; Langdell, "Memoranda Concerning Law School Students"; N. Holmes, *Journal*, 276; E. Washburn, "Harvard Law School," leaves 1b, 3.

78. Quotation is from E. Washburn, "Harvard Law School," leaf 1b. See Harvard University, Corporation Records, 11:254 (28 Oct. 1870); 12:137–38 (8 Nov. 1875); 12:149–50 (13 Dec. 1875).

79. C. Eliot, "Langdell," 521.

80. Langdell, Annual Report 1889–90, 133. See 133–35; Langdell, Annual Report 1870–71, 63–65.

all other schools of which I have any knowledge is the library . . . including the relation in which it stands to all the exercises of the School, the influence which it exerts directly and indirectly, and the kind and extent of use that is made of it by teachers and students. Everything else will admit of a substitute; or may be dispensed with; but without the library the School would lose its most important characteristics and indeed its identity."[81]

Beginning in fall 1870 several "radical" changes were made: increasing the budget, hiring a full-time librarian to provide constant supervision, restricting access to the general collection, and augmenting, rather than depleting, the collection each year.[82] Prompted by inductive teaching, student usage increased dramatically, and in 1873 Langdell personally donated ninety-eight volumes of law reports, costing about half his salary, because the school's budget could not provide for it. While he could have designated these volumes for the restricted general collection, the dean donated them instead to the "working library" used by students.[83] Throughout his tenure, Langdell carefully monitored the guidelines for acquisitions, and when the eminent Oxford law professor Dicey visited HLS in 1898, he found that the library's collection of English legal records far surpassed any other collection in the world.[84]

Finally, Langdell's most significant early curricular change was to ask the faculty in September 1871 to sequence the two-year program of study that had operated as a "merry-go-round" of introductory courses distributed over two years. Students started or finished at any point in either the "first-year" or "second-year" course of study, depending merely on the year they entered the school.[85] Langdell proposed that HLS offer both years of coursework annually and that the second-year courses truly presuppose first-year courses. Washburn and Nathaniel Holmes initially opposed upgrading the second-year courses, seeing only inconvenience to the students and themselves, but Eliot supported the proposal, and Washburn and Holmes acquiesced.[86]

As of 1873–74 the two-year sequence commenced with ten first-year hours in the "Big Five" courses—property, contracts, torts, criminal law, civil proce-

---

81. Langdell, Annual Report 1872–73, 63.

82. Quotation is from Langdell, Annual Report 1870–71, 64. See C. Eliot, Annual Report 1870–71, 18; Harvard University, Corporation Records, 11:251 (14 Oct. 1870); 320 (29 Sept. 1871); 401 (7 Aug. 1872).

83. Langdell to Eliot (4 Jan. 1873). See Langdell, Annual Report 1873–74, 67; 1874–75, 76.

84. Dicey, "Teaching of English Law," 423. See Haynes to Machen (10 Nov. 1874); Langdell to Eliot (28 June 1892).

85. James, *Charles W. Eliot*, 1:268.

86. E. Washburn, "Harvard Law School," preface, leaves 1, 4r–6r; N. Holmes, *Journal*, 275–76; C. Eliot, Annual Report 1870–71, 15–16; Harvard Law School, Faculty Minutes (28 Mar. 1871).

dure—that would endure at HLS for 130 years. In the ten hours of coursework required for the second year, the faculty ultimately decided to prescribe only two advanced courses: Thayer's Evidence (two hours) and Langdell's Equity Jurisdiction and Pleading (three hours). The remaining five hours were left to students' discretion, in keeping with Eliot's view that freedom of choice was the hallmark of university education.[87] Nevertheless, the sequencing of coursework into two ten-hour years in 1871 worked an "extraordinary revolution" by raising academic expectations at the school.[88]

These rapid changes, combined with Langdell's innovations in his own courses, led Eliot and other observers to conclude already in the early 1870s that no department in the university had undertaken "more radical reform than . . . the Law School."[89] Upgrading of the medical school lagged far behind, partly due to the fact that the average level of medical education in the United States at the time stood far below that of legal education. In addition, the Harvard medical faculty measured academic quality by the size of enrollments and valued practical experience above academic learning.[90] Since the medical school had no "radical" dean pushing tenaciously from inside, the president could not overcome the resistance of senior medical professors. Eliot therefore commenced to declare what became a litany over the next forty-five years: "The Law School is the most successful department of the entire university, and enjoys a reputation throughout the nation which is higher than that of any other department."[91]

Notwithstanding the president's judgment, the transformation of HLS was highly contentious, unfolding in two stages over sixteen years. The first stage began in 1870 and ended in 1876 with the retirement of Washburn, Langdell's primary opponent up to that point. The fundamental question during this period was whether HLS would embrace academic merit as the defining standard of student and faculty achievement, and the question arose primarily in regard to two controversial policies: establishing grading standards for year-end examinations and raising the admissions standard to the equivalent of a college degree.

87. Quotation is from Barnes, introduction, 8. The group of "Big Five" first appears in Harvard Law School, Catalog 1873–74. See Harvard Law School, Faculty Minutes (27 Apr. 1875); Harvard Law School, Catalog 1875–76, 1; C. Eliot, "Liberty in Education," 125–48.

88. Langdell, Annual Report 1873–74, 65.

89. "Harvard College Law School" (1874), 66. See C. Eliot, Annual Report 1871–72, 21; N. Holmes, Journal, 273.

90. Harrington, Harvard Medical School: A History, 3:989–1004, 1019–23, 1028–44, 1055–57.

91. Quotation is from C. Eliot to Dicey (2 May 1913). See also C. Eliot, Annual Reports 1871–72, 21; 1873–74, 28–29; 1876–77, 29; 1879–80, 15–16; Bonney to Eliot [circa 1886]; C. Eliot to Pritchett (13 Apr. 1915).

Beginning in 1876, the second stage lasted until the mid-1880s, when the newly created HLS alumni association met for the first time. During this period, the faction of Langdell and Ames opposed that of Gray and Thayer, although all four professors agreed that academic merit should be the standard of student and faculty success. What they disputed was the meaning of academic merit and, in particular, whether Langdell himself should be the norm. This question underlay the heated controversies arising over two related changes in academic policy: extending the degree program to three years and establishing an honor degree. In both stages, Langdell encountered determined opposition regarding both substance and procedure, for he was viewed as arrogant, inordinately tenacious, and willing to violate established procedure in order to accomplish his ends. He had not forgotten the tactics of the Erie Wars.

Establishing Academic Merit as the Standard

Following President Eliot's call for "strict annual examinations" in 1869, HLS established written end-of-year examinations, and Langdell introduced his new mode of posing complex, particular, hypothetical problems that tested students' understanding. Other professors did not generally adopt Langdell's approach. Washburn sometimes incorporated a few general hypotheticals, while Holmes and Charles Bradley requested only definitions, illustrations, and rules, as did Gray and Thayer. Even St. John Green, a full-time lecturer who has been considered a progressive legal thinker, did the same.[92] The only colleague embracing Langdell's mode was Ames, who may have been inspired while coteaching with Langdell during the 1870s.[93]

While the form of examination was a matter of choice, grading raised the question of whether to adopt the standard of academic merit, prompting sharp disagreement over the next six years. During the colonial era, Harvard College had ranked students through an obscure calculation of family pedigree, social standing, behavior, character, and academic performance. In the 1820s Harvard and other colleges established a numerical grading system, called the "Scale of Merit" at Harvard, whereby academic marks were reduced for behavioral and

92. C. Eliot, Inaugural Address 1869, 8. In Harvard Law School, Annual Examinations, see the exams of C. S. Bradley, Jurisdiction and Procedure in Equity 1873; Emory E. Washburn, Real Property 1873; Nicholas St. John Green, Torts 1873; John C. Gray, Property Sept. 1876; James B. Thayer, Criminal Law 1880. On Green, see appendix 1.

93. See, for example, in Harvard Law School, Annual Examinations: Ames, Torts June 1875, Oct. 1875, Sept. 1876, Trusts 1880. See Kimball, "'Warn Students That I Entertain Heretical Opinions,'" 62–65.

religious infractions.[94] In 1870 HLS introduced numerical grades based solely on the results of students' written examinations, thus narrowing the evaluation of students to their academic performance.[95]

However narrow, the new standard might have been acceptable to "the clique of courtly old professors" had the passing grade been generously set at a minimal competence that students could comfortably achieve, leaving time for other pursuits.[96] But the meritocrats wanted to identify an academic standard requiring students to work intensively, so a dispute immediately ensued. In late June, at a faculty meeting held in the evening at the president's house, as customary, it was moved and seconded (surely by Professors Washburn and Holmes) to adopt a minimum grade of sixty out of one hundred in each of the subjects examined to entitle a candidate to a degree. Among the four faculty, two (surely Dean Langdell and Lecturer St. John Green) opposed it. Eliot then broke the tie, voting the motion down, and a second motion setting the passing grade at seventy in each of the subjects was approved.[97]

Having lost the first round, Washburn and Holmes tried in the following year to weaken the standard by proposing to change the passing grade from a minimum of seventy on each exam to an *average* of seventy on all exams. After that motion was blocked, the two then made another motion to lower the passing grade to a minimum of sixty-five on each exam. Again they deadlocked with Langdell and Green, and Eliot cast the deciding vote against them. The minimum grade of seventy on each subject was then reaffirmed. In the third round, occurring in 1874 after the curriculum had been organized into a two-year sequence, a modest compromise was achieved, setting the minimum grade in second-year subjects at an *average* grade of seventy.[98]

Subsequently, Langdell and Washburn continued sparring, as over the question of whether a student who failed an exam could nevertheless have his competence certified by the dean or a professor. In July 1875 they compromised on an important issue when the faculty voted that an instructor "shall be entitled to divide [the grades] among the candidates in that subject and in such proportion as he

94. Each oral recitation was graded on a scale of 1–8; each written exercise, 1–24. Points were subtracted for missing morning daily prayers, a recitation, or a public church service, and for behavioral infractions. At the end of the term, points were tallied for each class. Shipton, *Biographical Sketches of Those Who Attended Harvard College*, 6:46; Morison, *Three Centuries of Harvard*, 260; Allmendinger, *Paupers and Scholars*, 122–24.

95. Harvard Law School, Grade Records, vol. 0, 1869–76.

96. Quotation is from Batchelder, "C. C. Langdell," 312n.

97. Harvard Law School, Faculty Minutes (26 June 1871).

98. Harvard Law School, Faculty Minutes (24 June 1872, 20 June 1874).

deems just."[99] This compromise, congenial to both hard and easy graders, allowed each professor to fail as many or as few students as he wished, and its significance appears in table 4, which presents the average grades awarded by HLS professors in first-year subjects during the first stage of transformation at HLS, before Washburn retired in 1876. Table 4 reveals that, at a time when the passing grade was 70 percent in each course, Washburn's grades averaged near the mid-80s, while Langdell's hovered about the mid-60s. Washburn thought most students worthy of passing; Langdell believed that most deserved to fail. Washburn's influence in resisting the standard of academic merit is shown by the fact that, before he retired in June 1876, the average annual passing rate of first-year HLS students examined was 80 percent. Immediately after he retired, the average dropped to 70 percent, as seen in table 5. Washburn's retirement did not end the debate over grading, although the gravamen shifted, marking the end of the first stage in the transition to academic meritocracy. Washburn was willing to assign grades that diverged sharply from Langdell's because he embraced the gentlemanly tradition, which had never ranked intellectual attainments first in the hierarchy of educational goals.[100] Washburn was not ashamed to appear academically lenient, because he believed that other attributes were more important than academic merit.

After Washburn's retirement, the passing grade stipulated by the faculty began to fluctuate dramatically: 65 percent in 1876, 40 percent in 1877, 50 percent in 1878, and so forth. More remarkably, the average grades assigned by each professor congregated around whatever new minimum was stipulated: Langdell and Ames generally just below; others generally just above.[101] This pattern emerged because Gray and Thayer, unlike Washburn, accepted the meritocratic standard, and did not want to appear less academically rigorous than Langdell. As Gray later wrote defensively to President Eliot, "It has been assumed that Mr. Langdell marks lower than any one else. . . . You will see that I mark at least as low as any one. I have *not* rejected as many men as some of my colleagues. . . . If it is deemed for the advantage of the school that I slash more severely, I shall be very glad to do so."[102] Consequently, the fluctuation of the minimal passing grade and the congregation of the average assigned grades after 1876 reflect faculty debate over how severe to make the standard of academic merit, not whether such a standard should be severe.

99. Harvard Law School, Faculty Minutes (2 July 1875). See 27 June 1874, 3 Oct. 1874.

100. Brauer, *Education of a Gentleman*, 52.

101. Annual faculty decisions on passing mark are recorded in front pages of Harvard Law School, Grade Records, vol. 0. See grades in vols. 0, 1.

102. Gray to Eliot (11 Mar. 1886).

TABLE 4 Average Grades in First-Year Subjects Awarded by HLS Faculty, 1869–76

Subject	1869–70	1870–71	1871–72	1872–73	1873–74	1874–75	1875–76
Property	77% [Washburn]	88% Washburn	86% Washburn	84% Washburn	85% Washburn	83% Washburn	82% Washburn
Contracts	63% [Langdell]	66% Langdell	67% Langdell	71% Langdell	62% Ames	68% Ames	61% Ames
Torts	71% [Green]	68% Green	67% Green	71% Green	80% Lathrop	73% Ames	67% Ames
Criminal Law	76% [Bennet]	77% Bennet	74% Green	74% Green	83% Washburn	85% Washburn	82% Washburn
Civil Procedure	66% [Langdell]	66% Langdell	60% Langdell	57% Langdell	64% Langdell, Ames	60% Ames	59% Langdell

Source: HLS, Grade Records, vol. o.

Note: The 1869–70 grades were assigned in the course for the 1870–71 academic year, because those entering HLS in 1869 apparently took these first-year courses in the 1870–71 school year.

TABLE 5　Results of Annual Examinations for First-Year Classes at HLS, 1870–80

Academic Year	First-Year Students Entering the School	First-Year Students Examined in June	First-Year Students Passing in June	Percentage of Examined Students Passing
1870–71	165	45	37	82
1871–72	92	26	19	73
1872–73	87	56	46	82
1873–74	95	52	39	75
1874–75	102	65	55	85
1875–76	119	75	62	83
Washburn retires				
1876–77	128	89	63	71
1877–78	111	66	46	70
1878–79	102	61	37	61

Source: HLS, Grade Records, vols. 0, 1.

The second dispute during the first stage of transition to academic meritocracy arose when Langdell proposed to require a bachelor's degree in the liberal arts for admission to the LL.B. course. This radical notion reflected his longstanding view of law as "a learned and liberal profession of the highest grade,"[103] and contrasted with the practice at HLS, and most other law schools, of requiring for admission "no examination, and no particular course of previous study," only a minimum age of nineteen and "testimonials of good moral character."[104] Not until 1896 did the American Bar Association recommend even a high school education as a minimum entrance requirement, which only a fraction of law schools had adopted by that point.[105] Therefore, Langdell's idea to require a college degree for admission

103. Langdell, Annual Report 1876–77, 89. Eliot and Langdell had this move in mind early on. C. Eliot, Annual Report 1871–72, 29. At HLS the fraction of college graduates among the students rose from about half in 1871 to two-thirds in 1879, four-fifths in 1895, to nine-tenths in 1900. C. Eliot, Annual Report 1879–80, 23–25; Ames, Annual Report 1899–1900, 168.

104. Harvard University, *Catalog 1869–70*, 59; Harvard University, *Catalog 1870–71*, 70; Harvard Law School, *Catalog 1871–72*, 2. The law schools of Boston University and Columbia University announced the expectation of a college degree for admission in the 1870s, but allowed the requirement to be easily evaded. See C. Warren, *History of the Harvard Law School*, 2:394n; Waltzer, "Harvard Law School under Langdell and Eliot," 53n79.

105. A. Reed, *Training for the Public Profession of the Law*, 319; Finnegan, "Raising and Leveling the Bar," 211. In the mid-1890s fewer than half of the law students at Columbia were college graduates, and the next highest fractions were found at Northwestern with 39 percent, Yale with 31 percent, and Michigan with 17 percent. In 1905 the percentages of college graduates among students at the law schools of certain

amounted to establishing academic achievement as the standard to enter HLS, and his aggressive push for this reform in 1875 met stiff opposition on both procedural and substantive grounds.

At a faculty meeting in February 1875 Langdell, Ames, Washburn, and Eliot began considering the requirement of a bachelor's degree for admission. Given the opposition of Washburn and the absence of Thayer, who had joined the faculty in the previous October, the dean was charged to "prepare a formal statement of the views of the majority of the Faculty on the subject, so far as they can be ascertained, and submit the same to the Faculty at the next meeting."[106] At the next faculty meeting on February 27, which Thayer also missed, the faculty voted to announce a new admissions policy in the HLS catalog of 1875–76, effective with the class entering in fall 1877: "*The course of instruction in the School is designed for persons who have received a college education*, and Bachelors of Arts will be admitted as candidates for a degree on presentation of their diplomas; but for the present, young men who are not Bachelors of Arts will also be admitted to the school as candidates for a degree upon passing a satisfactory examination."[107] Considering this an "important event in the history of the law school, and . . . in the history of legal education in the United States," Eliot immediately brought the new policy to the Corporation, which endorsed it two days later.[108] In May the Corporation strengthened this pathbreaking endorsement by voting to confer on Langdell an honorary LL.D. at commencement in June 1875.[109]

The adoption of this extremely high admission requirement was not only substantively radical, but procedurally suspect. Eliot had neglected to consult or inform the Overseers, whom he knew would oppose the measure, and Langdell had violated faculty process, it turned out. Both groups therefore revolted. In December 1875 the Overseers Visiting Committee to the Law School devoted its annual report to criticizing not only the new admissions requirement but also the other "radical and important" changes at the school. Meanwhile, Parsons and

---

leading universities were: Harvard 99, Columbia 82, Chicago 60, Yale 35, Pennsylvania 35, Northwestern 31, Michigan 13, Cornell 10, and Illinois 7. C. Eliot, Annual Report 1904–5, 41. Nationally in 1910, "only 8 percent of lawyers admitted to the bar were college graduates." Auerbach, *Unequal Justice: Lawyers and Social Change*, 95.

106. Harvard Law School, Faculty Minutes (17 Feb. 1875). See J. Thayer, "Memorial" [Feb. 1876], leaf 2; E. Washburn, "Harvard Law School," leaf 9r.

107. Harvard Law School, Faculty Minutes (27 Feb. 1875). Emphasis added. See Harvard Law School, *Catalog 1875–76*, 94.

108. Quotation is from C. Eliot, Annual Report 1874–75, 23. See [Langdell], Handwritten sheet stating HLS admissions policy [1875], in C. Eliot, Papers, box 67; Harvard University, Corporation Records, 12:102 (1 Mar. 1875).

109. Harvard University, Corporation Records, 12:113 (10 May 1875); Harvard College, Graduation Program, 1875.

Washburn were stoking discontent among the Overseers and influential alumni behind the scenes.[110]

On 27 December 1875 the HLS professors met at the president's house to discuss the critical report of the Overseers Visiting Committee. Langdell, Ames, and Thayer attended, along with Gray, who had joined the faculty in the previous April. Washburn was absent, having told the president that he would resign in 1876.[111] At the meeting, Thayer spoke at length, commencing with an ambiguous encomium for Langdell: "[The Overseers Committee] does not *know* evidently what a man we have in our dean. But . . . for one, I beg to say that whatever criticism I may make, I do it with the very greatest respect for him, and whatever I desire to have done or undone, I would not have him otherwise than just as he is."[112] These words are remarkably equivocal: Langdell himself is at issue as much as the new policies; he has great strengths and shortcomings; the new policies deserve praise and criticism; the dean may or may not be receptive to these observations.

Next, Thayer rebutted the Committee's support for the old methods of instruction: the Committee justified them only by appealing to tradition, neglected the fact that the old teaching methods were still employed at the school, and expressed "no appreciation of the remarkable qualities" of Langdell who had made significant improvements to examinations, the library, and other aspects of HLS. Nevertheless, Thayer suggested that the report's criticism "makes us . . . more free to criticize and oppose what we do not like."

Providing his own cue, Thayer then expressed his criticism. The teaching "method pursued by Mr. L. and Mr. A." deserves "strong praise" but there is "danger attending it." Regarding faculty hiring, "my experience leads me to attach a great deal of importance to . . . the advantage of some experience at the bar to one who is to teach." Regarding admissions, "I incline to think our specific requirements are *injudicious*. . . . If any of us could help in bringing here such a [student] as Judge Shaw or Marshall, would not the time [at HLS] be a vast addition to his merit?"[113]

---

110. The 1874–75 report is quoted in J. Thayer, "Memorial" [Feb. 1876], leaf 1. This report, about sixteen pages long, is missing from its place in the Harvard University, Overseers records, and it is replaced by a note saying that it was "put in the hands of Hon. Emory Washburn." Harvard University, Reports of the Overseers Visiting Committee, vol. 1, 1871–84. See E. Washburn, "Harvard Law School," leaves 11r, 20–21v. See "Reform in Legal Education" (July 1876).

111. Harvard Law School, Faculty Minutes (27 Dec. 1875).

112. The quotations and points here and below are drawn from six pages of written notes that Thayer entitled "Memorial" [Feb. 1876] and composed in preparation for his oral presentation.

113. U.S. Supreme Court Justice John Marshall (1755–1835) did not attend college and so would not have qualified to enter HLS under Langdell's new policy. Thayer's second example of Massachusetts Chief Justice Lemuel Shaw (1781–1861), who graduated from Harvard College in 1800 but did not attend law school, seems to confuse requiring a college degree to attend law school with requiring the LL.B. to practice law.

James B. Thayer,
circa 1880. Courtesy
of Special Collections
Department, Harvard
Law School Library.

After objecting to the substance of the new admissions policy, Thayer then made a startling accusation. While conceding that he favored an admissions examination and had missed the faculty meetings at which the new policy was discussed, Thayer accused the dean of manipulating the procedure to secure his end. The central issue "all com[es] to limit[ing] [admissions] to [college] graduates, and as we voted that down, it was, in my judgment, clearly not right to insert an announcement [in the HLS Catalog] which intimates that we contemplate it.... [as conveyed by the words] 'it is designed'. I was surprised to see it, and have always been amazed at it."

The surprising words that appeared in the faculty minutes of 27 February and then in the HLS catalog of 1875–76 were apparently never approved by the faculty, but entered into the minutes at a later time. Indeed, the passage in the faculty minutes is written in a different hand than the surrounding text. In particular, it seems that Langdell added the critical sentence that amazed Thayer and that radically changed the import of the policy: "*The course of instruction in the School is designed for persons who have received a college education.*" Thayer had understood the examination to be the threshold requirement for admission, from which a B.A. graduate could be exempted. Langdell turned this to mean that the B.A. degree was the threshold requirement and that the examination was a test of equivalency. Then he had his view written into the minutes even though, according to Thayer, "we voted that down." The dean apparently announced the policy ex cathedra in contradiction to the faculty's vote.

Four days after Thayer remonstrated Langdell at the HLS faculty meeting, the Overseers Committee on Reports and Resolutions did the same to Eliot by proposing a resolution declaring that the new HLS admissions policy was "injudicious"—employing the same word as Thayer—and "that the grave change attempted by the Faculty of the Law School, assented to by the Corporation, and published in the Catalog for the year 1875–76 . . . should have been submitted to the Board of Overseers for its approval." The full board then took these resolutions under consideration in the early months of 1876.[114]

The meritocrats were initially unrepentant. Ames wrote to the president: "the opposition of the Overseers of the leading university in this country to the proposed examination for admission to the Law School, . . . seems to me well nigh incomprehensible. . . . and the views of Massachusetts lawyers admit of but one explanation—the utter degradation of the legal profession in this country."[115] Here Ames echoed Langdell's link between academic standards and the quality and status of the legal profession. Eliot meanwhile proceeded with plans for administering the admissions examination of HLS and other departments in the university.[116] A month later, however, the reformers began to retreat. In late February the HLS faculty voted to eliminate Langdell's incendiary statement: "The course of instruction is designed for persons who have received a college education." Instead, they left the threshold ambiguous by adopting the policy: "At the beginning of the academic year 1877–78, and afterwards, candidates for a degree who are not graduates of a college will only be admitted upon passing a satisfactory examination. . . ."[117]

In response, the Overseers resolutions were withdrawn in April 1876,[118] although Langdell's opponents continued to press their advantage. In June the HLS faculty voted to reduce the passing grade in first-year courses to sixty-five, to convert it to an *average* of the courses, and to provide the loophole that a failing student could still be passed if the "respective examiners" agreed to it.[119] This outcome could only have been achieved through an alliance of Washburn, Thayer, and Gray outvoting Langdell and Ames. More significantly, the Corporation and Overseers chose Bradley to replace Washburn on the faculty despite the opposition

114. Quotation is from Report of the Committee of Reports and Resolutions (31 Dec. 1875), in Harvard University, Overseers Records, 11:225 (12 Jan. 1876). See 11:231, 233 (26 Jan., 9 Feb. 1876).

115. Ames to Eliot (25 Jan. 1876).

116. Harvard Law School, Faculty Minutes (28 Jan. 1876).

117. Harvard Law School, Faculty Minutes (26 Feb., 25 Mar. 1876). See Harvard Law School, *Catalog 1876–77*, 2.

118. Harvard University, Overseers Records, 11:237 (12 Apr. 1876).

119. Harvard Law School, Faculty Minutes (24 June 1876).

of Eliot, Langdell, and Ames. Having pushed the meritocrats back on their heels, the Overseers Visiting Committee declared a truce in November 1876, finding no fault at HLS and opining: "The condition of the School is excellent and the zeal and fidelity of the teachers and pupils is all that can be desired."[120]

The arrival of gentlemanly professor Bradley in 1876 meant that Langdell still did not have a favorable majority on the faculty, although Bradley's lack of engagement at HLS made him a more tractable opponent than Washburn. The offending language about admissions criteria had been excised, but the view that "the School is designed for persons who have received a college education" was never challenged again, and that became the unofficial policy of the school until 1893, when the admissions exam was formally eliminated as an option for those seeking to enter HLS as degree candidates.[121] By June 1876 Langdell had therefore succeeded in establishing academic merit as the primary standard of evaluation both to enter the school and to progress through the curriculum. The fundamental issue debated at HLS henceforth was not whether academic merit would be the primary standard, but how high or far that standard would be extended in various dimensions of "the *new system*."[122]

Thayer and Gray certainly embraced gentility, but they also advocated academic merit and would not concede the high ground to Langdell. In their minds, in fact, the issue became not academic policy but Langdell himself. The personal and principled dimensions of Langdell's rationale for academic meritocracy began to work against each other, because his personal identification with the academic standards belied the formal system of rational, disinterested policies and rules. Very soon, Thayer would no longer affirm, "I would not have [Langdell] otherwise than just as he is."[123]

The Meaning of Academic Merit

Beginning in 1876 after the departure of Washburn, the second stage of transformation intensified the conflicts by raising the question about the meaning of academic merit and, in particular, whether Langdell himself should be the norm. This question underlay the heated controversies arising over two related changes in academic policy: extending the degree program to three years and establishing an honor track. Here, too, the gravamen was not only substantive but also proce-

120. Harvard University, Report of the Overseers Visiting Committee, 1875–76, 1.
121. Harvard Law School, Faculty Minutes, 18 Apr. 1893; C. Eliot, Annual Report 1892–93, 30–31.
122. Emphasis in original. "Harvard College Law School," 67.
123. J. Thayer, "Memorial" [Feb. 1876].

dural, for Langdell practiced aggressive tactics that violated established process and prompted conflicting interpretations. Some thought that he arrogantly viewed himself as the sole arbiter of academic merit; others that he was defensively compensating for the unpopularity of his courses; still others that he was justifiably defending the meritocratic revolution against those seeking to compromise or reverse it.

The reform of extending the HLS program of study to three years—thereby adding another lap to the race for academic merit—initially prompted little opposition, even from those outside Harvard who derided Langdell's other changes.[124] By 1873 Langdell and Eliot were already calling for extending the program to three years, and in February 1876 the faculty approved the move. However, given the concurrent disputes over admissions standards and Washburn's replacement, Eliot delayed communicating the vote to the Corporation until April, when the faculty qualified the proposal by allowing students to spend the third year out of residence working in a law office and still earn the degree, if they returned at the end of the year and passed the exams.[125] This qualification placated critics who felt that the HLS program was becoming too academic and removed from practice. The Corporation then approved the revised proposal, and HLS announced in its catalog for 1876–77 that all students entering in fall 1877 would be required to complete the three-year program by passing examinations in the third-year courses to be introduced in 1879–80.[126]

But what was to be the curriculum of the new three-year program? During the entire 1876–77 academic year, the faculty could not reach agreement beyond adding courses in constitutional law, conflict of laws, and wills. The impasse arose because Langdell declined to modify the requirement that all second-year students had to take his Equity Jurisdiction and Pleading, even though Thayer agreed to relinquish the companion requirement to take his Evidence.[127] Equity was becoming the predominant subject of Langdell's teaching and writing, and he and others highly valued his expertise, which was "an accomplishment exceedingly rare in this country," especially concerning the most difficult and problematic aspects: jurisdiction and procedure.[128]

Langdell's refusal stemmed from the fact that students avoided his courses;

124. "Reform in Legal Education" (July 1876); "Higher Legal Education" (1876); E. Washburn, "Harvard Law School," leaf 17r–17v.

125. C. Eliot, Annual Report 1871–72, 22; Langdell, Annual Report 1872–73, 64; Harvard Law School, Faculty Minutes (26 Feb., 1 Apr. 1876).

126. Harvard University, Corporation Records, 12:173 (24 Apr. 1876); C. Eliot, Annual Report 1875–76, 28; Harvard University, *Catalog 1876–77*, 90.

127. Gray to Thayer (2 July 1877); Harvard Law School, Faculty Minutes (12 June 1877).

128. Quotation is from Langdell to Webster (15 Oct. 1857). See Frederick Pollock, quoted in J. Smith, "Christopher Columbus Langdell," 31.

his electives enrolled only a handful of students whereas all the other professors attracted at least five times as many.[129] Consequently, if the requirement was
eliminated, Langdell's enrollment in Equity also was certain to fall precipitously.
Nevertheless, Washburn, Gray, and others felt that protecting Langdell's enrollment in Equity was unfair to other faculty, as well as to the students forced to take
a course that "comprises only a part of what is commonly known in the profession
as equity."[130]

In fall 1877 prospective students first faced the new admissions requirement of
either a college degree or the passing of an examination, as well as the three-year
program of study. Not only were those two "very restrictive measures" daunting,
but the curriculum for the third-year was still not specified because the faculty
could not agree. As a result, the School "ran no small pecuniary risk" from declining
enrollments.[131] In the early 1870s the number of students at HLS had dropped due
to the unpopularity of Langdell's early reforms at HLS and to the founding of the
law school at Boston University in 1872 as an alternative to HLS. Enrollments then
recovered and rose by 1876–77 because many students tried to enter before the
two "very restrictive measures" went into effect.[132]

Table 6 summarizes the chronology of the key reforms, the overall enrollment, and the tuition during this period, revealing the financial problem faced by
Langdell and Eliot as they sought additional revenue in order to build the school.
Raising standards and tuition threatened enrollment according to the traditional
thinking about professional education, which presumed that low tuition and low
standards were necessary to attract students and maintain sufficient revenue. To
succeed, the Langdellian revolution required a new economic logic for professional education.

Langdell and Eliot certainly understood the market pressures driven by "the
recognized tendency of even the educated public to estimate the success and worth
of an educational institution by the number of students who resort to it."[133] They
anticipated the drop in enrollment and prudently banked reserves during the temporary influx of students prior to fall 1877 in order to offset the anticipated drop
in revenue in future years.[134] Then they annually "scanned with some anxiety
the statistics" about enrollment, hoping that the additional tuition from the new

129. Langdell, Annual Report 1876–77, 83.
130. [Gray], Six Points ([May 1878]). See E. Washburn, "Harvard Law School," leaves 20r, 19v; Gray
to Thayer (1 July 1877).
131. Quotations are from C. Eliot, Annual Report 1883–84, 34.
132. Langdell, Annual Report 1892–93, 135; C. Warren, History of the Harvard Law School, 2:382, 398,
502–3; Swasey, "Boston University Law School," 54–65; LaPiana, Logic and Experience, 17–18.
133. C. Eliot, Annual Report 1871–72, 28.
134. C. Eliot, Annual Report 1875–76, 28. In 1876–77 HLS realized a surplus of $5,366 on a budget of
$29,269. Harvard University, Treasurer Report 1876–77, 39.

TABLE 6   Chronology of Key Reforms, Enrollment, and Tuition at HLS, 1870–86

Academic Years	Major Reforms	Tuition for Full Course	Enrollment of All Students
1870–73	Introduction of two-year curriculum, written exams, and case method.	Rises from $100 to $250	Drops from 165 to 117
1872–75		$250	Rises to 144
1875–76	Catalog announces admissions requirement of bachelor's degree or passing examination.	$300	173
1876–77	Catalog announces three-year curriculum	$300	High point of 199
1877–78	Admissions requirements and three-year curriculum go into effect	$300	196
1878–79	Honor program established. (No graduating class due to three-year curriculum.)	$350	169
1879–80	(First three-year class graduates.)	$450	177
1880–82		$450	161
1882–83	Required hours of 2nd and 3rd years raised.	$450	Low point of 138
1883–86		$450	Rises to 158
1886–87	HLS alumni association formed	$450	188

Source: Langdell, Annual Reports.

third year would ultimately increase revenue unless overall enrollment declined by more than a third.[135] Meanwhile, their long-term plan for the school incorporated a paradoxical way of thinking about the market for professional education and its relationship to academic achievement. This new economic logic found its earliest full expression in response to an external threat during the critical 1877–78 academic year.

In September 1877, while the HLS professors commenced their second year of fruitless debate over the third-year curriculum, and Langdell and Eliot were

135. Quotation is from C. Eliot, Annual Report 1883–84, 34. See C. Eliot, Annual Report 1875–76, 28; Langdell, Annual Report 1875–76, 73.

anxiously scanning enrollment statistics, the highest court in New York issued new rules for admission to the state bar. These required three years of clerkship, two years of which could be substituted by the same number of years of study in a law school in New York State. This favoritism for New York schools (compounding the diploma privilege that Albany Law School and Columbia University law school already enjoyed) greatly disadvantaged HLS[136] by discouraging students who planned to practice in New York from enrolling, just at the time when the two "very restrictive measures" already threatened the financial solvency of the academic meritocracy. As one of the leading jurisdictions in the country, New York was also setting a dismaying example for others.

Langdell protested at length against New York's favoritism in his annual report, written in about December 1877, and Eliot followed suit in long letters to the chief justice of New York's highest court in March 1878. On the one hand, they argued that education for and admission to the practice of law should transcend the commercial pressures of the marketplace. A "Law School . . . is not a commercial establishment, and therefore is not amenable to the law of demand and supply." By favoring New York law schools, the bar admission rules acceded to the norms of the marketplace, treating lawyers "more as artisans than as professional men."[137] Langdell and Eliot thus indicted the low-tuition, low-standard, traditional logic of professional education and, concomitantly, any "rules which make discriminations in favor of the law schools of any particular state," for which HLS had "no desire."[138]

On the other hand, Langdell and Eliot nevertheless embraced a marketplace model for professional education by requesting "all that [HLS] has ever asked for, namely, a free field with no favors."[139] In this competition, however, professional schools would pursue "the interest of those Schools, well understood," which lay in cultivating academic merit.[140] "It is for the interest of the School and the profession" to raise academic standards,[141] because the traditional, commercial approach depreciated the profession, while academic meritocracy advanced its status as "a learned and liberal profession of the highest grade" and, in turn, increased its

136. LaPiana, *Logic and Experience*, 83–88. The "diploma privilege" denoted the entitlement that graduation from a law school automatically qualified the graduate to practice law in a particular jurisdiction.

137. Quotations are from Langdell, Annual Report 1876–77, 91, 89. See C. Eliot, Inaugural Address 1869, 20.

138. Quotations are from C. Eliot, Annual Report 1876–77, 30; C. Eliot to Church (9 Mar. 1878). See C. Eliot, Annual Report 1877–78, 38–39.

139. Langdell, Annual Report 1876–77, 88.

140. C. Eliot to Church (14 Mar. 1878), 146–47.

141. C. Eliot, Annual Report 1871–72, 22.

capacity to "render to the public the highest and best service in the administration of justice."[142] Here was Langdell's functionalist rationale for academic meritocracy: it served the legal profession which then served society.

It also benefited the professional schools, and in this respect Langdell and Eliot paradoxically invoked the discredited commercial justification. They believed that a professional school devoted to academic merit would prosper. "A more general principle" held that a school "will make a money profit by raising its standards, and that at once or in a very short time." The reason was that the school's "demand for greater attainments on the part of its students will . . . increase the reputation and influence of the institution as it makes its privileges and its rewards more valued and more valuable," attracting even more higher quality students.[143] Consequently, Eliot, in particular, sought validation for the academic changes in the growth of enrollments, writing "I am not content unless Harvard grows each year, in spite of the size which it has attained."[144]

The new economic logic of professional education developed by Langdell and Eliot was, therefore, paradoxical. It replaced student preferences and financial success with academic merit as the measure of quality, but ultimately maintained that student preferences and "money profit" would validate professional education based on academic merit. The dean and the president transformed the marketplace of professional education by reasoning that a more demanding and competitive academic system of legal education would attract more and better students. By the same token, New York law schools should not seek "more privileges" but "less," because, although lowering standards "may be temporarily [in] their interest. . . . it cannot, in the long run, be for the good of the Schools."[145]

The insightful analysis that professional schools prosper by disregarding "money profit" proved sound, particularly as the job market slowly began to favor academically meritorious students. By the mid-1880s HLS found itself "unable to fill all the places in lawyers' offices which have been offered . . . for third-year students just graduating."[146] By the early 1890s the appeal of academic training in Langdell's system was strengthened "by the success of recent graduates of the

142. Langdell, Annual Report 1876–77, 89, 91.

143. C. Eliot, Annual Report 1874–75, 26.

144. Quoted in Veysey, *Emergence of the American University*, 356n51. See C. Eliot, Annual Reports 1874–75, 27–29; 1890–91, 19; 1893–94, 23; C. Eliot to Gilman (13 Oct. 1885).

145. C. Eliot to Church (14 Mar. 1878), 146–47.

146. C. Eliot, Annual Report 1885–86, 13.

147. Note, *Harvard Law Review* (1891–92), 238. See Brandeis, *Letters*, 1:86; Bolles, *Harvard University*, 68; Hill, *Harvard College*, 254.

school ... spread through the profession."[147] In the early 1900s other university law schools, as at Yale and Chicago, began to embrace the new economic logic.[148]

But in the late 1870s it was merely an optimistic hope that high academic standards and prosperity could be harmonized. At that point, the nation's other leading law school, at Columbia University, remained, in effect, a proprietary school.[149] Even in the early 1890s the first medical school in the United States to require a bachelor's degree for admission adopted this measure reluctantly in order to satisfy a major donor, fearing that the high standard would depress enrollment.[150] Hence, in spring 1878 Eliot and Langdell ran counter to the prevailing economic logic of professional education when they rebutted discriminatory policies, such as the bar admission standards of New York, and advertised energetically for "meritorious students."[151]

Meanwhile, after two years of discussion about the three-year curriculum, the five HLS professors—Langdell, Ames, Thayer, Gray, and Bradley—set up a committee "to ascertain and report the views of the different members of the faculty." Headed by Gray, the committee adopted in May 1878 six points, which revealed Langdell's struggle to defend the requirement that students take his Equity Jurisdiction and Procedure for two hours, against the attack by the Gray-Thayer-Bradley faction.[152]

The committee decided that "1. Each member of the faculty should have sole control of his method of teaching a subject." This point reaffirmed the policy of tolerance that had prevailed ever since Langdell introduced case method. "2. Whether a subject should be required or elective should be decided by a majority of the faculty." Evidently, Langdell had enforced his personal intransigence by relying on his authority as dean. "3. The subject in question is Equity Jurisdiction and Procedure. 4. It comprises only a part of what is commonly known in the profession as equity." This charge that Langdell's equity course did not cover the field was made against his other courses taught by case method, and assumed that the

148. LaPiana, *Logic and Experience*, 145; Carrington, "Missionary Diocese of Chicago," 491.

149. LaPiana, *Logic and Experience*, 88. See Menken, "Methods of Instruction at American Law Schools," 168; Goebel, *History of the School of Law, Columbia University*, 90–133.

150. This school was Johns Hopkins University. Fleming, *William H. Welch*, 98–99. "In 1900 only John Hopkins required a college degree for admission, and in 1901 Harvard became the second school to institute this requirement ... as of 1900 only 15 or 20 percent of the [medical] schools even required a high school diploma for admission." Ludmerer, *Learning to Heal*, 113. In 1905 the percentages of college graduates among the students at medical schools of certain leading universities were: Harvard 87, Columbia 45, Chicago 45, Yale 14, Pennsylvania 31, Northwestern 19, Michigan 23, Cornell 15, and Illinois 15. C. Eliot, Annual Report 1904–5, 41.

151. *Quillets of the Law*, no. 1 (May 1878), 8.

152. Quotation is from Harvard Law School, Faculty Minutes (14 May 1878). For the following, see Harvard Law School, Faculty Minutes (30 May 1878); [Gray], Six Points ([May 1878]).

goal of teaching was to cover the subject matter, rather than to develop a method of thinking and analysis.[153]

"5. If any member of the faculty thinks that only one hour should be required to be devoted to the subject of Equity Jurisdiction and Procedure, he should vote so." This surprising point indicated both the gentlemanly reluctance to express open disagreement and Langdell's uncompromising insistence on his view. According to the code of the gentry, Langdell should have voluntarily acquiesced to the opinion of others, as did Thayer, without forcing them to insist on their way. Gentlemen deferred to each other, seeking to avoid open conflict or disagreement. Langdell's ungentle behavior forced others to act ungentle as well, and they resented it.

"6. The statement of a professor that he will not teach a subject unless it is made a required subject, should have no effect on the vote. To allow it to do so would be inconsistent with any organization or jurisdiction." Langdell had apparently threatened not to cooperate if the faculty voted to abolish the Equity requirement, indicating the highly personal and acrimonious character of the dispute.

Having rebutted Langdell with these ground rules, the faculty then voted on June 4 that second-year students had to take at least eight hours of course-work, all required, including Langdell's Equity Jurisdiction (one hour). In the third year, students had to choose at least six hours from a list of nine courses, including Langdell's Equity Procedure (two hours) and Langdell's Civil Procedure (two hours).[154] By this compromise, Langdell surrendered a required hour of his second-year equity course, while third-year students were required to take at least one of his advanced courses, unless additional courses were added to the third-year options, which seemed likely. To balance that possibility and to induce students to take Langdell's third-year Equity Procedure, the faculty agreed informally that students could earn a degree cum laude only if they had completed Equity Procedure. To that point, cum laude was a designation that the law faculty could vote to award to any student at its discretion.[155]

Notwithstanding this generous compromise, Langdell then tried to make his Equity Jurisdiction and Pleading the sine qua non of academic distinction. He proposed to establish an "Ordinary" program of study, in which enrollment in Equity would be wholly elective, and an "Honor" program, in which three hours of Equity, but no higher grade point average, would be required. In this way, Langdell's scholarly specialty and teaching would be uniquely identified with academic distinction

---

153. On this frequent criticism that Langdell and case method teaching failed to "cover" the subject matter, see Kimball, "Proliferation of Case Method," 226–27.

154. Harvard Law School, Faculty Minutes (4 June 1878).

155. Gray to Thayer [June 1878]; Langdell to Thayer (24 July 1878).

by "specially honoring those who pursued [equity] successfully to the full extent that it is taught."[156]

Langdell's aggrandizing proposal made Gray and others "sorry, surprised and disgusted. . . . To divide the school into two classes one of whom is to be entitled to a higher degree because they have studied equity procedure, though their marks may fall far below those attained by men who have not taken equity procedure, this I cannot consent to. . . . The matter would be emphasized and held up to . . . the *just* indignation and ridicule of the school and the profession."[157] Langdell may have believed that his course was the best indicator of academic merit, for he was known to be the most demanding professor. Nevertheless, by establishing his own specialty as the gateway to academic honor, he appeared to violate disinterested norms of academic merit and thus planted the seed of invidious discrimination in the putatively objective system of the academic meritocracy.

At a contentious faculty meeting held in the latter half of June to consider the dean's counterproposal, Langdell, Ames, and, likely, Eliot were strongly allied, to Gray's disgust, and the faculty voted to set aside the June 4 vote.[158] In subsequent weeks, they established a new compromise based on Langdell's proposal and the fact that the School could not staff the three ten-hour years that they had originally envisioned for the three-year curriculum. Instead, in the Ordinary program, they required fourteen total hours of entirely elective coursework in the second and third years and an average of 60 percent in examinations in order to earn a degree. The Honor program required fourteen total hours of coursework in the second and third years, including three hours of equity among ten stipulated hours. In addition, the Honor student had to average at least 75 percent without any failing grades. Thus, Langdell traded one hour of equity required of all students for three hours of equity required only of honor students.

Langdell's proposal had won, but he still was not satisfied. Although equity constituted only three of the required ten hours for the Honor program, and although higher grades were required for the honor degree, he proclaimed in his annual report that "the leading distinction" between the two programs was "that in the honor course all subjects having in them a large amount of equity are required, while in the ordinary course those subjects . . . are elective. A leading object of the measure . . . was to encourage the study of equity by specially honoring those who pursued it successfully to the full extent that it is taught."[159] This proclamation

156. Langdell, Annual Report 1877–78, 87–88.
157. Gray to Thayer [June 1878].
158. Gray to Thayer (27 July 1878); Harvard Law School, Faculty Minutes (28 June 1878).
159. Langdell, Annual Report 1877–78, 87–88.

about "the leading distinction" rested only on "the whims" of Langdell,[160] who persisted in treating his own specialty as more valuable and meritorious than that of his colleagues. Furthermore, he announced his viewpoint from the authoritative pulpit of his annual report as dean, implicitly presenting it as policy endorsed by the school and the faculty. The move resembled closely his announcement in the HLS catalog two years earlier that "the School is designed for persons who have received a college education."[161]

Far from conceding that equity was the "leading" characteristic of the Honor program, Gray and Thayer still maintained that Langdell's supposedly narrow course did not even deserve to be required at all. They considered the Ordinary/Honor distinction to rest on "a compromise which nobody approves or can defend."[162] In response, they attempted during July to marginalize the Honor program and the requirement to take Langdell's equity course. Ironically, the two ambivalent gentlemanly meritocrats therefore tried to raise the standards for Honor so that fewer students would enroll.

First, they successfully proposed the stricture that the 75 percent average minimum grade had to be achieved separately in each year, rather than overall. Second, they suggested raising the minimum grade for Honor in order to reduce enrollment. As Gray observed, "I hope practically the number will be small who take [the Honor program]. If it is large, I think we must shove the minimum [average grade] higher up." Third, in a lawyerly move, Thayer argued that, since the faculty had voted on a new course only for the cum laude degree, the summa cum laude degree was not governed by the cum laude requirements. Langdell replied that, logically, summa cum laude entailed all the requirements for cum laude, to which Thayer complained about "the impossibility of arguing logically from a compromise which nobody approves or can defend or which is adopted to meet the whims of one instructor." Invoking faculty process that he himself had violated, Langdell also maintained that a faculty vote was needed to establish any policy regarding summa cum laude, and Thayer's strategy ended there.[163]

In the end, Gray and Thayer could not prevent Langdell from making his Equity the jewel in the crowning Honor program atop the HLS curriculum. Focused on his law practice, Bradley provided no help, and Ames and Eliot supported Langdell in the crisis atmosphere of 1877 and 1878. The route to academic honor at HLS—and

160. Gray to Thayer (11 July 1878).
161. Harvard Law School, Faculty Minutes (27 Feb. 1875). See Harvard Law School, *Catalog 1875–76*, 94.
162. Gray to Thayer (11 July 1878).
163. Quotations are from Gray to Thayer (11 July 1878). See also Harvard Law School, Faculty Minutes (28 June 1878); Langdell to Thayer (24 July 1878); Gray to Thayer (26, 27 July 1878).

to a leading law firm—would go through Langdell's classroom. The 1878–79 HLS catalog therefore announced the long-awaited third-year program of study by way of introducing the new "Ordinary Course" and "Honor Course," which received an approving review in the *American Law Review*. From that point, the two programs gradually gained acceptance, and in June 1882, notwithstanding a continuing drop in enrollment, the faculty lengthened the race for academic merit by adding two hours to both the second and third years in both programs of study.[164]

Organizing the Alumni

In 1882 the decline in enrollment began to reverse, but the future of Langdell's system was still uncertain. Spring 1882 witnessed the intense fight over William Keener's appointment, while Thayer, flushed with his success in raising the endowment for the professorship of Oliver Wendell Holmes Jr. in January 1882, began soliciting money for the HLS library and met grudging resistance.[165] Thayer's personal appeals to HLS alumni in the Boston area netted no more than a few hundred dollars each. In New York City, senior HLS alumni, such as Joseph Choate, contributed like amounts and refused to involve themselves in the effort. In contrast, the recent alumni "all expressed tremendous willingness to do anything in their power. It is plain, however, that none of them have much hope. In fact, the whole outlook seems to me rather hopeless at present," wrote a young New York alumnus. "Why does not the law school or Mr. Langdell appeal directly to all the graduates who have flourished and grown rich?"[166]

Even if Langdell had been willing to join the soliciting, he and his policies did not generate enthusiasm among the older alumni, particularly in view of the serious business recession in the early 1880s. One recent alumnus who had hoped to raise ten thousand dollars in Chicago reported to Thayer: "But I found, on coming into close contact with the old gentlemen whom I had in mind, the hard stuff they are made of. . . . I feel very grateful to the Law School. [But] they criticize its methods as ill-adapted to a world where life is short and art is long." Appeals in Philadelphia and San Francisco were no more successful.[167] Consequently, solicita-

164. Harvard Law School, *Catalog 1878–79*, 2–4; "Harvard Law School" (1878), 159–61; Harvard Law School, Faculty Minutes (13 June 1882). See Harvard Law School, *Catalog 1879–80*, 3–5; Langdell, Annual Report 1877–78, 87–88.

165. J. Thayer, Correspondence and Memoranda, 3:108. See "The Law School at Cambridge," *Boston Advertiser*, 18 Jan. 1882; "The Law School at Cambridge," *Boston Evening Post*, 24 Jan. 1882, clippings in J. Thayer, Papers, box 20, f. 1.

166. Morawetz to Thayer (27 Mar. 1882). See other letters in J. Thayer, Papers, box 20, f. 1.

167. Quotation is from George F. Canfield to Thayer (19 Apr. 1882), J. Thayer, Papers, box 20, f. 1. See other letters in folder.

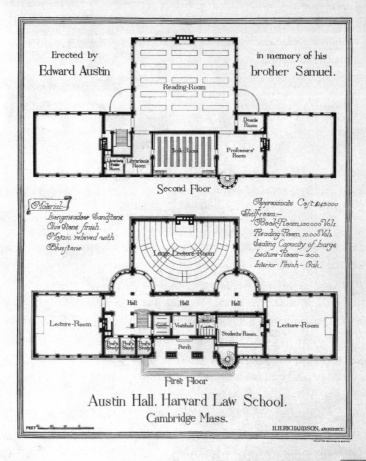

Erected by
Edward Austin

in memory of his
brother Samuel.

Reading-Room

Dean's Room

Book-Room

Professors' Room

Librarians' Room

Second Floor

Material:—
Longmeadow Sandstone.
Ohio Stone finish.
Mosaic relieved with
Bluestone.

Approximate Cost: $145,000
Shelfroom:—
Book-Room, 100,000 Vols.
Reading-Room, 10,000 Vols.
Seating Capacity of Large
Lecture-Room— 300.
Interior Finish— Oak.

Large Lecture-Room

Hall   Hall   Hall

Lecture-Room   Lecture-Room

Vestibule

Students' Room

Prof's Study   Prof's Study   Prof's Study

Porch

First Floor

Austin Hall. Harvard Law School.
Cambridge Mass.

H.H. RICHARDSON, ARCHITECT.

Austin Hall floor plan, 1883. The large semicircular classroom was built to accommodate case method teaching. Courtesy of Special Collections Department, Harvard Law School Library.

tions like Thayer's did not succeed in the early 1880s, apart from one large gift to build "the very handsome and commodious" Austin Hall, which opened in October 1883 and consumed the school's entire surplus for furnishings.[168]

The outlook changed in 1886, marking "the beginning of [a] period of rapid growth" in enrollment that was "coeval with the establishment of the Law School [Alumni] Association." In July 1886, at the prompting of Brandeis, a few of the original "Kit's freshmen" met with several older and recent alumni who ardently supported Langdell's reforms, and this group began to organize an association of HLS alumni. In conjunction with the effort, Langdell arranged for the University to publish a catalog of all HLS alumni and to send a copy to every living graduate of the school: "its natural friends and supporters."[169] In November 1886 the newly constituted HLS Association, comprising over five hundred graduates, held its inaugural meeting at an elaborate dinner that headlined the festivities commemorating the 250th anniversary of Harvard University. This billing officially confirmed the status of HLS as the paragon of a professional school at Harvard.[170]

The keynote speaker at the inaugural dinner was Massachusetts Supreme Judicial Court justice Holmes, now back in good graces, who offered personal testimony of the merits of "Mr. Langdell's way" of teaching. The dean himself met "with prolonged applause and three rousing cheers," and proceeded in his speech to explain his inductive teaching by making an analogy to the study of natural science. A decade later upon his retirement, he credited the HLS Association—guided primarily by Shattuck, James Carter, and Brandeis—with ensuring and enhancing the school's rapid growth thereafter.[171]

The formation of this alumni association culminated the series of reforms constituting the "new system" of academic meritocracy that Langdell designed and built between 1870 and 1886. By combining educational formalism with the goal of fostering academic merit, he introduced and effected in the face of great opposition: the admissions requirement of a bachelor's degree or its equivalent,

168. C. Eliot, Annual Report 1882–83, 27. See C. Eliot, Annual Reports, 1880–81, 26; 1883–84, 35.

169. Quotations are from Langdell printed in "Invitation from the Council of the Harvard Law School Association" [1890], in C. Eliot, Papers, box 79, f. 1890. See Langdell to Eliot (5 Sept. 1886), C. Eliot to Arnold (15 Sept. 1886); Harvard University, Corporation Records, 14:7 (27 Dec. 1886).

170. Devens, *Record of the Commemoration* (1887), 55–120, also printed as Harvard Law School Association, *Report* (1887). Long articles in the press highlighted the role of Harvard Law School: *Boston Evening Traveler*, 6 Nov. 1886; *Boston Evening Transcript*, 6 Nov. 1886; *Boston Post*, 6 Nov. 1886; *Boston Herald*, 6 Nov. 1886.

171. Quotations are from, respectively: Harvard Law School Association, *Report* (1887), 48; O. Holmes, Oration 1886, 38. See Langdell, Address 1886, 48; Langdell, Address 1895, 42–43. Beginning in 1914 with Josef Redlich, Langdell's analogy to natural science was frequently attacked during the twentieth century although critics did not understand the context of Langdell's remarks. See appendix 2.

the sequenced curriculum and its extension to three years, the inductive pedagogy of teaching from cases, the hurdle of written examinations for continuation and graduation, the examination posing written hypothetical problems, the program of study leading to academic honor, the independent career track for faculty, the transformation of the library from a textbook dispensary to a scholarly resource, and the national alumni association actively supporting the school.

In support of these new policies, Langdell and Eliot also introduced a new economic logic for professional education. Traditionally, professional schools had maintained low standards and low tuition in order to attract students and sufficient tuition to operate. Langdell and Eliot turned this thinking upside down, arguing that education for and admission to a liberal profession should transcend the commercial pressures of the marketplace. But, paradoxically, they also believed that a professional school devoted to academic merit would prosper. Higher standards would produce better graduates who would be more marketable, making the school more attractive to prospective students while elevating the standards in the profession. This new economic thinking was also part of the institutional system of academic meritocracy in professional education that originated during Langdell's deanship by 1886 and proliferated over the next century into other law schools, medical schools, business schools, and other types of professional schools.

Yet, while the alumni offered up "prolonged applause and three rousing cheers" for Langdell in 1886, it is doubtful that Gray and Thayer clapped enthusiastically. They had personally tasted the hubris accompanying the competition for academic honor. In theory, the formal system of academic meritocracy applied disinterested, objective standards through neutral, impersonal policies in order to identify and rank meritorious students. But from the inception of the system, the original and purest meritocrat—who, at enormous personal sacrifice, had tenaciously fought against the entrenched cultural system of the Brahmin gentry—enshrined his own specialty in the highest rank of academic honor. Langdell perhaps believed that his courses in equity were the crucial test of academic merit in law, but his pride and self-interest appeared to belie the principles of the formal system. A gentleman would have recoiled from this illiberal act of hubris, but a gentleman would never have designed the system and fought so tenaciously to build it.

CHAPTER 7

Students, 1876–1882

Like the HLS professors, students faced the choice of whether to make "the uncomfortable transformation of gentlemen into professionals."[1] Some were attracted to Langdell's vision of sorting students and lawyers by their academic merit; others held to the traditional norms of professional education. In either case, the current and prospective students of HLS had to decide whether and how to respond to the policies of "the *new system*," particularly during the second stage of the school's metamorphosis from 1876 to the early 1880s.[2]

The different paths of four representative individuals offer insight into students' decisions concerning that uncomfortable transformation: John R. Jones (1856–1913), who did not qualify under the new admission requirements, took the last opportunity to enter HLS before they were put in force. George Wigglesworth (1853–1930), who qualified to enter the "new system," nevertheless chose to circumvent its strictures by joining, with Jones, the last class before they took effect. William E. Russell (1857–96), a scion of the Harvard elite, also qualified for the "new system," but was too late to circumvent it, and so rejected it altogether and attended the law school at Boston University. Edmund M. Parker (1856–1938) also qualified, but, unlike Russell, chose to enter the "new system" and excelled. These four students attended law school during the transition to academic meritocracy between 1876 and 1882, and followed divergent but typical paths in negotiating that period of disconcerting change.

1876–77

Entering HLS in September 1876 as members of the last class before the two "very restrictive measures" went into effect,[3] Jones and Wigglesworth stood at opposite

1. Persons, *Decline of American Gentility*, 247.
2. Emphasis in original. "Harvard College Law School," 67.
3. C. Eliot, Annual Report 1883–84, 34. The two measures were extending the degree-course to three years and requiring a college degree, or its equivalent by examination, for admission.

poles of the HLS student body. Raised in a small town outside Scranton, Pennsylvania, Jones completed his secondary education during the early 1870s at nearby Wyoming Seminary, a Methodist school that did not offer the classical studies required by the new admissions exam that HLS introduced in fall 1877. He therefore enrolled in fall 1876 at the age of twenty, having worked as a clerk in a law office after receiving his diploma from Wyoming Seminary. Upon completing the LL.B., he returned to Pennsylvania and practiced law in Scranton until his death, serving as District Attorney of Lackawanna County from 1895 to 1901.[4]

While Jones typified the students who would be excluded by the new admission requirements in the future, Wigglesworth represented the type of student whom Langdell hoped to attract to his system.[5] George's father, Edward, was a graduate of both Harvard College and HLS, a successful lawyer, and a fellow of the American Academy of Arts and Sciences. During summers, the Wigglesworths visited the wealthy family of William F. Weld in Rye, New York, whose son "Willie" was George's playmate on the beach and future classmate at HLS. The Wigglesworths later summered in Bar Harbor, Maine, where Charles Eliot occasionally dropped by. George twice became the brother-in-law of Oliver Wendell Holmes Jr.; their wives were sisters and their siblings married. But Langdell's interest in such students as Wigglesworth stemmed not from their Brahmin background but rather their academic record.

Between 1865 and 1870, George excelled at the famous Dixwell Latin school, where the headmaster was the father of his future wife, Mary Dixwell, and one of his teachers in 1868–69 was James Barr Ames. At Harvard College, Wigglesworth rowed crew, joined an elite social club and a literary society, and was elected to both the Hasty Pudding Club and the editorial board of the *Harvard Advocate*. He also graduated third in his class of 158 in 1874, earning honors in classical languages. Even more impressive to Langdell, Wigglesworth exercised the new option of remaining for a postgraduate year to earn an M.A. by designing and completing "a course of liberal study" in political economy.[6] Wigglesworth thus contributed to the cultural shift from participating in "college life" to pursuing academic achievement that occurred among Harvard undergraduates during the final third of the nineteenth century.[7] Commensurate with that shift, Wigglesworth next embarked

4. Barber, "History of Wyoming Seminary"; Francis, "Mr. John R. Jones," 4.

5. Facts about Wigglesworth here and below are drawn from *New England Historical and Genealogical Register* (1930); Griffin, "Wigglesworth Family Papers"; Handwritten sheet of paper dated 1867, and letters to George Wigglesworth (summer 1876), in Wigglesworth Family Papers, boxes 5, 6.

6. Quotations are from Harvard University, *Catalog 1874–75*, 147–48. See Wigglesworth Family Papers, boxes 5, 13, 32, 35, 37.

7. Horowitz, *Campus Life*, 79; Townsend, *Manhood at Harvard*, 141.

on a "grand tour" of Europe, the final step prescribed by the received tradition of liberal education, but he incorporated into his itinerary four months of study in Germany, the customary pilgrimage for academically ambitious Americans at the time.[8] The strands of academic merit and Brahmin gentility were thus entwined throughout Wigglesworth's liberal education at Harvard and beyond.

In spring 1876 the HLS catalog for 1876–77 announced the admission requirement of a bachelor's degree (or its equivalent in passing an exam) and the three-year curriculum. These "very restrictive measures" entailed additional preparation, time, and expense in order for a student to earn the LL.B., and, after some discussion, the Wigglesworth family decided that George should not complete the traditional two years for his grand tour but return and enter HLS in fall 1876.[9] Meanwhile, young men with less education, fewer resources, and no Harvard contacts, such as Jones, also chose to enroll in this last class that was admitted via minimal requirements to complete the LL.B. in two years.

On Thursday, 28 September 1876, the academic year officially commenced for the diplomate from Wyoming Seminary in Pennsylvania and the Harvard B.A.-M.A., who had studied at Heidelberg. Jones and Wigglesworth's class of 116 first-year students included seventy who held bachelor's degrees: forty-seven from Harvard and twenty-three from other colleges. Rounding out the student body were sixty-five second-year students (who remained from the previous first-year class of ninety-eight) and six postgraduate bachelors of law. The total number of students enrolled at some point during the year reached 199, a historic high point that Langdell and Eliot interpreted as an anomalous bulge before the two "very restrictive measures" went into effect.[10]

Although the academic year at HLS officially commenced on the last Thursday in September, no classes met on that day or the next, when the examinations for "advanced standing" were held. These exams on the first-year courses served students who wished to enter directly into the second year due to prior legal study that they had completed either in a different school or in an office. The September exams also gave those who had failed in the previous June a second chance to pass and keep pace with their classmates. As the academic standards increased between 1876 and 1882 and more students failed, the latter purpose gradually displaced the former.

The last Thursday and Friday in September also provided time for students to

8. Letters to and from George Wigglesworth, Wigglesworth Family Papers, boxes 5, 6.

9. Quotation is from C. Eliot, Annual Report 1883–84, 34. See Harvard University, *Catalog 1876–77*, 90; Letters to and from George Wigglesworth (spring 1876), Wigglesworth Family Papers, box 6.

10. C. Eliot, Annual Report 1875–76, 28.

TABLE 7 Schedule of First-Year Courses for Jones and Wigglesworth, 1876–77

	Monday	*Tuesday*	*Wednesday*	*Thursday*	*Friday*
9–10 A.M.			Torts, Ames	Torts, Ames	Torts, Ames
10–11 A.M.	Criminal Law, Thayer	Civil Procedure, Langdell			
11 A.M.–noon	Real Property, Gray			Real Property, Gray	
Noon–1 P.M.			Contracts, Ames	Contracts, Ames	Contracts, Ames
3 P.M.–6 P.M.					moot courts
8 P.M.	Pow Wow Club				

Source: HLS, *Catalog 1876–77*

settle their living arrangements. Jones resided in one of the local rooming houses, which generally provided cheaper accommodations than the Harvard dormitories, and shared his quarters with a law student from Paris, France, and another from Kansas City, Missouri. Wigglesworth lived in Hollis Hall, occupied mostly by Harvard College graduates, and roomed with college classmates who were also attending HLS.[11] In addition to settling into their rooms, students arranged their accounts with the bursar and matriculated with Dean Langdell, who recorded in a notebook each student's full name and home town, educational background, capacity in languages, prior work in a law office, the name of the individual providing the character reference, any requests for advanced standing or special financial arrangements, and local living arrangements and landlord.[12] As first-year students in the two-year sequenced curriculum, Jones and Wigglesworth enrolled in the ten required hours of the "Big Five" core subjects, as presented in table 7.

The first meeting of the first course of Jones and Wigglesworth's first-year class was in Criminal Law and Criminal Procedure, taught by Thayer, whose opening lecture, on Monday, 2 October 1876, at 10 A.M., reveals the cultural shift at HLS. In the gentlemanly regime prior to Langdell's arrival, the opening lecture to the entering students had been a signal event of welcome and orientation, in which

11. Harvard Law School, *Catalog 1876–77*; Letters to and from George Wigglesworth (spring 1876), Wigglesworth Family Papers, box 6.

12. Langdell, "Memoranda Concerning Law School Students." At some point, the dean's interview was obviated by the admission requirements based on academic merit.

"one of the professors made a lecture explanatory of the course of study, its topics, and the aims of the school, at which the other professors were present." In fall 1870 after returning from his leave in the previous spring, Washburn resumed the custom, but his opening lecture did not meet the approval of Langdell, who terminated the practice.[13]

Assuming that the traditional practice continued when he joined the HLS faculty in fall 1874, Thayer prepared and delivered an extensive welcoming lecture to his class.[14] But by September 1876 he reluctantly acknowledged that school policy discouraged such opening lectures. For the first meeting of Criminal Law and Criminal Procedure, Thayer therefore began by drafting several hundred words of paternal and professional introductory advice, incorporating parts of the first lecture that he had given in fall 1874. Then he crossed it all out and substituted a shorter, less personal introduction, expressing to Jones, Wigglesworth, and their classmates his uncertainty about how, or whether, he should impart the paternal and practical advice that he felt obliged to offer despite his sense that it was no longer appropriate.[15]

> Only a day or two [has passed] since, [it was] arranged [that] I would meet you first. It is not [a] custom of recent [time] to make any formal [address of introduction]. [I] should have been glad to prepare [an address.] Haven't [done so] with any pol[ish.] But two or three things [ought] to be said.... This is the beginning of your study of law. [It is important] to you: one of the marked [phases of life].... [It is] impossible not to sympathize heartily with the good purposes and the honorable ambition that bring you here and to wish heartily for the fulfillment of your best hopes. I trust that when the hour comes for your leaving this room at the end of your course ... you will be able to look back upon a time when you have adhered with a good degree of fidelity to your best resolutions.

Another aspect of the transitional nature of Thayer's lecture appeared in his gentlemanly effort to quell dissent over case method teaching:

> the main [thing] to be done here is to study law, and [I] observe that you come here to study it *according to the programme of the school.* Your mind

13. Quotation is from E. Washburn, "Harvard Law School," leaves 1b, see 3v.

14. See J. Thayer, "Notes on Teaching Evidence," which was separated from Thayer's papers by historian Mark De Wolfe Howe, who, assuming that Thayer's lecture was typical of his day, published it as "First Law School Lecture" (1949).

15. Here and below the quotations are from J. Thayer, Criminal Law Teaching Notebooks, 1:1–2 (2 Oct. 1876) and from Thayer's "Notes on Teaching Evidence" of Oct. 1874, which he cross-references in the text. All emphasis is in the original.

therefore need not be perplexed by doubt as to [the] best way . . . to study this subject, and the method presented by the instructors in each department. . . . Let me say with emphasis that whatever else you do or leave undone, you will err greatly if you do not loyally adopt and follow in the case of each instructor the method which he shall point out in his own department. It may or may not be the method which you or your friends would individually prefer; but in as much as it is the method upon which the instructor founds all his efforts to help you, it is the best one for you under the circumstances of the case. It should be enough for you that it is the method adopted.

Yet another transitional characteristic appeared in Thayer's ambivalence over how much attention students should devote to interests outside of the formal curriculum. On the one hand, he felt that such outside interests—traditionally pursued and encouraged in the older system of gentlemanly acculturation—were beneficial and desirable; on the other hand, he feared that students might lose their focus on academic studies that would determine their professional career. Here was a palpable dilemma arising from the uncomfortable transformation to academic meritocracy. Hence, he advised:

You will probably find enough to do in keeping up faithfully in each subject. Such of you as have to teach [school], etc. should do as little of it as possible. It is probably necessary with some; but the result is nonetheless bad—less time and energy for your studies here. . . . Leave general studies or pursuits to [devote?] special attention to one particular department of science and affairs—law. Do it and steadily. Do not scatter your interest and energy. . . . But . . . do not give up all your private [interests] in other directions: natural science, psychology, languages, poetry, art or any [you are] happy enough to have, etc. Nay, go farther to acquire it. Have steady reading or study. . . . It must not be long, but it must not be omitted for the health of the mind and character. . . . The rule for this sort of thing, let me say again emphatically, is *subordination*, not *extirpation*.

After commenting on the extracurricular opportunities for learning—"Club courts. Converse with men. Moot courts. . . . *Use library* freely. Do not try to attend court much."—Thayer closed with the admonition: "Take notes. Attend lectures. Come freely to instructors. . . . You know at the end of the year comes an exam—a thorough one. The best preparation for that is to attend and to watch carefully the course of the lectures, especially to examine any doctrine or any case which is emphasized by the instructor."

Jones's diary from fall 1876 also reveals the cultural transition at HLS. In line with the gentlemanly tradition, Jones emphasized personal and professional self-improvement no less than academic achievement.[16]

I arose at the usual hour this morning, and attended my recitation in *Pleading*. When I returned to my room at 11 o'clock, I was pleasantly surprised by seeing a letter from my father laying on my table. . . . It was a welcome letter, in which he gave me some wise and judicious instructions, which have made a great effect on my mind. . . . "Make the best of your time—attend church on Sundays—keep out of bad company—set a mark in the future and endeavor to reach it—on that mark be stamped—a good moral character—an honest and virtuous life—integrity towards all men—abstinence from all intoxicating drinks—a good knowledge of law, and an honest and upright practice—a life of usefulness—then, if you should live to a ripe old age like your father, you can look back upon your history through life with satisfaction. . . ." These words are true and applicable to every young lawyer.

Beyond this earnest attention to self-improvement, Jones also took to heart Thayer's advice about ancillary reading in nonlegal topics, and explored "the *large, extensive,* and *comprehensive* Boston Public Library." Nevertheless, Jones also observed that the new prospect of "thorough and searching" final exams weighed on the students, who "walk up to the Librarian and hand in their slips for books, with frowns on their countenances or a worried and anxious look caused by turning over in their minds some knotty and intricate problem of real property."[17]

The shift in students' experience during 1876–77 appeared as well in the pedagogical variety they encountered, evident in Thayer's Criminal Law. Though promising that "I shall ask you questions pretty frequently and shall always expect you to ask questions in regard to any subject which is not understood," he proceeded during the fall by expounding on sections in Blackstone's *Commentaries* and Greenleaf's *Treatise on Evidence* and on assigned cases.[18] Thayer's few questions sought information or announced topics to be discussed, and Wigglesworth recorded no exchange of opinions in class.[19] In the spring, Thayer posed a few hypotheticals,

---

16. The following quotations are from Jones, Diary, 2–5. Emphasis in original.

17. Jones, Diary, 4–5.

18. J. Thayer, Criminal Law Teaching Notebooks, 1:1–2 (2 Oct. 1876). Blackstone, *Commentaries on the Laws of England* (1765–69); Greenleaf, *Treatise on the Law of Evidence* (1866).

19. Wigglesworth, Criminal Law 1876–77. Other students in Thayer's courses recorded Thayer's questions as topical headings, such as "What is the distinguishing characteristic of a crime?" or "What is the burden of proof of insanity?" after which complete answers follow immediately. Mack, Criminal Law 1880–81, 2, 5.

such as: "The punishment of rape being death [in the] law of United States and by imprisonment in state prison for any term of years [under state law], what is the condition of the dweller within the Navy Yard at Charlestown who is guilty of the offence there? Can he be punished by both jurisdictions? By whichever one gets him first? By only one, which?" But most class time was spent in elaborating sections of Blackstone or Greenleaf until, on June 4, Thayer began the notes for his final lecture by exclaiming with relief: "The Last!"[20]

Among the four other first-year courses, Gray's teaching in Real Property most closely resembled Thayer's approach. Assigning Washburn's traditional treatise, Gray lectured on topics under doctrinal headings, citing cases illustratively and spelling out their rules or implications didactically.[21] For his other three courses, taught by Ames and Langdell, Wigglesworth purchased not the large lined notebooks that he used in Thayer's and Gray's courses, but three thin, unlined notebooks, apparently anticipating that he would need less space and a freer hand to record notes.

On Tuesday, October 3, Langdell's one-hour Civil Procedure at Common Law commenced the three-part sequence that he had introduced in the previous academic year. Wigglesworth diligently recorded on the first two pages Langdell's succinct opening lecture that culminated in the steps of civil pleading: "Plaintiff's 1st = Declaration. Defendant's 1st = Plea by 1, 2, 3. Plaintiff's 2nd = Replication. Defendant's 2nd = Rejoinder. Plaintiff's 3rd = Surrejoinder. Defendant's 3rd = Rebutter. Plaintiff's 4th = Surrebutter. Denial raises question for court—others raise question for jury."[22]

On the following day at 9 A.M., Wigglesworth brought an identical empty notebook to the opening class of Torts and recorded Ames's opening lecture, beginning with a sharp distinction between legality and morality: "Law is science of legal rights and remedies for their infringement. Business of lawyer [is] to know what rights men possess and the procedure by which they may be enforced. Legal rights are those for violation of which wrongdoer is compelled [by] government to make compensation to party injured or to suffer punishment or both. There are also moral rights too, but not for lawyers.... So natural rights [as well]."[23] At noon on that same day, Wigglesworth carried his third empty notebook to the first class of Contracts, taught by Ames, and recorded an opening lecture in which Ames imparted several pathbreaking doctrines learned from Langdell, including

20. J. Thayer, Criminal Law Teaching Notebooks, 2:41 (22 Jan. 1877), 4:18–23 (4 June 1877).

21. See E. Washburn, *Treatise on the American Law of Real Property* (1876).

22. Wigglesworth, Civil Procedure 1876–77, leaf 1.

23. Wigglesworth, Torts 1876–77, leaf 1.

the distinction between unilateral and bilateral contracts and the definition of consideration as "detriment incurred by promisee at request of promisor."[24]

Over the next month, Wigglesworth's entries in each of these three notebooks devolved in a similar fashion. Through mid-October, at each meeting in the three case method courses, Wigglesworth dated an entry and recorded half as much as in the previous class: from two pages, to one page, to half a page, to three or four lines. By October 12 Wigglesworth was opening his notebook and dating the class meetings but making no record, except "Lunch at Mooney's" or "Bought my mare." On October 13 Wigglesworth gave up dating the class meetings in Ames's Contracts and began listing titles of cases with brief summaries, following the order of the casebook. After another ten pages, the case briefs cease as well.[25] A parallel devolution occurred in Ames's Torts and Langdell's Civil Procedure.

Conversely, the annotations in Wigglesworth's casebooks increase as the class notes decrease in the corresponding notebook, indicating that class discussion of cases rapidly displaced lectures in these three courses. In torts, for example, Wigglesworth converted to annotating Ames's *Cases on Torts* with comments derived from class discussion. These ranged from posing his own questions: "Why not plead by Confession and avoidance?"; to providing clarifications: "IMPORTANT. Question [in libel] is what the bystanders understand—not what the speaker meant"; to citing frequently what "Ames thinks . . ."; to objecting frequently to the decisions: "Not correct. . . . Not so"; to negating the objections: "~~Not True. . . . Not true~~," indicating an exchange of views in class.[26]

A special twist occurred in Langdell's course because he required students to find and read cases listed on a separate syllabus outside of the assigned casebook, Ames's *Cases on Pleading*, which did not present the broad view of civil procedure that Langdell had introduced. In addition, the dean employed in class the practical exercise "of giving out cases in Pleading, each case containing a statement of facts, and four counsel being assigned, two on a side, to plead against each other on those facts until they came to an issue of law or fact, when the case would be ready for a hearing and decision."[27]

Langdell's exercise in this course resembled the extracurricular mode of legal education: moot courts, which "ought to be most faithfully attended," Professor

24. Wigglesworth, Contracts 1876–77, leaves 1–2.
25. Quotation is from Wigglesworth, Civil Procedure 1876–77, front page. See Wigglesworth, Contracts 1876–77, leaves 1–12.
26. Wigglesworth, Annotations in Ames, *Select Cases on Torts*, 733m, 677marg, 363marg, 399marg, 481marg.
27. Langdell, Annual Report 1870–71, 60. See Langdell's nine-page, handwritten syllabus "Civil Procedure at Common Law. Second Year," 1876–77, in Langdell, Papers. A printed version is tucked in Langdell, "Civil Procedure," vol. 2.

Thayer advised.[28] In the 1870s moot courts were held on Fridays at 3 P.M., with professors rotating as the presiding judge and two students serving as co-counsel on each side of each case. These courts were serious and formal, as indicated both by the printing of statements of facts and students' briefs and by the detailed notes taken by Thayer on cases that he supervised and adjudged. Participating students were chosen by lot, and Wigglesworth and Jones were among the seventy-six students assigned roles in the nineteen moot court cases held during 1876–77.[29]

While faculty-run moot courts served the entire student body, the law clubs demanded more extensive legal research and attracted the most ambitious and talented students. Beginning in the 1820s, HLS students formed clubs to afford more opportunities to conduct moot courts, but these became dormant by the late 1860s.[30] Then in 1870 the small group of "Kit's freshmen," who staunchly supported Langdell's academic reforms, reinvigorated the institution by forming the Pow Wow Club. Its sole purpose was to pursue a demanding schedule of formally arguing and adjudging cases, including the preparation and presentation of extensive written pleadings, briefs, and decisions. Within a few years, Pow Wow was the most prestigious student organization at HLS.[31]

The full membership consisted of ten second-year students on the supreme court and ten first-year students on the superior court. At the beginning of the 1876–77 academic year, the Pow Wow supreme court comprised seven Harvard College graduates, one graduate each from Dartmouth and Brown, and one member without a bachelor's degree. In October 1876 Wigglesworth was one of the first-year students elected to the Pow Wow superior court, which comprised ten Harvard graduates and one from Brown.[32]

As suggested by the skew toward Harvard alumni, election to Pow Wow involved some degree of social connection, but the primary criteria were academic achievement and commitment. For example, the ten members of Wigglesworth's Harvard College class who eventually entered HLS and were elected to Pow Wow included the first-ranked in senior philosophy, the first-ranked in senior mathematics, the first-ranked in senior Greek, the first-ranked in French, the second-

28. Thayer, "Notes on Teaching Evidence," 20.

29. See moot court records in Wigglesworth Family Papers, box 13, f. 1876–78; J. Thayer, Papers, box 9, ff. 1–9; Harvard Law School, "Cases Argued and Determined in the Moot Court 1876–77." See Langdell, Annual Report 1876–77, 84.

30. Marshall Law Club, Record Book 1860–76, 1–2; C. Warren, *History of the Harvard Law School*, 2:319.

31. See "Pow Wow Records of Supreme Court 1870–82"; "Harvard Law School Clubs."

32. "Pow Wow Records of Supreme Court 1870–82," 29; "1873 Constitution" and "Revised/Amended Constitution of 1882," in "Pow Wow Records 1873–95 and 1934–69," leaves 1r, 10r, 22r–23r. The member without a bachelor's degree was Louis Brandeis.

ranked in modern languages, the second-ranked in modern-language grammar, the fifth-ranked in physics, the sixth-ranked in history, the third-ranked overall, and the winner of prizes in history and modern languages. Only one 1874 classmate was prominent in "theatricals" and not ranked high academically.[33] Thus, the selection criteria for Pow Wow were closely correlated with academic merit.

Wigglesworth's work for Pow Wow amounted to the equivalent of another major course. The first-year superior court generally prepared and heard cases for trial, while the second-year supreme court usually prepared and heard cases on appeal. A year-long docket was drawn up in the fall, and club members were assigned rotating roles as plaintiff's co-counsel, defendant's co-counsel, and judge. A fictitious case with a statement of facts was given to each group to argue on the appointed date. Wigglesworth had a case every month from November 1876 to June 1877—a heavier load than any other member of the superior court, and he related this club work to coursework as much as possible.[34]

The demanding academic pace in 1876–77 was broken by a few brief moments of respite, as Jones recorded: "Returned to my room early in the evening. Read a few chapters in Washburn's *Real Property*, then wrote a letter home. Drew my armchair up in front of the fire, smoked a cigarette, retired to bed at 10:30." In particular, Jones and many others relaxed on Sunday by attending church and strolling to Fresh Pond, "a pleasant spot . . . much frequented by the students."[35]

The first major break occurred during Christmas recess from December 24 to January 6. To save the expense of a trip home, Jones remained in Cambridge and recorded in his dairy:

> Christmas! Dec. 25. . . . Arose rather early this morning and was surprised to think that I forgot to hang up my stocking last night. . . . This day was unusually pleasant for December weather; the sleighing was good and nearly every person seemed able to procure some kind of a conveyance and skip over the crystal snow. . . . The church bells kept ringing and chiming all day. All the churches had service of some kind, and were attended by the more sanctimonious people. . . . The theaters were all crowded in the afternoon and evening, but this is nothing unusual, for they are nearly always filled and crowded. The people of Boston and Harvard students are great theater-goers. Today the streets of Cambridge seemed depopulated, and all the people seemed concentrated in the "Hub." Immense throngs pushed their

33. Harvard College Class of 1874 materials, in Wigglesworth Family Papers, boxes 32, 37.

34. Docket in "Pow Wow Records 1873–95 and 1934–69," leaves 10v, 11r. See Pow Wow Club, Records, box 4, ff. 4–6, 4–7; Wigglesworth, Contracts 1876–77.

35. Quotations are from Jones, Diary, 1–2, 7–8.

way along Tremont and Washington Streets.... Returned home, took my supper, passed the evening quietly in reading a Christmas legend and some of Tennyson's poetry. Retired to bed to rest my weary limbs, till I would be aroused in the morn by the usual rap upon my door, with the exclamation, "Mr. Jones—6 o'clock," made by my landlady.[36]

Wigglesworth surely visited his home in Boston, saddened by the memory of his father who had died on October 14 at the age of seventy-two. And he doubtlessly visited the home of Mary Dixwell, whom he had been courting since his college days.

Returning to coursework in January, Jones gave up his diary, and the remainder of his lone notebook relates only single-sentence reports of class meetings in various courses. In contrast, the expansive Wigglesworth ran out of pages in his first large notebook for Gray's lectures on real property and began taking notes in the nearly empty notebook originally devoted to Ames's course on torts. Gray's lectures were highly formalized into doctrinal categories incorporating titles of cases and their relevant rules, and Wigglesworth created an index on the inside back cover, listing pages in the notebook for the various categories. On February 26 Wigglesworth filled up the second notebook and moved on to a third.

Also in February, Langdell presided over his third moot court of the year, which concerned a plea under the Statute of Limitations that he had addressed in his *Cases on Sales* (1872). The co-counsel for the plaintiff included Jones; those for the defendant included Brandeis.[37] For Jones it was a chance to joust against the leading student in the class; for Brandeis the moot court may have contributed to securing the dean's assistance during a controversy in the early spring.

In mid-March the faculty held an open election among the second-year class to identify six candidates to deliver the student oration at the next commencement. Brandeis received the most votes, but two weeks later, on April 2, Langdell made this stunning announcement: "It appearing that Mr. Brandeis is not eligible as a candidate for the commencement part, Mr. [Samuel D.] Warren will be added to the list heretofore published, he having the next highest number of votes."[38] What had happened? Brandeis was not only a student leader but a faculty favorite who attained the highest grades earned by anyone in his class or any subsequent class at HLS. But Brandeis had entered HLS before his nineteenth birthday, and would not turn twenty-one, the required age for a student to earn a degree at HLS, until No-

36. Jones, Diary, 10–12.

37. Harvard Law School, "Cases Argued and Determined in the Moot Court 1876–77."

38. "Notice" (2 Apr. 1877), in Harvard Law School, Announcements. Warren subsequently became Brandeis's law partner and remained with him at HLS for a postgraduate year.

vember 1877.[39] Consequently, President Eliot declared Brandeis to be ineligible not only for a commencement oration but for graduation itself. Langdell apparently interceded with Eliot, however, and the Harvard Corporation granted an exception, allowing Brandeis to receive his cum laude degree at commencement.[40]

Meanwhile, in March, Wigglesworth had been appointed to the student committee formed to make arrangements for the funeral of former professor Washburn. On March 21 the school was closed in observance of the funeral, which all students were requested to attend.[41] Nevertheless, Wigglesworth had happier thoughts on his mind because he had been receiving a continuous stream of invitations to social events from Mary Dixwell. On April 29 they arranged to take a walk among the spring wild flowers near Fresh Pond and became engaged. When the engagement was officially announced on June 4, Ames, a former teacher at the Dixwell Latin school, sent flowers to Mary, as did the Pow Wow Club.[42] Those devoted to academic merit still made genteel gestures.

Looming over the happy announcement, however, was the prospect of "thorough and searching" exams at the end of the year.[43] On May 28 Langdell officially asked the second-year students "to give notice to the dean forthwith, by note in writing delivered to the Librarian, in what electives they intend to be examined." Of the seventy-two eligible second-year students on the rolls as of June, "sixty-one presented themselves for examination, of whom fifty-four passed and received degrees and seven were rejected."[44] Hence, 25 percent of the upperclassmen still enrolled in June would not graduate, and the first-year students realized that earning the degree could no longer be taken for granted. The pressure on HLS students to succeed in examinations, which was increasing as well at Oxford and Cambridge, was magnified by the fear of "disappointing one's family or special love interest."[45] Wigglesworth's fear was probably not assuaged when Mary wrote to him, "Can you go [for a walk] and not interfere with what you have to do? You must be honest with me and not let me interfere with the coming examinations, won't you?"[46]

39. Harvard Law School, Grade Records, vol. 0, 1875–76. In 1873–74 Harvard changed the rule that a law student must be at least nineteen years old to enter to the rule that a student could not receive the LL.B. before twenty-one years of age. C. Eliot, Annual Report 1873–74, 28.

40. Ford, "Boyhood of Brandeis"; Landis, "Mr. Justice Brandeis," 184–86; Strum, *Louis D. Brandeis*, 23–24; L. Baker, *Brandeis and Frankfurter*, 24.

41. Harvard Law School, Announcements.

42. Letters to and from George Wigglesworth (Apr.–May 1877), Wigglesworth Family Papers, box 6; Mary C. Dixwell, Bound notebook for engagement and wedding in Wigglesworth Family Papers, box 26.

43. Quotation is from Harvard University, *Catalog 1870–71*, 72.

44. Quotations are, respectively, from "Notice" (28 May 1877), in Harvard Law School, Announcements; Langdell, Annual Report 1876–77, 84–85.

45. Deslandes, "Competitive Examinations," 570.

46. Mary C. Dixwell to George Wigglesworth (27 May 1877), Wigglesworth Family Papers, box 6.

Of the 116 students originally enrolled in the first-year class, eighty-nine presented themselves for the final examinations. Two years later, Thayer still enjoyed recalling some of the hapless answers supplied by students in the Criminal Law course attended by Jones and Wigglesworth:

> [O]ne of my students in criminal law, to the question "whether it is crime at common law *to attempt* to commit suicide," wrote: "I do not so consider it. Of course, opinions differ." This was a California man.
>
>   Another, an Irishman, ... expatiated thus: "Suicide is no crime, but the attempt is, because society is injured by the loss of one of its individual members."
>
>   Another, to the question relating ... to the maxim that Christianity is part of the common law, went on to say: "The only way in which the common law enforces Christianity is by charitably giving the benefit of any doubt to the accused person."[47]

Other hapless answers apparently came from Willie Weld, Wigglesworth's childhood playmate and current classmate, whom Thayer failed, wealth and pedigree notwithstanding. In the end, sixty-three first-year students passed, 54 percent of the entering class, including both Jones and Wigglesworth.[48] The twenty-six who took the exams and failed still had the possibility of staying with their class by passing the exam for advanced standing in September.

The academic year then ended with requests to return books to the library and to reserve seats in the lecture room for the following year. The Wigglesworth family summered at Mt. Desert Island, where Mary visited, and the Dixwell family went to Breadloaf Inn in Vermont, where George visited. On September 20 Wigglesworth returned to Boston to prepare for his second and final year.[49]

1877–78

On the last Thursday and Friday in September, the two "very restrictive measures" took effect: the three-year curriculum and the entrance examination for applicants who did not have a bachelor's degree. Eleven nongraduates took the entrance exam; only two passed and were admitted as candidates for the LL.B. The nine

47. J. Thayer, Correspondence and Memoranda, 2:66 (28 Feb. 1879).

48. J. Thayer, Correspondence and Memoranda, 3:106–7 (Jan. 1882); Langdell, Annual Report 1876–77, 84–85.

49. Harvard Law School, Announcements; George Wigglesworth to Mother (12 Sept. 1877), Wigglesworth Family Papers, box 6.

failures, along with another thirteen nongraduates who did not take the exam, were admitted as special students, ineligible for the degree. Approximately eighty-six college graduates also entered the first-year class, including Abbott Lawrence Lowell, a paragon of the Brahmin gentry and successor to Eliot as president of Harvard.[50]

Joining the second-year class were eighteen students who passed the examinations for advanced standing, including some who had failed in the previous June, so the total number of degree candidates in Jones and Wigglesworth's second-year class was eighty-one as of early October. The grand total registered at some point throughout the year was 196 students, and the school again ran a surplus "in spite of a falling off in the fees from students and a considerable increase in expenditure for salaries."[51] Langdell took heart that "the establishment of an examination for admission, together with an extension of the course of study" had not resulted in "an immediate and material diminution of our numbers," as he had feared. But, he noted, "our large numbers this year are due in part...to the fact that the number of second-year students and postgraduate 'resident bachelors of law' is very large."[52] In other words, most of the students had enrolled before the third year became required.

That majority included both Wigglesworth, who moved into a rooming house with two fellow members of Pow Wow, and Jones, who lived in a rooming house with a special student. The much anticipated third-year course was not described in the 1877–78 catalog, since the faculty were still debating its content. Instead, Jones and Wigglesworth enrolled in the last offering of the second-year curriculum, comprising five hours of elective coursework, two required hours of Evidence taught by Thayer, and three required hours of Equity Jurisdiction and Procedure, cotaught by Ames and Langdell. For his electives, Jones chose Trusts and Mortgages taught by Bradley, second-year Real Property taught by Gray, and Corporations and Partnership taught by Bradley. Wigglesworth elected the two former courses, as well as Gray's Agency and Carriers and Ames's Bills of Exchange and Promissory Notes, amounting to an overload of eleven hours.

In Bradley's courses, Jones and Wigglesworth listened to lectures consisting of doctrinal rules supported by citations to cases and dogmatic appeal to authority.

50. Langdell, Annual Report 1876–77, 86–87; Langdell, Annual Report 1877–78, 86. Five Harvard undergraduates were also admitted as regular students, eligible for the degree based on examinations that they had completed at Harvard College. So the total of nongraduates admitted in September was twenty-nine: seven eligible for the degree, and twenty-two special students, four of whom soon withdrew.

51. Harvard University, Treasurer Report 1877–78, 5. See Langdell, Annual Report 1876–77, 84–85.

52. Langdell, Annual Report 1876–77, 85.

Questions were not encouraged, and "the outcome was unsatisfactory," observed the students.[53] Gray's courses differed little. In second-year Real Property, Jones recorded brief doctrinal rules, while Wigglesworth expansively recorded thirty-two lectures in 143 pages that were divided into highly formal doctrinal categories and sub-categories, with discussions of cases illustrating the rules and with a detailed index of the entire notebook.[54] This formal, didactic character also obtained in Agency and Carriers: Gray transmitted established doctrine as systematically as possible and rarely took issue with a decided case or addressed a conflict between authorities. Like Thayer's, his questions were usually rhetorical through the early 1880s, raising a topic and then immediately explaining it: "What legal acts may be done by Agent? [There are] very few things that one must do personally . . . , e.g. where woman releases dower, she must be personally examined."[55]

In the required second-year course on Evidence, Thayer assigned two traditional treatises,[56] but his lectures began to unfold the pathbreaking interpretation of judicial evidence for which he would later become famous. In particular, Thayer's long lecture on 8 October 1877 synthesized his thinking from the prior three years in neat, double-spaced pages, as if he were drafting an essay. Thayer here set forth his distinction between judicial inquiries and evidence, on the one hand, and scientific inquiries and evidence, on the other, which became renowned twenty-two years later in *A Preliminary Treatise on the Law of Evidence.*[57]

Jones and Wigglesworth's equity course presented the highly unusual arrangement of coteaching, as explained by Langdell in his first lecture on 4 October 1877: "Equity consists of three parts: 1. Equity Pleading. 2. Equity Procedure. 3. Equity Jurisdiction. Mr. L[angdell] will take the last two. Mr. A[mes] the first." Ames employed preprints of Langdell's *Cases on Equity Pleading*, formally published in summer 1878. For sixteen weeks, Langdell lectured on equity procedure, and on 7 February 1878, shifted to teach equity jurisdiction by case method, likely because he was beginning to assemble his casebook on this topic. Due to the fluid state of the course, Wigglesworth adopted a confusing format in his notebook of writing class notes mostly on the front of pages, sometimes on the backs, and sometimes skipping pages. Upon reaching the end of the notebook, he turned it upside down

53. Fessenden, "Rebirth of the Harvard Law School," 502. See Jones, Diary, 5–7; Wigglesworth, Trusts and Mortgages 1877–78.

54. Wigglesworth, Real Property 1877–78. Final examinations are in Wigglesworth Family Papers, box 13, f. 1876–78.

55. Wigglesworth, Agency and Carriers 1877–78, 7, 1–2.

56. Best, *Principles of the Law of Evidence* (1875–76); J. Stephen, *Digest of the Law of Evidence* (1877).

57. J. Thayer, Evidence Teaching Notebooks, 14:28–32 (8 Oct. 1877). See J. Thayer, *Preliminary Treatise on the Law of Evidence*, 263–76, 515–18; J. Thayer, *Select Cases on Evidence*, 1–4.

and began taking notes back to front on the backs of pages, skipping the backs of pages that had already been filled.[58]

Outside of the curriculum, moot courts were held as usual, though the number declined to sixteen during 1877–78,[59] as the law clubs attracted more interest among students. Brandeis, for example, remained active in Pow Wow even as a postgraduate "resident bachelor of laws." Wigglesworth moved up to the Pow Wow supreme court, which selected a new superior court comprising one Princeton graduate and eight Harvard graduates, including Lowell. In late November Thayer "was waited upon by A. L. Lowell" who asked, on behalf of Pow Wow, that the lecture on the Friday after Thanksgiving be postponed because "my one lecture was the only one to bring the club back" to school.[60] Such a petition from Pow Wow was not to be discounted as an evasion of academic rigor, and Thayer complied.

Both the dean and the president regarded Jones and Wigglesworth's class as inferior, for they were the group who had purposefully avoided the fully rigged "new system." And the class fulfilled these expectations in the annual examinations. Out of eighty-one eligible second-year students, sixty-six took the final exams, and forty-seven passed—58 percent of those eligible. In their public reports, Eliot called this "unsatisfactory," and Langdell labeled it a "very bad record."[61] In the examinations of the first-year class (the first to enter the three-year curriculum and to meet educational requirements for admission), forty-six passed, which was 69 percent of those eligible. Comparing these first-year exams with those of the inferior class from a year earlier, Langdell observed that the new first-years "were, upon the whole, distinguished for their excellence."[62] But Wigglesworth had earned excellent grades at the end of the first year, and the faculty nominated him in February 1878 to prepare an oration for the June commencement.

Wigglesworth became a life-long advocate of Langdell's system of competitive academic achievement, proclaiming in 1909: "At the head of all the Law Schools stands the Harvard Law School with the system of instruction introduced there by Prof. Langdell. In a law school the student's whole time is free for that work. He is aided by teachers skilled in giving instruction and whose interest and business it is to instruct, and more than this the student is surrounded by other students . . . eager

58. Quotation is from Wigglesworth, Equity 1877–78, 1. See Langdell, *Cases on Equity Jurisdiction* (1879).

59. Langdell, Annual Report 1877–78, 84.

60. J. Thayer, Evidence Teaching Notebooks, 17:119 (Nov. 1877); "Pow Wow Records of Supreme Court 1870–82," 29; "Pow Wow Records 1873–95 and 1934–69," 12; Wigglesworth, Pow Wow Records.

61. C. Eliot, Annual Report 1877–78, 37; Langdell, Annual Report 1877–78, 86.

62. Langdell, Annual Report 1877–78, 86. See Langdell, Annual Report 1878–79, 82.

to acquire the knowledge on which their future success depends. The constant intercourse and competition with these and the exchange of ideas furnish a stimulus and an aid to the study of law which must be felt to be appreciated."[63]

Nevertheless, Wigglesworth did not remain for a third year of postgraduate study as a Resident Bachelor of Laws, choosing instead to marry Mary Dixwell at her father's home in Cambridge on 20 June 1878. The wedding was the first of many, as Mary observed: "soon I shall find the road to Boston strewn with young lawyers and their Cambridge brides, and one couple behind the other in a procession."[64]

Though his academic record was undistinguished, Jones remained for a third academic year in 1878–79,[65] a decision perhaps prompted by the fact that this was the last year that third-year tuition was $50. In 1879–80 it rose to the rate of the first and second years, $150. In addition, Langdell would certainly have recommended that any HLS student remain for an optional third year. Whatever the reason, Jones's third year was fortuitous in providing Langdell an introduction to Margaret Ellen Huson.

1878–79

Born in 1856, Maggie Huson was Jones's cousin and the daughter of an Episcopal priest in Coldwater, Michigan, where she was raised. At Hellmuth College in Ontario, she received "a thorough, liberal, and useful education for young Ladies...based upon the soundest Protestant Christian Principles" and graduated with a diploma in 1875.[66] Moving to Boston at some point to study art, Maggie was visited by her mother, Patience (Jones) Huson, in 1879, and they evidently went to see Maggie's cousin, John R. Jones, at Harvard Law School.[67] No records describe the meeting or courtship between Maggie and Kit Langdell, or what attracted the twenty-four-year-old woman to the fifty-four-year-old dean of the law school. They shared Irish heritage, and Maggie may have feared becoming an "old maid," as some of her Hellmuth classmates were labeled.[68] Professionally and financially secure, Langdell was a prudent choice for a young woman, and they were wed in

63. Wigglesworth, "Law as a Profession" (1909). See "Notice" (Feb. 1878), in Harvard Law School, Announcements.

64. Mary C. Dixwell to Anna [?] (5 Feb. 1878), Wigglesworth Family Papers, box 6.

65. Cf. C. Warren, *History of the Harvard Law School*, vol. 3, s.v. "Jones, John R."; Harvard Law School, *Quinquennial Catalog*, s.v. "Jones, John R."

66. Hellmuth College, *Catalog 1871–72*, 9.

67. *Coldwater Courier*, 18 Sept. 1907; "Margaret Ellen Langdell" (1908); Huson, Will and Probate Papers (5 Sept. 1907).

68. Hellmuth College, *Catalog 1871–72*, signed by May Curtis (Nov. 3, '72), penciled annotation 5.

September 1880. Coldwater newspapers regarded Maggie's marriage as a coup,[69] while Boston newspapers gave slight notice to the wedding, though this was surely Langdell's doing, who requested that "no cards" be sent.[70] But he bought Maggie paintings, engravings, and other works of art for a wedding gift, and they settled into the house that the university had provided.[71]

Meanwhile, the faculty intensified the academic competition by adding the Honor program of study, even as prospective students were opting out of the tournament. In the academic year 1878–79 the enrollment dropped by 14 percent to 169 students. Just as Langdell had predicted, "this would be the year in which the School would suffer most from the combined effect of the examination for admission and the lengthening of the course to three years; for, while these measures would produce their full effect in reducing the numbers of the first-year class and second-year class, there would be no third-year class to make up for the diminished numbers in the other two classes. Still, the falling off in numbers was greater than had been anticipated." A deficit of $4,557, or 15 percent of the budget, required the administration to draw on the reserves that had been set aside.[72]

This "falling off in numbers" reflected the choices of students such as William E. Russell, who came from a prominent line of Harvard-educated lawyers skeptical of Langdell's reforms.[73] His father, Charles T. Russell, a graduate of both Harvard College and HLS during the 1830s, became a successful lawyer in Cambridge, where he employed his older son, Charles (Teddy) Russell Jr., in practice and served as mayor during the Civil War. William's uncle, William G. Russell, a distinguished Boston attorney, had studied at Harvard College and HLS during the 1840s, and in 1875 chaired the Overseers Committee that objected to Dean Langdell's ex cathedra announcement that HLS expected a bachelor's degree for admission.[74]

Russell enrolled in the Harvard College class of 1877 and belonged to the "college men" who found in sports teams, publication boards, literary societies, and

69. *Coldwater Republican*, 24 Sept. 1880; *Coldwater Courier*, 18 Sept. 1907.

70. *Boston Post*, 1 Oct. 1880; *Boston Daily Advertiser*, 30 Sept. 1880; *Boston Evening Transcript*, 30 Sept. 1880; *Boston Evening Traveler*, 30 Sept. 1880.

71. Receipts for purchases ordered 8 Sept. 1880 and paid 11 Oct. 1880, Langdell, Papers.

72. Quotation is from Langdell, Annual Report 1878–79, 83. Harvard University, Treasurer Report 1878–79, 5; C. Eliot, Annual Report 1878–79, 27–28. See figure 1, Student enrollment at Harvard Law School from 1870–71 to 1894–95, in chapter 9 below.

73. Here and below, see Gentile and Hyndman, "Guide to the William E. Russell Papers."

74. Report of the Committee of Reports and Resolutions (31 Dec. 1875) in Harvard University, Overseers Records, 11:225 (12 Jan. 1876). In 1883 William G. Russell chaired the Overseers Visiting Committee to the Law School that called for hiring "someone of large experience in the practice of the law and, if possible, of wide reputation in the profession," rather than W. A. Keener. William G. Russell, Harvard University, Report of the Overseers Visiting Committee, vol. 3, 1882–83 (Report read on 9 Jan. 1884).

social clubs the essence of college life.[75] The increased admission standard inaugurated at HLS in September 1877 would not have barred Russell, who could have entered HLS simply by showing his college diploma. But enrolling there would have placed him in the first class that was required to complete three years and to face ever rising academic expectations implemented through stringent examinations. Russell's personal inclinations combined with his father's and uncle's disgruntlement with HLS led him to enter the law school of Boston University.

Compared to law schools of the time, Boston University was among the most demanding, having established examinations and a three-year curriculum by 1876. But its requirements were not as high or as uniformly enforced as those at HLS, and its faculty "appreciated the fact that the students wanted practical information" rather than the strongly academic curriculum at HLS.[76] Russell was able to complete the course in two years, 1877–79, with significantly less effort than would have been required at Harvard. At the end of his first year, Russell wrote a long letter to a college classmate, expressing few worries about his academic merit and taking for granted that he would work in his father's law firm.

> As in my last [letter], I have parties numberless, victories glorious, and picnics riotous to tell you of.... We are all experiencing a decided relapse after some weeks of gaiety; the girls are beginning to leave us, and the prospect of spending nearly the whole blessed summer in this cursed hole is looming up with awful significance. Still, I am to run off for two weeks, but where, the Lord only knows. Just now I am seriously thinking, in spite of your well-meant caution, of taking in... a regular circus there, clown and all.... You want to hear of Class-day and [Harvard] Commencement; how the ladies conducted themselves on their day and the gentle men on theirs; what effect the crowds in Memorial [Hall] had on the dresses of your female friends and 52 gallons of punch... had on the heads of the male. Both gave out—dresses and punch, I mean, also a few heads; but as a rule the fellows behaved as decorously as the occasion would allow.... Speaking of business, I am going to enclose with this letter my first brief, just to show you that I am "working." The case was argued before the full bench last week. [Brother] Teddy has strong hopes of winning the case.... For picnics, we have had two since my last meeting—one with a peculiar crowd and rather a peculiar time; the other very select and correspondingly pleasant.... pardon this short and loose-jointed epistle. In haste, yours, Billy[77]

75. Quotation is found in Horowitz, *Campus Life*, 143; Townsend, *Manhood at Harvard*, 141.
76. Swasey, "Boston University Law School," 56, 57–58.
77. W. Russell to Parker (2 July 1878).

Despite the carefree tone, Russell did not lack talent or ambition. In 1879 he received the first summa cum laude degree awarded by Boston University law school, and went on to a prominent career, serving three terms as governor of Massachusetts in the early 1890s and nearly winning the Democratic nomination to succeed his good friend Grover Cleveland as president of the United States in 1896.

The defection of Harvard graduate Russell was matched by others, such as William C. Sanger. A classmate of Wigglesworth at Harvard, Sanger had also earned an M.A. during 1874–75 and embarked on the grand tour with Wigglesworth. When HLS announced in spring 1876 the extension of the course to three years, Sanger, rather than enrolling with Wigglesworth in the last two-year class at HLS, headed for Columbia University. There he completed the two-year law course during 1876–78 under the "Dwight System" of teaching by recitations, fashioned by undemanding and fee-driven Timothy Dwight, the best known competitor to Langdell's system at HLS.[78]

The desertion of Harvard College graduates, such as Russell and Sanger, was deeply worrisome to Langdell. In response to his first wave of reforms, including case method teaching, Boston University law school in 1872 attracted nearly one-third of its first entering class (12/37) and three-quarters of its college graduates (12/16) from Harvard College alumni. The second wave of more restrictive reforms at HLS in the late 1870s was expected to cause even more defections. Ironically revealing his anxiety, Langdell repeatedly tried to dismiss the decline in Harvard graduates as coincidental. When the number of Harvard graduates entering HLS dropped from forty-seven to thirty-eight in fall 1878, he wrote: "If this falling-off had been caused by the lengthening of the course to three years, it would have been a discouraging sign; but careful inquiry led to the conclusion that . . . the falling off was due to accidental causes."[79] Langdell's "careful inquiry" missed Russell and Sanger, at the least.

A rebound in the number of Harvard graduates during 1879–80 alleviated Langdell's anxiety, but, reporting on 1880–81, he again expressed both concern about the declining number of Harvard graduates and unwillingness to attribute it to the academic reforms.[80] This apprehension stemmed partly from worry about the financial viability of his system, which relied on the new economic logic that a more demanding and competitive academic system of professional education would attract more and better students. That reasoning would prove invalid if

78. In Wigglesworth Family papers, see correspondence of George Wigglesworth, box 5, f. 1875, and Diary (June–July 1875), box 18; Goebel, *History of the School of Law, Columbia University*, 33–89.
79. Langdell, Annual Report 1878–79, 83. See Boston University Law School, *Catalog 1872–73*, 65–67.
80. Langdell, Annual Report 1880–81, 73.

Harvard College alumni—who were among the best prepared college graduates and would naturally be inclined to continue their education at their alma mater—avoided Langdell's reforms and entered other law schools. In response, HLS increased the publicity and availability of its admissions exam, offering it twice annually in Cambridge and once in Cincinnati and in Chicago, where more HLS alumni lived than in any other city west of Pennsylvania.[81] Meanwhile, forty of the fifty-one members of the second-year class (the first to enter the three-year curriculum) attempted the second-year exam, and thirty-nine passed, including twelve who achieved the necessary average to enter the third year of the Honor program.[82]

1879–80

If the defection of Harvard College graduates to other law schools was a serious concern by September 1879, Langdell could have found no greater reassurance than the enrollment of Edmund M. Parker, eldest son of Joel Parker, the gentlemanly HLS professor who, after stepping down in 1868, wrote a long pamphlet sharply defending the condition of the school prior to Langdell's deanship.[83] When this somewhat bitter apologia appeared, Edmund was almost fifteen years old and said to resemble his father closely. After graduating from Harvard College with a distinguished academic record in 1877 and completing his liberal education with the traditional grand tour of two years in Europe, Edmund clerked in a lawyer's office during the summer of 1879 and showed no hesitation about enrolling at HLS in September in the third class entering the three-year curriculum.[84]

Parker's class numbered eighty-two, including seventy college graduates and fifty-nine Harvard alumni.[85] The total number of students rose to 177, and the school recorded a budget surplus due not only to the rise in enrollment but also to the increase in tuition for the third year from $50 to $150.[86] As a first-year student, Parker was required to schedule ten hours in the "Big Five" core subjects, as presented in table 8.

81. *Quillets of the Law*, no. 1 (May 1878), 8. Harvard Law School, *Catalog 1879–80*, 4; Brandeis, "Harvard Law School Association," 1.

82. Langdell, Annual Report 1878–79, 81–82.

83. J. Parker, *Law School of Harvard College*; [O. Holmes], "Harvard University Law School" (1870), 177; "Law School of Harvard College" (Oct. 1870–71), 563; *Centennial History of the Harvard Law School*, 22–23, 248, C. Warren, *History of the Harvard Law School*, 2:302–3, 366n.

84. Letters and papers in J. Parker, Papers, box 2; Harvard College Class of 1877, *Secretary's Report* (1890), 48.

85. Langdell, Annual Report 1879–80, 88. Langdell's account of the enrollment of Parker's class varies slightly. Cf. Langdell, Annual Report 1880–81, 74; Annual Report 1879–80, 83–88.

86. C. Eliot, Annual Report 1879–80, 10–11; Langdell, Annual Report 1879–80, 87.

TABLE 8 Schedule of First-Year Courses for Edmund M. Parker, 1879–80

	Monday	*Tuesday*	*Wednesday*	*Thursday*	*Friday*
9–10 A.M.		Torts, Howland	Torts, Howland		
10–11 A.M.	Torts, Howland	Contracts, Langdell	Contracts, Langdell	Contracts, Langdell	Criminal Law and Criminal Procedure, Thayer
11 A.M.–noon				Real Property, Gray	
Noon–1 P.M.	Real Property, Gray	Civil Procedure, Ames			
3 P.M.–6 P.M.					moot courts [suspended]
8 P.M.	Pow Wow Club meets				

Source: HLS, Catalog 1879–80

No records remain of Parker's courses on Real Property or Civil Procedure, but Langdell's teaching of Contracts in 1879–80 is conveyed by a student's account from the following year.

> I first saw [Langdell] as a teacher in the fall of 1880, at the opening of the Harvard Law School, in the course on Contracts.... His whole aspect was that of a modest, learned and kindly man. He ascended the platform...and opened the course with a brief statement of the nature of a contract. Then he called upon some student to state... the first case in his collection of cases.... After the case had been stated, a discussion followed of the point decided. This fairly broke the ice, and the students soon learned what was expected of them under the Langdell System.... His dominant purpose seemed to be to bring out not only the decision of each case, but the reason for the decision.... Although he had collected a number of volumes of cases, he...seemed to take up each case in the class as if he had never seen it before. He went over all the steps in the reasoning as new work.... His method was a daily object lesson to students in thoroughness and accuracy. Under his guidance discussions which would otherwise have been listless and unprofitable became stimulating and fruitful.... He was very hospitable to suggestions, but independent in his conclusions....

Professor Langdell was always willing to reconsider a conclusion in the light of new suggestions. Not infrequently in new courses with which he had not become thoroughly familiar, he would recant propositions which he had advanced as sound. A student recently informed me of a course in which Professor Langdell changed his opinion in regard to a case three times in the course of one week, each time advancing with positiveness a new doctrine. That he could do this without losing the respect or confidence of his students shows the esteem in which he was held. They knew well he was a teacher of originality and great industry, with no object but to discover and state truly the principles of the law.[87]

In Criminal Law and Criminal Procedure, Thayer continued as in the past, adumbrating prior years' lectures, while lamenting that "for this great subject, we have but one hour a week...while the other smaller subjects, except Pleading, have two or three hours per week.... What shall we do? Shall we skim it all?... Or shall we do some thoroughly and skim the rest? I shall try to do the last. It will be very imperfectly done, but we will do it as best...we can."[88] Parker's fifth required course, Torts, was taught with Ames's *Cases on Torts* by instructor Henry Howland, who gradually gained the confidence to challenge received authority. Only toward the end of the course did Howland offer evaluative or negative comments, such as "Bad law," "Wrong," or "Wild."[89]

Commensurate with the growing number of case method courses, the law clubs were flourishing, because their demands for legal research mirrored those of case method. Competition for membership in law clubs became intense, while their proceedings and documentation grew more elaborate and formal. Parker was elected to Pow Wow and participated in seven different cases between October and March.[90]

In June 1880 seventy-one of the entering eighty-two of Parker's classmates presented themselves for the final examinations; fifty-five passed, and seven of the failures tried again in September and all passed. Thus, sixty-two of the original eighty-two qualified to enter their second year as degree candidates, an improvement from earlier years that was attributed to the rise in admission standards.[91] Parker was among those who qualified for the Honor program.

87. Schofield, "Christopher Columbus Langdell," 275–77.

88. J. Thayer, Criminal Law Teaching Notebooks, 6:110 (29 Sept. 1884).

89. *PTorts74*, 352marg, 406marg, 581marg, 634marg, 647marg.

90. "Pow Wow Records 1873–95 and 1934–69," leaf 16r. See Pow Wow Club, Records, Superior Court, box 6, ff. 4–11.

91. Langdell, Annual Report 1879–80, 87.

1880–81

The anticipated problems of decreasing attendance and tuition arrived in full force, making this academic year "again one of comparative uncertainty and depression." The total number of enrolled students, along with tuition receipts, dropped to 161, the lowest since 1874–75.[92] Meanwhile, students began to make some unexpected choices that threatened the meritocratic system as much as did the decline in enrollment. They chose to enter as special students, to opt out of exams, and to leave before the third year.

Langdell and Eliot had always expected that the total number of those entering the school would fall, but they did not anticipate that many of those qualified to be degree candidates would enter instead "as special students."[93] The trend became particularly pronounced in 1880–81 when the first-year class of degree candidates fell to fifty-eight, compared to eighty-two during the previous year, when Parker entered. Since the number of special students in the school rose while the aggregate enrollment fell, the proportion of special students increased to more than 20 percent.[94] "It was not anticipated," Langdell observed, that the meritocratic reforms "would have their greatest effect in reducing the ratio of those who take the degree to the whole number who enter the School."[95] Ironically, in fact, the academic reforms were creating a haven for laggards and "ringers" recruited as athletes to play for the Harvard College teams. Because "only candidates for a degree were required to take the examination, . . . a special student in the Law School was in a very happy situation; there was no attendance required and no examination, and [by 1890] it had become . . . a very common way for men who wished to play football to connect themselves with the University, as in those days there were no restrictions requiring that men should be in the College only."[96]

In addition to the growing proportion of special students who avoided the competition for academic merit, a significant number of degree candidates were opting out of the examinations and this also contributed to "reducing the ratio of those who take the degree." In 1877–78, 13 percent (19/151) of the degree can-

92. Quotation is from C. Warren, *History of the Harvard Law School*, 2:416. See Langdell, Annual Report 1880–81, 68; Harvard University, Treasurer Report 1880–81, 7.

93. Langdell, Annual Report 1880–81, 73. Cf. Langdell, Annual Report 1876–77, 87.

94. Langdell, Annual Report 1880–81, 68–69; Langdell, Annual Report 1881–82, 85. The category of "special student," signifying nondegree candidate, formally appeared with the introduction of the admissions exam in 1877.

95. Langdell, Annual Report 1880–81, 75.

96. Holliday to Chafee (22 Nov. 1928). See Ames's correspondence concerning the University's Athletic Committee and football matters during the mid-1890s. C. Eliot, Papers, box 81, f. 1892, and box 100, f. 4.

didates in all three classes did not take the corresponding exams; in 1878–79 it was 20 percent (23/113); in 1879–80, 7 percent (9/132); in 1880–81, 13 percent (17/129). Eliot and Langdell were concerned if students took the exams and failed, but they worried more if students avoided the exams altogether, signifying disengagement from the competition for academic merit. Hence, "the ratio between those who enter the School as candidates for a degree and those who complete the course" indicated that "the success of the three-years' course ... has not been great," concluded Langdell. This trend worsened for Parker's class, which entered with eighty-two degree candidates, dropped to fifty-seven in the second year, and began the third with twenty-four.[97]

The last and most troubling choice was that students were not enrolling for classes in their third year. In deference to opponents of the three-year course of study, the faculty had provided the option for students not to enroll in classes or pay tuition in the third year, but to clerk in a lawyer's office and return at the end of the year and take the examinations in order to earn the degree.[98] This option, like that of entering HLS as a special student, was not originally regarded by Langdell as a serious possibility for many students and, therefore, no threat to the meritocratic system. But he identified it as a significant problem during 1880–81, while reflecting on the performance of the first three-year class during its final year, 1879–80. That class, including Lowell, had entered in September 1877, and, after two years, thirty-nine members remained eligible to earn the degree. But only sixteen enrolled at HLS to study for the third year, of whom twelve took the exams and passed, six with honor. The other twenty-three left, of whom five returned to take the exams and four passed, one with honor.[99]

In purely practical terms, students were able to forgo enrolling during the third year because the three-year curriculum required only twenty-four hours. Originally, the faculty had planned to add a third ten-hour year to the two ten-hour years required for the two-year course. Being understaffed, they instead set the total of required hours at twenty-four: ten in the first year, eight in the second, and six in the third. As a result, the dean observed, "the students ... have thought that it was possible to crowd the bulk of the work of three years into two years, and thus to save an entire year in time and expense ... Indeed, there is reason to believe that this has been with some an object not merely of economy, but of ambition. Certain it is that this object has been pursued by some of the most

97. Langdell, Annual Report 1880–81, 73–74.
98. Harvard Law School, *Catalog 1879–80*, 5.
99. Langdell, Annual Report 1879–80, 86–87.

ambitious men in the School, who could well afford both the time and expense of three years' study."[100]

In the bland genre of annual reports, those words reveal some heat, and Langdell was indeed outraged that the descendants of "Kit's freshmen" were foregoing the signature third year, a betrayal of the HLS system. Lowell, the future president of Harvard University, was perhaps the foremost traitor. Abundantly endowed with pedigree, wealth, and talent, he was precisely the kind of student whom Langdell needed to embrace the academic meritocracy. Instead, Lowell left during his third year, 1879–80, returned to take the exams and achieved the only honor degree among the defectors. But earning honor without studying in the third year only magnified the travesty. Brandeis later observed, "Langdell considered that A. L. [Lowell]...had committed an unpardonable sin by not staying for the third year."[101]

Indeed, Langdell maintained that student leadership was key, because, "if...the ten most prominent men in each class should remain in the School three years and take a degree, there is no doubt that the others would soon follow their example..., and the success of the three years' course would thus be complete."[102] In an effort to induce students with high ability and few resources to remain, Langdell called for endowments to fund additional scholarships, and Eliot sought another endowed professorship to amplify the required hours in the second and third years and force students to remain.[103]

Langdell's worries over these three ways of circumventing the HLS system—entering as special students, opting out of exams, and leaving before the third year—were somewhat assuaged by students such as Parker. During his second year, 1880–81, Parker pursued the Honor program of four required courses, including Equity Jurisdiction and Procedure with Langdell. In second-year Real Property, Gray assigned cases for students to read in advance, and then lectured on them in class. This new approach fit his later public defense of case method, which he defined as "the method of study by cases." Through such public pronouncements, Gray gradually became the most vocal HLS advocate for case method, although "in plain truth Gray does lecture," observers noted.[104] As a result, Parker's experience

100. Langdell, Annual Report 1880–81, 78.
101. Brandeis to Frankfurter (22 Feb. 1928).
102. Langdell, Annual Report 1880–81, 84–85.
103. *Quillets of the Law*, no. 1 (May 1878); Langdell, Annual Report 1880–81, 78; C. Eliot, Annual Report 1880–81, 27.
104. Dicey to Eliot (5 Dec. 1898). See E. Parker, Real Property 1880–81; Gray, "Cases and Treatises," 756–64.

in Gray's didactic classroom differed markedly from that in Langdell's or Ames's Socratic classes.

In his second-year course on evidence, Parker witnessed a further development in Thayer's analysis of the subject because, by 1880–81, Thayer was dispensing altogether with standard treatises and teaching with "no textbook." In 1883–84 he took a further step in clearing the ground for his own analysis by explicitly addressing the "very serious defects" of available treatises on evidence.[105] The balance of his course remained consistent during the late 1870s and 1880s. After setting forth his cardinal distinction between scientific inquiries and evidence, on the one hand, and legal inquiries and evidence, on the other, Thayer lectured on specific issues in the law of evidence and then employed Gray's "method of study by cases," which Thayer explicitly endorsed years later.[106]

In Trusts and Mortgages, Ames assigned his *Cases on the Law of Trusts* and expressed many more critical and evaluative judgments of received authority. Indeed, "Ames thinks . . ." is the most frequently repeated phrase in Parker's annotations in his casebook. Such comments as "Ames does not believe in this case" induced Parker to make his own judgments, as when he observed, "Ames thinks this amounts to a declaration of trust by the testator...Ames is probably right." Or, "Ames doubts this case. However, it may be sustained on two grounds not inconsistent with cases on p. 412n2."[107] Outside his coursework, Parker continued to participate in Pow Wow, stepping up to the supreme court[108] and editing and publishing a slim collection of English Statutes related to the law of property.[109]

In June 1881 Parker's second-year class of degree candidates numbered fifty-eight, of whom forty-nine presented themselves for examination, and forty-six passed. After the exams were graded, Langdell wrote to Parker the following letter, freighted with implications for the enrollment threats to his new system.

Dear Sir, I beg to inform you that you have passed satisfactory examinations in all the subjects of the Honor course. You are therefore admitted to the third year as a candidate for the Honor degree. If you become a member of the third year class, you will be entitled to write a commencement part, as you have obtained the required average in the studies of the first and second years. Yours truly, C. C. Langdell.[110]

105. J. Thayer, Evidence Teaching Notebooks, 20:153 (22–23 Nov. 1883). The 1880–81 course is found in Evidence, vol. 19.

106. J. Thayer, *Select Cases on Evidence*, iii; J. Thayer, *Cases on Constitutional Law*, vi; C. Warren, *History of the Harvard Law School*, 2:425.

107. PTrusts82, 309marg, 49marg, 413marg.

108. Pow Wow Club, Records, box 6, ff. 7–5, 7–6.

109. E. Parker and F. Bolles, *Collection of Important English Statutes* (1880, 1881).

110. Langdell to Parker (21 July 1881). See Langdell, Annual Report 1880–81, 69.

1881–82

On Thursday, September 29, Parker opted to pursue academic merit and began his third and final year at HLS. The overextended faculty still consisted of Professors Langdell, Ames, Thayer, and Gray, as well as instructor Howland. In November Thayer and Brandeis secured a commitment from young Willie Weld to endow a fifth professorship. Weld, who had come into his inheritance, still intended to earn a degree from HLS, and, far from bearing a grudge against Thayer for failing him, "knew it was his own fault" and actually "liked [Thayer] better than anybody" at the school.[111]

This new endowment alleviated some anxiety about finances, although the total enrollment remained at 161, the same as the previous year, and the other threats still loomed. The percentage of special students increased slightly, and only 54 percent (25/46) of second-year degree candidates returned for the third year.[112] Nevertheless, Parker not only remained to enroll fully in the Honor program, but actually took an overload in the following courses.

Jurisprudence, as well as Wills and Administration, were each taught one hour weekly by Gray, who largely lectured on cases,[113] as did Thayer in Agency and Carriers one hour weekly.[114] In Sales, which met two hours weekly, Thayer employed a more dialogical approach while assigning Langdell's *Cases on Sales*,[115] and in Bills of Exchange and Promissory Notes Ames made many evaluative judgments, recorded by Parker as "Ames agrees . . ." or "Ames doubts . . ." or "Ames denies . . ."[116] Ames thereby induced Parker to express his own opinions and challenges, which are not found elsewhere in his class notes or annotations: "Ames thinks that a note of this kind would be perfectly good if mortgagor was the maker. I don't in the case of an interest-bearing note."[117]

By the same token, more exchange and debate occurred in Ames's classroom than in Thayer's or Gray's: "Ames's idea is that 'An Acceptance is complete without Delivery.' (Question whether cases bear him out.) . . . Hodgkins thinks question is the same as to both, i.e. pure question of title not one of representation. A[mes]

111. J. Thayer, Correspondence and Memoranda, 3:106–8 (Jan. 1882).

112. Langdell, Annual Report 1881–82, 84–85.

113. Jurisprudence addressed a variety of topics, particularly the law of persons, rather than legal theory. I am grateful to Stephen Siegel for providing his summative analysis of Parker's class notes on Jurisprudence with Gray. See E. Parker, Jurisprudence 1881–82; E. Parker, Wills 1881–82; Mack, Wills 1882–83, 1–92.

114. E. Parker, Agency 1881–82.

115. See PSal72, 11marg, 694marg, interleaf, 700–701, 261marg, 202marg, 155marg, 214marg, 322marg.

116. PBills81, 45marg, 104marg, 74–5interleaf, 364marg. No class notes remain from Parker's two-hour course, Partnership and Corporations, taught by Ames with his *Cases on Partnership*.

117. PBills81, 99marg. See 287marg, 371marg.

thinks there is force in this, and confesses he has difficulty in distinguishing them." Finally, Ames often adopted an insulting and dismissive tone rarely found in other classes. One case was "Overruled in England but often absurdly followed in America." Another decision was "'Beneath criticism.' Ames."[118] Apart from this dismissive tone, Langdell's teaching in Equity Jurisdiction and Procedure resembled that of Ames, reflecting the techniques and purposes of his pedagogy, as described in chapter 4.[119]

Despite his overload of seven hours, Parker served as Chief Justice of Pow Wow, which had added a third court for third-year students, and he presided at the Club's annual dinner held at a Cambridge hotel at the end of March.[120] Final examinations followed in June, and the twenty-five enrollees from the third-year class were joined by another ten who had not enrolled but presented themselves for examination. Parker had anticipated the examinations throughout the year, noting at one point: "Be P[retty] D[amn] careful that you know exactly what this case decides. You may be asked that question on Exam Paper." All twenty-five enrollees passed, as did eight of the ten returnees. Of the thirteen eligible for honor, ten qualified, including Parker.[121]

Six days before commencement in June 1882, Parker was admitted to the bar in Massachusetts. After practicing law in a prominent Boston firm for several years, he opened his own office with one partner and joined the federal bar in 1885, thus contributing to the sterling employment record of honor graduates. But he never lost his inclination for scholarship and served as a lecturer on comparative administrative law at Harvard College from 1904 to 1910.[122] Parker thus personifies the shift in legal education from gentlemanly acculturation to competitive academic achievement. His father, HLS professor Joel Parker, had been the leading public apologist for the former regime, and a decade later Edmund elected to enter the new system and earn academic honor. Edmund's choices surely helped to validate the new system in the mind of Langdell, who studied under the father and taught the son.

The year 1882–83 began with five full-time professors, including the newly hired Oliver Wendell Holmes Jr. The faculty therefore raised the second-year requirement to ten hours for both the Ordinary and Honor programs, and the

---

118. *PBills81*, 207marg, 392marg, 307marg, 327marg.

119. See *PEqJur80*, 57marg, 111marg, 128marg, 146marg, 136–7interleaf, 144–5interleaf, 64marg, 70marg, 93marg.

120. Pow Wow Club, Records, box 7, ff. 5–7; "Pow Wow Records 1873–95 and 1934–69," leaf 21r.

121. Quotation is from *PSal72*, 195marg. See Langdell, Annual Report 1881–82, 85, 88. Langdell's figures do not appear consistent, but the categorization of the students is obscure.

122. J. Parker, Papers, box 2; Harvard College Class of 1877, *Secretary's Report, 1890*, 48.

third-year requirement to eight hours and ten hours respectively. These increases prevented students from doubling their course load in the second year and skipping enrollment in the signature third year, a stratagem that soon died out.[123] With the various threats of circumvention gradually abating, the enrollment trend began to reverse in 1883–84, as students seeking to enter leading firms began to flock to HLS. Meanwhile, alumni were making plans to launch an association, and graduates teaching at other law schools were beginning to proselytize on behalf of Langdell's "new system" of professional education.

123. C. Eliot, Annual Report 1889–90, 23.

CHAPTER 8

Triumph and Betrayal, 1886–1890s

Through the mid-1880s, "the Langdell system of study had not been adopted in any other law school."[1] Then, during the late 1880s HLS began surpassing even the most optimistic hopes of raising academic standards, attracting growing numbers of well-qualified students and producing well-trained graduates desired by leading firms. By 1895, when Langdell retired as dean, his system had triumphed, as ambitious, serious students crowded into HLS and as law schools at other universities began to adopt the model. Simultaneously, however, the leading meritocrats betrayed the HLS system by violating their own academic standards.

Despite its universalist principle, the practice of educational formalism was "gravely unjust,"[2] because the meritocrats explicitly categorized certain people—particularly women and graduates of Catholic colleges—apart from the rest of the applicants and then treated those categories invidiously as a matter of policy. Yet, the meritocrats believed that they had not violated formal standards of academic merit because the separate groups deserved distinctive treatment. In these two instances, the leading meritocrats—President Eliot, Dean Langdell, and his successor, Dean Ames—assumed different roles and adopted different positions. Yet, they all contributed to betraying Langdell's "just"[3] system, which, from the earliest moment of its triumph, never rendered judgments without some element of invidious discrimination.

Crowning Success

When Langdell rose to speak at the inaugural meeting of the HLS alumni association in November 1886, the "prolonged applause and three rousing cheers" that

---

1. *Boston Daily Advertiser*, 24 May 1895, 2.
2. J. Havens Richards to Charles W. Eliot (3 Aug. 1893), in Mahoney, Complete Primary Source, 23.
3. Jagemann to Eliot (6 Nov. 1899).

greeted him were totally "unexpected," he said.[4] Never one to feign modesty or praise, this positive reception surprised Langdell, because many alumni had relentlessly attacked his reforms for fifteen years. To be sure, skeptics of the system still lurked about,[5] but criticism was muted by the mounting evidence that "the *new system*"[6] of academic meritocracy was working and, in fact, exceeding the most optimistic projections.

By November 1886 enrollment had increased more than 35 percent to 188 from the low point of 138 in 1882, making the school "very prosperous."[7] Even Langdell admitted that "the success" of his reforms "no longer remained a question."[8] Over the next five years, the trend continued as enrollment more than doubled to four hundred by 1892, an increase that the president called "extraordinary" and others termed "astonishing."[9] The amazement stemmed not only from the sheer number of students, but also from their academic attainments. Over 70 percent were college graduates, who came from an ever larger number of institutions distributed ever more broadly across the United States, while also including a plurality of Harvard College graduates. More of the law students resided at the university, and more remained for three years.[10] By 1890 the first elite national professional school was rolling out of the "manufactory" of the university, as Eliot had envisioned in 1869.[11]

Langdell's design of academic meritocracy and concomitant economic logic were therefore proving valid for professional education: hire full-time faculty based on their academic accomplishments, raise admission standards, lengthen and sequence the curriculum, teach inductively from original sources, challenge the students in class, require stiff exams, grade them stringently, and rank the students by academic achievement. Then, after an anxious starving time, the school will attract many accomplished students, bringing "decided prosperity," which "is, of course, very welcome."[12]

The key to attracting students was "the prompt demonstration of the efficacy of

4. Quotations are, respectively from Harvard Law School Association, *Report* (1887), 48; Langdell, Address 1886, 48. See O. Holmes, Oration 1886, 38.

5. Schouler, "Cases without Treatises," 2; Batchelder, "1906—Notes for Langdell art[icle]."

6. Emphasis in original. "Harvard College Law School," 67.

7. C. Eliot, Annual Report 1886–87, 17–18. See Langdell, Annual Report 1885–86, 87.

8. Langdell, Annual Report 1886–87, 92.

9. Quotations are, respectively, from C. Eliot, Annual Report 1890–91, 19; Note, *Harvard Law Review* (1891–92), 238.

10. Langdell, Annual Report 1887–88, 104; Langdell, Annual Report 1888–89, 121–22; Ames, Annual Report 1896–97, 160; C. Warren, *History of the Harvard Law School*, 2:452.

11. C. Eliot, Inaugural Address 1869, 26.

12. Quotations are from C. Eliot, Annual Reports 1888–89, 19; 1890–91, 19.

the School's methods which its young graduates have supplied."[13] As the corporate law firm rose to the apex of the legal profession in the late nineteenth century, the primary workplace of elite lawyers moved from the courtroom to the office, and their most valuable expertise shifted from trial advocacy to legal counsel about complicated commercial transactions. Corporate firms found that academically trained law graduates—particularly those with skills in legal research and dialectic fostered by case method—could rapidly acquire the necessary expertise. Leading in this direction were the firms of Louis Brandeis in Boston and Paul Cravath in New York, which began to recruit "young lawyers, who had graduated from both college and law school . . . with high scholastic marks from elite universities."[14] In 1893 the secretary of Harvard reported that "honor graduates are certain to receive invitations to enter leading law offices in various parts of the country."[15] By the turn of the century elite law firms were routinely recruiting the strongest students, just as Charles O'Conor had hired Langdell for his expertise about wills in 1857.[16] As Brandeis wrote to Langdell, "it has been our custom to employ . . . young lawyers from the Harvard Law School" who rank "among the leaders of their respective classes."[17]

The shifts in the nature of legal expertise and in the hiring practices of elite law firms thus corresponded with changes in educational practice at HLS, as seen in the proliferation of case method teaching among the faculty and the popularity of law clubs among the students. Conversely, the shifts were correlated with the decline in moot courts during Langdell's administration. The tradition of mooting extended back centuries to the inns of court in London, and HLS professors Parsons, Parker, and Washburn had enthusiastically supervised six moot courts weekly during the mid-nineteenth century. When Thayer attended HLS in the 1850s, students wrote detailed pleadings, briefs, and judgments for the moot courts. Carrying on this tradition in the 1870s, Professor Thayer advised his students to attend moot courts "most faithfully" because "they give you the opportunity to apply your knowledge and to try your hand at the actual work of the profession."[18]

13. C. Eliot, Annual Report 1889–90, 24. See C. Eliot, Annual Report 1902–3, 20–21; Ames, Annual Report 1902–3, 168.

14. Hobson, "Symbol of the New Profession," 19.

15. Bolles, *Harvard University*, 68. See Hill, *Harvard College*, 254; Note, *Harvard Law Review* (1891–92), 238. In the early 1890s about twelve students were graduated with honors annually, or about one-sixth of the class. See Langdell, Annual Report 1893–94, 125.

16. Hobson, "Symbol of the New Profession," 3–19; Gawalt, "Impact of Industrialization on the Legal Profession," 107–9; R. Gordon, "Legal Thought and Legal Practice in the Age of American Enterprise," 82; R. Gordon, "Ideal and the Actual in the Law"; Galanter and Palay, *Tournament of Lawyers*, 4–19.

17. Brandeis to Langdell (30 Dec. 1889).

18. J. Thayer, "Notes on Teaching Evidence," 20. See J. Thayer, Papers, box 1, ff. 1–2; C. Warren, *History of the Harvard Law School*, 2:129; E. Washburn, "Harvard Law School," leaf 3v.

But the actual work of elite lawyers was changing as they went into corporate practice, and Langdell, who was among the first to establish himself at the bar by writing extensive briefs in complicated cases, said that he had "long doubted the utility" of the moot courts.[19] During the 1870s, as the dean introduced his academic reforms, the number of moot courts annually supervised by the faculty decreased steadily by more than 50 percent. In the 1879–80 academic year, the faculty voted to suspend moot courts altogether.[20] The suspension resulted, in part, from the heavy teaching load entailed by the introduction of the three-year curriculum. More significantly, student participation in moot courts had been declining, as both Langdell and Ames expressed little interest and the most am- bitious and energetic students devoted themselves to law clubs, which required extensive legal research similar to that involved in case method.[21] When moot courts resumed in the academic year 1880–81 Gray supervised four, Thayer two, Ames one, and Langdell none, a ratio corresponding with their fidelity to the gentlemanly mode of professional education and legal practice. In 1897 the moot courts were discontinued.[22]

By that point, other university law schools were subscribing to the paradoxical new credo that higher academic standards make a professional school more at- tractive. Thus, the dean of Yale Law School argued in 1904 to his skeptical presi- dent that the school should require a college degree for admission because "the reputation of every degree-granting institution depended on the public perception that its standards of admission and graduation are rigorous." In 1912 Yale finally adopted the requirement and also allowed faculty to teach by case method without special permission.[23]

Whatever vindication Langdell felt about these developments during the 1880s, he uttered scarcely a word of satisfaction or recrimination in his annual reports or remaining papers. It was left to Eliot to observe publicly in 1889, "Professor Langdell has now been dean of the Law School for almost twenty years. It has been a period full of fundamental changes, serious risks, grave criticisms, and severe anxieties; but the changes have proved wise, the risks have been run without

19. Langdell, Annual Report 1879–80, 83.

20. Harvard Law School, Faculty Minutes (11 Nov. 1879); E. Washburn, "Harvard Law School," leaf 3v; Harvard University, Report of the Overseers Visiting Committee 1877–78 (9 Jan. 1878). In 1870–71 the faculty supervised 32 moot courts; 1871–72, 28; 1872–73, 24; 1873–74, 19; 1874–75, 21; 1875–76, 21; 1876–77, 19; 1877–78, 16; 1878–79, 15; 1879–80, none. Langdell, Annual Reports.

21. Quotations are from Langdell, Annual Report 1879–80, 83. See Harvard Law School, Faculty Min- utes (11 Nov. 1879); E. Washburn, "Harvard Law School," leaf 3v; Harvard University, Report of the Over- seers Visiting Committee 1877–78 (9 Jan. 1878); C. Warren, *History of the Harvard Law School*, 2:416.

22. Langdell, Annual Report 1880–81, 68; "Harvard Law School Clubs."

23. Quotation is from LaPiana, *Logic and Experience*, 145. See Kimball, "Proliferation of Case Method."

disaster, the criticisms have been met or outgrown, and the anxieties have been forgotten in the crowning success of the last four years."[24] In 1892 the student editors of the *Harvard Law Review* likewise opined that the success of HLS "must be very gratifying... The dean especially must take great satisfaction in the prosperity of the school, and in the assured success and firm establishment of the method of instruction to which he has given so much thought and so many years of devoted effort."[25]

By the time he retired as dean in 1895, Langdell's system had succeeded, but also presented an ironic problem. The meritocratic engine was gaining too much speed, and Langdell could not find the brake. By 1891 HLS had outgrown "the very handsome and commodious" Austin Hall, built in 1883 to last fifty years. In 1892 the faculty divided the entering class in half and began to teach two sections of the first-year courses, which enrolled nearly 150 students.[26] Eliot saw only benefits to growth. After all, "if the Law School remain large, in spite of requiring every regular student to hold a good academic degree on admission, it will have made a valuable contribution to the better organization of professional education in the United States." But the faculty and dean were less sure. "The quality, not the size, of the school, is what they are chiefly proud of," observed Langdell.[27]

The number of students rose ever higher during the 1890s, as indicated by figure 1, Student Enrollment at Harvard Law School from 1870–71 to 1894–95. The faculty responded by closing various admission loopholes, hoping that the enrollment might decrease and be accommodated within Austin Hall. For example, they abolished the September examinations that allowed students to make up failures in exams from the previous June and continue in the school.[28] In particular, the faculty began raising admission standards.

From the outset in 1877, the HLS admissions examination had proved a demanding test of an applicant's knowledge of Blackstone's *Commentaries* and either Latin or an approved modern foreign language. The hurdle was much more difficult than that of Harvard's medical, dental, or veterinary schools, and by 1888 nearly half (99/212) of all the applicants examined had failed.[29] Nevertheless, the faculty

---

24. C. Eliot, Annual Report 1888–89, 21.

25. Note, *Harvard Law Review* (1891–92), 238.

26. Quotation is from C. Eliot, Annual Report 1882–83, 27. See C. Eliot, Annual Report 1890–91, 19; Langdell, Annual Report 1890–91, 114; 1892–93, 134; Langdell to Wambaugh (26 Mar. 1892).

27. Quotations are, respectively, from C. Eliot, Annual Report 1893–94, 23; Langdell, Annual Report 1893–94, 131.

28. Langdell, Annual Report 1891–92, 123; Langdell, Annual Report 1890–91, 115; J. Smith to Eliot (circa 1890).

29. Harvard Law School, Faculty Minutes (27 Feb., 2 July 1875); C. Eliot, Annual Reports 1885–86, 13; 1888–89, 20.

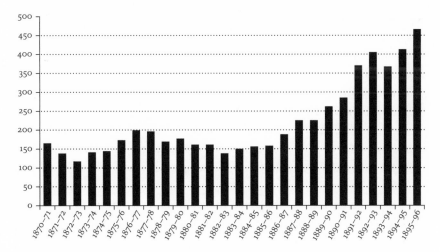

FIGURE 1. Student enrollment at HLS from 1870–71 to 1894–95. Data are drawn from Ames, HLS Annual Report 1894–95, 145.

voted in 1891, and again in 1892, to raise the bar higher and begin testing applicants' knowledge of Blackstone, Latin, *and* a modern foreign language. Intending by this move to reduce the enrollment of nongraduates, the faculty also sought to discourage special students by requiring them to take the admissions examination henceforth. In addition, those admitted as special students were now required to pass examinations in at least three courses annually in order to continue in the school.[30] No longer would HLS shelter "ringers" for the football team.

When the growth in enrollment still did not abate, the faculty again raised admission standards for "regular" students, those eligible to earn the LL.B. Since instituting the expectation of a college degree for regular students in 1877, the school had informally discriminated among such degrees. B.A. graduates were automatically admitted to degree candidacy, but graduates with other kinds of bachelor's degrees—B.S., Ph.B., B.Litt., and so forth—were admitted without examination only if the dean was "satisfied that [the degree] represents an amount of linguistic training equal to" the standard of the admissions examination.[31] In spring 1893 the faculty formalized and tightened this stricture by voting that, as of

30. See Harvard Law School, Faculty Minutes (23 Mar. and 10 Nov. 1891, 30 Sept. and 25 Nov. 1892); Harvard University, Corporation Records, 14:381 (13 Apr. 1891); Langdell, Annual Report 1890–91, 112; C. Eliot, Annual Report 1889–90, 24; 1890–91, 20; 1891–92, 24–25.

31. Quotation is from Harvard Law School, Faculty Minutes (2 July 1875); Harvard Law School, *Catalog 1877–78*, 2. See Harvard Law School, Faculty Minutes (27 Feb. 1875).

September 1896, admission as a regular student would be limited to those holding "respectable" degrees specified on a list in the annual catalog.[32]

Having introduced the expectation of a college degree for admission, while discriminating among the kinds of degrees, HLS here took the further step of discriminating according to the quality of the college granting the degrees. Faced with the choice between expanding the school with qualified students and selecting the most qualified, the HLS meritocrats "preferred selectivity" and pioneered the normative policy of elite, twentieth-century, professional education. Already in 1899 the Oxford University law faculty contemplated adopting the HLS policy.[33]

These moves in the early 1890s were intended "to reduce the number of students entering the school," explained Langdell. Yet, to the astonishment of all, the number did not decrease, but continued to climb. "The recent growth of the School . . . has been in spite of the constant efforts of the Faculty to reduce its numbers by increasing the standard of its requirements," wrote the dean, who could not slow down his meritocratic machine.[34] In fact, as standards rose, students enrolled in greater numbers, just as he and Eliot had envisioned.

By 1897 the meritocratic engine was highballing out of control. "The continued growth of the School . . . has upset all our calculations," wrote Ames, now dean. "Instead of the anticipated loss of at least 50 and possibly 100, in the first years after the change [in admission requirements], there has been a gain of 80 in the total registration," which surpassed 550.[35] The Overseers Visiting Committee therefore concluded that the overcrowding was nearing a "critical" situation in the school. In response, the faculty considered the radical step of selecting by class rank from the applicants with satisfactory degrees, but rejected this proposal because it would have discriminated against the more demanding colleges.[36]

During the 1890s the meritocratic machine therefore triumphantly generated not only prosperity but also "critical" overcrowding, to the consternation of the dean and faculty who were constantly looking for ways to reduce the flow of incoming students. Meanwhile, the increased selectivity yielded "a homogeneous body of men," without which "it would have been impossible to carry on such large classes."[37] This concern about excessive enrollments and the need for homogeneity set the stage for the betrayal of Langdell's new system.

32. Quotation is from C. Eliot, Annual Report 1892–93, 31. See Harvard Law School, Faculty Minutes (23 Mar., 31 Mar., 18 Apr. 1893).

33. Quotation is from Jencks and Riesman, *Academic Revolution*, 22. On Oxford, see Dicey to Eliot (14 Feb. 1899).

34. Langdell, Annual Report 1893–94, 129, 131.

35. Ames, Annual Report 1896–97, 164.

36. Quotation is from Harvard University, Report of the Overseers Visiting Committee 1896–97, 525.

37. *Centennial History of the Harvard Law School*, 49.

Categorical Discrimination

One of the basic tenets of academic meritocracy is justice, as Langdell expressed by "breathing out slaughter" when lawyers succeeded in practice due to "private and other '*influences*' with the judges and not...their abilities, learning, or experience!"[38] According to his educational formalism, students and faculty would be uniformly evaluated by reference to explicit objective standards of academic achievement, rather than irrelevant personal characteristics, such as social class. In this way, people would be treated justly, and by the end of the nineteenth century those at Harvard who administered various mechanisms of academic meritocracy assumed them to be "just."[39] Indeed, Langdell's system did operate more equitably in some respects than the preceding model of gentlemanly acculturation.

Langdell actively sought to admit and support students of limited means. When advocating more scholarships at one faculty meeting, he became filled with emotion and said "that he did not wish any deserving young man to be compelled to leave school for lack of financial assistance."[40] In addition, the academic meritocracy attracted to Harvard "students who grew up outside of New England" and challenged "the way New England students were dominating and conducting college affairs."[41] Furthermore, the new system was more ethnically and racially inclusive than the old regime. HLS began admitting Jews, among whom Brandeis became the exemplary meritorious student and successful alumnus. A number of East Asians attended the school, notwithstanding the passage of the Chinese Exclusion Acts, beginning in 1882.[42] The school also began to admit African Americans. Langdell's relationship to Harriet Jacobs may have induced Archibald Grimké to enroll in 1872, and the small number of African American students gradually increased.[43] In fact, special consideration was accorded to some individuals in order to counterbalance their disadvantages. In October 1894 the faculty voted

38. A. Russell to Machen (1 May 1868).

39. Jagemann to Eliot (6 Nov. 1899).

40. J. Smith, "Christopher Columbus Langdell," 28. See Harvard University, Corporation Records, 11:254 (28 Oct. 1870); 12:137–38 (8 Nov. 1875); 12:149–50 (13 Dec. 1875); 12:240 (29 Jan. 1877); 13:428–29 (19 Apr. 1886); Langdell, Annual Report 1880–81, 85–86; Harvard Law School, Faculty Minutes (5 Oct. 1897).

41. Du Bois, *Autobiography*, 139.

42. The first Asian student, from Japan, earned his law degree during the academic years 1872–73 and 1873–74. Cheng, "Untold Stories: Asian Pacific Americans at Harvard Law School." See J. Thayer, Correspondence and Memoranda, 3:54; in C. Eliot, Papers, see: Alexander Tison to Eliot (15 July 1889), box 77; John Wigmore to Eliot (10 Nov. 1890, 12 Dec. 1890, 27 Jan. 1890, 29 Mar. 1891, 3 May 1891), boxes 79, 81; J. M. Gardiner to Eliot (30 May 1890), box 124.

43. In the 1890s these included the graduates: Tolbert Fanning Sublett (1890), William H. Lewis (1895), Octavius V. Royall (1895), and Clement Garnett Morgan (1896). In Boston between 1874 and 1929, most of the black law students went to Harvard, while most Irish or female law students attended Boston University. Gawalt, "Impact of Industrialization on the Legal Profession," 106.

to remit the tuition fees for the current academic year of William B. Perry and Solomon J. Homer, ... it appearing that Perry has so lost his sight that he can acquire knowledge only through the sense of hearing, ... and the faculty believing him to be a man of marked ability and of much strength of character; it also appearing that Homer is an Indian, and that he has already given evidence of his being a man of much promise, and that his pecuniary circumstances will not permit of his remaining in the School unless he can be relieved from the payment of tuition fees.

In addition, the faculty voted

to remit the tuition fees for the current academic year of ... of William H. Lewis and Octavius V. Royall, who had scholarships last year, but whose records do not warrant their being recommended for scholarships for the present year ... and the Faculty regarding the cases of Lewis and Royall, both of whom are colored men, as so strong, though for different reasons, they believe it would not be right to require either of them to pay a tuition-fee during his remaining year in the School.[44]

Nevertheless, Harvard University and its law school were not immune to the pervasive "hardening of male chauvinism, racism, and xenophobia" during the late nineteenth century.[45] Even as Langdell's academic meritocracy became fully operational in the 1890s, categorical forms of invidious discrimination were established at the school. To be sure, the gentlemanly mode of professional education had incorporated manifest discrimination, but this was personalistic and idiosyncratic because access to professional education depended on the personal relationships developed among gentlemen, evidenced by the character reference required for admission. In contrast, the theoretically just system of academic meritocracy incorporated forms of unjust discrimination that relied on the "categorical thinking"[46] of educational formalism underlying the meritocracy.

This categorical discrimination did not occur simply by deception.[47] The sub-

---

44. Harvard Law School, Faculty Minutes, 12 Oct. 1894.

45. Laurie, *Artisans into Workers: Labor in Nineteenth-Century America,* 197. See Lewis, *W. E. B. Du Bois,* 98–100.

46. Horwitz, *Transformation of American Law, 1870–1960,* 17.

47. Cf. Auerbach, *Unequal Justice: Lawyers and Social Change,* 27; J. Foster, *Ideology of Apolitical Politics,* 12.

jectivity and prejudice were mediated by policies that appeared to preserve formal, disinterested academic judgments. First, the meritocrats distinguished certain categories of people—particularly women and graduates of Catholic colleges—from the other applicants. Then, they declared women an exception to the standard of academic merit and applied special scrutiny to the Catholic college graduates. These policies allowed the meritocrats to believe in their commitment to academic meritocracy notwithstanding their discrimination. They had not violated the standard of academic merit, they seemed to believe, because the distinctive categories deserved separate consideration. As a result, their belief in their commitment to academic meritocracy never wavered.

In each case, the categorical discrimination occurred amid a welter of motives, rationales, and misunderstandings that are often difficult to distinguish and sort. Further complicating the analysis, the leading meritocrats—Langdell, Eliot, and Ames—played separate roles and took different views in these two cases. Nevertheless, it is clear that categorical discrimination was enmeshed in the academic meritocracy from its inception; the two never existed apart. In fact, this discrimination became more deeply rooted and durable because its association with academic meritocracy made it appear legitimate.

This paradox was foreshadowed by Langdell's strong-armed insistence in the late 1870s that his own academic specialty of equity should be the sine qua non of the honor degree at HLS. To be sure, Langdell felt that his courses were the most demanding and gave the clearest indication of students' academic and legal talent. However, he still violated the most fundamental principle of his own system: that evaluation should proceed by disinterested, formal standards of academic merit. Even before 1880 the limitations of self-interest, cultural background, and inherent subjectivity were undermining the incipient educational formalism.

Entirely Unfit for the Feminine Mind

Beginning with the admission of women as baccalaureate candidates to Oberlin College in 1834, coeducation advanced slowly in American higher education, and by 1860 women could choose from about a dozen coeducational institutions and some one hundred women's colleges, half of which offered a liberal arts curriculum. During the 1860s women's access to higher education increased due to the dwindling enrollment of men during the Civil War and to the egalitarian impulse of land-grant universities founded under the Morrill Act of 1862. By the early 1870s, a few prominent universities—Michigan, Wisconsin, Cornell, and Boston—had adopted coeducation, though they still viewed it as experimental. At that point, about 30 percent of all college students were women, of whom about 40 percent were enrolled in coeducational institutions.[48]

In professional schools coeducation developed more slowly. In 1849 Elizabeth Blackwell became the first woman in the United States to graduate from a medical school, the Geneva Medical College in New York. In 1870 Ada Kepley became the first woman to earn a law degree when she graduated from the Union College of Law, later incorporated into Northwestern University. Also in 1870 the University of Michigan law school began admitting women, while the leading universities in the northeast hesitated. Cornell University president Andrew D. White, though an educational reformer, cautiously requested an evaluation of the Michigan innovation from law professor Thomas M. Cooley, who replied that coeducation was causing no problem or lowering of standards.[49]

In light of these events, President Eliot broached the question of educating women in his inaugural address of October 1869. Knowing the powerful opposition entrenched at Harvard, he recommended "a cautious and expectant policy" of maintaining the status quo due to "practical, not theoretical, considerations" inasmuch as "the world knows next to nothing about the natural mental capacities of the female sex." Though adopting this agnostic neutrality in public and observing that the issue was particularly "mooted" in regard to professional education, Eliot personally favored coeducation.[50]

This "cautious and expectant policy" anticipated the contradiction between the determined exclusion of women and the profound commitment to meritocracy that rapidly emerged at HLS. In September 1870 Langdell became dean and began instituting his meritocratic reforms. One year later, Helen M. Sawyer, a twenty-seven-year-old woman from New Hampshire, applied to study at HLS "trust[ing] that under the present liberal tone of Harvard, my sex will pose no misfortune to me."[51] Sawyer's trust reflected the assumption of women's rights activists that academic meritocracy would open doors previously closed to women. Activists embraced "the professional credo, that individual merit would be judged according

48. Ginzberg, "Joint Education of the Sexes," 68, Rosenberg, "Limits of Access: The History of Co-education in America," 108–10; Newcomer, *Century of Higher Education*, 23, 37, 46–49; Solomon, *In the Company of Educated Women*, 43–63.

49. Thomas M. Cooley to A. D. White (5 June 1871) Cooley, Papers, box 1. See Ludmerer, *Learning to Heal*, 14; Drachman, *Sisters in Law: Women Lawyers*, 37–51.

50. C. Eliot, Inaugural Address 1869, 17–18. Despite his support for coeducation expressed in personal correspondence, Eliot always remained circumspect in public. Even on the eve of his retirement, Eliot wrote that "the prime motive of higher education of women should be" not professional education, but "the development . . . of . . . family life and social life." C. Eliot, "Higher Education for Women," 522. See Hawkins, *Between Harvard and America*, 194–96.

51. H. Sawyer to Washburn (12 Sept. 1871).

to objective and verifiable standards," because "without the meritocratic pretensions of the professions women had no warrant for advancement or power within them."[52]

Sawyer's pedigree was impeccable. After graduating from college in upstate New York, she had worked in a law office for a year and "possess[ed] rare grades of mind and body."[53] Her father had served as a justice of New Hampshire's supreme court, authoring opinions that upheld the legal rights of women as circumscribed by their traditional roles, and President Franklin Pierce subsequently offered him the governorship of one of the U.S. territories.[54] Justice Sawyer wrote a brief letter approving his daughter's application, and William Barrett, an alumnus of HLS and Harvard College, wrote enthusiastically in support, "I have urged [Helen] to present herself to the Law School for admission, believing that the time has come when all the Schools of the University should be opened to all who desire to avail themselves of their privileges."[55]

Watched by the public press in New Hampshire, the HLS faculty passed Sawyer's request to Eliot who brought it to the Corporation, which turned her down in mid-October 1871. "No one expected a different result," asserted the *Woman's Journal*.[56] But the Corporation appeared to give the question serious consideration, engaging in "full discussion" that extended over two meetings.[57] In October 1872 another option appeared for Sawyer when Boston University established a law school that was more practical, less academically stringent, and also open to women.[58] But Sawyer pursued a legal career no further, and in 1873 married a druggist and moved to Ohio, where she raised three children.[59]

After barring Sawyer, Harvard persisted in its "cautious and expectant policy," while advocates for women's education commenced to petition the university from all sides. In spring 1872 James Freeman Clarke, a prominent Unitarian minister, Harvard Overseer, and staunch advocate of coeducation, arranged for the

---

52. Cott, *Grounding of Modern Feminism*, 234, 235. See Drachman, *Sisters in Law: Women Lawyers*, 4, 194, 199, 215.

53. *New Hampshire Patriot*, 27 Sept. 1871.

54. E. Day, *One Thousand Years of Hubbard History*, 234; *New York Times* (16 June 1882). See *Hall v. Young* (1857); *Livingston v. Pendergast* (1857); *Leith v. Leith* (1859); *Weeks v. Hill* (1859).

55. G. Sawyer to Washburn (13 Sept. 1871); Barrett to Washburn (12 Sept. 1871). See Bell, *Bench and Bar of New Hampshire*, 170.

56. *Woman's Journal*, 4 Nov. 1871. *New Hampshire Patriot*, 27 Sept. 1871.

57. Harvard University, Corporation Records (29 Sept., 16 Oct. 1871), 11:321, 325. See Greene, "Women in the Law" (1891).

58. Swasey, "Boston University Law School," 54–57; Boston University Law School, *Catalog 1872–3*, 65–67; Boston University, *Historical Register* (1911): 34–37.

59. *History of Seneca County, Ohio*, 787–88.

Overseers to appoint a committee to study coeducation at other institutions.[60] Four months later the committee reported that the requested study was pointless, because Harvard's "traditions and circumstances are so different" from coeducational institutions, because "the old and large colleges in the country" had "no disposition" to adopt coeducation, and because "the great body of the friends of Harvard College" did not want to discuss it.[61]

Even as the Overseers thus invoked tradition, convention, and political pressure in order to reject coeducation, the Corporation received a proposal that Harvard Medical School (HMS) should subsume the New England Female Medical College, "a school for educating nurses, midwives and female physicians." The Corporation referred the question to the Overseers, who voted to endorse the medical proposal so long as the arrangement "can be rescinded at any time." Faced with opposition on the medical faculty, however, the Corporation rejected the merger. The New England Female Medical College then turned to Boston University, which agreed to form a coeducational school of medicine in 1874.[62]

The opposition to coeducation among faculty and alumni of HMS was expressed most prominently over the next two decades by Edward H. Clarke, a noted physician and fellow of the American Academy of Arts and Sciences, who began teaching at HMS in 1855 when faculty were paid directly out of tuition. In 1870 and 1871 Clarke joined other senior professors in opposing the academic reforms that Eliot was advancing for the medical school along the lines of HLS. In 1872 Clarke resigned from the faculty in order to focus on his medical practice and was then elected to the Board of Overseers.[63] In this new role, Clarke opposed coeducation in general, especially in medical education and, above all, at the medical school of Harvard University.

As if responding to Eliot's statement that "the world knows next to nothing about the natural mental capacities of the female sex," Clarke published his own notorious assessment in *Sex in Education; or, A Fair Chance for the Girls* (1873). Claiming to draw his conclusions "from physiology, not from ethics or metaphysics," Clarke maintained that women must choose between higher education

60. Harvard University, Overseers Records (10 Apr., 8 May 1872), 11:39–40, 42. From 1867 to 1869, Clarke chaired the committee reporting to the Board of Overseers, which laid out the plan of reform for Harvard that resulted in the election of Charles W. Eliot as president in 1869.

61. Harvard University, Overseers Records (25 Sept. 1872), 11:69–70.

62. Quotations are from Harvard University, Overseers Records (7 Aug., 25 Sept. 1872), 11:65–66, 68. See Harrington, *Harvard Medical School: A History*, 1219–23; Nercessian, *Worthy of the Honor: A Brief History of Women at Harvard Medical School*, 38.

63. Harrington, *Harvard Medical School: A History*, 1051. See Nercessian, *Worthy of the Honor: A Brief History of Women at Harvard Medical School*, 33–36.

and bearing children, which is their natural function, because the physiological strain of doing both leads to mental and physical breakdown.[64] The first edition of Clarke's book sold out in a week, and fifteen more editions followed by 1890 as the work ignited a firestorm of public debate. Meanwhile advocates in every corner of Harvard attempted to introduce coeducation during the closing decades of the nineteenth century.

In June 1874 Harvard College had taken a small step toward coeducation when, in conjunction with the Women's Education Association of Boston, it began to offer examinations to teenage girls in surrounding towns who could earn a certificate signifying the completion of "a judicious programme of study." Though providing no instruction to girls, Harvard was clearly supporting their education in the liberal arts.[65] At the medical school, however, the faculty voted 7–6 against a resolution to provide analogous medical examinations to women in order to improve the training of local nurses.[66] Meanwhile, the U.S. Supreme Court ruled in 1873 that women had no right under the Constitution to practice law, and individual states could, therefore, prohibit them from becoming lawyers.[67] The question here was women's right to join not only the bar but also the judiciary and thereby to shape the nature of law. "Imagine women on the bench," wrote HLS professor Thayer in 1876. "Would not their peculiarities of sentiment, and difference in degree and measure and intensity with which they hold them, show itself in determining what is law?"[68]

Thayer's concern doubtlessly plagued the HLS meritocrats when, in 1878, another "request for the admission of a woman to the Law School was considered and denied" by the Corporation.[69] This decision apparently caused little dissent, inasmuch as neither the faculty nor the president left any record of the request. However, when a Boston woman offered in 1878 to donate ten thousand dollars to Harvard Medical School, if it would educate women on equal terms with men, fierce debate erupted. At a meeting of the Board of Overseers, Eliot himself moved that the donation be provisionally accepted. But the Overseers split on the ques-

64. Quotations are, respectively, from C. Eliot, Inaugural Address 1869, 17–18; Clarke, *Sex in Education*, 12–13. See Zschoche, "Dr. Clarke Revisited," 547, 547n6.

65. C. Eliot, Annual Report 1872–73, 26–28.

66. Harrington, *Harvard Medical School: A History*, 1223, 1236.

67. *Bradwell v. State of Illinois* (1873).

68. J. Thayer, Criminal Law Teaching Notebooks, 1:3 (30 Oct. 1876).

69. Harvard University, Corporation Records (7 Oct. 1878), 12:365. The identity of the female applicant is not recorded in any of the Harvard archives, but the chronology suggests that she may have been Lelia Robinson, who in 1879 began her studies at Boston University law school and in 1881 became the first woman to graduate, earning the LL.B. cum laude and ranking fourth out of thirty students. L. Robinson to the Equity Club (7 Apr. 1888); Drachman, *Women Lawyers and the Origins of Professional Identity*, 17.

tion, and the Corporation rejected the offer in deference to the medical faculty, who objected on the grounds that undertaking coeducation was "inexpedient" amid the meritocratic reforms that the president was forcing on them.[70] A month later, in July 1879, when the campaign to raise an endowment for HMS was stalled, Eliot wrote wistfully to a confidant that "this is just the time to offer a round sum of money to the university in order to procure the admission of women to the medical school."[71]

Although the barrier against women showed no sign of weakening at HLS or HMS, Eliot and the Corporation took another incremental step toward educating women in the college when, in 1879, the Women's Education Association of Boston sought to modify the examination of teenage girls in surrounding towns. Instead of the standard of "a judicious programme of study," the examination for the certificate was made "nearly identical with the examinations for admission to Harvard College."[72] This new standard actually decreased the educational requirements, but it conveyed greater legitimacy by explicitly indicating the girls' parity with the boys entering Harvard College. In addition, the Women's Education Association engaged Harvard faculty to offer college-level instruction to the girls who passed. In 1882 the Society for the Collegiate Instruction of Women was incorporated to raise money, purchase property, and retain Harvard faculty in order to offer these college-level courses. At that point, Harvard College began, in effect, admitting and instructing young women on a par with male undergraduates, but assumed no official responsibility for the academic work and conferred no academic credit.[73]

Also in 1882 the Corporation received another offer of a gift to support coeducation at HMS, when a group of female physicians promised $50,000. The fivefold increase over the prior offer multiplied commensurately the "vehemence and personal animosity" of the debate.[74] But the outcome was the same. Prompted by the threat of the medical faculty to resign, the Overseers voted 13–12 against the proposal, and the Corporation then turned it down. Justifying their opposition, the faculty said they were preoccupied with academic reforms, which they also opposed due, in part, to their conviction that raising academic standards would

---

70. Harvard University, Corporation Records (8 Apr. 1878, 9, 23 June 1879), 12:322, 409, 411; Harvard University, Overseers Records (10 Apr., 10 July, 25 Sept. 1878, 23 Apr., 7, 27 May 1879), 11:314–16, 332, 335, 354–56, 357, 360–61; C. Eliot, Annual Report 1878–79, 29–32. See Harrington, *Harvard Medical School: A History*, 1223–35; Nercessian, *Worthy of the Honor: A Brief History of Women at Harvard Medical School*, 40–43.

71. Quotation is from Nercessian, *Worthy of the Honor: A Brief History of Women at Harvard Medical School*, 43.

72. C. Eliot, Annual Report 1879–80, 444, appendix 5.

73. Morison, *Three Centuries of Harvard*, 392.

74. Harrington, *Harvard Medical School: A History*, 1217.

make the school unpopular and decrease enrollment.[75] While adhering to the traditional economic logic of professional education, the medical faculty thus behaved consistently in opposing both revolutions of academic meritocracy and coeducation in 1882, as they had in 1872. Conversely, women's rights activists, who favored both, also acted consistently, as did HMS dean Henry P. Bowditch in proposing in 1883 that HMS establish a separate department for the education of women. But the faculty rebuffed this as well.[76]

In this fashion, Eliot and "the progressive party in Harvard" thus were stymied during the early 1880s but hoped "to see progress resumed with moderation" as soon as possible.[77] Meanwhile, coeducation continued to spread across the country, and by 1890 nearly one hundred institutions were providing higher education to both women and men, including about seventy in the Midwest and the West. Overall, during the period of growth between 1870 and 1890, "women's educability had become what the abolitionist [cause] was before it and the suffrage [cause] after it."[78] Beginning in the 1890s, the national trend reversed, as prejudice against marginalized groups in American society increased dramatically.[79] A widespread reaction against coeducation arose and continued until about 1920, prompted by fears that higher education, the teaching profession, and public culture generally were becoming feminized.[80] Coeducation therefore advanced slowly and inconsistently.

In 1892 Johns Hopkins University agreed to admit women into the first class of its new medical school, despite the opposition of Hopkins president Daniel C. Gilman and founding professor William Welch. This radical step was taken in order to meet the condition of major gifts offered by female donors. At the same time, Johns Hopkins became the first medical school in the country to establish the admissions requirement of a bachelor's degree. This stricture, also opposed by Gilman and Welch, was required by the female donors and demonstrated again the consistency of women's rights activists in supporting both coeducation and

75. C. Eliot, Annual Report 1881–82, 37–38. See Harvard University, Corporation Records (26 Sept. 1881, 13 Mar., 10 Apr. 1882), 13:90, 127, 131–32; Harrington, *Harvard Medical School: A History*, 1238–46; Nercessian, *Worthy of the Honor: A Brief History of Women at Harvard Medical School*, 43–46.

76. Harvard University, Corporation Records (10 Dec. 1883), v. 13, pp. 264–65; Nercessian, *Worthy of the Honor: A Brief History of Women at Harvard Medical School*, 47.

77. C. Eliot to Gilman (28 June 1885).

78. Palmieri, "From Republican Motherhood to Race Suicide," 54. See Solomon, *In the Company of Educated Women*, 62–65.

79. Paul, *Conservative Crisis and the Rule of Law*, 2–7; Laurie, *Artisans into Workers: Labor in Nineteenth-Century America*, 197.

80. Rosenberg, *Beyond Separate Spheres*, 43–51; Rosenberg, "Limits of Access: The History of Coeducation in America," 111–16; L. Gordon, *Gender and Higher Education*, 43–45.

academic merit.[81] Watching these events from Harvard, Eliot refrained from expressing support publicly "because I feared it might exasperate some men in our
Medical Faculty who have been...much annoyed at my advocating the admission of women to our own Medical School. I still wish to bring that measure
about."[82]

Meanwhile, women sought continually to enter other departments at Harvard.
In October 1890 the Corporation voted to allow a female instructor at Wellesley
College to attend graduate courses, but not to register as a student of the University.[83] When other women made similar requests in November 1891, May 1892,
and September 1892, the Corporation denied them, however,[84] and in spring 1893
the Overseers rejected as "unwise and impracticable" a petition from alumni to
admit women to the divinity school.[85]

In November 1893 the Society for the Collegiate Instruction of Women proposed to change its name to "Radcliffe College," to cede full control to the Harvard Corporation, and to have the Harvard president countersign and "affix the
seal of Harvard University" to the diplomas.[86] The Harvard Overseers consented
to this plan, observing that the instruction of women would occur at Radcliffe
separately from the men, except for graduate courses in which "no possible harm
could be reasonably anticipated from 'the entrance of an occasional mature—and
scholarly—woman into small classes of men who are making study a serious business.'"[87] Radcliffe College was then legally incorporated in 1894.

In order to placate dissenting alumni, the governing boards insisted that the arrangement with Radcliffe did not constitute "an 'entering wedge' for coeducation,"
and rejected petitions that the Harvard degree be conferred on Radcliffe graduates. But the Corporation immediately blurred the distinction between the two
institutions by voting that Radcliffe students could attend certain undergraduate
courses at Harvard College.[88] Nevertheless, seeking to maintain the "compromise"

81. Fleming, *William H. Welch*, 98–99; Morantz-Sanchez, *Sympathy and Science: Women Physicians*,
85–88.

82. C. Eliot to Gilman (2 June 1890).

83. Harvard University, Corporation Records (1 Oct. 1890), 14:331.

84. Harvard University, Corporation Records (9 Nov. 1891, 9 May 1892, 27 Sept. 1892), 14:438, 485,
15:28.

85. Quotations are from Report of the [Overseers] Committee on the Admission of Women to the
Divinity School (17 May 1893) in Harvard University, Overseers Records, 13:92. See 31 May 1893, 13:103;
Boston Daily Advertiser, 29 June 1892.

86. Harvard University, Corporation Records (12 June 1893, 13 and 15 Nov. 1893), 15:104, 137–38,
134B.

87. Harvard University, Overseers Records, Special Committee on Radcliffe Degrees Report (7 Mar.
1894), 10.

88. Quotation is from A. Foster to Bonaparte (17 Jan. 1894), 25. See Harvard University, Overseers
Records, Special Committee on Radcliffe Degrees (7 Mar. 1894), 4; Harvard University, Corporation

between two "ardent" camps,[89] Eliot and the Corporation upheld the crucial distinction that women could not earn the Harvard degree.

Eliot's desire to maintain the delicate balance was challenged in the mid-1890s by incessant petitions seeking new exceptions and privileges for Radcliffe students.[90] One of these came to the law school during the 1896–97 academic year, asking that "Graduate women registered in Radcliffe" be permitted to attend courses. A straw poll of the HLS faculty yielded the following result:

DEAN [AMES]: Yes—but personally would regret it.

LANGDELL: Declined to express an opinion—the question not being before us.

THAYER: Yes—but personally does not want them.

GRAY: Yes—but does not want them to come, and does not advise.

[JEREMIAH] SMITH: Yes—thinks *some* women would make good lawyers.

[EUGENE] WAMBAUGH: Yes—does not advise women to study law and prefers not to have women in the school.

[JOSEPH H.] BEALE: Yes—separate instruction in first-year courses.[91]

With considerable ambivalence and with Langdell abstaining, the HLS faculty thus agreed to support the Radcliffe "compromise" and allow women enrolled at Radcliffe to obtain instruction but not the degree from HLS. Nothing came of this straw poll,[92] and two years later the issue of admitting women to HLS was officially confronted.

—⟂—

On 24 June 1899 the HLS faculty convened at 9 A.M. for the long, final meeting of the year at which the professors voted on all the candidates for degrees and acted on petitions for exceptions to the established policies of the school. For example, the faculty allowed the HLS students leaving to join the military and fight in the

Records (29 Jan. 1894), 15:163; Harvard University, Overseers Records (10 Jan., 7 Mar., 11 Apr., 2 May 1894), 13:143–44, 146–47, 149–50, 154–55.

89. C. Eliot to Brimmer (3 Nov. 1894).

90. See Harvard University, Overseers Records (25 Sept. 1895), 13:239; Harvard University, Corporation Records (15 Jan., 10 June, 29 Nov. 1895, 12 Oct. 1896, 11 Oct. 1897), 15:260, 290, 355, 435, 16:56.

91. "Opinions...taken in [HLS] Faculty meeting in 1896–97," in C. Eliot, Papers, box 124, f. 462. There is no other record of this straw poll in Harvard Law School, Faculty Minutes, Corporation Records, and Overseers records.

92. At its meetings of Apr. 8 and May 13, the faculty adopted some new restrictive policies on admissions, residency, and promotion of students, and the Corporation then resolved that the faculty should notify it of "any very material changes proposed" in academic or admissions requirements "before taking final action." Harvard Law School, Faculty Minutes (17 May 1897). This straw poll may have been the advance notice of a new policy that the faculty was contemplating.

C. C. Langdell, 1890s. Courtesy of Special Collections Department, Harvard Law School Library.

Spanish-American War to receive credit for their courses without taking exams during that academic year. Ever the purist, Langdell alone dissented. The HLS faculty also excused students who missed coursework or exams due to illness or the need to earn money, but these individuals, unlike the soldiers, were expected to take the exams at another time.[93] A number of such petitions were presented at the meeting of June 24 attended by Eliot, Ames, Langdell, Thayer, Smith, Gray, Ames, Brannan, Beale, and Williston.

The last petition came from Frances A. Keay, a graduate of Bryn Mawr College in history and economics who wished to enter HLS as a "regular student." Though her B.A. certainly met the standard of the HLS list of "respectable" bachelor's degrees that qualified applicants to be admitted as regular students, the faculty refused to admit Keay as a degree candidate. However, they voted "that if the Governing Boards of Radcliffe College admit her as a graduate student with a view to her attending this School, she may take the courses and examinations" but not receive the Harvard LL.B.[94] By this proposal—opposed only by Langdell—Keay would be admitted virtually to the status of a "special student" at HLS. Consistent with their straw poll from two years earlier, the HLS faculty apparently intended this arrangement to comport with the established "compromise" between Harvard and Radcliffe. On June 26 the Council of Radcliffe College assented to the HLS proposal,[95] and awaited action by the Corporation, whose members dispersed over the summer.

Meanwhile, the Harvard and Radcliffe administrations attempted to keep the matter confidential, fearing to stir up the opponents to coeducation. But a *Boston Herald* reporter learned about it, visited the law school, and found Gray, who imparted his understanding of the situation, observing that "if the Bryn Mawr girl . . . is admitted to the lectures next fall, she will come in for . . . all the celebrity that belongs to the first girl to attend the Harvard law school." The *Herald* eagerly published the story.[96] Summering in Maine, Eliot was dismayed that word was out, and rushed to correct the "very misleading" article, which "implies throughout that both Harvard and Radcliffe are seeking what is called coeducation. That is not true." By emphasizing the distinction between coeducation and the proposed

93. Harvard Law School, Faculty Minutes (May 1898–June 1899).

94. Quotation is from Harvard Law School, Faculty Minutes (24 June 1899). See Ballard, Questionnaire; Ames to Irwin (27 June 1899). Aspects of Keay's story have been told in C. Warren, *History of the Harvard Law School*, 2:467; *Centennial History of the Harvard Law School*, 55; Stevens, *Law School: Legal Education in America*, 83; Drachman, *Sisters in Law: Women Lawyers*, 138–40. This account draws on new archival evidence.

95. Council of Radcliffe College, Record (Nov. 1899).

96. *Boston Herald*, 19 July 1899, 7.

arrangement for Keay, which he supported, Eliot tried publicly to maintain the delicate "compromise."[97]

To make matters more complicated, in August Bryn Mawr president M. Carey Thomas communicated to Radcliffe some reservations about Keay's academic performance, writing that Keay showed "a rather unusual anxiety to defer examinations."[98] Because Keay was not "a strong enough student to be a good pioneer,"[99] Thomas feared that she would make a poor impression on professors who had not previously taught young women.[100] This judgment did not reach anyone at HLS, where it would certainly have raised concerns since academic pressure was continually increasing. Even advocates of coeducation on the HLS faculty and at Radcliffe may have balked at initiating a new policy for a woman whose performance under academic pressure was questionable.

Nevertheless, Keay's application seemed headed for approval. The petition fit the Radcliffe compromise, and the prospects for women in the legal profession had improved in the twenty years since the last woman had applied to HLS. In 1887 the dean of the University of Michigan Law School dismissed any doubt that women could study law. In 1888 Lelia Robinson, the first woman to gain admission to the bar in Massachusetts, observed "a great difference in the general public feeling concerning women attorneys now from that which prevailed when I first started.... Half a dozen years seem to have cleared away the fogs of doubt and hesitation through which I was viewed, and the idea of a woman in the law is no longer an uncomfortable novelty."[101] Consequently, while the Corporation consulted the Overseers during September 1899, Keay optimistically made living arrangements in Cambridge,[102] and another woman, Caroline J. Cook, submitted a petition making the same request as Keay.[103]

Born in Indiana in about 1863, Cook earned a B.A. from Wellesley College in 1884 and taught at the nearby Dana Hall School. In 1896 she entered Boston University law school and graduated in June 1899, writing a thesis entitled "Evidence as to Character."[104] Though Cook already held an LL.B., her application to HLS in September 1899 was not uncommon, given that law school graduates occasionally

97. *Boston Herald*, 26 July 1899, 7.

98. M. Thomas to Irwin (21 Aug. 1899).

99. M. Thomas to Bakewell (17 July 1899).

100. M. Thomas to Irwin (17 July 1899).

101. L. Robinson to the Equity Club (7 Apr. 1888).

102. Harvard University, Corporation Records (26 Sept 1899), 16:314; Harvard University, Overseers Records (27 Sept 1899), 13:442–43; Keay to Irwin (9 Sept. 1899).

103. Harvard Law School, Faculty Minutes (30 September 1899); Ames to Eliot (1 Oct. 1899).

104. C. J. Cook, "1942 Biographical Record"; Boston University, Commencement Program 1899; *Grand Forks Herald*, 7 Jan. 1906; *Boston Herald*, 9 Aug. 1947.

applied to HLS in order to obtain the Harvard degree. The articles in the *Boston Herald* during July likely piqued her interest to apply.

Cook's petition was to be heard by the HLS faculty on September 30, a meeting anticipated by advocates on both sides. On September 25 the Radcliffe College Council voted that it was willing to grant a law degree to women who completed the course of study at HLS.[105] But Langdell, hoping to reverse the June 24 vote in favor of Keay, composed a long memorandum that listed eight reasons against educating women at HLS:

1. Every Department of this University was founded for the education of men exclusively,... Therefore the plain and safe course for the governing bodies is to stand *super antiquas vias*.... To establish a system of coeducation would be to divert the funds of the University from the object for which they were given.

2. ... the founders of a new university may provide for the admission of men alone, or of women alone, or of both men and women indiscriminately, and the public is not entitled to any voice on the subject.

3. If this University were a state institution,... the question would be wholly different.

4. Assuming that the public is entitled to a voice,... the question therefore is, not whether a few women wish to be admitted to the University, but whether a majority of the public in weight—and influence—wish to have women admitted.

5. The question of admitting women to the Law School involves the question whether this University ought to aid or encourage women to become lawyers; and the governing bodies cannot decide the first question in the affirmative without assuming the responsibility of deciding the second question in the affirmative also.

6. The most pressing question in the Law School today is how to keep its numbers within manageable limits.... The [proper?] course would seem to be to leave the education of those women who wish to become lawyers to institutions which can take proper care of more students than they already have.

7. The planning and building of Austin Hall [in 1883]... settled in the negative the question of admitting women to the Law School until the time comes for erecting a new building.

---

105. Council of Radcliffe College, Record (25 Sept. 1899); Harvard University, Corporation Records (26 Sept. 1899), 16:314.

8. ...the founding of Radcliffe College...settled the question of coeducation for this University to this extent, namely, that...no woman can receive any of the instruction given by the University unless she be a member of Radcliffe College.[106]

While Langdell composed his memo in preparation for the September 30 meeting concerning Cook's application, Ames, having succeeded Langdell as dean, gathered data on the opposite side of the case. He compiled a table of forty "Law Schools not Admitting Women," and observed "thirty-three are Southern Schools," apparently pointing to their lower academic standards and to the stringent gender etiquette associated with the South. He also prepared a table of "Law Schools Admitting Women," listing thirty-eight institutions that enrolled 168 women, of whom eleven were college graduates. Ames evidently intended these data to indicate that many schools were admitting women and that few women could or would enter HLS, if permitted to do so.[107]

Ames's tables and Langdell's memorandum were circulated prior to the September 30 meeting, when Cook's application was discussed and "the opinions of the individual professors [were] taken down stenographically." As was his custom, Thayer prepared an oral presentation and rebutted certain points expressed in Langdell's memorandum and by professors at prior meetings:

The institution was founded and has received endowments not for the purpose merely of educating men, but...the question of sex did not really present itself....[M]en alone were received at first, but...it was really founded for the education of "youth." ...

The development of the times has made it the duty of a university to receive all persons who wish for an education, at least in its graduate courses.

It was not worth while to receive as members of the School one [woman] or six [women], but...if a sufficient number—say twenty or twenty-five—should present themselves,...they should be received....

It would not be agreeable to the young men...and...to the instructors at first. Personally, [I] would rather not have them present....but after a little while all that would disappear and no longer be thought of.

There is no reason why a woman who desires to study law, should not do so. It is for the women themselves to decide whether or not they want to

106. Langdell, Memorandum on Admitting Women to the Law School (30 September 1899).
107. Ames to Eliot (1 Oct. 1899). Ames also included a table of thirteen "doubtful schools," for which "the data at hand are insufficient" but "Probably women are admitted in a majority of them."

come.... This institution should announce that, *provided sufficient numbers want to be admitted*, the School should receive them as members.[108]

One by one, seven other professors endorsed Thayer's statement, with slight qualifications or elaborations, including Ames, who gave the most enthusiastic endorsement of admitting women: "It is desirable to open to women all possible avenues of intellectual development and for earning a livelihood. No harm can come to this institution from the admission of women to the Law School. The presence of women at other law schools has not caused any inconvenience, and any feeling of dissatisfaction on the part of the men-students is likely to be temporary."[109]

The lone dissent at the September 30 meeting came from Langdell, and the HLS faculty therefore voted to endorse Cook's petition, as they had Keay's.[110] Two weeks later, Eliot and the Corporation met and seemed poised to concur, for in the previous two decades they had prepared the way for the founding of Radcliffe College, supported the enrollment of female graduate students, and encouraged proposals to educate women in the medical school, despite staunch resistance by the faculty. Nevertheless, although the HLS faculty overwhelmingly agreed to admit women to their classrooms, the Corporation turned down Keay and Cook, voting that Harvard was "not prepared to admit women to the instruction of the Law School."[111]

Keay, having grown impatient with the delay, had already returned to Philadelphia and immediately enrolled at the University of Pennsylvania law school, "where they have had women students for a number of years, and where the experiment has proved so satisfactory that they are anxious of having as many as possible." In 1902 Keay graduated from the University of Pennsylvania Law School and opened a practice in Philadelphia, specializing in admiralty law. In 1907 she gave up practice, married, and moved to Cambridge, later working as a law librarian at HLS and at a law firm in Boston.[112] Cook meanwhile entered the Massachusetts bar in 1900 and engaged in private practice, while teaching part-time at local colleges and joining a number of progressive voluntary associations on behalf of women and working-class families. Elected the first president of the

---

108. Reported in Ames to Eliot (1 Oct. 1899). Emphasis added.

109. Reported in Ames to Eliot (1 Oct. 1899). Also attending were Beale, Brannan, Williston, Smith, Strobel, and Westengard.

110. Harvard Law School, Faculty Minutes (30 September 1899). See Ames to Eliot (1 Oct. 1899).

111. Harvard University, Corporation Records (16 Oct. 1899), 16:320. See Harvard University, Overseers Records (22 Nov. 1899), 13:445–46.

112. Quotation is from Keay to Irwin (23 Oct. 1899). See Keay's letters of 2, 29 Oct, 5 Nov. 1899; Ballard, Questionnaire; Ballard, Interview (18 Mar. 1920).

Massachusetts Association of Women Lawyers, she was widely recognized as "one of the most prominent women lawyers in Massachusetts."[113]

Keay and Cook apparently attributed the Corporation's rejection to Eliot, given his public rebuttal of the *Herald* story announcing coeducation at HLS.[114] But Eliot supported their petition, and the reason for their rejection must lie with Langdell. For thirty years, the president and the Corporation had been striving to convince a majority of the medical faculty to endorse any form of educating women, and here they had support from all but one of the law faculty. Yet, that one dissident guided the final decision. To be sure, Eliot and the Corporation heeded more than Langdell's personal stature as patriarch. HLS was Harvard's most successful professional school, which already had more students than it could handle, and those factors gave reason for pause. Beyond that, Langdell exercised influence because his arguments expressed the subliminal opposition of his colleagues, evident in two ways.

On the one hand, Thayer's requirement for "a sufficient number—say twenty or twenty-five"—of female applicants was clearly an eviscerating qualification in view of Ames's calculation presented at the meeting that, throughout the country, only eleven female law students were college graduates. Even these college graduates would not necessarily have qualified for admission to HLS as regular students, given the restrictive list of "respectable" degrees adopted in 1893. The faculty vote in favor of Keay and Cook was contradicted by Thayer's condition: "provided sufficient numbers want to be admitted." On the other hand, none of the HLS faculty actually desired coeducation or saw any benefit in it; most preferred not to admit women, but agreed to tolerate them. Only Beale, Brannan, and Ames were "perfectly willing that [women] should come." Westengard and Williston worried about "the restraint on class discussion." Smith, along with Thayer and Strobel, said that, personally, they "would very much prefer not to have the women there," though they agreed that women deserved admission.[115]

Consequently, Langdell expressed the preference of most of the faculty and guided the decision of the Corporation. His influence arose from reasons not appearing in his long memorandum, which contained only his formal arguments appealing to precedent and principle. He had more to say because, in addressing coeducation at HLS, Langdell employed his characteristic mode of reasoning.

113. Quotation is from *Dallas Morning News*, 23 Oct. 1911, 10. See C. J. Cook, "1942 Biographical Record"; *Grand Forks Herald*, 7 Jan. 1906; *Boston Herald*, 9 Aug. 1947.

114. Ballard, Interview (18 Mar. 1920); C. J. Cook, "Too Early for a Definite Answer," 36. See Drachman, *Sisters in Law: Women Lawyers*, 139.

115. Reported in Ames to Eliot (1 Oct. 1899).

In the memorandum, Langdell first drew from authority by appealing to the precedent of Harvard's founding purpose and maintaining that the university had a fiduciary and, possibly, legal obligation to "stand *super antiquas vias*" and devote its resources to "the education of men exclusively." The precedent had been confirmed, he said, in brick and mortar by building Austin Hall in 1883 without any provision for educating women. Finally, the precedent had been reconfirmed by "founding Radcliffe College" and thereby indicating "that no woman can receive any of the instruction given by the University unless she be a member of Radcliffe College."[116]

The memorandum also argued deductively from principle. If the founding purpose of Harvard could be changed, then the original goal of every "new university" was at risk. Even if the founding purpose of a state institution could be changed, then that did not apply to Harvard, being private. And even if Harvard were public, then the decision to change the founding purpose should broadly consider public opinion, not only the views of interested parties. Finally, admitting women to law school presumed that women should become lawyers, and Harvard had not examined that premise.

Langdell devoted his memorandum purely to this formal analysis of authority and principle, as if he considered no other factors. As in the treatment of vexing legal questions, however, Langdell employed his three-dimensional mode of reasoning, comprising a comprehensive yet contradictory integration of induction from authority, deduction from principle, and analysis of justice and policy. At the HLS faculty meeting on September 30, Langdell verbally added reasons drawn from justice and policy, in keeping with his standard approach of sublimating, while heeding, these considerations. At the meeting, "Professor Langdell, in addition to his written protest [in his memorandum], said that *the law is entirely unfit for the feminine mind—more so than any other subject*. . . . As to the suggestion made earlier in the meeting, that women make good use of the legal education acquired, by filling clerical positions, *he admitted that women had a special aptitude for clerical duties*, yet the study of the law would be not an improvement but an *injury* to them along this line. If they were to do practical work, the way to learn is by setting them at that work immediately, and not to give them a legal education."[117]

Hence, Langdell put "the feminine mind" in a separate category that was outside legal reasoning. In striking contrast to his treatment of working-class, Jewish, East Asian, American Indian, or African American men, women were an excep-

116. Langdell, Memorandum on Admitting Women to the Law School (30 September 1899).
117. Reported in Ames to Eliot (1 Oct. 1899). Emphasis added.

tion and had no standing in the tribunal of academic merit, and no credentials could qualify them. The tone of this misogynist statement suggests that Langdell's opposition to educating women at HLS had less to do with the formal analysis of authority and principle in his memorandum than with his depreciating assessment of their intellectual and psychological capacities and the vocation for which they were fitted. It was unjust, as well as impractical, to do women the "injury" of admitting them to a course of study that led to a profession for which they were "entirely unfit." Hence, "the idea that a course in the Law School would help [women] is entirely erroneous."[118]

In placing women in a separate category and declaring them an exception, Langdell thus adopted the three-dimensional mode of reasoning that he characteristically applied to difficult legal dilemmas. In this instance, he seems to have construed authority and principle to fit his judgments about justice and policy that arose fundamentally from his appraisal of women's intellectual and psychological capacities. But why did he make that appraisal?

—◦∿◦—

The source of Langdell's disparaging evaluation of women is not apparent in his personal background and experience. In his youth, it was his mother and her family who ignited his interest in education, while his older sister, Hannah, served as both a model and mentor for his pursuit of education. It was to Hannah that he "opened his heart . . . for the first time, and . . . made known his aspirations . . . for a college education."[119] As a student at Phillips Exeter Academy, he chose to read books written by Louisa M. Alcott and Harriet Beecher Stowe, as well as biographies of Mary, Queen of Scots, and Josephine, empress of Napoleon.[120] His wife, Margaret, graduated from Hellmuth College in Ontario with a diploma from the two-year "academical course" and the two-year "college course," far exceeding the normal educational attainments of women at the time.[121] And Margaret did not lose her identity in her husband, expressing her own judgments about Harvard policy and making philanthropic gifts in her maiden name, which were prominently recorded in public.[122]

118. Reported in Ames to Eliot (1 Oct. 1899).

119. Quotations are from Ames, "Christopher Columbus Langdell, 1826–1906," 466–67. See J. Smith, "Christopher Columbus Langdell," 27; Cogswell, *History of New Boston*, 170.

120. Golden Branch Society, Librarian's Book [1846–49].

121. Hellmuth College, *Catalog 1871–72*, 13; "Margaret Ellen Langdell" (1908), 20.

122. See Langdell to Eliot (17 Apr. 1904); Marble plaque in sanctuary of Christ Church, Cambridge, Massachusetts, 1907.

Despite these personal relationships with educated women and the widespread recognition by 1890 that women surpassed men in the academic rankings in most coeducational settings,[123] Langdell placed higher priority on education for men, as revealed in 1897, shortly before Keay applied to HLS. Serving as the trustee of a small fund for the family of the deceased custodian of HLS, Langdell was asked by the widow to authorize payment for the oldest child, Mabel Arnold, to complete her studies at Radcliffe College. But Langdell resisted, because, "as that [trust] fund is so small, and there are five other children, all younger than Mabel—*the youngest but one being a boy . . .*—I have very grave doubt whether it would be right to pay Mabel's tuition fee out of that fund." Not only did Langdell imply that the younger brother had a greater claim to the fund for education than the girls, but he also doubted the widow's idea that Mabel's education would be worthwhile either personally or financially.

"Mrs. Arnold, however, has no appreciation of my doubts," he wrote. "She thinks it the plainest case in the world; that it would be a calamity to have Mabel's college course interrupted; . . . that the fund could not be better employed than in helping her through; that money so used would not in fact be spent but invested, and invested to a great advantage with reference to the interest of the whole family. Mrs. Arnold appears to be a very nervous woman, is carrying a heavy burden, and I fear there is serious danger of her breaking down."[124]

Langdell proceeded to ask Eliot if the law school, rather than the trust fund, could pay for Mabel's tuition at Radcliffe. He was therefore willing to support the education of women, but he did so as a matter of extraordinary beneficence, not equity. The idea that Mabel's college education constituted an investment in a career was literally crazy to Langdell, though he had devoted his educational work to advocating the same investment for men.

Langdell's extreme appraisal of the "feminine mind" is linked closely to a gender distinction about vocation rooted in the widespread fear in Victorian culture that women were extinguishing the "manliness" of American men. "The whole generation is womanized," wrote Henry James, in *The Bostonians* (1886). "The masculine tone is passing out of the world; it's a feminine, a nervous, hysterical, chattering, canting age, an age of hollow phrases and false delicacy and exaggerated solicitudes and coddled sensibilities." Many other prominent books echoed the fear: *Manhood: The Causes of Its Pre-mature Decline* (1870), *Manliness in the Scholar* (1883), and *Manhood Wrecked and Rescued* (1900). Commensurately,

123. Hunter, *How Young Ladies Became Girls*, 228.
124. Langdell to Eliot (9 July 1897). Emphasis added.

efforts by women to establish themselves in new fields were seen as threats to manliness.[125] In the domain of education, when girls sought to compete with boys, as by entering debating clubs in the 1880s, the males moved on to make athletics the focus of academic life.[126]

This Victorian fear was pervasive at Harvard, which experienced a marked shift during the 1860s from a religious and beneficent ideal of manhood to that of "manliness": the ideal of a stronger, tougher, more physical man. In the 1880s and 1890s athletics emerged as the most popular outlet for students to demonstrate "manliness," while the competitive spirit increasingly infused academics. President Eliot and meritocratic professors argued that scholarly competition promoted "masculinity," a new word entering the language at this time. "*Scholarly manliness*"—achievement in a competitive academic system—was thus officially promoted as the means by which Harvard would build an "aristocracy" that was also "democratic" in admitting students from any social or economic background.[127]

No records remain of Langdell employing such masculinist language, and he discounted the most worrisome concern of his colleagues: that "mixed classrooms" of men and women would inhibit Socratic teaching or class discussion.[128] Nevertheless, his personal crusade for academic meritocracy certainly fit the new ideal of "scholarly manliness." In particular, the introduction of competitive examinations during the nineteenth century was associated with masculinity. By portraying "examinations as horrific ideals, tests of character, and sacred masculine rituals," students at Oxford and Cambridge, for example, created "a pervasive culture of extreme competition and struggle which enabled them to cast the successful victors in supremely masculine terms."[129] The terms of competition and struggle reverberate in Langdell's analysis of the benefits of providing scholarships for poor but able students: "if five out of the ten ablest men in each class had scholarships, and the other five had ample means, as the former would be sure to remain through the course and take their degree, the latter would do so also; for the ten would be each other's rivals, and able and ambitious men of means will never permit their rivals without means to enjoy better educational advantages than themselves."[130]

125. James, *Bostonians*, 333. See Miller, "Feminization of American Literary Theory," 20–39; Shi, *Facing Facts: Realism in American Thought and Culture*, 8–9, 215; Nercessian, *Worthy of the Honor: A Brief History of Women at Harvard Medical School*, 33.

126. Hunter, *How Young Ladies Became Girls*, 234–35.

127. Townsend, *Manhood at Harvard*, 17, 22, 89–97, 120–32. Emphasis in original.

128. Reported in Ames to Eliot (1 Oct. 1899).

129. Deslandes, "Competitive Examinations," 577–78. See Rothblatt, "Student Sub-Culture and the Examinations System"; Rothblatt, "Failure in Early Nineteenth-Century Oxford and Cambridge."

130. Langdell, Annual Report 1880–81, 85.

This scholarly manliness was particularly cultivated at university professional schools because, "as tests of manhood, ... examinations functioned as useful devices in steeling undergraduates for professional futures." The nature of professional preparation thus intensified scholarly manliness and helped "to preserve male prerogatives at institutions that were frequently characterized as under siege by women."[131] Within the domain of professional education, this masculine character was most intense at law schools.

In law, "masculinity was so fundamental to the profession's consciousness that for most of the [nineteenth] century it acted as an unarticulated first principle." In Victorian culture, "a man's admission to the bar and professional success depended on his conforming to these masculine values."[132] Consequently, "the deep conflict between femininity and professional identity ... plagued women lawyers in the nineteenth century."[133]

By 1899 and the debate over the petitions of Keay and Cook, Harvard had therefore become highly masculinized, fostering a competitive species of academic meritocracy particularly suited to an education that was conceived as preparation for the jousts of professional life. Among professional schools, none embraced more fully the masculine culture of competition and struggle than law schools, and among law schools, none more fully than those that adopted case method, which "requires struggle," as Carter stated in 1886.[134] In contrast, "the recitation method ... is not a virile system. It treats the student not as a man, but as a schoolboy," observed Ames.[135]

In following Langdell and adopting case method during the 1880s, the HLS professors thus "tapped the desire for the strenuous life," and some came to describe their endeavor as "Spartan education."[136] The students were eager to enlist, observing about their HLS training, "Of course, it was for blood. We were all competing. We all wanted to get into the best offices." By the same token, the law firms fought for the best graduates. In 1908 one accomplished HLS senior accepted a position with Cravath's prominent firm in New York, and found that the HLS network in Boston was not pleased. "Brandeis sent for me and asked me what I was going to do," the student later recalled. "I told him I was going to Cravath's. He wasn't at all enthusiastic about it. He didn't say anything, but I could see he

131. Deslandes, "Competitive Examinations," 569, 548. See 565–67.
132. Grossberg, "Institutionalizing Masculinity: The Law as a Masculine Profession," 134, 138, 148.
133. Drachman, "New Woman Lawyer and the Challenge of Sexual Equality," 228.
134. J. Carter, Address 1886, 27.
135. Ames, "Vocation of the Law Professor," 362.
136. Quotation is from LaPiana, *Logic and Experience*, 27. See E. Warren, *Spartan Education*.

wasn't enthusiastic." Soon thereafter the HLS professor who wrote *Spartan Education* pulled the student aside. "He said, 'Hello Kelley. What are you going to do?' I said, 'I've got a job at Cravath's.' He said, 'Kelley, I think you've made a damned fool of yourself.'"[137] In this milieu, it is not surprising that the emerging corporate law firms, staffed by the most competitive graduates from the leading case method schools, doubted the wisdom of hiring women.[138] By the same token, HLS would not admit women, and its "scholarly manliness" was vehemently expressed by Langdell on 30 September 1899: "the law is entirely unfit for the feminine mind—more so than any other subject."

Why did Langdell alone say it? Because he was not a gentleman. The other professors acted as gentlemen when, though believing "it would be extremely disagreeable to have women in the Law School,"[139] they set aside their personal preferences and entertained the ladies' petitions, since "the very notion of gentility or gentleness" incorporated "a respectful and appreciative attitude toward women."[140] Hence, in 1870 Helen Sawyer sent her petition to the gentleman Washburn, not the meritocrat Langdell.[141] By the same token, Smith, the least scholarly member of the faculty, who had been appointed largely due to his professional reputation on the bench and bar, was the most explicit in putting aside his own preference and generously assessing women's abilities: "So far as his personal comfort was concerned [Smith] would very much prefer not to have the women there. But . . . he would go even further than the other [professors] in believing in the ability of the women to distinguish themselves as lawyers."[142] In this way, the receptiveness of other HLS professors to the women's petition was prepared and fostered by the appreciation of "the lady" in the ideology of gentility embraced by the nineteenth-century Brahmin gentry.[143] Indeed, the very aspects of gentility that contributed to appreciation of women—gentleness, agreeableness, empathy—were precisely the characteristics that Langdell was often accused of lacking.[144]

The deep irony of women's exclusion from HLS, then, lay in these opposing contradictions. According to the neutral principles and objective standards of academic merit, women in the late nineteenth century had an absolutely just and

137. Quotations are from N. Kelly, Reminiscences, 39, 55. Nicholas Kelley attended HLS from 1905 to 1908.

138. Drachman, "New Woman Lawyer and the Challenge of Sexual Equality," 230–31, 236.

139. Reported in Ames to Eliot (1 Oct. 1899).

140. Persons, *Decline of American Gentility*, 80.

141. H. Sawyer to Washburn (12 Sept. 1871).

142. Reported in Ames to Eliot (1 Oct. 1899).

143. Persons, *Decline of American Gentility*, 93–95.

144. J. Carter to Eliot (20 Dec. 1869); E. Washburn, "Harvard Law School," leaf 12v; Batchelder, "C. C. Langdell," 312n1.

valid claim to be admitted to HLS, the self-professed champion of academic merit in legal education. But their petitions did not move Langdell, who betrayed his meritocratic commitment and gave voice to the subliminal opposition of the HLS faculty and the Harvard governing boards.[145] Meanwhile, the greatest receptivity to the women's petition came from the impetus of gentility—"a tradition that had always prided itself upon its masculinity"[146]—embraced by those who were least committed to the academic meritocracy that justified women's appeals.

This ironic outcome resulted from the Victorian masculinist ideology, which skewed the principles and standards of academic merit generally in higher education, particularly in professional education, and most especially in the leading law school in the nation. From the very moment of its triumphal inception, the system of neutral and objective standards within the academic meritocracy was betrayed by the subjective and culturally determined interpretation of male and female characteristics, which Langdell expressed quintessentially: "The law is entirely unfit for the feminine mind—more so than any other subject." Due to this distorted understanding of academic merit and to Langdell's ungentle character, his opposition to admitting women prevailed by giving voice to the tacit opposition of manly Harvard.

Certain Inferior Colleges

While categorizing women and excepting them from the standard of academic merit, HLS also classified graduates of Catholic colleges apart from other applicants and subjected them to special scrutiny.[147] This form of discrimination appeared in late spring 1893, soon after the HLS faculty voted that admission as a regular student would be limited, as of September 1896, to those holding "respectable" degrees specified on a list in the annual catalog.[148]

Based on "the colleges whose graduates have entered the School in recent

145. For example, the five Fellows of the Harvard Corporation who decided the petitions of Keay and Cook included HLS graduate Samuel Hoar, whom Eliot later eulogized as "a strong lawyer, ready for combat, eager in attack, firm in defense, a public-spirited citizen who believed in the New England liberties and New England democracy." Eliot, Annual Report 1903–4, 5.

146. Persons, *Decline of American Gentility*, 275.

147. This analysis builds on Mahoney, *Catholic Higher Education in Protestant America*, which presents exhaustive research in the Catholic archives. My interpretation diverges somewhat from Mahoney's and draws on some new archival materials related to the Harvard side of the story. I am grateful to Mahoney for supplying me with her typescript compilation of primary sources. See also Synnott, *Half-Opened Door: Discrimination and Admissions*, 40–44; O'Leary, "Jesuit Legal Education"; Scales, "Society of Jesus and Legal Education"; Kimball, "Paradox."

148. Quotation is from C. Eliot, Annual Report 1892–93, 30–31. Harvard Law School, Faculty Minutes (23 Mar., 31 Mar., 18 Apr. 1893).

years," the original list was apparently drawn up by Dean Langdell, and included the B.A. from sixty-five colleges and universities, the B.Lit. from seven institutions, the B.Phil. from twelve institutions, and the B.S. from seven institutions. This original list of April 1893 "will doubtless be enlarged from time to time," observed the faculty, who confided that responsibility to a standing committee composed of Langdell, Ames, and a recently appointed assistant professor in their mold, Samuel Williston.[149]

In order to enlarge the list, this HLS committee turned to the Committee on Admission from Other Colleges (COA) of Harvard College. COA evaluated the applications of transfer students and of graduates from other colleges who sought to enter Harvard College to earn a bachelor's degree. Harvard considered no other college to be its equal, so the best a graduate from another college could do was to be admitted to the Harvard senior class. HLS adopted the policy that if a student were admissible to the senior class at Harvard College, then the student could be admitted as a degree candidate directly into the law school. COA evaluated each application individually, but, in keeping with educational formalism, the law school wanted rules categorizing degrees and institutions as qualifying a student for admission or not. Consequently, HLS asked COA to generalize from its decisions about individual cases in recent years and to generate a list of institutions whose graduates had been and likely would be admitted to the Harvard senior class.[150]

In June 1893 after Langdell's original list was made public, the editor of the leading Catholic newspaper in Boston, the *Pilot*, protested to President Eliot that the list did not include any Catholic institutions, although there existed in the United States some sixty Catholic colleges, including about twenty-four Jesuit colleges, which generally had the best academic reputation.[151] Barring their graduates from HLS posed a significant threat to the leading Catholic colleges. During the 1890s these small colleges each graduated twenty or fewer students on average, and a total of between five and ten graduates annually entered HLS, constituting

149. Quotations are from Harvard Law School, Faculty Minutes (18 Apr. 1893). See Harvard Law School, Faculty Meeting (18 Apr. 1893).

150. Mahoney, Correspondence, 450–53. Cf. Mahoney, *Catholic Higher Education in Protestant America*, 72–79. Eliot attended the HLS faculty meeting that established this policy and likely suggested this mechanism. Harvard Law School, Faculty Minutes (18 Apr. 1893).

151. Applicants without a bachelor's degree or who held a bachelor's degree that was not on the list could still enter HLS as special students if they passed the admissions examination. Responding to criticism of their restrictive admissions policy, the faculty provided that special students could earn the LL.B. by attaining grades very close to those required for the honor degree. Given the difficulty of this standard, however, the new admissions policy meant that, in effect, those who did not graduate from a "respectable" college were barred from pursuing a degree at HLS. See *Chicago Legal News* (21 Oct. 1893), 62, 82; Lee to Thayer (30 Jan. 1894); *Centennial History of the Harvard Law School*, 50–51.

a significant fraction of the graduating classes at their alma maters, sometimes 10 percent or more. Exclusion from the leading law school in the country injured the career prospects of these graduates, made the Catholic colleges less attractive, and worsened their contemporaneous problem of declining or stagnant enrollments.[152]

Disavowing any anti-Catholic prejudice, Eliot justified Langdell's list on the grounds of academic merit, saying that undergraduate degrees in Catholic colleges "have, to a considerable extent, not been equivalent" to those "in leading Protestant or undenominational colleges." The *Pilot* then published the list on the front page with Eliot's explanation, though without his consent.[153] A few weeks later, in mid-July, the president of Jesuit-run Georgetown College wrote to Eliot, protesting Georgetown's exclusion from the list and sending its examination papers and catalogs for him to review. In response, Eliot and the HLS faculty committee decided to add Georgetown along with two other Catholic colleges in Massachusetts from which HLS drew a number of students: Boston College and the College of the Holy Cross. Nevertheless, in announcing the good news to the Georgetown president, Eliot observed that "the Catalog and examination papers of Georgetown College" indicated "very clearly" a "lack of equivalence" with leading Protestant or undenominational colleges.[154] Accordingly, those three were the only Catholic colleges among the 108 institutions and 131 bachelor's degrees appearing on the select list that was published in the HLS catalog in September 1893.[155]

Between 1893 and 1897 HLS added eighteen more degrees, including another one from a Catholic institution: the B.A. of the University of Notre Dame. In August 1897 a graduate of a Jesuit college not on the list appealed to Ames, who had succeeded Langdell as dean, arguing that his alma mater deserved to be on the list. Ames responded not only that additional Jesuit colleges were unworthy of being listed, but also that Georgetown, Boston College, and Holy Cross had "doubtless" been added to the list not on the basis of their academic merit but in order "not to appear sectarian."[156] Ames then took it upon himself to reconsider their status by asking the COA whether graduates of Georgetown, Boston College, and Holy

152. Mahoney, *Catholic Higher Education in Protestant America*, 14, 71–72, 102, 148, 192, 197.

153. *Boston Pilot*, 1 July 1893, repr., Mahoney, Correspondence, 418–19. See Mahoney, *Catholic Higher Education in Protestant America*, 6, 34–39.

154. Charles W. Eliot to J. Havens Richards (4 Aug. 1893), in Mahoney, Correspondence, 422. See 419–20.

155. Harvard Law School, *Catalog 1893–94*, 5–8.

156. Quotation is from James B. Ames to J. Frank Quinlan (10 Aug. 1897), in Mahoney, Correspondence, 435–36. See Harvard Law School, *Catalog 1897–98*, 5–8. Mahoney, *Catholic Higher Education in Protestant America*, 72, 287n48.

Cross were normally admitted to the Harvard College senior class. Informed that they were not, Ames removed Boston College and Holy Cross from the list, but retained Georgetown. The presidents of Holy Cross, Boston College, Georgetown, and Catholic University of America vigorously protested the decision to Ames and to Eliot.[157]

In the midst of this highly charged correspondence, Eliot increased Catholics' ire by writing an article in the *Atlantic Monthly* that cited Jesuit colleges as an example of retrograde education. The *Atlantic Monthly* then stoked Catholic outrage by refusing to publish a rebuttal from a former Boston College president, though it did publish a response from a Protestant professor at Princeton. In response to Ames's removal of Holy Cross and Boston College and to the *Atlantic Monthly* article, a great outcry arose from Catholics across the country charging Harvard and Eliot with bigotry or "intense anti-Catholic feeling." After some fruitless replies, Eliot withdrew from the controversy in February 1900 and ceased corresponding with the president of Boston College, who sent his entire correspondence with Eliot to the *Boston Globe*, which printed it.[158] Nevertheless, HLS held to its policy, and in June 1900, at the last faculty meeting attended by Langdell before his retirement as a professor, the faculty voted to deny the request of a B.A. graduate from a Jesuit college in Philadelphia to be admitted as a regular degree candidate.[159]

In 1904 HLS ceased publishing the list and directed prospective applicants to contact the secretary of the law school in order to ascertain whether their alma mater appeared on the select list of colleges. During the decade between 1893 and 1904, the list had been enlarged with nearly fifty other colleges and universities, but only two more Catholic colleges were added—the University of Notre Dame in 1894 and Manhattan College in 1900—and two of the original three Catholic colleges had been removed: Boston College and Holy Cross. As a result, only three of the 189 degrees listed in 1904 were from Catholic institutions.[160]

—⚬∿∿⚬—

This controversy over the HLS admissions policy reveals again that the standard of academic merit was enmeshed with categorical discrimination on religious and ethnic grounds. Until 1893 Catholics regarded Eliot as extremely liberal in reli-

157. Mahoney, Correspondence, 436–50; C. Eliot to Conaty (24 Oct. 1898); Mahoney, *Catholic Higher Education in Protestant America*, 74–76.

158. Quotation is from Timothy Brosnahan to J. Havens Richards (8 Mar. 1898), in Mahoney, Correspondence, 443–44. See C. Eliot, "Recent Changes in Secondary Education"; Mahoney, Complete Primary Source, 61–116; Mahoney, *Catholic Higher Education in Protestant America*, 88, 92–94.

159. Harvard Law School, Faculty Minutes (23 June 1900).

160. Harvard Law School, *Catalog 1903–4*, 4–7; Harvard Law School, *Catalog 1904–5*, 4.

gious matters and with good reason. For example, in December 1893 Eliot wrote privately to Johns Hopkins University president Daniel C. Gilman, "I sympathize with the Roman Catholics in their feeling that Roman Catholic children cannot be satisfactorily brought up in what we call secular schools."[161] Moreover, Eliot was widely credited with encouraging the enrollment of Catholics at Harvard and their participation in intellectual and religious affairs. During the 1890s, Harvard enrolled some three hundred Catholics—more than any other Catholic institution in the country. In a sense, Harvard was the largest Catholic college in the country. By the same token, Eliot, Ames, and other Harvard figures firmly denied any prejudicial motives throughout the controversy between HLS and the Catholic colleges. "Religious prejudice has nothing whatever to do with the matter," Eliot maintained. Catholic college leaders and observers therefore initially gave Eliot, Langdell, Ames, and their colleagues the benefit of the doubt.[162]

But in late 1897 and early 1898, when Ames reevaluated the standing of Boston College and Holy Cross, Jesuit leaders began to suspect "some very strong hostility to Catholic institutions" and "some intense anti-Catholic feeling" at Harvard.[163] After Boston College and Holy Cross were removed from the list, their alumni roasted Eliot in the public press, and Jesuit educators and hierarchs regarded Eliot as disingenuous and even suspected that Harvard wanted to steal precious enrollments away from Catholic institutions.[164]

The leading historical treatment of the controversy largely adopts the Catholic educators' view that their rebuttals bested the arguments of Eliot, whose prejudice—stemming from "Protestant-inspired modernism"—was thereby revealed.[165] However, it appears that, paradoxically, both the Catholic charges of sectarian bigotry and Eliot's denial of prejudice in defining academic merit are justified. In fact, anti-Catholicism was subtly entwined with valid, disinterested judgments about academic merit, but disentangling the prejudice from the academic judgments is extremely difficult for several reasons.

First is that Harvard administrators were elusive or ambiguous in communicating with the Catholic educators, who had great difficulty in obtaining precise explanations about the deficiencies of their colleges. Hence, Catholics complained about bigotry existing "somewhere in that Committee [on Admissions]"

161. C. Eliot to Gilman (2 Dec. 1893).

162. Quotation is from Charles W. Eliot to James Higgins (12 Jan. 1900), in Mahoney, Correspondence, 460. See 418–20, 474; Mahoney, *Catholic Higher Education in Protestant America*, 13, 21–59.

163. Mahoney, Correspondence, 442, 443.

164. Mahoney, Complete Primary Source, 98; Mahoney, Correspondence, 444–45, 471–74; Mahoney, *Catholic Higher Education in Protestant America*, 80, 107. See Auerbach, *Unequal Justice: Lawyers and Social Change*, 50.

165. Mahoney, *Catholic Higher Education in Protestant America*, 10. See 15, 82, 95–96, 123, 139, 145.

or "somewhere in Harvard." They requested specific points of criticism, and sent their catalogs and examination papers to Harvard officials for review.[166] But the Catholic educators could not even determine who was responsible for formulating or amending the list.

Langdell drew up the original list, and COA subsequently supplied the data, but HLS issued the list and then submitted it to the Harvard Corporation, which acceded without formally approving it. Meanwhile, the HLS standing committee charged to amend the list comprised Langdell, Ames, and Williston.[167] But Eliot personally decided to add the Jesuit colleges, and Ames personally decided to remove them. The diffuse responsibility for determining the list caused a good deal of frustration and uncertainty.[168] The COA chairman, after meeting with a delegation of Jesuits for several hours and trying to convince them of the validity of the list, complained to Eliot: "The list of colleges published by the law school has caused the [COA] considerable trouble.... If the law school adheres to the publication of its list, ... it alone should bear the responsibility for it and should not leave the task of defending it to" COA.[169]

Out of frustration, the Catholic educators always came back to Eliot demanding a justification for their exclusion from the list. But Eliot was elusive, usually describing the problems indirectly as a "lack of equivalence" to "leading Protestant or undenominational colleges." Beyond that, "it was not [the role] for a Protestant to make a public statement concerning the inferiority of the Jesuit colleges," Eliot wrote.[170] In fact, he maintained that Catholic educators were disingenuous, because they knew the problems with their curriculum. Nevertheless, Eliot's refusal to specify the defects of the Catholic colleges became a matter of public reproach in Catholic alumni associations and the newspapers. The problem of communicating with Harvard thus heightened the frustration of Catholic college leaders, and induced them to suspect bigotry more strongly.[171]

166. Quotations are from Mahoney, Correspondence, 442, 443. See 419–20, 436–39.

167. Harvard University, Corporation Records (29 May 1893), 15:94; Harvard Law School, Faculty Meeting (18 Apr. 1893). Langdell apparently had little further involvement in the controversy. He is not mentioned in Harvard College Committee on Admission from Other Colleges, Papers, including: correspondence, 1 folder, 1892–93; records, 1 vol., 1893–94; minutes, 5 vols., 1889–1905; letterbook, 2 vols., 1900–1902.

168. James B. Ames to Timothy Brosnahan (11 Mar. 1898), in Mahoney, Correspondence, 444. See 436–39, 450–51, 474, 480–81.

169. Jagemann to Eliot (6 Nov. 1899). One week later, the HLS faculty voted to end their reliance on the senior-class criterion as determined by the COA. Harvard Law School, Faculty Minutes (13 Nov. 1899). From that point on, HLS maintained its own separate list.

170. Quotations are, respectively, from Eliot's letters to James Roche (20 June 1893), J. Havens Richards (4 Aug. 1893), and John O'Brien (14 Feb. 1900), in Mahoney Correspondence, 417–18, 422, 470–71.

171. Mahoney, Complete Primary Source, 85–95, 111–12, 118; Mahoney, Correspondence, 456, 465, 467.

Charles W. Eliot, 1902.
Etching by John A. J. Wilcox.
Courtesy of Special Collections
Department, Harvard Law
School Library.

Despite this ambiguity and elusiveness in communication, the Harvard meritocrats did occasionally indicate what they considered to be the deficiencies in Catholic colleges. But here arises a second reason for the difficulty in disentangling the anti-Catholicism from disinterested judgments about academic merit. Both Catholic educators and those at Harvard adopted inconsistent positions regarding these deficiencies, which pertained to curricular content and to educational purpose.

In terms of content, Eliot wanted the Catholic colleges to reduce the amount of classical letters and increase that of modern subjects, above all, natural sciences. Trained as a chemist, Eliot believed that natural science was the essence of an up-to-date curriculum in the late nineteenth century.[172] But Eliot's insistence on this point was not consistent with the law school's position. The HLS admissions exam tested the applicant's "linguistic ability" in Latin and a modern language, and did not require content knowledge in any other modern subjects.[173] Why should Catholic colleges be barred from the list due to the failure to teach subjects that the law school did not require for admission?

While noting that inconsistency, the Catholic educators responded in two somewhat contradictory ways. On the one hand, they sometimes argued that they had added modern science and studies to their prescribed classical curriculum. On

---

172. C. Eliot, "Recent Changes in Secondary Education," 443. See Mahoney, Correspondence, 495; Mahoney, Complete Primary Source, 112.

173. Harvard Law School, *Catalog 1877–78*, 2; Harvard Law School, Faculty Minutes (10 Nov. 1891).

the other hand, they most often argued that their classical curriculum provided a much better undergraduate education than did the modern subjects at Eliot's Harvard.[174] Thus, Catholic educators argued both that they had already done what Eliot wanted, and that they did not need to and should not do what he wanted.

Furthermore, the Catholic educators were being somewhat disingenuous. While responding strenuously in public to the charge that their curriculum was retrograde, many Catholic college leaders privately conceded that they needed to add modern studies to their curricula. In fact, the enrollments at Catholic colleges were dropping or stagnating, because more and more Catholic parents were sending their children to Protestant or nonsectarian colleges, which offered more progressive education. Purely for the sake of institutional survival, the Catholic colleges had to modernize, and they knew it.[175]

The problem was that the Catholic educators, particularly the Jesuits, needed permission from Rome in order to change their uniform curriculum, but the Roman hierarchy was unsympathetic, and told the American Catholics not to bend to modern educational fads. Consequently, Catholic college leaders faced two contradictory demands.[176] Eliot and Harvard required that they modernize in order to get their graduates into the law school, and the Catholic and Jesuit hierarchy demanded that they resist any accommodation to modernity.

These inconsistencies in the debate over curricular content point to disagreement over the purposes of education, which lay at the heart of the dispute. The purposes guided the standards of academic merit and arose from religious values and philosophies of life. Here arises a third reason for the difficulty in disentangling the anti-Catholicism from disinterested judgments about academic merit: the disagreement over educational purposes was sublimated and addressed only obliquely.

The founders and reformers of the research universities in the final third of the nineteenth century generally believed that undergraduate education should foster intellectual autonomy and free inquiry in students. Eliot was the foremost

---

174. Cf. Brosnahan, "President Eliot and the Jesuit College," 3–30; Brosnahan, "Relative Merit of Courses in Catholic and Non-Catholic Colleges," 22–44. See Mahoney, Complete Primary Source, 90, 102–7, 112–13; Mahoney, Correspondence, 423–24, 437; Mahoney, *Catholic Higher Education in Protestant America*, 71, 115, 261. In making the latter argument, Catholic leaders generally took for granted that studying Greek and Latin letters and philosophy provided better mental discipline and better character development than did studies in modern humanities, social sciences, or natural sciences.

175. Mahoney, Correspondence, 426; Mahoney, Complete Primary Source, 29–30, 33, 48, 68, 107, 123, 126–27, 136; Mahoney, *Catholic Higher Education in Protestant America*, 7, 12–14, 102–3, 148, 192, 97, 195–238.

176. Mahoney, Complete Primary Source, 17, 40–46, 135; Mahoney, Correspondence, 428–29; Mahoney, *Catholic Higher Education in Protestant America*, 10, 15, 119, 134, 151–92.

proponent of this view, and therefore advocated the study of natural science and its "characteristic occupation..., namely, free, impartial, open-minded, truth-seeking."[177] Commensurately, he maintained that natural science should be taught by the laboratory method, and he championed the elective system, believing that electivism strengthened students' capacity for intellectual autonomy and free inquiry.[178]

Catholic college leaders did not recognize the fostering of intellectual autonomy and free inquiry as a primary, or even legitimate, goal of undergraduate education. In their view, undergraduate education aimed at relieving doubt and uncertainty by transmitting received truths. Thus, Catholic educators construed "science" as bodies of "special facts...recently discovered" about nature;[179] and they derided Eliot's elective system at Harvard as a "go as you please" approach, leading to educational anarchy. In fact, "electivism was Protestantism applied to education," a priestly alumnus of Holy Cross maintained.[180]

The disagreement over educational purpose was exemplified in opposing interpretations of "philosophy." What Catholic educators meant by "philosophy" was "a vast, compact, thoroughly reasoned, and tested body of philosophic truth" that can be "drilled into every graduate." Catholic educators therefore considered "philosophy" the heart of undergraduate education, built their curriculum around a "body of philosophic truth," and viewed that curriculum as vastly superior to all others.[181] Conversely, the Harvard meritocrats regarded "philosophy" to be a process or method of reasoned deliberation. Eliot maintained, "Philosophical subjects should never be taught with authority.... The very word education is a standing protest against dogmatic teaching. The notion that education consists in the authoritative inculcation of what the teacher deems true may be logical and appropriate in a convent, or a seminary for priests, but it is intolerable in universities and public schools, from primary to professional."[182]

This disagreement over educational purpose was fundamental, and leaders of other research universities concurred with Eliot. "Our experience accords with yours regarding the Jesuit colleges," wrote the president of the University of California to Eliot, "We find that their pupils are not inspired to think for themselves.

---

177. Charles W. Eliot to Thomas Dwight (8 Sept. 1908), in Mahoney, Complete Primary Source, 164.
178. Mahoney, Complete Primary Source, 144, 159; C. Eliot, "Liberty in Education," 125–48.
179. Mahoney, Complete Primary Source, 33. See 49, 113.
180. Mahoney, Complete Primary Source, 114, 115.
181. Quotations are from J. Havens Richards to Catholic Alumni Association of Boston (1897), in Mahoney, Correspondence, 433. See 401–16, 471–74.
182. C. Eliot, Inaugural Address 1869, 6.

I do not think this is due to the subjects they teach, but to the whole spirit of the instruction."[183]

Therefore, notwithstanding Catholics' charge of bigotry, there existed substantive grounds for Eliot's and Harvard's depreciation of the undergraduate education at Catholic colleges. Harvard's curricular content—particularly in modern studies and the natural sciences—was decidedly advanced beyond that of the Catholic institutions, by their own admission. Harvard's educational purpose of fostering students' capacity for intellectual autonomy and free inquiry was not supported or even recognized in the Catholic colleges. Nevertheless, the Harvard leaders did not apply these standards consistently, and their inconsistencies revealed deepseated sectarian prejudice.

Visiting Europe in the mid 1860s, young Eliot was repulsed by Catholic ritual and what he considered Catholics' uncritical and unthinking devotion to their rites, all of which reflected "the extraordinary contrast . . . between Catholicism and freedom of thought." In fact, he wrote, "I hate Catholicism as I do poison, and all the pomp and power of the Church is depressing and mortifying me. . . . Even the good which one recognizes in the mass of superstition and corruption is distressing, because it will lengthen the life and prolong the influence of the Mother of Abominations."[184]

Years later, near the end of the controversy over HLS admissions, Eliot reaffirmed his longstanding reservations about Catholicism:

> There have been moments in the life of the Catholic Church when it has desired to suppress scientific inquiry, and to prevent individuals from publishing the result of their own studies. . . . In general the Catholic Church has often been opposed to the modern spirit of inquiry. . . . The Church has not understood or been friendly to . . . free, impartial, open-minded, truthseeking. . . . How much more Protestant countries have contributed to the progress of science than the Catholic countries. . . . Have you considered how inevitably antagonistic to social and political freedom is the principle of absolute authority which is maintained by the Catholic Church in its own religious domain?[185]

Reflecting on his own Unitarian convictions in 1909, Eliot wrote: "I know I am in the habit of thinking that members of other Christian denominations cannot

183. Wheeler to Eliot (9 Nov. 1903).

184. Quotations are from Mahoney, Complete Primary Source, 2, 3. See Mahoney, *Catholic Higher Education in Protestant America*, 55–59, 82, 95–96, 123, 139, 145.

185. Charles W. Eliot to Thomas Dwight (8 Sept. 1908), in Mahoney, Complete Primary Source, 162, 164.

think much, or reason much, about the dogmas they accept; and when I encounter their defensive arguments they always seem to me weak and archaic.... but the[se] sentiments...make me fairly liable to the criticism...that I believe the Unitarians to be the only thinking, reasoning, and independent religionists."[186] Meanwhile, Langdell in a widely influential article stated that he "sincerely hoped" that residents of "ancient and thickly settled Spanish colonies" would never become citizens of the United States, thereby denigrating their ethnic and religious tradition.[187]

These views shaped the assessment of Eliot, Langdell, and Ames about the Catholic colleges and the eligibility of their graduates to enter HLS as regular students. This influence appeared not in judging the Catholic colleges deficient according to standards of academic merit, but rather in subjecting them to closer scrutiny than non-Catholic colleges and universities. The anti-Catholicism of Eliot, Langdell, and Ames operated in *selectively* applying the academic standards. "The degrees of all Catholic colleges are to be refused, while those of obscure protestant or undenominational institutions are accepted," complained the president of Georgetown.[188] "Petty mushroom colleges, born yesterday,... have been given the right hand of fellowship by Harvard" while Catholic colleges are excluded, noted the Catholic press.[189] "Certain inferior colleges were put [on the list] which no unbiased man would put on the same class with our colleges," observed the president of Boston College.[190] Harvard "has removed Boston C[ollege] and H[oly] C[ross] from its list.... At the same time other notoriously poor little colleges that cannot compete with ours are admitted," wrote the northeastern Jesuit Provincial to the Jesuit Superior General in Rome.[191]

This closer scrutiny was, therefore, "erroneous and gravely unjust," maintained the president of Georgetown.[192] Even the chairman of the COA, a Harvard College professor, echoed this view after meeting with a delegation from Boston College to explain the evidence and rationale underlying the list. COA "did not succeed in persuading the gentlemen that the list of approved colleges published by the law

186. Charles W. Eliot to Jerome D. Greene (2 July circa 1909), in Mahoney, Complete Primary Source, 177.

187. Langdell, "Status of Our New Territories," 386, 389–92. This point is discussed further in the following chapter.

188. J. Havens Richards to Charles W. Eliot (16 July 1893), in Mahoney, Correspondence, 419.

189. "Harvard and the Catholic Colleges," *Boston Pilot* (1 July 1893), quoted in Mahoney, Complete Primary Source, 21.

190. Timothy Brosnahan to J. Havens Richards (7 Nov. 1897), in Mahoney, Correspondence, 440–41.

191. Edward Purbrick to Luis Martín (Feb. 1899), in Mahoney, Complete Primary Source, 70.

192. J. Havens Richards to Charles W. Eliot (3 Aug. 1893), in Mahoney, Correspondence, 421.

school is *just*, because we had to admit that this list included some institutions ranking...no higher than Boston College."[193]

The selective and unjust application of academic standards appeared most clearly in Langdell's construction of the list and in Ames's removal of institutions from the list. The original list of April 1893 comprised "the colleges whose graduates have entered the School in recent years," and therefore included certain small, distant colleges that had sent one or two graduates to HLS in the previous five years, including Mount Union, Olivet, Racine, and DePauw.[194] But the original list did not include all such colleges. The dean—possibly in consultation with the president—culled through the colleges of past graduates.

Langdell was not a Brahmin from old Boston, and his rustic manners and rigid personality made him a social outsider throughout his tenure on the HLS faculty. But he had attended the Congregational Church in New Boston and married the daughter of an Anglican clergyman in 1880. He and Margaret then joined Episcopal Christ Church in Cambridge, and during the Catholic controversy in the 1890s, they became "devoted workers" at Christ Church and belonged to "that small nucleus of hard and loyal workers that kept the heart of the parish steadily beating."[195]

This Protestant background must have influenced the dean when, in 1893, he sorted through "the colleges whose graduates have entered the School in recent years" and eliminated all nine Catholic institutions that had sent graduates to HLS between 1885 and 1893, including Mount St. Mary's, Notre Dame, St. Xavier, College of the Sacred Heart, Manhattan, and the Jesuit institutions of Fordham, Boston College, Georgetown, Holy Cross, and Detroit. While only three of those eighteen Catholic graduates completed the LL.B., this graduation rate was not far below the rate of those entire classes at HLS.[196] This elimination of all the Catholic institutions indicates that some selective bias occurred in compiling the original list.

193. Jagemann to Eliot (6 Nov. 1899). Emphasis added.

194. Quotation is from Harvard Law School, Faculty Minutes (18 Apr. 1893). See Harvard Law School, Faculty Meeting (18 Apr. 1893); Harvard Law School, *Quinquennial Catalog*.

195. Quotation is from G. Day, *Biography of a Church*, 84–85. See M. Langdell, *Journey through the Years*, 56; Christ Church, Episcopal, "List of Voters before 1900."

196. Harvard Law School, *Quinquennial Catalog*. In addition, the compilers of the original list passed over a number of degrees and institutions such as the B.L. of the University of North Carolina; the B.S. of the University of Illinois, Worcester Polytechnic Institute, and Mississippi A.&M. University; and the B.A. of Wofford College, Virginia Military Institute, Missouri State University, Pacific Methodist College, Kansas Normal Institute, the University of New Brunswick, and Franklin and Marshall College. Many of the students with these backgrounds graduated successfully on time, and the graduate from Mississippi A.&M. University, Blewett Lee, was later offered a full professorship at HLS.

The process of removing institutions indicates the same selective bias. During the decade that the list was published between 1893 and 1904, only eight degree programs were dropped,[197] six for bookkeeping, nonsubstantive reasons. The B.A. of Adelbert College, the undergraduate college in Western Reserve University, was eliminated in 1893 because it duplicated the entry for Western Reserve. In 1896 the Wharton School of Finance and Economy and its B.Ph. were stricken, because the degree was subsumed by its parent institution, the University of Pennsylvania, which was added to the list at the same time. In 1896 the A.B. of Clark University was dropped after it was discovered not to exist. In 1897 the A.B. of Griswold College in Iowa was deleted when the degree became unfeasible after the college's preparatory school closed in 1895. In 1897 the Knox College B.Sc. degree was dropped in response to the elimination of the degree and the poor performance of one graduate at HLS. In 1903 the Centre College B.A. was deleted after the college was merged and briefly renamed Central University of Kentucky, whose bachelor's degree was added to the list at the same time.[198]

Only two institutions—Boston College and Holy Cross—were deleted from the list for substantive reasons, as happened when Ames decided to reexamine their credentials in August 1897. Ames had an impeccable Bostonian pedigree. After attending private schools, he entered Boston Latin School in 1858 at the age of twelve and then Harvard College in 1863, where he was president of the Hasty Pudding Club, captain of the baseball team, member of the Institute of 1770, president of Alpha Delta Phi literary society, and Class Day Orator, elected by his classmates. Following a "grand tour" of Europe, he entered HLS in September 1870 and never left after joining the faculty in 1873. Like Eliot, Ames was a Unitarian and attended the First Parish Church in Cambridge, while he also joined the Colonial Club, the Old Cambridge Shakespeare Society, and the Colonial Society of Massachusetts. Due to "the sweetness and charm of his personality" and "his amiable disposition and his cordial welcome," his students and colleagues at HLS regarded him with "esteem and love."[199] In the view of Jesuit educators, however, " Mr. Ames seems to be a testy fellow who, when confronted by a difficulty, cannot refrain from saying something disagreeable."[200]

197. Mahoney, *Catholic Higher Education*, appendix C.

198. Harvard College Committee on Admission from Other Colleges, Minutes, 3:8 (14 Oct. 1897); Mott Linn, Clark University Archives Staff, e-mail message to author, 26 Jan. 2006; Matthew D. Norman, Knox College Archives Staff, e-mail message to author, 26 Jan. 2006; "1865–1895 The Development Years," Davenport Public Library Special Collections (Davenport, Iowa) <http://www.qcmemory.org/> (20 Jan. 2006); "History of EKU," Eastern Kentucky University Libraries (Richmond, Kentucky) <http://www.library.eku.edu/collections/sca/eastern/history.php> (21 Jan. 2006).

199. S. Ames, "Memoir of James Barr Ames," 24–25. See also 4–7.

200. T. Brosnahan to J.H. Richards (8 Mar. 1898), in Mahoney, Correspondence, 443–44.

This difference in opinion mirrored the selective application of academic standards. Ames never reexamined any other colleges on the list for their academic merit, except the two Jesuit institutions. Closer scrutiny and more stringent academic standards were, therefore, applied to the category of Catholic colleges between 1893 and 1904, even while Ames, Langdell, and Eliot correctly believed that they employed neutral, objective measures of academic achievement.

—*mn*—

The 1890s were a triumphal decade, as Langdell's system of academic meritocracy exceeded all expectations in raising academic standards, attracting growing numbers of well-qualified students, producing well-trained graduates desired by leading firms, and prospering financially. In fact, the dean and the faculty, faced with limited space and teaching capacity, tried to restrict admissions and reduce enrollment, and these efforts set the stage for incorporating prejudicial discrimination into the academic meritocracy. Employing the "categorical thinking"[201] of educational formalism, the meritocrats classified women and graduates of Catholic colleges apart from the other applicants, and then declared the former an exception to the standard of academic merit and applied special scrutiny to the latter. Mediated by these policies, the invidious discrimination seemed invisible to the meritocrats, who continued to believe in their commitment to academic meritocracy, even as the "just" system discriminated against these categories of people during the triumphal inception of the system that should have, in principle, opened doors to admit them.

201. Horwitz, *Transformation of American Law, 1870–1960*, 17.

CHAPTER 9

Poor Old White-Whiskers, 1895–1906

Even while betraying its fundamental meritocratic principles, Langdell's system proliferated throughout university law schools, slowly during the 1890s and then rapidly after the turn of the century. In most schools, the system encountered opposition prompted by the "abomination"[1] of converting to case method teaching. This inductive pedagogy relied on Langdell's system because teaching with original sources demanded stronger academic preparation from both students and faculty. Hence, case method entailed "many of the organizational characteristics" of the meritocratic law school, and implied "Langdell's general theory of legal education."[2]

Beyond that functional link to the meritocratic reforms, case method assumed a powerful symbolic role in the campaign for higher academic standards. It was the "emblem" of Langdell's model, that is, "the specific figure which concentrates and intensifies a much more general reality."[3] Case method thus became "the badge of 'modernism' in the teaching world" and "the cachet of the crack law school."[4] By adopting case method, a law school signified that it had allied itself with the HLS-led movement to infuse legal education with the principles and policies of academic meritocracy. This alliance, though attractive to some, became for others a major reason to defend lecturing and recitation, to oppose "the Langdellian law curriculum...slavishly followed in the prestigious 'national' law schools,"[5] and, in a word, to resist "Harvardizing" themselves.[6]

---

1. *Centennial History of the Harvard Law School*, 35.

2. Quotations are, respectively, from Johnson, *Schooled Lawyers*, 126; C. Warren, *History of the Harvard Law School*, 2:511. See 504–14.

3. Quotations are from Williams, *Marxism and Literature*, 101–2.

4. Quotations are, respectively, from Kirkwood and Owens, "Brief History of the Stanford Law School," 16; Hicks, *Yale Law School: 1895–1915*, 45. See also Woodward, "Dimensions of Social and Legal Change," 246.

5. Boden, "Milwaukee Law School: 1892–1928," 16.

6. Frank, "Harvardizing the University" (1923), 1807.

But the advance of Langdell's new system of professional education was inexorable. By 1915, 40 percent of American law schools had adopted the emblematic case method, and another 24 percent had partially accommodated Langdell's method with the clear prospect of complete adoption on the horizon. Of the 36 percent of law schools that still rejected case method, the great majority were marginal or rapidly losing influence in American legal education, and most of these would convert during the next decade.[7] Already in 1898, Oxford professor Albert Dicey observed that "Harvard is quite ahead of the Universities of the U.S. . . ., and the Law School is their greatest triumph."[8] In 1904 Eliot concurred, "The Law School is the most successful of the University's professional Schools. And if there be a more successful school in our country or in the world for any profession, I can only say that I do not know where it is. The School seems to have reached the climax of success in professional education."[9]

This tidal wave was still welling up when Langdell wrote to Eliot on 17 June 1895:

> Dear Sir, Having now completed twenty-five and one half years of service as Dane Professor of Law, and twenty-five years of service as dean of the Law Faculty, and having reached the age of sixty-nine, I respectfully ask to be relieved from further services in the office of dean, and from one third of my duties as Dane Professor. I ask this, not because I find my present duties to be too heavy a burden, nor with a view to doing less work in the near future than I have done in the recent past, but in order that I may have more leisure to devote to the completing of other work.[10]

Langdell's retirement had been anticipated for some time. In the previous few years, Ames had gradually assumed some decanal duties and begun speaking on behalf of the school. In the previous months, the Harvard Law School Association had planned "a monster celebration" to honor the dean.[11] Speaking at the fête on 25 June 1895, were eminent jurists who had known Langdell over the course of his career, while he himself offered a typical "modest disclaimer" deflecting the praise.[12]

7. See Kimball, "Proliferation of Case Method," 240–47.

8. A. V. Dicey to Elinor M. Dicey (13–14 Nov. 1898), quoted in Rait, *Memorials of Albert Venn Dicey*, 164.

9. Eliot, Address 1904, 68.

10. Langdell to Eliot (17 June 1895).

11. *Boston Herald*, 7 July 1906, 3.

12. Quotation is from Gloag, "Christopher Columbus Langdell," 233. See Harvard Law School Association, *Report* (1895). Joseph Choate, typically, detracted from Langdell's accomplishments at the celebratory dinner, however. Choate, Address 1895, 63.

The Boston press gave prominent coverage to the event, though Langdell likewise avoided "all reference to his own activity" when speaking to reporters.[13]

Upon returning to the faculty, Langdell was given a two-thirds teaching load and allowed to continue residing in his university house.[14] His portrait had already been painted and hung in the HLS Library (and even displayed at the World's Columbia Exposition in Chicago), so the Overseers proposed to name the projected new HLS building "Langdell Hall," and the Corporation planned to establish a "Langdell Professorship" from the surplus funds of the school.[15] Yet, these honors and retirement from the deanship marked not the end of his academic work, but a new beginning.

Ever since 1880 his poor eyesight had been deteriorating, forcing him to lecture in his classes rather than teach Socratically because he could not see the students.[16] Increasingly, he avoided public gatherings because his virtual blindness caused him "much difficulty in getting about and in recognizing people."[17] In the last decade of his life, Langdell "could hardly see anything," observed Eliot. "His daily walks between Austin Hall and his house were terrifying to onlookers, particularly after the advent of the automobile. . . . Then he had to trust that the chauffeurs would see that a blind man was crossing the broad street. For several years he was quite unable to go alone on an unfamiliar path."[18] The sight of that "poor, old . . . white-whiskers . . . reeling his way along the streets" strengthened his reputation for eccentricity, particularly among young students who had not known him in his prime, such as Felix Frankfurter, and would contribute to molding Langdell's image in the twentieth century.[19]

Meanwhile, in order to continue his research, Langdell had to rely on a reader provided by the university.[20] In the reading room of the law school library, he

13. *Boston Journal*, 23 June 1895, 1. See Wingate, "Boston Letter" (1 June 1895); *Boston Herald*, 26 June 1895; *Boston Globe*, 26 June 1895; *Boston Morning Journal*, 26 June 1895; "Twenty-fifth Anniversary of Prof. C. C. Langdell," 1895.

14. C. Eliot, Address 1895, 72; C. Eliot to Langdell [circa Jan. 1898]; Langdell to Eliot (1 Feb. 1898).

15. Vinton to Eliot (30 Dec. 1892); Vinton to Wade (11 Jan. 1893); Ames to Eliot (31 Jan. 1898, 30 Dec. 1902); C. Eliot to Ames [circa Feb. 1898]; Harvard University, Report of the Overseers Visiting Committee 1896–97, 525, 528; Harvard University, Corporation Records, box 272–73, f. Apr.–May 1903 (27 Apr. 1903).

16. Schofield, "Christopher Columbus Langdell," 277; Beale, "Professor Langdell," 9–10; Ames, "Christopher Columbus Langdell, 1826–1906," 479, 481; Lee to Philbrick (18 Feb. 1926); Fessenden, "Rebirth of the Harvard Law School," 514.

17. Langdell to Haynes (5 May 1901).

18. C. Eliot, "Langdell," 525. Langdell's blindness is discussed in Kimball, "'*Warn Students That I Entertain Heretical Opinions*,'" 127–31.

19. Quotation is from Frankfurter to Frank (18 Dec. 1933).

20. "Treasurer's Statement, 1896," in C. Eliot, Annual Report 1895–96, 63; Langdell to Eliot (20 June 1895, 2 Feb., 3 Mar. 1897); Langdell to Wier (28 Feb. 1897); Ames to Eliot (9 Aug. 1895, 10 Dec. 1897);

occupied a separate table "piled high with foolscap on which he managed to get about two words on a line.... He had a large safety inkwell at which he used to make desperate jabs with a pen, not always successful." Occasionally, Langdell finished "with his right arm dripping with ink up to the elbow," and witnesses wondered "what became of all this manuscript."[21] This pathetic behavior contributed to the persistent image of Langdell as a "medieval-minded recluse," generating hopelessly arcane commentary on outmoded questions.[22]

However, on those pages of "foolscap"—most of which were discarded in the 1940s when Langdell's papers were archived and Oliver Wendell Holmes Jr. attained celestial stature[23]—Langdell scrawled the most publicly prominent and controversial writings of his career. In the decade after retiring as dean in 1895, he wrote provocative articles on two of the most significant constitutional questions in the following century: whether the U.S. Constitution follows the flag to all lands acquired or occupied by the United States, and whether corporate mergers that reduce competition violate the Sherman Anti-Trust Act (1890).

Three Periods of Academic Work

This final burst of publication was the third in Langdell's academic career, for his writing and teaching fall into three distinct periods, each characterized by the nature and venue of the publications as well as by the character and the subjects of his teaching. The end of each period was marked by an abrupt cessation in academic publishing and, except for the second, by a shift in his teaching. These periods are presented in table 9.[24]

During the early period from 1870 to 1883, Langdell published prolifically and produced a series of pedagogical works: seven casebooks or their installments, one revision of a casebook, two summaries of areas of law, and a revision of a summary. The early period ended in 1883 when Langdell abandoned his unfinished *Cases on Equity Jurisdiction* and temporarily ceased publishing, never producing another

---

C. Eliot, Papers, shorthand box 315—Dec. 30, 1896–June 24, 1897 and Oct. 1–Dec. 30, 1897, Legal Pad 6/97—15, pp. 3–4.

21. Anderson to Landis (24 Feb. 1938).

22. Quotation is from Beale, "Langdell, Gray, Thayer, and Ames," 523. See Sheppard, "Introductory History of Law in the Lecture Hall," 31.

23. The original shelf-list card from the "sampling" of Langdell's papers in the Harvard University archives reads: "Langdell's Papers, received from the Law School, 1941.... Includes a few letters. Bad writing, and very hard to identify. About six times as much thrown out." Langdell's papers have now been consolidated in Special Collections of Harvard Law School Library. See Kimball and Shapiro, Finding Guide.

24. Further discussion of this periodization is found in Kimball, "'Warn Students That I Entertain Heretical Opinions,'" 62–66.

TABLE 9 Periods of Langdell's Academic Publishing and Teaching, 1870–1906

Period	Dates	Academic Publications	Variety of Courses Taught
Early Period	1870–83	casebooks, doctrinal summaries	nine different courses, many taught with Ames
First Hiatus	1883–87	none	same three courses, no coteaching
Middle Period	1887–92	law review articles analyzing equity jurisdiction	same three courses, no coteaching
Second Hiatus	1892–97	none	same three courses, no coteaching
Late Period	1897–1906	law review articles on legal and policy topics	two courses 1895–1900, no teaching after 1900

casebook in the subsequent twenty-six years of his academic career.[25] In addition to the character of his publications, the nature of his teaching distinguished this period. After offering nine different courses between 1870 and 1883, he established a schedule of teaching the same three courses annually until he resigned as dean in 1895.[26] This shift was reinforced by the pattern of his collaborative teaching with his protégé and successor, Ames. Beginning in 1873, Langdell and Ames taught each other's courses, employed each other's casebooks, and cotaught courses in an unusually cooperative pattern. In 1880 their collaboration ceased abruptly, and Ames and Langdell henceforth taught their own courses with their own casebooks and never again cotaught or used each other's casebooks.[27]

Between 1883 and 1888, Langdell ceased his academic publishing and confined his teaching to three courses that the honor degree required or allowed as electives: suretyship, equity pleading, and equity jurisdiction.[28] One reason for these two shifts was the mounting demands of serving as dean of a revolutionary

25. Langdell and Ames produced the only casebooks in use at HLS until the academic year 1888–89, when John Gray and William Keener published their casebooks.

26. Those three courses were Suretyship and Mortgage; Jurisdiction and Procedure in Equity, using Langdell's *Cases in Equity Pleading* (1878); and Jurisdiction and Procedure in Equity, using his *Cases on Equity Jurisdiction* (1879–83) until 1890.

27. See Kimball, "'Warn Students That I Entertain Heretical Opinions,'" 62–65. Why Langdell and Ames ceased their collaborative teaching is open to speculation, but the collaboration may have ended because Langdell's deteriorating eyesight prevented him from engaging in Socratic discussion and forced him to lecture from a text, as he did increasingly during the 1880s.

28. Harvard Law School, *Catalog 1882–83*, 4; Harvard Law School, *Catalog 1886–87*, 2–3; Langdell, Annual Report 1885–86, 88–89.

professional school. Though burdened since the time he assumed the deanship in 1870, the crisis of falling enrollment in the late 1870s and early 1880s led him to observe that "circumstances beyond [his] control" were delaying his scholarship.[29] In addition, his deteriorating eyesight hampered his scholarship and teaching. Finally, he reined in his scholarship and teaching in order to recover from the bruising fights with the faculty during the 1870s, while finding refuge in his marriage to Maggie Huson in 1880. Though producing no children, their marriage was quite happy, for, as Eliot observed, Langdell's "relation to his wife, who was much younger than himself, and to her mother was so delicate and tender that it was a high privilege to witness it."[30]

In the early and mid-1880s Langdell therefore withdrew somewhat from academic pursuits and, perhaps, from the travails and conflicts besieging the law school. The extent of Langdell's alienation from his colleagues during this first hiatus appears in a letter that he wrote to an HLS classmate from Baltimore who had visited him and Maggie in 1883, likely to join a belated reception for their wedding. In the letter, Langdell first recalls his reticence at inviting the friend, whom he had known for thirty years, to visit: "When I wrote to you first, it was with much doubt and misgiving—first as to whether you would care to come; secondly, whether if you came, you would feel [gratified] for coming." Then, Langdell mourns the friend's departure, relating his feelings to his boyhood in a surprising way: "Nothing has happened since [your visit]...that so stirred me up. For days after you left, we felt more than the loneliness of Sunday. (You know that the idea which a New England boy associated with Sunday was chiefly that of loneliness.)"[31]

Langdell's allusion and parenthetical explanation are surprising. As shown by the diary of one of his college classmates, the predominant occupation of a rural New England boy on Sundays in the second quarter of the nineteenth century was to accompany his family to at least one, often two, church services.[32] Associated negative feelings, if any, concerned boredom or punishment. Most boys would have been happy to be left alone, rather than being dragged to church with their families. Just here arises the anomaly for Langdell. Each Sunday during his boyhood, he was reminded of his loss when other boys accompanied their families to church; hence, "the loneliness of Sunday" became an archetypal metaphor in his mind. In 1884 the boyhood feelings of loneliness and loss connected with his

29. Langdell, *Summary of Equity Pleading* (1883), iv. On the second edition of this work, see *Boston Daily Advertiser*, 20 Oct. 1883.
30. C. Eliot, "Langdell," 524.
31. Langdell to Machen (22 June 1884).
32. Gorham, Diary (7, 28 May, 4 June, 17 June, 9 July, 17 Sept., 1 Oct. 1848).

family still returned when someone close to him departed. Even at age fifty-eight, there was for Langdell no greater evidence of a personal bond than if the friend's departure stirred up in him "more than the loneliness of Sunday." Marriage could not heal the old wounds completely. Nor could the steadfast support of his sister, Hannah, who remained in Kansas and corresponded with Langdell throughout his life.

———◦∽∿∼◦———

In 1888 the middle period commenced as Langdell began publishing a series of articles for the *Harvard Law Review*, which had been founded by the Langdell Society of third-year students in 1887.[33] The venue and character of his writings thus shifted, although all these law review articles addressed equity jurisdiction and were collectively published as a treatise in 1905.[34] Meanwhile, his teaching did not change, despite the faculty's vote in 1886 to make all second- and third-year courses elective and eliminate the requirement that students take Langdell's courses. His enrollments held steady at about twenty and far exceeded the enrollments in several elective courses of other faculty: Thayer's Constitutional Law, Carriers, or Sales; Keener's Conflict of Laws; Gray's United States Courts or Advanced Property; and Ames's Legal History or Bills and Notes.[35] Even so, none of his classes were large, since most HLS students held it "advisable to arrange matters, as is so often done, by leaving out most of Langdell's courses,"[36] because "his teaching was preeminently fitted for the cleverest men in the school."[37]

After the middle period ended in 1892, a second hiatus in Langdell's writing lasted until 1897, prompted by the crisis of staggering increases in enrollment, detailed in chapter 8. In 1893 and 1894 he began to neglect certain administrative details, and Ames started to assume some decanal duties.[38] After unyoking himself from the deanship in 1895, Langdell rapidly published a second group of

33. Note, *Harvard Law Review* (1887–88): 100; *New York Times*, 21 Nov. 1886, 10.

34. In *Harvard Law Review*, see Langdell, "Brief Survey of Equity Jurisdiction: Classification of Rights," 1 (1888): 55–72; ". . . Classification of Wrongs," 1 (1888): 111–31; ". . . Specific Performance," 1 (1888): 355–87; ". . . Bills for an Account," 2 (1889): 241–67; ". . . Bills of Equitable Assumpsit," 3 (1890): 237–62; ". . . Creditors' Bills," 4 (1891): 99–127, 5 (1892): 101–38; ". . . Real Obligations," 10 (1897): 71–97; ". . . Classification of Rights and Wrongs [pts. 1–2]," 13 (1900): 537–56, 659–78; ". . . Equitable Conversion," 18 (1904): 1–22, 83–104, 245–70; 19 (1905): 1–29, 79–96, 233–49, 321–34. These articles were collected in *A Brief Survey of Equity Jurisdiction* (1905), which was then expanded in *A Brief Survey of Equity Jurisdiction* (1908).

35. Langdell, Annual Report 1885–86, 91. See Annual Report 1886–87, 88; Annual Report 1887–88, 93; Annual Report 1888–89, 112; Annual Report 1889–90, 127.

36. E. Thayer to J. Thayer (circa Sept. 1889).

37. Ames, "Christopher Columbus Langdell, 1826–1906," 486.

38. C. Eliot to Thayer (14 Feb. 1894); Brandeis to Eliot (25 Apr. 1893); Brandeis, *Letters*, 1:113–17; C. Eliot to Langdell [1893?]; C. Eliot to Brandeis (27 Apr. 1893); Ames to Eliot (29 June 1893).

law review articles during the late period between 1897 and 1906. His teaching schedule also changed, as he began offering two courses annually until 1900 when he relinquished teaching.

Though in this late period he taught entirely by lecturing, "the advance of old age did not in the least impair his power of concentrated thinking or his marvelous memory," observed his colleague Jeremiah Smith.[39] Nearly blind at age seventy-one, Langdell composed his essay "Discovery under the Judicature Acts of 1873, 1875" in one, nearly illegible draft in pen and ink, a remarkable feat for such a highly technical and intricate treatise.[40] When the eminent Oxford law professor Dicey lectured at Harvard in 1898, he was pleased that Langdell attended every lecture, though concerned because the "blind old gentleman ... knows more law than all of us put together" and was "sure to see the superficiality of my knowledge." Thus Dicey inquired into the significance of Langdell's offhand remark about one lecture, since "Langdell never says or writes a word which has not meaning in it."[41]

Not only did Langdell remain acute in the late period, but he branched out from his longstanding attention to equity and published articles on new topics. These articles, sometimes perplexing in themselves, were extracted from much longer manuscripts,[42] most of which are illegible or have been discarded. As a result, it is impossible to fathom his intellectual work in this closing decade, though it is certain that he explored new areas of jurisprudence and policy.

Our New Territories

One of Langdell's new explorations came in his article "The Status of Our New Territories," addressing the constitutional standing of the territories that the United States had seized from Spain as a result of the Spanish-American War. That conflict formally ended with the signing of the Treaty of Paris on 10 December 1898 and its ratification by the U.S. Congress on 6 February 1899. This treaty gave to the United States possession of the islands of Puerto Rico in the Caribbean and Guam

39. J. Smith, "Christopher Columbus Langdell," 31. See Whittier to Philbrick (10 Dec. 1925); Hand to Philbrick (17 Feb. 1926).

40. Langdell wrote out the original, which a secretary transcribed for the printer. Cf. Manuscripts Series 1.A.1–4, described in Kimball and Shapiro, Finding Guide, with "Discovery under the Judicature Acts of 1873, 1875," *Harvard Law Review* 11 (1897): 137–57, 205–19; 12 (1898): 151–75.

41. A. V. Dicey to Elinor M. Dicey (2 Nov. 1898), quoted in Rait, *Memorials of Albert Venn Dicey*, 159.

42. Cf. Manuscript 1.A.6, "Patents and Copyrights," 102 pp. [described in Kimball and Shapiro, Finding Guide], with the brief article "Patent Rights and Copy Rights," *Harvard Law Review* 12 (1899): 553–56. Also, cf. Manuscript 1.A.7 "C. Lan., Of Rights and Wrongs," 38 pp. [described in Kimball and Shapiro, Finding Guide] with "Classification of Rights and Wrongs," *Harvard Law Review* 13 (1900): 537–56, 659–78.

and the Philippines in the Pacific, as well as effective political control over Cuba. Compounded by the annexation of Hawaii five months earlier, the acquisition of these lands sparked intense debate across the nation, prompted, in part, by the competition among vested financial interests. The domestic sugar, fruit, and tobacco industries, as well as the labor movement, feared that the products and people of the new possessions would be allowed free access to the U.S. market. In addition, as the *New York Times* editorialized, "the chief cane-sugar-bearing lands of the world [that] have come into our possession...are in a bad way by reason of the competition of bounty-fed beet sugar."[43] The impoverished new possessions therefore needed revenue in order to pay for their governance and reconstruction.

In order to obtain this revenue and to protect U.S. markets, some argued for levying tariffs on these new territories, but this strategy ran into the constitutional stricture that "all duties, imposts, and excises shall be uniform throughout the United States."[44] Tariff proponents argued, however, that these new possessions belonged to a different category than existing territories of the United States, such as the Dakotas, Alaska, or Hawaii, which were presumed to be destined for statehood. Yet, the United States had never held territory exempt from constitutional authority and protection; therefore, the acquisition of the conquered lands sparked a crisis. Debate in Congress pitted the Democrats, who generally believed that the Constitution follows the flag, against the Republicans, who argued the new territories did not deserve the same constitutional status as prior territories. The latter view was regarded by many observers, such as prominent New York lawyer James Carter, as "a pretence only. The real motive is the love of [money]." Whatever the motives, the disagreement transcended the tariff dispute and rose to the question of whether the United States should hold colonial territories.[45]

Specific tariff disputes in the new territories thus gave rise to a series of cases, known collectively as the Insular Cases, which began to reach the U.S. Supreme Court in 1901. These Insular Cases engaged "the broader question of whether the revenue clauses extend of their own force to our newly acquired territories," as well as the fundamental issue of the constitutional status of the new possessions. In what came to be the leading case, *Downes v. Bidwell*, the majority opinion held that

---

43. *New York Times*, 27 Nov. 1898, 18. See Burnett and Marshall, *Foreign in a Domestic Sense*, xiii; Peralta, "Historical Analysis of the Insular Cases," 40; Sparrow, *Insular Cases and the Emergence of American Empire*, 57–78.

44. U.S. Constitution, article I, sec. 8.

45. Quotation is from J. Carter to Thayer (17 Feb. 1899). See Peralta, "Historical Analysis of the Insular Cases," 40; Levinson, "Canon(s) of Constitutional Law," 246; Sparrow, *Insular Cases and the Emergence of American Empire*, 57–78.

full constitutional standing extended only to the states of the United States, not to its territories, which were "appurtenant" to the United States and received only such constitutional protection as the federal government chose to accord to each of them individually.[46] However, the court subsequently treated as authoritative the concurring opinion of Justice Edward D. White, who reasoned that a territory received constitutional protection after it was explicitly "incorporated" into the United States. White adopted this concept and language directly from an article in the *Harvard Law Review* written two years earlier by Abbott L. Lowell.[47]

Published among the flood of commentary concerning the Insular Cases, Lowell's essay belonged to a group of five articles that were the most frequently cited contributions to the debate and that appeared in the *Harvard Law Review* in late 1898 and early 1899. These articles took up the question of the constitutional status of the newly acquired lands by asking, as the U.S. Supreme Court did subsequently, whether the meaning of "United States" in the Constitution included territories possessed by the United States. If not, then the federal government could govern such possessions and their inhabitants as it chose, even as colonies, unfettered by the Constitution. Two of the articles answered negatively, effectively endorsing colonialism; two answered affirmatively, extending constitutional protection to all U.S. territories. Several months later in the next volume of the *Review*, Lowell proposed his intermediate "third view" that the Supreme Court ultimately adopted.

Answering negatively were Langdell and his colleague Thayer, a leading authority on constitutional law. Thayer maintained that the United States must abandon the "childish" notion that "all men, however savage and however unfit to govern themselves, were oppressed when other people governed them." Instead, the nation must accept its "new and inevitable" role as a colonial power, recognizing that constitutional rights and limitations apply only to the states and not to territories. Meanwhile, the United States should preserve the sanctity of its homeland and "never . . . admit any extracontinental State into the Union."[48] Answering affirmatively was Carman F. Randolph, a prominent lawyer, who argued that any territory acquired by the United States receives the same constitutional standing and privileges as all previous territories, because U.S. territories are presumed destined for statehood "according to the spirit of the Constitution."[49] Professor

46. Quotations are from *Downes v. Bidwell* (1901), 284–85, 287.

47. *Downes v. Bidwell* (1901), 287, J. White concurring; Lowell, "Status of Our New Possessions." Here and below, see Burnett and Marshall, "Between the Foreign and the Domestic," 5–8; Torruelia, *Supreme Court and Puerto Rico*, 24–31, 44; Cabranes, "Some Common Ground," 43; B. Thomas, "Constitution Led by the Flag: The *Insular Cases*," 82–103; Sparrow, *Insular Cases and the Emergence of American Empire*, 40–55.

48. Quotations are, respectively, from J. Thayer, "Our New Possessions," 475, 485, 484.

49. Randolph, "Constitutional Aspects of Annexation," 292.

Simeon Baldwin of Yale Law School agreed with Randolph that constitutional purview extends beyond the states of the Union, because "a power to rule [a territory] without restriction, as a colony or dependent province, would be inconsistent with the nature of our government," as Chief Justice Taney had argued in the infamous *Dred Scott* case.[50]

Though disagreeing over whether the United States could legitimately hold colonies, Baldwin and Randolph actually concurred with Langdell and Thayer about the nature of these acquisitions from the Spanish-American War. None of the four wanted any of these lands to become a full-fledged part of the nation, and their disagreement arose from the changed political situation at the time when each article was composed. Writing during the public debate over whether Congress should ratify the Treaty of Paris, Randolph and Baldwin projected the unpalatable outcome that the new lands would have to become states because the two authors wanted to discourage ratification and acquisition of the conquered lands. Writing after the public and political debate had been resolved, Langdell and Thayer recognized that "we no longer have before us the question of whether we will take on extracontinental colonies or not. We have them now. Our real question is what to do with them."[51] Considering how "to undertake the government of dependent countries," Langdell decided that they fell outside of constitutional purview,[52] and Thayer frankly considered them colonies. For Randolph and Baldwin, this "real question" was still hypothetical and avoidable.

The four articles thus clearly presented the doctrinal dilemma between extending constitutional purview to every land acquired by the United States, as Randolph and Baldwin argued, and confining it narrowly to the states, as Langdell and Thayer recommended. Attempting to resolve the dilemma in November 1899, Lowell's "Third View" distinguished between the "acquisition" of territories and their "incorporation" into the United States. Lowell thus sought to reconcile the "two opposing theories" by maintaining that, until new territories were "incorporated into the union," they were not covered by the Constitution, and their inhabitants were not entitled to the rights of citizens. This distinction between incorporated and unincorporated territory was then adopted by Justice White and, ultimately, the U.S. Supreme Court.[53]

50. Quoted in Baldwin, "Constitutional Questions," 401. See *Scott v. Sandford*, 60 U.S. 393 (1857).

51. J. Thayer, "Our New Possessions," 483. Congress ratified the treaty on 6 February 1899, and Langdell completed his essay late in January 1899. Apparently, he moved from a position opposing annexation of any territory during spring and summer, 1898, to his ultimate position endorsing colonialism when faced with the "real question" in January and February 1899. See J. Thayer, Papers, box 17, ff. 17–18.

52. Langdell, "Status of Our New Territories," 392.

53. Lowell, "Status of Our New Possessions," 171–76, 156. *Downes v. Bidwell* (1901), 287, J. White concurring.

—⌇∿⌇—

Each of the authors of these five prominent articles was accustomed to engaging in public controversy, except Langdell. Why did he enter this controversy? As a student at Exeter and Harvard, he had actively debated such political questions in the literary societies, and, upon returning to Harvard to join the faculty, he had sought to participate in the social and intellectual life of the university. But after the wounding disputes of the 1870s at HLS, he increasingly withdrew, refusing to speak or appear at professional meetings, even the American Bar Association meeting on legal education, despite urging by President Eliot and leading lawyers.[54] Nor did the legal issues draw Langdell to the dispute over the new territories. He had little expertise or interest in constitutional law, which the HLS curriculum long treated as ancillary. Nevertheless, in the period between the December 10 signing and the February 6 ratification of the Treaty of Paris, when public debate on the constitutional status of the new possessions reached a fever pitch, rumors circulated among the HLS students that Langdell was preparing an essay on the controversy.[55] The reason for Langdell's unusual commentary on this public issue may lie in Dicey's visit to HLS during the two months leading up to the Treaty of Paris.

One of the most famous law professors in England at the time, Dicey's reputation rested particularly on his expertise concerning the unwritten British constitution. At the invitation of Eliot and the HLS Association, he visited Harvard in October and November 1898 and delivered a series of eleven public lectures analyzing the development of legislation in England during the nineteenth century.[56] Several factors suggest that Dicey's visit to Harvard induced Langdell to write "The Status of Our New Territories."

The two legal scholars respected each other's work, having met during Dicey's first trip to the United States in 1870 and corresponded frequently since that time.[57] In 1880 Dicey, with "the most unfeigned admiration," ranked Langdell's *Cases on Contracts* among the great American legal writings.[58] Subsequently, Dicey praised Langdell's "immense analytical power" and his "unrivalled acquaintance with the history of English case law."[59] Dicey also extolled HLS and ranked its library,

---

54. See Rawle to Eliot (1 July 1899); C. Eliot to Langdell [circa July 1899]; Langdell to Eliot (11 July 1899).

55. E. Thayer to J. Thayer (circa Feb. 1899).

56. Ames to Eliot (10 Dec. 1897, 7 July, 31 Oct. 1898); *Boston Globe*, 1, 5 Oct. 1898. The following account draws on Rait, *Memorials of Albert Venn Dicey*, 145–74; Cosgrove, "A. V. Dicey," 325–28; MacMahon, "Dicey at Harvard Law School."

57. A. V. Dicey to Elinor M. Dicey (4 Oct. 1898), quoted in Rait, *Memorials of Albert Venn Dicey*, 151.

58. Dicey, "English View of American Conservatism," 229.

59. Dicey, "Teaching of English Law," 429.

Langdell's pride, as the best collection of English legal records in the world.[60] Conversely, Langdell greatly esteemed Dicey's stature in English jurisprudence and attended every one of his lectures at Harvard, sending a congratulatory letter upon their completion, though he did not regard legislation to be "law" per se. When Dicey later had trouble finding a publisher for the lectures, Langdell tried to arrange publication through the HLS Association, and when Dicey's book finally appeared, Langdell devoted great effort to reviewing it.[61]

In addition to their mutual regard, another factor indicating Dicey's influence on Langdell was that Dicey was "the preeminent theorist of the British Empire" and the foremost advocate that England should keep its colonies.[62] Arriving in Massachusetts soon after the cessation of hostilities between Spain and the United States, Dicey heard "all sorts of opinions about the war" throughout his visit, which coincided with the public debate and treaty negotiations over the prospective new territories. Doubtlessly, he expressed his imperialist views to his hosts, including Langdell, with whom he had lunch soon after arriving at Harvard.[63]

Apart from advocating imperialism, Dicey may have interested Langdell in the constitutional implications of the territories controversy through the series of four lectures that he delivered contemporaneously at the Lowell Institute in Boston. Entitled "A Comparative Study of Constitutions," these lectures are not extant, but Dicey offered comparisons to the Swiss and Prussian constitutions and, likely, to the French and the British constitutions, drawn from his acclaimed book on the subject.[64] The influence of Dicey's comparative lectures is reflected in Langdell's extensive research into international peace treaties, statutes, and cases pertaining to the development and formation of the United States and its territories, beginning with the 1763 Treaty of Paris and extending through Federal legislation of 1898.[65] Hence, Dicey's comparative method may have inspired Langdell's approach in his essay.

Shortly after Dicey's departure from Cambridge, Langdell commenced preparing his unprecedented public commentary on the Territories controversy.

60. Dicey, "Teaching of English Law," 423. See 422–40.

61. A. V. Dicey to Elinor M. Dicey (2 Nov. 1898), quoted in Rait, *Memorials of Albert Venn Dicey*, 159; Ames to Eliot (20 July 1899); C. Eliot to Dicey (15 Jan. 1906). See Langdell, "Dominant Opinion in England," 151–67.

62. MacMahon, "Dicey at Harvard Law School," 17.

63. A. V. Dicey to Elinor M. Dicey (24–25 Nov. 1898), quoted in Rait, *Memorials of Albert Venn Dicey*, 167. See 151, 154, 155, 166–68.

64. Dicey, *Lectures Introductory to the Law of the Constitution* (1885). A. V. Dicey to Elinor M. Dicey (2 Nov. 1898), quoted in Rait, *Memorials of Albert Venn Dicey*, 159; *Boston Evening Transcript*, 10 Nov. 1898, 10.

65. Langdell, "Manuscript 4.B.2 Research Notes on States of the U.S.," in Langdell, Papers.

In this effort, he addressed constitutional law, advocated an imperialist policy, and employed a comparative method, all indications that Dicey's visit in October and November 1898 prompted Langdell to write "The Status of Our New Territories."

Though falling outside his longstanding areas of expertise, Langdell's article attracted significant attention due to his position as the elder statesman of the nation's leading law school. During debate in the U.S. House of Representatives, one congressman quoted Langdell and Thayer to show that "Harvard University was on the side of" President McKinley and the Republicans in maintaining that the Constitution does not extend to the newly acquired territories.[66] In the U.S. Senate, one senator similarly invoked "two learned professors of law in Harvard University, Thayer and Langdell."[67] In the earliest Insular Cases, U.S. Supreme Court justices may have drawn certain arguments from Langdell's article.[68] Apart from exercising this political and judicial influence, the article demonstrates the continuity of Langdell's mode of reasoning throughout his intellectual work.

Scholars have interpreted the article in contradictory ways: as an exemplar of legal formalism wholly devoted to deductive consistency and internal textual analysis, as an example of contemporary racial and ethnic prejudice, and as an effort to achieve just administration of economic policy.[69] In fact, Langdell's argument in his Territories article comprises all these contradictory elements. This inconsistency stems from the fact that his mode of reasoning remained three-dimensional, incorporating a comprehensive yet contradictory integration of induction from authority, deduction from principle, and analysis of justice and policy.

Typically foregoing all introductory formalities, Langdell's article begins abruptly by posing the legal question: does "legislation which the Constitution requires to be uniform throughout the United States" apply to the territories captured by the United States in the Spanish-American War? More generally, does the Constitution cover new lands acquired by the United States? In order to answer this question, he attempted to "ascertain the meaning of the term 'United States'" in all its usages in the Constitution and to ask whether the term comprehended "our new territories" as well as "states." His answer was no. "The Constitution of the United States as such does not extend beyond the limits of the States which are united by and under it."[70]

---

66. *New York Times*, 23 Feb. 1900, 3.

67. Belmont, "Constitution and the Presidential Campaign."

68. Torruelia, *Supreme Court and Puerto Rico*, 42–44, 49n–50n.

69. Cf. Amar, "Intratextualism," 783–86; Grey, "Langdell's Orthodoxy," 34n130; Torruelia, *Supreme Court and Puerto Rico*, 26–27; W. Carter, "Reconstructing Langdell," 121–24.

70. Langdell, "Status of Our New Territories," 389, 365, 371.

Of the twenty-seven pages in the article, Langdell devoted twenty-four to this semantic approach, manifesting the formalistic, deductive, and "intratextual" character that some have identified in the essay. Yet, Langdell's deductions from principle relied on a comprehensive, inductive analysis of authority. Continuing his tireless research into original sources to the end of his career, Langdell examined some 230 peace treaties, constitutions, statutes, and cases pertaining to the development and formation of the United States and its territories from 1763 to 1898 and recorded his findings in a sheaf of 462, double-sided, manuscript sheets. As in his footnotes on cases for Parsons's *Law of Contracts*, these research notes demonstrate that Langdell's "intratextual" deductions from principle rest on prior inductive investigation into original authority, far surpassing the dozen treaties and cases discussed in the article.[71]

In keeping with his three-dimensional mode of reasoning, Langdell also considered the two extralegal factors of justice and policy. In fact, Langdell states that these factors explain why Congress in the past did not follow his interpretation of doctrine, and instead treated territories as states and uniformly applied to territories the same rules on taxes, duties, naturalization, and bankruptcy that applied to the states. This historical uniformity "proves nothing" about the doctrinal principle of whether the Constitution covers new lands acquired by the United States. Rather, "there were many reasons in favor of the course adopted," including contiguity of the territories, similarity of their soil and climate, the expectation that they would become states, and the absence of competition between the territories' products and those of the States, among other things. However, "with the acquisition of Hawaii and the Spanish Islands, . . . all these conditions are radically changed," including potential economic losses prompted by the decline in import duties and "ruinous" competition "with home products."[72]

Clearly, these "many reasons" are matters of policy or convenience. They also include an appeal to justice and a balancing of the interests of both parties, because "abandoning totally . . . the practice which has hitherto prevailed of extending to territories the revenue system of the United States . . . is required as well in justice to them as in justice to this country." Our importation of duty-free products from the new territories and their importation of our manufactured goods would cause economic harm to both, Langdell argued. Beyond justice, he suggested that treating "our new territories" differently from the old is a benevolent obligation,

71. Cf. Langdell, "Manuscript 4.B.2 Research Notes on States of the U.S.," in Langdell, Papers, 104, 105, 125, 180, 182, 188–89, 194, 222v; Langdell, "Status of Our New Territories," 378, 391, 380–82, 386n1, 390.

72. Quotations in this paragraph and the following two paragraphs are from Langdell, "Status of Our New Territories," 386, 389–92.

"if we are to undertake the government of dependent countries, with any hope of gaining credit for ourselves."

Consequently, what Langdell himself calls "the strongest possible reasons" in support of his position appear in the final three pages of the essay and derive from concerns for justice and policy. In fact, Langdell goes further to indicate that Congress previously treated territories as states due to the ethnic similarity of their populations (setting aside the native inhabitants of those territories). However, "with the acquisition of Hawaii and the Spanish Islands, ... all these conditions are radically changed." The U.S. government could not expect to govern "ancient and thickly settled Spanish colonies" while observing the U.S. Bill of Rights, and, conversely, "it is to be sincerely hoped that ... they will never be permitted ... to be represented in the United States Senate."

Langdell's reasoning thus incorporated not only deduction from principle, induction from authority, and justice and policy, but also the ethnic and racial prejudice that pervaded contemporary debate. Randolph had observed, "The United States ... ought not to annex a country ... irredeemably unfit for statehood because ... the character of its people and ... the climatic conditions forbid the hope ... to elevate its social conditions and ultimately justify its admission as a State." Baldwin also opposed extending the Constitution to "the half-civilized Moros of the Philippines, or the ignorant and lawless brigands that infest Puerto Rico, or even the ordinary Filipino of Manila."[73] Lowell doubted the capacities of the territories' inhabitants in the "art of self-government," and justified distinguishing between the political capacities of different territories' inhabitants by observing that, even within the United States, the "theory of universal political equality does not apply to tribal Indians, to Chinese, or to negroes under all conditions."[74]

Lowell's words reveal how the racial implications of the Insular Cases appear "as a logical extension of domestic racism so prevalent in the era of Jim Crow."[75] Just as they had determined his judgments of the academic merit of women, cultural and personal prejudices shaped Langdell's understanding of justice and policy, which provided "the strongest possible reasons" for his legal conclusions.[76] His analysis of "the status of our new territories," prompted by the visit of Dicey, therefore fits his characteristic three-dimensional mode of reasoning, exhibiting a comprehensive yet contradictory integration of induction from authority, de-

---

73. Randolph, "Constitutional Aspects of Annexation," 304; Baldwin, "Constitutional Questions," 415.

74. Lowell, "Colonial Expansion of the United States," 153, 152.

75. B. Thomas, "Constitution Led by the Flag: The *Insular Cases*," 94–95.

76. Langdell, "Status of Our New Territories," 391.

duction from principle, and analysis of justice and policy, shaped by personal and cultural values and prejudices.

Holmes and Northern Securities

Two years after the decision in *Downes v. Bidwell* (1901), Langdell addressed the trust-busting efforts of President Theodore Roosevelt in two essays that attracted the greatest notoriety during his lifetime. Analyzing the famous *Northern Securities* case, Langdell's essays demonstrate his continued engagement with prominent public issues, the continuity of his three-dimensional mode of reasoning, and the deep respect of Holmes for Langdell's legal acumen.[77] In fact, Holmes borrowed much of the analysis for his dissent in *Northern Securities*—his first written opinion as a justice on the U.S. Supreme Court—from Langdell's articles that had been published a few months earlier.

According to the predominant interpretation, Holmes's jurisprudence is distinctly different from and highly critical of Langdell's, although some scholars have considered Holmes to be essentially formalistic and therefore closer to the received view of Langdell.[78] The predominant view draws a line of interpretation through the two points when Holmes sharply criticized Langdell: in 1880–81 and in 1895–97. But those two points were outliers, coinciding with the two instances when Holmes felt vulnerable and disappointed in his own career. Apart from those two anomalies stimulated by Holmes's frustrated ambitions, he respected and consulted Langdell's work and repeatedly borrowed from it over the thirty-six years of their relationship.

—◦◦◦—

Having known of each other through reputation and mutual acquaintances, their professional association commenced in October 1870, a few weeks after Langdell became dean, when Holmes editorialized in the *American Law Review* that HLS was now on course to become "what it ought to be." Soon thereafter Langdell published the 1870 edition of *Cases on Contracts*, which Holmes extolled in an anonymous review. When the full casebook appeared in October 1871, Holmes repeated his praise in another review, as well as in a review of a different work. In 1872 Langdell's *Cases on Sales* elicited an even more complimentary review from

77. *Northern Securities v. United States* (1904); Langdell, "The Northern Securities Case and the Sherman Anti-Trust Act," *Harvard Law Review* 16 (1903): 539–54; "The Northern Securities Case under a New Aspect," *Harvard Law Review* 17 (1903): 41–44. Additional discussion and documentation of this subject appear in R. Brown and Kimball, "When Holmes Borrowed from Langdell."

78. See Kimball, "Langdell Problem."

Holmes.[79] Conversely, Langdell embraced all of Holmes's recommendations for improvement, and in 1877 he sent Holmes the advance page proofs of his *Summary of Equity Pleading* and a final copy when it appeared in print. Holmes responded with another glowing review.[80]

Their relationship was clearly positive and mutually appreciative until 1880, when Holmes suddenly published sarcastic criticism of the "summary" that Langdell appended to the second edition of *Cases on Contracts* (1879).[81] Holmes later minimized the sarcasm as "a slight touch of irony in my sincere appreciation of Langdell,"[82] and softened his criticism considerably in *The Common Law* (1881). Nevertheless, why did Holmes suddenly erupt, given their past relationship and his borrowing of doctrinal insights from that same appended summary, which he described as "most suggestive and instructive" a few months later?[83]

Vastly ambitious, Holmes was driven to elevate himself, even if he had to detract from others to do so.[84] In 1880 he was almost forty, the age by which a successful man should have made his mark, he said. Having neither established a career path nor authored a masterpiece, Holmes deeply feared that his great ambitions would be unfulfilled.[85] Meanwhile, Langdell—the New Boston rustic from outside the Brahmin circle of the Olivers, the Wendells, and the Holmeses—had achieved national distinction in legal scholarship. The inevitable comparison surely ignited Holmes's latent inclination to advance himself at the expense of others. To be sure, Holmes also sought to rebut formalistic jurisprudence, and his reductive interpretation of both German jurists and Langdell served that end.[86] But, in addition to the jurisprudential critique, Holmes's barbs stemmed from his "ambition . . . combined with an equally burning sense that he was being unappreciated."[87]

79. Quotation is from [O. Holmes], "Harvard University Law School" (1870), 177. [O. Holmes], Review (1871); [O. Holmes], Review of *American Reports* (1871); [O. Holmes], Review (1872a); [O. Holmes], Review (1872b). On Holmes's authorship, see Kimball, "Langdell on Contracts and Legal Reasoning," appendix 1.

80. O. Holmes to Langdell (3 Mar. 1877); [O. Holmes], Review (1877).

81. [O. Holmes], Review (Mar. 1880).

82. O. Holmes to Hohfeld (21 Mar. 1914). See Howe, *Justice Oliver Wendell Holmes*, 2:231.

83. O. Holmes to Pollock (10 Apr. 1881).

84. J. Thayer, Correspondence and Memoranda, 3:143–44; Touster, "Holmes a Hundred Years Ago: The Common Law," 683, 687; G. White, *Justice Oliver Wendell Holmes*, 89, 94, 113–15, 476; Alschuler, *Law without Values*, 31–40; G. White, "Looking at Holmes," 63.

85. Howe, *Justice Oliver Wendell Holmes*, 2:135; G. White, *Justice Oliver Wendell Holmes*, 148–49, 297.

86. In "Holmes's *Common Law*," Reimann brilliantly demonstrates that Holmes misrepresented German jurists as formalists, but assumes that Holmes represented Langdell correctly. In fact, Holmes misrepresented Langdell just as he did the Germans.

87. G. White, "Looking at Holmes," 80.

Stung by the sarcasm, Langdell abstained from efforts in January 1882 to create a professorship at HLS for Holmes. When Holmes joined the faculty in fall 1882, he nevertheless adopted Langdell's method in teaching both torts and suretyship,[88] and employed case method with greater fidelity and enthusiasm than professors Gray or Thayer ever would. In December 1882 Holmes fell out of favor at Harvard when he abruptly resigned the professorship to accept what he considered a more distinguished position as a justice on the Massachusetts Supreme Judicial Court. But in 1886 he was back in good graces and publicly extolled Langdell's inductive method in an oration at the organizational meeting of the alumni association.[89] Consequently, Holmes appeared to be trying to reconcile with Langdell after the eruption of 1881 and Holmes's sudden decision to leave the HLS faculty in December 1882.

Nevertheless, in the mid-1890s Holmes once again targeted Langdell, beginning at the celebration held in honor of Langdell's retirement as dean of HLS in 1895. Addressing the four hundred attendees at the gala event, Holmes was the only speaker who did *not* refer to the guest of honor. Instead, Holmes warned against three hallmarks of Langdell's jurisprudence: learning, logic, and history. "Learning...is liable to lead us astray," he said, because "the law, so far as it depends on learning, is indeed,...the government of the living by the dead." He also warned against "a peculiar logical pleasure in making manifest the continuity between what we are doing and what has been done before," because "historic continuity with the past is not a duty, it is only a necessity."[90]

Combined with neglecting to mention Langdell, Holmes's critical remarks at the retirement celebration were virtually insulting, and soon thereafter he accepted an invitation to deliver an address at the dedication of a new law building at Boston University. During his preparations, he conceived the speech as a treatment of "legal education," while bearing in mind "old Langdell," who "is most instructive when filtered through the mind of a beloved disciple, who will piece out his aperçus and drop his system."[91] In January 1897 at Boston University Holmes delivered the address that became famous under the title "The Path of the Law." In the first half of the speech, he attacked what he considered the fallacy of associating law with morality; in the second half he dismissed both logic and history as standards for deciding cases. While scholars have often observed that the latter part

88. O. Holmes, Oration 1886, 39; Mack, Suretyship, Fall 1883.
89. O. Holmes, Oration 1886, 29, 38; Brandeis, "Harvard Law School," 21–22.
90. O. Holmes, Oration 1895, 60–61.
91. Quotations are, respectively, from O. Holmes to Castledown (17 Sept. 1897); O. Holmes to Gray (2 Oct. 1896). See Seipp, "Holmes's Path," 549–50.

of "The Path" criticizes the logical formalism generally associated with Langdell,[92] the relationship is much closer, because the direct antecedent of that second half is Holmes's rebuke to Langdell at the retirement dinner eighteen months before.

Holmes's formalist caricature of Langdell served as a subliminal foil and stimulus for "The Path of the Law," just as it did for the introduction to *The Common Law* sixteen years earlier. But why target Langdell for a second time in 1895–97, after apparently reconciling with HLS in the mid-1880s? For an explanation, one must look beyond the formal reasons to contextual factors, as recommended by "The Path of the Law," which has appropriately been considered Holmes's "vocational address."[93]

In 1895 Holmes encountered his second great vocational crisis. After sitting on the Massachusetts Supreme Judicial Court for twelve years, he badly wanted an appointment to the U.S. Supreme Court, but two Massachusetts justices in their mid-sixties were sitting on the court and his objective seemed "unattainable."[94] Frustrated ambition led Holmes to demean the accomplishments of others at times, and the "monster celebration" honoring Langdell likely prompted Holmes's critical remarks at the retirement dinner.[95] If Holmes could never become a U.S. Supreme Court Justice, then Langdell did not deserve to be lionized.

Indeed, Holmes's statement at Langdell's fête is remarkably like the speech he gave, while still frustrated, a few years later at a ceremony marking the centennial of John Marshall's appointment to the U.S. Supreme Court. The ceremony was part of a nationwide series of tributes to Marshall, but, rather than celebrate the former chief justice, Holmes took the opportunity to depreciate Marshall's accomplishments. As at Langdell's retirement dinner, Holmes's "ambition, when combined with an equally burning sense that he was being underappreciated, made him incapable of publicly acknowledging the gifts of others."[96]

When Holmes's pangs of ambition were allayed, he returned to the norm of expressing appreciation for Langdell. Soon after Holmes was appointed chief justice of the Massachusetts Supreme Judicial Court in 1899, he listed Langdell "among the best of the young men" at Harvard in his generation, "men of the highest type, who all attained distinction."[97] Then, after he joined the U.S. Supreme Court in

---

92. See O. Holmes, "Path of the Law," 457–65, 465–78. See Burton, *Path of the Law and Its Influence*, 2; Grey, "Holmes on the Logic of the Law," 133–57; S. Perry, "Holmes vs. Hart," 187.

93. R. Gordon, "Law as a Vocation: Holmes and the Lawyer's Path," 7.

94. Holmes, quoted in Seipp, "Holmes's Path," 551. See G. White, *Justice Oliver Wendell Holmes*, 148–49, 297.

95. Quotation is from *Boston Herald*, 7 July 1906, 3. See G. White, *Justice Oliver Wendell Holmes*, 193.

96. G. White, "Looking at Holmes," 80.

97. O. Holmes, *Memoir of George Otis Shattuck* (1900), 6.

Oliver Wendell Holmes Jr., circa 1902. Courtesy of Special Collections Department, Harvard Law School Library.

1902, Holmes borrowed from Langdell's articles most of the analysis for his dissent in *Northern Securities*, just as he had borrowed doctrinal insights on contract for *The Common Law* and inductive teaching when on the faculty of HLS.

—⟋⟍⟍—

The *Northern Securities* case arose when industrialist James J. Hill and financier J. Pierpont Morgan attempted to consolidate two major competing railways—the Great Northern Railway and the Northern Pacific Railway—under a holding company in New Jersey. This Northern Securities Company created a powerful railroad monopoly stretching from Chicago to the Pacific, and in February 1902 President Theodore Roosevelt ordered his attorney general to file suit to break up the Northern Securities Company under two sections of the Sherman Anti-Trust Act (1890). Section 1 declared illegal "every contract, combination . . ., or conspiracy, in restraint of trade or commerce"; Section 2 prohibited acts that "monopolize, or attempt to monopolize, or combine or conspire . . . to monopolize any part of the trade of commerce among the several States."[98] In April 1903 a federal circuit court

98. An act to protect trade and commerce against unlawful restraints and monopolies, 2 July 1890, ch. 647, §26 Stat. 209, 15 U.S.C.A. §§1–7, 15 (1890).

unanimously decided in favor of the government,[99] and the defendants appealed. By the time the appeal reached the U.S. Supreme Court, the case had generated over eight thousand pages of transcripts, evidence, and arguments, prompting *The Nation* to observe that "no case has come before the Supreme Court of the United States since the *Dred Scott* decision fraught with graver consequences."[100]

In March 1904 the court issued its decision and in a 5–4 vote upheld the circuit court's finding in favor of the federal government. In his majority opinion, Justice Harlan emphasized the monopolistic effect of the merger, inasmuch as "the entire commerce of the immense territory in the northern part of the United States between the Great Lakes and the Pacific at Puget Sound will be at the mercy of a single holding company, organized in a state distant from the people of that territory." Rebutting the appellants' argument that the *Sherman Act* was a criminal statute and should be construed narrowly, Harlan asserted that the case arose from "a suit in equity," and that the court, "in virtue of a well-settled rule governing proceedings in equity, may mould its decree so as to accomplish practical results,—such as law and justice demand."[101]

The four dissenting justices joined both of the two dissents, one authored by Justice Holmes and the other by Justice White. Holmes's dissent attracted little notice at the time or subsequently, apart from observations that it deviated from his reputation as a social progressive and antiformalist. These two points were closely associated, as the *American Law Review* observed: "The dissenting opinions are closely logical,... narrow and technical," and thus "ignore the main fact, which is that the creation of the 'holding company' was a mere device or trick invented... for the mere purpose of evading the provisions of the Antitrust Law."[102]

Holmes's dissent therefore seemed uncharacteristic, and it displeased both Roosevelt, who appointed him, and most of the public press. The *Boston Daily Globe* called his dissent the "surprise of the day," because Holmes "was supposed to be the friend of the common people, the student of socialism, the champion of labor," but he produced "an opinion... in favor of the capitalistic contention." *Outlook* observed that Holmes leaned toward "the hopelessly antiquated laissez-faire school of political economy."[103] Not only did his substantive judgment seem

---

99. *United States v. Northern Securities* (1903).

100. "Hearing in the Northern Securities Case," (1903), 499.

101. *Northern Securities v. United States* (1904), 327–28, 360.

102. "Constitutional Law: Regulation of Interstate Commerce" (1904): 430. See Novick, *Honorable Justice: The Life of Oliver Wendell Holmes*, 272; Letwin, *Law and Economic Policy in America: The Evolution of the Sherman Antitrust Act*, 229; Peritz, *Competition Policy in America, 1888–1992*, 41.

103. *Boston Globe*, 15 Mar. 1904, 2; "Northern Securities Case" (1904): 726. See also Logan, "Supreme Court in the Northern Securities Case" (1904).

unusual, but the technical arguments, the circumstances, and the testimony of observers at the time all indicated that Holmes relied on Langdell in formulating his opinion.

Throughout his career, Langdell had refrained from commenting on public controversies until 1898 when Dicey's visit prompted him to address the Territories question. In 1903 Langdell again broached a prominent policy issue by writing two essays on *Northern Securities*. The notoriety of his Territories articles may have stimulated him to do so, but more likely the reason was that *Northern Securities* involved longstanding personal and academic interests. Langdell had conducted meticulous research into the financial prospects of railroads and had purchased stock in several lines.[104] In addition, he possessed extensive experience in civil litigation from his work on Wall Street, including serving as sole counsel on behalf of the Northern Railroad Company in its appeal of an order to dissolve.[105] Both the interests of investors and the problems of breaking up and reorganizing railroads are discussed in his articles. However, the major reason impelling Langdell to weigh in was likely that a central issue in *Northern Securities*, as he understood it, was equity jurisdiction, which had become his primary scholarly interest in the previous fifteen years. Indeed, he was outraged that the courts were invoking equity doctrine to interpret the case, even though the statute's provision to issue an injunction was authorized by legislative authority, not by equity doctrine.

Moreover, in 1900 Langdell had addressed public policy regarding railway monopolies and mergers, arguing that the government should ensure that competition among entities that provide public services, such as railways, is not destructive. He observed that in England many public services were retained under the authority of the king and operated as state monopolies in order "to secure the efficient performance of such services for a fixed and reasonable compensation." Alternatively, the government delegated the performance of the service to private persons or corporations, which were granted "a monopoly commensurate, as nearly as possible, with the duty imposed," because when "the State itself undertakes the performance of a service for the general public, it always maintains a monopoly of such service,—for example, that of carrying the mails." Under either approach adopted in England—government operation or private control—the public benefited from monopoly, Langdell argued.[106]

104. Langdell, Will and Probate Papers (1906); Beale, "Langdell, Gray, Thayer, and Ames," 387–88; C. Eliot, "Langdell," 524.

105. *New York v. Northern Railroad* (1869).

106. Langdell, *Brief Survey of Equity Jurisdiction* (1905), 234–36. Langdell's analysis originally appeared in "Classification of Rights and Wrongs," *Harvard Law Review* 13 (1900): 537–56, 659–78.

American legislators, however, had been slow to learn the lessons of the English experience. "In this country a strong disposition has been shown to delegate the power of the State, not to particular persons or corporations selected by the legislature, but to any persons who shall voluntarily organize themselves into corporations, and comply with certain prescribed conditions." Langdell appreciated that this approach was founded "upon the principle of granting equal rights to all," but it led to the "abandonment of all attempt to protect from unjust and ruinous competition those who have invested their money irrevocably in providing means and facilities for serving the public. For example, when one set of men have built a railway from A to B, the State does nothing to prevent another set of men from building another railway between the same points, and as near to the former as they please."[107]

The reluctance in the United States to control or moderate competition in public services was thus fraught with potential difficulties, according to Langdell. Such problems were particularly common to the railroad industry. Langdell lamented that state legislatures had "passed statutes authorizing railway companies to mortgage all their property and 'franchises'; and hence receiverships and reorganizations of railway companies, which are entirely unknown in England, have become disastrously familiar in this country."[108]

Convinced, then, of the necessity of regulating large-scale public services, Langdell opposed on policy grounds the government's attempt to break up the Northern Securities Company. Langdell believed that railways were natural monopolies, and that the public was harmed by the government policy that had initially permitted the Northern Pacific and Great Northern railways to be built parallel to one another. Consequently, Langdell's distinctive ideas about monopolies of public services, as well as his expertise on the central issue of equity jurisdiction, induced him to publish his views on *Northern Securities*.

Between the time that the lower court issued its judgment in April 1903 and the Supreme Court handed down its decision in March 1904, a myriad of articles appeared on the case. Langdell's two essays in June and November attracted considerable attention due to their unorthodox views on policy and jurisprudence. On June 14 the *New York Daily Tribune* reported the publication of Langdell's first article, stating that "Professor Langdell, the jurist of the Harvard Law School, says the United States circuit court decision on Northern Securities is not good constitutional law." The following day, the *New York Times* devoted one-and-a-half columns on the editorial page to summarizing Langdell's article, observing that

107. Langdell, *Brief Survey of Equity Jurisdiction* (1905), 236.
108. Langdell, *Brief Survey of Equity Jurisdiction* (1905), 236. These were the circumstances that Langdell had litigated in *New York v. Northern Railroad* (1869).

Langdell attacked the lower court decision on "new grounds" and presented "quite the severest criticism . . . which has come to our notice." The *United States Investor* and the *Boston Globe* subsequently concurred that Langdell "was the first to challenge the circuit court's decision from the ultra legal point of view." Langdell's comments were also reported by such industry publications as *Railway World*.[109]

In addition to press coverage, Langdell's heretical views received prominent notice in legal journals. In July 1903 the *Albany Law Journal* maintained that Langdell provided the "most incisive and vigorous criticism of . . . the Northern Securities case," as did a scholar in the *Michigan Law Review*.[110] In the *Yale Law Journal*, Daniel Chamberlain, a former governor of South Carolina, offered a scholarly rebuttal to Langdell that was reported in the *New York Times*. Conversely, the counsel for Morgan cited one of Langdell's articles in his brief to the Supreme Court, a highly unusual citation at the beginning of the twentieth century.[111] The notoriety and novelty of Langdell's essays must have brought them to the attention of Holmes, who was corresponding with Frederick Pollock about the latter's essay on *Northern Securities* that the *Harvard Law Review* had asked him to write after it published Langdell's second article.[112]

A few days after the Supreme Court issued its decision, the *United States Investor*, a business periodical published in Boston, New York, and Philadelphia, observed that "the reasoning of Mr. Holmes's dissenting opinion runs exactly parallel with a review of the merger decision . . . from the pen of Professor C. C. Langdell," leading to "the firm conviction" that Holmes had drawn his argument from Langdell. Four days later, the *Boston Globe* endorsed and reprinted the *Investor*'s article.[113] The most likely source of these reports is Franklin Fessenden, a Massachusetts superior court judge and one of the original "Kit's freshmen," who later published a defense for his teacher.[114] Beyond Fessenden's testimony, the evidence for Holmes's borrowing lies in the symmetry between his dissent and Langdell's analysis that presented "new grounds" and "the severest criticism" of

109. *New York Daily Tribune*, 14 June 1903, 7; *New York Times*, 15 June 1903; *United States Investor*, 19 Mar. 1904, 414; *Boston Globe*, 23 Mar. 1904, 6. See Langdell, "Northern Securities Case."

110. Quotation is from "Current Topics" (1903): 201. See Wilgus, "Need of National Incorporation Law," 390.

111. Chamberlain, "Northern Securities Case," 58, 65; *New York Times*, 30 Nov. 1903; Brief for Appellants Morgan, Bacon, and Lamont in *Northern Securities v. United States* (1904), 293–96, citing Langdell, Northern Securities I.

112. Pollock, "Merger Case and Restraint of Trade," 155n1; O. Holmes to Pollock (2 Jan. 1904); Pollock to Holmes (11 May 1904). Scholars have suggested that Pollock influenced Holmes, but see R. Brown and Kimball, "When Holmes Borrowed from Langdell," 316–19.

113. *United States Investor*, 19 Mar. 1904, 413–14; *Boston Globe*, 23 Mar. 1904, 6.

114. See Kimball, "Langdell Problem." In his defense of Langdell's work, Fessenden made an extraneous reference to "the final decrees in the Northern Securities case," seeming to suggest that Langdell had some connection to the U.S. Supreme Court decision. ("Rebirth of the Harvard Law School," 512n.)

the government's case.[115] Langdell's argument was novel both in method and substance, raising points that had not been addressed in the circuit court's decision.

Adopting formalistic reasoning, Langdell, followed by Holmes, invoked the literalist principle "that a lawgiver is supposed to mean only what he says"; the two authors therefore considered only the "exact words" of the *Sherman Act*, explicitly ignoring the supposed intent of Congress.[116] In addition, they both formalistically adopted "the ultra legal point of view,"[117] meaning that they evaluated the statute solely in light of the doctrines of common law and equity, setting aside policy considerations, which dominated discussion of the case at the time. Based on this approach, Langdell, and then Holmes, concluded that the act was "a criminal statute," deriving its authority from the legislature, not from equity doctrine or common law, and that the defendants' actions did not fit the definition of the stipulated crimes, as provided by accepted canons of statutory interpretation.[118] Langdell applied this reasoning to the *Northern Securities* case through the following steps, which Holmes adopted.

The *Sherman Act* instructed the government to institute proceedings in equity—that is, to seek an injunction—to prevent and restrain violations of the Act.[119] But what jurisdiction did the court possess to grant an injunction? According to equity doctrine, Langdell observed, one "may maintain a suit in equity" for an injunction in order "to prevent the commission of a civil tort." But no civil tort had occurred, stated Langdell, because, by definition, a "civil tort must necessarily be an injury to some person in respect to his personal rights or his rights of property." Here no "person," including the federal government, had claimed or could claim to be injured, because no one's property rights could be harmed until someone was actually forced to pay unreasonable rates by one of the railroads. As a result, "no court of equity could have entertained any suit founded upon the Act." Consequently, the authority to seek an injunction came not from equity doctrine but from the legislature, so "the Sherman Anti-Trust Act is a criminal statute pure and simple."[120] Holmes likewise affirmed, "The statute of which we have to find

---

115. Quotations are from *New York Times*, 15 June 1903, 6. No papers of Holmes remain that indicate exactly how he wrote his dissent in *Northern Securities v. United States* (1904).

116. Quotations are respectively from Langdell, Northern Securities I, 551, and from O. Holmes in *Northern Securities v. United States* (1904), 403.

117. *United States Investor*, 19 Mar. 1904, 413–14; *Boston Globe*, 23 Mar. 1904, 6.

118. Quotation is repeated in Langdell, Northern Securities I, 543; *Northern Securities v. United States* (1904), 401. See 402; Langdell, Northern Securities II, 41.

119. An act to protect trade and commerce against unlawful restraints and monopolies, 15 U.S.C.A. §§1–7, 4 (1890).

120. Langdell, Northern Securities I, 540–43.

the meaning is a criminal statute," and it is "vain to insist that it is not a criminal proceeding."[121]

The significance of this conclusion was that "a criminal statute" had to be interpreted strictly, without the latitude granted by equity practice or doctrine. Such latitude to "mould its decree so as to accomplish practical results" is precisely what Justice Harlan invoked in the majority opinion.[122] The effect was to import the flexibility of equity into the arena of criminal law where it did not belong, according to the interpretation of Langdell and Holmes.

Employing the literalist method, Langdell next examined whether railroads were denoted by Section 2 of the Act, which sought to punish those who monopolized, or sought to monopolize, "any part of the trade or commerce among the several states." Now, Langdell wrote, "railways are by far the most important of all instruments on inland trade and commerce, but an instrument by means of which a thing is done . . . is not the thing itself." Thus, "the only thing that a railway company can monopolize is the carriage of goods and passengers for hire," and because "such carriage does not constitute trade or commerce, it follows that railway companies are not within section 2 of the Act." Indeed, the *Sherman Act* has not "a single word that can lead any one to think that its authors had either railways or railway companies at all in their contemplation."[123]

Langdell's point here was so heretical that the *American Law Review* dismissed it as a "hare-brained proposition,"[124] but Holmes sympathetically observed that "there was even a reasonable doubt whether [the *Sherman Act*] included railroads until the point was decided by this court." If the court accepted that the government could regulate "an indirect effect upon commerce not shown to be certain and very great," then "I can see no part of the conduct of life with which, on similar principles, Congress might not interfere."[125] Though sympathetic to the point, Holmes did not rely on this argument, which had already been negated by the court.

Having shown that equity had no jurisdiction in the case according to established doctrine and that the court derived the authority for its injunction only from the "criminal statute," Langdell and Holmes then had to consider the crimes identified in the statute, namely "monopoly" and "restraint of trade." Adhering to the accepted canons of statutory interpretation, they began by observing that the

121. *Northern Securities v. United States* (1904), 401.
122. *Northern Securities v. United States* (1904), 360.
123. Langdell, Northern Securities I, 543–44.
124. "Combinations in Restraint of Interstate Commerce" (1903): 461.
125. *Northern Securities v. United States* (1904), 402–3.

key term, "restraint of trade," in Section 1 of the *Sherman Act* must be interpreted in its "legal sense," that is, according to common-law doctrine. Interpreted in this way, "restraint of trade" meant that two or more parties contracted not to compete, and since the facts did not fit that meaning, no "criminal" offence should have been found. Instead, the court erroneously defined "restraint of trade" as "to destroy or lessen the motive for competition between two or more persons."[126]

Langdell and Holmes likewise construed "monopoly" narrowly according to common-law doctrine. Referencing its English origins, Langdell stated that monopoly exists only when "one person excludes [all] others from . . . his trade by procuring them to . . . contract not to carry on that kind of trade."[127] While adverting to the English origins, Holmes took a slightly different route,[128] but reached the same outcome, maintaining that the charge of "monopoly" against the Northern Securities Company "rests on a popular instead of an accurate and legal conception of what the word 'monopolize' in the statute means."[129]

The popular meaning of monopoly was so broad that it could apply to every railway and even every business. Langdell pointed out that "every railway company necessarily has a monopoly of the carriage of by far the greater part of goods carried by it, and no railway company could live without such monopoly." Holmes used very similar language.[130] In fact, wrote Langdell, it was impossible to distinguish what were popularly called "monopolies" from "a partnership which has been formed among several tradesmen for the purpose of taking over the business of each" because "such a partnership differs from the greatest of the so-called trusts only in size." Holmes likewise observed that, based on the popular meaning of monopoly, the Sherman Act "would send the members of a partnership . . . to prison."[131]

Reinforcing their distinctive symmetry, Langdell and Holmes then departed from literalism and ultralegalism in order to discuss the intention and policy of the *Sherman Act*. Having declared these issues irrelevant, Langdell typically reversed himself in order to explain why his views would not expose the public to the putative "rapacity of railroad monopolists."[132] Holmes likewise stated that, among

126. Quotations are from Langdell, Northern Securities II, 41–42. See *Northern Securities v. United States* (1904), 403–4.

127. Langdell, Northern Securities II, 42–43.

128. *Northern Securities v. United States* (1904), 403–4.

129. *Northern Securities v. United States* (1904), 409. See Langdell, Northern Securities II, 43–44.

130. Langdell, Northern Securities I, 545. See *Northern Securities v. United States* (1904), 406–7.

131. Langdell, Northern Securities II, 43–44; *Northern Securities v. United States* (1904), 406.

132. Langdell, Northern Securities I, 553.

the extraneous issues "mentioned in argument," he would address "the supposed attempt to suppress competition."[133]

According to Holmes, such suppression would create an atomized, hypercompetitive, and inefficient economy and society, and the *Sherman Act* should "not be construed to mean the universal disintegration of society into single men, each at war with all the rest." Furthermore, some kinds of businesses needed to be large in order to function properly. "Size, in the case of railroads, is an inevitable incident."[134] This analysis of Holmes echoed that of Langdell both in the *Northern Securities* articles and in his writing on equity jurisdiction published in 1900.

Recognizing that railways might charge "unreasonable rates," Langdell maintained that the state could remedy this injury through "its unquestioned power to regulate and control railway rates." In contrast, the policy implications of the circuit court's decree were undesirable and unworkable. The underlying purpose of fostering unlimited competition would produce "the greatest evils to the public as well as to the railways," including enormous increases in expenses, capital costs, and rates. This is shown by the fact that "every railway company necessarily has a monopoly of the carriage of by far the greater part of the goods carried by it, and no railway company could live without such monopoly." For the most part, "the only competition possible among railway companies is at competing points." The paradoxical effect of "unrestrained competition" would be unreasonably low rates at hubs where many railroads competed, which had to be counterbalanced by excessively high rates in remote areas served by few lines. As he had done four years earlier, Langdell noted that if the state operated railroads as a public utility, it would demand a monopoly. Consequently, rather than fostering "unlimited competition," the state should afford railways the same protection against competition that it would enjoy. Langdell therefore proposed that the government could establish a public agency to closely monitor the private railway companies and their rates according to "such rules and regulations as the state from time to time sees fit to make."[135]

———❦———

Langdell's writings on *Northern Securities* demonstrate that, in the final years of his life, he greatly expanded the scope and readership of his legal scholarship. He also employed his characteristic three-dimensional mode of reasoning, including

133. *Northern Securities v. United States* (1904), 409.
134. *Northern Securities v. United States* (1904), 407. See Waller, "Antitrust Philosophy of Justice Holmes," 316; O. Holmes to Pollock (25 May 1906, 30 Apr. 1910), O. Holmes to Einstein (1, 30 Aug. 1908).
135. Langdell, Northern Securities I, 545, 551n2, 553.

an explicit commitment to formalist analysis and deduction from legal principles, inductive consideration of authorities, and sublimated consideration of policy and justice after denying its relevance to the legal issue. Despite the contradictory methodological standards, Langdell sought consistency and coherence among all three dimensions of his analysis.

Another important continuity demonstrated by Langdell's writing on *Northern Securities* was Holmes's respect for and reliance on Langdell's analysis, notwithstanding his typical failure to credit Langdell. Despite the two anomalous, insulting critiques of Langdell in 1880–81 and 1895–97, Holmes predominantly expressed appreciation for Langdell or borrowed from his work over the thirty-six years of their relationship. Even at the very end of his life, Langdell's novel and severe criticism of the circuit court's decision was largely adopted by Holmes, whose dissent in *Northern Securities* is accordingly regarded as unusual because "its reliance on common-law terms and doctrines seems so archaic as to be difficult to understand."[136]

In fact, the difficulty here arises because Holmes borrowed from Langdell and because Langdell's ultralegal arguments consisted with prudent policy considerations. Furthermore, it is difficult to determine, as was typical, whether Langdell began with convictions about proper public policy for railroads and adopted a legal analysis to support those, or vice versa, or whether he worked from both ends toward a reconciliation of the two. In any case, it is certain that he practiced Holmes's jurisprudential "paradox of form and substance" to the end of his career.

Resignation and Death

Despite the growing attention given to his writings, the "blind white-whiskers" increasingly refrained from traveling to public gatherings, being "very dependent on an accustomed knowledge of his surroundings."[137] In 1899 and 1900 he declined fervent invitations to attend the American Bar Association meetings on legal education, the fiftieth reunion of his College class of 1851, and the annual Old Folks' Days in New Boston. Indeed, Langdell was so reluctant to venture outside of his accustomed surroundings that he slept in his house for three nights while Harvard moved it to make way for a new building.[138] His increasing debility and rigidity

---

136. Novick, *Honorable Justice: The Life of Oliver Wendell Holmes*, 461n64.

137. Quotations are from Frankfurter to Frank (18 Dec. 1933); C. Eliot to Robinson [circa 1901].

138. Rawle to Eliot (1 July 1899); C. Eliot to Langdell [circa July 1899]; Langdell to Eliot (11 July 1899); M. E. Huson to F. A. Atwood (1908), quoted in F. Atwood, *Old Folks' Day*, 22, 11–12; S. Atwood to Batchelder (8 Aug. 1906); Langdell to Haynes (5 May 1901).

reinforced his paradoxical mode of reasoning in disputes, exacerbating the difficult negotiations over his retirement.

In 1900 Langdell asked to stop teaching and, rather than retire, to reformulate his position in line with that of today's nonteaching "research professor." The University offered to pay his full salary if he retired, so this request was purely a matter of whether he would formally be categorized as "retired" or as actively engaged in research. Eliot could not divorce teaching from the definition of a professor and therefore considered Langdell's request to be self-contradictory and indicative of his "pathetic" health. Ames, then dean, was even less comprehending. "Professor Langdell's wish to be and not to be a full professor at the same time is certainly embarrassing," he wrote. "I think it would be more dignified on his part to accept the handsome [arrangement] which would be made for him and become Professor Emeritus."[139] Having pioneered the role of full-time professor, Langdell was now proposing a different set of responsibilities for the occupation, whereas Eliot and Ames held that the category of "professor" must be uniform.

Langdell responded in typically formal terms that "the theory" and the precedent of pension arrangements did not fit his case. A pension is "a compensation for services already rendered and not yet fully paid for." But he would continue to work by writing articles; therefore, a pension and the title "emeritus" were not appropriate, and he should be paid his salary in "compensation for my services." As an afterthought, he adverted to the "sentimental" rationale of maintaining his self-respect and, second, to fairness, in that people should not think he had "been laid upon the shelf" when he was still working hard by writing articles.[140] In this way, Langdell persisted to the end in emphasizing the formal definitions framing a dispute while invoking, but sublimating, fairness and "sentimental" reasons that seemed to carry more weight. In response, Eliot took the matter to the Corporation, which considered Langdell's proposal "inexpedient" and instead reaffirmed their commitment to pay his full salary if he resigned. Langdell then submitted his resignation on 8 October 1900.[141]

After spending the next five years engaged in writing essays and articles, Langdell died of heart failure at home during his sleep on 6 July 1906. In his will, he left 480 acres of land and an annuity to his sister, Hannah, then eighty-two years old and still living in Kansas. Apart from some small benefactions, the bal-

---

139. Quotations are, respectively, from C. Eliot to Ames [17 Aug. 1900]; Ames to Eliot (17 Sept. 1900). See Langdell to Eliot (12 Aug. 1900); Ames to Eliot (15 Aug. 1900).

140. Langdell to Eliot (20 Aug. 1900).

141. Quotation is from C. Eliot to Langdell (27 Sept. 1900). See Langdell to Eliot (26 Aug., 28 Sept, 8 Oct. 1900). See *Boston Journal*, 20 Sept. 1900.

ance of his estate valued at more than five million dollars in today's money he left to his wife Maggie, who died thirteen months later.[142] Prominent law journals throughout the United States, Canada, and Britain noted his passing, and eminent lawyers and professors associated with HLS attended the funeral and carried his casket to the burial site at Mount Auburn Cemetery in Cambridge.[143] No eulogy was offered at the time. Perhaps now is the occasion.

—⁓⁓—

Raised on a hardscrabble farm in a small New Hampshire town, Christopher Columbus Langdell was virtually orphaned by age ten and mired in rural poverty. Drawing on earnings from menial jobs, contributions from his faithful sisters, and scholarships awarded for academic achievement, he earned a diploma from Phillips Exeter Academy, completed two semesters at Harvard College, clerked in the law offices of prominent attorneys in New Hampshire, and studied at Harvard Law School for three-and-a-half years. In 1855 Langdell entered the New York City bar and practiced on Wall Street until 1870, building a successful practice and gaining a reputation among lawyers as an extremely learned, upright, and effective counselor who kept a low profile.

Deciding to change careers in 1870, Langdell accepted a professorship at Harvard Law School and, during three distinct periods over the next thirty-six years, made significant scholarly contributions to jurisprudence and to legal doctrine in the fields of common-law contract and equity procedure and jurisdiction. In jurisprudence, Langdell's emphasis on parsimonious abstraction led scholars in the century after his death to associate him with a sterile approach to legal study known as "legal formalism" or "classical legal thought." But his characteristic mode of reasoning in law, and other domains, was three-dimensional, exhibiting a comprehensive yet contradictory integration of induction from authority, deduction from principle, and analysis of justice and policy. The contradiction lies in Langdell's combining all three while claiming to emphasize logical consistency and to disregard justice and policy. Langdell's mode of reasoning therefore fits not the Procrustean interpretation of Oliver Wendell Holmes Jr., but the "paradox of

142. Langdell, Will and Probate Papers (1906); Huson, Will and Probate Papers (5 Sept. 1907). Langdell also owned another two hundred acres in Gage County, Nebraska, that remained from his investments in midwestern farm mortgages. When Hannah disposed of the property in 1909 for $9,900, it had appreciated sixty-six times since Langdell had purchased it thirty years earlier. *Standard Atlas of Gage County, Nebraska*, 65; Petition for Probate of Foreign Will [of Christopher C. Langdell] (4 May 1907); Quit-Claim Deed from Elizabeth P. Boyer to Hannah Warner (20 Aug. 1909); Warranty Deed from Hannah Warner to Jacob S. Patterson (29 Dec. 1909).

143. *Boston Morning Journal*, 7 July 1906; *Boston Evening Transcript*, 6 July 1906, 4, 8; *Boston Globe*, 7 July 1906; *Boston Post*, 7 July 1906.

form and substance" that has been considered one of Holmes's greatest insights about judicial reasoning.

Recognition of Langdell's influence on legal doctrine was limited by several factors. Holmes received credit for Langdell's seminal contributions to contract law; much of Langdell's legal research addressed the soon outmoded fields of equity pleading and jurisdiction; and he did not study or discuss prominent constitutional disputes until the very end of his career. Nevertheless, he remained an authority of surprising duration and range. His publications have been cited in more than twenty cases decided by the U.S. Supreme Court, thirty-six cases decided by U.S. Courts of Appeals or Circuit Courts, and some five hundred cases decided in other courts in the United States.[144]

But Langdell's most profound and enduring influence lies in instituting the fundamental principle, or ideology, of professional education in America: that one's professional worth depends on where one goes to professional school and how one performs there. By inventing and building a revolutionary educational "system," Langdell instantiated and credited the principle of academic meritocracy, which nearly all professional schools and professions in the United States came to embrace during the twentieth century.

Meritocracy has generated a great deal of commentary and scholarly analysis[145] since the term was coined in 1958 by socialist Michael Young, who served as the head of research for the Labor Party in Britain. Young welded a Greek suffix to a Latin root to create "this unpleasant term." Jarring both to the tongue and to the social theories of many observers, meritocracy has generated conflicting responses. Young himself believed that meritocracy had come to prevail over other forms of social and political organization. "Today...democracy can be no more than aspiration," he wrote, for we have "rule not so much by the people as by the cleverest people; not an aristocracy at birth, not a plutocracy of wealth, but a true meritocracy of talent." Nevertheless, Young anathematized meritocracy, believing that it drew the most talented people from the working classes into the elites of Britain and thereby robbed the lower classes of the leaders necessary to revolt against the elites and achieve a truly democratic society.[146] Meritocracy undermined social justice precisely because it worked so well.

---

144. I am grateful to Jason Blokhuis for gathering these data.

145. See, for example, Herrnstein, *I.Q. in the Meritocracy* (1973); Husén, *Talent, Equality and Meritocracy* (1974); Klitgaard, *Elitism and Meritocracy in Developing Countries* (1986); Wooldridge, *Meritocracy and the "Classless Society"* (1995); Lerman, *Meritocracy without Rising Inequality* (1997); Lemann, *Big Test: The Secret History of the American Meritocracy* (1999); Arrow, Bowles, and Durlauf, *Meritocracy and Economic Inequality* (2000); McNamee and Miller, *Meritocracy Myth* (2004).

146. Quotations are from Young, *Rise of the Meritocracy*, 153n2, 17–18. See Lemann, *Big Test: The Secret History of the American Meritocracy*, 115–20.

Subsequent critics have focused on the question of whether meritocracy works at all, whether it is an illusion and indirectly serves the hidden interests of elites, who employ the ideas of "talent" and "equal opportunity" in order to legitimate their essentially inherited privileges in society. Wealthy scions prepare for examinations, score well, and ascend to positions of prestige and power ostensibly justified by their demonstrated talent. Debates over such issues about the meaning and measure of merit and about socioeconomic opportunity intensified in the second half of the twentieth century, contributing to the historiographical judgment that "American meritocracy" was created by its "founders" in the decades following World War II when the "modern bureaucratic state" emerged and required "administrative and scholarly service."[147]

But the idea and the practice of meritocracy had earlier origins in the examinations established by Cambridge and Oxford universities in the first half of the nineteenth century. Furthermore, much earlier antecedents exist in other cultures.[148] Nevertheless, in the 1870s and 1880s C. C. Langdell made several distinctive innovations that, for better or worse, resulted in the vast proliferation of academic meritocracy throughout professional education over the course of the twentieth century.

Most fundamentally, Langdell conceived a new set of legitimating relationships between a profession, its domain within society, the expertise of the professionals, and their education. Specifically, Langdell maintained that the just working of the legal system relies on the effectiveness of the legal profession, which depends on lawyers' expertise derived, in turn, from their academic achievement in law school. Academic merit determines the effectiveness and the integrity of the members of "a learned and liberal profession of the highest grade," who will then "render to the public the highest and best service in the administration of justice."[149] These relationships between professional education, expertise, practice, and virtue presented a new understanding of professional legitimacy.

Evidence of Langdell's influence is shown by the fact that these relationships, while pervasive throughout professional education, are strongest in the legal profession. Within medicine and business, the other two most powerful domains of graduate professional education, the correlation between the ranking of the professional schools and the status, authority, and prospects of the professionals is less strong. This is because the admissions threshold in medical schools is higher than

---

147. Quotations are from Lemann, *Big Test: The Secret History of the American Meritocracy*, 344.

148. See, for example, Twitchett, *Birth of the Chinese Meritocracy: Bureaucrats and Examinations in T'ang China*.

149. Langdell, Annual Report 1876–77, 89, 91.

in any other field, while entry to the field of business does not require graduation from business school. Hence, in both of those domains the ranking of a professional school is less salient to the perception of professionals' effectiveness than in law. Within the so-called minor or semi-professions, the correlation remains positive but weakens as one moves down the hierarchy of status and influence of the professions.[150] In law, however, the ranking of the schools and one's academic performance are closely related to the ranking in the profession: one's achievement in law school determines to a great extent one's professional prospects. Being closest to its source, law schools are more thoroughly steeped in the ideology of academic meritocracy.

Langdell's commitment to this principle derived from his experience of advancing himself through self-discipline, adherence to the established rules, and academic achievement. As a pauper scholar at Exeter and Harvard, he developed a firm conviction in the idea that personal and professional advancement is achieved by excelling within the established rules of the formal system of academic merit. His experience practicing on Wall Street strengthened and extended his conviction that professional success requires strong legal science acquired through demanding legal education. Langdell's conviction that academic achievement should determine one's professional fortunes also entailed a commitment to "democracy" in the sense that the principle ensured equal opportunity to succeed in the profession. Consequently, professional expertise, academic merit, professional success, and democracy coincide, in Langdell's view.

Langdell's second distinctive innovation was to integrate his commitment to fostering professionals' academic merit with the formalism of his legal expertise. Based on this new conceptual integration, he then created—or engineered—a coherent "new system" of institutional mechanisms devoted to advancing and assessing academic merit. That formal system included: the admissions requirement of a bachelor's degree, the sequenced curriculum and its extension to three years, the inductive pedagogy of teaching from cases, the hurdle of written examinations for continuation and graduation, the written examination posing hypothetical problems, the program of study leading to academic honor, the independent career track for faculty, the transformation of the library from a textbook dispensary to a scholarly resource, and the national alumni association actively supporting the school.

Thirdly, Langdell presented a financial justification for those two innovations by positing a direct functional relationship between his "new system" and the

150. See Etzioni, *Semi-Professions and Their Organization*; Glazer, "Schools of the Minor Professions," 346–64.

emerging expertise of the profession. While practicing on Wall Street, he had leaped far above the third tier of Edward Bogardus and the second tier of Addison Brown, and helped to establish a new role in litigation: crafting the extensive written brief that was beginning to displace the weight of oral argument in complicated cases arising from large, intricate commercial transactions. Commensurately, the skills that his system developed in legal research, in analysis of original sources, and in dialectical inquiry were precisely those that the leading, corporate firms began to demand. By the mid-1880s HLS found itself "unable to fill all the places in lawyers' offices which have been offered" for its graduates.[151] At the same time, the leading firms in Boston and New York began to recruit "young lawyers, who had graduated from both college and law school . . . with high scholastic marks from elite universities,"[152] and by the turn of the century elite law firms were actively recruiting the strongest students.[153]

This outcome was not at all evident in 1870. In the history of higher education, a tension or outright conflict has generally prevailed between financial imperatives, on the one hand, and academic standards or aspirations, however defined, on the other. This tension or conflict might be said to arise inevitably from the distinction between the material and intellectual dimensions of human experience. Nevertheless, in times and places where the financial and academic forces have been aligned or mutually reinforcing, fundamental changes have occurred in the institutional configuration of higher education.

During the thirteenth century in Western Europe, for example, the intellectual life of the *studia*, vitalized by Greek and Islamic philosophy and sciences, combined with the local economic engines of the guilds of faculty and masters to form the new institution called the *universitas*. In subsequent centuries there emerged the "college," another new institution that was often endowed by wealthy burghers to provide safe domiciles at universities for students living far from their homeland or belonging to religious sects or orders at odds with the university authorities. Simultaneously, the colleges provided the desired instruction in academic studies that were excluded from the formal university curriculum and constituted, in part, the *studia humanitatis* or "the humanities," which served the burgher class by cultivating the "Christian gentleman." Centuries later, in recent time, the funding of scientific research at universities by government and industry, which began in World War II and increased in subsequent decades, radically transformed the cul-

151. C. Eliot, Annual Report 1885–86, 13.

152. Hobson, "Symbol of the New Profession," 19. See Brandeis, *Letters*, 1:86.

153. Bolles, *Harvard University*, 68. See Hill, *Harvard College*, 254; Gawalt, "Impact of Industrialization on the Legal Profession," 107–9.

ture and purposes of American universities as such funding shaped the "natural" organization for scientific and technological fields. The virtue and the value of such new configurations in higher education are open to question, but the significance of their impact is not.

Similarly, Langdell coupled a new functional and financial logic to his emphasis on academic merit in professional education. Traditionally, professional schools maintained low standards and low tuition in order to attract students and obtain sufficient revenue to operate and to gain some profit. Both Langdell and Eliot argued that education for and admission to a liberal profession should transcend the commercial pressures of the marketplace, while they also maintained, paradoxically, that a professional school devoted to academic merit would prosper. Higher standards would produce better graduates who would be more marketable, making the school more attractive to prospective students and elevating the standards in the profession.

Though uncompromising, Langdell was a practical Yankee and prudent investor, and he knew the system would fail if it were not economical and marketable. "If the Law School remain large, in spite of requiring every regular student to hold a good academic degree on admission, it will have made a valuable contribution to the better organization of professional education in the United States," observed Eliot.[154] In other words, if HLS dramatically increased *both* its standards and its market, then other schools would follow and the revolution of professional education would be underway. And Langdell's analysis that professional schools prosper by disregarding "money profit" proved sound.[155]

Langdell's "new system" therefore triumphed in professional education. When he joined the HLS faculty, no one in the school believed in academic meritocracy. Upon his death, "both instructors and students in the Law School . . . [were] firmly convinced that rank in the School furnishes the strongest evidence of the coming professional career."[156] Looking back upon this transformation in 1915, Eliot adjudged that selecting Langdell was one of the three best things he did in his forty-year tenure as president of Harvard.[157]

Nevertheless, the universalist premise of educational formalism proved no more valid than that of legal formalism. The meritocrats at HLS explicitly classified women and graduates of Catholic colleges apart from other applicants, and

---

154. The quotation is from C. Eliot, Annual Report 1893–94, 23. See Langdell, Annual Report 1893–94, 131.

155. C. Eliot, Annual Report 1874–75, 26.

156. Lowell, Annual Report 1908–9, 8.

157. C. Eliot to Pritchett (13 Apr. 1915).

then declared women an exception to the standard of academic merit and applied special scrutiny to the Catholic college graduates. These policies allowed the meritocrats to believe that they had not violated the standard of academic merit, because the special categories deserved distinctive treatment. As a result, their belief in their commitment to academic meritocracy never wavered, although the categorized peoples saw a blatant contradiction between that commitment and the invidious policies.

Prominent studies of the movement toward academic meritocracy in American higher education have sometimes assumed it to be virtually "inevitable."[158] Even critical studies of the prejudicial operation of the movement have sometimes assumed that it once operated without bias and might therefore again.[159] The assumption appears as well in prominent legal arguments about how the system could be fixed to operate fairly and justly. The judicial expectation that professional schools can repair the system and realize Langdell's dream "twenty-five years from now,"[160] implies that it originally worked and broke at some point along the way. Otherwise, why the expectation to fix something that has not worked?

However, Langdell's life and work reveal that there has never existed a moment, even at its inception, when the formal system of academic meritocracy in professional education operated free of the interests, values, and prejudices of those who conceived, built, and operated the system. But in drawing up an indictment, we must apply equal scrutiny to the alternatives, which critics of the "Langdellian orthodoxy" have often neglected to propose.[161] In Langdell's mind, the alternatives to his bench and bar were those of Edward Bogardus or Boss Tweed. We must therefore consider whether, like democracy in political life, academic meritocracy may still be the best of the worst ways of organizing professional life.

---

158. Jencks and Riesman, *Academic Revolution*, 12.

159. See Karabel, *Chosen: The Hidden History of Admission and Exclusion*, 1. Cf. Auerbach, *Unequal Justice: Lawyers and Social Change*, 27–29.

160. *Grutter v. Bollinger* (2003), 343.

161. Quotation is from Konefsky and Schlegel, "Mirror, Mirror on the Wall," 837. See 831–51; Kennedy, "How the Law School Fails"; Seligman, *High Citadel: The Influence of Harvard Law School*; Hathaway, "Mythical Meritocracy of Law School Admissions"; Roithmayr, "Deconstructing the Distinction between Bias and Merit"; Kahlenberg, *Broken Contract: A Memoir of Harvard Law School*.

APPENDIX 1

Nicholas St. John Green

Born in 1835, Nicholas St. John Green graduated from Harvard College in 1851 and from HLS in 1853 and became a prominent Boston lawyer and a member of the intellectual circle that developed the philosophy of pragmatism. In 1870 he began serving as one of the lecturers at HLS whose teaching supplemented that of the three professors: Langdell, Emory Washburn, and Nathaniel Holmes. Green's courses in criminal law and torts were well received, and he began publishing a steady stream of highly regarded writings.[1] Of the nine lecturers, he was the only one who voted on key questions decided by the HLS Faculty in 1871 and 1872, before Ames joined the faculty.

By voting in support of Langdell's reforms in 1871 and 1872, Green played a critical role in parrying the opposition of Washburn and Holmes and allowing Eliot to cast critical swing votes. As a result, Green was perfectly positioned to be appointed a professor at HLS by 1873. He had been a successful lawyer; his teaching and writing were exemplary; he alone among the adjunct lecturers was already accorded faculty status; and he had allied himself with Langdell and Eliot in elevating academic standards. Why were Ames, Bradley, and Gray offered professorships instead, and why did Green leave HLS for a position at the new law school at Boston University?[2]

One possible explanation lies in Green's personality, which was no less eccentric than Langdell's is reputed to have been.[3] But the most credible explanation is suggested by the circumstances of Green's premature death in 1876 while

1. *Centennial History of the Harvard Law School*, 214; Swasey, "Boston University Law School," 57.
2. The leading scholarly interpretation posits personal antipathy and intellectual disagreement between Green and Langdell, but relies on the views of Green's son seventy years later, and does not square with the original records. Wiener, *Evolution and the Founders of Pragmatism*, 152–71, 154n, 275n57.
3. Green's confrontational manner exhibited "a Socratic coarseness." "Nicholas St. John Green," in AAAS, *Proceedings*, 12 (1877): 291. See also *Boston Evening Transcript*, 30 Jan. 1877. Professor David J. Seipp of Boston University Law School has suggested to me that descriptions of Green's teaching style at B.U. indicate that he was far less tolerant of received authority than was common on law faculties.

serving as dean of Boston University law school.[4] Several laudatory memorials and obituaries attribute Green's early death to a mistaken overdose of laudanum, an alcoholic tincture of opium.[5] But other newspaper reports at the time suggested suicide as the cause, and handwritten marginalia in the Harvard archival file on Green call him a "drunkard."[6] These latter possibilities provide a more plausible explanation for Green's departure from HLS, because Eliot refused to appoint two other brilliant members of the pragmatist circle—Chauncey Wright and Charles Peirce—to anything more than occasional lectureships due to their unorthodox lifestyles, including excessive drinking.[7] Consequently, personal problems likely barred Green's promotion (in front of Bradley and Gray) to professor at HLS, and led ultimately to his tragic death.[8]

4. When the founding dean of B.U. law school became ill during 1874–75, Green assumed the duties of dean and continued until his death "after the close of the school year 1875–76." Swasey, "Boston University Law School," 57.

5. Wiener, *Evolution and the Founders of Pragmatism*, 233n2; *Oxford English Dictionary*, s.v. "laudanum."

6. *Boston Evening Transcript*, 9 Sept. 1876; two handwritten notes and untitled transcriptions of obituaries in Green, Biographical File.

7. J. Thayer, *Letters of Chauncey Wright*, 137–38.

8. According to Wiener's longstanding prominent interpretation, Green decided to leave HLS in 1873 for the new law school founded at Boston University because Langdell expected Green to convert to case method, which supposedly consisted of didactic commenting on cases, and because Green was "most intimate" with Chauncey Wright and other members of the Pragmatist philosophical circle, who were intellectually opposed to Langdell. Wiener's source for this inaccurate approving portrayal of Green at the expense of Langdell is Green's own son, with whom Wiener corresponded in the 1940s, the period when Holmes's stature and his deprecating caricature of Langdell were reaching their apogee. Quotation is from Wiener, *Evolution and the Founders of Pragmatism*, 231–32. See 154n, 275n57. Cf. LaPiana, *Logic and Experience*, 100–119.

Langdell's Analogies between Law and Natural Science

While dean at HLS, Langdell made three brief analogies between the law and natural science that were widely quoted in the twentieth century, prompting much criticism of his conception of "legal science."[1] The first appeared in Langdell's famous preface to his first casebook, published in 1871:

> Law, considered as a science, consists of certain principles or doctrines.... Each of these doctrines has arrived at its present state by slow degrees; in other words, it is a growth, extending in many cases through centuries. This growth is to be traced in the main through a series of cases.... Moreover, the number of fundamental legal doctrines is much less than is commonly supposed.... *If these doctrines could be so classified and arranged that each should be found in its proper place,* and nowhere else, they would cease to be formidable from their number.... It seemed to me, therefore, to be possible ... *to select, classify, and arrange all the cases which had contributed in any important degree to the growth, development, or establishment of any of its essential doctrines.*[2]

Three years later, in a second brief analogy, Langdell began to specify the disciplines: "The work done in the Library is what the scientific men call original investigation. The Library is to us what a laboratory is to the chemist or the physicist, and what a museum is to the naturalist."[3] In 1886 Langdell made a third analogy that was reprinted in prominent journals:

1. Friedman, *History of American Law* (1985), 617; Hurst, *Growth of American Law*, 261–64; Wiener, *Evolution and the Founders of Pragmatism*, 153; Sutherland, *Law at Harvard*, 174–78; Horwitz, Review, 49–50; Stevens, *Law School: Legal Education in America*, 52–53; Sheppard, "Introductory History of Law in the Lecture Hall," 60n275; Siegel, "Joel Bishop's Orthodoxy," 222; Speziale, "Langdell's Concept of Law as Science," 1–37; Grey, "Langdell's Orthodoxy," 16–24; Schweber, "'Science' of Legal Science," 455–64; Hoeflich, "Law and Geometry," 95–121; W. Carter, "Reconstructing Langdell," 75–80; Schweber, "Before Langdell: The Roots of American Legal Science," 629–33; P. Kelley, "Holmes, Langdell, and Formalism," 35–40.
2. Langdell, *Cases on Contracts* (1871), preface. Emphasis added.
3. Langdell, Annual Report 1873–74, 67.

It was indispensable to establish at least two things—that law is a science, and that all the available materials of that science are contained in printed books.... My associates and myself, therefore, have constantly acted upon the view that law is a science and that a well-equipped university is the true place for teaching and learning that science.... We have also constantly inculcated the idea that the library is the proper work-shop of professors and students alike; that it is to us all *that the laboratories of the university are to the chemists and physicists, the museum of natural history to the zoologists, the botanical garden to the botanists.*[4]

Much of the attention given to these analogies during the twentieth century derives from the attention paid to them in 1914 by Josef Redlich. An Austrian scholar, Redlich wrote a report for the Carnegie Foundation and, eager to dispel the idea that law is an inductive discipline, stressed "this favorite [idea] of Langdell's" in order to rebut it.[5] However, Redlich's supervisor at the Carnegie Foundation, Alfred Z. Reed, regarded Redlich's attack as unfounded, observing that "Redlich takes great pleasure in exploding this theory [that law is like a natural science.] But I can find nowhere that Langdell states this evidently heretical view."[6]

Indeed, Langdell placed little weight upon his comparisons between natural science and jurisprudence. Throughout the rest of his published works, his letters, and about ten thousand pages of loose or bound manuscripts, I have not found another such analogy. If natural science was the polestar of his jurisprudence, it seems extraordinary that it would be glimpsed so rarely.

In contrast, in his annual report for 1880–81 Langdell devoted as much attention to discussing "law as a science," as in the three instances quoted above, without making any reference to natural science. If the comparison to natural science were critical to his thinking, it seems that he would have made an analogy in the 1880–81 report.[7] Moreover, in another annual report, he asserted, "Law has not the demonstrative certainty of mathematics ... nor does it acknowledge truth as its ultimate test and standard, like natural science."[8] Consequently, Langdell's three analogies between jurisprudence and natural science in 1871, 1874, and 1886 seem to be anomalous, notwithstanding the attention that they received in the twentieth century.

---

4. Langdell, Address 1886, 49–50, repr., *Law Quarterly Review* 9 (1887, London): 123–25; *American Law Review* 21 (1887): 123–25. Emphasis added.

5. Redlich, *Common Law and the Case Method*, 15. See 15–18, 54–66.

6. A. Reed to Thayer (5 Nov. 1914).

7. Langdell, Annual Report 1880–81, 83–84.

8. Langdell, Annual Report 1876–77, 96–97.

Why would Langdell state the three evocative analogies if he gave them little weight? Each one was presented in a popular rather than a technical statement that he knew would be read by Harvard president Eliot, who fancied the allusions to natural science. In fact, Langdell addressed the explicit 1874 analogy to Eliot, and Langdell delivered the 1886 analogy at a podium he shared with Eliot, who expressed his hearty approval.[9] In 1874 and 1886, Dean Langdell was apparently voicing the language of his president's "vision." Surely he was not the last dean to do this.[10]

The source material for his famous analogies between natural science and legal science, teaching and research, lie in the taxonomic disciplines of Asa Gray's botany and Louis Agassiz's zoology that he had encountered in his sophomore class in natural history. To these sources were overlaid references to evolutionary theory and to chemistry and other laboratory sciences, which arose from the "immediate and cataclysmic change in outlook" prompted by Darwin's *The Origin of Species* in 1859;[11] from Holmes's allusion to "tracing the growth of a doctrine" in his 1871 review,[12] which Langdell read carefully and assimilated; and from the local and personal influence of Harvard president and chemist Eliot.

9. C. Eliot, Oration 1886, 62–63.

10. Redlich later observed, "To an enthusiastic scientist like Eliot it was an illuminating and attractive idea that the law ought to be studied from its own concrete phenomena, from law cases, in the same way that the laws of the physical sciences are derived from physical phenomena and experiments." *Common Law and the Case Method*, 15.

11. Ghiselin, *Triumph of the Darwinian Method*, 1.

12. [O. Holmes], Review (1871).

BIBLIOGRAPHY

Arranged Alphabetically by Abbreviated Titles

Anonymous newspaper articles are listed under the title of the newspaper and the date of the issue. Legal cases appear in the list of cases following the bibliography. Citations to the Charles W. Eliot Papers in the Harvard University Archives follow the citation system obtaining until 2007. See the cross-references in "Charles William Eliot, 1834–1926. Papers and records: obsolete call numbers: a guide," available at Harvard University Archives (2007).

AAAS, Archives
     American Academy of Arts and Sciences, Archives (Cambridge, Mass.)
AAAS, Proceedings
     American Academy of Arts and Sciences, *Proceedings*, vols. 8–12 (1873–77).
Ackerman, *Gold Ring: Jim Fisk, Jay Gould, and Black Friday*
     Kenneth D. Ackerman, *The Gold Ring: Jim Fisk, Jay Gould, and Black Friday 1869* (New York: Dodd, Mead, 1988).
ACon71
     James Barr Ames, annotated copy of Christopher C. Langdell, *A Selection of Cases on the Law of Contracts* (Boston: Little, Brown, 1871), Special Collections, Harvard Law School Library.
Adams, C., "Chapter of Erie"
     Charles F. Adams Jr., "A Chapter of Erie," *North American Review* 109 (July 1869): 30–106.
Adams, C., "Erie Railroad Row"
     Charles F. Adams Jr., "The Erie Railroad Row," *American Law Review* 3 (1868): 41–86.
Adams, C., and H. Adams, *Chapters of Erie*
     Charles F. Adams Jr. and Henry Adams, *Chapters of Erie and Other Essays* (1886; repr., New York: Henry Holt, 1966).
Adams, H., *Education*
     Henry Adams, *The Education of Henry Adams* (1906; repr., Boston: Houghton Mifflin, 1961).
Adams, H., *Letters*
     Henry Adams, *The Letters*, ed. J. C. Levenson et al., 6 vols. (Cambridge, Mass.: Harvard University Press, 1988).

Adams, J., to Thayer (9 Jan. 1883)
  John Q. Adams Jr. to James B. Thayer (9 Jan. 1883), James B. Thayer Papers, Special
  Collections, Harvard Law School Library, box 27.

AEq1
  James Barr Ames, annotated copy of Christopher C. Langdell, *Cases in Equity*
  Pleading, Selected with Special Reference to the Subject of Discovery ... [Part
  I] (Cambridge, Mass.: Printed for the Author, [1875]) and *Cases in Equity*
  Pleading ... [Part II] (Cambridge, Mass.: Printed for the Author, [1876]), bound
  together, Special Collections, Harvard Law School Library.

AEq2
  James Barr Ames, annotated copy of Christopher C. Langdell, *Cases in Equity*
  Pleading, Selected with Special Reference to the Subject of Discovery ... [Part
  I] (Cambridge, Mass.: Printed for the Author, [1875]) and *Cases in Equity*
  Pleading ... [Part II] (Cambridge, Mass.: Printed for the Author, [1876]), bound
  together with Langdell, *A Summary of Equity Pleading* (Cambridge, Mass.: Charles
  W. Sever, 1877), Special Collections, Harvard Law School Library.

Allen to Town Clerk, New Boston (28 July 1924)
  Agnes May (Langdell Warner) Allen to Town Clerk, New Boston (28 July 1924)
  Vault of Whipple Free Library, New Boston, N.H., f. "Beard."

Allmendinger, *Paupers and Scholars*
  David S. Allmendinger Jr., *Paupers and Scholars: The Transformation of Student Life in*
  Nineteenth-Century New England (New York: St. Martin's Press, 1975).

[Alpha Delta Phi], *A. D. Club*
  [Alpha Delta Phi Society], *The A. D. Club of Harvard University, 1837–1906*
  (Cambridge, Mass.: [privately printed], 1906).

Alpha Delta Phi, *Catalog*
  Alpha Delta Phi Society, *Catalog* (Cambridge, Mass.: Metcalf, 1851).

Alschuler, *Law without Values*
  Albert W. Alschuler, *Law without Values: The Life, Work, and Legacy of Justice Holmes*
  (Chicago: University of Chicago Press, 2000).

Altschuler, *Andrew D. White*
  Glenn C. Altschuler, *Andrew D. White: Educator, Historian, Diplomat* (Ithaca, N.Y.:
  Cornell University Press, 1979).

Amar, "Intratextualism"
  Akhil Reed Amar, "Intratextualism," *Harvard Law Review* 112 (1999): 747–827.

Ames, Annual Report (date varies)
  James Barr Ames, "[Annual Report of the Dean of] the Law School," *Annual Reports*
  of the President and the Treasurer of Harvard College, 1896–1910 (Cambridge, Mass.:
  Harvard University, 1896–1910).

Ames, "Christopher Columbus Langdell"
  James Barr Ames, "Christopher Columbus Langdell," *Harvard Graduates' Magazine*,
  15 (Dec. 1906): 209–12.

Ames, "Christopher Columbus Langdell, 1826–1906"
  James Barr Ames, "Christopher Columbus Langdell, 1826–1906," in *Great*
  American Lawyers, ed. William D. Lewis (Philadelphia: John C. Wilson, 1909),

8:465–89. [Repr., Ames, *Lectures on Legal History and Miscellaneous Legal Essays* (Cambridge, Mass.: Harvard University Press, 1913), 467–82.]

Ames, "Professor Langdell"
James Barr Ames, "Professor Langdell—His Services to Legal Education," *Harvard Law Review* 20 (1906): 12–13.

Ames, "Vocation of the Law Professor"
James Barr Ames, "The Vocation of the Law Professor," in *Lectures on Legal History and Miscellaneous Legal Essays* (Cambridge, Mass.: Harvard University Press, 1913), 354–69.

Ames to Eliot (date varies)
James Barr Ames to Charles W. Eliot (1870–1905), Charles W. Eliot Papers, Harvard University Archives, boxes 69, 78, 100, 268–9 [*sic*].

Ames to Irwin (27 June 1899)
James Barr Ames to Agnes Irwin (27 June 1899), Correspondence and Papers of the Council of Radcliffe College, Radcliffe College Archives, Harvard University, folder "Papers re Admission to Law School."

[Ames, S.], "Memoir of James Barr Ames
[Sarah R. Ames], "Memoir of James Barr Ames," in *Lectures on Legal History and Miscellaneous Legal Essays*, James Barr Ames, 2–26 (Cambridge, Mass.: Harvard University Press, 1913).

Anderson to Landis (24 Feb. 1938)
Robert B. Anderson to James M. Landis (24 Feb. 1938), repr., "A Memoir: Inside the Law School, 1892–1938," *Harvard Law School Bulletin* (Mar. 1965): 9.

Anson, *Principles of the English Law of Contract* (1879)
William R. Anson, *Principles of the English Law of Contract and of Agency in its Relation to Contract* (Oxford: Clarendon Press, 1879).

Anson, *Principles of the English Law of Contract* (1883).
William R. Anson, *Principles of the English Law of Contract and of Agency in its Relation to Contract*, 2nd ed. (Oxford: Clarendon Press, 1883).

Arrow, Bowles, and Durlauf, *Meritocracy and Economic Inequality*
Kenneth Arrow, Samuel Bowles, and Steven N. Durlauf, *Meritocracy and Economic Inequality* (Princeton, N.J.: Princeton University Press, 2000).

ASal72
James Barr Ames, annotated copy of Christopher C. Langdell, *A Selection of Cases on Sales of Personal Property* (Boston: Little, Brown, 1872), vol. 1, Special Collections, Harvard Law School Library.

ASSA, "Department of Jurisprudence"
American Social Science Association, "Department of Jurisprudence," *Journal of Social Science* 5 (1873): 207.

ASSA, "General Intelligence"
American Social Science Association, "General Intelligence. I. Home," *Journal of Social Science* 3 (1871): 199.

ASSA, "List of New Members"
American Social Science Association, "List of New Members," *Journal of Social Science* 2 (1870): 296.

Atiyah, *Essays on Contract*
  Patrick S. Atiyah, *Essays on Contract*, 2nd ed. (Oxford: Clarendon Press, 1990).
Atiyah, *Introduction to the Law of Contract*
  Patrick S. Atiyah, *An Introduction to the Law of Contract*, 4th ed. (New York: Oxford University Press, 1989).
Atwood, F., *Old Folks' Day*
  F. A. Atwood, *Old Folks' Day, New Boston, N.H.* (Manchester, N.H.: John B. Clarke, 1908).
Atwood, S. to Batchelder (8 Aug. 1906)
  Solomon D. Atwood to Samuel F. Batchelder (8 Aug. 1906), Samuel F. Batchelder Papers, Cambridge Historical Society, Cambridge, Mass., box 5.
Auerbach, *Unequal Justice: Lawyers and Social Change*
  Jerold S. Auerbach, *Unequal Justice: Lawyers and Social Change in Modern America* (New York: Oxford University Press, 1976).
Axtell, *Educational Writings of John Locke*
  James T. Axtell, *The Educational Writings of John Locke* (Cambridge: Cambridge University Press, 1968).
Bailyn, *New England Merchants*
  Bernard Bailyn, *New England Merchants* (Cambridge, Mass.: Harvard University Press, 1955).
Baker, J., *Introduction to English Legal History* (1979)
  John H. Baker, *An Introduction to English Legal History*, 2nd ed. (London: Butterworths, 1979).
Baker, J., *Introduction to English Legal History* (1990)
  John H. Baker, *An Introduction to English Legal History*, 3rd ed. (London: Butterworths, 1990).
Baker, J., *Law's Two Bodies*
  John H. Baker, *The Law's Two Bodies: Some Evidential Problems in English Legal History* (Oxford: Oxford University Press, 2001).
Baker, J., Review
  John H. Baker, review of *The Rise and Fall of Freedom of Contract*, by P. S. Atiyah, *Modern Law Review* 43 (1980): 467–69.
Baker, L., *Brandeis and Frankfurter*
  Leonard Baker, *Brandeis and Frankfurter: A Dual Biography* (New York: Harper and Row, 1984).
Baldwin, "Constitutional Questions"
  Simeon E. Baldwin, "The Constitutional Questions Incident to the Acquisition and Government by the United States of Island Territories," *Harvard Law Review* 12 (1899): 393–416.
Baldwin, "Readjustment of the Collegiate to the Professional Course"
  Simeon E. Baldwin, "The Readjustment of the Collegiate to the Professional Course," *Yale Law Journal* 8 (1898): 1–23.
Ballard, Interview (18 Mar. 1920)
  Frances Keay Ballard, Interview (18 Mar. 1920), Bureau of Vocational Information Records, Radcliffe College Archives, Harvard University, B-3/M-118, f. 144.

Ballard, Questionnaire
   Frances Keay Ballard, Questionnaire, Bureau of Vocational Information Records,
      Radcliffe College Archives, Harvard University, B-3/M-118, f. 153.
Barber, "History of Wyoming Seminary"
   Denny Barber, "History of Wyoming Seminary" (2001), <http://www
      .wyomingseminary.org/general info>, 14 June 2004.
Barnes, "Introduction"
   Thomas G. Barnes, introduction to *A Selection of Cases on the Law of Contracts*, by
      Christopher Columbus Langdell (1871; repr., Birmingham, Ala.: Legal Classics
      Library, 1983).
Barrett to Washburn (12 Sept. 1871)
   William Barrett to Emory Washburn (12 Sept. 1871), Charles W. Eliot Papers,
      Harvard University Archives, box 67.
Batchelder, "1906—Notes for Langdell art[icle]"
   Samuel F. Batchelder, "1906—Notes for Langdell art[icle]," Samuel F. Batchelder
      Papers, Cambridge Historical Society, Massachusetts, box 5.
Batchelder, "C. C. Langdell"
   Samuel F. Batchelder, "C. C. Langdell, Iconoclast," in *Bits of Harvard History*
      (Cambridge, Mass.: Harvard University Press, 1924), 301–23.
Batchelder, "Christopher C. Langdell"
   Samuel F. Batchelder, "Christopher C. Langdell," *Green Bag* 18 (1906): 437–43.
Baylies, *Questions and Answers for Law Students*
   Edwin Baylies, *Questions and Answers for Law Students* (Albany, N.Y.: William Gould,
      1873).
Beale, "Jens Iverson Westengard"
   Joseph H. Beale Jr., "Jens Iverson Westengard," *Harvard Law Review* 32 (1918):
      93–97.
Beale, "Jeremiah Smith"
   Joseph H. Beale Jr., "Jeremiah Smith," *Harvard Law Review* 35 (1921): 1–8.
Beale, "Langdell, Gray, Thayer, and Ames"
   Joseph H. Beale Jr., "Langdell, Gray, Thayer, and Ames: Their Contribution to the
      Study and Teaching of Law," *New York University Law Quarterly Review* 8 (1931):
      385–95.
Beale, "Professor Langdell"
   Joseph H. Beale Jr., "Professor Langdell—His Later Teaching Days," *Harvard Law
      Review* 20 (1906): 9–11.
Bell, *Bench and Bar of New Hampshire*
   Charles H. Bell, *The Bench and Bar of New Hampshire* (Boston: Houghton, Mifflin,
      1894).
Bellefontaine, "Social Law Library"
   Edgar J. Bellefontaine, "The Social Law Library: 175 Years of Service to the Bench
      and Bar of Massachusetts," *Boston Bar Journal* 24, no. 10 (1980): 5–27.
Belmont, "Constitution and the Presidential Campaign"
   Perry Belmont, "The Constitution and the Presidential Campaign," *New York Times*,
      8 Apr. 1900, 25.

Benjamin, *Treatise on the Law of Sale*
> Judah P. Benjamin, *A Treatise on the Law of Sale of Personal Property* (London: H.
> Sweet; Washington, D.C.: Morrison, 1868).

Bergan, *History of the New York Court of Appeals*
> Francis Bergan, *The History of the New York Court of Appeals, 1847–1932* (New York:
> Columbia University Press, 1985).

Beringause, *Brook Adams*
> Arthur R. Beringause, *Brook Adams: A Biography* (New York: Alfred A. Knopf, 1955).

Bernstein, *New York City Draft Riots*
> Iver Bernstein, *The New York City Draft Riots: Their Significance for American Society
> and Politics in the Age of the Civil War* (New York: Oxford University Press, 1990).

Best, *Principles of the Law of Evidence*
> William M. Best, *The Principles of the Law of Evidence*, 6th ed. (New York: J.
> Cockcroft, 1875–76).

Bishop, *Doctrines of the Law of Contracts*
> Joel P. Bishop, *The Doctrines of the Law of Contracts in Their Principal Outlines, Stated,
> Illustrated, and Condensed* (St. Louis, Mo.: Soule, Thomas & Wentworth, 1878).

Black, *Dictionary of Law* (date varies)
> Henry C. Black, *A Dictionary of Law*, 1st ed. (1891; repr., New York: Lawbook
> Exchange, 1991).

Blackburn, *Treatise on the Effect of the Contract of Sale*
> Colin Blackburn, *A Treatise on the Effect of the Contract of Sale on the Legal Rights
> of Property and Possession in Goods, Wares and Merchandise* (London: William
> Benning, 1845).

Blackstone, *Commentaries on the Laws of England*
> William Blackstone, *Commentaries on the Laws of England*, 4 vols. (Oxford:
> Clarendon Press, 1765–69).

Blake to Warren (9 July 1907)
> Henry N. Blake to Charles Warren (9 July 1907), Charles Warren Papers, Special
> Collections, Harvard Law School Library, box 37.

Bloomfield, *American Lawyers*
> Maxwell Bloomfield, *American Lawyers in a Changing Society, 1776–1876* (Cambridge,
> Mass.: Harvard University Press, 1976).

Boden, "Milwaukee Law School: 1892–1928"
> Robert F. Boden, "The Milwaukee Law School: 1892–1928" (bound typescript,
> Marquette University Law School Library, [1977]).

Bolles, *Harvard University*
> Frank Bolles, *Harvard University: A Brief Statement of What Harvard University Is,
> How It May Be Entered and How Its Degrees May Be Obtained* (Cambridge, Mass.:
> Harvard University, 1893).

Bone, "Mapping the Boundaries of a Dispute: Conceptions of Ideal Lawsuit Structure"
> Robert G. Bone, "Mapping the Boundaries of a Dispute: Conceptions of Ideal
> Lawsuit Structure from the Field Code to the Federal Rules," *Columbia Law
> Review* 89 (1989): 1–118.

Bonney to Eliot [circa 1886]

Charles C. Bonney to Charles W. Eliot [circa 1886], Charles W. Eliot Papers, Harvard University Archives, box 74.

Boston Daily Advertiser (30 Sept. 1880)
  [Wedding Announcement for Christopher C. Langdell and Margaret Huson], *Boston Daily Advertiser*, 30 Sept. 1880, 4.

Boston Daily Advertiser (20 Oct. 1883)
  "New Publications," *Boston Daily Advertiser*, 20 Oct. 1883, 2.

Boston Daily Advertiser (29 June 1892)
  "The Divinity Alumni," *Boston Daily Advertiser*, 29 June 1892, 9.

Boston Daily Advertiser (24 May 1895)
  "Just Honors," *Boston Daily Advertiser*, 24 May 1895, 1–2.

Boston Daily Atlas (22 July 1853)
  "Affairs in and About the City," *Boston Daily Atlas*, 22 July 1853, 1.

Boston Evening Transcript (9 Sept. 1876)
  "Death of a Well-Known Lawyer," *Boston Evening Transcript*, 9 Sept. 1876, 4.

Boston Evening Transcript (30 Jan. 1877)
  "Literary Matters," *Boston Evening Transcript*, 30 Jan. 1877, 4.

Boston Evening Transcript (30 Sept. 1880)
  [Wedding Announcement for Christopher C. Langdell and Margaret Huson], *Boston Evening Transcript*, 30 Sept. 1880, 4.

Boston Evening Transcript (13 Sept. 1886)
  "Professor E. W. Gurney," *Boston Evening Transcript*, 13 Sept. 1886, 2.

Boston Evening Transcript (6 Nov. 1886)
  "Harvard Celebration," *Boston Evening Transcript*, 6 Nov. 1886, 10.

Boston Evening Transcript (10 Nov. 1898)
  "Prussian Constitutionalism," *Boston Evening Transcript*, 10 Nov. 1898, 10.

Boston Evening Transcript (6 July 1906), 4
  "Was a Law School Leader. Prof. Langdell Passes Away," *Boston Evening Transcript*, 6 July 1906, 4.

Boston Evening Transcript (6 July 1906), 8
  "Professor Langdell's Contribution to Legal Study," *Boston Evening Transcript*, 6 July 1906, 8.

Boston Evening Traveler (30 Sept. 1880)
  [Wedding Announcement for Christopher C. Langdell and Margaret Huson], *Boston Evening Traveler*, 30 Sept. 1880, 4.

Boston Evening Traveler (6 Nov. 1886)
  "Harvard's Celebration," *Boston Evening Traveler,* 6 Nov. 1886, 7.

Boston Globe (26 June 1895)
  "Array of Talent Dean Langdell Honored by Alumni," *Boston Globe*, 26 June 1895, 1, 9.

Boston Globe (1 Oct. 1898)
  "Prof. Dicey Will Lecture at Harvard," *Boston Globe*, 1 Oct. 1898, 7.

Boston Globe (5 Oct. 1898)
  "Prof. A. V. Dicey Speaks at Harvard," *Boston Globe*, 5 Oct. 1898, 4.

Boston Globe (15 Mar. 1904)

"Northern Securities Company an Outlaw," *Boston Globe*, 15 Mar. 1904, 2.

Boston Globe (23 Mar. 1904)
"View of Justice Holmes," *Boston Globe*, 23 Mar. 1904, 6.

Boston Globe (7 July 1906)
"Prof. Langdell of Harvard, Dean, Aged 80," *Boston Globe*, 7 July 1906, 3.

Boston Herald (6 Nov. 1886)
"The First Day," *Boston Herald*, 6 Nov. 1886, 1.

Boston Herald (26 June 1895)
"Feast of Wit and Wisdom: Dean Langdell Honored by Harvard Law School Alumni; Quarter Centennial Celebrated," *Boston Herald*, 26 June 1895, 1, 4, 8.

Boston Herald (19 July 1899)
"A Coeducation Step," *Boston Herald*, 19 July 1899, 7.

Boston Herald (26 July 1899)
"Co-Education Not Intended," *Boston Herald*, 26 July 1899, 7.

Boston Herald (7 July 1906): 3
"Dean of Harvard Law School Dies," *Boston Herald*, 7 July 1906, 3.

Boston Herald (7 July 1906): 6
"Prof. Langdell," *Boston Herald*, 7 July 1906, 6.

Boston Herald (9 Aug. 1947)
"Rites Here Today for Caroline Cook, Woman Attorney," *Boston Herald*, 9 Aug. 1947, 22.

Boston Journal (23 June 1895)
"Law School's Dean," *Boston Journal*, 23 June 1895, 1.

Boston Journal (20 Sept. 1900)
"Dean Langdell Out," *Boston Journal*, 20 Sept. 1900, 1.

Boston Morning Journal (26 June 1895).
"Teacher of Lawyers," *Boston Morning Journal*, 26 June 1895, 1, 7.

Boston Morning Journal (7 July 1906)
"Professor Langdell, As a Law Teacher, Was Famous," *Boston Morning Journal*, 7 July 1906, 2.

Boston Post (20 Dec. 1855)
"Deaths," *Boston Post*, 20 Dec. 1855, 20.

Boston Post (1 Oct. 1880)
[Wedding Announcement for Christopher C. Langdell and Margaret Huson], *Boston Post*, 1 Oct. 1880, 4.

Boston Post (6 Nov. 1886)
"Harvard Law School," *Boston Post*, 6 Nov. 1886, 1.

Boston Post (7 July 1906)
"Professor Langdell of Harvard Dies at Cambridge Home," *Boston Post*, 7 July 1906, 7.

Boston University, Commencement Program 1899
Boston University, Commencement Program 1899 [(Boston: Boston University, 1899)], Rare Books and Archival Research Center, Boston University.

Boston University, *Historical Register*

Boston University, *Historical Register...Fifth Decennial Issue 1869–1911* (Boston: Boston University, 1911).

Boston University Law School, *Catalog 1872–73*
Boston University Law School, *Catalog 1872–73* (Boston: Boston University, 1872).

Bouvier, *Law Dictionary*
John Bouvier, *A Law Dictionary Adapted to the Constitution and Laws of the United States of America*, 12th ed., 2 vols. (Philadelphia: George W. Childs, 1868).

Bozeman, *Protestants in an Age of Science*
Theodore D. Bozeman, *Protestants in an Age of Science: The Baconian Ideal and Antebellum American Religious Thought* (Chapel Hill: University of North Carolina Press, 1977).

Bradley to Eliot (date varies)
Charles S. Bradley to Charles W. Eliot (1869–76), Charles W. Eliot Papers, Harvard University Archives, boxes 66, 67, 69.

Bradley to Thayer (9 Dec. 1873)
Charles S. Bradley to James B. Thayer (9 Dec. 1873), James B. Thayer Papers, Special Collections, Harvard Law School Library, box 20.

Brandeis, "Harvard Law School"
Louis D. Brandeis, "The Harvard Law School," *Green Bag* 1 (1889): 10–25.

Brandeis, "Harvard Law School Association"
Louis D. Brandeis, "Harvard Law School Association" (Cambridge, Mass.: Harvard Law School, 12 June 1890).

Brandeis, *Letters*
Louis D. Brandeis, *Letters of Louis D. Brandeis*, ed. Melvin I. Urofsky and David W. Levy (Albany, N.Y.: State University of New York Press, 1971).

Brandeis to Brandeis (30 May 1883)
Louis D. Brandeis to Adolph Brandeis (30 May 1883), *Letters of Louis D. Brandeis*, ed. Melvin I. Urofsky and David W. Levy (Albany, N.Y.: State University of New York Press, 1971), 1:65–66.

Brandeis to Eliot (25 Apr. 1893)
Louis D. Brandeis to Charles W. Eliot (25 Apr. 1893), Charles W. Eliot Papers, Harvard University Archives, box 137B.

Brandeis to Frankfurter (22 Feb. 1928)
Louis D. Brandeis to Felix Frankfurter (22 Feb. 1928), *Letters of Louis D. Brandeis*, ed. Melvin I. Urofsky and David W. Levy (Albany, N.Y.: State University of New York Press, 1971), 5:324.

Brandeis to Langdell (30 Dec. 1889)
Louis D. Brandeis to Christopher C. Langdell (30 Dec. 1889), *Letters of Louis D. Brandeis*, ed. Melvin I. Urofsky and David W. Levy (Albany, N.Y.: State University of New York Press, 1971), 1:86.

Brandeis to Wehle (date varies)
Louis D. Brandeis to Otto A. Wehle (1875–76), *Letters of Louis D. Brandeis*, ed. Melvin I. Urofsky and David W. Levy (Albany, N.Y.: State University of New York Press, 1971), 1:7–8.

Brannan to Thayer (3 June 1897)

Joseph D. Brannan to James B. Thayer (3 June 1897), James B. Thayer Papers, Special Collections, Harvard Law School Library, box 17.

Brauer, *Education of a Gentleman*
George C. Brauer Jr., *The Education of a Gentleman: Theories of Gentlemanly Education in England, 1660–1775* (New Haven, Conn.: College and University Press, 1959).

Bronaugh, "Secret Paradox of the Common Law"
Richard Bronaugh, "A Secret Paradox of the Common Law," *Law and Philosophy* 2 (1983): 193–232.

Brosnahan, "President Eliot and the Jesuit College"
Timothy Brosnahan, "President Eliot and the Jesuit College," *Sacred Heart Review* 23 (13 Jan. 1900): 3–30.

Brosnahan, "Relative Merit of Courses in Catholic and Non-Catholic Colleges"
Timothy Brosnahan, "The Relative Merit of Courses in Catholic and Non-Catholic Colleges for the Baccalaureate," in *Proceedings of the Second Annual Conference of the Association of Catholic Colleges of the United States,* 22–44 (Washington, D.C.: Association of Catholic Colleges of the United States, 1900).

Brown, A., *Autobiographical Notes*
Addison Brown, *Autobiographical Notes for His Children* (Boyce, Va.: Carr, 1972).

Brown, E., *Legal Education at Michigan*
Elizabeth G. Brown, *Legal Education at Michigan, 1859–1959* (Ann Arbor: University of Michigan, 1959).

Brown, G., *Consent of the Governed*
Gillian Brown, *The Consent of the Governed: The Lockean Legacy in Early American Culture* (Cambridge, Mass.: Harvard University Press, 2001).

Brown, R., and Kimball, "When Holmes Borrowed from Langdell"
R. Blake Brown and Bruce Kimball, "When Holmes Borrowed from Langdell: The 'Ultra Legal' Formalism and Public Policy of *Northern Securities* (1904)," *American Journal of Legal History* 45 (2002): 278–332.

Bruce, D., *Archibald Grimké*
Dickson D. Bruce Jr., *Archibald Grimké: Portrait of a Black Independent* (Baton Rouge: Louisiana State University Press, 1993).

Bruce, R., *1877*
Robert V. Bruce, *1877: Year of Violence* (New York: Bobbs-Merrill, 1959).

Bryce, *American Commonwealth*
James Bryce, *The American Commonwealth*, new ed. (New York: Macmillan, 1924).

Buck, *Social Sciences at Harvard 1860–1920*
Paul H. Buck, ed., *Social Sciences at Harvard 1860–1920: From Inculcation to the Open Mind* (Cambridge, Mass.: Harvard University Press, 1965).

Burnett and Marshall, "Between the Foreign and the Domestic"
Christina Burnett and Burke Marshall, "Between the Foreign and the Domestic: The Doctrine of Territorial Incorporation, Invented and Reinvented," in *Foreign in a Domestic Sense: Puerto Rico, American Expansion, and the Constitution,* ed. Christina Burnett and Burke Marshall, 1–36 (Durham, N.C.: Duke University Press, 2001).

Burnett and Marshall, *Foreign in a Domestic Sense*

Christina Burnett and Burke Marshall, eds. *Foreign in a Domestic Sense: Puerto Rico, American Expansion, and the Constitution* (Durham, N.C.: Duke University Press, 2001).

Burton, *Path of the Law and Its Influence*

Steven J. Burton, ed. *The Path of the Law and Its Influence: The Legacy of Oliver Wendell Holmes Jr.* (New York: Cambridge University Press, 2000).

Buswell and Walcott, *Practice and Pleading in Personal Actions*

Henry F. Buswell and Charles H. Walcott, *Practice and Pleading in Personal Actions in the Courts of Massachusetts* (Boston: George B. Reed, 1875).

Cabranes, "Some Common Ground"

José A. Cabranes, "Some Common Ground," in *Foreign in a Domestic Sense: Puerto Rico, American Expansion, and the Constitution*, ed. Christina Burnett and Burke Marshall, 39–47 (Durham, N.C.: Duke University Press, 2001).

Callow, *Tweed Ring*

Alexander B. Callow Jr., *The Tweed Ring* (New York: Oxford University Press, 1966).

Carmalt to Warren (10 Oct. 1907)

James E. Carmalt to Charles Warren (10 Oct. 1907), Charles Warren Papers, Special Collections, Harvard Law School Library, box 37.

Carrington, "Hail! Langdell!"

Paul D. Carrington, "Hail! Langdell!" *Law & Social Inquiry* 20 (1995): 691–760.

Carrington, "Missionary Diocese of Chicago"

Paul D. Carrington, "The Missionary Diocese of Chicago," *Journal of Legal Education* 44 (1994): 467–518.

Carrington, "Teaching Civil Procedure"

Paul D. Carrington, "Teaching Civil Procedure: A Retrospective View," *Journal of Legal Education* 49 (1999): 311–32.

Carter, J., Address 1886

James C. Carter, Address, in *Report of the Organization and of the First General Meeting, 1886*, Harvard Law School Association, 24–29 (Boston: Harvard Law School Association, 1887).

Carter, J., Address 1895

James C. Carter, Address, in *Report of the Ninth Annual Meeting at Cambridge, June 25, 1895*, Harvard Law School Association, 40–41 (Boston: Harvard Law School Association, 1895).

Carter, J., to Eliot (20 Dec. 1869)

James C. Carter to Charles W. Eliot (20 Dec. 1869), Charles W. Eliot Papers, Harvard University Archives, box 66.

Carter, J., to Thayer (17 Feb. 1899)

James C. Carter to James B. Thayer (17 Feb. 1899), James B. Thayer Papers, Special Collections, Harvard Law School Library, box 17.

Carter, W., "Reconstructing Langdell"

W. Burlette Carter, "Reconstructing Langdell," *Georgia Law Review* 32 (1997): 1–139.

"Case System of Teaching Law"

"The Case System of Teaching Law," *Virginia Law Register* 1 (1896): 299.

Centennial History
> *The Centennial History of the Harvard Law School, 1817–1917* (Cambridge, Mass.:
>   Harvard Law School Association, 1918).

Chafee to Perry (6 Mar. 1929)
> Zechariah Chafee Jr. to Ralph B. Perry (6 Mar. 1929), Zechariah Chafee Jr. Papers,
>   Harvard Law School Library, microfilm edition.

Chamberlain, "Northern Securities Case"
> Daniel H. Chamberlain, "The Northern Securities Case; A Reply to Professor
>   Langdell," *Yale Law Journal* 13 (1903): 57–65.

Chandler, *Visible Hand: The Managerial Revolution in American Business*
> Alfred D. Chandler Jr., *The Visible Hand: The Managerial Revolution in American
>   Business* (Cambridge, Mass.: Harvard University Press, 1976).

Chase, "Birth of the Modern Law School"
> Anthony Chase, "The Birth of the Modern Law School," *American Journal of Legal
>   History* 23 (1979): 329–48.

Chase, "Origins of Modern Professional Education"
> Anthony Chase, "Origins of Modern Professional Education: The Harvard Case
>   Method Conceived as Clinical Instruction in Law," *Nova Law Journal* 5 (1981):
>   323–63.

Cheng, "Untold Stories: Asian Pacific Americans at Harvard Law School"
> Andrew Cheng, "Untold Stories: Asian Pacific Americans at Harvard Law School"
>   (unpublished paper, Daniel R. Coquillette's Legal Education Seminar, Harvard
>   Law School, Cambridge, Mass., spring 2000).

Chicago Legal News (21 Oct. 1893): 62
> "The Harvard Idea," *Chicago Legal News* (21 Oct. 1893): 62.

Chicago Legal News (21 Oct. 1893): 82
> "The Harvard Departure," *Chicago Legal News* (21 Oct. 1893): 82.

Chitty, *Treatise on Pleading*
> Joseph Chitty, *A Treatise on Pleading, and Parties to Actions*, 10th Am. ed.
>   (Springfield, Mass.: Merriam, 1847).

Choate, Address 1895
> Joseph H. Choate, Address, in *Report of the Ninth Annual Meeting at Cambridge, June
>   25, 1895*, Harvard Law School Association, 63–65 (Boston: Harvard Law School
>   Association, 1895).

Choate to Batchelder (18 July 1906)
> Joseph H. Choate to Samuel F. Batchelder (18 July 1906), Samuel F. Batchelder
>   Papers, Cambridge Historical Society, Massachusetts, box 5.

Choate to Warren (18 Oct. 1907)
> Joseph H. Choate to Charles Warren (18 Oct. 1907), Charles Warren Papers, Special
>   Collections, Harvard Law School Library, box 37.

Christ Church, Episcopal, "List of Voters before 1900"
> Christ Church, Episcopal (Cambridge, Massachusetts), Archives, folder C-09-4,
>   "List of Voters before 1900."

Clark, *Handbook of the Law of Code Pleading*

Charles E. Clark, *Handbook of the Law of Code Pleading*, 2nd ed. (St. Paul, Minn.: West Publishing, 1947).

Clarke, *Sex in Education*
Edward H. Clarke, *Sex in Education; or, A Fair Chance for the Girls* (1873; repr., Boston: James R. Osgood, 1874).

Codman to Warren (24 Oct. 1907)
Charles R. Codman to Charles Warren (24 Oct. 1907), Charles Warren Papers, Special Collections, Harvard Law School Library, box 37.

Cogswell, *History of New Boston*
Elliott C. Cogswell, *History of New Boston, New Hampshire* (Boston: Ran, Avery, Cornhill, 1864).

Coldwater Courier (18 Sept. 1907)
"Mrs. M. Langdell: Some Facts Concerning a Good Woman," *Coldwater Courier*, 18 Sept. 1907.

Coldwater Republican (24 Sept. 1880)
[Wedding Announcement for Christopher C. Langdell and Margaret Huson], *Coldwater Republican*, 24 Sept.1880.

"Combinations in Restraint of Interstate Commerce"
"Combinations in Restraint of Interstate Commerce," *American Law Review* 37 (1903): 461.

"Constitutional Law: Regulation of Interstate Commerce"
"Constitutional Law: Regulation of Interstate Commerce—Validity and Interpretation of the Sherman Anti-Trust Act," *American Law Review* 38 (1904): 430.

Cook, C. J., "1942 Biographical Record"
Caroline J. Cook, "1942 Biographical Record," Records of Wellesley College Alumnae Association, Wellesley College Archives, Wellesley, Mass.

Cook, C. J., "Too Early for a Definite Answer"
Caroline J. Cook, "Too Early for a Definite Answer," *Boston Daily Globe* (24 Nov. 1907): 36.

Cook, C. M., *American Codification Movement*
Charles M. Cook, *The American Codification Movement: A Study of Antebellum Legal Reform* (Westport, Conn.: Greenwood, 1981).

Cooley, Papers
Thomas M. Cooley, Papers, 1850–98, Michigan Historical Collections, Bentley Historical Library, University of Michigan.

Coquillette, *Anglo-American Legal Heritage*
Daniel R. Coquillette, *The Anglo-American Legal Heritage* (Durham, N.C.: Carolina Academic Press, 1999).

Cordasco, *Shaping of American Graduate Education*
Francesco Cordasco, *The Shaping of American Graduate Education: Daniel Coit Gilman and the Protean Ph.D.* (Totowa, N.J.: Rowman and Littlefield, 1973).

Corning, *Amos Tuck*
Charles R. Corning, *Amos Tuck* (Exeter, N.H.: News-Letter Press, 1902).

Cosgrove, "A. V. Dicey"

Richard A. Cosgrove, "A. V. Dicey at the Harvard Law School, 1898: A Study in the Anglo-American Legal Community," *Harvard Library Bulletin* 26 (1978): 325–35.

Cosgrove, *Our Lady the Common Law*

Richard A. Cosgrove, *Our Lady the Common Law: An Anglo-American Legal Community, 1870–1930* (New York: New York University Press, 1987).

Cott, *Grounding of Modern Feminism*

Nancy F. Cott, *The Grounding of Modern Feminism* (New Haven, Conn.: Yale University Press, 1987).

Council of Radcliffe College, Record (date varies)

Council of Radcliffe College, Record of Meetings and Votes (1898–99), Charles W. Eliot Papers, Harvard University Archives, box 268–269 [*sic*].

Crocker to Warren (30 Jan. 1908)

George C. Crocker to Charles Warren (30 Jan. 1908), Charles Warren Papers, Special Collections, Harvard Law School Library, box 37.

"Current Topics"

"Current Topics," *Albany Law Journal* 65 (1903): 201.

DAB

Dictionary of American Biography (New York: Charles Scribner's Sons, 1931–).

Dallas Morning News (23 Oct. 1911)

"Rise of Women to Legal Powers," *Dallas Morning News*, 23 Oct. 1911, 10.

Daniels, *American Science in the Age of Jackson*

George H. Daniels, *American Science in the Age of Jackson* (New York: Columbia University Press, 1968).

Davis, N., *Return of Martin Guerre*

Natalie Zemon Davis, *The Return of Martin Guerre* (Cambridge, Mass.: Harvard University Press, 1983).

Davis, W., *Bench and Bar of Massachusetts*

William T. Davis, *Bench and Bar of the Commonwealth of Massachusetts*, 2 vols. (Boston: Boston History, 1895).

Day, E., *One Thousand Years of Hubbard History*

Edward W. Day, *One Thousand Years of Hubbard History 866 to 1895* (New York: Harlan Page Hubbard, 1895).

Day, G., *Biography of a Church*

Gardiner M. Day, *The Biography of a Church: A Brief History of Christ Church, Cambridge, Massachusetts* (Cambridge, Mass.: Riverside Press, 1951).

Day, H., to Langdell (31 Jan. 1870)

Henry Day to Christopher C. Langdell (31 Jan. 1870), Lord Family Papers, 1807–1961, Special Collections, Harvard Law School Library.

Dedham, Mass., School Committee, *Report 1849–50*

Dedham, Massachusetts, School Committee, *Report . . . 1849–50* (Dedham, Mass.: privately printed, 1850).

Deslandes, "Competitive Examinations"

Paul R. Deslandes, "Competitive Examinations and the Culture of Masculinity in Oxbridge Undergraduate Life, 1850–1920," *History of Education Quarterly* 42 (2002): 544–78.

Devens, *Record of the Commemoration*
    Charles Devens, *A Record of the Commemoration... on the Two Hundred and Fiftieth
    Anniversary of the Founding of Harvard College* (Cambridge, Mass.: John Wilson,
    1887).
Dicey, "English View of American Conservatism"
    Albert V. Dicey, "An English View of American Conservatism," *The Nation*, 25 Mar.
    1880, 229.
Dicey, *Lectures Introductory to the Law of the Constitution*
    Albert V. Dicey, *Lectures Introductory to the Study of the Law of the Constitution*
    (London: Macmillan, 1885).
Dicey, "Teaching of English Law"
    Albert V. Dicey, "The Teaching of English Law at Harvard," *Harvard Law Review* 13
    (1900): 422–40.
Dicey to Eliot (date varies)
    Albert V. Dicey to Charles W. Eliot (1898–99), Charles W. Eliot Papers, Harvard
    University Archives, box 126A.
Dodge, "Lawyers of New Boston"
    Perley Dodge, "The Lawyers of New Boston—At Home and Abroad," in *History
    of New Boston, New Hampshire*, ed. Elliott C. Cogswell, 199–201 (Boston: Ran,
    Avery, Cornhill, 1864).
Dorman B. Eaton, 1823–1899
    [n.a.], *Dorman B. Eaton, 1823–1899* (New York: [privately printed], 1900).
Douglas to Warren (1908)
    J. C. Douglas to Charles Warren (1908), Charles Warren Papers, Special Collections,
    Harvard Law School Library, box 37.
Dowley, *Law in a Nut-Shell*
    Morris F. Dowley, *The Law in a Nut-Shell, Comprising Concise and Lucid Answers to
    Five Hundred Leading Legal Questions* (New York: Warn & Peloubet, 1878).
Drachman, "New Woman Lawyer and the Challenge of Sexual Equality"
    Virginia B. Drachman, "The New Woman Lawyer and the Challenge of Sexual
    Equality in Early Twentieth-Century America," *Indiana Law Review* 28 (1995):
    227–57.
Drachman, *Sisters in Law: Women Lawyers*
    Virginia B. Drachman, *Sisters in Law: Women Lawyers in Modern American History*
    (Cambridge, Mass.: Harvard University Press, 1998).
Drachman, *Women Lawyers and the Origins of Professional Identity*
    Virginia B. Drachman, *Women Lawyers and the Origins of Professional Identity in
    America: The Letters of the Equity Club, 1887 to 1890* (Ann Arbor: University of
    Michigan Press, 1993).
Du Bois, *Autobiography*
    W. E. B. Du Bois, *The Autobiography* (New York: International Publishers, 1968).
Dumas, "Naming of Children in New England"
    David W. Dumas, "The Naming of Children in New England, 1780–1850," *The New
    England Historical and Genealogical Register*, 132 (1978): 196–210.
Dunbar, "President Eliot's Administration"

Charles F. Dunbar, "President Eliot's Administration," *Harvard Graduates' Magazine* 2 (June 1894): 449–76.

Dupree, *Asa Gray*

A. Hunter Dupree, *Asa Gray: American Botanist, Friend of Darwin* (1959; repr., Baltimore: Johns Hopkins University Press, 1988).

Duxbury, *Frederick Pollock*

Neil Duxbury, *Frederick Pollock and the English Juristic Tradition* (Oxford: Oxford University Press, 2004).

Dwight, "Law lectures 1871–2"

Theodore W. Dwight, "Law lectures recorded by George A. Miller, senior year, 1871–2, Columbia College Law School," Special Collections, Columbia University Law School Library.

Eliot, C., Address 1895

Charles W. Eliot, Address, in *Report of the Ninth Annual Meeting at Cambridge, June 25, 1895,* Harvard Law School Association, 69–73 (Boston: Harvard Law School Association, 1895).

Eliot, C., Address 1904

Charles W. Eliot, Address, in *Report of the Eighteenth Annual Meeting . . . June 28, 1904* Harvard Law School Association, 68–70 (Boston: Harvard Law School Association, 1904).

Eliot, C., Annual Report (date varies)

Charles W. Eliot, *Annual Reports of the President and Treasurer of Harvard College, 1869–1909* (Cambridge, Mass.: Harvard University Press, 1870–1910).

Eliot, C., "Higher Education for Women"

Charles W. Eliot, "The Higher Education for Women," *Harper's Bazaar*, June 1908, 519–22.

Eliot, C., Inaugural Address 1869

Charles W. Eliot, Inaugural Address, repr. as *A Turning Point in Higher Education: The Inaugural Address of Charles William Eliot as President of Harvard College, Oct. 19, 1869* (Cambridge, Mass.: Harvard University Press, 1969).

Eliot, C., "Langdell"

Charles W. Eliot, "Langdell and the Law School," *Harvard Law Review* 33 (1920): 518–25.

Eliot, C., "Liberty in Education"

Charles W. Eliot, "Liberty in Education" (Feb. 1885), in *Educational Reform: Essays and Addresses*, 125–48 (New York: Century, 1898).

Eliot, C., "Methods of Instruction"

Charles W. Eliot, "Methods of Instruction," in *University Administration, [A. W. Harris Lectures at Northwestern University]*, 174–213 (Boston: Houghton Mifflin, 1908).

Eliot, C., Oration 1886

Charles W. Eliot, Oration, in *Report of the Organization and of the First General Meeting, 1886,* Harvard Law School Association, 60–63 (Boston: Harvard Law School Association, 1887).

Eliot, C., Papers

Charles W. Eliot, Papers, Harvard University Archives.

Eliot, C., "Recent Changes in Secondary Education"
  Charles W. Eliot, "Recent Changes in Secondary Education," *Atlantic Monthly*,
    October 1899, 433–44.
Eliot, C., to Ames [circa Feb. 1898]
  Charles W. Eliot to James B. Ames [circa Feb. 1898, Charles W. Eliot Papers,
    Harvard University Archives, shorthand box 317, legal pad 28/98-10/98.
Eliot, C., to Ames [circa June 1898]
  Charles W. Eliot to James B. Ames [circa June 1898], Charles W. Eliot Papers,
    Harvard University Archives, shorthand box 317, legal pad 8/98-20.
Eliot, C., to Ames [17 Aug. 1900]
  Charles W. Eliot to James B. Ames [17 Aug. 1900], Charles W. Eliot Papers, Harvard
    University Archives, shorthand box 320, legal pad 25 Sept. 1899.
Eliot, C., to Arnold (15 Sept. 1886)
  Charles W. Eliot to J. H. Arnold (15 Sept. 1886), Charles W. Eliot Papers, Harvard
    University Archives, box 74.
Eliot, C., to Brandeis (27 Apr. 1893)
  Charles W. Eliot to Louis D. Brandeis (27 Apr. 1893) Louis Dembitz Brandeis
    Papers, University of Louisville, Kentucky, microfilm version, reel 1.
Eliot, C., to Brandeis [1893]
  Charles W. Eliot to Louis D. Brandeis [1893], Charles W. Eliot Papers, Harvard
    University Archives, shorthand box 306, book 17 19/93.
Eliot, C., to Brimmer (3 Nov. 1894)
  Charles W. Eliot to [?] Brimmer (3 Nov. 1894), in Harvard University Corporation
    Records, Harvard University Archives, box 15.
Eliot, C., to Church (date varies)
  Charles W. Eliot to Sanford E. Church (1877–78), Charles W. Eliot Papers, Harvard
    University Archives, box 89, letterbook, 139–52.
Eliot, C., to Conaty (24 Oct. 1898)
  Charles W. Eliot to Thomas J. Conaty (24 Oct. 1898), Charles W. Eliot Papers,
    Harvard University Archives, box 92.
Eliot, C., to Dicey (15 Jan. 1906)
  Charles W. Eliot to A. V. Dicey (15 Jan. 1906), Charles W. Eliot Papers, Harvard
    University Archives, box 95, letterbook, 130.
Eliot, C., to Dicey (2 May 1913)
  Charles W. Eliot to A. V. Dicey (2 May 1913), Charles W. Eliot Papers, Harvard
    University Archives, box 401.
Eliot, C., to Dunbar (11 Jan. 1883)
  Charles W. Eliot to Charles F. Dunbar (11 Jan. 1883), Charles F. Dunbar
    Correspondence, Harvard University Archives.
Eliot, C., to Fessenden (3 Mar. 1919)
  Charles W. Eliot to Franklin G. Fessenden (3 Mar. 1919), Charles W. Eliot Papers,
    Harvard University Archives, box 382.
Eliot, C., to Gilman (date varies)
  Charles W. Eliot to Daniel C. Gilman (1876–93), Daniel Coit Gilman Papers, Milton
    S. Eisenhower Library, Johns Hopkins University, ms. 1, box 1.13.

Eliot, C., to Holmes (4 Nov. 1881)
  Charles W. Eliot to Oliver W. Holmes Jr. (4 Nov. 1881), Charles W. Eliot Papers,
    Harvard University Archives, box 70.
Eliot, C., to Holmes (18 Nov. 1916)
  Charles W. Eliot to O. W. Holmes Jr. (18 Nov. 1916), Oliver Wendell Holmes Jr.
    Papers, Harvard Law School Library, microfilm version.
Eliot, C., to Holmes (28 Mar. 1924)
  Charles W. Eliot to Oliver W. Holmes Jr. (28 Mar. 1924), Oliver Wendell Holmes Jr.
    Papers, Harvard Law School Library, microfilm version.
Eliot, C., to Lane (2 Oct. 1922)
  Charles W. Eliot to William C. Lane (2 Oct. 1922), Charles W. Eliot Papers, Harvard
    University Archives, box 68.
Eliot, C., to Langdell [1892?]
  Charles W. Eliot to Christopher C. Langdell [1892?], Charles W. Eliot Papers,
    Harvard University Archives, shorthand box 305, book 23/92.
Eliot, C., to Langdell [1893?]
  Charles W. Eliot to Langdell [1893?], Charles W. Eliot Papers, Harvard University
    Archives, shorthand box 306, book 17 19/93.
Eliot, C., to Langdell [circa 1894a]
  Charles W. Eliot to Christopher C. Langdell [circa 1894a], Charles W. Eliot Papers,
    Harvard University Archives, shorthand box 310, book 30 25/94.
Eliot, C., to Langdell [circa 1894b]
  Charles W. Eliot to Christopher C. Langdell [circa 1894b], Charles W. Eliot Papers,
    Harvard University Archives, shorthand box 310, book 37.
Eliot, C., to Langdell [circa 1895]
  Charles W. Eliot to Christopher C. Langdell [circa 1895], Charles W. Eliot Papers,
    Harvard University Archives, shorthand box 311, legal pad 19.
Eliot, C., to Langdell [circa Jan. 1898]
  Charles W. Eliot to Christopher C. Langdell [circa Jan. 1898], Charles W. Eliot
    Papers, Harvard University Archives, shorthand box 317, legal pad 17/98-10/98.
Eliot, C., to Langdell [circa July 1899]
  Charles W. Eliot to Christopher C. Langdell [circa July 1899], Charles W. Eliot
    Papers, Harvard University Archives, shorthand box 319, legal pad 6/99-13.
Eliot, C., to Langdell (27 Sept. 1900)
  Charles W. Eliot to Christopher C. Langdell (27 Sept. 1900), Charles W. Eliot
    Papers, Harvard University Archives, box 92, letterbook, 85.
Eliot, C., to Lee (13 Mar. 1897)
  Charles W. Eliot to Blewett Lee (13 Mar. 1897), Charles W. Eliot Papers, Harvard
    University Archives, box 91, letterbook, 167a–168.
Eliot, C., to Pritchett (13 Apr. 1915)
  Charles W. Eliot to Henry S. Pritchett (13 Apr. 1915), Correspondence of Charles W.
    Eliot, Special Collections, Harvard Law School Library.
Eliot, C., to Robinson [circa 1901]
  Charles W. Eliot to Mr. Robinson [circa 1901], Charles W. Eliot Papers, Harvard
    University Archives, shorthand box 324, book Aug. 30–Oct. 1, 1901.

Eliot, C., to Smith (5 Jan. 1907)
  Charles W. Eliot to Jeremiah Smith (5 Jan. 1907), Charles W. Eliot Papers, Harvard
    University Archives, box 96, letterbook, 7–8.
Eliot, C., to Strobel (19 May 1898)
  Charles W. Eliot to Edward H. Strobel (19 May 1898), Charles W. Eliot Papers,
    Harvard University Archives, box 92, letterbook, 9.
Eliot, C., to Thayer (date varies)
  Charles W. Eliot to James B. Thayer (1874–94), James B. Thayer Papers, Special
    Collections, Harvard Law School Library, boxes 18, 20, 22.
Eliot, C., to Wambaugh [circa May 1892]
  Charles W. Eliot to Eugene Wambaugh [circa May 1892], Charles W. Eliot Papers,
    Harvard University Archives, shorthand box 305, book 23/92.
Eliot, C., to Williston (23 Apr. 1890)
  Charles W. Eliot to Samuel Williston (23 Apr. 1890), Charles W. Eliot Papers,
    Harvard University Archives, box 90, letterbook, 7a–8.
Eliot, S., "Some Cambridge Pundits"
  Samuel A. Eliot, "Some Cambridge Pundits and Pedagogues," *Proceedings of the
    Cambridge Historical Society*, 13–35 (Cambridge, Mass.: Cambridge Historical
    Society, 1940).
Etzioni, *Semi-Professions and Their Organization*
  Amitai Etzioni, *The Semi-Professions and Their Organization* (New York: Free Press,
    1969).
Everett to Warren (date varies)
  William A. Everett to Charles Warren (1907–8), Charles Warren Papers, Special
    Collections, Harvard Law School Library, box 37.
Exeter News-Letter (23 Mar. 1888)
  "William Weir Stickney," *Exeter News-Letter*, 23 Mar. 1888, 3.
Faler, *Mechanics and Manufacturers in the Early Industrial Revolution*
  Paul G. Faler, *Mechanics and Manufacturers in the Early Industrial Revolution: Lynn,
    Massachusetts, 1780–1860* (Albany, N.Y.: State University of New York Press,
    1981).
Farnsworth, "Contracts Scholarship"
  E. Allan Farnsworth, "Contracts Scholarship in the Age of the Anthology," *Michigan
    Law Review* 85 (1987): 1406–62.
Fessenden, "Rebirth of the Harvard Law School"
  Franklin G. Fessenden, "Rebirth of the Harvard Law School," *Harvard Law Review* 33
    (1920): 493–517.
Finnegan, "Raising and Leveling the Bar"
  Dorothy E. Finnegan, "Raising and Leveling the Bar: Standards, Access, and the
    YMCA Evening Law Schools, 1890–1940," *Journal of Legal Education* 55 (2005):
    208–33.
Fleming, *William H. Welch*
  Donald Fleming, *William H. Welch and the Rise of Modern Medicine* (1954; repr.,
    Baltimore: Johns Hopkins University Press, 1987).
Flexner, *Daniel Coit Gilman*

Abraham Flexner, *Daniel Coit Gilman* (New York: Harcourt, Brace, 1946).

Ford, "Boyhood of Brandeis"
Bert Ford, "Boyhood of Brandeis," *Boston American*, 4 June 1916, 7–8.

Foster, A., to Bonaparte (17 Jan. 1984)
Alla W. Foster to Charles J. Bonaparte (17 Jan. 1984), in *Special Committee on Radcliffe Degrees Report* (7 Mar. 1894), appendix D, Harvard University Board of Overseers Records, Harvard University Archives.

Foster, J., *Ideology of Apolitical Politics*
James C. Foster, *The Ideology of Apolitical Politics: The Elite Lawyers' Response to the Legitimation Crisis in American Capitalism, 1870–1920* (New York: Associated Faculty Press, 1986).

Fox, "Professor Langdell"
Austen G. Fox, "Professor Langdell—His Personal Influence," *Harvard Law Review* 20 (1906): 7.

Francis, "Mr. John R. Jones"
Harold Francis, "Mr. John R. Jones Is at Rest," *Scranton Telegram*, 14 Dec. 1913, 4.

Frank, "Harvardizing the University"
David A. Frank, "Harvardizing the University," *Alcalde* 10 (Feb. 1923): 1807–9.

Frankfurter, "Joseph Henry Beale"
Felix Frankfurter, "Joseph Henry Beale," *Harvard Law Review* 56 (1943): 701–3.

Frankfurter to Frank (18 Dec. 1933)
Felix Frankfurter to Jerome N Frank (18 Dec. 1933) Jerome N. Frank Papers, Yale University Archives, series 2, box 12.

Fried, "Lawyer as Friend"
Charles Fried, "The Lawyer as Friend: The Moral Foundations of the Lawyer-Client Relation," *Yale Law Journal* 85 (1976): 1060–89.

Friedman, *Contract Law in America*
Lawrence M. Friedman, *Contract Law in America* (Madison: University of Wisconsin Press, 1965).

Friedman, "Formative Elements in the Law of Sales"
Lawrence M. Friedman, "Formative Elements in the Law of Sales: The Eighteenth Century," *Minnesota Law Review* 44 (1960): 411–60.

Friedman, *History of American Law*
Lawrence M. Friedman, *A History of American Law*, 2nd ed. (New York: Simon & Schuster, 1985).

Friedman and Macaulay, "Contract Law and Contract Teaching"
Lawrence M. Friedman and Stewart Macaulay, "Contract Law and Contract Teaching: Past, Present, and Future," *Wisconsin Law Review* (1967): 805–20.

Galanter and Palay, *Tournament of Lawyers*
Marc Galanter and Thomas Palay, *Tournament of Lawyers: The Transformation of the Big Law Firm* (Chicago: University of Chicago Press, 1991).

Gawalt, "Impact of Industrialization on the Legal Profession"
Gerard W. Gawalt, "The Impact of Industrialization on the Legal Profession in Massachusetts, 1870–1900," in *The New High Priests: Lawyers in Post–Civil War America*, ed. Gerard W. Gawalt, 97–123 (Westport, Conn.: Greenwood, 1984).

Gentile and Hyndman, "Guide to the William E. Russell Papers"
Richard H. Gentile and Nancy R. Hyndman, "Guide to the William E. Russell Papers, 1846–1920," unpublished typescript (1982), Massachusetts Historical Society, Boston.

Ghiselin, *Triumph of the Darwinian Method*
Michael T. Ghiselin, *The Triumph of the Darwinian Method* (Berkeley: University of California Press, 1969).

Gilman, Papers
Daniel Coit Gilman, Papers, Milton S. Eisenhower Library, Johns Hopkins University.

Gilman to Eliot (28 Feb. 1906)
Daniel Coit Gilman to Charles W. Eliot (28 Feb. 1906), Charles W. Eliot Papers, Harvard University Archives, box 214.

Gilmore, *Ages of American Law*
Grant Gilmore, *Ages of American Law* (New Haven, Conn.: Yale University Press, 1977).

Gilmore, *Death of Contract*
Grant Gilmore, *The Death of Contract* (Columbus: Ohio State University Press, 1974).

Ginzberg, "Joint Education of the Sexes"
Lori Ginzberg, "The 'Joint Education of the Sexes': Oberlin's Original Vision," in *Educating Women and Men Together: Coeducation in a Changing World*, ed. Carol Lasser, 67–81 (Urbana: University of Illinois Press, 1987).

Glazer, "Schools of the Minor Professions"
Nathan Glazer, "The Schools of the Minor Professions," *Minerva* 12 (1974): 346–64.

Gloag, "Christopher Columbus Langdell"
Ralph W. Gloag, "Christopher Columbus Langdell," *Albany Law Journal* 68 (1906): 231–33.

Goebel, *History of the School of Law, Columbia University*
Julius Goebel Jr., *A History of the School of Law, Columbia University* (New York: Columbia University Press, 1955).

Golden Branch Society, Librarian's Book [1846–49]
Golden Branch Society, Librarian's Book [1846–49], bound manuscript, Phillips Exeter Academy Archives, Exeter, N.H.

Golden Branch Society, Records 1841–50
Golden Branch Society, Records 1841–50, Phillips Exeter Academy Archives, Exeter, N.H.

Gordley, "Natural Law Origins of the Common Law of Contract"
James Gordley, "Natural Law Origins of the Common Law of Contract," in *Towards a General Law of Contract*, ed. John Barton, 367–465 (Berlin: Duncker & Humboldt, 1999).

Gordley, *Philosophical Origins of Modern Contract Doctrine*
James Gordley, *The Philosophical Origins of Modern Contract Doctrine* (Oxford: Clarendon Press, 1991).

Gordon, J., *Scarlet Woman of Wall Street*

John S. Gordon, *The Scarlet Woman of Wall Street: Jim Fisk, Jay Gould, Cornelius Vanderbilt, the Erie Railway Wars, and the Birth of Wall Street* (New York: Weidenfield & Nicholson, 1988).

Gordon, L., *Gender and Higher Education*
Lynn D. Gordon, *Gender and Higher Education in the Progressive Era* (New Haven, Conn.: Yale University Press, 1990).

Gordon, R., "Holmes's *Common Law*"
Robert W. Gordon, "Holmes's *Common Law* as Legal and Social Science," *Hofstra Law Review* 10 (1982): 719–46.

Gordon, R., "Ideal and the Actual in the Law"
Robert W. Gordon, "'The Ideal and the Actual in the Law': Fantasies and Practices of New York City Lawyers, 1870–1910," in *The New High Priests: Lawyers in Post–Civil War America*, ed. Gerard W. Gawalt, 51–74 (Westport, Conn.: Greenwood, 1984).

Gordon, R., "Law as a Vocation: Holmes and the Lawyer's Path"
Robert W. Gordon, "Law as a Vocation: Holmes and the Lawyer's Path," in *The Path of the Law and Its Influence: The Legacy of Oliver Wendell Holmes Jr.*, ed. Steven J. Burton, 7–32 (New York: Cambridge University Press, 2000).

Gordon, R., "Legal Thought and Legal Practice in the Age of American Enterprise"
Robert W. Gordon, "Legal Thought and Legal Practice in the Age of American Enterprise, 1870–1920," in *Professions and Professional Ideologies in America*, ed. Gerald L. Geison, 70–110 (Chapel Hill: University of North Carolina Press, 1983).

Gorham, Biographical File
Jason M. Gorham, Biographical File, Harvard University Archives.

Gorham, Diary
Jason M. Gorham, Diary (May 1848–Nov. 1849), bound manuscript, Harvard University Archives.

Gould, *Treatise on the Principles of Pleading*
James Gould, *Treatise on the Principles of Pleading in Civil Actions*, 4th ed. (Albany, N.Y.: W. Gould, 1876).

Grafton to Warren (28 Oct. 1907)
Charles C. Grafton to Charles Warren (28 Oct. 1907), Charles Warren Papers, Special Collections, Harvard Law School Library, box 37.

Grand Forks Herald (7 Jan. 1906)
"A Wife's Business Dealings," *Grand Forks Herald*, 7 Jan. 1906, 3.

Granger to Warren (Oct. 1907)
Moses M. Granger to Charles Warren (Oct. 1907), Charles Warren Papers, Special Collections, Harvard Law School Library, box 37.

Grant, "Art of Living"
Robert Grant, "The Art of Living," *Scribner's Magazine*, 17 (Jan., May, June 1895): 3–15, 615–27, 752–66.

Gray, "Cases and Treatises"
John C. Gray, "Cases and Treatises," *American Law Review* 22 (Sept. 1888): 756–64.

[Gray], Six Points

[John C. Gray], Six Points ([May 1878]), loose manuscript sheets, James B. Thayer
Papers, Special Collections, Harvard Law School Library, box 20.

Gray to Eliot (28 Dec. 1882)
John C. Gray to Charles W. Eliot (28 Dec. 1882), Charles W. Eliot Papers, Harvard
University Archives, box 70.

Gray to Eliot (3 Jan. 1883)
John C. Gray to Charles W. Eliot (3 Jan. 1883), Charles W. Eliot Papers, Harvard
University Archives, box 71.

Gray to Eliot (11 Mar. 1886)
John C. Gray to Charles W. Eliot (11 Mar. 1886), Charles W. Eliot Papers, Harvard
University Archives, box 74.

Gray to Thayer (date varies)
John C. Gray to James B. Thayer (1877–80), James B. Thayer Papers, Special
Collections, Harvard Law School Library, box 20.

Green, Biographical File
Nicholas St. John Green, Biographical File, Harvard University Archives.

Greene, "Women in the Law"
Mary Greene, "Women in the Law," *Woman's Journal*, 22 (14 Feb. 1891): 56.

Greenleaf, *Treatise on the Law of Evidence*
Simon Greenleaf, *A Treatise on the Law of Evidence*, 12th ed. (Boston: Little, Brown,
1866).

Gregg and Hippauf, *Birth of the Republican Party*
Hugh Gregg and Georgi Hippauf, comps., *Birth of the Republican Party: A Summary
of Historical Research on Amos Tuck and the Birthplace of the Republican Party at
Exeter, New Hampshire* (Nashua, N.H.: Resources of New Hampshire, 1995).

Grey, "Holmes on the Logic of the Law"
Thomas C. Grey, "Holmes on the Logic of the Law," in *The Path of the Law and Its
Influence: The Legacy of Oliver Wendell Holmes Jr.*, ed. Steven J. Burton, 133–57
(New York: Cambridge University Press, 2000).

Grey, "Langdell's Orthodoxy"
Thomas C. Grey, "Langdell's Orthodoxy," *University of Pittsburgh Law Review* 45
(1983): 1–53.

Griffin, "Wigglesworth Family Papers"
Katherine H. Griffin, "Wigglesworth Family Papers...A Guide to the Collection,"
unpublished typescript (1988), Massachusetts Historical Society, Boston.

Grinnell, "Unpublished Conversation with President Eliot"
Frank W. Grinnell, "An Unpublished Conversation with President Eliot at the
Beginning of Langdell's Teaching" (n.d.; typescript, 1 p.) in Christopher
Columbus Langdell, Biographical file, Harvard University Archives.

Grossberg, "Institutionalizing Masculinity: The Law as a Masculine Profession"
Michael Grossberg, "Institutionalizing Masculinity: The Law as a Masculine
Profession," in *Meanings for Manhood: Constructions of Masculinity in Victorian
America*, ed. Mark C. Carnes and Clyde Griffen, 133–51 (Chicago: University of
Chicago Press, 1990).

Grossman, "James Coolidge Carter"

Lewis A. Grossman, "James Coolidge Carter and Mugwump Jurisprudence," *Law and History Review* 20 (2002): 577–629.

Gruning, review (2001)
David Gruning, review of *Droit Anglais des Affaires*, by Oliver Moreteau, *Loyola Law Review* 47 (2001): 981–92.

Gurney to Eliot [3 Jan. 1883]
Ephraim W. Gurney to Charles W. Eliot [3 Jan. 1883], Charles W. Eliot Papers, Harvard University Archives, box 71.

Hand to Philbrick (17 Feb. 1926)
Learned Hand to Francis S. Philbrick (17 Feb. 1926), Francis S. Philbrick Papers, Harvard University Archives, box 1.

Harper, "Situation of the Small College"
William R. Harper, "The Situation of the Small College" (1900), in *The Trend in Higher Education in America* (Chicago: University of Chicago Press, 1905), 349–89.

Harrington, *Harvard Medical School: A History*
Thomas F. Harrington, *The Harvard Medical School: A History, Narrative and Documentary*, ed. James G. Mumford (New York: Lewis, 1905), 3 vols. paginated continuously.

Harvard College, Graduation Program, 1875
Harvard College, Graduation Program, 1875, "Commencement, Class Day, Exhibitions [1875]," Harvard University Archives, box 161.

Harvard College, *Monthly Returns* (date varies)
Harvard College, *Monthly Returns, Examinations, and Term Aggregates* (1848–50), Harvard University Archives.

Harvard College, "Performance for Exhibition"
Harvard College, "Performance for Exhibition" (16 Oct. 1849), Charles F. Dunbar Correspondence, Harvard University Archives.

Harvard College Class of 1851, Class Book
Harvard College Class of 1851, Class Book, Harvard University Archives.

Harvard College Class of 1851, Records
Harvard College Class of 1851, Records, Harvard University Archives.

Harvard College Class of 1877, *Secretary's Report, 1890*
Harvard College, Class of 1877, *Secretary's Report, no. 4, 1890* (Cambridge, Mass.: Riverside Press, 1890).

Harvard College Committee on Admission from Other Colleges, Papers
Harvard College, Committee on Admission from Other Colleges, Papers, Harvard University Archives.

"Harvard College Law School"
"Harvard College Law School," *Magenta*, 4 Dec. 1874, 67.

"Harvard Law School"
"Harvard Law School," *American Law Review* 13 (Oct. 1878): 159–61.

Harvard Law School, Announcements
Harvard Law School, Announcements, Tabular Views, Examination Papers 1869–91, Special Collections, Harvard Law School Library.

Harvard Law School, Annual Examinations (date varies)
    Harvard Law School, Annual Examinations: 1871–1971, Special Collections,
        Harvard Law School Library.
Harvard Law School, "Cases Argued and Determined in the Moot Court 1876–77"
    Harvard Law School, "Cases Argued and Determined in the Moot Court of Harvard
        Law School during the Academic year, 1876–77," Harvard University Archives.
Harvard Law School, *Catalog* (date varies)
    Harvard Law School, *Catalogs* (1848–1910) (Cambridge, Mass.: Harvard University,
        18–).
Harvard Law School, Faculty Meeting (18 Apr. 1893)
    Harvard Law School, Faculty Meeting with Charles W. Eliot (18 Apr. 1893),
        manuscript record, Charles W. Eliot Papers, Harvard University Archives, box
        264–265 [sic].
Harvard Law School, Faculty Minutes (date varies)
    Harvard Law School, Faculty Minutes (1870–1910), Special Collections, Harvard
        Law School Library.
Harvard Law School, Grade Records
    Harvard Law School, "Grade Records: Book of Marks," 1869–1971, Harvard
        University Archives, Cambridge, Mass., 69 vols., numbered 0–68.
Harvard Law School, *Quinquennial Catalog*
    Harvard Law School, *Quinquennial Catalog of the Law School of Harvard University,
       1817–1934*, ed. Guy H. Holliday (Cambridge, Mass.: Harvard Law School, 1934).
Harvard Law School Association, *Report* (1887)
    Harvard Law School Association, *Report of the Organization and of the First General
       Meeting, 1886* (Boston: Harvard Law School Association, 1887).
Harvard Law School Association, *Report* (1895)
    Harvard Law School Association, *Report of the Ninth Annual Meeting at Cambridge,
       June 25, 1895* (Boston: Harvard Law School Association, 1895).
"Harvard Law School Clubs"
    "Harvard Law School Clubs," *Harvard Alumni Bulletin*, 5 Feb. 1922, 441.
Harvard University, *Catalog* (date varies)
    Harvard University, *Catalog, 1848–1910* (Cambridge, Mass.: Metcalf, 18–).
Harvard University, Corporation Records (date varies)
    Harvard University, Corporation Records, Harvard University Archives.
Harvard University, Overseers Records (date varies)
    Harvard University, Board of Overseers Records, Harvard University Archives.
Harvard University, Report of the Overseers Visiting Committee (date varies)
    Harvard University, Reports of the Board of Overseers Visiting Committee to the
       Law School, 1871–84, vols. 1–3, Harvard University Board of Overseers Records,
       Academical Series II, Harvard University Archives.
Harvard University, Treasurer Report (date varies)
    Harvard University, "Annual Report of the Treasurer of Harvard College," appended
       to *Annual Reports of the President and the Treasurer of Harvard College (1876–81)*
       (Cambridge, Mass.: Harvard University, 1877–82).
Haskell, *Emergence of Professional Social Science*

Thomas L. Haskell, *The Emergence of Professional Social Science: The American Social Science Association and the Nineteenth-Century Crisis of Authority* (Urbana: University of Illinois Press, 1977).

Hathaway, "Mythical Meritocracy of Law School Admissions"
James C. Hathaway, "The Mythical Meritocracy of Law School Admissions," *Journal of Legal Education* 34 (1984): 86–96.

Hawkins, *Banding Together: The Rise of National Associations*
Hugh Hawkins, *Banding Together: The Rise of National Associations in American Higher Education* (Baltimore: Johns Hopkins University Press, 1992).

Hawkins, *Between Harvard and America*
Hugh Hawkins, *Between Harvard and America: The Educational Leadership of Charles W. Eliot* (Cambridge, Mass.: Harvard University Press, 1972).

Hawkins, *Pioneer: A History of the Johns Hopkins University*
Hugh Hawkins, *Pioneer: A History of the Johns Hopkins University, 1874–1889* (Ithaca, N.Y.: Cornell University Press, 1960).

Haynes to Langdell (10 Feb. 1870)
Robert W. Haynes to Christopher C. Langdell (10 Feb. 1870), Christopher Columbus Langdell Papers, Special Collections, Harvard Law School Library.

Haynes to Machen (10 Nov. 1874)
Robert W. Haynes to Arthur W. Machen (10 Nov. 1874), Lewis H. Machen and Family Papers, Manuscript Division, U.S. Library of Congress, Washington, D.C., box 18.

"Hearing in the Northern Securities Case"
"The Hearing in the Northern Securities Case," *The Nation*, 24 Dec. 1903, 499.

Hellmuth College, *Catalog 1871–72*
Hellmuth Ladies' College, *Catalog . . . 1871–72* (London, Ontario: Hellmuth Ladies' College, 1872).

Herrnstein, *I.Q. in the Meritocracy*
Herrnstein, Richard. *I.Q. in the Meritocracy* (Boston: Little Brown, [1973]).

Hicks, *Yale Law School: 1895–1915*
Frederick C. Hicks, *Yale Law School: 1895–1915* (New Haven, Conn.: Yale University Press, 1938).

"Higher Legal Education"
"The Higher Legal Education," *Central Law Journal* [St. Louis] 3 (1876): 540.

Hill, *Harvard College*
George B. Hill, *Harvard College by an Oxonian* (London: Macmillan, 1895).

Hilliard, *Law of Contracts*
Francis Hilliard, *The Law of Contracts*, 2 vols. (Philadelphia: Kay, 1872).

Hilliard, *Treatise on the Law of Sales*
Francis Hilliard, *A Treatise on the Law of Sales of Personal Property* (New York: Halsted and Voorhis, 1841).

History of Seneca County, Ohio
[n.a.], *History of Seneca County, Ohio* (Chicago: Warner, Beers, 1886).

Hoar, "Remarks"
E. R. Hoar, "Remarks," in *Minutes of the Suffolk County, Massachusetts Bar Meeting*

held *June 7, 1889, in memory of Peleg W. Chandler*, 10 [Boston: Suffolk County Bar
Association, 1889].

Hobson, "Symbol of the New Profession"
Wayne K. Hobson, "Symbol of the New Profession: Emergence of the Large Law
Firm, 1870–1915," in *The New High Priests: Lawyers in Post–Civil War America*, ed.
Gerard W. Gawalt, 3–27 (Westport, Conn.: Greenwood, 1984).

Hoeflich, "Law and Geometry"
Michael H. Hoeflich, "Law and Geometry: Legal Science from Leibniz to Langdell,"
American Journal of Legal History 30 (1986): 95–121.

Holden to Whiton (17 June 1869)
D. E. Holden to William H. Whiton (17 June 1869), Lord Family Papers, 1807–1961,
Special Collections, Harvard Law School Library.

Holdsworth, *History of English Law*
William Holdsworth, *A History of English Law*, ed. A. L. Goodhart and H. G.
Hanbury (London: Methuen, 1965).

Holliday to Chafee (22 Nov. 1928)
Guy H. Holliday to Zechariah Chafee Jr. (22 Nov. 1928), Zechariah Chafee Jr.
Papers, Harvard Law School Library, microfilm edition.

Holmes, N., *Journal*
Nathaniel Holmes, *Journal: A Genealogy of the Holmes Family of Londonderry, N.H.*,
[circa 1900] typescript transcribed by Marie Hedrick from the original in
Peterborough Town Library, Peterborough, New Hampshire.

Holmes, N., Papers
Nathaniel Holmes Papers, Special Collections, Harvard Law School Library.

Holmes, O., *Collected Works*
Oliver W. Holmes Jr., *The Collected Works of Justice Holmes*, ed. Sheldon M. Novick,
5 vols. (Chicago: University of Chicago Press, 1995).

Holmes, O., "Common Carriers"
Oliver W. Holmes Jr., "Common Carriers and the Common Law," *American Law
Review* 13 (1879): 609–31.

Holmes, O., *Common Law*
Oliver W. Holmes Jr., *The Common Law* (Boston: Little Brown, 1881).

[Holmes, O.], "Harvard University Law School" (1870)
[Oliver W. Holmes Jr.], "Harvard University Law School," *American Law Review* 5
(Oct. 1870): 177.

Holmes, O., *Memoir of George Otis Shattuck*
Oliver W. Holmes Jr., *Memoir of George Otis Shattuck* (Cambridge, Mass.: John
Wilson and Son, 1900).

Holmes, O., Oration 1886
Oliver W. Holmes Jr., "Oration," in *Report of the Organization and of the First General
Meeting, 1886*, Harvard Law School Association, 29–42 (Boston: Harvard Law
School Association, 1887).

Holmes, O., Oration 1895
Oliver W. Holmes Jr., Oration, in *Report of the Ninth Annual Meeting at Cambridge,
June 25, 1895*, Harvard Law School Association, 60–61 (Boston: Harvard Law
School Association, 1895).

Holmes, O., "Path of the Law"
   Oliver W. Holmes Jr., "The Path of the Law," *Harvard Law Review* 10 (1896–97):
      457–78.
[Holmes, O.], Report of Board of Overseers (9 Jan. 1878)
   [Oliver W. Holmes Jr.], "Report of Board of Overseers Visiting Committee to the
      Law School, 1877–78," Harvard Overseers Records, Harvard University Archives,
      Cambridge, Mass., Academical Series II, vol. 2 (9 Jan. 1878).
[Holmes, O.], Review (1871)
   [Oliver W. Holmes Jr.], review of *A Selection of Cases on the Law of Contracts...*, by
      Christopher C. Langdell...1870 (Part I), *American Law Review* 5 (1871): 539–40.
[Holmes, O.], Review (1872a)
   [Oliver W. Holmes Jr.], review of *A Selection of Cases on the Law of Contracts...*, by
      Christopher C. Langdell...1871, *American Law Review* 6 (1872): 353–54.
[Holmes, O.], Review (1872b)
   [Oliver W. Holmes Jr.], review of *A Selection of Cases on Sales of Personal Property...*,
      by Christopher C. Langdell...1872, *American Law Review* 7 (1872): 145–46.
[Holmes, O.], Review (1877)
   [Oliver W. Holmes Jr.], review of *A Summary of Equity Pleading*, by Christopher C.
      Langdell...1877, *American Law Review* 11 (1877): 763–64.
[Holmes, O.], Review (Mar. 1880)
   [Oliver W. Holmes Jr.], review of *A Selection of Cases on the Law of Contracts with a
      Summary...*, by Christopher C. Langdell...1879, *American Law Review* 14 (Mar.
      1880): 233–35.
[Holmes, O.], Review (Sept. 1880)
   [Oliver W. Holmes Jr.], review of *A Summary of the Law of Contracts*, by Christopher
      C. Langdell...second edition...1880, *American Law Review* 14 (Sept. 1880): 666.
[Holmes, O.], Review of *American Reports* (1871)
   [Oliver W. Holmes Jr.], review of *The American Reports*, *American Law Review* 5
      (1871): 550.
Holmes, O., to Castledown (17 Sept. 1897)
   Oliver W. Holmes Jr. to Clare Castledown (17 Sept. 1897), Oliver Wendell Holmes
      Jr. Papers, Harvard Law School Library, microfilm edition.
Holmes, O., to Einstein (date varies)
   Oliver W. Holmes Jr. to Lewis Einstein (1908), Oliver Wendell Holmes Jr. Papers,
      Harvard Law School Library, microfilm edition.
Holmes, O., to Eliot (date varies)
   Oliver W. Holmes Jr. to Charles W. Eliot (1880–81), Charles W. Eliot Papers,
      Harvard University Archives.
Holmes, O., to Gray (2 Oct. 1896)
   Oliver W. Holmes Jr. to Anna L. (Mrs. John C.) Gray (2 Oct. 1896), Oliver Wendell
      Holmes Jr. Papers, Harvard Law School Library, microfilm edition.
Holmes, O., to Hohfeld (21 Mar. 1914)
   Oliver W. Holmes Jr. to Wesley N. Hohfeld (21 Mar. 1914), Oliver Wendell Holmes
      Jr. Papers, Harvard Law School Library, microfilm edition.

Holmes, O., to Langdell (3 Mar. 1877)
Oliver W. Holmes Jr. to Christopher C. Langdell (3 Mar. 1877), Oliver Wendell Holmes Jr. Papers, Harvard Law School Library, microfilm edition.

Holmes, O., to Pollock (date varies)
Oliver W. Holmes Jr. to Frederick Pollock (1881–1904), Oliver Wendell Holmes Jr. Papers, Harvard Law School Library, microfilm edition.

Honnold and Reitz, *Sales Transactions*
John O. Honnold and Curtis R. Reitz, *Sales Transactions: Domestic and International Law: Cases, Problems, and Materials*, 2nd ed. (New York: Foundation Press, 2001).

Hook, "Brief Life of James Bradley Thayer"
Jay Hook, "A Brief Life of James Bradley Thayer," *Northwestern University Law Review* 88 (1993): 1–8.

Horowitz, *Campus Life*
Helen Lefkowitz Horowitz, *Campus Life: Undergraduate Cultures from the End of the Eighteenth Century to the Present* (1987; repr., Chicago: University of Chicago Press, 1990).

Horwitz, Review
Morton J. Horwitz, review of *Ages of American Law*, by Grant Gilmore, *Buffalo Law Review* 27 (1978): 47–53.

Horwitz, *Transformation of American Law, 1870–1960*
Morton J. Horwitz, *The Transformation of American Law, 1870–1960: The Crisis of Legal Orthodoxy* (New York: Oxford University Press, 1992).

Howe, "First Law School Lecture"
Mark De Wolfe Howe, "The First Law School Lecture of James Bradley Thayer," *Journal of Legal Education* 2 (1949): 1–23.

Howe, *Justice Oliver Wendell Holmes*
Mark De Wolfe Howe, *Justice Oliver Wendell Holmes*, vol. 2, *The Proving Years, 1870–1882* (Cambridge, Mass.: Harvard University Press, 1963).

Hunter, *How Young Ladies Became Girls*
Jane E. Hunter, *How Young Ladies Became Girls: The Victorian Origins of American Girlhood* (New Haven, Conn.: Yale University Press, 2002).

Hurst, *Growth of American Law*
James Willard Hurst, *The Growth of American Law: The Law Makers* (Boston: Little, Brown, 1950).

Hurst, *Law and the Conditions of Freedom*
James Willard Hurst, *Law and the Conditions of Freedom in the Nineteenth Century* (Madison: University of Wisconsin Press, 1950).

Husén, *Talent, Equality and Meritocracy*
Torsten Husén, *Talent, Equality and Meritocracy: Availability and Utilization of Talent* (The Hague: Martinus Nijhoff, 1974).

Huson, Will and Probate Papers (5 Sept. 1907)
Margaret E. Huson, Will and Probate Papers, filed 5 Sept. 1907, Middlesex County Courthouse, Cambridge, Mass. (no. 75545).

Jagemann to Eliot (6 Nov. 1899)

Hans C. G. von Jagemann to Charles W. Eliot (6 Nov. 1899), Charles W. Eliot
Papers, Harvard University Archives, box 114.

James, *Bostonians*
Henry James, *The Bostonians* (New York: Macmillan, 1886).

James, *Charles W. Eliot*
Henry James, *Charles W. Eliot: President of Harvard University, 1869–1909*, 2 vols.
(Boston: Houghton Mifflin, 1930).

Jencks and Riesman, *Academic Revolution*
Christopher Jencks and David Riesman, *The Academic Revolution* (Chicago:
University of Chicago Press, 1968).

Johnson, *Schooled Lawyers*
William R. Johnson, *Schooled Lawyers: A Study in the Clash of Professional Cultures*
(New York: New York University Press, 1978).

Johnston, and Savoy, *Statistical Records, Town of New Boston*
Lisa Johnston and William Savoy, *Statistical Records, Town of New Boston, New
Hampshire . . . through 1894* (New Boston, N.H.: [privately printed], 1994).

Jones, Diary
John R. Jones, Diary and Class Notes of a Harvard Law School Student, 1876–77,
Special Collections, Harvard Law School Library.

Kahlenberg, *Broken Contract*
Richard D. Kahlenberg, *Broken Contract: A Memoir of Harvard Law School* (Amherst:
University of Massachusetts Press, [1999]).

Kalman, *Legal Realism at Yale*
Laura Kalman, *Legal Realism at Yale, 1927–1960* (Chapel Hill: University of North
Carolina Press, 1986).

Kansas State Historical Society, *Transactions 1905–1906*
Kansas State Historical Society, *Transactions . . . 1905–1906* (Topeka, State Printer,
1906).

Karabel, *Chosen: The Hidden History of Admission and Exclusion*
Jerome Karabel, *The Chosen: The Hidden History of Admission and Exclusion at
Harvard, Yale and Princeton* (Boston: Houghton Mifflin, 2005).

Kaufman, *Women Teachers on the Frontier*
Polly Welts Kaufman, ed. *Women Teachers on the Frontier* (New Haven, Conn.: Yale
University Press, 1984).

KCon71
William A. Keener, annotated copy of Christopher C. Langdell, *A Selection of
Cases on the Law of Contracts* (Boston: Little, Brown, 1871), Special Collections,
University of Virginia Law Library.

Keasbey, "Origin and Nature of Consideration"
Edward Q. Keasbey, "The Origin and Nature of Consideration in the Law of
Contract," *New Jersey Law Journal* 6 (1883): 296–335.

Keay to Irwin (date varies)
Frances Keay to Agnes Irwin (1898–99), Correspondence and Papers of the Council
of Radcliffe College, Radcliffe College Archives, Harvard University, folder
"Papers re Admission to Law School."

Keener to Eliot (date varies)
>   William A. Keener to Charles W. Eliot (1882–83), Charles W. Eliot Papers, Harvard University Archives, boxes 70, 71.

Kelley, N., Reminiscences
>   Nicholas Kelley, Reminiscences, 1952–53, Transcript of Interviews Conducted by Wendell Link, Columbia University Oral History Collection, Lamont Library, Harvard University, microfiche W 286, no. 101.

Kelley, P., "Critical Analysis of Holmes"
>   Patrick J. Kelley, "A Critical Analysis of Holmes's Theory of Contract," *Notre Dame Law Review* 75 (2000): 1681–1773.

Kelley, P., "Holmes, Langdell, and Formalism"
>   Patrick J. Kelley, "Holmes, Langdell, and Formalism," *Ratio Juris* 15 (2002): 26–51.

Kennedy, "How the Law School Fails"
>   Duncan Kennedy, "How the Law School Fails: A Polemic," *Yale Review of Law and Social Action* 1 (1970): 71–90.

Kennedy, "Toward an Historical Understanding of Legal Consciousness"
>   Duncan Kennedy, "Toward an Historical Understanding of Legal Consciousness: The Case of Classical Legal Thought in America, 1850–1940," *Research in Law and Sociology* 3 (1980): 3–24.

Kent, *Commentaries on American Law*
>   James Kent, *Commentaries on American Law*, 4 vols. (New York: O. Halsted, 1826–30).

Kiddle and Schem, *Cyclopaedia of Education*
>   Henry Kiddle and Alexander J. Schem, eds. *The Cyclopaedia of Education* (New York: E. Steiger, 1877).

Kimball, "Langdell on Contracts and Legal Reasoning"
>   Bruce A. Kimball, "Langdell on Contracts and Legal Reasoning: Revising the Holmesian Caricature," *Law & History Review* 25 (2007): 345–99.

Kimball, "Langdell Problem"
>   Bruce A. Kimball, "The Langdell Problem: Historicizing the Century of Historiography, 1906–2000s," *Law & History Review* 22 (2004): 277–337.

Kimball, "Law Students' Choices and Experience"
>   Bruce A. Kimball, "Law Students' Choices and Experience during the Transition to Competitive Academic Achievement, 1876–1882," *Journal of Legal Education* 55 (2005): 163–207.

Kimball, "Paradox"
>   Bruce A. Kimball, "The Paradox of Prejudicially Applying Valid Academic Standards: A Historical Case Study in the Ethics of Academic Administration," in *Ethical Challenges in Academic Administration*, ed. Elaine Englehardt, Michael S. Pritchard, Kerry Romesburg, and Brian E. Schrag (New York: Springer, forthcoming).

Kimball, "Principle, Politics, and Finances"
>   Bruce A. Kimball, "The Principle, Politics, and Finances of Introducing Academic Merit as the Standard of Hiring for 'the teaching of law *as a career*,' 1870–1900," *Law & Social Inquiry* 31 (2006): 617–48.

Kimball, "Proliferation of Case Method"
  Bruce A. Kimball, "The Proliferation of Case Method Teaching in American Law
    Schools: Mr. Langdell's Emblematic 'Abomination,' 1890–1915," *History of
    Education Quarterly* 46 (2006): 192–247.
Kimball, *True Professional Ideal*
  Bruce A. Kimball, *The "True Professional Ideal" in America, A History* (Oxford: Basil
    Blackwell, 1992).
Kimball, *"Warn Students That I Entertain Heretical Opinions"*
  Bruce A. Kimball, *"Warn Students That I Entertain Heretical Opinions, Which
    They Are Not to Take as Law'*: The Inception of Case Method Teaching in the
    Classrooms of the Early C. C. Langdell, 1870–1883," *Law & History Review* 17
    (1999): 57–140.
Kimball, "Young Christopher Langdell"
  Bruce A. Kimball, "Young Christopher Langdell: The Formation of an Educational
    Reformer 1826–1854," *Journal of Legal Education* 52 (June 2002): 189–239.
Kimball and Brown, "Highest Legal Ability"
  Bruce A. Kimball and R. Blake Brown, "'The Highest Legal Ability in the Nation':
    Langdell on Wall Street, 1855–1870," *Law & Social Inquiry* 29 (2004): 39–104.
Kimball and Reyes, "First Modern Civil Procedure Course"
  Bruce A. Kimball and Pedro Reyes, "The 'First Modern Civil Procedure Course,' as
    Taught by C. C. Langdell, 1870–78," *American Journal of Legal History* 47 (2005):
    257–303.
Kimball and Shapiro, Finding Guide
  Bruce A. Kimball and Molly McGinn Shapiro, Finding Guide to the Papers of
    Christopher Columbus Langdell (1826–1906), Harvard Law School Library,
    Special Collections (2004), 40 pp.
Kimball and Shull, "Ironical Exclusion of Women"
  Bruce A. Kimball and Brian S. Shull, "The Ironical Exclusion of Women from
    Harvard Law School, 1870–1900," *Journal of Legal Education* 58 (2008): 3–31.
Kirkwood and Owens, "Brief History of the Stanford Law School"
  Marion R. Kirkwood and William B. Owens, "A Brief History of the Stanford Law
    School, 1893–1946" (unpublished typescript, Stanford Law School Library, Mar.
    1961).
Klitgaard, *Elitism and Meritocracy in Developing Countries*
  Robert Klitgaard, *Elitism and Meritocracy in Developing Countries: Selection Policies for
    Higher Education* (Baltimore: Johns Hopkins University Press, 1986).
Konefsky and Schlegel, "Mirror, Mirror on the Wall"
  Alfred S. Konefsky and John Henry Schlegel, "Mirror, Mirror on the Wall: Histories
    of American Law Schools," *Harvard Law Review* 95 (1982): 833–51.
Lafferty, "Founding of the College of Law of the University of Kentucky"
  W. T. Lafferty, "The Founding of the College of Law of the University of Kentucky,"
    Kentucky Law Journal 11 (1923): 51–58.
Landis, "Mr. Justice Brandeis"
  J. M. Landis, "Mr. Justice Brandeis and the Harvard Law School," *Harvard Law
    Review* 55 (41): 184–86.

Langdell, Address 1886
> Christopher C. Langdell, Address, in *Report of the Organization and of the First General Meeting, 1886*, Harvard Law School Association, 49–50 (Boston: Harvard Law School Association, 1887).

Langdell, Address 1895
> Christopher C. Langdell, Address, in *Report of the Ninth Annual Meeting at Cambridge, June 25, 1895*, Harvard Law School Association, 41–48 (Boston: Harvard Law School Association, 1895).

Langdell, Annual Report (date varies)
> Christopher C. Langdell, "[Annual Report of the Dean of] the Law School," in *Annual Reports of the President and Treasurer of Harvard College* (1870–95) (Cambridge, Mass.: Harvard University Press, 18—).

Langdell, *Brief Survey of Equity Jurisdiction* (1905)
> Christopher C. Langdell, *A Brief Survey of Equity Jurisdiction, being a series of articles reprinted from the Harvard Law Review* (Cambridge, Mass.: Harvard Law Review Association, 1905), comprising *Harvard Law Review* 1 (1888): 55–72, 111–31, 355–87; 2 (1889): 241–67; 3 (1890): 237–62; 4 (1891): 99–127; 5 (1892): 101–38; 10 (1897): 71–97.

Langdell, *Brief Survey of Equity Jurisdiction* (1908)
> Christopher C. Langdell, *A Brief Survey of Equity Jurisdiction, being a series of articles reprinted from the Harvard Law Review* (Cambridge, Mass.: Harvard Law Review Association, 1908), combining Langdell, *A Brief Survey of Equity Jurisdiction* (1905), and Langdell, "Equitable Conversion," *Harvard Law Review* 18 (1904): 1–22, 83–104, 245–70; 19 (1905): 1–29, 79–96, 233–49, 321–34.

Langdell, *Cases in Equity Pleading* (1875)
> Christopher C. Langdell, *Cases in Equity Pleading, Selected with Special Reference to the Subject of Discovery . . . [Part I]* (Cambridge, Mass.: Printed for the Author, [1875]).

Langdell, *Cases in Equity Pleading* (1876)
> Christopher C. Langdell, *Cases in Equity Pleading . . . Part II* (Cambridge, Mass.: Printed for the Author [by the Press of John Wilson], 1876).

Langdell, *Cases in Equity Pleading* (1878)
> Christopher C. Langdell, *Cases in Equity Pleading, Selected with Special Reference to the Subject of Discovery . . . [Part I]* and *[Part II]* (Cambridge, Mass.: Printed for the Author, 1878).

Langdell, *Cases on Contracts* (1870)
> Christopher C. Langdell, *A Selection of Cases on the Law of Contracts* (Boston: Little, Brown, 1870).

Langdell, *Cases on Contracts* (1871)
> Christopher C. Langdell, *A Selection of Cases on the Law of Contracts* (Boston: Little, Brown, 1871).

Langdell, *Cases on Contracts* (1879)
> Christopher C. Langdell, *A Selection of Cases on the Law of Contracts with a Summary of the Topics Covered by the Cases*, 2nd ed. (Boston: Little, Brown, 1879), 1 vol. in 2 parts, with a summary appended.

Langdell, *Cases on Equity Jurisdiction* (1879)
    Christopher C. Langdell, *Cases on Equity Jurisdiction* ([Cambridge]: [1879–80?]),
        missing front pages and including parts 1–5.
Langdell, *Cases on Equity Jurisdiction* (1883)
    Christopher C. Langdell, *Cases on Equity Jurisdiction* ([Cambridge, Mass.: [1879–
        83?]), missing front pages and including parts 1–5, plus pp. 242–369.
Langdell, *Cases on Sales* (1872)
    Christopher C. Langdell, *A Selection of Cases on Sales of Personal Property*, vol. 1
        (Boston: Little, Brown, 1872).
Langdell, Check Ledger 1871–75
    Christopher C. Langdell, Check Ledger, 1871–75, Christopher Columbus Langdell
        Papers, Special Collections, Harvard Law School Library.
Langdell, "Civil Procedure"
    Christopher C. Langdell, "Civil Procedure at Common Law, 1871–76," 4 manuscript
        notebooks, Special Collections, Harvard Law School Library.
Langdell, "Classification of Rights and Wrongs"
    Christopher C. Langdell, "Classification of Rights and Wrongs," *Harvard Law Review*
        13 (1900): 537–56, 659–78.
Langdell, "Creation and Transfer of Shares"
    Christopher C. Langdell, "The Creation and Transfer of Shares in Incorporated
        Joint-Stock Companies," *Harvard Law Review* 11 (1898): 536–38.
Langdell, "Discovery under the Judicature Acts of 1873, 1875"
    Christopher C. Langdell, "Discovery under the Judicature Acts of 1873, 1875,"
        Harvard Law Review 11 (1897): 137–57, 205–19; 12 (1898): 151–75.
Langdell, "Dominant Opinion in England"
    Christopher C. Langdell, "Dominant Opinion in England during the Nineteenth
        Century in Relation to Legislation . . . ," *Harvard Law Review* 19 (1906): 151–67.
Langdell, "Equitable Conversion"
    Christopher C. Langdell, "Equitable Conversion," *Harvard Law Review* 18 (1904):
        1–22, 83–104, 245–70; 19 (1905): 1–29, 79–96, 233–49, 321–34.
Langdell, *Forms of Procedure*
    Christopher C. Langdell, *Forms of Procedure in the Court of King's Bench* (Cambridge,
        Mass.: Wilson [circa 1875]).
Langdell, "Harvard Celebratory Speeches"
    Christopher C. Langdell, "Harvard Celebratory Speeches: Professor Langdell," *Law
        Quarterly Review* 9 (1887): 123–25.
Langdell, "Harvard Law School, 1869–1894"
    Christopher C. Langdell, "The Harvard Law School, 1869–1894," *Harvard Graduates'
        Magazine*, 2 (June 1894): 490–98.
Langdell, "Lecture Notes in Suretyship Class, 1892–93"
    Christopher C. Langdell, "Lecture Notes taken by an Unidentified Student in
        Suretyship Class taught by C. C. Langdell in 1892–93," Special Collections,
        Harvard Law School Library.
Langdell, "Memoranda Concerning Law School Students"
    Christopher C. Langdell, "Memoranda Concerning Law School Students, Sept.

1870 to July 1873," bound manuscript, Special Collections, Harvard Law School Library.

Langdell, Memorandum on Admitting Women to the Law School (30 Sept. 1899)
Christopher C. Langdell, Memorandum on Admitting Women to the Law School (30 Sept. 1899), Charles W. Eliot Papers, Harvard University Archives, box 268–69 [*sic*].

Langdell, Memorial for George Arnold (circa Dec. 1893)
Christopher C. Langdell, Memorial for George Arnold (circa Dec. 1893), one manuscript sheet, in Charles W. Eliot Papers, Harvard University Archives, box 130.

Langdell, "Mutual Promises as a Consideration for Each Other"
Christopher C. Langdell, "Mutual Promises as a Consideration for Each Other," *Harvard Law Review* 14 (1901): 496–508.

Langdell, Northern Securities I
Christopher C. Langdell, "The Northern Securities Case and the Sherman Anti-Trust Act," *Harvard Law Review* 16 (1903): 539–54.

Langdell, Northern Securities II
Christopher C. Langdell, "The Northern Securities Case under a New Aspect," *Harvard Law Review* 17 (1903): 41–44.

Langdell, "Northern Securities Case"
Christopher C. Langdell, "The Northern Securities Case and the Sherman Anti-Trust Case," *Railway World*, 29 (1903): 847, 850–52, 875, 878–79.

Langdell, Lectures on Partnership and Commercial Paper
Christopher C. Langdell, Lectures on Partnership and Commercial Paper (1870–71), 2 manuscript notebooks, Special Collections, Harvard Law School Library.

Langdell, Papers
Christopher Columbus Langdell, Papers, Special Collections, Harvard Law School Library.

Langdell, "Patent Rights and Copy Rights"
Christopher C. Langdell, "Patent Rights and Copy Rights," *Harvard Law Review* 12 (1899): 553–56.

Langdell, "Status of Our New Territories"
Christopher C. Langdell, "The Status of Our New Territories," *Harvard Law Review* 12 (1899): 365–92.

Langdell, *Summary of Equity Pleading* (1877)
Christopher C. Langdell, *A Summary of Equity Pleading* (Cambridge, Mass.: Charles W. Sever, 1877).

Langdell, *Summary of Equity Pleading* (1883)
Christopher C. Langdell, *A Summary of Equity Pleading*, 2nd ed. (Cambridge, Mass.: Charles W. Sever, 1883).

Langdell, *Summary of the Law of Contracts*
Christopher C. Langdell, *A Summary of the Law of Contracts* (Boston: Little, Brown, 1880).

Langdell, Will and Probate Papers (1906)

Christopher C. Langdell, Will and Probate Papers, filed Jan.– Sept. 1906, Middlesex
County Courthouse, Cambridge, Mass. (no. 71864).

Langdell to Cogswell (22 June 1863)
Christopher C. Langdell to E. C. Cogswell (22 June 1863), in *History of New Boston,
New Hampshire*, ed. Elliott C. Cogswell, 250 (Boston: Ran, Avery, Cornhill, 1864).

Langdell to Day (26 Jan. 1871)
Christopher C. Langdell to Henry Day (26 Jan. 1871), Lord Family Papers, 1807–
1961, Special Collections, Harvard Law School Library.

Langdell to Eliot (date varies)
Christopher C. Langdell to Charles W. Eliot (1869–1905), Charles W. Eliot Papers,
Harvard University Archives, boxes 67, 82, 130, 225, 264–65 [*sic*].

Langdell to Haynes (5 May 1901)
Christopher C. Langdell to Henry W. Haynes (5 May 1901), Harvard College Class
of 1851, Manuscript Class Book, Harvard University Archives, 532.

Langdell to Machen (date varies)
Christopher C. Langdell to Arthur W. Machen (1856–84), Lewis H. Machen and
Family Papers, Manuscript Division, U.S. Library of Congress, Washington, D.C.,
boxes 17, 18.

Langdell to Parker (21 July 1881)
Christopher C. Langdell to Edmund M. Parker (21 July 1881), Joel Parker Papers,
1848–1939, Massachusetts Historical Society, Boston, box 2.

Langdell to Shattuck (date varies)
Christopher C. Langdell to George O. Shattuck (1856–60), Peleg W. Chandler
and George O. Shattuck Papers, New England Lawyers Collection, Historical
Collections, Harvard Business School Library, case 2.

Langdell to Thayer (24 July 1878)
Christopher C. Langdell to James B. Thayer (24 July 1878), James B. Thayer Papers,
Special Collections, Harvard Law School Library, box 20.

Langdell to Wambaugh (26 Mar. 1892)
Christopher C. Langdell to Eugene Wambaugh (26 Mar. 1892), Charles W. Eliot
Papers, Harvard University Archives, box 82.

Langdell to Webster (date varies)
Christopher C. Langdell to Joseph R. Webster (1856–80), Christopher Columbus
Langdell Papers, Special Collections, Harvard Law School Library.

Langdell to Whiton (date varies)
Christopher C. Langdell to William H. Whiton (1869–71), Lord Family Papers,
1807–1961, Special Collections, Harvard Law School Library.

Langdell to Wier (28 Feb. 1897)
Christopher C. Langdell to Miss Wier (28 Feb. 1897), Charles W. Eliot Papers,
Harvard University Archives, box 130.

Langdell to Woolsey (6 Feb. 1871)
Christopher C. Langdell to Timothy D. Woolsey (6 Feb. 1871), Theodore Dwight
Woolsey Papers Yale University Archives, box 23.

Langdell and Lord, "Surrogate Court" (24 July 1869)
Christopher C. Langdell and George D. Lord, "Surrogate Court . . . In the matter of

the Last Will and Testament of Rufus L. Lord, Dec." (24 July 1869), Lord Family
  Papers, 1807–1961, Special Collections, Harvard Law School Library.
Langdell and Porter, "Petition of Eleazar Lord" (28 June 1869)
  Christopher C. Langdell and J. K. Porter, "Petition of Eleazar Lord, to Surrogate
    Court of County of New York" (28 June 1869), Eleazar Lord Papers, Special
    Collections, Harvard Law School Library.
Langdell, M., *Journey through the Years*
  Marion E. Langdell, *A Journey through the Years* (Cudahy, Wis.: [privately printed],
    1978).
LaPiana, "Just the Facts: The Field Code and the Case Method"
  William P. LaPiana, "Just the Facts: The Field Code and the Case Method," *New York
    Law School Law Review* 36 (1991): 287–336.
LaPiana, "Langdell Laughs"
  William P. LaPiana, "Langdell Laughs," *Law & History Review* 17 (1999): 141.
LaPiana, *Logic and Experience*
  William P. LaPiana, *Logic and Experience: The Origin of Modern American Legal
    Education* (New York: Oxford University Press, 1994).
Lasser, ed., *Educating Women and Men Together*
  Carol Lasser, ed., *Educating Women and Men Together: Coeducation in a Changing
    World* (Urbana: University of Illinois Press, 1987).
Laurie, *Artisans into Workers: Labor in Nineteenth-Century America*
  Bruce Laurie, *Artisans into Workers: Labor in Nineteenth-Century America* (New York:
    Noonday Press, 1989).
"Law School" (1892)
  "The Law School," *Harvard Law Review* 6 (1892): 150.
"Law School of Harvard College" (Oct. 1870–71)
  "The Law School of Harvard College," *American Law Review* 5 (Oct. 1870–71): 563.
LCon70
  Christopher C. Langdell, annotated copy of Christopher C. Langdell, *A Selection of
    Cases on the Law of Contracts* (Boston: Little, Brown, 1870), Special Collections,
    Harvard Law School Library.
Leake, *Elements of the Law of Contracts*
  Stephen M. Leake, *The Elements of the Law of Contracts*, 1st ed. (London: Stevens
    and Sons, 1867).
Lee to Eliot (15 Mar. 1897)
  Blewett Lee to Charles W. Eliot (15 Mar. 1897), Charles W. Eliot Papers, Harvard
    University Archives, box 139A.
Lee to Philbrick (18 Feb. 1926)
  Blewett Lee to Francis S. Philbrick (18 Feb. 1926), Francis S. Philbrick Papers,
    Harvard University Archives, box 1.
Lee to Thayer (30 Jan. 1894)
  Blewett Lee to James B. Thayer (30 Jan. 1894), James B. Thayer Papers, Special
    Collections, Harvard Law School Library, box 17.
Lemann, *Big Test: The Secret History of the American Meritocracy*

Nicholas Lemann, *The Big Test: The Secret History of the American Meritocracy* (New York: Farrar, Straus and Giroux, 1999).

LEq75

Christopher C. Langdell, annotated copy of Christopher C. Langdell, *Cases in Equity Pleading, Selected with Special Reference to the Subject of Discovery . . . [Part I]* (Cambridge, Mass.: Printed for the Author, [1875]), Special Collections, Harvard Law School Library.

Lerman, *Meritocracy without Rising Inequality*

Robert Lerman, *Meritocracy without Rising Inequality: Wage Rate Differences Are Widening by Education and Narrowing by Gender and Race* (Washington D.C.: Urban Institute, 1997).

Lerner, "From Popular Control to Independence: Reform of the Elected Judiciary"

Renee Lettow Lerner, "From Popular Control to Independence: Reform of the Elected Judiciary in Boss Tweed's New York," *George Mason Law Review* 15 (2007): 109–160.

Letwin, *Law and Economic Policy in America: The Evolution of the Sherman Antitrust Act*

William Letwin, *Law and Economic Policy in America: The Evolution of the Sherman Antitrust Act* (New York: Random House, 1965).

Levinson, "Canon(s) of Constitutional Law"

Sanford Levinson, "The Canon(s) of Constitutional Law: Why the Canon Should Be Expanded to Include the Insular Cases and the Saga of American Expansionism," *Constitutional Commentary* 17 (2000): 241–328.

Lewis, *Great American Lawyers*

William D. Lewis, ed., *Great American Lawyers*, 8 vols. (Philadelphia: John C. Winston, 1907).

Lewis, *W. E. B. Du Bois*

David L. Lewis, *W. E. B. Du Bois: Biography of a Race, 1868–1919* (New York: H. Holt, 1993).

Lind, "Economic Analysis of Early Casebook Publishing"

Douglas W. Lind, "An Economic Analysis of Early Casebook Publishing," *Library Law Journal* 96 (2004–6): 95–126.

Little, Brown, Papers

Little, Brown, Co., Papers, Houghton Library, Harvard University.

Llewellyn, "Across Sales on Horseback"

Karl N. Llewellyn, "Across Sales on Horseback," *Harvard Law Review* 52 (1939): 725–46.

Llewellyn, *Common Law Tradition*

Karl N. Llewellyn, *The Common Law Tradition: Deciding Appeals* (Boston: Little, Brown, 1960).

Llewellyn, "First Struggle to Unhorse Sales"

Karl N. Llewellyn, "The First Struggle to Unhorse Sales," *Harvard Law Review* 52 (1939): 873–904.

Locke, *Some Thoughts Concerning Education*

John Locke, *Some Thoughts Concerning Education*; and, *Of the Conduct of the Understanding* (Indianapolis: Hackett, 1996).

Logan, "Supreme Court in the Northern Securities Case"
  Walter S. Logan, "The Supreme Court in the Northern Securities Case," *Arena* 31
    (1904): 473.
Long to Warren (7 Oct. 1907)
  John W. Long to Charles Warren (7 Oct. 1907), Charles Warren Papers, Special
    Collections, Harvard Law School Library, box 37.
Lord to Lord (18, 20, 24 May 1869)
  Letters between Eleazar Lord and Thomas and David Lord (18, 20, 24 May 1869),
    Lord Family Papers, 1807–1961, Special Collections, Harvard Law School Library.
Lothrop to Warren (1 Oct. 1907)
  Thornton K. Lothrop to Charles Warren (1 Oct. 1907), Charles Warren Papers,
    Special Collections, Harvard Law School Library, box 37.
Lowell, Annual Report (date varies)
  Abbott L. Lowell, *Annual Reports of the President and Treasurer of Harvard College,
    1909–1932* (Cambridge, Mass.: Harvard University Press, 1910–33).
Lowell, "Colonial Expansion of the United States"
  Abbott L. Lowell, "The Colonial Expansion of the United States," *Atlantic Monthly*,
    Feb. 1899, 145–55.
Lowell, "Status of Our New Possessions"
  Abbott L. Lowell, "The Status of Our New Possessions—A Third View," *Harvard Law
    Review* 13 (1899–1900): 155–76.
Lowell Daily Citizen and News (3 Mar. 1873)
  "The Commonwealth Understands," *Lowell Daily Citizen and News*, 3 Mar. 1873, 1.
Ludmerer, *Learning to Heal*
  Kenneth Ludmerer, *Learning to Heal: The Development of American Medical Education*
    (Baltimore: Johns Hopkins University Press, 1985).
Lurie, *Louis Agassiz*
  Edward Lurie, *Louis Agassiz: A Life in Science* (1960; repr., Baltimore: Johns Hopkins
    University Press, 1988).
Mack, Criminal Law 1880–81
  Alfred Mack, Criminal Law 1880–81, in Mack, Class Notebooks, 1880–83, 4 bound
    notebooks, Special Collections, Harvard Law School Library.
Mack, Suretyship Fall 1883
  Alfred Mack, Suretyship Fall 1883, in Mack, Class Notebooks, 1880–83, 4 bound
    notebooks, Special Collections, Harvard Law School Library.
Mack, Wills 1882–83
  Alfred Mack, Wills 1882–83, in Mack, Class Notebooks, 1880–83, 4 bound
    notebooks, Special Collections, Harvard Law School Library.
MacMahon, "Dicey at Harvard Law School"
  Paul MacMahon, "Dicey at Harvard Law School: A Comparative Study in the
    Development of Legal Education" (unpublished paper, Daniel R. Coquillette's
    Legal Education Seminar, Harvard Law School, Cambridge, Mass., spring 2006).
Madden, *Chauncey Wright*
  Edward H. Madden, *Chauncey Wright and the Foundations of Pragmatism* (Seattle:
    University of Washington Press, 1963).

Mahoney, *Catholic Higher Education in Protestant America*
　　Kathleen A. Mahoney, *Catholic Higher Education in Protestant America: The Jesuits and Harvard in the Age of the University* (Baltimore: Johns Hopkins University Press, 2003).
Mahoney, Complete Primary Source
　　Kathleen A. Mahoney, Complete Primary Source Summary related to the Law School Controversy, typescript on file [circa 2000]. Some letters are translated from Latin. On file with author.
Mahoney, Correspondence
　　Kathleen A. Mahoney, "Correspondence related to the Law School Controversy," Appendix D in Mahoney, "Modernity and the Education of American Catholics: Charles W. Eliot, Harvard Law School, and the Jesuits" (Ph.D. diss., University of Rochester, 1995).
Main, "Naming Children in Early New England"
　　Gloria L. Main, "Naming Children in Early New England," *Journal of Interdisciplinary History* 27 (1996): 1–27.
Mandelbaum, *Boss Tweed's New York*
　　Seymour J. Mandelbaum, *Boss Tweed's New York* (New York: John Wiley, 1965).
"Margaret Ellen Langdell"
　　"Mrs. Margaret Ellen [Huson] Langdell," *Bulletin of the Phillips Exeter Academy*, Mar. 1908, 20–21.
Marshall Law Club, Record Book 1860–76
　　Marshall Law Club, Record Book 1860–76, Special Collections, Harvard Law School Library.
Martin, A., *Civil Procedure at Common Law*
　　Alexander Martin, *Civil Procedure at Common Law* (Boston: Boston Book, 1899).
Martin, E., *Life of Joseph Hodges Choate*
　　Edward S. Martin, *The Life of Joseph Hodges Choate [1832–1917] . . . Including His Own Story of His Boyhood and Youth*, 2 vols. (New York: C. Scribner's, 1920).
Martin, G., *Causes and Conflicts*
　　George Martin, *Causes and Conflicts: The Centennial History of the Association of the Bar of the City of New York, 1870–1970* (1970; repr., New York: Fordham University Press, 1997).
Marvin, *Legal Bibliography, or a Thesaurus of Law Books*
　　John Gage Marvin, *Legal Bibliography, or a Thesaurus of American, English, Irish, and Scotch Law Books* (Philadelphia: T. & J. W. Johnson, 1847).
Maury, *Collections*
　　William A. Maury, *The Collections and Recollections of William A. Maury*, ed. Alice M. Parmalee (Washington, D.C.: [privately printed], 1938).
May, *History of the University of Rochester*
　　Arthur J. May, *A History of the University of Rochester, 1850–1962*, ed. Lawrence E. Klein (Rochester, N.Y.: University of Rochester, 1977).
[McCormick] Presbyterian Seminary, *General Catalog*
　　[McCormick] Presbyterian Theological Seminary, *General Catalog* (Chicago: Presbyterian Theological Seminary, 1939).

McFarland, "Partisan of Nonpartisanship: Dorman B. Eaton"
Gerald W. McFarland, "Partisan of Nonpartisanship: Dorman B. Eaton and the
Genteel Reform Tradition," *Journal of American History* 54 (1968): 806–22.

McIntyre, "Percentage of College-Bred Men in the Medical Profession"
Charles McIntyre, "The Percentage of College-Bred Men in the Medical Profession,"
The Medical Record 22 (16 Dec. 1882): 682.

McManamon, "History of the Civil Procedure Course"
Mary B. McManamon, "The History of the Civil Procedure Course: A Study in
Evolving Pedagogy," *Arizona State Law Journal* 30 (1998): 397–440.

McNamee and Miller, *Meritocracy Myth*
Stephen J. McNamee and Robert K. Miller Jr., *The Meritocracy Myth* (New York:
Rowman & Littlefield, 2004).

Meade, *Judah P. Benjamin*
Robert D. Meade, *Judah P. Benjamin, Confederate Statesman* (London: Oxford
University Press, 1943).

Menken, "Methods of Instruction at American Law Schools"
S. Stanwood Menken, "Methods of Instruction at American Law Schools. II.
Columbia College, in the City of New York," *Columbia Law Times* 6 (1893):
168–70.

Metcalf, *Principles of the Law of Contracts*
Theron Metcalf, *Principles of the Law of Contracts: As Applied By Courts of Law* (New
York: Hurd and Houghton, 1867; repr., Cambridge, Mass.: Riverside Press, 1874).

Millar, *Civil Procedure of the Trial Court*
Robert W. Millar, *Civil Procedure of the Trial Court in Historical Perspective* (New
York: Law Center of New York University for the National Conference of Judicial
Councils, 1952).

Miller, "Feminization of American Literary Theory"
Elise Miller, "The Feminization of American Literary Theory," *American Literary
Realism* 23 (1990): 20–39.

Milton, *Poetical Works*
John Milton, *The Poetical Works of John Milton, a New Edition with Notes and A
Life of the Author by John Mitford* (Lowell: D. Bixby, 1848), 2 vols. [Inscribed to
Christopher C. Langdell by Jared Sparks] Harvard Law School Library Special
Collections.

Montgomery, *Examinations: An Account of Their Evolution*
R. J. Montgomery, *Examinations: An Account of Their Evolution as Administrative
Devices in England* (London: Longmans, Green, 1965).

Morantz-Sanchez, *Sympathy and Science: Women Physicians*
Regina Markell Morantz-Sanchez, *Sympathy and Science: Women Physicians in
American Medicine* (New York: Oxford University Press, 1985).

Morawetz to Thayer (date varies)
Victor Morawetz to James B. Thayer, James B. Thayer Papers, Special Collections,
Harvard Law School Library, box 20.

Morison, *Three Centuries of Harvard*

Samuel E. Morison, *Three Centuries of Harvard, 1636–1936* (Cambridge, Mass.: Harvard University Press, 1936).

Mushkat, *Tammany: The Evolution of a Political Machine*
Jerome Mushkat, *Tammany: The Evolution of a Political Machine, 1789–1865* (Syracuse, N.Y.: Syracuse University Press, 1971).

Myers, G., *History of Tammany Hall*
Gustavus Myers, *The History of Tammany Hall*, 2nd ed. (1917; repr., New York: Dover, 1971).

[Myers, J.], "Harvard Law School" (5, 19 Feb. 1875)
[James J. Myers], "The Harvard Law School," *Harvard Advocate*, 5 Feb. 1875, 146–47; 19 Feb. 1875, 8–9.

M[yers, J.], "Langdell's 'Selected Cases on Contracts [A reply]"
[James J. Myers], "Langdell's 'Selected Cases on Contracts' [A reply]," *Southern Law Review* 6 (1880): 449.

[Myers, J.], "'Law Schools vs. Lawyers' Offices'"
[James J. Myers], "'Law Schools vs. Lawyers' Offices,'" *Harvard Advocate*, 1 Apr. 1873, 33–35; 11 Apr. 1873, 50–51.

Nelson and Howicz, *Williston on Sales*
Deborah K. Nelson and Jennifer L. Howicz, *Williston on Sales*, 5th ed. (Deerfield, Ill.: Clark, Boardman, Callaghan, 1994).

Nercessian, *Worthy of the Honor: A Brief History of Women at Harvard Medical School*
Nora N. Nercessian, *Worthy of the Honor: A Brief History of Women at Harvard Medical School* (Cambridge, Mass.: Harvard University, 1995).

New Boston, *Annual Report for 1871*
New Boston, *Annual Report of the Town…for 1871* (Manchester, N.H.: Campbell and Hanscom, 1871).

New Boston, "Family Records"
New Boston, "Family Records" (1791–1860), 2 vols., recopied in 1883, Office of Town Clerk, New Boston, N.H.

New Boston, "Register of Interment"
New Boston, "Register of Interment, New Boston Cemetery" [1772–1870], Whipple Free Library, New Boston, N.H.

New Boston, Tax Inventory (date varies)
New Boston, Tax Inventory, manuscript books (1806–1885), Whipple Free Library, New Boston, N.H.

New Boston, Town Records, Third Book
New Boston, Town Records, Third Book (1824–39), Whipple Free Library, New Boston, N.H.

New Boston School Committee, *Reports* (date varies)
New Boston, School Committee, *Reports of the Superintending School Committee*, Whipple Free Library, New Boston, N.H.

Newcomer, *Century of Higher Education*
Mabel Newcomer, *A Century of Higher Education for American Women* (New York: Harper, 1959).

New England Historical and Genealogical Register (1863)

"Marriages and Deaths," *New England Historical and Genealogical Register* 17 (1863): 178–79.

New England Historical and Genealogical Register (1930)
[Wigglesworth Family], *New England Historical and Genealogical Register* 84 (1930): 214–15.

Newfield, *Ivy and Industry*
Christopher Newfield, *Ivy and Industry: Business and the Making of the American University, 1880–1980* (Durham, N.C.: Duke University Press, 2003).

New Hampshire Gazette (20 Apr. 1820)
"Married, in New Boston, Mr. John Langd[ell] to Lydia Beard," *New Hampshire Gazette*, 20 Apr. 1820, 3.

New Hampshire Patriot (27 Sept. 1871)
"Blackstone and Petticoats," *New Hampshire Patriot*, 27 Sept. 1871, 2.

New York Daily Tribune (14 June 1903)
"Northern Securities Decision," *New York Daily Tribune*, 14 June 1903, 7.

New-York Historical Society, *Charter and By-Laws 1858*
New-York Historical Society, *Charter and By-Laws . . . 1858, with a List of Members* (New York: Historical Society, 1862).

New York Law Institute, *Catalog*
New York Law Institute, *Catalog . . . of the Library of the New York Law Institute* (New York: Martin's Steam Printing House, 1874).

New York Law Institute Library
New York Law Institute Library [New York: [privately printed], 1918].

New York State, *Code of Civil Procedure*
New York State Commissioners on Practice and Pleadings, *The Code of Civil Procedure of the State of New-York, Reported Complete* (Albany, N.Y.: Weed, Parsons, 1850).

New York Times (23 July 1853)
"Phi Beta Kappa Annual Meeting," *New York Times*, 23 July 1853, 8.

New York Times (29 May 1855)
"Law Intelligence," *New York Times*, 29 May 1855, 3.

New York Times (3 May 1858)
"Public Meetings," *New York Times*, 3 May 1858, 5.

New York Times (16 June 1882)
"Obituaries," *New York Times*, 16 June 1882, 51.

New York Times (21 Nov. 1886)
"Harvard's New Law Club: A New Organization of Third Year Men," *New York Times*, 21 Nov. 1886, 10.

New York Times (27 Nov. 1898)
"To Make the Sugar Islands Pay," *New York Times*, 27 Nov. 1898, 18.

New York Times (23 Feb. 1900)
"Puerto Rico Bill May be Beaten," *New York Times*, 23 Feb. 1900, 3.

New York Times (15 June 1903)
"The Securities Decision," *New York Times*, 15 June 1903, 6.

New York Times (30 Nov. 1903)

"Defends Merger Decision," *New York Times*, 30 Nov. 1903, 5.

New York Times (10 Apr. 1913)
"Addison Brown Dies, Ex-District Judge," *New York Times*, 10 Apr. 1913, 11.

Noble to Eliot (20 Apr. 1883)
J. C. Noble to Charles W. Eliot (20 Apr. 1883), Charles W. Eliot Papers, Harvard
University Archives, box 71.

North American and United States Gazette (16 Dec. 1871)
"Literary Notices," *North American and United States Gazette*, 16 Dec. 1871, 1.

"Northern Securities Case"
"The Northern Securities Case," *Outlook*, 26 Mar. 1904, 726.

Norton, *Philosophical Discussions by Chauncey Wright*
Charles E. Norton, *Philosophical Discussions by Chauncey Wright, with a Biographical
Sketch* (1877; repr., New York: Burt Franklin, 1971).

Note, *Harvard Law Review* (1887–88)
Note, *Harvard Law Review* 1 (1887–88): 100.

Note, *Harvard Law Review* (1891–92)
Note, *Harvard Law Review* 5 (1891–92): 89, 238.

Novick, *Honorable Justice: The Life of Oliver Wendell Holmes*
Sheldon M. Novick, *Honorable Justice: The Life of Oliver Wendell Holmes* (Boston:
Little, Brown, 1989).

Nyquist, "Contract Theory"
Curtis W. Nyquist, "Contract Theory, Single Case Research, and the Massachusetts
Archives," *Massachusetts Legal History* 3 (1997): 3–87.

Oakley and Coon, "Federal Rules in State Courts"
John B. Oakley and Arthur F. Coon, "Federal Rules in State Courts: A Survey of
State Court Systems of Civil Procedure," *Washington Law Review* 61 (1986):
1367–1434.

"Obituaries [of Jeremiah Smith]"
"Obituaries [of Jeremiah Smith]," *Bulletin of the Phillips Exeter Academy*, Jan. 1922,
18–19.

O'Leary, "Jesuit Legal Education"
David E. O'Leary, "Jesuit Legal Education at Boston College Law School,
Perspectives" (unpublished paper, Daniel R. Coquillette's Legal Education
Seminar, Harvard Law School, Spring 2005).

Oleson and Voss, eds. *Organization of Knowledge in Modern America*
Alexandra Oleson and John Voss, eds. *The Organization of Knowledge in Modern
America, 1860–1920* (Baltimore: Johns Hopkins University Press, 1979).

Oliphant, "Parallels in the Development of Legal and Medical Education"
Herman Oliphant, "Parallels in the Development of Legal and Medical Education,"
Annals of the American Academy of Political and Social Science 167 (May 1933):
156–64.

Palmieri, "From Republican Motherhood to Race Suicide"
Patricia A. Palmieri, "From Republican Motherhood to Race Suicide: Arguments on
the Higher Education of Women in the United States, 1820–1920," in *Educating*

Women and Men Together: Coeducation in a Changing World, ed. Carol Lasser, 49–66 (Urbana: University of Illinois Press, 1987).

Parker, E., Agency 1881–82

    Edmund M. Parker, Agency 1881–82, in Parker, Class Notes, Special Collections, Harvard Law School Library.

Parker, E., Jurisprudence 1881–82

    Edmund M. Parker, Jurisprudence 1881–82, in Parker, Class Notes, Special Collections, Harvard Law School Library.

Parker, E., Real Property 1880–81

    Edmund M. Parker, Real Property 1880–81, 2 vols., in Parker, Class Notes, Special Collections, Harvard Law School Library.

Parker, E., Wills 1881–82

    Edmund M. Parker, Wills 1881–82, in Parker, Class Notes, Special Collections, Harvard Law School Library.

Parker, E., and F. Bolles, *Collection of Important English Statutes*

    Edmund M. Parker and Frank Bolles, eds., *A Collection of Important English Statutes, showing the principal changes in the law of Property* (Cambridge, Mass.: [J. S. Cushing printer], 1880; repr., Boston: Soule and Bugbee, 1881).

Parker, F., to Adams (18 Dec. 1882)

    Francis E. Parker to John Q. Adams (18 Dec. 1882), Charles W. Eliot Papers, Harvard University Archives, box 71.

Parker, J., *Law School of Harvard College*

    Joel Parker, *The Law School of Harvard College* (New York: [privately printed], 1871).

Parker, J., Papers

    Joel Parker, Papers 1848–1939, Massachusetts Historical Society, Boston.

Parsons, Ta., "Professions"

    Talcott Parsons, "Professions," *International Encyclopedia of the Social Sciences* (New York: Macmillan and Free Press, 1968), 12:536–47.

Parsons, Th., *Law of Contracts*

    Theophilus Parsons, *The Law of Contracts*, 2 vols. (Boston: Little, Brown, 1853, 1855).

Parsons, Th., to Eliot (1 Dec. 1869)

    Theophilus Parsons to Charles W. Eliot (1 Dec. 1869), Charles W. Eliot Papers, Harvard University Archives, box 66.

Parsons, Th., to Machen (13 Mar. 1855)

    Theophilus Parsons to Arthur W. Machen (13 Mar. 1855), Lewis H. Machen and Family Papers, Manuscript Division, U.S. Library of Congress, Washington, D.C., box 17.

Patterson, "Langdell's Legacy"

    Dennis Patterson, "Langdell's Legacy," in "Symposium, Reconsidering Grant Gilmore's *The Death of Contract*," *Northwestern University Law Review* 90 (1995): 196–203.

Paul, *Conservative Crisis and the Rule of Law*

    Arnold Paul, *Conservative Crisis and the Rule of Law: Attitudes of Bar and Bench, 1887–1895* (1960; repr., Gloucester, Mass.: Peter Smith, 1976).

PBills81

Edmund M. Parker, annotated copy of James B. Ames, *A Selection of Cases on the Law of Bills and Notes and Other Negotiable Paper* (Boston: Soule and Bugbee, 1881), Special Collections, Harvard Law School Library.

PEqJur80

Edmund M. Parker, annotated copy of Christopher C. Langdell, *Cases on Equity Jurisdiction* ([Cambridge]: [1879–80?]), parts 1–5, Special Collections, Harvard Law School Library.

Peralta, "Historical Analysis of the Insular Cases"

Carlos I. Gorrín Peralta, "Historical Analysis of the Insular Cases: Colonial Constitutionalism Revisited," *Revista del Colegio de Abogados de Puerto Rico* (1995): 31–55.

Perillo, "Origins of the Objective Theory of Contract Formation"

Joseph M. Perillo, "The Origins of the Objective Theory of Contract Formation and Interpretation," *Fordham Law Review* 69 (2000): 427–77.

Peritz, *Competition Policy in America, 1888–1992*

Rudolph J. R. Peritz, *Competition Policy in America, 1888–1992: History, Rhetoric, Law* (New York: Oxford University Press, 1996).

Perry, R., to Chafee (28 Feb. 1929)

Ralph B. Perry to Zechariah Chafee Jr. (28 Feb. 1929), Zechariah Chafee Jr. Papers, Harvard Law School Library, microfilm edition.

Perry, S., "Holmes vs. Hart"

Stephen J. Perry, "Holmes vs. Hart: The Bad Man in Legal Theory," in *The Path of the Law and Its Influence: The Legacy of Oliver Wendell Holmes Jr.*, ed. Steven J. Burton, 158–96 (New York: Cambridge University Press, 2000).

Persons, *Decline of American Gentility*

Stow Persons, *The Decline of American Gentility* (New York: Columbia University Press, 1973).

Petition for Probate of Foreign Will [of Christopher C. Langdell] (4 May 1907)

Petition for Probate of Foreign Will [of Christopher C. Langdell], 4 May 1907, Gage County Courthouse, Nebraska.

Phelps to Warren (29 Sept. 1907)

Charles E. Phelps to Charles Warren (29 Sept. 1907), Charles Warren Papers, Special Collections, Harvard Law School Library, box 37.

Phillips Exeter Academy, *Catalog 1847–8*

Phillips Exeter Academy, *Catalog 1847–8*, Phillips Exeter Academy Archives, Exeter, N.H.

Phillips Exeter Academy Dean of Students, *Register 1830–54*

Phillips Exeter Academy Dean of Students, *Register 1830–54*, Phillips Exeter Academy Archives, Exeter, N.H.

Pollock, "Afterthoughts on Consideration"

Frederick Pollock, "Afterthoughts on Consideration," *Law Quarterly Review* 17 (1901): 415–22.

Pollock, "Merger Case and Restraint of Trade"

Frederick Pollock, "The Merger Case and Restraint of Trade," *Harvard Law Review* 17 (1904): 151–55.

Pollock, *Principles of Contract*
  Frederick Pollock, *Principles of Contract at Law and in Equity* (London: Stearns,
    1876).
Pollock, "Vocation of the Common Law"
  Frederick Pollock, "The Vocation of the Common Law," in *Report of the Ninth Annual
    Meeting at Cambridge, June 25, 1895*, Harvard Law School Association, 11–34
    (Boston: Harvard Law School Association, 1895).
Pollock to Holmes (11 May 1904)
  Frederick Pollock to Oliver W. Holmes Jr. (11 May 1904), Oliver Wendell Holmes Jr.
    Papers, Harvard Law School Library, microfilm version.
Porter, "Biographical Sketch of the Pastors"
  W. C. Porter, "Biographical Sketch of the Pastors," in the Committee on History and
    Publication, *History of the First Presbyterian Church of Fort Scott, Kansas*, 14–16 (Ft.
    Scott, Kans.: Monitor Binding & Printing, 1909).
Potts, "Curriculum and Enrollment"
  David B. Potts, "Curriculum and Enrollment: Assessing the Popularity of
    Antebellum Colleges," in *The American College in the Nineteenth Century*, ed.
    Roger L. Geiger, 37–45 (Nashville, Tenn.: Vanderbilt University Press, 2000).
Pound, "Joseph Henry Beale"
  Roscoe Pound, "Joseph Henry Beale," *Harvard Law Review* 56 (1943): 695–98.
Pound, "Law School, 1817–1929"
  Roscoe Pound, "The Law School, 1817–1929," in *The Development of Harvard
    University since the Inauguration of President Eliot 1869–1929*, ed. Samuel Eliot
    Morison, 472–97 (Cambridge, Mass.: Harvard University Press, 1930).
Powell, *From Patrician to Professional Elite*
  Michael J. Powell, *From Patrician to Professional Elite: The Transformation of the New
    York City Bar Association* (New York: Russell Sage Foundation, 1988).
Pow Wow Club, Records
  Pow Wow Club, Records, Special Collections, Harvard Law School Library.
"Pow Wow Records 1873–95 and 1934–69"
  "Pow Wow Club Records, 1873–95 and 1934–69," bound manuscript, Pow Wow
    Club Records, Special Collections, Harvard Law School Library.
"Pow Wow Records of Supreme Court 1870–82"
  "Pow Wow Club Records and Case Reports of Supreme Court 1870–82," bound
    manuscript, Pow Wow Club Records, Special Collections, Harvard Law School
    Library.
Prude, "Social System of Early New England Textile Mills"
  Jonathan Prude, "The Social System of Early New England Textile Mills: A Case
    Study, 1812–40," in *The New England Working Class and the New Labor History*, ed.
    Herbert G. Gutman and Donald H. Bell, 90–127 (Urbana: University of Illinois
    Press, 1987).
PSal72
  Edmund M. Parker, annotated copy of Christopher C. Langdell, *A Selection of
    Cases on Sales of Personal Property* (Boston: Little, Brown, 1872), vol. 1, Special
    Collections, Harvard Law School Library.

PTorts74
> Edmund M. Parker, annotated copy of James B. Ames, *Select Cases on Torts* ([Cambridge, n.p.], 1874), Special Collections, Harvard Law School Library.

PTrusts82
> Edmund M. Parker, annotated copy of James B. Ames, *A Selection of Cases on the Law of Trusts* (Cambridge, Mass.: J. Wilson, 1881–82), Special Collections, Harvard Law School Library.

Purcell, *Crisis of Democratic Theory*
> Edward A. Purcell Jr., *The Crisis of Democratic Theory: Scientific Naturalism and the Problem of Value* (Lexington: University Press of Kentucky, 1973).

Putnam to Eliot (25 Apr. 1891)
> William L. Putnam to Charles W. Eliot (25 Apr. 1891), Charles W. Eliot Papers, Harvard University Archives, box 81.

Quillets of the Law
> *Quillets of the Law*, advertising brochure (May 1878), Little, Brown Papers, Houghton Library, Harvard University, box 4.

Quit-Claim Deed from Elizabeth P. Boyer to Hannah Warner (20 Aug. 1909)
> Quit-Claim Deed from Elizabeth P. Boyer to Hannah Warner (20 Aug. 1909), Registry of Deeds, Gage County, Nebraska, book 94, p. 72.

Rait, *Memorials of Albert Venn Dicey*
> Robert S. Rait, ed. *Memorials of Albert Venn Dicey: Being Chiefly Letters and Diaries* (London: Macmillan, 1925).

Randolph, "Constitutional Aspects of Annexation"
> Carman F. Randolph, "Constitutional Aspects of Annexation," *Harvard Law Review* 12 (1898–99): 291–315.

Rawle to Eliot (1 July 1899)
> Francis Rawle to Charles W. Eliot (1 July 1899), Charles W. Eliot Papers, Harvard University Archives, box 119.

Redlich, *Common Law and the Case Method*
> Josef Redlich, *The Common Law and the Case Method in American University Law Schools* (New York: Carnegie Foundation for the Advancement of Teaching, 1914).

Reed, A., *Training for the Public Profession of the Law*
> Alfred Z. Reed, *Training for the Public Profession of the Law* (New York: Carnegie Foundation for the Advancement of Teaching, 1921).

Reed, A., to Thayer (5 Nov. 1914)
> Alfred Z. Reed to Ezra Ripley Thayer (5 Nov. 1914), Ezra Ripley Thayer Papers, Special Collections, Harvard Law School Library, box 8.

Reed, G., *Bench and Bar of Michigan*
> George I. Reed, ed., *Bench and Bar of Michigan: A Volume of History and Biography* (Chicago: Century Publishing and Engraving, 1897).

"Reform in Legal Education"
> "Reform in Legal Education," *American Law Review* 10 (July 1876): 626–41.

Reid, "Life at the Law School"

John P. Reid, "Life at the Law School When Charles Doe Was a Student," *Harvard Law School Bulletin* (June 1959): 9–10.

Reimann, "Holmes's *Common Law*"

Mathias W. Reimann, "Holmes's *Common Law* and German Legal Science," in *The Legacy of Oliver Wendell Holmes Jr.*, ed. Robert W. Gordon, 72–114 (Stanford, Calif.: Stanford University Press, 1992).

Review of Langdell's *Selected Cases on Contracts* (1880)

[n.a.], review of Langdell's *Selected Cases on Contracts . . .* 1879, *Southern Law Review*, n.s., 5 (1880): 872–73.

Richardson, *William E. Chandler*

Leon B. Richardson, *William E. Chandler, Republican* (New York: Dodd Mead, 1940).

Risjord, *Chesapeake Politics*

Norman K. Risjord, *Chesapeake Politics, 1781–1800* (New York: Columbia University Press, 1978).

Ritchie, *First Hundred Years*

John Ritchie, *The First Hundred Years: A Short History of the School of Law of the University of Virginia for the Period 1826–1926* (Charlottesville: University Press of Virginia, 1978).

Roach, *Public Examinations in England*

John Roach, *Public Examinations in England, 1850–1900* (Cambridge: Cambridge University Press, 1971).

Robinson, E., *Ministerial Directory*

Edgar S. Robinson, ed., *The Ministerial Directory of the Ministers of the Presbyterian Church of the United States* (Oxford, Ohio: Ministerial Directory, 1898).

Robinson, L., to the Equity Club (7 Apr. 1888)

Lelia Robinson to the Equity Club (7 Apr. 1888), Mary Earhart Dillon Collection, Radcliffe College Archives, Cambridge, Mass.

Roeber, *Faithful Magistrates and Republican Lawyers*

A. G. Roeber, *Faithful Magistrates and Republican Lawyers: Creators of Virginia Legal Culture, 1680–1810* (Chapel Hill: University of North Carolina Press, 1981).

Roithmayr, "Deconstructing the Distinction between Bias and Merit"

Daria Roithmayr, "Deconstructing the Distinction between Bias and Merit," *California Law Review* 85 (1997): 1449–1507.

Roscoe, *Outlines of Civil Procedure*

Edward S. Roscoe, *Outlines of Civil Procedure* (London: Longmans, 1876).

Rosenberg, *Beyond Separate Spheres*

Rosalind Rosenberg, *Beyond Separate Spheres: Intellectual Roots of Modern Feminism* (New Haven, Conn.: Yale University Press, 1982).

Rosenberg, "Limits of Access: The History of Coeducation in America"

Rosalind Rosenberg, "The Limits of Access: The History of Coeducation in America," in *Women and Higher Education in American History*, ed. John Mack Faragher and Florence Howe, 107–29 (New York: W. W. Norton, 1988).

Ross, *Origins of American Social Science*

Dorothy Ross, *The Origins of American Social Science* (Cambridge: Cambridge University Press, 1991).

Rothblatt, "Failure in Early Nineteenth-Century Oxford and Cambridge"
  Sheldon Rothblatt, "Failure in Early Nineteenth-Century Oxford and Cambridge,"
    History of Education 11 (Mar. 1982): 1–21.
Rothblatt, "Student Sub-Culture and the Examinations System"
  Sheldon Rothblatt, "The Student Sub-Culture and the Examinations System in
    Early 19th Century Oxbridge," in *The University and Society*, ed. Lawrence Stone
    (Princeton, N.J.: Princeton University Press, 1974), 1:247–303.
Roy, *Socializing Capital: The Rise of the Large Industrial Corporation*
  William G. Roy, *Socializing Capital: The Rise of the Large Industrial Corporation in
    America* (Princeton, N.J.: Princeton University Press, 1997).
Rudy, "Eliot and Gilman"
  S. Willis Rudy, "Eliot and Gilman: The History of an Academic Friendship," *Teachers
    College Record* 54 (Mar. 1953): 307–18.
Russell, A., *Avoidable Causes of Delay*
  Alfred Russell, *Avoidable Causes of Delay and Uncertainty in Our Courts* (Philadelphia:
    Danda, 1891).
Russell, A., to Machen (1 May 1868)
  Alfred Russell to Arthur W. Machen (1 May 1868), Lewis H. Machen and Family
    Papers, Manuscript Division, U.S. Library of Congress, Washington, D.C., box 18.
Russell, W., to Parker (2 July 1878)
  William E. Russell to Edmund M. Parker (2 July 1878), Joel Parker Papers, 1848–
    1939, Massachusetts Historical Society, Boston, Mass., box 2.
Samuels, *Henry Adams*
  Ernest Samuels, *Henry Adams* (Cambridge, Mass.: Harvard University Press, 1989).
Samuels, *Young Henry Adams*
  Ernest Samuels, *The Young Henry Adams* (Cambridge, Mass.: Harvard University
    Press, 1948).
Sawyer, G., to Washburn (13 Sept. 1871)
  George Y. Sawyer to Emory Washburn (13 Sept. 1871), Charles W. Eliot Papers,
    Harvard University Archives, box 67.
Sawyer, H., to Washburn (12 Sept. 1871)
  Helen M. Sawyer to Emory Washburn (12 Sept. 1871), Charles W. Eliot Papers,
    Harvard University Archives, box 67.
Scales, "Society of Jesus and Legal Education"
  Daniel Scales, "The Society of Jesus and Legal Education: Perspectives on Boston
    College Law School's Jesuit Identity" (unpublished paper, Daniel R. Coquillette's
    Legal Education Seminar, Harvard Law School, spring 2003).
Schlegel, "Between the Harvard Founders and the American Legal Realists"
  John H. Schlegel, "Between the Harvard Founders and the American Legal
    Realists: The Professionalization of the American Law Professor," *Journal of Legal
    Education* 36 (1985): 311–25.
Schofield, "Christopher Columbus Langdell"
  William Schofield, "Christopher Columbus Langdell," *American Law Register*, n.s.,
    46 (1907): 273–96.
Schouler, "Cases without Treatises"

James Schouler, "Cases without Treatises," *American Law Review* 23 (1889): 1–10.

Schweber, "Before Langdell: The Roots of American Legal Science"
Howard Schweber, "Before Langdell: The Roots of American Legal Science," in *The History of the American Law School: A Comprehensive Selection of Essays*, ed. Steve Sheppard, 606–57 (Pasadena, Calif.: Salem Press, 1999).

Schweber, "'Science' of Legal Science"
Howard Schweber, "The 'Science' of Legal Science: The Model of the Natural Sciences in Nineteenth-Century American Legal Education," *Law and History Review* 17 (1999): 421–66.

Scudder to Hoar (9 June 1883)
Henry J. Scudder to E. R. Hoar (9 June 1883), Charles W. Eliot Papers, Harvard University Archives, box 71.

Searby, *History of the University of Cambridge*
Peter Searby, *A History of the University of Cambridge*, vol. 3, *1750–1870* (Cambridge: Cambridge University Press, 1997).

Sebok, "Misunderstanding Positivism"
Anthony J. Sebok, "Misunderstanding Positivism," *Michigan Law Review* 93 (1995): 2054–95.

Seeley and Petticrew, *Seeley's Question Book*
Levi Seeley and Nellie G. Petticrew, *Seeley's Question Book: Containing Methods of Teaching All Subjects* (Danville, N.Y.: F. A. Owen, 1905).

Seipp, "Holmes's Path"
David J. Seipp, "Holmes's Path," *Boston University Law Review* 77 (1997): 515–58.

Seligman, *High Citadel: The Influence of Harvard Law School*
Joel Seligman, *The High Citadel: The Influence of Harvard Law School* (Boston: Houghton Mifflin, 1978).

Shapiro, "'Discovered Places': A History of the Academy Library"
Robert N. Shapiro, "'Discovered Places': A History of the Academy Library," *Phillips Exeter Bulletin*, Summer 1985, 3–4.

Shattuck to Eliot (17 Dec. 1869)
George O. Shattuck to Charles W. Eliot (17 Dec. 1869), Charles W. Eliot Papers, Harvard University Archives, box 66.

[Shearman], "New York City Judiciary"
[Thomas G. Shearman], "The New York City Judiciary," *North American Review* 105 (1867): 145–67.

Sheppard, "Introductory History of Law in the Lecture Hall"
Steve Sheppard, "An Introductory History of Law in the Lecture Hall," *The History of Legal Education in the United States*, ed. Steve Sheppard (Pasadena, Calif.: Salem Press, 1999), 1:1–71.

Shi, *Facing Facts: Realism in American Thought and Culture*
David E. Shi, *Facing Facts: Realism in American Thought and Culture, 1850–1920* (New York: Oxford University Press, 1995).

Shipton, *Biographical Sketches of Those Who Attended Harvard College*
Clifford K. Shipton, *Biographical Sketches of Those Who Attended Harvard College* (Boston: Massachusetts Historical Society, 1930–92).

Shryock, *Unique Influence of the Johns Hopkins University*
  Richard H. Shryock, *The Unique Influence of the Johns Hopkins University on American Medicine* (Copenhagen: Ejnar Munksgaard, 1953).
Siegel, "Joel Bishop's Orthodoxy"
  Stephen A. Siegel, "Joel Bishop's Orthodoxy," *Law and History Review* 13 (1995): 215–59.
Siegel, "John Chipman Gray"
  Stephen A. Siegel, "John Chipman Gray and the Moral Basis of Classical Legal Thought," *Iowa Law Review* 86 (2001): 1513–99.
Simpson, *Legal Theory and Legal History*
  A. W. B. Simpson, *Legal Theory and Legal History: Essays on the Common Law* (London: Hambledon Press, 1987).
Slafter, *Schools and Teachers of Dedham, Massachusetts*
  Carlos Slafter, *The Schools and Teachers of Dedham, Massachusetts, 1644–1904* (Dedham, Mass.: [privately printed], 1905).
Smith, D., "Child-Naming Practices"
  Daniel S. Smith, "Child-Naming Practices, Kinship Ties, and Change in Family Attitude in Hingham, Massachusetts, 1641–1880," *Journal of Social History* 18 (1985): 541–66.
Smith, D., "Continuity and Discontinuity in Puritan Naming"
  Daniel S. Smith, "Continuity and Discontinuity in Puritan Naming: Massachusetts, 1771," *William and Mary Quarterly*, 3rd ser., 51 (Jan. 1994): 67–91.
Smith, J., "Christopher Columbus Langdell"
  Jeremiah Smith, "Christopher Columbus Langdell '45," *Bulletin of Phillips Exeter Academy*, Sept. 1906, 27–32.
Smith, J., "Prof. Christopher C. Langdell"
  Jeremiah Smith, "Prof. Christopher C. Langdell," *Proceedings of the New Hampshire Bar Association*, n.s., 2 (1904–8): 340–48.
Smith, J., to Eliot (date varies)
  Jeremiah Smith to Charles W. Eliot (1890–1907), Charles W. Eliot Papers, Harvard University Archives, boxes 79, 130, 247.
Smith, S., "Believing Like a Lawyer"
  Steven D. Smith, "Believing Like a Lawyer," *Boston College Law Review* 40 (1999): 1041–1137.
Social Law Library, *Act of Incorporation and By-laws*
  Social Law Library, *Act of Incorporation and By-laws* (Boston: Alfred Mudge & Son, 1875).
Soffer, *Discipline and Power, 1870–1930*
  Reba N. Soffer, *Discipline and Power: The University, History and the Making of an English Elite, 1870–1930* (Stanford, Calif.: Stanford University Press, 1994).
Solomon, *In the Company of Educated Women*
  Barbara M. Solomon, *In the Company of Educated Women* (New Haven, Conn.: Yale University Press, 1985).
Soltow, *Men and Wealth in the United States, 1850–1870*

Lee Soltow, *Men and Wealth in the United States, 1850–1870* (New Haven, Conn.:
   Yale University Press, 1975).
Sparrow, *Insular Cases and the Emergence of American Empire*
   Bartholomew H. Sparrow, *The Insular Cases and the Emergence of American Empire*
      (Lawrence: University of Kansas Press, 2006).
Speziale, "Langdell's Concept of Law as Science"
   Marcia Speziale, "Langdell's Concept of Law as Science: The Beginning of Anti-
      formalism in American Legal Theory," *Vermont Law Review* 5 (1980): 1–37.
Sprague to Warren (20 Feb. 1908)
   Henry H. Sprague to Charles Warren (20 Feb. 1908), Charles Warren Papers,
      Special Collections, Harvard Law School Library, box 37.
Sproat, *Best Men: Liberal Reformers in the Gilded Age*
   John G. Sproat, *The Best Men: Liberal Reformers in the Gilded Age* (New York: Oxford
      University Press, 1968).
Standard Atlas of Gage County, Nebraska
   Standard Atlas of Gage County, Nebraska, including a Plat Book (Chicago: Geo. A.
      Ogle, 1906).
Starks, "Christopher Columbus Langdell"
   G. E. Starks, "Christopher Columbus Langdell," one-page typescript in biographical
      file of Christopher C. Langdell, Phillips Exeter Academy Archives, Exeter, N.H.
Starr, *Social Transformation of American Medicine*
   Paul Starr, *The Social Transformation of American Medicine* (New York: Basic Books,
      1982).
Stephen, H., *Treatise on the Principles of Pleading*
   Henry J. Stephen, *A Treatise on the Principles of Pleading in Civil Actions*, 8th Am. ed.
      (Philadelphia: Kay, 1859).
Stephen, J., *Digest of the Law of Evidence*
   James F. Stephen, *A Digest of the Law of Evidence*, 3rd ed. (London: Macmillan,
      1877).
Sterns, *Genealogical and Family History*
   Ezra S. Sterns, ed., *Genealogical and Family History of the State of New Hampshire,
      1908* (New York: Lewis, 1908).
Stevens, *Law School: Legal Education in America*
   Robert Stevens, *Law School: Legal Education in America from the 1850s to the 1980s*
      (Chapel Hill: University of North Carolina Press, 1983).
Stevens, "Law Schools and Legal Education, 1879–1979"
   Robert Stevens, "Law Schools and Legal Education, 1879–1979: Lectures in Honor
      of 100 Years of Valparaiso Law School," *Valparaiso University Law Review* 14
      (1980): 179–259.
Story, R., *Forging of an Aristocracy*
   Ronald Story, *The Forging of an Aristocracy: Harvard and the Boston Upper Class,
      1800–1870* (Middletown, Conn.: Wesleyan University Press, 1980).
Story, W., *Treatise on the Law of Contracts*
   William W. Story, *A Treatise on the Law of Contracts Not under Seal* (Boston: Little
      and Brown, 1844).

Story, W., *Treatise on the Law of Sales*
  William W. Story, *A Treatise on the Law of Sales of Personal Property* (Boston: Little and Brown, 1847).
Story and Bigelow, *Treatise on the Law of Contracts*
  William W. Story, *A Treatise on the Law of Contracts*, 5th ed., prepared by Melville M. Bigelow (Boston: Little, Brown, 1874).
Strong, *Diary*
  George Templeton Strong, *The Diary [1835–75]*, ed. Allan Nevins and Milton H. Thomas, 4 vols. (New York: Macmillan, 1952).
Strum, *Louis D. Brandeis*
  Philippa Strum, *Louis D. Brandeis: Justice for the People* (Cambridge, Mass.: Harvard University Press, 1984).
Subrin, "David Dudley Field and the Field Code"
  Stephen N. Subrin, "David Dudley Field and the Field Code: A Historical Analysis of an Earlier Procedural Vision," *Law and History Review* 6 (1988): 311–73.
Subrin, "How Equity Conquered Common Law"
  Stephen N. Subrin, "How Equity Conquered Common Law: The Federal Rules of Civil Procedure in Historical Perspective," *University of Pennsylvania Law Review* 135 (1987): 909–1002.
Sutherland, *Law at Harvard*
  Arthur E. Sutherland, *The Law at Harvard: A History of Men and Ideas, 1817–1967* (Cambridge, Mass.: Harvard University Press, 1967).
Sutherland, "One Man in His Time"
  Arthur E. Sutherland, "One Man in His Time," *Harvard Law Review* 78 (1964): 7–22.
Suzzallo, "Lecture Method"
  Henry Suzzallo, "Lecture Method," in *A Cyclopedia of Education*, ed. Paul Monroe (New York: Macmillan, 1911), 3:671.
Swasey, "Boston University Law School"
  George R. Swasey, "Boston University Law School," *Green Bag* 1 (1899): 54–65.
Synnott, *Half-Opened Door: Discrimination and Admissions*
  Marcia Graham Synnott, *The Half-Opened Door: Discrimination and Admissions at Harvard, Yale, and Princeton, 1900–1970* (Westport, Conn.: Greenwood, 1979).
Taft to Thayer (11 June 1898)
  William H. Taft to James B. Thayer (11 June 1898), Charles W. Eliot Papers, Harvard University Archives, box 268–69 [*sic*].
Taggart, "David Cross"
  D. A. Taggart, "David Cross," *Proceedings of the New Hampshire Bar Association*, n.s., 3 (1910–16): 434–43.
Tebbets, *Memoir of William Gibbons*
  Theodore Tebbets, *A Memoir of William Gibbons* (New York: privately printed, 1862).
Teeven, *History of the Anglo-American Common Law of Contract*
  Kevin M. Teeven, *A History of the Anglo-American Common Law of Contract* (Westport, Conn.: Greenwood, 1990).
Teeven, "Conventional Moral Obligation"
  Kevin M. Teeven, "Conventional Moral Obligation Principle Unduly Limits

Qualified Beneficiary Contrary to Case Law," *Marquette Law Review* 86 (2003): 701–52.

Thayer, E., to J. Thayer (date varies)

Ezra R. Thayer to James B. Thayer (1889–99), James B. Thayer Papers, Special Collections, Harvard Law School Library, boxes 17, 18, 19.

Thayer, J., *Cases on Constitutional Law*

James B. Thayer, *Cases on Constitutional Law, with Notes* (Cambridge, Mass.: Charles W. Sever, 1894–95).

Thayer, J., Correspondence and Memoranda

James B. Thayer, Correspondence and Memoranda, 1871–83, Special Collections, Harvard Law School Library, 6 vols.

Thayer, J., Criminal Law Teaching Notebooks

James B. Thayer, Criminal Law Teaching Notebooks, James B. Thayer Papers, Special Collections, Harvard Law School Library, box 3.

Thayer, J., Evidence Teaching Notebooks

James B. Thayer, Evidence Teaching Notebooks, James B. Thayer Papers, Special Collections, Harvard Law School Library, boxes 5–6.

Thayer, J., *Letters of Chauncey Wright*

James B. Thayer, *Letters of Chauncey Wright with Some Account of His Life* (Cambridge, Mass.: J. Wilson, 1878).

Thayer, J., "Memorial" [Feb. 1876]

James B. Thayer, "Mem[orial] about Law School 1875–76 Winter" [Feb. 1876], James B. Thayer Papers, Special Collections, Harvard Law School Library, box 20.

Thayer, J., "Notes on Teaching Evidence"

James B. Thayer, "Notes on Teaching a class of evidence law" [6 Oct. 1874], Harvard Law School Library, Special Collections.

Thayer, J., "Our New Possessions"

James B. Thayer, "Our New Possessions," *Harvard Law Review* 12 (1898–99): 464–85.

Thayer, J., Papers

James B. Thayer, Papers, Special Collections, Harvard Law School Library.

Thayer, J., *Preliminary Treatise on the Law of Evidence*

James B. Thayer, *A Preliminary Treatise on the Law of Evidence* (Boston: Little Brown, 1898).

Thayer, J., Sales Teaching Notebook no. 1

James B. Thayer, Sales Teaching Notebook no. 1, James B. Thayer Papers, Special Collections, Harvard Law School Library, box 7.

Thayer, J., *Select Cases on Evidence*

James B. Thayer, *Select Cases on Evidence at the Common Law with Notes* (Cambridge, Mass.: Charles W. Sever, 1892).

Thayer, J., "Teaching of English Law"

James B. Thayer, "The Teaching of English Law at Universities," *Harvard Law Review* 9 (1895): 169–84.

Thayer, J., to Eliot (date varies)

James B. Thayer to Charles W. Eliot (1869–89), Charles W. Eliot Papers, Harvard University Archives, boxes 66, 77.

Thayer, J., to Everett (28 May 1890)
James B. Thayer to Charles C. Everett (28 May 1890), James B. Thayer Papers, Special Collections, Harvard Law School Library, box 18.

Thayer, J., to Forbes (15 Sept. 1854)
James B. Thayer to Mrs. Edith Forbes (15 Sept. 1854), James B. Thayer Papers, Special Collections, Harvard Law School Library, box 15.

Thernstrom, *Poverty and Progress*
Stephan Thernstrom, *Poverty and Progress: Social Mobility in a Nineteenth-Century City* (Cambridge, Mass.: Harvard University Press, 1964).

Thomas, B., "Constitution Led by the Flag: The *Insular Cases*"
Brook Thomas, "A Constitution Led by the Flag: The *Insular Cases* and the Metaphor of Incorporation," in *Foreign in a Domestic Sense: Puerto Rico, American Expansion, and the Constitution*, ed. Christina Burnett and Burke Marshall, 82–103 (Durham, N.C.: Duke University Press, 2001).

Thomas, M., to Bakewell (17 July 1899)
M. Carey Thomas to Dr. Bakewell (17 July 1899), M. Carey Thomas Papers, Radcliffe Institute, Harvard University, microfilm edition.

Thomas, M., to Irwin (17 July 1899)
M. Carey Thomas to Agnes Irwin (17 July 1899), M. Carey Thomas Papers, Radcliffe Institute, Harvard University, microfilm edition.

Thomas, M., to Irwin (21 Aug. 1899)
M. Carey Thomas to Agnes Irwin (21 Aug. 1899), Correspondence and Papers of the Council of Radcliffe College, Radcliffe Institute, Harvard University, f. "Papers re Admission to Law School."

Thomas, W., *Lawyering for the Railroad*
William G. Thomas, *Lawyering for the Railroad: Business, Law and Power in the New South* (Baton Rouge: Louisiana State University Press, 1999).

Thurston, Review
Edward S. Thurston, review of *A Selection of Cases and Statutes on the Principles of Code Pleading . . .*, by Charles M. Hepburn, *Harvard Law Review* 14 (1901): 554.

Torruelia, *Supreme Court and Puerto Rico*
Juan R. Torruelia, *The Supreme Court and Puerto Rico: The Doctrine of Separate and Unequal* (Río Piedras, Puerto Rico: Editorial de la Universidad de Puerto Rico, 1985).

Touster, "Holmes a Hundred Years Ago: *The Common Law*"
Saul Touster, "Holmes a Hundred Years Ago: *The Common Law* and Legal Theory," *Hofstra Law Review* 10 (1982): 673–717.

Towne, *Memorial of Rev. Theodore Tebbets*
Edward C. Towne, *A Memorial of Rev. Theodore Tebbets: A Sermon . . . Feb. 8, 1863* (Boston: Walker, Wise, 1863).

Townsend, *Manhood at Harvard*
Kim Townsend, *Manhood at Harvard: William James and Others* (Cambridge, Mass.: Harvard University Press, 1996).

Turner, *Liberal Education of Charles Eliot Norton*
James Turner, *The Liberal Education of Charles Eliot Norton* (Baltimore: Johns Hopkins University Press, 1999).

"Twenty-fifth Anniversary of Prof. C. C. Langdell"
"The Twenty-fifth Anniversary of Prof. C. C. Langdell as Dean of Harvard Law School," *American Law Review* 29 (1895): 605.

Twitchett, *Birth of the Chinese Meritocracy: Bureaucrats and Examinations in T'ang China*
Dennis C. Twitchett, *The Birth of the Chinese Meritocracy: Bureaucrats and Examinations in T'ang China* (London: China Society, 1976).

U.S. Census of 1850
U.S. Department of the Interior, *Seventh Decennial Census of the United States, 1850* (Washington, D.C.: U.S. Office of the Census, 1850).

U.S. Constitution
United States Constitution.

United States Investor (19 Mar. 1904)
[Report on *Northern Securities v. United States* (1904),] *United States Investor* (19 Mar. 1904): 413–14.

Vanderbilt University Law Department, *Register 1904–1905*
Vanderbilt University Law Department, *Register 1904–1905: Announcement 1905–1906* (Nashville, Tenn.: Vanderbilt University, 1905).

Veysey, *Emergence of the American University*
Laurence R. Veysey, *The Emergence of the American University* (Chicago: University of Chicago Press, 1965).

Vinton to Eliot (30 Dec. 1892)
Frederic P. Vinton to Charles W. Eliot (30 Dec. 1892), Charles W. Eliot Papers, Harvard University Archives, box 264–65 [*sic*].

Vinton to Wade (11 Jan. 1893)
Frederic P. Vinton to Winthrop H. Wade (11 Jan. 1893), Charles W. Eliot Papers, Harvard University Archives, box 264–65 [*sic*].

VNEq75
George W. Van Nest, annotated copy of Christopher C. Langdell, *Cases in Equity Pleading, Selected with Special Reference to the Subject of Discovery . . . [Part I]* (Cambridge, Mass.: Printed for the Author, [1875]), Special Collections, Harvard Law School Library.

Wait, *Law and Practice in Courts of New York*
William Wait, *The Law and Practice in . . . Courts in the State of New York*, 3rd ed. (Albany, N.Y.: W. Gould, 1874).

Walker, *Everyday Life in Victorian America*
Robert H. Walker, *Everyday Life in Victorian America, 1865–1910* (1967; repr., Malabar, Fla.: Krieger, 1994).

Waller, "Antitrust Philosophy of Justice Holmes"
Spencer W. Waller, "The Antitrust Philosophy of Justice Holmes," *Southern Illinois University Law Journal* 18 (1994): 283–328.

Waltzer, "Harvard Law School under Langdell and Eliot"
Kenneth Waltzer, "The Harvard Law School under Langdell and Eliot: Example

and Leadership in the Professionalization of Legal Education 1870–1900"
(unpublished seminar paper submitted to Paul H. Buck, Harvard University
Archives, Cambridge, Mass., 1965).

Wambaugh, "Professor Langdell"
Eugene Wambaugh, "Professor Langdell—A View of His Career," *Harvard Law
Review* 20 (1906): 1–4.

Wambaugh to Eliot (date varies)
Eugene Wambaugh to Charles W. Eliot (1891–92), Charles W. Eliot Papers, Harvard
University Archives, box 83.

Wambaugh to Thayer (date varies)
Eugene Wambaugh to James B. Thayer (1889–92), James B. Thayer Papers, Special
Collections, Harvard Law School Library, boxes 20, 27.

Ware, "Remarks"
Darwin E. Ware, "Remarks," in *Minutes of the Suffolk County, Massachusetts Bar
Meeting held June 7, 1889 in memory of Peleg W. Chandler*, 16 [Boston: Suffolk
County Bar Association, 1889].

Warner, Report of Superintendent of Public Instruction 1864
Austin Warner, Report of Superintendent of Public Instruction for Bourbon
County, in *Third Annual Report . . . Topeka, Dec. 31, 1864*, Superintendent of Public
Instruction of the State of Kansas (Lawrence, Kans.: Public Printer, 1865).

Warranty Deed from Austin and Hannah Warner to Christopher C. Langdell (10 Feb.
1877)
Warranty Deed from Austin and Hannah Warner to Christopher C. Langdell (10
Feb. 1877), Registry of Deeds, Gage County, Nebraska, book S, p. 13.

Warranty Deed from Hannah Warner to Jacob S. Patterson (29 Dec. 1909)
Warranty Deed from Hannah Warner to Jacob S. Patterson (29 Dec. 1909), Registry
of Deeds, Gage County, Nebraska, book 96, p. 343.

Warren, C., *History of the Harvard Law School*
Charles Warren, *History of the Harvard Law School and of Early Legal Conditions in
America*, 3 vols. (New York: Lewis, 1908).

Warren, E., *Spartan Education*
Edward H. Warren, *Spartan Education* (Boston: Houghton Mifflin, 1942).

Warren, J., to C. Warren (2 June 1908)
Joseph Warren to Charles Warren (2 June 1908), Charles Warren Papers, Special
Collections, Harvard Law School Library, box 37.

Washburn, E., "Harvard Law School"
Emory Washburn, "Harvard Law School" (draft manuscript circa 1877), 44 pp.,
Samuel F. Batchelder Papers, Cambridge Historical Society, Massachusetts,
box 2.

Washburn, E., *Treatise on the American Law of Real Property*
Emory Washburn, *A Treatise on the American Law of Real Property*, 3 vols. (Boston:
Little, Brown, 1876).

Washburn, E., to Eliot (1 Apr. 1876)
Emory Washburn to Charles W. Eliot (1 Apr. 1876), Charles W. Eliot Papers,
Harvard University Archives, box 74.

Washburn, J., to Thayer (5 Dec. 1873)
John D. Washburn to James B. Thayer (5 Dec. 1873), James B. Thayer Papers, Special Collections, Harvard Law School Library, box 20.

Weare, N.H., School Committee, *Report 1853–54*
Weare, New Hampshire, School Committee, *Report…1853–54* (Manchester: J. H. Goodale, 1854).

Webb to Langdell (20 Mar. 1881)
Benjamin H. Webb to Christopher C. Langdell (20 Mar. 1881), Christopher Columbus Langdell Papers, Special Collections, Harvard Law School Library.

WEq75
Charles L. B. Whitney, annotated copy of Christopher C. Langdell, *Cases in Equity Pleading, Selected with Special Reference to the Subject of Discovery… [Part I]* (Cambridge, Mass.: Printed for the Author, [1875]), Special Collections, Harvard Law School Library.

Wheeler to Eliot (9 Nov. 1903)
Benjamin I. Wheeler to Charles W. Eliot (9 Nov. 1903), Charles W. Eliot Papers, Harvard University Archives, box 257.

White, G., *Justice Oliver Wendell Holmes*
G. Edward White, *Justice Oliver Wendell Holmes: Law and the Inner Self* (New York: Oxford University Press, 1993).

White, G., "Looking at Holmes"
G. Edward White, "Looking at Holmes Looking at Marshall," *Massachusetts Legal History* 7 (2001): 63–80.

White, G., "Revisiting James Bradley Thayer"
G. Edward White, "Revisiting James Bradley Thayer," *Northwestern University Law Review* 88 (1993): 55–60.

White, M., *Social Thought in America: The Revolt against Formalism*
Morton White, *Social Thought in America: The Revolt against Formalism*, 2nd ed. (Boston: Beacon, 1957).

White, T., Review
Thomas R. White, review of *A Selection of Cases and Statutes on the Principles of Code Pleading…*, by Charles M. Hepburn, *University of Pennsylvania Law Review*, n.s., 40 (1901): 314–15.

[Whiton], "Substance of the communication" (30 June 1869)
[William H. Whiton], "Substance of the communication between Thomas Lord and William H. Whiton at 38 Exchange Place, June 30, 1869," Lord Family Papers, 1807–1961, Special Collections, Harvard Law School Library.

Whiton to Langdell (14 Sept. 1871)
William H. Whiton to Langdell (14 Sept. 1871), Lord Family Papers, 1807–1961, Special Collections, Harvard Law School Library.

Whiton to Lord (date varies)
William H. Whiton to David Lord (1869–71), Lord Family Papers, 1807–1961, Special Collections, Harvard Law School Library.

Whiton to Porter and Langdell (25 June 1869)
William H. Whiton to John K. Porter and Christopher C. Langdell (25 June 1869),

manuscript copy of original, Lord Family Papers, 1807–1961, Special Collections, Harvard Law School Library.

Whittier to Philbrick (10 Dec. 1925)

Clarke B. Whittier to Francis S. Philbrick (10 Dec. 1925), Francis S. Philbrick Papers, Harvard University Archives, box 1.

Wiebe, *Search for Order, 1877–1920*

Robert H. Wiebe, *The Search for Order, 1877–1920* (New York: Hill & Wang, 1967).

Wiecek, *Lost World of Classical Legal Thought*

William W. Wiecek, *The Lost World of Classical Legal Thought: Law and Ideology in America, 1886–1937* (New York: Oxford University Press, 1998).

Wiener, *Evolution and the Founders of Pragmatism*

Philip Wiener, *Evolution and the Founders of Pragmatism* (Cambridge, Mass.: Harvard University Press, 1949).

Wigglesworth, Agency and Carriers 1877–78

George Wigglesworth, Agency and Carriers 1877–78, in Wigglesworth, Class Notes, Special Collections, Harvard Law School Library.

Wigglesworth, Annotations in Ames, *Select Cases on Torts*

George Wigglesworth, Annotated copy of [James Barr Ames], *Select Cases on Torts* ([Cambridge, n.p.], 1874), part 2, Harvard University Archives.

Wigglesworth, Civil Procedure 1876–77

George Wigglesworth, Civil Procedure 1876–77, in Wigglesworth, Class Notes, Special Collections, Harvard Law School Library.

Wigglesworth, Class Notes

George Wigglesworth, Class Notes, Special Collections, Harvard Law School Library.

Wigglesworth, Contracts 1876–77

George Wigglesworth, Contracts 1876–77, in Wigglesworth, Class Notes, Special Collections, Harvard Law School Library.

Wigglesworth, Criminal Law 1876–77

George Wigglesworth, Criminal Law 1876–77, in Wigglesworth, Class Notes, Special Collections, Harvard Law School Library.

Wigglesworth, Equity 1877–78

George Wigglesworth, Equity 1877–78, in Wigglesworth, Class Notes, Special Collections, Harvard Law School Library.

Wigglesworth, "Law as a Profession"

George Wigglesworth, "The Law as a Profession," speech to the Milton Academy Trustees (17 Dec. 1909), typescript, Wigglesworth Family Papers, 1682–1966, Massachusetts Historical Society, Boston, box 34.

Wigglesworth, Pow Wow Records

George Wigglesworth, Pow Wow Records, in Wigglesworth, Class Notes, Special Collections, Harvard Law School Library.

Wigglesworth, Real Property 1877–78

George Wigglesworth, Real Property, second year, 1877–78, in Wigglesworth, Class Notes, Special Collections, Harvard Law School Library.

Wigglesworth, Torts 1876–77

George Wigglesworth, Torts 1876–77, in Wigglesworth, Class Notes, Special
    Collections, Harvard Law School Library.
Wigglesworth, Trusts and Mortgages 1877–78
    George Wigglesworth, Trusts and Mortgages 1877–78, in Wigglesworth, Class
    Notes, Special Collections, Harvard Law School Library.
Wigglesworth Family Papers
    Wigglesworth Family Papers, 1682–1966, Massachusetts Historical Society, Boston.
Wilby to Eliot (11 June 1898)
    Charles Wilby to Charles W. Eliot (11 June 1898), Charles W. Eliot Papers, Harvard
    University Archives, box 268–269 [*sic*].
Wilder to Warren (11 Oct. 1907)
    Daniel W. Wilder to Charles Warren (11 Oct. 1907), Charles Warren Papers, Special
    Collections, Harvard Law School Library, box 37.
Wilgus, "Need of National Incorporation Law"
    H. L. Wilgus, "Need of National Incorporation Law," *Michigan Law Review* 2 (1904):
    358–95.
Williams, *Marxism and Literature*
    Raymond Williams, *Marxism and Literature* (New York: Oxford University Press,
    1977).
Williston, "Jeremiah Smith"
    Samuel Williston, "Jeremiah Smith," *Harvard Graduates Magazine* 30 (1921): 157.
Williston, "Joseph Henry Beale"
    Samuel Williston, "Joseph Henry Beale: A Biographical Sketch," *Harvard Law
    Review* 56 (1943): 686–89.
Williston, *Life and Law: An Autobiography*
    Samuel Williston, *Life and Law: An Autobiography* (Boston: Little, Brown, 1940).
Williston, "Successive Promises"
    Samuel Williston, "Successive Promises of the Same Performance," *Harvard Law
    Review* 8 (1894): 27–38.
Williston to Eliot (22 Apr. 1890)
    Samuel Williston to Charles W. Eliot (22 Apr. 1890), Charles W. Eliot Papers,
    Harvard University Archives, box 79.
Wilson to Warren (3 Oct. 1907)
    Alexander Wilson to Charles Warren (3 Oct. 1907), Charles Warren Papers, Special
    Collections, Harvard Law School Library, box 37.
Wingate, "Boston Letter"
    Charles E. L. Wingate, "Boston Letter," *The Critic* (1 June 1895): 410.
Wise, *Italian Boy: A Tale of Murder and Body Snatching*
    Sara Wise, *The Italian Boy: A Tale of Murder and Body Snatching in 1830s London* (New
    York: Henry Holt, 2004).
Woman's Journal (4 Nov. 1871)
    "News and Notes," *Woman's Journal*, 4 Nov. 1871, 349.
Woodward, "Dimensions of Social and Legal Change"
    Calvin Woodward, "Dimensions of Social and Legal Change: The Making and

Remaking of the Common Law Tradition in Nineteenth-Century America," *New Literary History* 17 (Winter 1986): 233–48.

Wooldridge, *Meritocracy and the "Classless Society"*
Adrian Wooldridge, *Meritocracy and the "Classless Society"* (London: Social Market Foundation, 1995).

Wylie, *Self-Made Man in America*
Irvin G. Wylie, *The Self-Made Man in America: The Myth of Rags to Riches* (New Brunswick, N.J.: Rutgers University Press, 1954).

Yeazell, *Civil Procedure*
Stephen C. Yeazell, *Civil Procedure*, 5th ed. (New York: Aspen Publishers, 2000).

Yeazell, "Teaching Supplemental Jurisdiction"
Stephen C. Yeazell, "Teaching Supplemental Jurisdiction," *Indiana Law Journal* 74 (1998): 241–50.

Yellin, *Harriet Jacobs*
Jean Fagan Yellin, *Harriet Jacobs: A Life* (New York: Basic Civitas, 2004).

Young, *Rise of the Meritocracy*
Michael Young, *The Rise of the Meritocracy, 1870–2033: The New Elite of Our Social Revolution* (London: Thames & Hudson, 1958).

Zschoche, "Dr. Clarke Revisited"
Sue Zschoche, "Dr. Clarke Revisited: Science, True Womanhood, and Female Collegiate Education," *History of Education Quarterly* 29 (1989): 545–69.

Zunz, *Making America Corporate, 1870–1920*
Oliver Zunz, *Making America Corporate, 1870–1920* (Chicago: University of Chicago Press, 1990).

CASES CITED

Arranged Alphabetically by Abbreviated Titles Used in the Notes

Adams v. Lindsell (1818)
   Adams v. Lindsell, 1 B. & Ald. 681, 106 Eng. Rep. 250 ([King's Bench] 1818).
Banorgee v. Hovey (1809)
   Banorgee v. Hovey, 5 Mass. 11 ([Massachusetts] 1809).
Beane v. Middleton (1797)
   Beane v. Middleton, 4 H. & McH. 74 ([Maryland] 1797)
Bradwell v. State of Illinois (1873)
   Bradwell v. State of Illinois, 83 U.S. 442 ([U.S. Supreme Court] 1873).
Campbell v. Holt (1885)
   Campbell v. Holt, 115 U.S. 620 ([U.S. Supreme Court] 1885).
City Bank v. Perkins (1859)
   City Bank of New Haven v. Perkins, 4 Bosworth's Rep. 420 ([N.Y. Superior Court]
      1859).
City Bank v. Perkins (1864)
   City Bank of New Haven v. Perkins, 29 N.Y. 554 ([N.Y. Court of Appeals] 1864).
Crapo v. Kelly (1872)
   Crapo v. Kelly, 83 U.S. 610 ([U.S. Supreme Court] 1872).
Davis v. Wells (1881)
   Davis v. Wells, 104 U.S. 159([U.S. Supreme Court] 1881).
Delafield v. Parish (1857)
   Delafield v. Parish, 1 Redf. Surr. 1 (N.Y. Surrogate's Court 1857).
Delafield v. Parish (1862)
   Delafield v. Parish, 25 N.Y. 9 ([N.Y. Court of Appeals] 1862).
Demarest v. Daig (1865)
   Demarest v. Daig, 32 N.Y. 281 ([N.Y. Supreme Court] 1865).
Downes v. Bidwell (1901)
   Downes v. Bidwell, 182 U.S. 244 ([U.S. Supreme Court] 1901).
Grafton v. Cummings (1879)
   Grafton v. Cummings, 99 U.S. 100 ([U.S. Supreme Court] 1879).
Grutter v. Bollinger (2003)
   Grutter v. Bollinger, 539 U.S. 306 ([U.S. Supreme Court] 2003).
Hall v. Young (1857)
   Hall v. Young, 34 N.H. 134 ([New Hampshire] 1857).

Hallett v. Wylie (1808)
> *Hallett v. Wylie*, 3 Johns 44 ([New York] 1808).

Hart v. Sansom (1884)
> *Hart v. Sansom*, 110 U.S. 151 ([U.S. Supreme Court] 1884).

Hunt v. Jackson (1866)
> *Hunt et al. v. Jackson*, 12 F.Cas. 924 ([Federal Circuit Court] 1866).

Kelly v. Crapo (1864)
> *Kelly v. Crapo*, 41 Barbour's 603 (N.Y. Supreme Court 1864).

Kelly v. Crapo (1871)
> *Kelly v. Crapo*, 45 N.Y. 86 (N.Y. [Court of Appeals] 1871).

Kuhn v. Webster (1858)
> *Kuhn, Administrator v. Webster & Others*, 78 Mass. (12 Gray) 3 ([Massachusetts] 1858).

Leith v. Leith (1859)
> *Leith v. Leith*, 39 N.H. 20 ([New Hampshire] 1859).

Livingston v. Pendergast (1857)
> *Livingston v. Pendergast*, 34 N.H. 544 ([New Hampshire] 1857).

Madison v. Baptist (1865)
> *Madison Avenue Baptist Church v. Baptist Church in Oliver Street*, 19 Abbott's Pr. 105 ([N.Y. Superior Court] 1865).

Madison v. Baptist (1866)
> *Madison Avenue Baptist Church v. Baptist Church in Oliver Street*, 26 N.Y. Super. Ct. 570 ([N.Y. Superior Court] 1866).

Madison v. Baptist (1867)
> *Madison Avenue Baptist Church v. Baptist Church in Oliver Street*, 2 Abbott's Pr. (n.s.) 254 ([N.Y. Superior Court] 1867).

Madison v. Baptist (1869)
> *Madison Avenue Baptist Church v. Baptist Church in Oliver Street*, 31 N.Y. Super. Ct. 109 ([N.Y. Superior Court] 1869).

Madison v. Baptist (1871)
> *Madison Avenue Baptist Church v. Baptist Church in Oliver Street*, 46 N.Y. 131 ([N.Y. Court of Appeals] 1871).

Madison v. Madison (1863)
> *Madison Avenue Baptist Church v. Madison Avenue Baptist Church et al.*, 26 How. Pr. 72 ([N.Y. Supreme Court] 1863).

McCulloch v. Eagle (1822)
> *McCulloch v. Eagle Ins. Co.*, 18 Mass. (1 Pick.) 278 ([Massachusetts] 1822).

Milbank v. Crane (1863)
> *Milbank v. Crane*, 25 How. Pr. 193 (N.Y. [Supreme Court] 1863).

New York v. Northern Railroad (1869)
> *People of the State of New York v. Northern Railroad Co.*, 53 Barb. 98 (N.Y. [Supreme Court, New York County] 1869).

New York v. Northern Railroad (1870)
> *People of the State of New York v. Northern Railroad Co.*, 42 N.Y. 217 (N.Y. Court of Appeals, 1870).

Northern Railroad v. New York (1870)
   Northern Railroad Co. v. People of the State of New York, 79 U.S. 384 ([U.S. Supreme
      Court] 1870).
Northern Securities v. United States (1904)
   Northern Securities Co. v. United States, 193 U.S. 197 ([U.S. Supreme Court] 1904).
Offord v. Davies (1862)
   Offord v. Davies, 12 C.B.N.S. 748 ([England] 1862).
Osgood v. Laytin (1867)
   Osgood v. Laytin, 1867 WL 5776 (N.Y. [Supreme Court, New York County] 1867).
Parish v. Parish (1858)
   Parish v. Parish, 42 Barbour's 274 ([N.Y. Supreme Court] 1858).
Paul v. Frazier (1807)
   Paul v. Frazier, 3 Mass. 71 ([Massachusetts] 1807).
Payne v. Cave (1789)
   Payne v. Cave, 3 *Term Reports* 148 ([England, King's Bench] 1789).
Scott v. Sandford (1857).
   Dred Scott v. Sandford, 60 U.S. 393 ([U.S. Supreme Court] 1857).
Sterling v. Jaudon (1867)
   Sterling & Bunting v. Jaudon et al., 48 Barbour's 459 (N.Y. [Supreme Court, New York
      County] 1867).
Thompson v. Insurance Co. (1881)
   Thompson v. Insurance Co., 104 U.S. 252 ([U.S. Supreme Court] 1881).
In the matter of Turfler (1865)
   In the matter of the petition of George C. Turfler, 44 Barbour's 46 (1865) (N.Y.
      [Supreme Court, New York County] 1865).
United States v. Northern Securities (1903)
   United States v. Northern Securities Co., 120 Fed. R. 721 ([Federal circuit court] 1903).
Weeks v. Hill (1859)
   Weeks v. Hill, 38 N.H. 199 ([New Hampshire] 1859).
Wilkie v. Roosevelt (1802)
   Wilkie v. Roosevelt, 3 Johns Cas. 206 ([New York Superior Court] 1802).

INDEX

Academic merit, meaning of, 219–29

Academic merit hiring standard. *See* Hiring standard of academic merit for faculty

Academic meritocracy: acceptance and success of, 2–5, 7–8, 219, 224–25, 264–70, 308, 309–10; overview, 3, 6–8; founding principles, 5; CCL's vision of and commitment to, 5–6; economic logic of, 7, 221–24, 232, 265, 279, 292; betraying principles of, 7–8, 220, 225–29, 232, 264, 273, 308; justice of legal system reliant on, 83, 129, 271, 342, 343; criticism of and resistance to, 194, 197, 207–9, 212, 215, 216, 219, 309, 341–42, 347; gentlemen vs. scholars and, 194–201, 226; supporters of, 200–201, 202, 206, 207, 209, 210, 212, 219, 345; elements of formal system, 201–6, 222, 343; establishing at HLS, 210–19; threats to, 221–23, 225, 252–53, 257–59, 261, 263; circumventing, methods of, 258–59; enduring influence of, 341–46. *See also* Discrimination and academic meritocracy

—institutional mechanisms of: sequenced curriculum, 6, 7, 39, 130–40, 208–9, 232, 343; written examinations posing hypothetical problems, 6, 131, 160–64, 210, 232, 343; alumni association support, 6, 229–32, 343; degree or continuation requirements, 7, 209, 211–12, 218, 232; three-year curriculum, 7, 39, 210, 219–22, 232, 343; library as scholarly resource, 33, 207–8, 232, 320–21, 343; admission requirements, 39, 209–10, 214–18, 231, 235, 268–70, 343; independent career track for faculty, 168, 207, 232, 343; Honor program, 210, 219, 226–29, 232, 343. *See also* Case method of teaching

Academic merit standard, development of: overview, 2–5, 7–8; influences on, 6–7, 11, 192, 196, 203, 205–6; beginnings, 206–10; functionalist rationale for, 223–24

Academic standards: Harvard Law School (1868–82), 130, 161, 211–12, 213, 214–18, 219, 226, 235, 268–70; traditional commercial approach to, 223–24; of Harvard Law School (1880–1910), 269–72, 283, 295–96, 301, 315; Harvard College (1870–90s), 281, 296, 300, 305

Adams, Brooks, 197, 200–201

Adams, Charles Francis, Jr., 72

Adams, Henry, 200

Adams, John Quincy, Jr., 183

Adams v. Lindsell (1818), 112

Adelbert College, 307

Agassiz, Louis, 11, 25–26, 351

Albany Law School, 223

Alcott, Louisa M., 290

Almy, Charles, 154–56

Alpha Delta Phi, 28

American Academy of Arts and Sciences, 197, 234, 276

American Bar Association, 191, 214, 320, 338

American Social Science Association, 197–98

Ames, James Barr: criticism of bench and bar, 146–47; HLS student, reconstructed class discussion, 149–53; HLS faculty appointment, 171–72, 174–75, 187, 190, 200, 347; photograph, 172; resignation, 177; Holmes's HLS faculty appointment and, 180; Eliot and, 185; on teaching law as profession, 191–92; on Washburn, 196;